The Etruscans Begin to Speak

THE
ETRUSCANS
BEGIN TO
SPEAK

ZACHARIE MAYANI

Docteur de l'Université de Paris
Former Pupil of the École du Louvre

TRANSLATED BY
PATRICK EVANS

Souvenir Press

First published by Arthaud, Paris,
as *Les Éstrusques Commencent à Parler*
First British edition published
1962 by Souvenir Press Ltd.,
34 Bloomsbury Street,
London, W.C.1, and simultaneously in
Canada by The Ryerson Press,
Toronto 2, Canada

Printed in Great Britain
by Richard Clay and Company, Ltd.,
Bungay, Suffolk

To Simon Shargo
in friendship

The combinatorial method has yielded the little
which was to be expected of it, and we must accept
the fact that it can now yield no more.

The comparative etymological method fell into
bad repute only because it was badly applied. In
the discovery of truth it is not enough that the
method should be, as far as can be seen, rigorous;
intuition and luck are needed too.

In any case, the right method in any search for
truth is the method which gets results.

ALFREDO TROMBETTI, *La lingua etrusca* (1928).

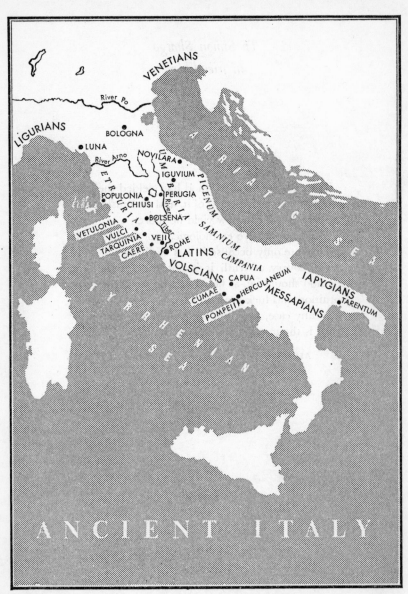

VENETIANS

River Po

LIGURIANS

BOLOGNA

LUNA

River Arno

NOVILARA

ETRURIA

IGUVIUM

UMBRIA

PICENUM

POPULONIA

PERUGIA

CHIUSI

BOLSENA

Tiber River

VETULONIA

VULCI

VEII

SAMNIUM

TARQUINIA

CAERE

ROME

LATINS

CAMPANIA

VOLSCIANS

CAPUA

IAPYGIANS

CUMAE

HERCULANEUM

MESSAPIANS

POMPEII

TARENTUM

ADRIATIC SEA

TYRRHENIAN SEA

ANCIENT ITALY

CONTENTS

7

PHOTOGRAPHS

FIGURES
Drawn by the author

ABBREVIATIONS AND PRONUNCIATION

ABBREVIATIONS

A—indicates an Etruscan word or phrase whose meaning is known for certain.

B—indicates an Etruscan word or phrase whose probable meaning is known.

CIE—Corpus of Etruscan Inscriptions.

CII—Corpus of Italic Inscriptions, A. Fabretti, 1867.

CIL—Corpus of Latin Inscriptions.

LM—the Book of the Mummy, *Liber Linteus;* text of Zagreb (Agram).

M.—Stuart E. Mann, *A Historical Albanian–English Dictionary*, 1948.

NRIE—Mario Buffa, *Nuova Raccolta di iscrizioni etrusche*, Florence, 1935.

P.—Massimo Pallottino, *Testimonia linguae etruscae* (a selection of Etruscan inscriptions and glosses), Florence, 1954.

SE—*Studi Etruschi*, Florence.

PRONUNCIATION

Etruscan letters:

c—k, g, q, (tz?) (tch?)
e—e, i
f—b, bh, ph, f
p—b, p
sc—sh
ś—sh (Fr. *ch*)
t—d, t
θ—hard th (as in "think"), soft th (as in "though"), dz, tz
u—u, o
χ—ch as in Scots "loch"

Albanian letters:

c—tz, ts
ç—tch
ë—like Fr. "mute" e
j—consonantal y, or like *ille* in Fr. *taille*, *feuille*
sh—sh (Fr. *ch*)
x—dz

PREFACE TO THE ENGLISH EDITION

WHEN I came to publish the results I had obtained in deciphering the Etruscan language by comparing it with Albanian (or, to be precise, with the Illyrian nucleus preserved in Albanian), I knew there were many readers who always found the history of any discovery almost as interesting as the discovery itself.

Consequently I gave an autobiographical, chronological turn to much of my exposition. I have tried to re-create an elusive intellectual process: the gradual forward movement of chaotic ideas, and the transition from these early gropings to a world of clarity and equilibrium.

But this treatment has caused a number of the arguments in favour of my method to be scattered here and there in the text and even, in some cases, relegated to the closing sections of the book. Moreover, I have not been concerned to quote all these arguments in full; I have frequently been content to give the author's name and the title of the work in which the argument was more amply set out. I said to myself: The battle of the Etruscan language has gone on so long, so vast a heap of abortive theories and unsuccessful translations has been accumulated, that any serious critic, especially if he be an Etruscologist, who wants first and foremost *to understand Etruscan*, will forgive me this omission. He will check my assertions by referring to the sources I mention—just as I myself, for the last thirty years, have gone gleaning wherever I could, on the alert for any helpful allusion, however slight, and grateful for the smallest pointer to the road ahead. He will then meet afresh the striking and indeed astounding similarities—phonetic and morphological as well as semantic—which I have pointed out between Albanian and Etruscan.

However, to satisfy any reader who is less interested in the story of the discovery than in the data on which the discovery is based, I will summarise the evidence briefly here, warning him at the same time that most of it will also be found in the main body of the book.

This study, then, is concerned with *Albanians, Illyrians, Etruscans and their respective languages.*

Tomaschek wrote:

Ptolemy, the celebrated geographer of the 2nd century B.C., mentions an Illyrian people of the province of Macedonia, east of

13

Dyrrachium (Durazzo). . . . Plainly this was the primitive nucleus of the present-day Albanians. . . . As these Albanians begin to be frequently mentioned only from about 1040 onwards, Mannert believed this observation of Ptolemy's to be an interpolation by a later hand. . . . But almost no falsifications of this kind are to be found in the text of Ptolemy, where the only glosses are explicitly designated as such, and in which a number of ancient ethnic names emerge again after a long lapse of time . . . (Pauly-Wissowa, 1893).

Moreover, the Albanian town of Skodra is mentioned already by Livy (end of 1st century B.C.), XLIV, 31.

Here, then, we have the ancient nucleus of the Albanian people. That people's language can only have been an Illyrian idiom (or Thraco-Illyrian).

Such authorities as Pauly-Wissowa, Sandfeld, N. Jokl, S. E. Mann, M. Lambertz, C. S. Coon and others confirm that the Albanians are of Illyrian stock (377–9).[1] According to Coon, no other stock has inhabited Epirus and Albania from ancient times onwards.

It is true that modern Albanian contains a large number of words borrowed from the languages which the Albanians have heard in the course of their history: Greek, Latin, Gothic, Slavonic, Turkish, etc. But the language's ancient nucleus constitutes an independent linguistic treasure. Gustav Meyer devoted himself to the task of perceiving and delimiting this "Erbfund", as he conceived it to be, an "inherited stock" *whose substance was Indo-European.* Similarly, N. Jokl and the other authors just mentioned have established the fact that this linguistic stock is an independent branch of the great family of Eastern Indo-European languages. It is true that G. Meyer was not concerned to establish the links connecting Albanian with Illyrian, the latter of which was known only in small fragments in his time. But Jokl, Walde-Pokorny, S. E. Mann and others have proved that G. Meyer narrowed down the "inherited stock" to an unnecessary degree and that in many cases he alleged a borrowing from Greek, Latin, Slavonic or elsewhere when in fact he was dealing unawares with a single, common, primitive source. I have therefore, in my scrutiny of Albanian words, constantly consulted the works of all these authors (61, etc.).

In his important work, *Studien zur albanischen Etymologie und Wortbildung* (1911), Jokl has shown the incontestable antiquity of the following Albanian words which, moreover, I have been able to use as a

---

[1] The figures in brackets refer to pages in the present book.

foundation in the deciphering of numerous Etruscan Texts, and as points of reference:

> *njöme* (tender), *blé* (to buy), *bageti* (cattle), *banoj* (to inhabit, dwell), *bote* (world), *det* (sea), *dukem* (to appear), *therras* (to call), *err* (dark), *gdhin* (to become light), *gjerë* (broad), *idhnak* (irascible, etc.), *kap* (to seize), *kem* (aromatic substance), *kreme* (feast), *ljumë* (happiness), *marr* (to take), *madh* (great, big), *ruaj* (to keep, guard), *shkoj* (to go), *tund* (to shake), *zi* (misfortune), etc.

To this list may be added *shokh, shov, shof,* "to see" (discussed by Walde-Pokorny), and many others.

Jokl also makes it clear that a number of terms in Albanian reflect the most primitive features of early economy. Thus Albanian *djathë*, "cheese", is connected with Sanskrit *dadhi*, "curdled milk", and thus with the very beginnings of cheese-making. Jokl proves that the Latin *grosa*, "plane", which is etymologically isolated in that language, derives from a word preserved in Albanian: *geruaj*, "to grate", and *gerrusë*, "plane". He also proves, contradicting Meyer, that Albanian *idhnak*, "choleric", a word which has been invaluable to me in the decipherment of four texts (204), is connected with Sanskrit *inddhe*, "inflamed".

Finally, it is above all to Jokl that we owe an important step towards the decipherment of Etruscan: it was he more than anyone else who established the *continuity* between Illyrian and Albanian and proved the presence of an ancient Illyrian *nucleus* in Albanian.

It had long been known that the Illyrian roots occurring in place-names and the names of ancient heroes: *mal*, "mountain", *bardh*, "white" (Sandfeld, 378), *dardë*, "pear" (whence Dardania), *delma*, "sheep" (whence Dalmatia), *brini*, "antlers" (whence Brindisi), etc., were preserved in Albanian unchanged in either form or meaning. Dozon had already recognised in *vend*, which is frequently found in ancient place-names, the Albanian *vend*, "place, country". But Jokl broke open the restricted circle of proper names by establishing that Illyrian *treg*, "market", whence *tregeste*, "Trieste", survived in Albanian *treg*, with the same meaning (170), and that Illyrian *Balizae* was perpetuated by Albanian *baltje*, "marsh" (379), etc. In 1950 C. S. Coon noted that the ancient Illyrian roots *plak*, "old", *madh*, "great", and *mal*, "mountain", were still current, unaltered, in Albanian (382). Jokl ended his study, *Albaner*, in these terms:

> The linguistic patrimony of the ancient Balkan peoples, both Illyrians and Thracians, is intimately bound up with the language of the Albanians.

(EBERT, *Reallexikon*, I)

To recapitulate: G. Meyer "crystallised" ancient Albanian but over-looked its connections with Illyrian. Jokl broadened these ancient foundations and built a bridge between Illyrian and Albanian. But although he brought out the striking phonetic resemblances between Albanian and Etruscan, he did not make any special study of Etruscan.

Following the lead of these great masters, I have succeeded, as far as my abilities allowed, in making a third, purely empirical, step in the same direction. Guided in the first place by intuition, I eventually approached the Etruscan enigma by the route traced by Ascoli, Trombetti, G. Meyer, Jokl, Thomopoulos, Buonamici, Devoto, S. E. Mann and Lambertz.

I placed ancient Albanian (the linguistic stock inherited from Illyrian) alongside Etruscan—whose camouflage, as it were, or disguises, I had first to penetrate,[1] and was then able to proceed systematically with the work of deciphering.

There was all the more reason for undertaking this work in that the path had been smoothed by the discoveries made by a constellation of scholars who, without having Albanian in mind, had detected the Indo-European character of Etruscan.

Pauli, O. Müller and Deecke recognised the Indo-European characteristics of Etruscan grammar (28).

Torp (in 1906) saw the connection between the Etruscan word *pevakh*, "beverage, beer", and the Indo-European root *pi*, "to drink" (63). Axel Persson found the same word in Albanian and Cretan. Bugge pointed out the Indo-European provenance of Etruscan *zivas*, "life". Hammarstrom-Justinien has proved that Etruscan *radh* is identical with Latin *ordo*, "order" (64). I, in turn, have succeeded in discovering several Etruscan words derved from that important root (181, 224, 330). And in the field of phonetics close links between Etruscan and Albanian have been pointed out by Moratti (in 1887), Jokl, Ribezzo, Devoto, Thomopoulos (66), Buonamici and others.

A total of several dozen inscriptions has now been deciphered. These texts, now that they are transparent to us, constitute so many windows through which we see the very thoughts, emotions, hopes, joys and sorrows of the Etruscans. And at the same time the exact meaning of a large number of Etruscan words has been established, words of which it had previously been possible to infer, *via* glosses and analogies, only the general implication. The reason why the month of May was called Ampiles in Etruscan is made clear by Albanian *amble*, "sweet". The

---

[1] The Etruscans wrote *pecse* for Pegasus, *utuse* for Odyssey, etc. By no means all the necessary inferences have yet been drawn from this characteristic. In addition, Etruscan words are often run into one another. It is only with the help of Albanian that I have been able to separate them.

word *gur, cur,* which is both Oscan (written on a slinger's missile) and Etruscan (included in a list of building materials), is explained by Albanian *gur,* "stone" (228). M. Pallottino conjectured that the Etruscan word *vrath,* also written on a slinger's missile, might mean "Kill!" or "Wound!", on the analogy of similar inscriptions in Latin. And Albanian answers: "*Vras* means 'Kill!'" Until now any unknown word in an Etruscan inscription has tended to be taken for a proper noun, and a number of imaginary individuals have been created in this way; a certain Pava-Tarkhies, for example.[1] But Albanian tells us that *pava* means "has seen"; hence "Tarkhies has seen" (97).

Thus we have learnt that the Etruscans were Illyrians and that their language was essentially Illyrian. In this there is nothing astonishing. That great family of peoples and tribes, those of Pannonia, Illyria itself, Dalmatia, Epirus and Albania, to whom in different degrees were related the Macedonians, Thracians, Phrygians, Lydians, some of the Cretans, the Philistines, etc., and whose destinies have been studied by Professor F. Altheim and other authors, is like a whole Atlantis emerging from oblivion. Its ramifications in ancient Italy have long been known. Many of the Etruscans' contemporaries and neighbours were Illyrians: the Venetians, Picenians, Iapygians, Messapians, Calabrians and others.

Illyrian tribes were on the move from the Balkans into Asia Minor as early as the 2nd millennium B.C. The Tursha, the Etruscans' ancestors, are heard of about 1200 B.C. Aeneas, the ally of the Trojans, subsequently annexed by the Roman imperial legend as a new founder of Rome, was, according to L. Malten, the personification of an Illyrian tribe, the Dardanians, some of whom settled in Sicily (cf. Strabo, XIII, 53). In Malten's view this tradition reflects an Illyrian migration parallel to that of the Etruscans, who came by way of Lemnos. We may note that Aeneas goes to live at Sagesta, a Sicilian town with an Illyrian name (cf. Tergeste, etc.). (Malten, "Aineias", *Archiv für Religionswiss.,* XXIX, 1931.)

But, to come back to our Etruscans and Albanians, these historical splendours, however colourful, are less impressive than the following extraordinary fact: the identity of *grammatical* forms (as seen in the article, in nouns and their declinations, in the past participles and passive voice of verbs, etc.) in Etruscan and Albanian, a feature to which I have devoted much attention (57, 86, 230, 256, 267, 451–3).

Ribezzo, in 1953, voiced his distress thus: "Redetermination by final *-u,* as in *atiu, tularu,* is an obscure point." Today, we can reply that it is

---

[1] Other such phantom characters are Tretu (194), Adhets (54) and Krankru (151).

obscure no longer; this *u* is the definite article in postposition exactly as in Albanian—as in, for example, Albanian *dushk-u*, "the oak". And to make matters perfect, this very same word *dushku* occurs in Etruscan (232).

To sum up, what was my working tool?

I had a certain "capital" of *ancient* Albanian words at my disposition at the outset of my deciphering. These were words already registered by other authors; they fall into the following categories:

(a) Albanian words from the "inherited stock" collected by G. Meyer (e.g., *anë*, "side", 72; *mui*, "to be able", 149; *miluar*, "sheep", 300; *turizë*, "muzzle", 166; *thom*, "to say", 348; *shterunë*, "heifer", 281, etc.).

(b) Albanian words added to this stock by Jokl, as quoted above; and those added by Coon, Pauli and Hammarstrom, also quoted.

(c) Albanian words which are sufficiently exact equivalents of Etruscan words preserved in glosses (*dru-hem*, "to fear", 99; *kuqerem*, "red", 174; *kreme*, "feast", 213, etc.).

(d) Albanian words equivalent to elements of known ancient languages. Such are *tre, mal, plak, madh*, which are found in Illyrian; *cenis*, "price, reward" (109), Scythian; *gjaset*, "fitting" (199), Osco-Umbrian; *balle*, "forehead, front" (396), Phrygian; *gardh*, "enclosure" (112), which has a counterpart in Hittite, etc.

The antiquity of some sixty Albanian words was thus assured. I was to meet them again in Etruscan. But, in turn, my deciphering of a considerable quantity of Etruscan inscriptions eventually imposed a wider conception of the Illyrian nucleus preserved in Albanian.

It is obvious that the sum of these words, and of the thirty or forty Etruscan words which were already known, and of my own contribution of over 200 newly deciphered Etruscan words, constitutes the first stage only. In many matters darkness still reigns. But how many joyful, vivid pictures have already risen out of this darkness to show us a daily life of which we had no inkling! At last the Etruscans are telling us candidly what they felt and thought.

Z. M.

PART ONE

Confronting the Etruscan Problem

INTRODUCTION

WHAT is the best way of presenting a discovery which, on the face of it, may seem improbable: the successful deciphering of a large number of Etruscan words and inscriptions?

In this book I shall have to bring forward much that is new; and, because of the very nature of the subject, this new material at once upsets established theories and, on occasion, poses exciting but tantalising problems.

I shall therefore not spend too much time in reviewing what has already been written, by competent authors, about the Etruscans. The history of the people, and their art and religion, have been closely studied for years past, so far as such studies were possible without an understanding of the language. Moreover, the language was not a completely closed book. On the one hand, Greek and Roman authors have preserved a few fragments of it. Thus it was known that, for example, *aïs, eis*, meant "god", and *aisar, eiser*, "gods"; the names of several Etruscan deities were known too, the names of some of the months and so on. And, on the other hand, a comparison of epitaphs, Etruscan and Roman, enabled Pauli and other scholars to deduce the meaning of several words: *clan*, "son"; *clenar*, "sons"; *avil*, "year"; *ril*, "age"; *svalce*, "lived"; *suθi (suthi)*, "tomb", etc. But the words deciphered in this way were few.

Etruscan texts look easy to read, because the Etruscan alphabet is the same as the Greek. Nevertheless, an almost total darkness enveloped the meanings of the words found on sarcophagi, the walls of tombs and objects fashioned as votive offerings to the gods, such as statuettes, cups and vases. The same was true of the twelve short chapters of the only Etruscan "book" which we possess, the famous text written on the linen bandages wound round the mummy of an Etruscan woman, a mummy now preserved in the Museum at Zagreb (Agram).

It is therefore to these texts, till now obscure, that the present work is devoted. Even today, they have not all been elucidated with equal success. The translation of some fragments is correct beyond dispute; of others, no more than probably correct. Accordingly, each word or text deciphered will be labelled with a letter, A or B. Category A will comprise those whose meaning is certain; category B, those whose meaning seems very likely to be right. The meaning of any words or phrases which have no letter appended to them is merely conjectural. Obviously, it has been the accumulation of A and B which has led me to publish the results of my work; and, with this publication, the Etruscans' two thousand years of silence are broken at last. Those colourless figures who at one time glided dumbly before our gaze now pause and let us hear them speaking.

What they will say is not very like the contents of most ancient inscriptions. We shall not be listening-in to the orders of kings or historic records of victories—on the contrary, we shall be surprising Etruscan *man* in his daily life, in peace or war, in temple or tavern, in his kitchen or in a doctor's consulting room; a normal Etruscan, a man like ourselves, someone who is very close to us, and endowed with that astonishing vitality which the works of his people's art have long caused us to expect. All our documents will be human ones, sometimes of a heart-stirring spontaneity.

Of course, in our progress we shall encounter here a stumbling-block and there a gap, which I shall neither conceal nor minimise; my object being not merely to brandish the trophies of a fantastic hunt but also to admit, in all candour, my own inadequacy and the hesitations, meanderings and false trails which, so often, have led me astray and after which I have had to "go back to the start". Nor shall I gloss over the inevitably unforeseeable character of the texts to be deciphered. I would have infinitely preferred to entrench myself safely in a single category of inscriptions, any little group which I could have treated methodically and of which I could have produced a clear, exhaustive rendering! Instead, I have had to rescue the truth little by little from the shadows, clutching now at an intuition, an analogy or some remembered allusion, now at a suspicion or a chance resemblance.

Four years ago I found myself in the heart of this Etruscan jungle, of which, as it were, all the previous surveys and maps, however imposing, had proved false. But I had an axe in my hand: a single, dawning intuition. I wanted to make a straight, unencumbered trail. So I hacked away as if for dear life. But my progress through the underbrush went zigzagging about in the most lamentable fashion, sometimes making a detour round a pitfall, sometimes crawling and sometimes jumping as I avoided one danger after another.

If only the results of the battle were in every case clear and convincing! I cannot say they are. No doubt I have contributed my own share to the large collection of ridiculous blunders with which, as we shall see, the path of Etruscology is strewn. But could one have hoped for better? Do you expect to see the dead wake to life in their beautiful sculptured sarcophagi and the soothsayers resume their hieratic gestures, in a perfectly orderly fashion, without an inconsistency or contradiction anywhere, and with every word rescued from the realm of inarticulate sound?

No; inevitably, mistakes will still occur. And, in any case, there is no question of wounded pride. At every frontier post of Etruscology a large notice ought to be erected: "Abandon pride, all ye who enter here." What would be really ridiculous would be to hope to solve the problem by a wave of the wand; to look for a key which would open every door and make everything clear.

And yet there is a key; I have recently found it; it is highly effective, and the purpose of my book is to place it in the hands of every student of things Etruscan. Nevertheless, the process of reconstructing a language forgotten from the beginning of the Christian era is going to demand a long struggle, careful discernment and constant perseverance. Has any branch of knowledge been exempt from mishaps and disappointments in its early stages? Etruscology merely follows the general rule.

I must pause here to ask a question: is the reader really familiar with the main difficulties involved in deciphering Etruscan texts? Some of these difficulties are hardly ever mentioned. If you read books or articles which purport to convey what we know about the Etruscans to the general public you will often see the problem of decipherment relegated to a shadowy, marginal position. The author who, but a moment before, was so copious and lively, painting for us with such dash and brilliance his picture of Etruscan civilisation, appears embarrassed as soon as he has to deal with the language. He gives a little cough, assumes an air of mystery and gestures to us to keep our voices down, walk on tiptoe and not linger over this delicate point, as if we were outside the room of someone gravely ill, who must not be disturbed.

The problem of decipherment has, in fact, become the sensitive spot in Etruscan studies. Not only has Etruscan been compared with various other languages, ancient and modern, in the hope of unravelling its secrets, but in vain; there are special technical difficulties which confuse the issue.

Here are some of them:

(1) In many cases we do not know where a word begins or ends. We see a group of letters and are unable to say whether it makes a word, or two shorter words, or a whole sentence. To quote one example, a scene engraved on a looking-glass shows, among other things, a young

FIG. 1. pava tarχies, "Tarχies (the augur) has seen"

soothsayer examining the liver, the traditional seat of omens. The inscription says: *pavatarχies*. *Tarχies* having been recognised as Tarquin, the whole has been interpreted as a new proper noun, *Pava-Tarχies*. But I have succeeded in proving that *pava* means "has seen", as will appear later. We thus have a sentence: "*Tarχies* has seen." Since the legend the artist was dealing with was well known, he expressed himself briefly (Fig. 1).

(2) The alphabet used by the Etruscans was only borrowed, and although they modified it here and there, it did not correspond satisfactorily to the phonetics of their speech. That is why they had recourse to different letters to express the same sounds. The scribes took little trouble to adhere to a single system. They used *p* to express *p*, *b* or *bh*; their *c* stands for *k*, *g*, *q*, *tz* or *tch*. The vowel *u* can mean *o* as well as *u*. And *v* is often used for *u*.

(3) Lastly, and still confining ourselves to the immediate obstacles, the Etruscans, especially in the last centuries before the Christian era, took to imitating a vexatious habit of the Semites, that of leaving out certain vowels when writing. In Phoenician, for example, the word *malkat* (queen) is written *mlkt* and the missing parts have to be guessed. Similarly, the Etruscans wrote *Elχsntre* instead of Alexander. This offers no difficulties when the word is a known proper name, but at other times it produces a stumbling-block.

The result is that we often do not know the exact pronunciation of an Etruscan word. On meeting it we have to ask two questions: Is this word complete or abbreviated? Do its consonants and vowels express it exactly or only approximately?

Perhaps I shall be told that the technical difficulties enumerated here are of slight importance beside the main fact, namely that Etruscan is a unique linguistic "island" in that no analogy can be established between it and any other known language; a splendid isolation which, if real, must cause all our attempts at deciphering it to be frustrated.

I am not of this opinion, for reasons soon to be made clear. But here meanwhile is a miniature demonstration of the difficulties. We possess an inscription: *put*. The word is English; but the man who wrote it used a phonetic script so that for *through*, for example, he always wrote *thru*. But in addition to this he used *p* for *b* as well as *p*; and *u* for *u* or *o* or *oa* or *oo*; and *t* for either *t* or *d*.

Unless you have some external clue to guide you there is no hope of getting the solution. You can interpret *put* as *put*; but it might equally well be *but*, *boot*, *boat* or *bode*. You are now in the position of an Etruscologist.

I have said that Etruscan texts look easy to read. You can see that this appearance is often dangerously misleading. If it were not so we would not have been faced with a poignant spectacle, that of an incomprehensible, hermetically sealed language, at the heart of our old European civilisation, which has been the object of such masterly studies, baffling the scholars of every country for the last three centuries.

The problem would be less painful if it concerned the dialect of some obscure tribe. But the language in question was that of a vigorous population, the "twelve peoples of Etruria", tireless cultivators, founders of cities, bold navigators, deft craftsmen; soldiers, traders, builders of temples, dykes and forts. They drained their marshes, canalised the Po, planted vines, worked in metals. It was they who transformed the hamlet of Rome into a fortress where the Roman shepherds, always on the alert to pillage any Greek or Etruscan heavy wagon which ventured near their boundaries, were finally initiated into urban life and the benefits of organised society.

This was the language which gave us a number of terms still in use in our daily life: *fenêtre*, lantern, cistern, tavern, ceremony, person, letter, etc. It was the Etruscans who laid the foundations of religious and political organisation in Italy, of Roman military organisation, and of art, sculpture and the theatre as the Romans knew them. It was the Etruscans who gave a start to literary and scientific endeavour in Italy, a role in which they were succeeded only by the new masters of mankind, the Greeks, whose intellectual supremacy the Etruscans unreservedly admitted.

What methods were used in attempting to recover this language whose meaning was lost but whose vitality could still somehow be felt? The history of Etruscan studies begins with a crime of passion. In the 15th century, having unearthed a few Etruscan inscriptions, a Dominican, Annio de Viterbo, decided that it must be possible to interpret them with the aid of Hebrew, which he believed to be the source of all other languages. To ensure the triumph of his own views, this enthusiast inscribed Hebrew words, in Etruscan letters, on tablets, and buried these tablets in a place where genuine inscriptions had previously been found. Luckily for us, this species of imitative magic was not adopted by other scholars of his time. Moreover, Etruscan studies had acquired erudite status long before the 15th century; various ancient writers had discussed the language and origins of the Etruscans. One of the most eminent Etruscologists of all ages, the emperor Claudius (1st century A.D.), devoted to this subject a work in twenty volumes which was studied in the Library of Alexandria; but unfortunately the whole of it has disappeared. What remains to us is such testimonies as, for example, that of the Greek historian Denys of Halicarnassus (1st century B.C.) on the unique nature of the Etruscan language. The Etruscans, he declares, differ from all other peoples in their language and their customs. It is curious to observe to what an extent this gratuitous assertion has bedevilled the progress of modern Etruscology.

Since the 15th century many solutions to the problem have been propounded. In turn, the origin of the Etruscans has been said to be American, Semitic, Celtic, Slav, Ugro-Finnish, Armenian, Berber and even Sumerian. J. Martha, towards the close of the last century, wrote: "They have been turned into Celts, Semites . . . Thraco-Illyrians, Hittites. . . . There can be no certainty till we have the key to the language. . . ."

Trombetti regarded Etruscan as a Mediterranean language, intermediate between the Basque–Caucasian and Indo-European groups. In 1940 the situation was summarised by M. Renard in these terms: "The answer has been sought in vain in almost every language on the globe, from Finnish to Coptic and from Basque to Japanese."

As the more outlandish conjectures gradually fell away, the scale began, during the 19th century, to tilt in favour of an Indo-European character for the Etruscan language. However, the pioneers of this tendency had at their disposal neither proven epigraphic results nor methods of established efficacy. Hence it was possible for deciphering to produce some very odd twists in the hands of Corssen. This eminent philologist, who, it must be admitted, discovered a number of interesting things, was apt to seize on an Etruscan word which bore some resemblance to a Greek or Latin word and to conclude, there and then, that the two were identical. Thus his pen briskly transformed the Etruscan θaura, "tomb, grave", into a bull (taurus) in prime condition for the corrida. Zilc, which means an Etruscan magistrate, was taken for silex (flint). As several Etruscan sarcophagi or funerary urns are inscribed with a stock formula: (So-and-so) . . . zilc . . . avils . . . (aged so-and-so many years) lupu (died), Corssen took avils for a proper noun and assimilated lupu to the Greek root meaning "cut, carve" (whence "glyptic"), and translated the formula: "In stone . . . Avils carved . . ."—What did he carve? Well, a sarcophagus, of course. Fine fellows, these Etruscans! said Corssen to himself. On their sarcophagi they put not only the name of the deceased but the sculptor's name too. What respect for craftsmanship!

Meanwhile, on another sarcophagus, he would find another Avils: avils maχs semfalχls (i.e., "died, aged 71 years"), and would thereupon take this for another sculptor, by name Avils Maχs. But then along came a third Avils, and a fourth; a whole brood of Avils. Not a single sarcophagus but had this name on it! The name had the dickens of an attraction for these sculptors. So they must have been a powerful family, Corssen concluded, a highly respected clan with many branches. Think what you please of their art, but it must at all events be noted that their names occur side by side with those of nobles buried in the most aristocratic vaults in Perugia and Volsinia. More than twenty of these accredited sculptors in Southern Etruria, but only six in Northern. . . .

And these fruitful cogitations were followed by a masterly discourse on the probable organisation of the workshops of those master-craftsmen, proud of their art, handing on the torch from father to son. . . .

And do you think that considerable progress must have been made since 1875? Not much, actually; we are still at the foot of the mountain. And, in any case, a heavy plea in extenuation can be entered on Corssen's behalf: in his day there were still several Indo-European languages, such as Hittite, which were completely unknown.

A method of quite a different order was followed by such great philologists as O. Müller, Pauli, Deecke and others, who, after making a minute analysis of certain grammatical forms displayed by Etruscan (final *a* as one of the signs denoting the feminine; final *s* as one sign of the genitive; the suffix *-ce* for verbs in the past: *zilaχce*, "he administered", etc.), concluded that Etruscan belonged to the great Indo-European family of languages. Corssen added his own deduction that it belonged to the Italic branch of that family. But an article thirty-nine pages long, by Deecke, sufficed, according to M. Pallottino, to overthrow "like a house of cards" the edifice built up by Corssen.

So far, so clear; but the matter did not end there. If Deecke began by doubting that Etruscan was Indo-European in character he subsequently swung right round and agreed that it was. He re-read, revised and extended Otto Müller's excellent work, *The Etruscans* (1877), whose orientation in that direction is quite definite. No other construction can be placed on the final conclusion of Müller and Deecke: "This [i.e., the Etruscan] people belonged to the Greek family of peoples, though it was certainly an outlying member of that family."

Deecke's position became ever more firmly fixed in this quarter. In his *Forschungen und Studien* (Studies and Researches), Vol. II (1882), he mentions the suffix *a* of the feminine, and adds: "*Dies ist specifisch indogermanisch.*"

In 1952, however, MM. Meillet and Cohen observed that Etruscan could "not so far be assimilated to any linguistic family". In 1942, noting the failure of all attempts to discover a relationship between Etruscan, on the one hand, and, on the other, the Italic dialects, and Greek, Armenian, Basque, the Caucasian and Ugro-Finnish languages and even Dravidian, M. Pallottino had given a wider and more detailed development to a formula first suggested by Buonamici. According to Pallottino, Etruscan was a composite language, essentially non-Indo-Germanic; Tyrrhenian or pre-Hellenic in origin, from somewhere in the Aegean region; it had been influenced, during its formation, by an autochthonous substratum, and could also be shown to have received a powerful infusion of Indo-Germanic elements. The author's conclusion was that the problem of Etruscan origins was less important than that of the growth and shaping of the Etruscan people, which, as such, first became a distinct entity in Italy itself.

In the last few decades special attention has been paid to the morphology of Etruscan: verbs, the accidence of nouns, the evolution of vowel-sounds, and so on have been scrutinised, but most of this work has been done blindfold; only in a very few cases could any meaning be assigned to the enigmatic words which scholars handled and classified in accordance with purely external indications. Consequently, nothing but hypothetical solutions could be put forward where the origin and development of the Etruscan people were concerned.

Equally dubious was the lively debate dividing Etruscan students into two opposite camps, one continuing the search for a language similar to Etruscan (the comparative method), the other maintaining that such a language probably did not exist and that the only hope lay in the "combinatorial" method, the analysis and comparison of what could be deduced from Etruscan alone. The second of these courses was that chosen by M. Pallottino, according to whom the Etruscan people and language were produced by conditions which appeared in Italy during the 2nd millennium B.C., and which could not have arisen elsewhere.

In view of the fact that the combinatorial method, which had set up its flag on the ruins of the comparative method, was equally disappointing where deciphering was concerned, several researchers began to take a somewhat gloomy view of the situation.

F. Messerschmidt observed in 1935: "The state of the problem is more confused than formerly. The philological, historical and archaeological material so far discovered is insufficient to provide a solution."

In a courageous article, "A che punto siamo con la interpretazione dell'etrusco", published in the important review *Studi Etruschi* (1953), edited by M. Pallottino, F. Ribezzo sent up a distress signal:

> According to Eva Fiesel, the contribution made by the First International Conference on Etruscology is confined to the elucidation of a single word (*tular*, "boundaries, limits"). . . . Does this represent a general impasse? (P. 105.)
>
> In Etruscan . . . logical links are implied rather than expressed; anyone who tries to supply them from extraneous sources, in a language whose meaning is unknown, is taking big risks. (P. 108.)
>
> Progress to date has been discouraging. The studies made by Etruscologists of the generations of Bugge, Lattes, Torp and Trombetti belong to philology, glossology and etymology rather than to Etruscology. (P. 110.)
>
> It has to be admitted that, as yet, the interpretation of texts has consisted mainly of interpreting inscriptions . . . and therefore of lexicology, the recognition of words. . . . This was the task which gave rise to the combinatorial method.

But, by way of a final titbit, the author gives us this exhortation:

> It is only in this way—by slowly unravelling words, and the elements of their roots, and grammatical categories, and syntactical expressions—that the Sphinx can be forced to give up its secret.

But had not the same ideas been expressed, with even greater frankness, by M. Trombetti, in 1928?

> *Si e girato attorno alla fortezza senza tentare de penetrarvi* . . . This [i.e., the combinatorial] method has yielded the little which was to be expected of it, and we must accept the fact that it can now yield no more. It was already recognised by Skutsch that "despite the acquisition of new materials the combinatorial possibilities, or at least the easier ones, are exhausted". (*La lingua etrusca*, p. viii.)

To continue this rapid review, here is the testimony of M. R. Bloch, dated 1956:

> The combinatorial method, even when applied with the greatest caution and ingenuity, has not yet thrown any real light on words designating ideas. . . . The translation of texts is still the weak point. . . . (*Le Mystère Étrusque*, pp. 77–8.)

Finally, M. Pallottino, in his own book *The Etruscans*, referring to comparatively lengthy texts, such as the Book of the Mummy or the Tile of Capua, has made the straightforward admission that—

in this field the combinatorial method, taken all in all, has produced inconclusive results.

It is to this widespread but comprehensible feeling of disappointment that, ultimately, I attribute a curious phenomenon, tragicomical more than anything else, which has become evident of recent years not so much in the study of the Etruscan language (which, for the moment, we shall continue to leave untroubled in its monumental, marmoreal stillness), but, rather, on the frontiers of that study.

I am thinking of the defensive revolt which has taken place against the "Etruscomaniacs", the enthusiastic amateurs who offer their kind help to Etruscan studies by writing things some of which, it must be owned, are decidedly comic.

M. Pallottino devotes several pages of his book *The Etruscans* to these disturbers of public order, but deals with them fairly indulgently. He notes that, as early as 1936, a rapid succession of ephemeral "discoveries" made by amateurs had ended by actually misleading those who were interested in Etruscan; to such an extent, indeed, that sceptics began regarding the Etruscan problem as the chosen playground of cranks, the comedy sector of linguistic studies. The author goes on to deplore the activities of those who, without possessing the necessary training for the task, think they have discovered the solution to the problem; and he pays homage to the hard and painstaking work of those scholars to whom we owe the slow but real progress which Etruscology has made during the last two centuries.

The same opinion is expressed by M. R. Bloch, in his short book which gives an outline of the Etruscan problem:

All attempts to throw light on Etruscan by comparing it with a known language have, so far, failed lamentably, and these failures, many of which have been caused by a lack of linguistic training and the naïve pretensions of amateurs dazzled by the seeming success of their own essays in translation, have done little more than to attract unmerited scorn from a few intelligent people. (*Les Étrusques*, 1954, p. 59.)

In short, amateurs and cranks are blamed for their baneful success in misleading the public and surrounding the subject with confusion and discredit. But are things really as bad as that?

It all depends on the view you hold of the public. If you think of it as a heroine in the style of *Uncle Tom's Cabin*, a languorous lady feebly reclining on a sofa and succumbing under the weight of her imaginary ailments, and constantly reproaching her slaves with their neglect of her, then, indeed, it will be easy to demoralise the public and divert its capricious attention from Etruscan problems.

But for my own part I see the public in a different light. I believe there are plenty of educated people who, without trying to become Etruscan specialists, attentively read press accounts of discoveries in Ancient Etruria, go to exhibitions of Etruscan art, admire its master-pieces and are delighted whenever they get a chance of increasing their knowledge in this field. Certainly they must be amused to follow, in the newspapers, any account of an unsuccessful attempt at deciphering. What is less certain is that these failures have devastating emotional effects or provoke any special animosity.

It seems to me that the touchy susceptibilities of Etruscologists are to be explained by the atmsophere of gloom which, in recent years, has come to surround everything Etruscan. Almost every article or mono-graph devoted to the Etruscan riddle has the word "gloomy" pro-minently displayed. The Etruscans loved good food and drink, but their outlook is supposed to have been gloomy. Etruscan religion was gloomy. Inevitably, then, their idea of the next world, with its population of demons, must have been gloomier still! This is as realistic as to imagine that, in our own times, the window displays of undertakers are decorated with pin-up girls and that funerals are conducted to the sound of jazz.

I am not trying to make out that gloomy elements had no place in the Etruscan conception of life. The Etruscans practised human sacrifice (though only rarely; and in any case so did the contemporary Greeks and Romans); they made use of blood (almost invariably animal blood) in libations for the dead; and they portrayed demons, who were the prototype of the medieval devil. None of this can be gainsaid, but, in compensation, this extraordinary people felicitously counterbalanced their dark side through their exuberance and love of life, and indeed sensuality.

My own belief is rather that Etruscologists, discouraged in some degree by the intractable resistance which their subject offers to research, have been overcome by gloomy feelings themselves and have then projected those feelings on to the Etruscans.

There is, moreover, a psychological factor at work which influences us without our being aware of it. An archaeologist comes to love the ancient civilisation, country and people which he is studying; so much so that he identifies himself with that people and its loves and hates and sorrows. He becomes a Greek of the 5th century B.C., or an Egyptian of the 2nd millennium B.C., with all the virtues and vices of the Greeks or the Egyptians. I had occasion to muse on this phenomenon when I was studying the problem of the Hyksos invasion of Egypt (18th century B.C.). Among the contributions of these alien conquerors to the empire of the Pharaohs were bronze, horses, the wheel and the chariot, and the seeds of a primitive monotheism. But for Mr ——, an eminent Egyptologist, the one hundred and thirty years of their dominion were a kind of temporary misunderstanding, a bad moment which was quickly over and to which it would be ridiculous to attach any importance. Egypt, for that learned man, was something so grandiose and radiant that these interlopers were no more than a fly which settles on a beautiful face and is immediately brushed off.

"The Hyksos? No such people ever existed."

"But what about the invasion of Egypt?"

"Well, perhaps, yes. But it was the Egyptians themselves who did it."

"But how on earth——?"

"The Egyptians of the Delta, of course!"

Tendencies of this sort have frequently manifested themselves in archaeology. Has it not been written that the Israelites' exodus from Egypt was not "historically attested", whereas that of the Philistines was an incontrovertible historical fact? Those who put the Philistines into the Exodus story, instead of the Hebrews, forgot that the Philistines were never reduced to slavery, and, moreover, that the Egyptian borderlands of Palestine were actually ceded to them by the Pharaohs.

The result of continuing this line of reasoning would be to deny that any people ever migrated anywhere. The Norman invasion of England, for example, would be a mere fable; the fact was that the English dandies of that day, already impressed by Paris fashions, sent an urgent message across the Channel and imported a certain Guy the Tailor, who happened to be a Norman. . . .

However that may be, I fear that Etruscologists may, in their turn, have become imbued with the mentality of the ancient Italic people whom they study. In which case they would interpret the stubborn resistance of the Etruscan citadel as an infallible sign of the anger of the gods. What, then, must be done? Well, of course, that anger must be appeased. But how? In the time-honoured way: by sacrifice. Of what? Everyone knows what to sacrifice, and has done ever since Neolithic times: a stranger, an interloper. However, burning is no longer the fashion, so the best that can be done is to issue a communiqué:

The Regular Etruscological Army, which has been besieging the Etruscan fortress for the last three centuries, hereby gives warning

B

that if any unattached sharpshooters not embodied in the said Army, should try to insinuate themselves into its ranks, they will be rigorously excluded and will be conducted back to the academic disciplines from which, respectively, they set out.

One word more in favour of free discussion. A negative attitude towards the amateurs would have been comprehensible enough if they had had any monopoly of ineffectual deciphering. Unfortunately this is not the case. There have been many times when the same ill fortune has pursued eminent Etruscologists, well versed in the subject. We have seen how things went with Corssen. J. Martha, who wrote a well-documented contribution on Etruscan art for the Dictionary of Daremberg-Saglio, was an established expert; yet his translation of the Book of the Mummy is a confection which bears no relation whatsoever to the Etruscan text. It would be easy to extend the list. And is it to be thought that so many failures, all the more serious in that they were the work of accredited scholars and the result of long and careful study, have neither led the public astray nor brought Etruscology into disrepute?

Finally, on the subject of the public's reactions, I may perhaps be allowed to mention my own experience. It is limited, because I was working on my own and was being careful to avoid making any premature confidences of my results. Nevertheless, over those four years, I told several people of my acquaintance what was the subject, though no more, of my investigations. All these individuals expressed interest, but did not fail to emphasise the difficulties of such an undertaking. Some warmly encouraged me to publish my early findings, considering that even if I did not actually manage to decipher anything, my remarks would at least be judicious enough to contribute to the progress of Etruscan studies. Others, again, showed such enthusiasm at the prospect of my deciphering even *one* hitherto undeciphered Etruscan word, let alone two or three words, that I was excited and felt encouraged to persevere in my labours.

But there were shadows in the picture, too. I called on the editorial secretary of a Parisian weekly to suggest that I write an article on Oriental archaeology. I took the occasion of showing him my latest book. The title seemed to interest him. We chatted for a little while; then I got up, and he walked a few steps with me towards the door to show me out. He was a thoughtful, intelligent young man, with excellent manners. At this moment I told him point-blank that I was working at present on the deciphering of an Etruscan text. The result was electrifying. He tottered as if I had punched him on the jaw. For a fraction of a second the earth seemed to tremble beneath his feet; he had to lean against the mantelpiece. His whole torso pivoted at the waist, and his head, as it pointed towards me, described a perfect circle, as happens to someone swallowing down a large pill. This rapid circular movement enabled him to suppress a burst of uproarious laughter which was threatening to break him in two. I watched him with a poker face. Finally, raising his head like a swimmer coming up after a dive, he contented himself with saying: "Ah! So you're working on Etruscan!"

That "Ah!" was worth hearing; it contained a whole symphony of compassionate understanding. It certainly did not imply that I was on a straight line *AB*, where the point *A* represented a seeker of the philosophical stone (myself), and the point *B*, a gentleman handing out blank cheques at regular intervals. Nobody who had not written a *History of Antiquity* in three volumes, or who was not at least the occupier of a professorial chair, could possibly be allowed to mention Etruscan deciphering in the young man's presence. Its being mentioned by an ordinary person, one, moreover, who wanted to place a short article in his journal, was obviously a shock. I understood. I took no offence. Clearly, I was engaged in dangerous work.

The conclusion I have reached is that the fund of public sympathy towards Etruscan studies is by no means exhausted. The amateurs can do no more harm to the patient, detailed work of professional Etruscan scholars than they can in other fields of knowledge. Effervescence of the sort they provoke from time to time is the daily bread of 20th-century man. Archaeologists, in any case, ought to remember what a milestone in the study of antiquity was set up by an amateur: Schliemann, the first man to conceive the idea of excavating historic sites. Till then, the only digging to have been done was in libraries and archives.

However, students of Etruria will feel stronger, better immunised against their real or supposed vexations, as soon as the deciphering of the language proceeds along a healthier and more spacious road than hitherto. They will then be able to escape at last from the vicious circle in which one feels them to be wearing themselves out at present. It is with this purpose in mind that I am publishing my own contribution in the following pages.

If the public's attitude towards Etruscan really were one of irritable suspicion, I should have had to surround myself with precautions before exhibiting the gains I have made in decipherment. I would have had to move softly, taking the utmost care to avoid giving offence by contradicting existing views; above all, I should have had to avoid using so compromising a word as "adventure", even in its noblest sense—as we speak, for example, of Columbus's adventure.

I trust the reader does not expect me to indulge in any such petty hypocrisies.

For I have indeed enjoyed a wonderful adventure. And now the reader shall enjoy it with me.

I

DECIPHERING

1. TOWARDS DISCOVERY

IT happened in 1932 or perhaps 1933. I was an archaeological student in Paris, and did my reading at the Bibliothèque Mazarine.

A summer day. Framed in the tall windows which gave on to the Seine there appeared an incredible landscape by Bonnard, streaming with gold and blue. Its warm shimmerings were beginning to come between my eyes and my open book. My attention was disarmed; I began musing.

Not far from me, at the big table in the middle of the room, was a gentleman I did not know, possibly a professor; he had pince-nez, a moustache and a little beard and was studying a book with startling illustrations. I could no more refrain from casting a furtive glance in his direction than one can from reading an open newspaper over one's neighbour's shoulder in the subway train. He noticed my wondering gaze and smiled at me. I made bold to ask, "Is that Etruscan?" He made a gesture in the affirmative. Like me, he was taking a moment's relaxation. Almost without meaning to, I added, "What *is* Etruscan?"

You would have said my neighbour had been waiting for just this question. He seized a scrap of drawing-paper and a pencil; three minutes later he was holding out the paper, which was now covered with some twenty Etruscan words each accompanied by its meaning in French. He had laid them out in firm, bold writing, without needing to stop and think, as if they were always in the forefront of his mind. "Here you are," he said, "this is all that is known on the subject."

I never saw him again or found out who he was. But I still have the paper.

I was studying the Ancient East, and Etruscan was no part of my concerns. But at odd moments, turning the pages of a volume of an encyclopaedia, or a learned periodical, I strayed briefly into the company of the Etruscans. But I had other things to think about, and from one occasion to the next I almost forgot what I had read on the subject.

One day, however, I went through Skutsch's great article in Pauly-Wissowa's encyclopaedia, a sober, substantial summary, still useful today, of the Etruscan problem. I retained, though vaguely, the statement that Etruscan could not be deciphered by way of any other language; but this made no impression on me. Moreover, I took no notes on the article. I cannot now understand why it was that, finding myself confronted one day by the text of the Book of the Mummy, I copied it out, from the first word to the last, in a separate notebook. I was particularly struck by words which looked like Hebrew: *caveθ* was so very like *kaved*, "the liver"; and then *enaś*—could this mean "man"? It was peculiar. In the course of their maritime expansion, surely the Etruscans, who for generations and indeed centuries were allies of the Carthaginians, must have borrowed a few words from them, a few nautical terms, some phrase or other?[1]

Was I holding (I wondered) the end of Ariadne's thread? No, these fragmentary clues were, rather, bits of gossamer floating in the air and would disappear without trace.

Months passed, and years. In my rare leisure moments I would take down the Etruscan Book of the Dead from the out-of-the-way corner in which I kept it, and plunge into a perusal as fascinating as it was disappointing. It never occurred to me to wonder why I did this.

The pleasure I got from it was a strange one, mixed with melancholy. The experience was that of suddenly detaching oneself from the world of reality, from everything, and diving into a dream at once soothing and frightful. It was like walking in the streets of a city which had never been built, touching the walls of houses which had never been made of stone—or even papier mâché, and watching people pass of whose features, and even of whose faces, one could get not a glimpse; and hearing litanies, prayers and chants whose rapid rhythms one could feel, but not a sound of which one could hear.

These people were going about their business all round me, yet were unaware of my presence. They walked or ran straight through me as if I had not been there. In this world of ghosts I myself was turning into a ghost.

I had a vague expectation that, one day, I would feel something drawing me closer to that hidden life whose heart had never stopped beating; but I entertained no hopes of getting results by following such attempts at deciphering as had so far been made and the arguments to which they had given rise.

[1] It may be noted in passing that I later came on the *Albanian* word, possibly of ancient origin, *anije*, "ship" (M. 8), which is identical with *aniyah*, at once the Hebrew and the Phoenician word for "ship". G. Meyer, indeed, considers *anije* to be a loanword from Hebrew. Phoenician seems more likely. However, it is not yet established whether the word occurs in any Etruscan text.

As soon as I shut the notebook I came back to reality. But, at night, whole sentences would go on rolling through my head, like so many waves of mocking absurdity:

> ceia hia etnam ciz . . . vacl aisvale . . . cisum pute tul θans haθec
> repinec . . . θuflθaś . . aperucen . . . satiriasaχiia . . .
> vacl lunasie . . .

Lunar landscapes!

About 1950 I returned to Paris after a long absence. I was preparing to publish my researches on the Hyksos, which, however, did not appear until 1956. In leisure moments I was able to resume an old amusement of mine: idling along the quays and poking about in the booksellers' boxes there. Without going so far as to imitate one o Murger's heroes, whose coat had an enormous pocket which was set aside for foreign languages, I did not fail to bring home with me from time to time some thoroughly useless book. It was in this way that I acquired a little Albanian–German dictionary by L. Arbanas. I had really no need of it. I knew almost nothing of Albania and had no intention of going there, or of studying any of the Balkan languages. Leafing my way through this little book, I merely noted the presence of a few Slav roots encrusted in an unaccustomed context. The book was cheap, anyway. Once home, I thrust it away among others of its kind, and for a long time never thought of opening it again.

My studies had drawn me towards the ancient steppes of Euro-Asia, from which the first waves of Indo-European migration had started. It was to these waves that I attributed the emergence of the Hyksos. But the steppes forced me to concern myself with the Scythians. And so, in 1956, I embarked on a new series of researches, devoted exclusively to that curious group of peoples, who were contemporary with the Etruscans. It thus came about that my attention was gradually diverted from the Ancient East to Eastern Europe.

One point, among others, was of special interest to me: the remains of the Scythian language. Copious material was to hand on this subject in two bulky volumes published in German by a Russian professor with a French name, Bonnel.[1]

But, between the Hyksos and the Scythians, I needed a holiday.

I had a long, wearisome task in front of me. I decided that before submitting my neck to the yoke I would indulge in a short interlude, uncontaminated by any utilitarian purpose: a holiday among the Etruscans. I began rereading the works which gave an outline of the

[1] E. Bonnell, *Beiträge zur Alterthumskunde Russlands*, St Petersburg, 1882.

problem. One thing led to another, and I soon found myself wanting
to acquire a thorough documentation. But some of the books I needed
were not available in Paris. A simple solution suggested itself: why not
take my vacation on the spot, in Etruscan Italy? The obvious place to
go was Florence. But I knew only too well that, once there, I would
succumb to an overwhelming temptation to renew my acquaintance
with the city's artistic treasures. This would have torpedoed my plans,
so, on second thoughts, I took a ticket for Bologna.

And in fact the seductions of the Etruscan Felsina, the modern
Bologna, turned out to be less subversive. I responded promptly to the
call of Bolognese art by visiting the Pinacotheca to see the pictures of
the brothers Carraccio, those strangely pre-romantic painters so close
to Delacroix. After that I was free to concentrate on the Etruscans. To
my great pleasure I was given access, without formalities and in spite
of having no letter of introduction, to the library of the ancient
University of Bologna.

Thus, deaf to every attraction from outside, I was able at last to
give my attention to the works of Pallottino, Nogara and other writers.
There were few people about; religious silence reigned in the long
reading-room lined with enormous volumes in rust-red bindings,
stamped with venerably bristling armorial bearings. Naturally, I
supplemented my reading by examining the precious Etruscan relics
in the Museo Civico. I was particularly struck by the large funerary
crocks which go under the courtesy title of "urns". It was somewhat
disconcerting to visualise worthy priests and brave warriors finding
their last resting-places in these bulky pots.

The Etruscan language, as I pondered on it during my return
journey, made me think of some vast, silent plain piled with ruins
and debris, the only traces left by a horrible battle in which the con-
tending parties had annihilated each other.

Not only did there seem to be no solution; I had also been put on
my guard against looking for a solution without thinking very carefully
first.

However, I had made a precious find at Bologna. I had jotted long
before in my notebook: "One of the most important things to be discovered in archaeology is a museum." This time, I had unearthed in a
bookshop a new book by M. Pallottino, of which I had not heard
before. It was a small but substantial collection containing more than
850 important Etruscan inscriptions: *Testimonia linguae etruscae*. These
texts, all scrupulously checked, had hitherto remained scattered in
various publications, and not all of them had been gathered into the

large Corpus of Etruscan Inscriptions, which was inconvenient for keeping at home. Pallottino's work, in short, was pricelessly useful; research would have been almost impossible without it. This valuable tool was now at my disposal.

None the less, I had to abandon my Etruscans, in the hope of escaping to them again at some future date; meanwhile I must confine myself to the concrete world and the Scythians.

All that the Etruscans had given me was a powerful, inarticulate feeling of distress.

Back in Paris, I tried to dismiss them from my mind. I set myself to the study of Bonnell with redoubled ardour. But Bonnell's ideas were as vast as the steppes he described. The Scythians being separated from the Phrygio-Thracian world only by the Danube, and having, moreover, invaded Asia Minor (in the 6th century B.C.), Bonnell had crossed the great river at a bound and straddled the Black Sea and the Caucasus. He had forgotten his drinkers of mare's milk for a moment to establish himself in his new dominions. He took in the Macedonians, the Epirots, Albanians and Illyrians, and the ancient Pelasgians. I learnt that Illyrian names might wander almost anywhere. The name of Cape Malea in the island of Lemnos, which had once been inhabited by the Pelasgians, was to be explained by the Illyrian or Albanian root *mal*, "mountain". The name of an Illyrian tribe, the *Triballoï*, and the Phrygian royal title *ballen*, came from the Albanian word *ballë* and meant "the people of the Three Peaks" and "he who is at the head of things" (just as from the Slav word *tchelo*, "forehead", come *tchelnik*, *natchalnik*, "chief"). Very interesting; but I felt I had been given a cold shower when I found Bonnell tacking on to all this, for no reason, the Semitic word *baal*, "master", which had no business there at all.

In Bonnell's quotations the name von Hahn occurred frequently. He had been an Austrian consul in Eastern Greece and had written a voluminous work on the language and customs of the Albanians. This phase of consular history had been a fortunate one for Europe's museums, when Clermont-Gannaud had been French consul in Jerusalem and when the consuls of the great nations were continually sending whole caravans of masterpieces of ancient art to the Louvre, the British Museum and elsewhere. Other consuls, who were not archaeologists, addressed themselves to the study of little-known languages of the Levant.

In order to check Bonnell's statements I found myself compelled, willy-nilly, to delve into von Hahn. It was natural to suppose that the wild mountains and inaccessible passes of Epirus should have retained some vestiges of a remote past, as have so many other natural museums: the hot sands of Egypt and Mesopotamia, the frozen subsoil of Siberia, the Caucasus, and the inhospitable forests of Lithuania. Johann Georg von Hahn was not only a philologist but also an industrious ethnographer. He had spent years collecting and comparing the vocabulary of the Albanian language, studying the folklore, noting down the songs, folk-tales and proverbs, and describing the traditions and customs of the country to which he had been posted.[1] Though, by profession, he was neither a historian nor a philologist, I was later to find a good many of his deductions reproduced by authorities of our own day, such as F. Altheim, for example. Von Hahn was, moreover, capable of taking a broad view. He sought to elucidate several Albanian place-names by studying the ancient peoples of the Balkans, the Danube and Asia Minor. I was always on the lookout for my Scythians, whose name cropped up frequently.

Meanwhile I took note of several elementary facts: that the name Dalmatia was to be explained by *dele*, the Albanian for "sheep"; that Dardania was to be explained from the same Illyrian source, by *dardhe*, "pear"; that terms related to Albanian words had been used by the Messapians, an ancient Illyrian tribe in Italy, and were found abundantly in Apulia and Calabria. The name Brindisi was to be explained by the Messapian *brendos* and, surprisingly, also appeared in the Albanian *bri*, plural *brini*, "antlers". Von Hahn had tracked out an obscure ancient Illyrian people, the Iapodes of Istria, and had occupied himself with their colonies in Italy, in Picenum, next door to both Romans and Etruscans. The name of one of their tribes, Lopsi, was presented as being derived from the Albanian *lope*, "cow"; and in Tirol, the Rhaetia of antiquity, the cow was called *lobé*. All this seemed well enough, but matters took a turn for the worse when von Hahn connected the name Ioppé (Jaffa) with the Iapodes; for Ioppé meant "beautiful" (fem.) in the Canaanite language and had nothing to do with the aforesaid cows.

On the other hand, the Albanian funeral customs, which von Hahn faithfully described, undoubtedly bore the stamp of very ancient times. We shall mention them again later.

Von Hahn's Albanian–German dictionary is placed after the historical and literary sections of his book. My glance was arrested by a strange, isolated word: *shekh*, of which, however, the author had not managed to give a satisfying explanation. *Shekh*, he said, meant "abandoned". It was a word to which the speaker would add the name of a person still alive, and in this form was used by Albanian

[1] *Albanesische Studien*, Jena, 1854.

women as something to swear by. A mother would say: *"Shekh djal!"*; and since *djal* was "child" or "son", that meant, apparently, "May I be abandoned by my child!"

A sister would swear by her elder brother; if she had no elder brother she would swear by her father: *"Shekh babaï!"*

Reading this, I could not help remembering the Etruscan word *šeχ*, which is phonetically exactly the same and means "daughter". There are numerous Etruscan inscriptions in which, say, a woman called Tanaqvil or Pumpuii is named as the *šeχ* of a woman called Sentinei.

"But what of it?" I said to myself. "There's nothing to be inferred from this."

The two words were, indeed, quite distinct. The Etruscan word meant "daughter"; the Albanian, "abandoned". The Etruscans applied it to any deceased woman, whereas among the Albanians it was a forbidden word. Were, then, the two ideas completely foreign to one another, coinciding phonetically but in no other way?

But during the course of its survival down the centuries, surrounded by a kind of taboo, an armour of superstition, might not this Etruscan word have totally changed its substance, like a fossilised shell? That is, might not the Albanian women, preserving a distant echo of Etruscan invocations, have kept the word in their own objurgations and given it a new sense?

For such objurgations and exorcisms are sometimes adorned with archaic words which no one understands any more.[1]

Such were my thoughts; which, however, I shrugged off even while I was thinking them, deprecating them as mere guesswork. But these protracted musings did have the effect of riveting my attention and receptivity on a curious phenomenon: the Albanian language.

That language, certainly, was only a siren. I must make myself clear—and, at the same time, avail myself of this opportunity of bringing a modicum of order into our knowledge of this minor, yet too-long neglected, branch of the great mammalian family. For sirens, having so far eluded classification, can cause a great deal of trouble.

Essentially, these graceful creatures can be divided into two categories: the sirens of Odysseus and those of Columbus. The first are as pernicious, deceptive and misleading as the second are gentle and beneficent. The latter rise up before the gaze of all who seek to widen the horizons of mankind. That was why, during his first expedition,

[1] This Etruscan *shekh* may be simply Albanian *shekh*, the present of *shoh*, "to see".

Columbus and his company thought they saw sirens. The daring navigator sincerely believed in their existence. Previously, his men had been overwhelmed by the terrible loneliness, the vacant immensity, of the sea surrounding their carvels. Suddenly to encounter sirens, those familiar creatures whose enticing charms were frequently carved on ships' prows or tavern doors, was almost like meeting a friend or a brother in the middle of a desert. The solitude was dispelled and everyone breathed again.

Sirens first, and knowledge after.

Thus it is that sirens make their appearance during research, as an almost inevitable stage in the development of any new branch of science.

Von Hahn was an enthusiast. In his eyes the Albanians were directly descended from the ancient Illyrians and, moreover, belonged to the same family of that race as the Etruscans. He considered the name of the great tribe of Southern Albania in our day, the Tosk, to be perfectly identical with Tuscan-Etruscan, while the name of the Albanian town of Tirana was identical with the Etruscans' other designation, Tyrrhenians. To me, this looked too good to be true. I could not help observing that modern Etruscologists had discarded these bold conclusions and that the name of von Hahn never appeared in their discussions. At that time I did not know that a philologist of repute, Ascoli, had supported von Hahn's theses. But the fact remained: the Etruscan language was still obdurately unknown.

Von Hahn had gone back to Strabo, Polybius and the literature of antiquity in general. I began completing his documentation by reading the works of later, better-informed scholars. Little by little a picture began forming itself under my eyes, that of a vast family of peoples and tribes whose languages were related to Illyrian and who had spread towards the Adriatic and the Mediterranean, into Italy, Crete and Palestine: Illyrians, Venetians, Iapygians, Macedonians, Phrygians, etc.

This spectacle had divided philologists and historians into two camps. The members of the first camp were quick to seize on any sign of Illyrian expansion. Their main supporting evidence was two languages, one ancient and the other modern, Messapian and Albanian, both of which had kept an Illyrian basis, whereas Thracian and Macedonian contained only a few scraps of Illyrian; and the intention was to use this basis as the foundation of future discoveries, notably the recovery of Etruscan.

This was the camp of the "Illyriophiles".

Facing it was the other, that of the "Illyriophobes", irritated by this hail of Illyrian names which were shot at them from all sides, so much so, indeed, that a good half of the ancient world seemed to have been peopled by cohorts of Illyrians, with a population-density as high as that of present-day New York. The Illyriophobes might well have asked: "How could such a horde have subsequently dispersed like a flock of sparrows?" And they disputed every little point, denied the reality, antiquity and cohesion of the Illyrian deluge, and withdrew into the sacred Etruscan strongpoint, reputedly impregnable.

It is safe to say that no decisive battle between the two camps has ever taken place; only skirmishes in isolated sectors.

On one occasion, however, the Illyriophobic positions suffered a rather severe bombardment from Jokl, in Ebert's *Reallexikon*. But at the approach of night Jokl, with due respect for the established hierarchy, ceased his cannonade, consulted his watch, yawned and said: "The sequel doesn't concern me. I'm not an Etruscologist. I'm off to bed."

So the armies were able to maintain their respective positions.

In all this there was something which left me rather puzzled: in discussing the role which Illyrian might play in the deciphering of Etruscan, contemporary authors stayed inside the charmed circle of the *names* of deities and legendary heroes, or of places commemorated in myth or tradition. No one was trying to extract a root from these names, some element common to several of them, and to compare it with such and such an Etruscan word. Methods of this kind were continually extolled but never applied. The staple of scholarly diet consisted of highly ingenious suggestions.

Meanwhile, as I went on reading von Hahn, I was gradually initiating myself into the Albanian tongue. It is hard, crystalline, with clearly cut facets, markedly more virile than melodious, abundantly supplied with evidently Indo-European formations, inclining at one moment towards abrupt abbreviations and at another towards copious discursiveness. Heavily incrusted with Latin, Greek, Slavonic, Turkish and other roots, the accumulated borrowings of centuries, the language gave me the impression that, where its original nucleus was concerned, it was like no other. And it was full of traps for anyone who tried to determine where this primitive nucleus ended and where the amalgam of borrowings began.

As for the utility of Albanian from the archaeological point of view, I soon came up against the barrier erected by Professor G. Petrotta:

Endeavours to explain Lycian, Thracian and *Etruscan* inscriptions with the help of Albanian have so far yielded no results. . . . This is an indication that Albanian possesses insufficient affinities with these languages to provide a key to them. . . .

In any case, we are confronted by the spectacle of the *barren toil* of scholars searching in Albanian, a unique Balkan language of unknown origin, for some small part of the veil of profound mystery behind which the ethnography of this region lies concealed. (Our italics.)

This warning neither encouraged nor discouraged me. I saw no reason for regarding the question as closed.

It is true that in *The Etruscans* Professor Pallottino also declares: "We may exclude the possibility of deciphering Etruscan *completely* with the aid of some exterior factor." But, to begin with, we are not necessarily so proud as to demand completeness. After so long a famine, shall we not be glad to decipher even a half or a quarter?

Moreover, has not the same writer been lavish with good advice on methods of research in Etruscan studies; has he not written that one cannot "dispense with rigorous self-criticism, methodical doubt, cold detachment in the evaluation of results obtained"?

Agreed. And, as for detachment, I had no blinding passion, no predilection for one camp or the other. And as for the healthy effects of doubt, there could be no argument. But no doubt is unilateral. Fresh air must be let in on every side. Self-doubt does not go well with blind veneration for others' authority. Thus, I could not uncritically accept current opinions on the connection between Etruscan and Albanian; I had to check them.

But (I shall be asked) must one check *all* the sources, examine *all* the languages which have been suggested for the elucidation of Etruscan?

Perhaps. But there is no need to make a rigid principle of it. Room must be left for intuition. My intuition told me that it was still necessary to try Albanian; no other language gave me any such feeling. If someone had assured me that the secret of Etruscan lay in the Berber language no force in the world would have led me to study Berber; rather, indeed, would I have renounced Etruscan. Albanian attracted me, and others' opinions inspired me with—doubts. Whoever believed in Berber was welcome to study Berber.

Without knowing why, I found myself once more reading and re-reading the *Testimonia*, the collection of Etruscan inscriptions.

Among these formless remains, these lifeless ruins of a language reputed to have fallen silent for ever, which I had vowed more than once to abandon to its fate, there were a few things to which I reacted more energetically than to the rest, things which set up a resonance in my mind. These were certain words preserved by Hesychius of Alexandria, that benefactor of all students of Etruscan, whom Skutsch unjustly appreciated at less than his true value; and also a few words often used in epitaphs.

Could *suplu*, "flautist", fail to remind me of the old Russian word *sopiel, sopilka*, "a shepherd's pipe"? Could *capys*, "falcon", raise any other echo in me than *kobietz, kobtchyk*, "falcon", in the Slav languages? Was not *sval-ce*, "has lived", the same as *zival, zhyval*, "was living"—the word which every child in a Slav country learns when he hears a story for the first time?

Surely these words, and so many others for which similar parallels could be found, were part of Etruscan, because Etruscan belonged to the *satem* linguistic group, the Oriental Indo-European languages? And surely many of the Albanian words, whose provenance has been labelled Slav or Lithuanian, must be equally old? Their appearance in the Balkans used to be attributed to Slav penetration of the right bank of the Danube, in the 6th century of our era. But Hrozny's deciphering of Hittite has drawn our attention to a number of roots in that language which are still flourishing in Eastern Europe today. These words were therefore current in Anatolia in the 15th century B.C. Albanian could have inherited them from Illyrian, and, as Kretschmer, Jokl and Vasmer have observed, the Danube has nothing to do with the matter.

To paraphrase the well-known English proverb, I was getting rather tired of thinking about the pudding so much and hearing the pudding talked about so often, when all the time the great thing was to taste the pudding. I opened one of my notebooks at random and looked at the first Etruscan inscription which met my eye. It was a famous bilingual, Etrusco-Latin specimen. We possess very few of these and, unfortunately, do not know whether the Etruscans took the trouble to be accurate in translating their texts into Latin. What was before me was the epitaph of an augur and *fulguriator*, Cafates; someone, that is, whose function it was to examine the entrails of sacrificial victims and observe lightning. These two functions were expressed in Etruscan by three words: *netśvis trutnvt frontac*. The third of these words having already been interpreted, by analogy with a Greek root, as being connected with thunder, I concentrated my attention on *netśvis*, which was as obscure as anyone could have wished. I extracted Arbanas' little Albanian–German dictionary from its hiding-place, and began

looking: *i, j, k*, . . . *m*, . . . The letter *n* begins on p. 98—and there
was nothing there. Well, really, at this rate . . .

Discouraged, I gazed at the little book which had so disappointed
me. Its cover is adorned with an old-fashioned vignette representing
the principal races of mankind. In the centre, squatting *à la Turque*,
is a majestic person equipped with a patriarchal beard and a *tchibouk*.
He appears to be conversing on transcendent matters with an East
Indian athlete with a naked torso. Perhaps they are discussing the
prices of little slave boys. On their left are to be seen an impassive
Chinese and a frowning Caucasian. To the right there is a little group
of Europeans. An imperial, like Napoleon III's, distinguishes a
Frenchman. Standing beside him is Phileas Fogg in person, provident
and perspicacious, as is shown by the telescope firmly held in one
hand. Above the whole floats a lady with an ample bust, worthy of
Rodin, and censored, *in extremis*, with a few roses. Crowned with a
small globe, she represents the Muse of Geography.

Obviously, the publisher of these little dictionaries was thinking of
busy travellers; he was not concerned with Etruscologists in distress.

Still, I was beginning to get used to the whims of Albanian verbs.
Some of them mean the same thing with, or without, an *n* at the beginning. One such couple is *ndëgjoj* and *dëgjoj*. Both of these mean "to
hear". At first I could not understand why. But everything comes out
clear in the end. This *n*-prefix is a kind of preposition. The two words
are something like the French *porter*, "to carry", and *emporter*, "to carry
off, carry away". To a Frenchman these two verbs are as different as
two worlds. But put yourself inside the skin of a foreigner knowing less
than a dozen words of French, and imagine yourself standing be-
wildered in a French Custom house. Whichever of these three you hear
will be all the same to you: "*Portez——*" or "*Emportez——*" or
"*Transportez votre valise.*" You have understood "*portez*", you know you
have got to carry your case somewhere, and that is good enough; the
rest is mere unnecessary refinement. *Ndëgjoj* and *dëgjoj* are a similar
case.

Suppose, then, I apply the same principle to *netśvis*? That is to say,
since it is not to be found, suppose I look for *tśvis*?

I open my *Wörterbuch* once more. There are plenty of words beginning with *t*, including numerous verbs beginning with *tch* (*tsh*), the
letter which in Etruscan may be denoted by *c* or *s* or *ś*, even in the same
word (as was established by D. Lattes). Here on p. 121 is a verb
tśtoiś, "to continue". It is strange to note how like this is to *tśvis*, the

word I want to find. Here is *tśroïs̆*, "to widen". But no *tśvis*. My eyes
come to rest in the left-hand column of p. 121. Here we are: *tśovis*,
"*voraussehen*", "to foresee"; and just above is *tśoïs*, "to see, notice".
I am stupefied.

True, this solution might have been just right. Since the Albanian
ne means "in", my verb *ne-tśvis* would have meant "to see inside".
Introspection, perhaps? Just right for an augur. No. Too good to be
true. I refuse to believe in it.

I know that L. Barthou [1] once picked up from a secondhand bookseller, on the quays, a school textbook with annotations in Bonaparte's
writing. But to have a similar stroke of luck was beyond me. No little
book, as I passed a bookseller's stall, grabbed at my coat-tails, shouting,
"Buy me! You'll find an Etruscan word inside me!"

This first sally, which I looked on as a failure, gave me a shock.

I began to understand the vital importance of dialects in Albanian.
The difficulty, and the richness, of this language are caused by the
survival of regional variations. From time immemorial the Albanians
have not only striven heroically for their independence but have also
been divided into rival clans, always at daggers drawn with one
another under the influence of the insatiable vendetta. This has caused
a large number of old idioms to remain in use, each refusing to give
way to any other.

Thus I had deciphered nothing. Yet, in spite of these uncertain
gropings, all my other problems had retreated into the background,
and Etruscan was once more assuming the principal place in my
thoughts.

I had the good luck to obtain, as an aid in my work,[2] a precision
instrument without which I should have been able to make no head-
way. This was the excellent Albanian–English dictionary by Stuart E.
Mann, published in London in 1948. This book was to von Hahn's
dictionary what a modern pneumatic drill is to a common or garden
spade. What a difference! In von Hahn's time Albanian had not even
had a universally recognised alphabet. In transcribing Albanian words
von Hahn had used Greek letters, adapting them to the requirements
of Albanian phonetics by means of diareses and by various markings
invented by himself. Since 1850 the language had been progressively
consolidated, purified and unified. The Latin alphabet had been
definitively adopted, with *sh* as pronounced in English, *c* for *tz*, and

---

[1] The French politician and writer who was assassinated (1934) at the same time as
King Alexander I of Yugoslavia, in Marseille. (*Tr.*)
[2] Thanks to S. E. Mann,

ç for *tch* and *tsh*. A great task had been accomplished by Albanian experts of various nationalities, and by the Albanians themselves, in collecting all the existing materials relative to the history and grammar of the language. Good dictionaries appeared. Mann's, the result of patient industry and a long period of residence in the country, reflects this new order of things. Mann has faithfully recorded all the delicate distinctions and local variations of the language. I admired his book and pondered on its possible usefulness to me in my investigations.

One winter's day, at the Bibliothèque Nationale, I was studying for the first time the pictures adorning Greek and Etruscan vases, collected

FIG. 2. *enqten:* "Conqueror"

and published 120 years before by E. Gerhard.[1] They may have been the same old engravings as I had glimpsed twenty-five years ago at the Bibliothèque Mazarine. They consisted of exquisite little scenes, taken from Greek mythology and in many cases vigorously drawn. Some of them were accompanied by short inscriptions in Etruscan. Plate CXXIV attracted my attention most of all. It showed a fight between two heroes, the one on the left being armed with a bow and a club, and the one on the right with a lance, a sword and a shield. The result of the struggle might appear uncertain; however, the general move-

[1] *Griechische Vasenbilder*, 1840.

ment and emphasis seemed to indicate that the man on the left, with
a head-dress in the form of a wolf's head with open mouth, had just
shot an arrow and that his opponent had been hit by it; this detail
had been left out; the Etruscan figurative gift is no slave to detail
(fig. 2).

This drawing, displaying such mastery, was accompanied by three
words. Two of them denoted the heroes: Adethes (or Aθets) and
Kaon; but the mythological context of the scene does not matter to us
at the moment. The third word, *enqten*, beside the hero on the left, set
me wondering. Gerhard had been unable to explain it; he had neither
found a meaning nor suggested an analogy.

My need, clearly, was to lie in wait for lonely Etruscan words on
narrow paths; to trap them, jump out on them in places where they had
little chance of escape. Had not such a moment now come? Here
was a word which was the name of neither a place nor a person. For
more than two thousand years it had been slumbering on this vase.
It concealed some clear, simple, obvious meaning. But what was that
meaning?

Asking myself this question, I reminded myself at the same time that,
as yet, I had not interpreted a single word of Etruscan. Only one
point had been gained: I had acquired the habit of never opening a
book on Etruscan studies, in my daily reading at the Bibliothèque
Nationale, without having Mann's dictionary in front of me. It is true
that it was there in the role of a fetish rather than a tool, since I was
not yet sure how to set about using it. It seemed to be nothing but a
silent witness of my angry impotence, my inability to draw oracular
information from it. But this witness was soon to start contributing.

I seized the dictionary; opened it, probably, with the same tremors
as the Etruscan soothsayers felt when they examined some unlucky
quadruped's liver in order to read the will of the gods.

I said to myself, "Let's look up *enqten*."

"*Enqten?* . . . It's not there."

"Very well, we'll have a look at *engden*."

"*Engden?* . . . No, there's no entry for that."

"All right, then, *enkten*."

"*Enkten?* . . . Nothing doing."

"Then try *enkthen*."

"*Enkthen?* . . . That's not there either."

I shut the dictionary. This little dialogue was getting too depressing.

My discouragement was short lived. I was already beginning to feel
that in such cases it was not just a matter of reading as one reads a
newspaper, or of simply looking words up in the dictionary. No, one

had to put on dark glasses and an apron, put out the light and start up the X-ray machine. One must see the skeleton of the word and, in the skeleton, the parts which mattered most; for, if Albanian really had consented to preserve some of the ancient substance of Illyrian, it would be absurd to expect every word to have been kept in its entirety, with its soft, perishable parts, its finer contours, its folds, and its moles or warts.

I opened the dictionary again. I said to myself, persuasively: *enqt.*, *engd.*, *nkt.*, *ngd.* That is the spinal column of the word I am looking for; the main line; everything else is mere frills.

I went right through the letters beginning with *e*. Nothing there. But there was still a small group of words beginning with *ë*. On p. 98 I found:

ëngadhënjenj, a verb (which for my purposes boiled down to *engdnn*); and

ëngadhënjim, a noun (amounting to *engdnim*). IM is one of the suffixes for abstract nouns and was therefore unimportant.

But what did all this mean? I was referred to p. 317 to see *ngadhnjej*, *ngadhnjim*. I turned up this fateful page and found:

Ngadhnim (obsolete): conquest, victory.

Ngadhnoj or *ngadhnjëj*: to conquer.

Ngadhnuer: victorious.

And so on. But *engd*?

At a loss, I gazed for the tenth time at *ngadhnoj* and the frightful *ëngadhënjenj* (*engdnn*), so inflated and elongated,[1] which was rushing out at me like a bear hardly awoken from its winter sleep, escaping noisily from its lair, its coat bristling with bits of twig, fir cones, tufts of grass, pebbles—perhaps the word in the engraving meant "conqueror", "victorious", something on those lines? The man who had drawn the picture had obligingly put it in the appropriate place so that the spectator should waste no time trying to guess the result of the battle.

I looked about me as if an earthquake had just shaken the Rue de Richelieu. But everything was in its proper place. As firm as rock, the pillars of the reading-room were still supporting the glazed vaulting above the heads of us zealous readers, and in the frescoes along the walls the sky was still blue and the rustling of the painted trees barely audible.

I longed to shout to my neighbours, intent on *L'Illustration* for 1911 or *The History of Byzantine Art*, "I'm on the trail of Etruscan!"

I could not at that moment recall, it is true, any regulation saying,

---

[1] Cf. Albanian *engushullim* and *ngushullim*, "consolation" (M. 322); *ëngënjenj* and *ngënjenj*, "to deceive" (M. 319), etc. The *ë* is prothetic.

"Readers succeeding in deciphering an ancient language are requested
to refrain from any expression of their emotions such as could disturb
other users of the reading-room." But my feeling for order told me
that such a regulation might well be in force.

So all I did was to slump back lounging in my chair. There was no
point in exposing myself to ostracism. Besides, who would have
believed me?

I was at the foot of a craggy mountain, on whose side, for the first
time, a little path could be faintly discerned. I had premonitions of
the rock-faces, torrents and screes which were going to bar my way.
But I had to start climbing.

Had I really scored a success? It was more like a casual accident.
At the same time, though, it gave me a healthy shock and enabled me
to overcome the most serious obstacle still encumbering my path as a
decipherer, namely myself.

I had been gradually coming to a decision: to drop everything else
and give a thorough trial to Albanian. I could feel that *tshovis* and
enqten were waiting within arm's length. Materially speaking, a journey
was necessary and had to be made by the shortest possible route, from
the Rue de Richelieu to the courtyard of the Louvre, over the bridge
and along the Rue des Saints-Pères to the School of Living Oriental
Languages. But would I find Albanian there?

I did.

During one of my first lessons Mr N., who was in charge of the
beginners' course, mentioned the word *dëgjoj*, "to hear". I plucked
up my courage and asked shyly whether there was not also another
form, *ndëgjoj*? Mr N. cast a disapproving glance in my direction.
The language was by no means an easy one to learn, its difficulties had
to be smoothed over for the three young students who had set about it
with such laudable determination, and now here was a new pupil who
insisted on aggravating the difficulties by asking awkward questions.

And Mr N. replied: "We don't say *ndëgjoj* any more. It's archaic."

Like all Albanians, he was proud of his language and wanted it to be
modern, right up to date, swept clean of the cobwebs of the past. He
did not know that in my ears his answer sounded like a melody by
Mozart. He had done just what I wanted; he had confirmed that all
these *n*'s and *ë*'s at the beginning of verbs had fallen into disuse. Mann
had said as much in black and white, and I had no reason to doubt it;
yet, all the same, I was devoured by doubts and anxieties. And now
these verb-forms turned out to be obsolete! What a bit of luck!

Later, I was to understand that the word *enqten* was a difficult case;

consequently, its Albanian counterpart seemed almost impossible to identify. But again and again I was able to find Albanian words in which the Etruscan root was clearly and faithfully reproduced.

As for *enqten*, I thought at first that it was enough to cut off the initial *ë* to get the root *nqt*. But the whole syllable *en* was the prefix; so the verb was reduced to *qten*. And this *qten* is found in Albanian: *kthen(em)*, "to turn, return", etc.; *kthenej ndë dhet*, "to return to the earth" (Job xxxiv. 15, "Man shall turn again unto dust"); *përkthej*, "to refract (light)", etc. We shall subsequently meet the Albanian

FIG. 3. A plea for mercy

ën-begatem, "to become rich", and the Etruscan *em-fepame*, "to surprise" (p. 134), and also the Lydian *en-slifid* (p. 389). Thus *enqten* would mean "returns (the blow)" or "repulses (the adversary)"; it may form part of the vocabulary of war. The man with the club, moreover, is Hercules. *Aθets* would be his exclamation: *Aθets!* *Aθ* is Hades, *ets* is "go" (cf. Albanian *ec*, "go", M. 93). Thus: "Depart to Hades!"

Another combat-scene, which did not take me long to decipher, confirmed that I was on the right track. The Etruscan caption accompanying it is, moreover, easier to recognise and, in addition, is clearly illustrated by the drawing. Table CCCXCI, 2, in Gerhard's collection of Etruscan mirrors [1] shows the final stage of a curious combat (fig. 3).

[1] *Estruskische Spiegel*, Vol. IVa, Berlin, 1865.

One of the fighters, with raised sword, is threatening the other, who is disarmed and has obviously had the worst of it. Gerhard observes:

> If the inscription *eln*, which relates to this youth, were comprehensible, we should be enlightened as to the meaning of this scene and of others like it.

No one will deny the pertinence of this observation, but it does not get us much farther.

But on examining the inscription in question I found that Gerhard's reading was inaccurate. The word between the two combatants was not *eln* but *epn*. This enabled me to find the solution, thanks, once again, to Albanian. The verb "to give, to give oneself", a basic word, is somewhat fluid in Albanian, probably because of dialectal influences, but is easy to recognise. The root is *ap, ep, ip, jap, jep* (M. 95). In addition to the active forms there is a middle voice, *ipem, epem*, "to surrender" (M. 167).[1] The final *n* corresponds to the Albanian suffix *ni*, denoting the plural of the imperative. The meaning of the Etruscan word is perfectly clear, even if there are still details to be debated: "Surrender!" Moreover, the beaten fighter is seen to be raising his right hand and asking for mercy.

The following examples of words deciphered are arresting, and will allow me to bring this introduction to a speedy close and pass on to a systematic exposition of the texts elucidated. There is, for example, a whole series of inscriptions in Etruscan taken from the leaden or stone projectiles which Tuscan soldiers despatched with their murderous slings at their enemies' heads or over the walls of beleaguered towns. These inscriptions are short; lapidary, as we may indeed call them. Inscriptions of the same sort made by Roman soldiers are a help in reading them. The Romans used to inscribe their slingstones with insults, sarcastic quips, curses or injunctions: "Kill!", "Strike!" and so on.

M. Pallottino's collection includes several of these inscriptions. For instance, the first part of an inscription on a leaden missile (p. 256) reads

$$vra\theta$$

If we consult Mann's dictionary (or any other, such as Leotti's) we find a verb *vras*, "to kill" (M. 564).

Thus the Etruscan inscription means "Kill!" and is an appeal uttered by the slinger to his missile, or, if you prefer, a charm whose

---

[1] Cf. *jipen mbas punimit artistik*, "they devote themselves to artistic pursuits" (M. Lambertz, *Albanishes Lesebuch*, Leipzig, 1948, I, p. 294).

impetuous, laconic style is exactly that of a soldier; a spell concentrated in a single word.[1]

Here is another and still more arresting example. This time we shall not be satisfied with a "bewitched" stone; we need a thunderbolt, no less. It will be handled by Tinia-Jupiter in person, in authentic Etruscan style.

I will come to it by stages.

Recently Professor Glori has tried to decipher some Etruscan texts and to explain the name of Rome. Observing that "Roman" in Etruscan was *rumaχ* (*romakh* or *romak*) and that the Hebrew for "spear" is likewise *romakh*, M. Glori has worked up a legendary episode: Romulus, an Etruscan chieftain in the service of King David, arrives on the banks of the Tiber, chooses the site of the future city, sticks his spear into the ground as a sign of ownership and says: "There, ladies and gentlemen! Here I take my stand and here shall be *Romaχ*."

Now, there was no need to cross the Mediterranean to discover the origin of the word. It would have been enough to cross the Adriatic. Or even to cross nothing at all, but merely to open Leotti's Albanian–Italian dictionary and seek out the Albanian word *romak*, "Roman". The ending -*ak* is not part of the root, but is a purely Etruscan termination with an ethnic reference. In the same way Etruscan has *rumaχ* (inhabitant of Rome), *velznaχ* (inhabitant of Felsina), *cusiaχ* (of Chiusi), *svetimaχ* and so on. In the word *frontac*, the soothsayer's title which we have already encountered, the same termination denoted an occupation, profession or the like. The same suffix is found in the Lydian word *sfardak* (inhabitant of Sardis) and in the name Spartac, which is of Thracian origin. But this is also a characteristic of Albanian: Romak, Durrësak (inhabitant of Durazzo), Ishmiak (of Ishmia), Ulqinak (of Dulcigno, or Ulqi), *fusharak* (plain-dweller, *fushë*, "plain"). This Albanian -*ak* often denotes a quality, habit or character-trait: *zemerak*, "courageous" (from *zemer*, "heart"), *hollak*, "thin", etc. It is, moreover, a feature common to several Eastern Indo-European languages. In Russian we find -*ak* or -*iak*: *sibiriak* (a Siberian), *polak* (a Pole), *toulak* (an inhabitant of Toula), *permiak* (an inhabitant of Perm), etc. It also stands for habitual occupation or for character-traits: *rybak*, "fisherman", *prostak*, "a simpleton", etc. The same is true of the language of the Scythians: *wayag*, "courser", *marak*, "assassin", etc.[2] This, therefore, is the linguistic family to which Etruscan is related.

In addition, so early an authority as F. Bopp, in his *Comparative*

---

[1] M. Pallottino translates *vraθ* by "to strike, to kill", by analogy with Latin inscriptions and without mentioning Albanian (*Elementi di lingua etrusca*, p. 91).

[2] Abayev, *Ossetic Language and Folklore*, Moscow, 1949, p. 221 (in Russian).

Grammar of the Indo-European Languages, pointed out the role (sometimes perfectly clear, at other times slightly veiled) which is played by the suffix *ak* in Sanskrit: *partak-as*, "dancing", *savak-a*, "child", *madrak-as*, "from the region of Madra", etc.; in Latin: *edax*, genitive *edacis*, "voracious", *tenax*, "tenacious", etc.; and in Lithuanian: *degikas*, "incendiary", etc.

Moreover, Krahe has noted the same suffix in Illyrian, both in place-names—Draudacum, Kerak—and in personal names—Barac-o, Theutac-o, etc. (*Lexikon altillyr. Personennamen*, pp. 148 and 115).

These indications would appear to invalidate C. Tagliavini's recent attempt to explain the Albanian suffix -*ak* as a borrowing from the Slavonic languages.

It is by this route that we approach an association of two words which occurs frequently in the Book of the Mummy: *ais cemnac*. *Ais* is god; *cemnac*, with the familiar -*ak* termination, is an epithet characterising the god or a whole group of gods.

The meaning of *cemnac* came to me while I was reading a singular book published in 1814 by an Englishman, William Martin-Leake, in which he described his Albanian journey of three or four years earlier. He had been entrusted with a confidential mission, that of frustrating the plans of Napoleon in the Near East.[1]

Martin-Leake, one of the first Western travellers to visit Albania, made some interesting observations. According to him, the Albanians had borrowed many words from modern Greek; during the 5th century they had taken certain terms from the Goths, who at that time held Epirus; in the 11th, from the Franks, who held Durazzo; and subsequently many from the Slavs. The national hero G. Kastrioti (Iskander Bey) was in power from 1443 to 1467. Until 1648 the Albanians remained Christian, part of the population being thereafter converted to Islam, under Turkish pressure; but they have remained indifferent to religious problems. They are poor, energetic, insensitive and make excellent soldiers. They played a prominent part in the liberation of Greece. Lord Byron enrolled a number of them in his service and wrote down several of their songs.

Both the country and the language were little known in those days. Martin-Leake's preface reflects the attitude current in his time:

> By many persons the author may be thought to have bestowed more attention than it deserves upon the poor and barbarous dialect of Albania. It must be considered curious, however, as holding a distinct character in the midst of the languages by which it is

[1] *Researches in Greece*, London, 1814.

surrounded, being in all probability the ancient Illyrian, with some alterations of the same kind, as Latin and Greek have undergone from the Teutonic and Slavonian conquerors of Southern Europe (p. iii).

As for the Albanians:

A nation, irregular and undisciplined as soldiers, but possessing a perfect familiarity with the use of arms; ferocious and ignorant, and uncivilised, but cherishing an enthusiastic partiality for their native mountains (p. iv).

Finally, our learned traveller took copious notes on the Albanian language. It would seem that he got a peasant to talk in his presence, noting down his speech sentence by sentence and transmitting it to the reader with translations into Bulgarian, Roumanian and English. His interlocutor delivered himself of a number of homely truths:

Intelligent men do not stand about with folded arms but take oxen and go and plough and sow. . . . If a sick man wishes to get well, let him not eat walnuts and filberts; let him eat almonds, apples and pears and eschew chestnuts, cucumbers, melons and water-melons. . . .

I was savouring these precepts of popular wisdom when my eyes were arrested by a phrase: *"Gemon kelia"*, translated by Martin-Leake as "thunders the sky". *Kelia* comes from Latin, of course; *gemon*, on the other hand, belongs to the very heart of the language. Mann gives: *gjëmoj*, "to thunder"; *gjëmim*, "thunder" (p. 146). In M. Lambertz we read: *gjëmo-nine maletë*, "the mountains were thundering".[1] I ought to add that the difference between Mann's *gjëm* and Martin-Leake's *gem* is unimportant, since the Albanian *j* merely has the effect of soften-ing the consonant which precedes it; *e* and *ë* are interchangeable as between dialects; the two words are thus the same.

For some reason I was charmed by *gemon kelia*. I repeated it several times in an undertone. My thoughts were about to climb an unknown path step by step:

> *gemon kelia* . . . thunders the sky
> *gemon* . . .   thunders
> *gemn* . . .
> *kemn* . . .
> *cemn* . . .
> *cemnac* . . .
> *ais cemnac* . . . god thundering!

[1] *Op. cit.*, Vol. I, p. 132.

Issuing from the mouth of an Albanian mountain-dweller 150 years ago, recorded with a goose-quill pen by a scholarly Englishman, the expression gave me a tingling shock; it was like an electric spark released from the silent centuries. Tinia the god of thunder and lightning stood before me, and I was thunderstruck indeed. Tinia, *ais cemnac*, with the same termination -*ak* in his epithet as in the words *rumaχ*, *velznak*. *Ais cemnac*, an habitual appellation . . . Well, he had certainly kept his habit of thundering, had Tinia-Jupiter.

We have seen, however, that the idea of thunder appears to be clothed in the Etruscan word *frontac*. It may therefore be that, despite the indication given by the Albanian verb *gemoj*, the Etruscan *cemnac* is an epithet denoting lightning rather than thunder. That the word preserved in Albanian should have undergone this slight alteration in meaning is, of course, quite possible.

It must be observed, moreover, that the root *gjëm* has a Latin counterpart, *gemo*, translated by Ernout and Meillet as "to groan, moan, weep". One notes that M. Ernout adds: "Etymology uncertain." There is plainly no proof that *gjëm* is copied from *gemo* just as the number *θu*, which is common to Latin and Albanian, does not of itself constitute proof of borrowing. In any case, the meaning "groan, moan or weep" is in no way consonant with the character of Tinia-Jupiter and cannot throw any doubt on the meaning of the epithet *cemnac*, *cemnaχ*.

As for the addition of the letter *n* to the root *gem*, we shall revert to it in the chapter on Etruscan art.

As we know, Tinia is often represented in Etruscan art with a stylised representation of a thunderbolt in his hand. One of the characteristics of the Etruscans is that they were great consumers of electric current, which they squandered all the more blithely in that meters and inspectors had not yet been invented. One Etruscan priest, an unsung predecessor of Franklin, had made rash experiments and paid for them with his life. However, the electricity in question was provided only by the sky, and its use was confined to the requirements of religion. But the religious needs of the Ancients were identified with all their activities. Putting it briefly, the Etruscans had classified lightning, labelled and listed it according to what direction it came from, its colour and where it struck. These distinctions enabled them to decide which god had sent the flash and what it meant. It might convey pleasure, refusal, a warning; but it could also chastise. O. Müller explained the frequency of thunderstorms in maritime Etruria by its marshy soil and its warm, unhealthy air. The lightning-lore of the Etruscans was still extant in the year 408 *of our era*, when the "fulgurators" of the town of Narnia proposed using lightning to repulse the Goths, who were menacing Rome as well as Narnia. These descendants of the Etruscans insisted on one condition: that Bishop Innocentius should give his blessing on their public ceremony and solemn incantations. But it would appear that he preferred the darkness of Gothic barbarism, which descended on Europe for the space of some ten centuries.

In sum, lightning, in all its various modes, was a kind of "celestial nail" which any of the nine gods, all of whom had thunderbolts at their disposal, could drive into the earth to communicate whatever decision he might have made. But I had had the luck to extend the list of signs in this celestial Morse code. *Ais cemnac* had woken from its long sleep to hurl at me a thunderbolt of a new species, unknown to the old augurs. This time it was a sign of benevolence, a lexicological lightning, an encouragement to any who were prepared to subject themselves to "barren toil" for the sake of interpreting the hieratic language to which it belongs.

I could no longer doubt that my method of deciphering was valid; I therefore set out resolutely on this road, knowing well that it was not devoid of pitfalls and stumbling-blocks. I shall mention here only one other word which I had deciphered, and shall mention it, moreover, because it concerns one of the intrinsic notions of Etruscan civilisation, one of the very pivot-points of Etruscan religious life, deeply connected as it was with the worship of ancestral shades; and because these shades or *manes* are depicted in tomb-frescos such as, for example, the François Tomb, which shows a sacrifice being made to the shade of Patrocles; and, finally, because the word "shade" plays the leading role in the Book of the Mummy. The word in Etruscan is *hia*. It is also a thoroughly Albanian noun, *hie, hija*, with the definite article appearing as a post-position, just as in Etruscan (*hija*, M. 159); and it is related to the Greek *skia*. To convince oneself one has only to open any Albanian book or newspaper. In the Albanian translation of Ecclesiastes vi. 12 we read that man "passes like a shadow", *shkon si hie*, the brief days of his life. But we shall see later that the Albanian verb *shkon* is also thoroughly Etruscan, and has the same meaning in that language. The proof will be afforded by what appears to be a single word but is in fact a double or composite word, which I take from the Book of the Mummy: *scuχie*, that is, "Come (go, pass, etc.) O shades!" We shall be forced to concede that the Etruscan expression *scuχie* and the Albanian expression *shkon si hie* are, as it were, built of the same materials, and have the same meaning.

A final observation. The Albanian *hije* means not only "shade, shadow" but also "image; likeness; god"; which suits us very nicely. So, in Mann's Albanian grammar: *i ka hijë një bir mbreti*, "(he) has the *air* of a king's son" (p. 106).[1] Thus the Etruscan *hia* was also "image, likeness, appearance".

We can go forward. The shades of the Etruscans are beside us.

2. MY PREDECESSORS

My method of decipherment was built up as follows: I noted certain of Bonnell's allusions; I verified them with the help of material collected by von Hahn; and having perceived the possible relevance of Albanian, I began studying that language. To get an idea of its ancient nucleus I consulted Gustave Meyer's etymological dictionary of Albanian. But certain warnings could not be overlooked. Jokl affirms that G. Meyer went too far in denying the antiquity of many Albanian roots and regarding them as borrowings from foreign sources. Stuart E. Mann, in the preface to his Albanian–English dictionary, writes as follows:

> G. Meyer, in his *Etymol. Wörterbuch* . . ., discovered only 400 radicals whose Indo-European origin could be proved. This number can now be multiplied by five at least . . . [G. Meyer] failed to perceive most of the abundant original material of this language . . . His identification and interpretation of the Indo-European elements in Albanian are at once naive and inconsistent.

Nevertheless, S. E. Mann admits that some of Meyer's interpretations of Albanian words are brilliant.

I also compared G. Meyer's conclusions with the views of Kretschmer, Jokl and Vasmer. Once sieved in this fashion, the vocabulary could be compared with that of Etruscan.

It goes without saying that this external framework did not of itself hold any guarantee of success. It was the exception to find, from time to time, an Albanian word which was an exact copy, miraculously preserved, of a corresponding Etruscan word. Thus, for instance, when I saw for the first time the Albanian word *lart*, "high, elevated", it was easy to recognise in it the widely diffused Etruscan proper noun. The same is true of *mantisa*, an Etruscan commercial term, and of several other glosses preserved by Hesychius and other authors. We shall discuss *mantisa* in due course.

But most of the time there was a perceptible gap between the word

---

[1] *mbret* comes from *imperator*.

I deciphered and its Albanian counterpart. Sometimes the Etruscan word would turn out in reality to be a coupling of words, such as *pava Tarχies* (Tarχies has seen) or *θuluter* (two men praying) or several others which we shall be looking at later; sometimes the word has become unrecognisable through some slight deviation or modification which, at first sight, confused the issue. Moreover, I was, so to speak, thinking within the categories of Albanian syntax; but Albanian is a modern, composite language, the product of a long development, and it would be illogical to expect its syntax to take us back 2,500 years.

And so Etruscan words often seemed to me to be like nutshells made of well-tempered steel. Time after time their toughness would compel me to give up; and if they did sometimes yield to my teeth they did so with an alarming crunch, which always left me disconcerted. They demanded not only a concentration of my will-power and intellectual energy but also a stroke of intuition, something largely fortuitous and, alas, to be neither commanded nor conjured to appear.

Thus, in conditions so complicated and so little dependent on my own will, I felt myself happy to achieve a pioneer's task and blaze a trail for conquests which my successors would make. I knew that where I was working with a penknife, others would come armed with electronic equipment.

Nevertheless, at the outset of my work I was ingenuous enough to believe that I had discovered an epigraphical California. Lying in wait for me, however, was a surprise of a less agreeable nature than the discovery of an archaeological museum. I had already deciphered more than half of the Etruscan words which are presented in this book when I began—as I went on familiarising myself with the history of Etruscan studies, always closely bound up with the study of Etruscan texts—to become aware of an unexpected fact: my California had been discovered long before. Worse: it had been thoroughly explored and had been the setting for a "boom", and an abortive one at that. Dozens of other prospectors had thronged into the territory, some a hundred, others fifty, others thirty years before my own arrival.

But after disembarking and sniffing the air a little they had merely raked the topsoil here and there and struck a few casual blows with their pickaxes; after which they had declared the region unhealthy, barren and uninhabitable, and had departed towards other horizons. A few, indeed, had proclaimed their enthusiasm and predicted a great future for the country; but they had been unable to produce any proof of their words. The end-result was that my California remained deserted, plunged in lethargic sleep.

I did not know how lively had been the debate about the part which might be played by Albanian in the elucidation of Etruscan, and how many clear, explicit pointers had been relegated to oblivion.

To my astonishment, I perceived that without knowing it I had been responding to a call which had been sounded long ago; that I was merely continuing an endeavour which had long been adumbrated, but prematurely abandoned; with this difference, of course, that I am now able to bring forward such irresistible proofs, and so many of them, that any possibility of chance coincidence must be set aside.

Let us take a glance back. As early as 1877 Ascoli, developing von Hahn's suggestions, had written:

If anyone were to attempt, with the help of Albanian, to decipher the *misteriosissime* inscriptions of the Etruscans, we certainly would not be in a position to say that he was setting out from flimsier premises than those already chosen by many scholars of well-tried ability.[1]

In 1883 S. Bugge analysed the Etruscan word *zivas* (which he interpreted as meaning "alive") and connected it with the Sanskrit *givas*, Lithuanian *gyvas*, Slav *zivu*, etc., noting at the same time that the Etruscan plural termination -*ar*, -*er* was also to be found in Danish (*Sönner*, "sons");[2] summing up, he concluded that Etruscan was an Indo-European language. This was the first step towards connecting it with Albanian.

In 1887 Moratti affirmed that the Etruscans, Messapians and Albanians had originated in Asia Minor. He associated the Etruscan word *ri(l)*, "age", with the Albanian root *rri*, "to grow".

In 1889 E. Schneider declared that Etruscan could be deciphered with the aid of Old Albanian, but according to G. Buonamici his application of this principle left much to be desired.[3]

In 1906 A. Torp, a Danish scholar, after several unsuccessful interpretations, managed to isolate an important Etruscan word, *pevaχ*, which occurs in the Book of the Mummy in juxtaposition with *vinum*, and judiciously inferred that *pevaχ* meant "beverage".[4] This Indo-European root, which is also found in the Balto-Slavonic languages (*pivo*, "beer") and in Albanian (*pi*, "to drink"; *piva*, "has drunk"), did not, however, incite anybody to undertake research in this direction.

In 1909, in the article which has already been quoted, Skutsch pointed out analogies between Etruscan and Albanian, but did not lay special emphasis on them.

[1] Quoted by Petrotta, in the article already mentioned.
[2] *Etr. Forschungen u. Studien*, IV Heft, p. 57.
[3] *Di alcune vere od apparente analogie fra l'etrusco e l'albanese*, 1919, p. 82.
[4] *Etruskische Beitrage*, II, p. 11.

In 1919 Buonamici, in his article already quoted, contributed greatly to the understanding of the problem. The article takes note of a book by a Greek author, Thomopoulos, who found several points of contact between Etruscan, on the one hand, and Albanian, ancient Greek and Hittite, on the other. Buonamici describes Thomopoulos's essay as "powerful", adding that Thomopoulos poses "extraordinary erudition" and that some of his comparisons are ingenious. But these are little more than formal compliments, since one sees that Buonamici is far from regarding the problem as having been illuminated; the arguments marshalled by Thomopoulos have not convinced him and, while he does find a little truth in them, he evidently considers that Thomopoulos has not succeeded in casting his demonstration in a scientific mould; he therefore decides to adopt Thomopoulos' line of inquiry himself in order to render it worthy of general attention.

He then proceeds to indicate several points which Etruscan and Albanian possess in common:

1. Transition from *a* to *e*: *Patruni*, *Petruni*, in Etruscan; *amble*, *emble*, "sweet", in Albanian; and the same relationship, in both languages, between *a* and *u*, *e* and *i*; *e* and *u*, *i* and *l*, etc.
2. The termination -*ak*, which we have already seen (here Buonamici mentions Etruscan *rumaχ* but overlooks Albanian *romak*).
3. The final -*s* of the Etruscan genitive and the final -*s* of the same case of feminine nouns in Albanian.

From all these comparisons Buonamici draws only a very circumspect conclusion, saying that he observes in Etruscan and Albanian "a tendency to evolve analogously", resulting either from a common origin or from analogous reaction to substrata, "*sostrati omoglotti preistorici*". He does, however, recognise Albanian as offering "materials for a useful comparison with Etruscan". The phrase is as carefully calculated as the final communiqué of a diplomatic conference. The matter rested there.

A thunderclap resounded, however, in the form of a short but brilliant article by M. Hammarström-Justinien, published in the *Studi Etruschi* (Vol. XI, p. 250). This writer had read a short Etruscan inscription on a drinking-cup,

(P. 488) *ta θafna raθiu cleusinśl*

of which he proposed to discuss only the third word.

It was already known that *ta* meant "this", that *θafna* meant "cup", and that the last word referred to the city of Clusium. Quoting a similar Latin inscription ("*ordo et cives Tarquiniensium*"), the author interpreted the word *raθiu* as the equivalent of the Latin *ordo*, "line, order", and, by extension, "council". His grounds were the analogy between the Etruscan word *raθ*, on one hand, and *rad*, *radh* (Swedish and Danish), *rata* (Persian), *radq* (Ossetic), on the other hand.

Hence: "This is the cup of the Council of Clusium."

The demonstration was a just one. And we may note that it would not have been difficult to proceed from thence to Albanian, since in that language the same word makes its appearance as *"radë"* (M. 106). But no one made this comparison, and darkness reigned as before. The word is nevertheless found in other Etruscan inscriptions, with the sense of "line", and we shall touch on it again in our chapter on Etruscan religion.

Later on, the same author points out the existence in Etruscan of a "possessive termination" *-u* (as, for example, in *tular-u*, "boundary"), an ending which can be seen in *raθiu*, *hinθiu*, etc. If he made a single further step forward he would have recognised in this *u* the Etruscan *definite article*, just as in Albanian we see *dushk-u*, "the oak", *si-u*, "the eye", etc. (In other cases there is a terminal *i*.)

Let us mention the subsequent observation, in 1924, by Jokl, that *in Albanian* there exist consonantal groups *br*, *dr*, *gr* which tend to soften into *pr*, *tr*, *kr*, a fact which connects them with identical phenomena in the consonantal changes *in Etruscan*. But Jokl took the matter no further.

Parallel to the problem of the connections between Etruscan and Albanian, attention was paid to the relationship between Illyrian and Albanian, on the one hand, and, on the other, the languages of various Italian peoples. Pauli asserted a close kinship between Messapian, Illyrian and Albanian. Ribezzo recognised substantial resemblances between proper names in Albanian and those in the Venetian–Iapygian–Illyrian group. Trombetti observed that the Illyrian race extended the whole length of the Apennine peninsula, from the country of the Veneti right down into Apulia and Calabria. Lattes admitted to having "no adverse feelings towards an Illyrian origin for any Italic population",[1] words which attest the objectivity of that devoted Etruscologist. I do not think Lattes would ever have consented to add, "except for the Etruscans".

Finally, Devoto judged that, on the one hand, the ancient inhabitants of Picenium were related to the Etruscans and that, on the other hand, they (especially the Liburnians) belonged to the great Illyrian family. These are the terms in which the views of Devoto are summed up by Buonamici, in *Studi Etruschi*, Vol. XVI, 1942, pp. 334–5. What does this amount to, in plain language, if not to saying that the Etruscans belonged to the Illyrian family, a fact which no one dared admit? Was

---

[1] In Buonamici, *L'interpunzione sillabica*, *Studi Etruschi*, XVI, 1942, p. 337.

C

not that the reason why scholars had found themselves penned in a vicious circle of inconsistency and hesitation?

As I followed these zigzags of Etruscology in the past, my attention was drawn willy-nilly to the unfortunate Thomopoulos, who had earned a few compliments and then been completely forgotten by all concerned with the subject. It occurred to me to glance at his book. To my surprise there was a copy at the Bibliothèque Nationale. It was a bulky volume, published in Athens in 1912; its title was *Iacobou Thomopoulou. Pelasgika.* Written in modern Greek, the book was almost as incomprehensible to me as an Etruscan text. I armed myself with dictionaries and gleaned what I could from it. I did at least gather how the author had contrived, with the help of Albanian, to decipher several Etruscan words. To my disappointment, I saw that at least half a dozen words, which I had hitherto regarded with legitimate satisfaction as my own authentic finds, had already been understood in the same way as by me and had been published, as it were behind my back, forty-five years earlier! But it was really obvious that Thomopoulos could not have reacted differently from myself to such words as *mantisa*, or *capys*, or *ci* ("three"), or *lart*, rendered by him as the Greek *ypsistos*, "supreme".

What was more, I found in his pages, with sincere admiration in this case, some ten Etruscan words whose meaning eluded me or at least left me wavering, and for which he had supplied convincing interpretations. I therefore made haste to accept his point of view, which will be duly acknowledged below, as occasion arises.

Finally, I noticed about twenty doubtful or faulty interpretations, cases in which the solution suggested by Thomopoulos appeared unacceptable to me. He sometimes let himself be led astray by mere phonetic resemblances. In this way such an elementary word as *θaura*, "tomb", was turned by him into "father-in-law", because of its resemblance to the Greek word *daér*. In the same way, Thomopoulos thought he had found in an epitaph a mention of an Etruscan civil officer, "*agoranomos*" (superintendent of a market). Nothing of the kind, alas; for the tomb was that of a little girl. Child prodigies exist, certainly, but this one was rather too prodigious.

Thomopoulos tended to refer Etruscan words to ancient Greek or pre-Hellenic Pelasgic, rather than to Illyrian. It is not part of my task to discuss this problem. I shall simply observe that some of Thomopoulos's deficiencies have not escaped the notice of Buonamici, who, however, has simply ignored most of Thomopoulos's propositions, without separating the wheat from the tares. Broadly speaking, he has thrown out the baby with the bath water. The ideas of Thomopoulos

have remained hidden under a bushel. Nevertheless, some of his views
and discoveries were perfectly correct, and there is no doubt that he
was one of the precursors of the genuine decipherment. We must
hope that his work will be studied once more and that a translation,
or at least a detailed summary of it, will appear. My own recon-
naissance of this private ground having been very superficial, the value
of Thomopoulos's conjectures might then emerge clearly.

In one way and another, by Ascoli and Bugge, by Jokl, Thomopoulos and Hammarström, the Albanian key to the Etruscan language
had been suspected, suggested, indicated and even offered to investi-
gators of the Etruscan enigma. But they ignored all these approaches
and passed on. Some preferred to look for a solution in a supposititious
archaic Egypt, others in Iberia, and so forth, while yet others declared
simply that Etruscan could not be explained by means of any other
language. But the combinatorial method, based on the internal laws
of the Etruscan language, was bound to fail for want of a sufficiently
wide lexicological basis. My intention in the present work is precisely
to widen that basis, and thus to throw the road open to the decipherment of all the Etruscan epigraphic materials we possess. But that will
demand still more, and much more, co-operative effort by Etruscologists, experts in Albanian, Latinists, Hellenists, and specialists in the
Caucasian and Oriental Indo-European languages.

The Etruscan Bastille has been taken. But we must remember that
the fall of the Bastille was only the first step towards the founding of a
new order.

FIG. 3A. Winged thunderbolt,
Etruscan symbol of the god
Tinia, ais cemnac

II

PRELIMINARY REMARKS ON ETRUSCAN
NUMBERS

BEFORE embarking on a number of subjects which reflect the daily life
of the Etruscans, as seen through their written remains, I must establish
certain basic notions; notably, that of numbers.

This section of our study is a comparatively barren region. It has
to be traversed before one can reach the land flowing with milk and
honey.

The problem of numbers being decidedly complex, what is presented
here is mainly of a suggestive nature. But, as we proceed, we shall
concern ourselves with various other topics, of historical, religious or
literary interest.

A certain quantity of *numbers* are to be recognised here and there in
Etruscan inscriptions. But the identification of these numbers remains
difficult. The six first numbers, however, form a group apart. One
finds them not only in epitaphs (in which the age of the deceased or the
number of his children is given) and the Book of the Mummy (which
specifies, for example, the dates of the periodical religious ceremonies
and the size of the various offerings) but also on Etruscan *dice*. On a
pair of them, known as the dice of Campanari or the Tuscan dice,
there are inscribed not the usual numbers but the following six words,
which I shall give here in alphabetical order and which correspond
(but we do not know in what order) to the numbers 1, 2, 3, 4, 5, 6:

$$ci, \; hu\theta, \; ma\chi, \; \acute{s}a, \; \theta u, \; zal.$$

Thus, instead of invading mathematics, we find ourselves beginning by
entering the realm of games, which were much in vogue among the
Etruscans. Sometimes they invested games with a special meaning,
using them to fathom the will of the gods. Horace jestingly relates how
an old Samnite woman predicted his future after rattling her dice in a
dicebox. However that may be, it was by throwing dice that the
Etruscans decided, before a banquet, who was to preside over it: a
transitory presidency, to be sure, but an important one, for this dictator
of the table would decree how much each guest was to drink. It is to
be hoped that they did not resort to the same method when they had

to choose a lucumon.[1] Generally speaking, no doubt, they played at dice as lightheartedly as people do now, in the din of a tavern, meanwhile helping themselves to a cup of good wine from Luna, brought to them by the nimble and obliging serving-girls, of whom we shall have more to say later. They played without any premonition that on these little cubes would one day be erected the complicated theories of Etruscologists.

The dice at our disposal do not, indeed, belong to a single type. On another pair of dice, the so-called dice of Autun, the following Etruscan words have been found:

> *i   va   est   urti   caius   volote*

Finally, there are three types of dice marked with dots, as ours are, from 1 to 6 in number, but differing in the way the dots are arranged. All these variations for some ten dice in all! Notably, according to the number of dots marked on their opposite faces, these dotted dice can be divided into the following categories:

(a) 1 and 6; 2 and 5; 3 and 4. The sum of each pair of opposed numbers is 7.

(b) 1 and 2; 3 and 4; 5 and 6.

(c) On a single example, we find 1 and 6; 2 and 4; 5 and 3.[2]

To which category do the Tuscan dice belong? That is the problem.

Here is a graphic representation of these Tuscan dice, which have been the centre of a long, stern battle in which Etruscologists have taken part:

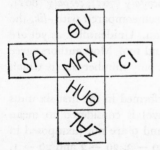 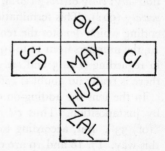

FIG. 4

Our illustration gives a simplified picture of these dice, Etruscan letters having been replaced by a Latin transcription. The fact which immediately catches attention is that only the word *max* is written in

---

[1] An Etruscan chieftain. (*Tr.*)
[2] Buonamici, *Epigrafia etrusca*, p. 406.

the same direction on both dice; the orientation of all the other numbers varies. From which the conclusion was drawn that *maχ* may have meant "one", the number from which it was usual to begin when marking the facets of dice.

Here, by way of contrast, are the two aspects of one of the dice of Autun:

FIG. 5

"The meanings of all these words elude us," writes Buonamici. But it has not escaped notice that they arrange themselves naturally in a series of which each member is longer than the preceding one. The numbers of letters are in arithmetical progression, with *i* corresponding to 1, *va* to 2, *est* to 3, *orti* to 4, *caius* to 5 and *volote* to 6; which is to say that these words symbolise the first six numbers. The meanings of the words will be elucidated at the end of this chapter, but their numerical values will not thereby be changed. It remains meanwhile to add that the marking of opposite faces of these Autun dice puts them into the category 1:6; 2:5; 3:4. The sum of any two opposite faces is 7.

The other numbers which are known but not yet certainly identified are *semf* (7?), *cezp* (8?), *nurf* (9?). The tens are expressed by a termination -*alχ*: *cialχ* or *cealχ* (30?), *sealχ* (40?), *semfalχ* (70?), *cezpalχ* (80?), *muvalχ* (90?). This termination -*alχ* has been compared with -*lik*, the ending which denotes the tens in Lithuanian. Unidentified as yet are 10, the numbers from 11 to 19, and 50, 60 and 100. Most authors agree in regarding *ci* as 3 and *cealχ* as 30. The only number about which there is really no doubt is *zaθrum*, 20.

In the tens the adding-on of units is performed in the first six units by juxtaposition. Thus *ciś cealχlś* (genitive) is considered to mean "(of) 33". But, according to Torp, 7, 8 and 9 are not juxtaposed in this way. 17, 18 and 19 are expressed as 20 — 3, 20 — 2 and 20 — 1. Similarly, 27, 28 and 29 are expressed as 30 — 3, 30 — 2, 30 — 1. This, indeed, explains why as well as *ciś cealχlś* (33, the age of the deceased) there is another combination of the same numbers, *ciem cealχlś* (in L.M.). Since the particle -*em* indicates a *subtraction*, what we have here is 30 — 3 (27). This form occurs in the Book of the Mummy and represents a *date*. Since there is no such date as the thirty-third day of a month, we are bound to fall back on the twenty-seventh as the answer; all the more so in that these numbers sometimes occur in association with nouns which, thanks to the glosses we possess, have been identified as the names of certain months.

Now there are, in all, three numbers which are regularly subtracted in this fashion: *θu, ci, zal*. With the sign of subtraction incorporated, they appear as *θunem, ciem, eslem*: less one, less two, less three. From which it is concluded that *θu, ci, zal* in a certain order, must represent 1, 2, 3.

But what is the order?

It has been observed that, in funerary inscriptions, after the numbers *ci* and *zal* the word "sons" occurs in the plural: *clenar* (instead of *clan*), in which *-ar* is the sign for the plural. It follows from this that each of these numbers is greater than unity; so that the role of 1 falls to *θu*.

But how are we to allot the right values to *ci* and *zal*? It is a matter of observation that *ci* occurs frequently in the Book of the Mummy, especially in Chapter VII, in which it is thought that certain rites are described. The conclusion drawn from this is that *ci* must be a sacred number. Now it is known that the Etruscans consecrated three gates of each town to their gods and that their temples were often divided into three parts, which seems to indicate the worship of a divine triad. From this it is deduced that *ci* was "three". We thus have *θu* = 1, *zal* = 2, *ci* = 3. If this is correct, *θunem* must be "less 1", *eslem* "less 2" and *ciem* "less 3". By applying the rule that "opposite faces add up to 7", we get *śa* = 4, *maχ* = 5 and *huθ* = 6. Therefore, say both Torp and Trombetti, our Tuscan dice is arranged as follows:

```
      ┌───┐
      │ 1 │
  ┌───┼───┼───┐
  │ 4 │ 5 │ 3 │
  └───┼───┼───┘
      │ 6 │
      ├───┤
      │ 2 │
      └───┘
```

This is the current view among Etruscologists. But I am bound to say that, at first sight, the arrangement seems rather arbitrary to me. The central position, the position allotted to *maχ*, as Skutsch declares, could have been occupied only by 1 or 6. What reason could there be for putting 5 there? Round this 5, on the four adjacent faces of the cube, the numbers 1, 3, 6 and 4 are supposed to have been arranged—

but in accordance with what principle? However, let us go on to examine the number *θu*. Can we be sure that it means "one"? Let us look at the documents.

We have, to begin with, a bas-relief representing *two* men standing firmly one beside the other, like two soldiers on parade, with a short inscription: (P. 208, CIE 5180) *θuluter* (A). Very early in my study of Albanian I learnt that *lus* means "to pray" and that this verb possesses a middle-voice form *lutem*, while "he who prays" is designated by *lutës* (M. 253). In Etruscan one would expect this to be *lut*, plural *luter*; whence *θuluter* would seem to mean "two individuals praying" or "two men at prayer".

However, those who hold that *θu* = 1 could object that *θu* denotes in the present instance a *common* action on the part of these two individuals, on the lines of *com* in the word "combatants", for example. So the question remains undecided.

Now let us examine an Etruscan inscription of the 3rd century B.C. engraved on the wall of a funerary cave at Perugia. In this study of numbers only the first words of the inscription concern us:

(P. 619, CIE 4116) *cehen suθi hinθiu θués sianś etve θaure* . . . (A).

This is the beginning of an inventory of the contents of the cave. This inventory would have pleased a museum curator, anxious both to satisfy the curiosity of visitors to his establishment and, at the same time, to impress upon them that the objects displayed had been set out under scrupulous supervision:

cehen: Thomopoulos recognised in this word the Albanian *keha, kehan*: "here, this way" (Pelasgika, p. 547). This word is also to be found in Mann, *khâ, këhâ*, with the same meaning (p. 197).

suθi, "tomb, sepulchre": the final *i* is the definite article in postposition, as in Albanian: *mal, mali*, "the mountain".

hinθiu: this word is to be explained by the Osco-Umbrian *hondomu*, "lower", whence *hunte, Hondo*, a chthonic god; *aisna hinθu* are infernal gods. In the present context we have to do with a *subterranean* tomb.

θues: this is our word *θu*, in the genitive. "Of two"?

sianś: this is two words: (1) *si* is the Albanian "to her, from her" (M. 450); (2) *anś* is the Albanian *anë*, with the *ś* of the genitive (M. 7). *θues sians* therefore means "from its two sides, on both sides". It may be noted that, in Albanian, *anë* is accepted by G. Meyer as one of the words forming the native basis of the language.

The importance of the word *anë* in Etruscan inscriptions makes a brief digression necessary. We meet this old Illyrian word in the Tomb of the Inscriptions of Tarquinia, which was reproduced by Luigi Canina.[1] (Fig. 6.)

FIG. 6. "Put (that) beside the gods"

This tomb is decorated with eight frescos, two on each of the four walls. The subjects of the frescos are games and sporting contests in honour of the deceased. The pictures are full of life; horsemen with their mounts capering just before the start of a race, and scenes from boxing and wrestling matches. Amid this throng, in a separate fresco, we see a character as heavily bearded as a Cuban, standing rather stiffly; badly drawn, moreover, with his left arm looking like a set square. He appears to be the master of ceremonies, and is in the act of giving orders to a servant or slave. The latter is running up to him holding laurel branches, which are probably intended for crowning the victors in the games.

Near the head of the bearded character there is a short inscription. There are many inscriptions in this tomb, but it seems that they deteriorated quickly after the discovery of the tomb in 1827, and that they were copied only after some time had elapsed. They are consequently not easy to read. M. Pallottino gives only one of them, taken from a scene of sacrifice. However, the text referring to the picture with which we are concerned has suffered comparatively little.

L. Canina gives it as *veiiiuaniies*; the CIE gives it as *ve...aniees*; but after the *ve* there is, I think, a syllable *ce*. Still, the meaning of the inscription is clear enough: *ve* or *veii* is the Albanian verb *ve*, "to put", "put" (second person singular imperative) (M. 547); *ie*, with the

[1] *L'Antica Etruria Marittima*, 1851, tav. LXXXVII.

definite article *iu*, is Albanian *hie*, "gods", *hiu*, "the gods" (M. 159), the initial *h* being unimportant in Illyrian; finally, the word which principally interests us, *anies*, is *anë*, "side", in an oblique case. The meaning of the short sentence which we are studying is therefore: "Put (that) beside the gods", that is to say, "beside the statues of the gods". The servant makes no reply; but in other scenes, alongside this one, there are verbal exchanges which are full of humour and observation of character, as we shall see in later chapters. Nothing could be more marvellous than these ingenuous dialogues recorded fresh from life which enliven the walls of these tombs and which take us to the very heart of the Etruscan city and its day-to-day existence.

We can now return to the opening sentence of our inscription from Perugia:

> *etve*: I read this word as *edue*, since in Etruscan *u* and *v* are often used interchangeably, just as *θ* and *t* are interchangeable. The word is thus connected with *θu*; it emerges as *tue*, *θue*, the feminine of *θu*, "two". Let us recall that in the Slav languages, for example, this number possesses two genders: *dva* in the masculine and *dvé* (*dvié*) in the feminine. The initial *e* would be either prothetic (like the *e* of *eslem*, for example) or a conjunction "and".
>
> *θaure*, "tombs": a word we have seen already, in the plural.

The meaning of the sentence as a whole is therefore: "Here is a subterranean tomb. On two of its sides there are two tombs . . ."

This interpretation is corroborated by a graphical document. On consulting a *compte rendu* by G. Conestabile of the excavations made at Perugia, I received a pleasant surprise in the form of a plan of the underground chamber in question, thus:

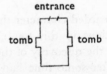

Conestabile writes: "On the longer sides of the chamber are to be seen two [funerary] niches, facing each other."

Surely the text under review now becomes explicit?

Need we go on looking for evidence that *θue*, *tve* might mean "one"? *θaure* being in the plural, our sense of objectivity must not be allowed to sway us to the point of accepting unlikely solutions.

In the opinion of an Albanian *savant*, however, *etve* is "paternal, belonging to the parents" ("to the father and mother"), *et* being a plural form of *at*, "father". *Etve* is an oblique case, cf. *maleve, maluve, malave* (p. 229).

Let us now note two other cases of the number "two", one from the Etruscan world, the other from among Illyrian place-names.

(*a*) In a funerary inscription from Vulci (P. 324, CIE 5315) it is recorded of an Etruscan nobleman how many times in his life he held the office of chief magistrate (prytanis): *θunz purtsvana*. *θunz* is evidently "twice", for why should the fact be underlined if he had held the honour only once?

(*b*) Von Hahn and other writers cite an Illyrian locality called Dimallum, the interpretation of which is "*dy-male*", "two mountains". Nobody, indeed, would think of inventing such an absurd name as "*one* mountain".

We must pause, finally, to look at a particularly interesting case of the Etruscan *θu*, the case where this number is incorporated into the name of a deity, *θuflθa*.

The problem is a very tissue of duplicity.

As soon as we invoke *θuflθas* we find ourselves in the presence of half a dozen equivocal deities, closely related to each other and perhaps representing, in antiquity, so many divine persons of a single divine unity. They are as follows: Janus (Ani, in Etruscan), Culśan, Culśu, Cul(alp), *θuflθa*. They are almost the Dr Jekyll and Mr Hyde of the Etruscan pantheon.

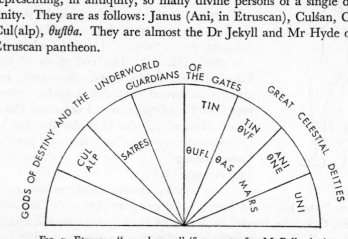

FIG. 7. Etruscan "sacred space" (fragment, after M. Pallottino)

Ani-Janus-Bifrons, the god with two faces, is reminiscent of a Sumero-Babylonian deity, the Gate-keeper who opens the celestial gates to Shamash, the Sun. The Roman Janus is likewise a "porter", his name being derived from the Latin *janua*, "door, house-door".[1] He would

_____
[1] More especially, a vaulted passage.

seem to have been a Latin or Italic deity borrowed by the Etruscans. A door being both entrance and exit, this god presided over all beginnings and all endings.

Culśan, according to Nogara and other writers, is the Etruscan Janus. It is probably he who appears on the bronze liver of Piacenza, which is an "almanach" of the Etruscan gods, under the name of *Cvl alp*. But Ani and Culśan are lodged in different sectors of that liver, and of the Etruscan *"mappa mundi"* or *"sacred space"* which is reproduced in our Fig. 7. While the first of these gods occupies a place beside the great celestial deities, Tinia and Juno, the second is among the gods of destiny and the Underworld. Culśu is a guardian-goddess of the gates of hell; but it is important to notice that she is mentioned neither on the liver nor on the map. Let us note in any case that Culśan is a god with two faces, a Janus, as is proved by a bronze statuette (Fig. 8) bearing the following inscription:

(P. 640, CIE 437) *v cvinti arntiaś culśanśl alpan turce*

—of which the translation is: Velia Cvinti, wife of Arnth, to Culśan (this) offering (?) has given.

We may observe that *turce* (A) is the past of the Etrucans verb which is connected with the Albanian *dorzoj*, "to give" (M. 81), and *dhuroj*, "to offer" (M. 93). The ending *-ce* of the Etruscan aorist (*svalce, lupuce, zilaχce*, etc.) reappears in several Albanian irregular verbs: *thacë*, "said", *mbetçe si gur*, "I remained like a stone" (Dozon, p. 85). It is also the past in Old Slavonic: *kovashe*, "was forging", *poyashe*, "were singing", etc. (*The Epic of Prince Igor*, 12th century A.D.)

FIG. 8

As for *θuflθa*, Deecke considers her as a goddess "who heals and blesses" and compares her with the Earth goddess, Ops, "the Sower", while Janus himself also bore the title of "the Sower". The form *θuflθa* is found neither on the bronze liver nor on the "map"; instead, we find *θuflθas*. Is this the genitive of the same name? Divine names occur both in the nominative (*Tin, Leθn*) and in the genitive (*Tins, Leθns*). If not, it might, perhaps, be the name of a deity not known from any other source.

Let us briefly examine a few inscriptions in which the goddess *θuflθa* appears:

(a) (P. 652, CIE 446). Votive inscription to *θuflθas* (with this noun in the dative) on a statuette of a child.

(b) (P. 558, CIE 2341). *eiseras θufiθi cver* "to the goddess *θuflθa*, to the treasure (of the temple)". We shall encounter *cver* again later. This inscription figures on a statuette representing a naked man holding a patera and making a libation (Gori, *Museum Etruscorum*, 1737, Tab. C).

(c) (P. 740, CII 2603 bis.) *eiseras θuflθicla trutvecie* "to the goddess *θuflθa*, an appeal, to the guardian of faith (?)". I suppose that *cla* can be explained by the Albanian verb *klaj, qaj*, "to shout, call by name" (M. 199 and 411). The word *trutvecie* will be studied later. This dedication is inscribed on a statuette representing a beautiful young woman with a Greek profile who is making a gesture with her right hand, probably a gesture of adoration.[1]

Thus prayers were addressed to *θuflθa* for the well-being of men, women and children. The life of a child, then as now, was truly a "beginning".

(d) (P. 447). A dedication to *θuflθa*, in which a woman, θania Cencnei, implores the goddess *θuflθal cauzna* (of Clusium): *śuv lusi* (A) "look thou upon my prayer"; here we can recognise two words we have already seen, *shov (shuf)*, Etruscan and Albanian, "to see", and *lus*, "prayer", with the definite article.

(e) (P. 654). Consecration of a candelabrum to *θuflθas* (of Clusium?).

(f) (P. 149). Votive inscription *θuflθas cver* on a bronze spear.

With all this we must bear in mind that, in the Etruscan map of the world, the name *θuflθas* is inscribed partly in the sector of the *Guardians of the Gates* and partly among the gods of heaven, beside Tinia and in direct proximity to *Ani-Janus*. *This proximity confirms that the deity in question belongs to the Bifrons family.* It is, however, remarkable that neither the goddess *θuflθa*, nor *Culśu*, is ever shown with a double head. On the contrary, this honour is reserved to a male deity who appears frequently on the coinage of the Etruscan town of Velathri. The coins show a dolphin on one side and an unmistakable Bifrons on the other.

FIG. 9

In Gori's *Museum Etruscorum* two other coins from the same town are illustrated, both of them with a Bifrons (fig. 9); in one instance both faces are bearded, in the other, both

[1] *Annali dell'Inst. archeol.*, XXXIII, 1861, Tav. T.

youthful (Table CXCVI, I and II). Who was this god? Ani, Culśan, or perhaps a masculine θuflθa, since we already know a pair of this kind, Culśan and Culśu? Or did the goddess θuflθa have the special function of protecting maternity? While all this remains obscure, the name (or rather the epithet) θuflθa-θuflθas can be completely explained with the help of Albanian.

And here is the explanation:

θuflθas is θu-flθas
This f is a b (bh), as in frontac-bronté.
The word is therefore Du-blθas.
Du is "two".
balθash is "frontal, foreheads, of foreheads" in Albanian.

The word "forehead" exists in Albanian in two forms: ball (masculine) and ballë (feminine); whence baj ballë, "to face, confront"; ballaballë, "face to face"; ballinë, "frontispiece"; balaballët, "opposite", ballet being the plural form of the noun (M. 18).

The ending -ash, in θuflθaś, is that of the ablative plural. Thus from dega, "branch", comes degash (Mann, Gram., p. 50). The noun ballëz (diminutive of balle, M. 18) would give ballëzash (baldzash, which probably contracted into -blθaś, -flθaś).

Du-balθas is Bifrons.

Janus-Bifrons in person.

The reality of a name of this kind is confirmed by an analogous case: the name of the Thraco-Illyrian people already mentioned, the Triballoï, the inhabitants of the mountainous region of the "Three Foreheads (Three Peaks)".

We thus stand before the very source of the Latin Bifrons, who, with all respect to him, was only a translation from the Etruscan.

These are our positive arguments in favour of θu = "two". There is a negative argument which can be added to them. It is derived from a sentence in the Book of the Mummy:

θunem cialχus etnam iχeslem cialχus θanal (XI, 17)

There are two dates in this, and there is no reason to suppose that different months were implied. The first date is θunem cialχus; according to Trombetti and his predecessors, θu being "one", this means "30 — 1", the 29th of the month. Next, there comes an event: etnam iχ. It will appear in due course that this means: "The ancestors set out." But the nature of the event does not concern us for the moment. Now comes the second date: eslem cialχus, when something else will happen, though what is to happen has never yet been elucidated.

According to Trombetti, this second date means (*eslem* being "minus two") "30 — 2", the 28th of the month. Why should the 29th come before the 28th? Would it not be more natural for the 28th (*θunem cialχus*) to be mentioned before the 29th, *eslem cialχus*, which is just what does happen if we accept $θu = 2$?[1]

θu being "two" (cf. Albanian "*dy*", and Latin, etc.), what is *unity*? Is it *ci* or *zal*? But we have seen that after both of them comes a word in the plural (*clenar*): in inscriptions P. 98 and P. 169, after *ci*; but apparently only in one inscription, after *zal*. Here the words are (P. 170, CII 2056): *clenar zal arce*, "he begot *zal* sons." It is on this inscription that all the following writers—Fabretti, Pauli, Deecke, Skutsch, Goldmann, Cortsen, Torp, Buonamici, Trombetti and Pallottino—base their arguments in asserting that *zal* is greater than one.

If, by chance, there had been a copyist's mistake, which is improbable but not impossible, *zal* could mean 1, and *eslem*, "less one". I have not seen the original of the text, but it has apparently come down to us in good condition. Then what is the derivation of *eslem*? Has anyone given us any real warrant for believing that it comes from *zal*? May there not be some other word, *sal* let us say, which resembles *zal* and from which *eslem* is derived; a word which means "one" but does not appear on the Campanari die, where "one" is probably represented by *maχ*? This would be possible if there were two different words for "one" in Etruscan, as, for example, there are in so many languages words for "two", "pair" and "couple", all expressing the same idea; and as, in Slavonic, there are words for "one" and "once"; or as, in Lithuanian, there are two words for "ten", *deshimt* and *-lik* (the ending of numbers greater than ten such as *trylika*, "thirteen", etc.). We should note that Etruscan does possess an enigmatic word *sal* which is floating loose, unattached to any meaning as yet, in the Book of the Mummy and elsewhere. I have only suggestions to offer in connection with this word, and the verse in question: *sal cus eluce caperi zamtic* (LM, XII, 12) will be studied in one of the closing chapters.

Let us now pass to the number *huθ*. In the Torp-Trombetti arrangement the value of this number is 6. There is, however, one piece of evidence from antiquity (preserved by Stephanus of Byzantium) which has given occasion for a different interpretation. Trombetti writes:

> Oŝtir, followed in this by Kretschmer, argued from the name of a pre-Hellenic town Huttenia, later rendered as Tetrapolis ("four towns"), that *huθ* corresponded to *four*.[2]

[1] M. Pallottino, at least, believes that these dates are arranged progressively (SE, XI, 1937, p. 215).
[2] *La lingua etrusca*, p. 40.

It seems that a bitter battle developed round this idea. Vetter
defended it. E. Meyer would not accept it. Trombetti was also against
it. A. von Blumenthal wrote that *Hut-tenia* came from *hut* and the pre-
Hellenic *ten*, meaning "town". Goldmann retorted that this was
"groundless", since there was not one town, Tetrapolis, but a federation, founded in Greek times, of four towns of Attica (Marathon,
Tricorinthos, Oïnoe and Probalinthos). Eva Fiesel wrote in 1931 that
comparisons of this sort were based only on resemblances and that this
translation of Huttenia was in no way certain, because the meaning of
*hu*θ had not been established.

And yet, *ten* has an exact counterpart in the Albanian *ndenjë* (*ndenj-*,
denj-), "residence", which we shall encounter shortly. It was therefore
an Illyrian noun.

Does *hu*θ occur elsewhere?

My attention was attracted by an inscription on a receptacle for
wine, an "amphoria vinaria", as M. Pallottino describes it:

(P. 73) *.n hu*θ*te anaes*

The first letter of the first word is missing. It seems reasonable
enough, to me, to suppose that an "amphoria vinaria" would contain
wine, and that the first word indicated that important product; and
this leads to the idea that the word was *en*, which also occurs in, for
example, the group *lena haustiś enac eśi* (LM, X, g.4). In this fragment
lena is "libation", as we shall eventually see, *haustiś* is connected with
the Underworld, *eśi* is usually understood as "blood" (because of its
resemblance to the same word in Hittite), and *en* or *ena* is probably one
of the names for wine, related to the Italic *vinum*; *enac eśi*, with the well-
known Etruscan conjunction *c*, therefore indicates that the libation
consisted of "wine with blood" ("wine and blood").

The word *hu*θ*te*, evidently, is derived from *hu*θ.

The word *anaes* is already familiar to us in θ*ues si anś*, which we have
already examined ("its two sides"); *anś* and *anaes* are exactly the same,
the second being spelt out more completely and showing even more
clearly its identity with the Albanian *anë*.

What can *hu*θ mean in the formula "wine from *hu*θ sides"? "Five
sides" or "six sides" makes no immediate appeal. What we are
looking for, of course, is a stock phrase, a *cliché*, something with the
authority of a bilingual inscription. One therefore thinks of the "four
sides of the horizon" and "four sides of the world", as the expression
goes in the Slav languages, and the "four winds of heaven" in the Old
Testament. Are not the four cardinal points the common basis of all

ABOVE: The Tuscan dice. On the upper one can be read (*from right to left*) the word *maχ*, written diagonally. On the lower die: *huθ*.

OVERLEAF: *Velθur Partunus*: inscription on the sarcophagus of the *zilχ* of Tarquinia.

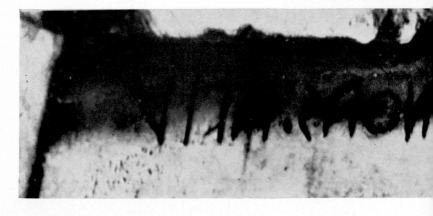

Venθ, the goddess with outspread wings. She is presiding over a
sacrifice to the shade of Patroclus.

PRELIMINARY REMARKS ON ETRUSCAN NUMBERS

civilisations? We thus have a brand of wine called "Wine of the four sides".

But why should a wine be called that? A "wine from the South" or "wine from the East" would have been more natural. Perhaps some Etruscan tradesman was trying to eclipse his competitors by going one better than any of them? The reader doubtless remembers that Etruscan foreign trade took in the four quarters of the civilised world of the time, from the shores of the Baltic (whence came amber and where there arrived, for example, an Etruscan bronze receptacle of the 8th century, found in Denmark) to Egypt and Urartu. So much for the economic aspect. As for the Etruscans' religious life, the phrase "four points of the horizon" occurred even more frequently in it. It is enough to recall the Etruscan "templum", the sacred square in which the omens were consulted and which was laid out in concordance with the four quarters of the horizon. The Etruscans were the people, above all other peoples, for whom "the four sides" were a daily preoccupation.

To this I add the opinion of two eminent scholars: Kretschmer and Vetter. Paul Kretschmer vigorously defended Oštir's argument, finding it "impeccable".[1] E. Vetter wrote:

> Oštir's assimilation of the pre-Hellenic Huttenia to $hu\theta$, a thesis accepted by Kretschmer and sharply contested by others, . . . should not be dismissed as having been controverted, given that other attempts at explaining the word $hu\theta$ are by no means convincing.[2]

On another occasion the same writer noted: "If Oštir's identification of $hu\theta$ is correct, it is of great significance for the problem of the origins of the Etruscans."[3]

Vetter meant that a concentration in Greece, in pre-Hellenic times, of a people speaking a language related to Etruscan, would throw light on the stage preceding the Etruscans' settlement in Italy.

We cannot concern ourselves with this problem here. But the question of the number $hu\theta$ seems to be decided in favour of 4.[4]

---

[1] *Glotta*, XVIII, pp. 110 *et seq.*
[2] *Glotta*, XVIII, p. 306.
[3] *Glotta*, XVII, 299.
[4] The Albanian *anë* also means "receptacle". Did the Etruscan *ane* mean "measure" ("one quart")? If so, the meaning of inscription P. 73 is that the amphora contained: "Wine. Four measures." Finally, *anë* also means "region" (M. 7). This leads one to a hypothesis which finds an echo in the history of Rome. Ancient Rome was known as *Roma Quadrata*, Rome of the Four Regions. Is, then, *huθte anaes* the Etruscan for *Quadrata*, "Of the Four Regions"? In this event, *(e)n huθte* would be a "wine of Rome". The amphora comes from Caere, which was near Rome and in alliance with it. However one approaches the matter, *huθ* is "four".

We shall now go back a step to discuss the meaning of the word ci. Not only do I accept 3 as its value; I shall also explain how I conceive the nature of the word in my own mind. Ci is 3 by virtue of its phonetic form as well as by interpretation. It should be pronounced "tchi" (like the Italian ci). It is connected with the Indo-European tre, tri. I sensed this by way of the Polish $trzy$, "three"; and I was later surprised to find the same idea in Thomopoulos. He probably did not know Polish, but had read the word somewhere. I will explain matters.

ci is connected with tre, tri in the following way: In the Slav languages, 3 is generally "tri" But in Polish and Czech this becomes "$trzy$"; the r becomes a double consonant, rz, which in this case is pronounced ch, sh. Thus $trzy$, while retaining the structure of tri, is pronounced $tshi$; this pronunciation is rather like the Italian ci. Skutsch perceived clearly that ci should be pronounced in similar fashion; he was guided by comparing the Etruscan number $cial\chi uz$ with $sial\chi veis$ in the related dialect of Lemnos. The variation in the first letter proved to him that it could not be pronounced k.

Etruscan writing, stretched on the Procrustean bed of an alien alphabet, was, in addition, phonetic. Consequently, the Etruscan ci, unlike $trzy$, displays no outward and visible sign of its organic connection with tri; it is nevertheless the same word. These little disguises are a typical feature of Etruscan writing.

Here is a further consideration in favour of $ci = 3$. An expression which occurs frequently in LM, in connection with a sacrifice to Hades, is $cisum pute$. Since Thracian is very close to Illyrian, I believe that $pute$ is the same as Thracian pod, "foot" (Tomaschek, $Die alt. Thraker$, II, I, 30). $cisum$ is 3. $cisum pute$ would thus be a sacred tripod, as among the Romans, the Greeks and the Cretans, all of whom called it $tripus$ ($tripudis$).

In proposing to identify $ma\chi$ with "one", Pauli emphasised that $ma\chi$ was part of the word $me\chi lum$, by which the community of the "twelve peoples of Etruria" were designated. But $me\chi lum$ ($me\theta lum$) could just as well mean "league, confederation", etc., without the specific idea of "one" being present at all. Ellis attested that in Georgian "one" had two names, one of which was $mkholo$, "once, one only". Bugge stressed that an ancient Cretan word $amakis$, "once", as also Armenian meg, $miak$, were strongly reminiscent of the Etruscan $ma\chi$.[1] The relations of Etruscan to the Aegean and Anatolian world deserve the closest attention. Skutsch, as has been mentioned earlier,

[1] $Etr. Forschungen u. Studien$, IV, p. 148.

held that $ma\chi$, "one", might occupy the position on the die from which the numbering of its faces was begun. So if we take $ma\chi$, "1", as centre, and have established the values of θu, "2", and ci, "3", in the top and the right-hand compartments respectively of our Tuscan die, and of $hu\theta$, "4", in the compartment below $ma\chi$, we find that if we move in the direction indicated by 2, 3, 4 (that is to say, clockwise), 5 occupies the compartment belonging to $\acute{s}a$, to the left of $ma\chi$. Therefore, and pending further information, we present our Tuscan die thus:

Tesinθ is probably the complete form of the number "ten" in Etruscan, and *tesne* its abbreviated form. It displays a kinship to the Slavonic *diesentj, dziesientj, diesiat*. Pauli pointed to the Indo-Iranian *daçan* in connection with it. Deecke and Bugge were of the same opinion. We shall occupy ourselves with the word *tesinθ* in the chapter on the Kitchen. The Albanian word is *dhetë*.[1] *zaθrum* (A), 20, has a counterpart in Albanian, as follows: *njiëzet*, "a score", 20; *dyzet*, "two score", 40, in which *një* is 1 and *dy* is 2. Thus the essential part of *zaθrum* reappears in *zet*.

χimθm is probably 100, already identified as such by Deecke, by analogy with Latin "centum". M. A. Cuny presented the prototype of the Indo-European "cent" in the form **kmtom*, which is close to the Etruscan *χimθm*.

But that author simultaneously gave an exposition of his point of view concerning the nature of Etruscan:

> Lydo-Etruscan seems to be closer to early Chamitic than to Semitic. . . . Analogies should be sought in the first place with a language anterior to Chamitic, Semitic or Southern Caucasian. . . . Ancient Egyptian lends itself particularly to the establishment of such analogies.[2]

---

[1] It is permissible to wonder whether the number *ten* is not present in the suffix of the multiples of ten, *-alχ. cialχ* would then be "three times ten", 30 (as *triginta = tri(de) cemta = 3 × 10 = 30*, in Latin; or as *tri-dzat = 3 × 10 = 30*, in Slavonic). *alχ* also exists as a separate word in Etruscan (*alχu*, P. 2, 10 and 18), but its meaning is not yet clear.

[2] *Etrusque et lydien*, R.E.A., pp. 107-12.

In view of the fact that the origins of Semitic take us back to the dawn of the ages of the Pharaohs, I shall never be courageous enough to associate myself with any such far-ranging venture in search of the secret of Etruscan; all the more so in that, since 1923, Ancient Egyptian, which "lends itself particularly" to the establishment of analogies with Etruscan, has not helped anyone to elucidate a single Etruscan word.

However that may be, $\chi im\theta m$ occurs in an interesting inscription of the 4th century B.C., engraved on a strip of lead known as the Magliano fragment. It begins like this:

(P. 359, CIE 5237)

cauθas tuθiu avilś LXXX ez χimθm casθialθ lacθ . . .

The interpretation of this text is as follows:

cauθas, "to the god Cauθa", *Caθ*, a solar deity: the final *s* is, as in Albanian, the sign of the dative and also of the genitive.

tuθiu, "of the town": a word common to several ancient Italic languages.

avilś, "annually, per annum".

LXXX ez, "80 times"?: I take as my clue here the Hittite *-iš*, "time, occasion", in the expression *20-iš*, which means "20 times" (J. Friedrich, *Hith. Wörterbuch*, p. 304) (the entry concludes with a question-mark). In any case, the Hittite *-iš* does not denote a date (unlike the Etruscan *huθis*, "the fifth"), for it is also found in *50-iš*, *70-iš*, etc.

lacθ is probably "libation", as will be shown shortly.

χimθ casθialθ is probably a number. We are guided by an analogy which comes in a later part of the same text: *cialaθ χimθm avilsχ*, in which we can recognise *ci*, "three", *χimθm*, "hundred", and *avils(χ)* "per annum"; *cialaθ* is the same as *cialχ*, "thirty", since *χ* and *θ* are interchangeable in Etruscan (*meχlum, meθlum*). Thus *cialaθ χimθm* is "a hundred and thirty". But what is *casθialθ*?

casθi inevitably reminds me of *gjashtë*, the Albanian for "six" (the *j* in this word is of secondary importance). This obliges me to postulate at least a partial co-existence of two categories of numbers in Etruscan usage: Indo-European (Illyrian) and Anatolian numbers (such as *maχ*). As a pendant to ancient Illyrian *tri*, discussed above, mention can be made of Illyrian and Indo-European *pes* (5); for on the Danube there used to be a town named Aquincum which, according to Ptolemy, was also called Pession (von Hahn).

It may be that this number *pes*, "five", is present in the word *peslialχ* which appears in an incomplete epitaph (P. 195, CII 2100) and which is followed by a lacuna. The word does not express the age of the deceased; he died at the age of 36, as the remainder of the inscription clearly shows. The meaning of *peslialχ* therefore remains unknown; but its form evidently puts it into the same class as *cialχ*, *cezpalχ*, *muvalχ*, etc. It must therefore mean "50" or convey some idea connected with 50. A "leader of 50 men"?

χimθ casθialθ thus emerges as 160. This number has the recommendation of being related to the LXXX of the same text. The sense is perhaps "80 times . . . 160 libations", that is to say 80 ceremonies each consisting of 2 libations. The whole phrase may mean: To Cauθas of the City, 80 times a year, 160 libations.

Finally, we must remember that the Etruscan for 60 is still unknown. It need hardly be said that the interpretation put forward here is hypothetical.

lacθ (A) is interpreted by way of Albanian *lag*, "to sprinkle, water", and *lagët*, "watered" (M. 233), and also by Hittite *lahura*, "vase for making libations" (B. Hrozny, *Histoire de l'Antiquité*, p. 290). Therefore, "libation". All the more certainly so, in that the word also occurs in the forms *laχuθ*, *laχθ* in the cippus of Perugia.

Our elementary course of Etruscan arithmetic will conclude with a fraction. Can any normal language dispense with fractions? To think that Etruscan did would be to insult the Etruscans' adroitness in trade, and also their care for precision in general. It is my belief that the word "half" is to be found engraved on a leaden plaque. These metal tablets were used for recording important agreements and contracts, and an Etruscan lawyer's office must have borne a distant resemblance to a hardware shop. The example in question is the inscription P. 380, CIE 5211, which mentions a large number of men and women who appear to be taking part in a ceremony. We shall come back to this later. For the moment we shall point to one fact only, namely that contributions are mentioned, among them being *ceś zeriś ims* (line 6) and *ceś zeriś* (line 9). *Ceś* would seem to be the genitive of *ci*, "three"; *zeriś* perhaps "gold, gold coin", by analogy with the Scythian word for gold, *zirin*, and the Ossetic *zarand* (see V. Abayev, *La langue et le folklore ossètes*, Moscow, 1949, p. 190). Finally, *ims*, the keystone of our hypothesis, is the Albanian *gjymsë*, "half" (M. 151). There are thus individuals who are contributing three "golden guineas" and others contributing three and a half. If I am on the right track this elimination of the initial *gj* of *gjymsë*, to yield the Etruscan *ims*, is extremely interesting.

Let us note also that the Macedonians, who were related to the Etruscans, called Aphrodite *Zeirene*, while the Greeks called her *chryse*, "golden"; from which it follows that *zeirene* means "golden". In Avesta *zari* is "gold". However, *zeri* seems to possess more than one meaning.

Involved in this problem of fractions is a certain Etruscan gloss whose meaning, fortunately, is clear. The gloss is concerned not with a number but with the verb "to divide". A Latin author, Macrobius, has handed down to us its Etruscan equivalent: *iduare* (A). The Ides of the Ancients (the days which *divide* certain of the months into halves) are connected with this verb. I verified the etymology of the word thanks to the Albanian verb *daj*, "to divide"[1] (M. 305), and to the ending *-uar*, which, in Albanian, denotes the past participle; thus from the verb *dëgjoj*, "to hear", which we have already encountered, comes *dëgjuar*, "heard" (M. 72), and from the verb *kërkoj*, "to seek", comes *kërkuar*, "sought, sought after". The first letter of *iduare*, *i*, is simply the article, however incredible that may sound in speaking of Etruscan. But here is the reason for my being able to assert it; and we shall subsequently find another instance.

In Albanian *i* is the definite article placed *before* abstract nouns. *iduare* meant "division, divided or dividing".

And here is an excellent proof of the antiquity of the Illyrian article. Identifying the Albanian tribes of antiquity with those of today, Carleton S. Coon recalls an ancient tribal name, Emathia, whose interpretation is provided by Albanian *e madhia*, "the Great" (*The Mountains of the Giants*, 1950, p. 41).

A general remark can be inserted here. In spite of the fact that, in Etruscan, "hundred" was probably *kmtom*, *χimθm*, the language belonged to the Eastern, the so-called "satem", group of the Indo-European languages, not to the "kentum" or Western group. The same paradox is presented by Albanian, whose word for "hundred" is *qind*, but which nevertheless belongs to the "satem" group.

We can now come back to a secondary problem, the meaning of the phrase *i va est orti caius volote*, which was chosen for inscribing on dice solely because of the respective lengths of its words.

It is an oddity—an Etruscan proverb in praise of the efficient training

---

[1] Cf. Greek *daiō*.

of horses. No doubt the Etruscans knew plenty about that. It certainly makes a refreshing change from our arithmetical toils. Deciphered, the inscription on the Autun dice runs as follows:

i: the definite article, already studied.

va, "ford", in Albanian: G. Meyer connects it with the Latin *vadum*.

est: the *"est"* of Latin, French and Albanian (*âsht*).

orti: in Albanian, *urt-i*, an archaic word, means "intelligence, prudence"; *urtë* is "intelligent, docile, tractable (of animals)" (M. 541).

The use of *o* is a sign showing that the text belongs to a late stage in the development of the language.

caius: probably Albanian *kalush*, "pony", from *kal*, "horse".

Later, we shall encounter the Etruscan words *calusin*, "horseman", and *Kalukasu*, both from this root *cal*. But perhaps the derivation may seem dubious. Perhaps I shall be told, "This *cal* of yours is certainly only a borrowing from Latin *caballus*; as an Albanian word, therefore, it is of late origin. So how can you identify it with an Etruscan word?"

However, this is what Krahe has to say about the matter (in *Die Sprache der Illyrier*, 1955): "The Latin word *caballus*, Greek *kaballes* (packhorse), has already been traced back to its Illyrian origin on several occasions—recently by V. Cocco (*Caballum*, Coïmbra, 1945). The view that Illyrian is the native soil of this word is confirmed by several personal names derived from the root *cabal*: Caballus, Caballius, Cabalionius, Kabaletus, etc." (p. 115).

volote: is reminiscent of a number of Albanian words. I select a root which is common to all the Indo-European languages: *volitsi*, "convenience, ease"; *volicem*, "convenient, suitable" (M. 563). These are related to the Latin *volo* and Slavonic *vole*, "to wish". *te* is probably a suffix denoting an adjective.

The general meaning is: "To a docile horse, the ford is pleasant."

It need hardly be said that there may be further details to be explored in the meaning of this sentence, and that there may be a play on words in it; the Etruscans liked puns, as we shall see, indeed, and they did absolutely nothing to aid the Etruscologist in his task. They had a sense of humour; I have noticed it, just as others have noticed their "gloom". In topical language, I have succeeded in observing the hitherto concealed side of the Etruscan moon.

In conclusion, I would remark that the best exposition of previous endeavours towards a knowledge of numbers in Etruscan is that furnished by Trombetti. Why did that author, who proved himself to be so intelligent, objective and patient, fail to unravel the Etruscan enigma? It is quite clear that the fault lay in his method. Guided solely by external resemblances, he would take, for example, two words such as *cemnaχ* and *raχ* and make them into two nouns belonging to the same category. A dangerous illusion, since in the first of them *-aχ* (*ak*) is a suffix added to a verb (*gem, gemn*, "to thunder"), while the second is a root *raχ*, "to smite, slaughter". It is sufficiently obvious that these two words cannot be grouped together. But how could such misunderstandings be avoided when he was given to erecting purely hypothetical morphological compartments, without penetrating to the meanings of the words in question?

In spite of such errors, *La lingua etrusca* contains a wealth of highly valuable information. Such as, for example, that on the points of contact between Etruscan and the languages of Asia Minor and the Caucasus, as we shall see later.

If only Trombetti had been willing to content himself with scrutinising the Indo-European languages and those of Asia Minor, which would certainly have afforded him an immense domain! Unfortunately, he left no language in the world untouched in his attempt to throw light on Etruscan. He mobilised Tasmanian, Malagasy, Lappish, Tungu, etc. Does there exist anywhere a language so synthetic as to have affinities with other languages from all over the world? Etruscan was a natural language, with its own accidents of growth and those capricious and inconsequential features which produce the difficulty but also much of the charm of any living language. Trombetti was not the only writer to believe that there must therefore be a substantial relationship between Basque and the dialects of New Zealand, so that these and any other languages could always be called upon to contribute their mite towards the elucidation of Etruscan. Was not this belief as ingenuous as that of the earliest students of Etruscan, who regarded Hebrew as "the mother of all languages"?

When someone is anxious to prove that such and such a linguistic root is diffused throughout the world, and when, in support of his thesis, he quotes Mordvin and Kaffir simultaneously, I am apt to be reminded of an experiment in physics which I witnessed as a schoolboy. The master would line up his pupils and tell them to hold each other's hands, so as to make a human chain. Then, using a familiar apparatus, he would send through this living chain a weak electric current. Provided one was not one of the links oneself, it was amusing to see how each pupil would give a start in turn, as the current reached him. Well, I think that if you made a similar chain consisting of a Tasmanian, a Lithuanian, a Kaffir, a Yakut, an Aztec, a Hittite, a Copt and whom you will, and then uttered a few quotations of the kind in question, each member of the chain would give a start; he would be hearing his own language, but disfigured. The situation can hardly be otherwise so long as one simply plucks words out of the dictionary, without paying attention to their linguistic ambiance in each case, and the linguistic families to which they belong.

And the ambiance of Etruscan is, above all, Illyrian.

Nevertheless, it was Trombetti who wrote the following very sensible words:

> The etymological method [i.e., the method of comparison with other languages] fell into bad repute only because it was badly applied. . . . For the rest, when it is a question of discovering truth . . . the right method is the one which yields results. . . . In the conquest of truth, it is not enough to possess a method and that this should be rigorous, as far as can be seen; luck and intuition are needed too. . . . Thus Bopp, using a method which would nowadays be considered the last word in unsoundness, founded the comparative grammar of the Indo-European languages.
>
> (*La lingua etrusca*, p. X.)

PART TWO

The Etruscan Texts

III

THE PEOPLE AND THE CITY

THE origins of this people, known variously as the Tursci, Tusci and Etrusci, are partly bound up with the Tursha, that warlike tribe which during the 13th and 12th centuries B.C., together with the Lycians and other wandering tribes, made attacks by sea on the Egypt of the Pharaohs. Eventually, some five or six centuries later, the Tursha settled in what was to be known as Etruria. The importance of this fact seems to have been underrated by several authors, according to whom the development of civilisation in the districts inhabited by the Etruscans displays no sudden, violent change. Other authors emphasise that the civilisation of the Etruscans was predominantly agricultural, as against the presumably maritime civilisation of the Tursha, and that the majority of the Etruscan cities are not on the Mediterranean coast. However, none of these authors has any explanation to offer for the identity of the ethnic names, Tursha and Tursci, or, for instance, of the fact that the national patronymic of the Etruscans, Tarquin, is that of a deity of Asia Minor, Tark or Tarkon.

When an alien group settles among an autochthonous population, especially a group as dynamic and aggressive as the Tursha, matters do not always proceed in a pacific and friendly way. This kind of settlement often proclaims itself to the attention of archaeologists by the traces of fire and destruction it has left behind it.

Thus, for example, C. F.-A. Schaeffer has established the fact that a whole series of sites, throughout Northern Mesopotamia, Syria and Phoenicia, display at a certain level, that is to say at the same period in each case, a layer bearing witness to destruction and fire. This scholar attributed these strata, which are everywhere the same, to a single initial cause. Thanks to his insight the chaotic picture presented by the excavations made in the "land of the fertile crescent" was suddenly charged with meaning. Just what was the initial cause of this wave of destruction had still to be defined. For my part, I saw in it the traces of devastation left by the Hyksos as they advanced on their way towards Egypt.

This was all the more likely in that a succession of similar strata had been created three centuries earlier, in the West this time, by another movement of Indo-European expansion, travelling likewise from north to south:

93

All settlements in central Greece and the Peloponnesus were brutally destroyed. Eutresis and Orchomenus in Boeotia, and Zygouries or Asine in Argolis, show signs of having been burnt; some sites in the Peloponnesus were abandoned for ever.

(F. Chapoutier, *Les Premières Civilisations*, 1950, p. 262)

Now the Tursha, who make their appearance in Italy about the 9th or 8th century B.C. and whose own name for themselves is *Rasna*, undoubtedly bring with them several new elements pertaining to Anatolian civilisation: rites, features of funerary architecture, artistic motifs, a certain touch of Eastern luxury and also the name Tarkon, whose introduction into Etruria cannot be explained by commercial intercourse alone; but the appearance of these elements in Italy is neither preceded nor accompanied by arson and violence and other signs of a break with the past. I by no means infer from this that the settlement of the Tursha never took place. It did, but peacefully; for which there was a good reason. The names of some of the places in Lydia from which the Tursha came—Malea (from Albanian *mal*, "mountain"), Plakia (from *plak*, "old")—were Illyrian. On reaching Italy, their new homeland, the Tursha encountered a population of the same ancestry as themselves and speaking the same language, Illyrian, and they integrated themselves with that population without much difficulty. Moreover, there is nothing to show that they came over in a single wave. It was a matter, rather, of separate groups, like bands of Norsemen; but, in this instance, attracted overseas, and thereafter absorbed, by the ambiance of their own kin. Although they were a minority, they probably made themselves felt as a more active element than their predecessors, and were the leaven producing a new civilisation. The old population of Etruria, more primitive and essentially agricultural, was not autochthonous either: like the Messapians, for example, it preceded the Tursha by only a few centuries, gradually establishing itself among the Osco-Umbrians and other local peoples and acquiring the ways of their rather rudimentary civilisation. Thus it comes about that the Etruscan language is a well-defined organic unity; though it shows dialectal variations, it does not reflect the participation of heterogeneous *ethnic* elements. As will be pointed out, several terms brought over from Asia Minor bear witness only to certain cultural differences. As for the siting of Etruscan cities, and the objection which is sometimes made that they are remote from the sea, the same could be said of Athens, and the conclusion could be drawn that the Greeks of Attica were not a sea-faring race. But this remoteness was only relative and, in Etruria, was imposed by fear of pirates,

Etruscan pirates as well as others. Caere, Tarquinia, Vulci and Vetulonia are near the sea; and Populonia is right on the coast.

The Etruscans never constituted a nation. Each city was a little country in itself, with its own political organisation. A single common sanctuary, that of the god Vertumnus (Veltuna), near Volsinia, was periodically visited by gatherings of delegates from the "twelve peoples of Etruria" for religious ceremonies; at which, however, questions of common interest were debated.

Rome trembled before these formidable warriors clad in bronze and, in the 6th century, was compelled to bow to their rule. The Etruscans were in occupation of the Po valley and Campania (Capua, Pompeii). From the 8th century onwards they exploited the iron mines on the isle of Elba and exported marble, wine, pottery and footgear, etc. The Greeks were afraid to venture into the Tyrrhenian Sea and maintained contact with Cumae and Massilia (Marseilles) only with great difficulty. At the height of its power Etruria occupied almost 27,027 square miles and had a population of 2 million people (7th–5th centuries).[1] But, hemmed in among youthful, aggressive peoples, the Samnites, Volsci, Latins, Greeks and Carthaginians, on the sea, a threat soon to be augmented on land by the Gauls, and already torn internally by the struggle between nobles and bourgeoisie, Etruria could counter the situation only by concluding alliances with her neighbours. But these alliances were always precarious. The appearance of the Greeks of Corinth in Sicily (4th century), and the advance of the Gauls, were disastrous for Etruria. It was this latter danger which made almost all the cities of Etruria remain deaf to the appeal of Veii during its ten years' siege by the Romans. The Gauls, for their part, continually proposed an alliance with the Etruscans against the Romans. But there was no Etruscan common policy. Veii succumbed in 396 B.C. In the end the Romans subdued Etruria, after centuries of struggle. Roman colonies on Etruscan soil undermined the political framework of Etruria.

The Etruscan inscriptions available to us bear but few traces of all these events. They sound a faint echo of wars, even desperate wars; but no historical fact and almost no name known to the ancient world is mentioned by them, except in one fresco of the François Tomb, which illustrates an episode in the Etruscan domination of Rome. Nevertheless, in some of the inscriptions we shall find important material relating both to the legendary past and to public life among

[1] M. Renard, *La question étrusque*, Brussels, 1941.

the Etruscans, in addition to the importance of these texts for deciphering the language.

Let us begin with the scene engraved on the Tuscan Mirror, which
consists essentially of a group of people gathered round a young man
examining a liver, in which omens were commonly sought. The
inscription says: *veltune ucerseia* (A) *vl tarχunus raθ lθ pava tarχies* (A).

Despite one or two doubtful places in the script, the general meaning
is clear. Veltune is the god Vertumnus. His presence indicates that
the subject is not a local event but something on the national plane.
Ucerseia is the woman standing in the centre. Vl Tarχunus is the
bearded man on her right. The words *raθ lθ* beside the youth, towards
the left, do not seem to refer specifically to him. Finally, *pava Tarχies*
is placed over the soothsayer's head.

M. Pallottino has identified the scene as a lesson in the art of
divination. P. Ducati has interpreted it as a study of the omens relating
to the foundation of the city of Tarquinia. Nothing has been said about
Ucerseia. This is most surprising, for it is she who plays the leading
part in the scene. We are confronted here by one of the most important
features of Etruscan legend.

To begin with, Ocresia is known to have been an Etruscan proper
name, one which existed in both the masculine and the feminine.
Bugge cites a *larθi heli cainal ucrsa* and also a *θania veleθnei ucurs*.[1] In the
second place, the name figures in a tradition which connects the
Etruscan past with the early days of Rome. The legend is one which
has come down to us in several versions; only two will be mentioned
here:

(*a*) Ocresia was a slave in the house of Tarquinius Priscus, king of
Tarquini and later of Rome. One day, as she was making an offering
on the domestic hearth, she saw an apparition, a phallus. This was
immediately recognised as a revelation by the lar or genius of the royal
family, predicting an extraordinary birth in the house. The king
therefore ordered Ocresia to dress as a bride and go to the hearth.
She became pregnant. Her son, Mastarna, became one of the Etruscan
military leaders who were settled in Rome. He became king of Rome
under the name Servius Tullius, his memory being subsequently
glorified by the emperor Claudius (in his speech to the senate in
defence of the rights of the Gaulish nobility).

(*b*) According to Plutarch, one Tarcheties, a cruel king of the
Albans, having seen the prodigy, ordered his daughter to offer herself
in union with the genius of the dynasty. But this princess had no

[1] *Etruskisch und Armenisch*, Christiania, 1890, p. 128.

particular liking for Etruscan mythology, so sent her slave Ocresia instead.

To come back to the inscription, *pava*, the key word in the puzzle, is a past tense (aorist) of the Illyrian (and therefore Etruscan and Albanian) verb *shof, shoχ, shoh,* which we have studied already, "to see". Opening Mann, p. 488, we find: *shof*, aorist *pava*. This ending *-va* for the past is very frequent in Etruscan: *marunuχva*, "he was administering", *eprθieva*, "he was a prytanis", etc.

In Albanian the suffix *-va* is the sign of the aorist in several verbs: *blej*, "to buy", *bleva*, etc. (M., *Albanian Grammar*, p. 28). Thus, *pava Tarχies*, "Tarχies saw". According to the legend, the meaning of the apparition was explained by Tanaquil, the king's wife. But according to our mirror, Tarχies, an augur, a soothsayer, consults the liver of a victim so as to interpret the original prodigy, to which Ocresia is required to pay tribute in her own person. This may be a variant of the legend.

Vl Tarχunus is therefore king Tarquinius Priscus. Finally, *rθ lθ* is a hard nut to crack. I am inclined to regard it, not as the name of the youth who is placed on the left to ensure symmetry in the general design (a constant preoccupation with Etruscan artists) but, rather, as the completion of the short sentence, "Tarχies saw". Perhaps the artist wanted to make the meaning of the oracle more explicit, just as *enqten* shows which of the two fighters is winning. Simply as a conjecture, mention may be made of *rad*, "destiny" (M. 421) and *ledhë*, "flattery", *ledhatoj*, "to flatter" (M. 239–40); thus, perhaps, a "flattering destiny" predicted for the future Etruscan condottiere? But the end of the inscription is in a poor state and other suggestions are possible.

Let us retain the essential fact: an omen was read from the appearance of a liver; a remarkable birth was predicted.

Innumerable pages have been written already on this custom of the Etruscans. Omens were the very pivot of their religion, which, through the Lydo-Hittite civilisation, went back to Assyrio-Babylonian sources. We recall the model of a liver found at Piacenza, divided into different sectors, on which the names of several Etruscan deities are written. Making a summary of the progress so far achieved in Etruscan studies, K. Olzscha recently observed that this bronze model of a liver must have been used for teaching the soothsayers' art, but was also a model with which any animal's liver could be compared so that any unusual features in the latter could be detected and conclusions drawn from them ("Schrift u. Sprache der Etrusker", *Historia*, Wiesbaden, VI, 1957, p. 34).

D

Yet there is something to be added on this subject of divination.
Before setting out on the road which leads from Etruria to Mesopotamia, ought we not to pause for a moment in Albania?
We shall receive a curious reminder of the past.
A party sent out by Harvard University published in 1950 an excellent report on its investigations in Albania. It had studied anthropo-
logical and demographic problems, taken anthropometrical measurements of a thousand Northern Albanians (Ghegs), concerned itself
with the folklore of the country and so on. One of Carleton S. Coon's
observations runs as follows:

> They are also great believers in omens and in divination. Men
> versed in this skill read the future by observing the sternal bones of
> fowl and the scapulae of sheep. I have witnessed a performance of
> the latter. The bone has its special divisions, each of which has
> meaning. On the sheep's scapula the joint socket is the house, and
> its depth or shallowness indicates whether the house will be empty
> or full of wealth. This can be used to predict success or failure of
> crops. The ridge on the blade shows whether or not flocks will
> multiply. Small holes on the blades are cradles, and the diviner can
> tell how close to the family, i.e. the "house", the birth will be.
>
> (*The Mountains of the Giants*, Papers of the Peabody Museum,
> p. 37 *ss*.)

Coon quotes authors of earlier generations, according to whom the
conditions of Albanian life recalled the Iron Age of the Hallstatt
culture. At the same time this prophecy of a *birth* from signs on the
shoulder-blade of a ewe takes us back, by a remarkable short cut, to
the Tarχies of our *pava Tarχies*.
One overriding impression will be conveyed by the inscriptions set
before the reader in this chapter: although there were as many mother-
countries in Etruria as there were large towns, the conception of
country was already established in their scale of moral values.
There is, to begin with, the fact that the founding of the city was
accompanied by religious rites; its very ramparts, as well as its
boundaries, were sacred. The boundaries were designated as *tular
spural*. *spura* is "city", which invites us to recall in passing that the
Slavonic word *sbor*, *sobor* means "assembly, gathering". The earth
itself acquires sanctity through the presence of the ancestors.
This is made clear by Fustel de Coulanges:

> According to tradition, Romulus, to found Rome, digs a trench
> and throws into it a sod of earth brought from Alba. Each of his

companions likewise throws into it a little earth from his own home country. For every one of them these handfuls of earth symbolised "the sacred soil in which his ancestors were buried and to which the ancestral shades were attached". "They believed that, by placing earth from their own countries in the trench, they had enclosed the spirits of their ancestors there."

(*La Cité antique*, p. 154)

This brings us to the very source of the idea of a country or fatherland. We shall take up the point again when we come to speak of the goddess Venθ.

The attachment the Etruscans felt for their Italic homeland can be seen from the names they gave to some of its rivers, mountains and valleys. The origin of the name Tiber (B), indeed, can be seen in the Albanian *thepuer*, *thepore*, "notched" (M. 534). The word aptly expresses the river's winding course.

From this very attachment resulted, after all, the remarkable organisation and the beauty of the cities of Etruria, with their wide, paved streets intersecting at right angles, their artificial watercourses and so on. Veii, after being captured, pillaged and partly burnt, was still so much more beautiful than Rome that a proportion of the Romans conceived a desire to leave their own town and settle in the Etruscan city; which caused the young patricians to go down into the popular quarters and implore the inhabitants not to leave the ancestral soil.

Before we discuss city administration, let us briefly consider the general idea of power as expressed in Etruscan. Hesychius has preserved the word *drouna* (P. 829) (A). His Greek rendering conveys the sense of "domination, command, power". But, thanks to Albanian, we can lay bare the primitive idea which underlies the noun *drouna*, and which is "to cause to fear". It is connected with an Albanian irregular verb, the intransitive verb *drue*, *drua*, "to fear"; *druen*, "they fear"; *druhem*, "to be afraid", etc. (M. 84). To *command*, in the Etruscan way of thinking, was above all to inspire a salutary fear. An offender had always to reckon with the risk of physical punishment.

We may add that, in an article which we shall be quoting again in our chapter on the family, M. J. Heurgon expresses this regret:

But we search in vain, in our inscriptions, for the word **truna* or **druna* which would correspond to it.

(*Historia*, VI, p. 75)

It is obvious that the syllable *na* of this word is only a suffix (cf. *rasna*, etc.). What we have to look for is the root *dru, tru*. We shall find it in the word *truisie*, included in a scene engraved on a mirror, a scene which will be studied in the same chapter (on the Family). Very probably it is also to be found in the word *trutnot*, a soothsayer's title, which we shall look at in our discussion of Etruscan religion.

Etruscan administration is well known to us from epitaphs. Civil officers' prerogatives, like every other official element in Etruscan life, bore a sacred character, which was indeed grounded in the very fact that every such officer took part in certain sacrifices and in some cases directed them. One of the commonest terms connected with this official class was *zilaθ* (A). It is instructive to find that this word has been preserved almost intact in Albanian: *zyrtar*, "functionary" (M. 585), in which the final *-ar* is simply the customary termination denoting a profession or habit (a feature which we shall encounter in Etruscan too). *Zyrë* is an "urgent matter". The Albanian–Russian dictionary gives *zirtar*. Under *zyrë*, Mann notes: "obsolete word". What, it is only 2,500 years since this little word, still fresh, just out of the bud, was current in the spacious streets of Tarquinii; and already it is being relegated to the archives? It's hard to believe how fast these Illyrian words wear out and fall into disuse!

Let us devote a few lines to the word *zilc, zilχ*, which in more than one instance has been saved for us by a sarcophagus and a handsome inscription which have been spared by the ravages of time. The individual concerned in the instance chosen here was an official in Tarquinii, one Velθur Partunus (Bardhunus)—"a Mr V. White, an official of the Borough Council", as it might be—concerning whom we read:

> (P. 126, CIE 5423) *velθur partunus larisalisa clan*
> *ramθas cuclnial*
> *zilχ ceχaneri tenθas*
> *avil sval as LXXXII*
> V.P., of Laris son
> (and of) Ramθa Cuclnia
> (was) *zilχ ceχaneri tenθas*.
> (deceased in) year of (his) life 82

What rung did he occupy in the city hierarchy?

According to our interpretation of *huθ-tenia*, "four cities", *ten* is "city" and *tenθas* would be "of the city".

The word *ceχaneri* has given rise to a large number of hypotheses. The root *ceχa* might, in accordance with Thomopoulos's intuitive solution, be identified with the Albanian këha, "here" (M. 197). Thus, in the epitaph of a certain Larθ Velθas (P. 90, CIE 5385), the word ceχari has been interpreted as ceχa ri, "here lies"; for the Albanian rri means "is, dwells" (M. 439). We turn next to a small votive figure of Apollo which is preserved at the Bibliothèque Nationale. The inscription on it includes the words: trce clen ceχa (P. 737, CII 2613). They mean that this image was "given (in order) to be here"; for clen (A) is the Albanian klenë, the infinitive of the verb jam, "to be" (M. 199). Finally, we appeal to the Cippus of Perugia, P. 570, to which we shall return in another context, and which ends with the words: iχ ca ceχa ziχuχe. Broadly, the meaning of these words is: "(That) will go (i.e. will happen) in accordance with what is written here" (?).

ceχane is an adjective derived from ceχa; we recognise the suffix -ne, as in rasne ("Etruscan") and siiane ("savoury"). What must be the meaning of zilχ ceχane? I believe it refers to a civil officer responsible for a section of the population of Tarquinii. One thinks of the Roman "tribune of the people", for example. ceχaneri would be a collective or plural form, like manimeri ("fruit, posterity"), which has been encountered already. The part of the population known as ceχaneri were, perhaps, "those who have always lived here, the locals, the natives", the autochthonous element in the city, those who were there before the Etruscans.

Note that the word neri occurs in LM, where it quite clearly means "people, individuals"; cf. Albanian nieri (M. 330) and Greek aner, "man". So perhaps ceχaneri means "the people of this place"? This seems too much like a coincidence.

Whatever the answer may be, Velθur Partunus must have been an important person, and the name by which his sarcophagus is known, del Magnate, is doubtless right.

But another approach is possible: we can postulate that Thomopoulos was wrong and that ceχa is connected with θaχ, zaχ, zac, "blood" (Albanian gjak), just as Etruscan etnam, "fathers" (Albanian etna) comes from at, "father" (in both languages), and as clenar comes from clan.

In that case, ceχa would be "bloody sacrifice" (or perhaps just "sacrifice"), and ceχaneri would become "consanguineous, native". Thus, in Polish, krewny, "relative", is derived from krew, "blood". zilχ ceχaneri tenθas, in our text P. 126, will now be "zilχ of the native city, zilχ of the city of his birth". And on the same supposition, trce clen ceχa (P. 737) would mean "gave (in order) to be (at the place of) sacrifice". And the closing words of P. 570 would indicate a sacrifice (ziχuχe) and blood (ceχa) shed in honour of the dead.

Finally, in inscription P. 90, CIE 5385, *ceχasieθur* would become "the line of kin", "of the same blood".

Marun (A), another administrative title, of frequent occurrence in inscriptions, is well explained by the Albanian verb *maroj* (*mbaroj*, *ënbaronj*), "to perfect, complete, finish off" (M. 268), which is connected (and this is remarkable) with another verb, *mbarshtoj*, "to arrange, administer, control" (*ibid.*). This is abundance indeed! We have got right inside Etruscan administration and seen how the wheels go round; and (thanks to Albanian) we can observe that it was decidedly unlike other administrations: it considered its business as "urgent" and liked getting it finished!

There was also a grade of supreme officials, whose name probably comes from an archaic vocabulary. The word is *purθ* (A). This official was the same as the Greek *prytanis*, the leader of the priests. In Greece the word was also a synonym for "king". According to Hammarström, in the 9th and 8th centuries B.C. the *prytaneis* were mainly in evidence in the islands, Asia Minor and Eastern Greece, that is to say in the territories regarded as "Pelasgic".

But the *prytanis*, at once a magistrate and a high priest in classical antiquity, is a figure belonging to an advanced epoch which tended to forget its own modest antecedents. Daremberg relates it to those antecedents by reminding us that the Prytaneum was a building which housed the common *hearth* of the state, the altar of Hestia; a fire was kept perpetually alight there, and it was from that altar that a colony would take a portion of the sacred fire of the mother country. In other words, it was a place where the sacred fire of the tribe was maintained, and the task of the *prytanis* in early times was to look after the fire.

Once again it is Albanian, that guardian of Illyrian antiquities, which allows us, as it were, to put a fingertip on the very stuff of these terms, with no decorative superfluities intervening. There is a verb, *purris*, "to stir the fire" (M. 409); *prush*, "brazier" (Albanian–Russian dictionary, p. 345): *prushis*, "I stir the fire" (von Hahn, III, p. 106); *posi prushi ndënë hi*, "like embers under the ashes" (Leotti's Albanian–Italian dictionary, p. 1113).

In the same way, the *flamen* (a Roman priest) had his name from Latin *flare*, "to blow the fire".

There is one more important personage for us to identify, and the search this time will take us back at one leap to Roman days. This character is *camθi*, whom previous interpretations have mistakenly sought to enrol in the ranks of the Etruscan priesthood. Our own inclination is to see him as a worthy *centurion*, for *camθ* is reminiscent of *χimθ*, "hundred", a number already discussed, and also of *cnticnθ*

(Book of the Mummy, Chapters VII and IX), which will be studied below. The dependence of Roman military organisation on that of the Etruscans, in Rome's early days, makes this connection permissible. There is, moreover, an interesting epitaph, P. 99, CIE 5526, which confirms our interpretation of *camθi*. It refers to Larθ Ceisinis, son of Velus, who *cizi zilaχce meθlum*, "was three times *zilaθ* of the league" (perhaps not the general Etruscan confederation but a league consisting of Tarquinii and the small towns round it) and who *nurfzi canθce calusin* (B):

> *nurfzi*, "nine times"
> *canθce*, "served as *canθi*" (*camθi*)
> *calusin*, "horsemen, of the horsemen", from *cal*, "horse".

It is easier to believe that the famous Etruscan cavalry was commanded by centurions rather than by priests.

However, it was not the administrative organisation of these citystates which constituted their strength, but, much more, an atmosphere in which courage, devotion and sacrifice for one's country were habitually cultivated. In Gerhard's collection of drawings from mirrors (*Etruskische Spiegel*, V, 127) there is a most expressive picture of an Etruscan boy listening to someone playing the harp and apparently musing, while his book lies open in his lap. The cause of his reverie is not the music but the book. The text is, I grant, almost indistinguishable; nevertheless, I have succeeded in picking out the word *iraś*, on the higher of the two open pages. The boy's name, Artile, is a diminutive. *iraś*, a word borrowed from Greek, is, of course, "hero". It is cheering to find that *irash*, borrowed from the same source, also exists in Albanian, where it is an adjective, "virtuous, heroic" (M. 167). It is even more cheering to be able to interpret the name Artile by means of Albanian. It comes, in all likelihood, from the radical *arti*, "brave" (M. 12).

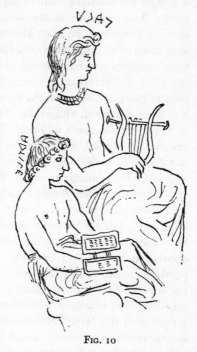

FIG. 10

Thus, this Etruscan schoolboy with the symbolic name is imbuing himself, young as he is, with ideas of courage and heroism. Is he dreaming of Homer's heroes? Or Alexander the Great, whose stock is related to his own? Or the Trojans, another kindred race?

There is an inscription on a bronze vase which, it seems to me, indicates a prize awarded to the brave by a city:

(P. 241) mi zpurana talape

mi is "this" (or else "I am"). zpurana comes from śpura, "city"; it is worth adding that the Etruscan quarter of Rome was called Subura. The ending -na, already encountered (as in suθina, "funerary"), denotes pertaining or belonging; this spurana is therefore "municipal". talape consists of tal and ape; tal is Albanian dalë, "courageous" (M. 66), and ape embodies the root (already noted) ap, "to give". So that the whole means: "Gift of the city to the brave man".

Bravery was required, in case of need, to extend even to the sacrifice of life itself. Things could hardly have been otherwise, indeed, among a people the Romans used to say was one of the most pious on the earth. And religion was inseparable from sacrifice. No prophet ever arose in Etruria to say, like Hosea: "Mercy, and not sacrifice." The idea of sacrifice must have saturated the very air of Etruria. At every step, sacrifices had to be made to the celestial or the infernal gods, to the gods of vegetation, to the gods of rivers, springs and rain, to the gods of gates and doors, to the ancestral shades, on whom divine status had been conferred, and so on. The consumers of these offerings were as many as the needs of man. The mouths of the deities, whether celestial or infernal, were open on every side, invisible hands were ever stretched out, both from above and from below, for their daily pittance, and while these demands might be discreetly hinted at by means of a clap of thunder, they might equally well be underlined by a drought, an epidemic or a defeat in war. Consequently, about an Etruscan banqueting table there could be felt the presence of as large a company of divine guests as of mere mortals; but the feeling was rendered less oppressive by the fact that the gods were willing to accept token portions instead of life-sized ones, and that on the whole the gods had the same tastes and inclinations as human beings. This similarity even created a kind of family atmosphere round the table, though the lower members of this large family were obliged to submit in silence to the incomprehensible tyranny of the higher.

In very difficult circumstances the supreme offering, that of human blood, was required. It was something like a "blood-bank"; with this difference, that contributions to it were made not for the sake of other people but for the divine shades of the ancestors. And an Etruscan noble was capable of sacrificing his life not only on the field of battle but also in a solemn religious ceremony, as we shall see. Obviously, it was preferable to sacrifice an alien life if one could.

Human sacrifice to the shades of heroes was practised by all the peoples of classical antiquity. Among the Homeric Greeks, the Etruscans and the Romans, this often took the form of massacring some of the prisoners captured in war. According to Herodotus (I, 166), pirates from Phocaea who had settled in Corsica ravaged the neighbouring coasts until, eventually, the Tyrrhenians and Carthaginians, upon whom these incursions fell most heavily, united to launch a large-scale attack on the Phocaeans. After the battle the allies stoned their prisoners to death. But the following fact has been specially singled out as an example of Etruscan cruelty: after a victory over the Romans, in 355 B.C., the Tarquinians cut the throats of 307 Roman prisoners. Four years later it was the Romans' turn; they massacred the population of Tarquinii, all except 358 members of the high aristocracy, who were taken to Rome, beaten with rods and beheaded. But we should also remember that in 405, at the end of the fratricidal Peloponnesian War, the Spartans, after overcoming the Athenian fleet, slaughtered 4,000 citizens of Athens whom they had taken prisoner. The Etruscans were no better or worse than other people. But, little by little, human sacrifice died out among the Etruscans and was replaced by games, boxing matches and, as we shall see, contests in which a man fought a large dog.

In any case, in our own times, when more than six million men, women and children have been herded into gas chambers because of their religion and nobody stayed the murderers' hands, who would dare to speak of Etruscan "cruelty"?

On the walls of tombs the Etruscans used to depict the sacrifice of Trojan prisoners to the shade of Patroclus, an episode recounted in the *Iliad*. But in the François Tomb, by the side of the fresco representing that sacrifice, there is a painting of another episode, taken from the annals not of Greece but Etruria. Several Etruscan heroes are depicted massacring several other heroes, who are Etruscans too. The picture concerns a struggle between two clans for supremacy in Rome. Caile Vibenna and his men have been taken prisoner by Tarχunies Rumaχ and his companions. But Mastarna, whom we have mentioned earlier, comes to the rescue and liberates Caile. Claudius's mention of Mastarna, and also a tile on which a brother of Caile is named, prove that these two are historical characters. But there is a detail in this second fresco which has not hitherto been explained.

One of the victors, as he plunges his sword into an enemy's breast, cries:

(P. 299) *venθical . . . ś . . . plsaχs* (fig. 11).

This inscription, unfortunately much damaged, deserves close attention. Its main lines can be unravelled thus:

venθi is the dative of a noun *venθ*, which designates a goddess of death. She is directly related to the earth, which is sacred because it harbours the spirits of the ancestors. Now, the term *vend* is an important element in Illyrian and Indo-European to-ponymy; its diffusion extends as far

FIG. 11

as Lycia (Kaduanda, Pudvandos, according to Pauli and Bugge) Iran. *In Albanian*, vend *means "place, country, homeland"*.

cal, in this context, is probably the Albanian *gjallë*, "life" (or, more properly, "living" and "to live", M. 141).

. . . pl remains obscure; cf. *ep, nep* "to give".

saχs breaks down into *sa*, "how much", and *kesh*. The latter word comes from the Albanian verb *kam*, "to have"; (të) *kesh*, "may thou have"; *kishe*, "thou wast having". Phrases beginning with "how much, so much, as much" are of frequent occurrence in Etruscan epigraphy; we shall return to them later.

What was the sense of the whole exclamation? Despite the lacunae, it would seem to be translatable as: "You shall give to Venθ (of) your life as much as you have." The victor is dedicating his victim's life to Venθ.

I find an excellent confirmation of my interpretation in the following lines of Mommsen, which have to do with Roman religion:

> The execution of the criminal condemned to death was as much an expiatory sacrifice offered to the divinity as was the killing of an enemy in just war; . . . just as the enemy paid [the penalty] to mother earth and the good spirits on the field of battle.
>
> (*History of Rome*, Bk. I, Ch. 12.)

Let us now inquire more closely who Venθ was. She figures in the first of these two frescos, the one portraying a sacrifice to the shade of Patrocles. With outspread wings she stands beside Achilles, who is sacrificing a Trojan. It is surprising to note that she has not the down-cast air of an infernal spirit, despite the two serpents, her attributes.

An important contribution to our knowledge of her has been made by F. Poulsen, who has given such an authoritative description of a number of Etruscan tombs decorated with frescos.[1] In his study of the François Tomb he reaches the conclusion that Venθ was one of the *Lasa*, who were *benevolent* spirits of life after death. Her tutelary role comes out more prominently in the Golini Tomb, which Poulsen has also described. (Fig. 12.)

FIG. 12. Venθ, protectress of the dead

The two snakes at the goddess's girdle indicate her connection with the Underworld. It is nevertheless she who receives or accompanies the young nobleman, a Larth, who has just arrived, driving his chariot, in the other world. With her left hand the goddess is making a gesture of reassurance; in her right she holds a rolled-up scroll, which Poulsen conjectures to contain an enumeration of the good deeds which this Larth accomplished in his brief existence; no doubt a list whose reading is to mollify the severity of the god Hades, that Jupiter of the infernal realms.

However, on the strength of the similar scroll of Laris Pulena, already mentioned, and from other inscriptions, it may be suggested that in this case and others of the same kind the list was chiefly one of services rendered to the city and the country. These services would therefore be proclaimed by the goddess whose very name means "native country, native city". In that country it is she who receives

[1] *Etruscan Tomb Paintings*, 1932, p. 54, fig. 40.

and protects the souls of the ancestors. It is to her that a considerable proportion of the sacrifices appears to have been devoted. We thus get a glimpse of how, from these various indications, the idea of the country and of patriotism begins to emerge, an idea which is progressively elevated and purified as its development proceeds.

This appears to me to be corroborated by another portrayal, examined elsewhere, in the domain of Roman archaeology: the winged Roman goddess of Glory, who probably inherited the functions of Venθ, holding a scroll on which the merits of the deceased are recorded.

In conclusion, let us note that in Chapter VII of the Book of the Mummy, Venθ figures with the name of Vanθ.

Now the soil which engendered Venθ, that Etruscan Glory, is originally no other than the native earth to which the souls of the

FIG. 13. Two Etruscan nobles allowing themselves to be sacrificed

ancestors remain attached. These souls must be supported so that in their turn they will support the country in times of danger. In times of acute danger they need some exceptional guarantee of this solidarity between the past and the present. The blood of prisoners is inadequate, in this supreme sacrifice; and Etruscan nobles are consequently prepared to give up their own.

We are here contemplating one of the darkest pages in our perusal of Etruscan antiquity. However, there is no question of "delight in cruelty", but, rather, of an act of faith, an archaic rite.

A striking engraving published by G. Körte in 1890 (*I rilievi delle urne etrusche*, Rome, pl. CXV, I) depicts a scene in which a twofold voluntary sacrifice of this kind is taking place (fig. 13). In the centre are two young patricians, one kneeling, the other standing. The face of the first displays an impressive serenity. Behind them are to be seen two sacrificants with up-raised daggers, ready to immolate them. On the right of the group is a flute-player; on the left are two men-servants carrying tools and a ladder; the servant on the extreme left, in his emotion, has grasped his comrade's arm. According to Körte, the ladder is required for the ritual incineration which will follow.

The author writes that the bas-relief in question belongs to the 3rd or 2nd century B.C., when such barbarous ceremonies no longer took place:

> Our bas-reliefs, therefore, do not refer to contemporary funeral rites, but rather to some famous event in [Etruscan] mythology, some incident in which individuals of noble birth offered themselves as sacrifices for the salvation of their country, thus also obtaining for themselves a place of honour in the memory of posterity. (P. 260.)

So the tutelary Venθ and the patriotic conception of country make their appearance as notions which had evolved and been purified, notions which had originally been developed in the ancient Italic civilisation under the influence of Etruscan beliefs.

I think the same goddess can be identified in the Thracian *Bendis*. The Thracians identified Bendis with Artemis; but Artemis was confused with Hecate, the goddess of the Underworld.

Let us return to the rewards offered for virtue in daily life. Here, first, is a conjectural interpretation of an inscription from a decorated vase:

(P. 65) *cena mi kalaturus fapenas cenecuhe θieze*

cena (A), "price, value, recompense". An old Indo-European root, to be grouped with *kaena* (in the Avesta), *kaïna* in Scythian, Greek *poïne*, Slavonic *tzena*, Albanian *cenis* "to evaluate".

calaturus presumably means "cup".

fapenas, a noun in the dative.

cuhe is probably the Albanian *kohe*, "time" (M. 202). According to G. Meyer, this term is indigenous, not a loan-word (*loc. cit.*, p. 194).

θieze is difficult. It is perhaps connected with the notion of "ten, about ten", already discussed.

The meaning of the whole is perhaps: "This vase is a reward to Fabena for the period of his decade."

A much more spectacular rise to glory was commemorated by the erection of the effigy of an Etruscan *orator* in the temple of the god Sancus. This is a handsome bronze statue, an early prefiguration of the austere spirit of Roman sculpture. It bears an inscription (P. 651, CIE 4196):

> *auleśi meteliś ve vesial clenśi cen flereś*
> *tece sanśl tenine tuθineś χisvlics*

Like some other authors, M. Pallottino has translated the first part of this inscription as follows: "To Aule Meteli, son of Vel and his wife Vesi, this statue has been erected . . ." For, in fact, the ending *si* indicates the dative, *cen* is the accusative of *ca* ("this", adjective or pronoun), and *fleres* is accepted as meaning an ex-voto or image. *tece* is probably equivalent to Albanian *tek*, "in".

It is known that *sanśl* can mean "of Sancus" or "of the god Sancus". *tenine* is simply a derivative of the root *ten*, which we have seen already in the words *huθ-tenia* and *tenθas* ("of the town"). We have also noted Albanian *ndenjë*, "residence" (M. 306). In a number of Albanian words beginning with *nd* the *n* can disappear (thus *ndek* develops into *tek*, and *nderi* into *deri*, M. 306; and *ndez* into *dhez* M. 307). This *tenu* or *tenine* comes down to *den* and is equivalent to our *ndenjë*. *tuθines* is an Italic noun whose meaning is already known to be "of the citizens". The two closing words of the inscription, *χiś vlicś*, have not hitherto been explained. *xiś* can be interpreted through Albanian *hieshi*, "adornment" (M. 159); *vlicś* is Albanian *vluk*, "peak, summit, crowning" (oblique case) (M. 561). In short, and conjecturally, this word can be translated as "the most beautiful thing".

The text appears to mean: "To Aule Meteli, son of Vel and Vesi. This statue (is), in the house of Sancus, from (his) fellow-citizens a supreme adornment." If, however, *cen* means "prize", the reading will be: "To Aule . . . this statue is a prize; in the house of Sancus", etc.

After these texts, which leave us undecided on various points, we shall be rewarded by the study of an inscription of great historical importance, one which reminds us that, in the state of division which obtained in ancient Italy as a whole and also in Etruscan territory, wars frequently occurred. The inscription is taken from a cippus, a tombstone, in Perugia, and glorifies an action of outstanding heroism. Let us start by recalling what we know about the origins of military organisation among the Etruscans, and among the Romans:

The names of the three tribes of ancient Rome or the three centuries of knights, Ramnes, Luceres and Tities, were Etruscan denominations, and it cannot be doubted that a similar division had taken place in Etruria itself.

(O. Müller, *loc. cit.*, p. 355)

The introduction in Rome of the satellites or bodyguards was due to the Etruscan leaders ... especially Tarquinius Superbus. ... Now there are two terms pertaining to the army for which there is no plausible etymology: *miles* and *veles* ... Varro ... indicates that the *milites* were provided originally by three Etruscan tribes, the *Titienses*, *Ramnes* and *Luceres* ...

(A. Ernout, *Les éléments étrusques du vocabulaire latin*, 1930, p. 117)

There were therefore in Rome three bodies of cavalry whose names (italicised by us in the second of the two quotations above) were certainly disfigured versions of Etruscan names, but must originally have possessed meanings denoting the characteristics or functions of those bodies respectively.

It is with this in mind that we shall examine our Perugian inscription. Here is a preliminary observation: it contains neither proper names nor the word *clan* ("son"). My conclusion, reached in spite of several lacunae in the text, is that it refers to the common grave of several mounted warriors who fell during a victorious attack on an enemy city. Here is the text (P. 572, CIE 4539):

> *ca suθi nes [l]* . . . *amcie titial canl restiaś*
> *cal caraθsle aperucen ca θui ceśu lusver etva*
> *ca .urane cares. caraθsle se* . . .

ca suθi: "This is the tomb".

nesl: I explain this by Albanian *nejshëm*, "joined" (M. 313) (coming from *nye*, "joint, articulation"); the meaning will be "conjoint, common".

There is another possibility, through an alternative form of *ndenjë*, "dwelling-place", with the meaning of "place of rest".

amcie may be the past of the verb "to be", whose present tense in Albanian is conjugated as follows:

jam	*jemi*
je	*jini*
asht	*janë*

The initial *j* is of secondary importance; *amcie* would correspond to *amce*, the past tense of the verb; and the meaning of the Etruscan might be "it was".

titial (A): here are our Etruscan Tities, in the genitive. There is a

choice of two Albanian words, either of which may offer the
etymology of their name: *thitë*, the plural of *thi*, "wild boar"
(M. 354) and *dhitë*, the plural of *dhi*, which in modern Albanian
means "goat" (M. 91); but since *dhi e egër* means "chamois", it is
possible that the Etruscan *dhi* means "chamois". But I am
inclined to think that these Etruscan hussars had a boar as their
standard.

canl (B) is Albanian *gjanë* (with the -*l* of the genitive, *gan-l*), "wide".

restiaś: an interesting word; it is easy enough to interpret, but alas!
in three different ways at once:

> (a) by Albanian *resht*, "rank, line" (M. 435), which gives to
> *canl restiaś* the sense of "in an extensive line";
>
> (b) by Albanian *rrëshitë*, "gliding" (M. 438). "Dash"?
>
> (c) by *resitje*, "act of obliterating, destroying" (M. 426). An
> attack or charge? See P. 758, Additions to Chapter III
> (LM), 4.

cal is probably Albanian *cal*, "horse", a parallel formation to Latin
caballa, "mare". If not, one thinks of *gjallë*, "living", in the sense
of "lively".

caraθsle is a thing of beauty. I recognise in it two words, a noun
and a verb, connected without any valid reason from our point of
view at the present day; but the silence of Etruscan grammarians
on such matters must not be construed as meaning that their
outlook coincided with ours.

caraθ (A) comes from an ancient and well-tried Indo-European
source, *garad*, etc., since it is found in Hittite as *gurta*, "town"
(Friedrich, *Hit. Wört.*, p. 119); in Oscan, *hurtin*, "sacred grove"
but also "enclosure"; in "Pelasgic", *Curtu, Cortona*; in Albanian,
"enclosure" (M. 122); and in Slavonic, *grad, ograda, gorod*, "enclosed place, town".

sle (A) is the Albanian verb *shlej, shlyej*, "to efface, obliterate"
(M. 486); here used in the sense of "to rase". It occurs in other
Etruscan texts.

aperucen: this also consists of two words joined together.

ape (B) is Albanian *hap*, "to open". The initial *h* is secondary.
Compare *ha*, "he eats", and *a*, with the same meaning. Thus,
in Etruscan, we find *hercle* and *ercle*, both meaning Hercules.

I find it difficult to equate *ap* with the Roman verb *aperire*, "to
open" (Meyer-Lübke, no. 515), because of the suppression of
the *r*.

rucen (B) corresponds to an accusative form of Albanian *rrugë*,
ruga, "street, road". G. Meyer considers this word to be "Old

Italian". But the same author held that the word *raθ*, for example, was "Romanic"; Hammarström, however, has demonstrated the antiquity of this Etruscan word. *Ruga* is therefore either ancient *Italic*, or Etruscan.

ca is Albanian *ca*, "a little, a few".

θui: "here".

ceśu will be Albanian *këso*, "such, so" (M. 197).

lusver (A): having met the Etruscan Hussars we now have the luck to fall in with the Uhlans as well. In the first place it should be remembered that *a* and *u* are sometimes alternative to one another: *Aclinei*: *Ulcnal*; *aχale*: *uχule* (Buonamici, *Di alcune vere*, etc., p. 85); and that *v* often appears instead of *u*. Thus, we shall read our word as *luśuer* or *laśuer*. I have no hesitation in identifying it as the Hittite (Friedrich, *loc. cit.*, p. 123) and Illyrian verb *lâ*, "to leave, loose", with imperfect tense *lishë*, aorist *lashë*, etc. *laśuer* has the same ending, denoting the past participle, as we have already found in the gloss *iduare*, and as occurs in the Albanian *dashur*, "loved", from the root *due*, "to love, to wish". These men who were "loosed" or unleashed are no other than the daring Etruscan horsemen, Luceres, here seen in the honourable company of *titial*, the Tities.

The third body of cavalrymen, the Ramnes, seem to have been absent from the battle—unless perhaps they lie buried somewhere beneath the ruins of the text.

etva ca: "and two", or "several"?

.urane: the truncated remains of the word *spurane*, "of the town". Here, we are on the edge of an interesting problem. If two letters of the word are missing the natural supposition is *spurane*. If only one is missing, *turane* suggests itself. In Lydia *tura* was the word for "fortress, walled city". Some authors have seen in this word the origin of the name of the *Tyrrhenians*. We shall return to the subject when we come to deal with the Lydian language. If *turane* should be the answer it would be the only mention of *tura* in the whole of Etruscan epigraphy. But nothing can be constructed on the basis of a mere lacuna.

cares may make us think either of the Albanian *garre*, "trench" (M. 123), or of Latin *carrus*, "wagon, chariot", the second of which is not of Latin but of Celtic origin. We shall meet the word again in the Stele of Novilara.

It is obvious that no one as yet can claim to interpret every word and every different shade of meaning in an Etruscan text. We shall be glad enough to render the general meaning, which, in the example now under review, presents itself as follows:

"This is the common (?) grave of the Tities, who, in a great cavalry charge, razed the ramparts (caraθsle) and opened the way (aperucen), and of the Luceres who (with) the chariots of the city mowed down the obstacles. . . ."

There is much that is not clear. We should like to know the name of the town which was assaulted. Still, the document is an interesting one.

The history of Etruscan military activities is further illuminated by other references. M. Ernout writes:

Trossuli, another early term denoting cavalry, according to Pliny, is Etruscan. Thus we appear to have, in celeres, trossuli, flexuntes, three vestiges of the Etruscan domination in Rome, three names given by the Etruscans to different cavalry formations.

(Loc. cit., p. 105)

If these three words are Etruscan, an explanation may be suggested for celeres by way of Albanian qell, "to conduct, stop, delay" (M. 413); for flexuntes, through flakë, "flame";[1] and, finally, for trossuli through turshij, "to strike, shatter" (M. 530). This arrangement would amount to a judicious distribution of combat roles among the respective detachments: to halt the enemy, to shake him by a daring attack and finally to break up his forces.

It may be added that, thanks to caraθ(sle), we are able to understand two other inscriptions in the Testimonia. The first of them has been preserved only in part:

(1) (P. 532, CIE 3202). Written on a stone. Two out of the four words are missing; the remainder is: . . . iucurte at (A). But we can elucidate this much.

iu: Albanian hyu, "god, divine", a word which occurs frequently. "Sacred", perhaps? (M. 164).

curte: equivalent to caraθ; here, "sequestered space, enclosure, sacred grove".

at: "mother" (as will be seen below).

This fragment therefore means: ". . . sacred enclosure (of the) Mother . . ." Thus the stone designated a temenos or grove consecrated to a Mother Goddess, Turan, Juno or Latona.

[1] Derived from Greek floks?

(2) (P. 644, CIE 471). On the plinth of a statuette:

tinścvil me unial curtun

tinś: "of the day".
cvil: "brilliance, light", as we shall see in the chapter on the Tavern.
tinscvil: an epithet for Aurora, the dawn?
mi: "this".
unial curtum: "Juno's precincts".

The sense of the inscription is: "This (is a statuette of) Aurora from the grove of Juno."

Much clearer than these two are some of the inscriptions on Etruscan missiles. We have already seen one sample. Fortunately for us there are plenty more. Bugge deciphered long ago one of the words occurring on them, *harc*, by comparing it with Armenian *harkanem*, "struck, wounded". Etruscan does in fact present points of contact with Armenian, and so does Albanian. But another inscription of this ballistic genus, which I shall analyse, keeps us inside the Illyrian frame of reference. The word is *cresmie*, which Buonamici has collected from one of these projectiles. I explain it through Albanian *krismë*, "crash", *kris*, "to crack, shatter" (M. 215). The meaning, then, is: "Shatter!"

These inscriptions are not always so sanguinary. The Etruscan warriors sometimes informed them with blunt humour. This is proved by an amusing inscription on another "bullet": (P. 493) *mi katekril* (A). This little document is admirably clear; and, once again, we find two words coupled together.

For, in fact, *katek* is the Albanian *katoc*, which has two meanings: (1) "a nut"; (2) "a piece, a head" (as we say, for example, a head of garlic) (M. 189). I take this word to be related to Russian *katatj, katitj*, "to roll", which includes the idea of something round or rounded. The distinction between final *k* and *ç (tsh)* is unimportant in Albanian, as is shown by, for instance, *gjumaç* and *gjumak*, "sleeper" (M. 149), or *haliq* and *haliç*, "ruin" (M. 428). So the inscription means: "Here is a pea!", or, if you want to add a condiment to this verbal dish, you can translate it as: "Do you like peas?" or something of the kind. By despatching to the inhabitants of a besieged town, who were likely to be underfed in any case, these sly allusions inscribed on an indigestible substance, the Etruscan soldiers were teasing them in the most effective way possible. But I fear their "vegetables" may seem equally indigestible to lovers of the "gloomy" and to those who deny the Illyrian and Indo-European character of the Etruscan language.

There is another inscription in the same style, also on a leaden sling-stone: (P. 401) *hurtu* (B). It should probably be read as *hurdhu*, with the definite article -*u* at the end. The word *hurdhë* is found in Albanian, and the explanation of it given by Mann (p. 164) fits the Etruscan *hurtu* as well as the glass slipper fitted Cinderella. *Hurdhë*, he tells us, is an Albanian game, "the door-game", in which "the players try to throw certain objects into the mouth of one of them".

This is hardly a game, it seems to me, for chairmen of financial corporations and other ornaments of society; by which I mean that there are more elegant ways of amusing oneself. But, to compensate us for that, the game has an archaic touch about it. The drift of our terse inscription might be conveyed thus: "Would you like to play with me? Open your mouth, then. Here it comes!" That was just the Etruscan style. Moreover, in his description of the wars between the Romans and the Veiians, Livy frequently mentions the jeers and insults which the two camps used to exchange with one another.

There are many inscriptions of this kind, for the Etruscan slingers very often wrote something on their missiles. We must excuse these ebullient young men; perhaps the quartermaster was slack and did not hand out an issue of writing-paper with the proper regularity. For my own part, I not only appreciate their humour and the freedom they enjoyed in the indulgence of it (at a time when, alas, their lives were in danger); I also highly approve of their having written so much. And it shows they did know how to write.

Some of the other inscriptions in this category are more difficult. The one which says *har* (B) (P. 377) must, I think, be understood by means of the Albanian verb *harr*, "to weed". If this is a joke, it is a sombre one. The missile was adjured to "pull up the weeds". A comparable inscription (P. 649), *semnissi* (B), is evidently made up of two words: *shême*, the Albanian for "ruin" (M. 471), and *nis*, a verb, "to begin" (M. 325). The meaning is therefore: "Begin to ruin!" or: "Sow ruin!" Another inscription (P. 617): *mi cuicna*, probably belongs to the same category; unless it is a proper name, it can perhaps be explained as an insult: *koje*, *kue* means "skin" in Albanian (M. 203); *kna* may be "dog"—cf. Albanian *qen*, Latin *canis*, Greek *kuon*, and, especially, Lydian and Carian *kan* (see Chapter VIII, "A Visit to the Doctor"). It would therefore be an apostrophe: "Dog-skin!"

To bring this little treatise on the epistolary art among the Etruscans to a worthy end, I have chosen an edifying inscription whose meaning is confirmed by something concrete and tangible, namely the very shape of the leaden missile on which it is scrawled. This missile (Fig. 14, after Fabretti, CII) is peculiarly slender and elongated. Its inscription is: *strevc* (A) (P. 784, CII 2635). This is not one word but two, and indeed a whole sentence: *stre* is the Albanian verb *shtrij*, "to stretch, extend, lie down at full length" (M. 503); *vc* (uk) I finally recognised as Albanian *ujk*, "the wolf" (M. 503), which takes us straight into the world of totems and into Lycia, the "country of the wolves". *strevk*, *shtreuk* means: "Stretch out like a wolf [running]!" "Leap like a wolf!" The words are a spell laid on the missile. The wolf was an important element in Balkan and Aegean mythology three thousand years ago, and it remained a basic theme in the folklore of the region almost until our own day.

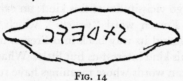

FIG. 14

At the last moment I am unable to resist the temptation to include two more of these "missives" sent by Etruscan slingers.

One of them is caustic: (CII, no. 2639) *putist ic* (B). By analogy with the verbal forms *pultis* ("to consent", p. 212) and *puris* ("stir the fire", p. 207) I assimilate *putis* to Albanian *puth*, *puthës*, "to embrace, kiss" (M. 410); *t* denotes an adjective or "in, as"; *ic* is Albanian *ik*, "run!" (M. 166). The rendering, therefore, is: "Go with (my) kiss!" or "Go (as, in the role of, a) kiss!"

The other is savage (*ibid.*, no. 2640): *θkikθ*. *θk* is Albanian *dzak*, "blood, to bleed"; *ik* is "run!"; final *θ* is "in". Thus: "Draw blood in your course!"

It remains to examine two or three military terms which the Romans inherited from the Etruscans along with other features or conceptions associated with the life of the state. In the article already quoted, M. Ernout mentions the Latin word *turma*, "squadron of horsemen, crowd":

> ... *Turma*, a word whose appearance is not Indo-European, and whose use, on Varro's testimony, seems to have been due to the Etruscans ...
>
> (*Loc. cit.*, p. 118) [1]

Where the "Indo-European" aspect is concerned, I should like to remark that the question will probably have to be reconsidered in the light of the facts already set out, and of those to be set out subsequently, throughout this study. Etruscan contains a certain number

[1] A. Ernout, "Les éléments étrusques du vocabulaire latin", *Bulletin de la Société de Linguistique*, XXX, 1930, p. 118.

of Anatolian words which are possibly not Indo-European. But in the
majority of cases its vocabulary is Illyrian and related to Hittite,
Lithuanian and the Slav languages, etc.; it is therefore essentially an
Indo-European language.

We next note that *turmë* appears in Albanian, with the same sense of
"mass, crowd, band" (M. 530). Of course, this does not mean that
the word is automatically to be included among those inherited directly
by Albanian from Illyrian. It passed from Etruscan into Latin; it may
later have been borrowed from Latin by Albanian. It is quite normal
for words to undergo vicissitudes of this kind; an example closer to our
own times is the French word *"fleurette"*, which was borrowed by
English and later found its way back into French in the English form
"flirt". Cases of this kind interest us but little. What we are concerned
with here is Etruscan words whose meanings have remained unknown,
and which can be explained with the help of Albanian.

To this category belongs another Roman military term of Etruscan
origin, which has been preserved in a gloss: (P. 816) *balteus*, "belt,
shoulder-belt", especially a sword-belt. Thomopoulos explained this
with the help of *balea*, *balitsea* (*Pelasgika*, p. 504). These words are
given in Mann's dictionary as *"insignium*, handkerchief" (M. 18). For
my part, I link *balteus* (B) with the Albanian root *baj*, "to bear, support" (M. 17). The infinitive of this verb is *bajtun*, *bajtur*; *bajtës* is
"carrier"; *bajtshëm* means "portable". The difference between the *i*
and the *l* is no obstacle, this fluctuation being characteristic of both
Etruscan and Albanian. Etruscan has *ziiace* and *zilace*, *piute* and *plute*.
And in Albanian we find *fle*, "to sleep", and *fjetun* (M. 110); *mbiej*, "to
milk", and *mbiel* (M. 270); *gjobë*, "fine" (in the sense of penalty), and
globë (M. 128); and so on. Thus the Etruscan and Illyrian *bajtës* or
baltës, the "carrier" of the sword, is the father of Latin *balteus*.

In the same way, we shall see a number of "Etruscan glosses", which
in the last two thousand years have become as desiccated as the roses
of Jericho, coming back to life and regaining their colour and scent;
and we shall marvel at the fidelity with which the ancients, especially
the wise Hesychius, preserved them.

IV

THE FAMILY

CLAN, lineage, family; such was the basis of Etruscan society. Accordingly, funerary inscriptions scrupulously catalogue, after the name of the deceased, the names of his father and mother, his grandparents and sometimes that of an uncle. His administrative career is briefly described, and the number of his children is recorded.

Woman was surrounded with affection and respect, and, in contrast to Greek usage, the mistress of the house was admitted on equal terms at the banqueting table. Certain priestly functions were reserved to a particular noble family; and since civil offices were always tied to religious functions, certain positions of responsibility were inaccessible to anyone not of noble birth. Hence the accentuated importance of lineage as a factor in social life. This situation changed only when the expansion of sea-borne trade, and the exploitation of the colonies (Corsica and Sardinia) and of mines (on Elba and in Spain), brought into being a rich and liberal bourgeoisie. This class was to oust the aristocracy from a number of positions.

As early as 1883, Bugge interpreted the word θur, θura (whose terminal a we regard as the definite article, as in Albanian) to mean "*gens*, family, line". Thus

(F. 2033) *vel leinies arnθial θura*

is rendered: "Vel Leinies, of the family of Arnth." [1]

It can be observed that this θura (A), the very foundation-stone of the life of society in Etruria, has been preserved intact in that vehicle of Illyrian tradition, the Albanian language: *dorë*: (1) hand; (2) kind, sort, social class (Leotti, p. 124); class, rank, kind (M. 80).

We come back to the impressive Laris Pulena of Tarquinia, who is always preparing to take part in a feast of the gods, but who receives us nevertheless with his usual patience, and asks us with a touch of irony, as he shows us his parchment: "Well, you've learnt to read, have you? Then pray do so!"

But, but—— It's rather embarrassing. We really thought we had begun to understand a bit. But we shall manage to dissect this

[1] *Etr. Forsch.*, IV, p. 191.

treasured inscription only piece by piece, as if it was a sort of epigraphical artichoke. On this occasion we shall extract a tasty morsel from it: Laris Pulena (P. 131) *parniχ amce*. He was a *parniχ* (A). Albanian *paranik*, "ancestor" (M. 350), of which the root is *par*, "first", can be recognised here. In Etruscan the meaning would be "patrician".

Let us continue our round of visits to Etruscan noblemen. Another inscription, that of Alethnas (P. 169, CII 2065), informs us for a start that he was *zilaθ parχis* (A).

Deecke, whose studies, according to Skutsch, together with those of Corssen, had established the Indo-European character of the Etruscan language, was tempted one day by the Father of Lies to translate *parχis* by "park, enclosed place". Corssen translated it by "equestrian". Torp supposed that *par* meant "father". And F. Leifer worked up a theory according to which *parc* meant "thunder", a sign of power!

M. J. Heurgon, from whose account this résumé is partially borrowed, adopts the explanation put forward by S. Mazzarino: *zilaθ parχis* was a magistrate of the *patricians* ("L'Etat étrusque", *Historia*, VI, 1957, p. 94).

Substantially, this conclusion is both elegant and accurate; but it is based on erroneous etymology, which in turn was based on faulty method. In fact, *parχis* means "of noble lineage". But the word springs from a primitive and material notion: "belly", *uterus*. We have already pointed out that Etruscan words are sometimes slightly disguised. The root to be sought out was not *parc* but *bhark* or *bark*. And we find it, fresh and alive, in Albanian: *bark*, "belly, womb, generation, race, lineage, family" (M. 21). *parχis*, that is to say, *barkis*, will mean: "from generations, for generations".[1] Therefore, a hereditary *zilaθ*, as it were. There is no difficulty in finding Indo-European cousins for this word *bark*: Russian *briukho*, Polish *brzuch*, "belly".

The father was called *at* (A) in Etruscan. It is curious that this word is not always easy to discern in the inscriptions. It exists in Albanian and has several forms of plural: *atën(it)*, *atër(it)*, (M. 14), *ateri* (M. 27) and *etna* (M. 97). *Etna*, in all probability, is present in the word *etnam*,[2] "ancestors", which occurs frequently in the Book of the Mummy. It will be discussed later. In P. 100 we find *θnam* for *etnam*.

Atër is, I think, represented in an expression which crops up several times: *hels atraś* (P. 293, P. 301, P. 317, P. 318). The most explicit

---

[1] The word is an ablative and makes a perfect parallel with the Albanian ablative plural: *nerzish*, "from men"; *motis*, "from times" (Cimochowski, *Le dialecte de Dushmani* 1951, p. 50.)

[2] Cf. *cletra*, "litter" (Osco-Umbrian), and *cletram* (Etruscan).

example is an inscription of the François Tomb which is accompanied
by the figure of a woman surrounded by effigies of the dead:

(P. 301, CIE 5278) *θanχvil verati helś atrś* (B)

The first two words are her own name and her family name. *hell* is
explained by Albanian *ila* (cf. *ijë*, "of the entrails", M. 165) in the
sense of "bosom" or "midst"; "in the bosom of the ancestors". This is
illustrated by a fresco of the ancestral shades which is to be seen in the
same tomb. All this is in agreement with the deductions of Trombetti,
who recalls Latin *atta*, "father", and Skutsch, for whom *ati* means
"mother".

I have found confirmation in the decipherment of two short but
interesting inscriptions:

(*a*) On a mirror: *Turan ati* (A) (P. 754), "Aphrodite the Mother".
(*b*) On a statuette of a goddess: *vnat* (A) (P. 456, CIE 303).

This is as charming as it is brief: *Un at*, "Juno the Mother". Perhaps
in both cases we should see a dative: offerings to goddesses.

An epitaph on the side of a sarcophagus announces the last resting-
place of a certain *Elnei Ramθa* (P. 159) who was *ati θuta* of an Aule Velu
θansina. *ati θuta* is "mother beloved". *θuta* is the past participle of
the verb *due*, "to love" (M. 35), although G. Meyer holds that *due*
comes from Latin *debeo*, "to owe"; but at the same time he compares
desh (the past tense of the verb *due*) with the verb *zush*, from the Avesta,
and with an ancient Indian word *jush*.

In Albanian there are two words for "mother": *nuna* (Arbanas,
p. 99) and *amë*, *ëma* (M. 5). Now it seems that these two nouns, in
addition to *ati*, occur in Etruscan:

A. *ame*: the deciphering of this Etruscan word is not without its
pitfalls, for there is also a root *am*, "to be", whence *amce*, "was"
(aorist or imperfect), and thus we must be on the watch for words whose
literal form is the same but whose meanings are different. But let us
note a few cases in which *ame* seems to mean "mother" rather than
anything else—

(1) *Uni at* is Juno-Mother. It therefore seems logical to identify
    this surname of Juno in another phrase which appears to mean
    the same as this one. There is a vessel (*askos*) bearing the
    following inscription:

(P. 213, NRIE 530) *turis mi une ame*

Goldmann has incorrectly interpreted *turis* as equivalent to
Greek *turos*, "cheese"; and Corssen was wrong in inferring that

une denoted a liquid. It is likelier that *turis* is "gift, offering" (cf. *turce*, "gave") and that *une ame* is "Juno-Mother". So the whole reads: "This is an offering to Juno the Mother."

(2) In LM, VII, 14, we read: *acil ame etnam*. *Acil* is "urn", *etnam*, "fathers". The phrase says, therefore, "the urns of the mothers and the fathers". If our translation is correct it will be noticed that the mothers are mentioned first.

(3) On the Cippus of Perugia (P. 570) we read: *ipa ama hen naper*. *Naper* is known to mean a measure of land; and we have seen already that *ipa* is connected with the verb *ip*, *ap*, *ep*, "to give". *Ama*, in this instance, is a mother or mother-in-law, who is giving or bequeathing lands or assigning them towards the expenses of worship. According to E. Vetter, however, *ame* is connected with the verb *am-*, "to be", and means "may it be, let it be".

B. *nuna*, with the sense of "mother", appears to be used in a confused inscription on a vessel. This inscription (P. 29, CIE 8412) begins with these words: *ipas ikam ar nuna turani ria* . . .

ipas: denotes the receptacle itself; cf. Greek *ibé*, suggests Corssen.
ikam: *i-* is the sign of the direct object; *kam*, in Albanian, is "to have" (M. 178).
ar: "altar", as will be shown later.
nuna: "Mother"?
turani: to Turan-Aphrodite?
ria: new, new-made, young, fresh, etc.
Is the receptacle consecrated to Aphrodite the Mother?

On the same subject we may quote another inscription, this time from Veii: (P. 46, NRIE 885) . . . *mi nunai*. It is evidently a votive inscription, and we are tempted to reconstitute it as *uni mi nunai*, or as *Aritimi nunai* (the latter in view of the fact that these two nouns, *Aritimi* and *nuna*, are found together on another vase, also from Veii; P. 45, NRIE 867). The meaning would be either "To Uni the Mother" or "To Aritimi (Artemis) the Mother".

Concerning Alethnas (who was mentioned a little earlier) we are told that he begot three sons: *clenar ci acnanasa* (P. 169). Although the meaning of the third word is in no doubt, its composition is not easily determined. It is built up of three elements: *a-cnana-sa*. The first *a* is, I believe, a direct object coming before the verb (as in Albanian): (he) *them* begot. *cnan* is the Albanian verb *qënun*, "to be", but used transitively here: "to cause to be, to create"; it is also the word for mother in Lycian: *knna*. The third part, *asa*, should perhaps be connected with Albanian *asaj*, "to her"; but in Etruscan the word could equally well mean "to him, for him".

Similarly, inscription P. 87, *ati nacnuva*, means "the mother who created us". *ati* is "the mother"; *na*, "us"; *cnuva* is the past of the same verb *qënun*; *va* is a suffix of the past tense in Etruscan (cf. *pava, marunuχva*, etc.).

Let us enlarge the family circle somewhat. In LM, among the shades who are called to the funeral feast, we see:

$$arθ \ vaχr \ ceuś \ (VII, 7) \ (A)$$

arθ is Albanian *ardhë*, the subjunctive of the irregular verb *vij*, "to come" (M. 10). A proper name (Arth = Arnth) is hardly a possibility here.

vaχr is a characteristically Indo-European word. It is, of course, Albanian *vjehër*, Russian and Bulgarian *svekor*, etc. (M. 559); in short, "father-in-law"; though it should be noted that in Etruscan it could also mean "parents-in-law".

This deduction concerning the meaning of *vaχr* is rendered possible by the fact that the word occurs on the Cippus of Perugia (P. 570, CIE 4538), the very first line of which makes mention of the donatrix we have already encountered, Tanna Larez(ul), who is described as *ame vaχr lautn velθinas*. The first two words denote a family relationship, of course. *ame* means "mother" (M. 5), like *ati*. Is Tanna "the mother of the father-in-law of Veliθna, the freedman"? Or, on the other hand, does the expression *ame vaχr* simply mean "the mother-in-law", in Etruscan? One may also wonder why *vaχr* is mentioned here at all. But while these details are still undecided, there is no doubt about the meaning of *vaχr*.

So let us welcome these Etruscan fathers-in-law and mothers-in-law. Their entry into the "Indo-European family", in the literal and the figurative sense, is both seemly and irrevocable.

ceus is Albanian *gjysh*, "grandfather", *gjushë*, "grandmother" (M. 151).

This word occurs in another inscription, on the wall of a tomb in Tarquinii (P. 98, CIE 5525), which mentions a lady, *ramθa matulnai*. The epitaph enumerates her family relationships: she was *seχ* (daughter) of *A*, *puia* (wife) of *B*, and *ceus* (grandmother) of *C, D, E, ...* The order in which these data are given leaves no doubt as to the meaning of *ceus*.

The three words in question (LM, VII, 7) therefore mean: "May they come, the parents-in-law and grandparents!"

An epitaph (P. 630) mentions a man named Arnt, qualified as *veliak hapiśnei* (B). The second of these words is a woman's name. *veliak* recalls Albanian *vlla*, "brother".

We should note that *nefs*, "nephew" in Etruscan, has an exact counterpart in Albanian: *nipash* (M. 325). And the Latin word of Etruscan origin, *talea*, "shoot, sprig", which I take from the article by M. Ernout, previously quoted, is nicely interpreted by means of the Albanian root (already encountered) *dal*, "to issue, come out"; thus, "what comes out from a tree", i.e., "a sprig".

This brings us round to the subject of youth. We shall seize this chance of regaling ourselves with a votive inscription whose meaning is limpidity itself.

The following Albanian words facilitated my understanding of it:

> *djalë*, "boy"
> *djalosh*, "boy"
> cf. *djaloshar*, adj. "youthful"
> *djaleri*, "youth, childhood" (M. 77).

Let us observe at once that this old Illyrian word *djalë* is clearly of high interest. We shall have occasion to devote a few lines to it at the end of this study.

On the statuette of a goddess, we read:

> (P. 734, CIE 302) *mi fleres atisiliθiial* (A)

M. Buffa considered that the name of the goddess Ilizia was to be discerned in the third word. For my own part, I translate this text as follows:

mi fleres: "this is an ex-voto" (or "effigy").
ati: "of the Mother".
sili: is the Albanian verb *siell*, among whose meanings are "to bear bring, produce" (M. 450).
θial: "children".

Thus: "This is the effigy of the Mother who causes children to be born." We have previously seen "Aphrodite the Mother" and "Juno the Mother". All these are so many different hypostases of the Great Mother of Asia Minor, the fertility-goddess *par excellence*, whom women used to supplicate to make them fruitful.

Another *djalë* is preserved in a slightly dilapidated gloss of Hesychius. It concerns childhood: (P. 802) *agaletora*. Thomopoulos very justly explained this word by reference to the Albanian *djalë*. My glance strayed past this judicious parallel without my recognising its value. In order to appraise it better I had first to study the problem of the various dialects of Albanian, already elucidated by the work of M. Lambertz, Carlo Tagliavini and Cimochowski. I was then able to see that, for example, the word *gjak*, "blood", might occur in another dialect as *dzjak*, and in another as *ziak*. It is therefore hardly surprising to meet it in Etruscan in the form of θac (P. 612). Coming back to *agaletora*, it may fairly be supposed that this gloss has been mishandled by copyists in the course of centuries, and that its termination *ora* is the particle *eri*, denoting the plural or (as in Albanian) an abstract noun; the initial *a* may be prothetic. The only part of the word we can salvage in this affair is *galet*, which is an oblique case of *gjale*. This *gjalë* is a dialectal variation of *djalë*, just as *gjak* is a variant of *dzjak*.

Thus the original word must have been *a-djalëtori*.

A slight complication arises in the epitaph of our friend *aleθnas zilaθ parχis*, already studied. The inscription goes on to say:

(P. 169) . . . *zilaχnu θeluśa ril XXVIIII* . . .

The translation is: (1) "he was a zilaθ" or "he became a zilaθ"; (2) "[at the age] of 29 years". But what is the word *θeluśa* doing between these two pieces of information? My first interpretation was that it was an equivalent of *θialiśa*, "boy, young" (P. 93) (discussed above), and my translation ran: "He became *zilaθ* while still young: at the age of 29 years." My reasoning was that, in principle, this office was conferred only on men of mature years and that Aleθnas was an exception; however, a man of twenty-nine is no longer in his first youth. I must therefore mention another possible interpretation: *θeluśa* may be connected with Albanian *dallueshëm*, "distinguished" (M. 66) (derived from the basic root *dal*, "to issue", and the derived root, *dalloj*, "to distinguish"). In which case the fragment would mean: "He served as zilaθ, with distinction, for 29 years." As a matter of figures this is not impossible, for this high-born Etruscan died at the age of sixty-six.

Before finishing with this problem of *djalë* and divesting ourselves, for the moment, of these swaddling-bands of Antiquity, we have one more case to deal with; a really complicated one this time. Its difficulty is all the more regrettable in that we are faced with two imposing bas-reliefs which seem to promise us information about the family life of the Etruscan nobility (fig. 15). Of these two reliefs, the one on the left shows a warrior taking leave of a woman; that on the right, a group of two or three people who seem to be exchanging two legal documents of great importance, duly set out on stamped paper. These characters face us as solemnly as those painted by the *douanier* Rousseau. But this does nothing to dissipate our bewilderment, which is all the greater in that

FIG. 15. Hero and freedwoman

the right-hand bas-relief has no inscription. As for the inscription on the left, G. Körte, who published it, expresses himself very cautiously:

> Its interpretation is difficult and uncertain . . . not, however, the transcription, which seems to contain the names of two of the people represented. They are doubtless husband and wife, and their appearance proves that they belong to the Etruscan nobility.[1]

Here is the inscription. On the bas-relief it is divided into two fragments (P. 390, CIE 144):

θafaalki laθunikai θania iiulaθilin

[1] *I rilievi delle urne etrusche*, II, 1890, p. 159; Table LXV.

I asked myself in vain which of the characters in this family "diptych" was still alive at the time, and which lay dead and buried under this stone; and I found only one thing in the inscription which was clear: θania, in Etruscan, is a woman's name which is widely used.

One may add with equal assurance that iiulaθilin does not look in the least like a proper name.

Looking at the left-hand scene, we may conjecture that the young warrior is setting out on his last journey. His horse is waiting ready in the background, and the young woman, to console him, has placed her hand on his shoulder. Is he going to the battlefield on which he will meet his death, or is he about to travel directly into the beyond? We have no means of knowing. Are the words a dialogue, or, on the contrary, are they all spoken by him to θania? It is hard to say. It is certainly he, in any case, who says iiulaθilin; this is a word which can be deciphered and which will add to our stock of acquisitions:

iiu: "god" or "gods", connected with Albanian hie, "god" (the same word as means "shade"; and, in Etruscan, it perhaps indicates the *divine shade* of a hero or ancestor, not just an ordinary shade); it is also connected with hyj, "god" (M. 159 and 164).

la: the Albanian la, "to leave", which has been seen already.

θilin: this is djalë again; "child, children", in the accusative.

Putting all this together, it means: "I entrust the children to the gods." What appeared to be a word is in fact a sentence. Such are the surprises Etruscan epigraphy springs on us.

Let us now turn our attention to laθunikai. This word gave me a good deal of trouble. I tried various fruitless expedients, such as linking it with the goddess Latona. But I finally hit on a simpler solution. It is, in fact, enough to observe the delightfully free and easy way in which the Etruscan scribes wrote the well-known word for "the freed-woman"; every scribe followed his own fancy:

1. lautna (P. 560)
2. lautni (P. 393, etc.)
3. *latni* (P. 443)
4. *lautuni* (P. 606)
5. lautniθa (P. 550)
6. *lautnic* (P. 550)

On comparing these variants with one another I think our *latunikë* should be added to the set, for it is related more or less to numbers 3, 4 and 6.

There remains the first word of the inscription. If it is a proper name this is probably the only example of its occurrence. It looks more like a sentence. In which case, its meaning may be:

θa: "says", in Albanian (tha).

fa must be read as ba; this f is like the f in θuflθa, frontac and several important words which we shall come to later: fufluns, fanuse, etc. ba would come from the Albanian verb bâj, "to make, to do"; here in a passive sense: "to happen, to take place".

alki may be the Albanian haliq, "ruin, collapse" (M. 151); cf. Hittite ualχ, "to strike"? (Friedrich, loc. cit., p. 252)

Thus the inscription would mean: "A catastrophe has taken place, O θania the freedwoman! I entrust the children to the gods." But one can look at the same text as constituting a dialogue, with one speech written close to the warrior's head: θafaalki laθunikai, "He says: A catastrophe has taken place, [O] freedwoman!", and the other speech, written close to the woman's head: θania iiulaθilin, "θania says: Entrust [thy] children to the gods!"

Obviously, both conjectures are far from satisfactory. For one thing, we have still not succeeded in finding the hero's name. But the word (or sentence) θafaalki looks nothing like a man's name. The only acquisition which this inscription has yielded is iiulaθilin. If my interpretation of laθunikai were confirmed it would give interesting testimony on how important a part could be entrusted to a freedwoman in the Etruscan family. But no deduction can be built on such shaky foundations. The same word could mean, "You are leaving the house in mourning", as we shall see in Chapter XII.

lautniθa brings us up against an important problem: the word lautni, "a freedman", probably carries the designation of "family" hidden within it. As early as 1883, Deecke had seen that this word was connected with the Latin concepts "domesticus, gentilicus, familiaris"; its meaning is therefore "one who has been admitted into the family". The same author emphasised that the expression suθi lautni could not be translated as "a liberated tomb", but must be rendered as "a family vault"; and at the same time he stressed the close relationship between lautni, lutni (P. 589) and the Slavonic and Teutonic laudhni, ludini, ludi, Leute, "people",[1] which is one more indication of the Indo-European character of the Etruscan language. It is notable that the term "freedman", in a Lycian bilingual inscription studied by Kretschmer, is translated as "belonging to the family".

---

[1] Forsch. und Stud., V, 44.

Let us look now at another concept, that of a "client". He was a former "free man" or former "freedman". Mommsen says:

> The clients are among the constituent members, along with the slaves properly so called, of the family ruled by the will of the *citizen* (patronus).

But on becoming a member of the family the "client" was far from acquiring the same rights as the other members: he could not leave his *patronus* or enter the service of another *patronus*. Like a serf, he remained attached to the family and was handed down from father to son.[1] He was part of inheritance and the patrimony.

These dates will help us to establish the identity of an important Etruscan word: *eteri, etera*. In the inscriptions we often find: *suθi etera, lautn eteri* (P. 450). I shall interpret this word through the root *at*, "father" (already discussed), and notably through Albanian *atëri*, "paternity" (M. 14), which, for the ancients, would mean "patrimony" and perhaps "inheritance". In this case *lautn(i) eteri* would be an "inherited" freeman or client, forming part of the family patrimony. In the same way Aleθnas, discussed earlier in this chapter, being *zilaθ eterav* (that is to say *eterau*, with the definite article), inherited his title of *zilaθ* with his patrimony.

Finally, there is the problem of "descendants, posterity". Unless I am mistaken, this idea is expressed by the words *mani* (P. 730, CIE 304), *manim* (P. 169, CII 2055), *manimeri* (P. 170, CII 2056). The third of these inscriptions ends with the following phrase:

eθl matu manimeri

eθl can be divided into *e* and *θl*. *e* would be a particle of some kind, e.g., demonstrative. These shifting particles are current in Albanian too; and sometimes they confuse the situation.

θl would correspond to the Albanian verb "to go out", understood in a wide sense.

matu seems to be perfectly identical with Albanian *madh*, "great"; and *-u* is a definite article in postposition.

manimeri: "posterity"? My guide here is Albanian *mane*, the name for several kinds of berry (mulberry, etc.) (M. 262). Perhaps in the sense of "fruit", "seed"?

So Arnθ Aleθnas was one who *clenar zal arce*, "begot six sons", and "from whom sprang a numerous posterity".

This interpretation seems to me to be confirmed by inscription

---

[1] Fustel de Coulanges, pp. 307-8.

E

P. 169, where it is stated that another Aleθnas *VI manin arce,* "begot six descendants".

There was something special about Etruscan family life: it was based on affection. This feeling was expressed not only in frescos and carvings, where husband and wife gaze trustingly at one another, but also in a word which is found in epitaphs and which was at first taken to mean "spouse, married person" because, in a charnel-house inscription, it occurs after the names of two married people: (P. 586, CIE 3538) *tuśurθi* (B). I think the basis of the word is *dusur,* equivalent to Albanian *dashur,* "love" (M. 68); *tuśurθi* would therefore mean "in love". Later the word may have come to be used for "married man or woman".

Engraved on an Etruscan gem is a child's head, with this inscription: (P. 780) *num* (A). This I recognise as Albanian *njom,* "tender"; *njomje,* "tenderness" (M. 333).

Going up in the age-scale, we find an amusing nickname which was applied to schoolboys. No specialised knowledge, indeed, is required to understand it. The word is *apcar,* inscribed on a gem on which there is an engraving of a boy holding an abacus, a bead-frame for doing sums with (P. 779, CII 2578 *ter*). The Etruscan word *apc* (*abak*) is a borrowing from Greek. The ending *-ar* is the same as in *capesar* ("cobbler") and other nouns of the kind, which denote profession or habit, and which we shall examine later. *apcar* is the name for a pupil who finds it necessary to have constant recourse to his abacus.

In a charnel-house at Tarquinii the remains of a girl were discovered. Her father was called Velus, her mother Larθi. Her grandparents' names are given too. The epitaph ends as follows:

(P. 193, CII 2104) . . . *avils śas amce uples* (A)

The word which enabled me to work out the meaning, namely *uples,* is extremely important, not only because it depicts the ambiance but also as regards Etruscan grammar. *uples* is a verb in the mediopassive mood; I was able to deduce this, obviously, from the initial *u,* which characterises that mood in Albanian verbs in the aorist and in the subjunctive, and also from the terminal *s* (Albanian *sh, sha*). Thus, in Albanian:

bâj: to make
bahem: to be made, to make oneself, to become
ûba: he has become
u-bâjsh: (optative) may you become

Cases of this kind are not numerous in Etruscan, but, naturally, it would not have been possible to understand them without knowing the rule. Our word *uples* demonstrates this. The root we find in it is the Albanian *fle*, "to sleep", with the optative inflection: "Mayest thou go to sleep!" The preceding words in the text mean: "She was [aged] 5 years."

This word *fle* occurs in other instances as well. Among the drawings given by Fabretti in his CII I noticed a bronze figurine representing a woman with a conical head-dress who is gathering her skirt with one hand, after the manner of the crinoline-wearing ladies of Renoir. With her right hand she is making a gesture which may well mean: "Peace!" Between her shoulder-blades the artist has engraved the word *flezru* (A). M. Pallottino has read this as *flezrl* (P. 629, CIE 4562), and remarks laconically: "Bronze statuette of a woman (5th century)." Her pose is hieratic, as befits a sacred personage. She seems to be giving a blessing or extending her

FIG. 16. Aphrodite and dove (detail)

protection. Now, the term *flezru* falls apart to make two words: *flesh*, which is the (*u*)*ples* of the preceding text; and *rue*, which is Albanian *ruej*, "to protect" (M. 430). She is a divinity who *protects sleep*, an Etruscan tutelary angel. No doubt her aid was effective against night-noises, mosquitoes and depressing thoughts.

If *flez* is an oblique case of the noun *fle*, *ple*, "sleep", *flez-ru* will mean "protectress of sleep". We may add that Jokl studied this Albanian verb *ruej* and established its antiquity, rejecting G. Meyer's attempt to explain it as a borrowing from Slavonic (*loc. cit.*, p. 75).

So this little world of the Etruscan woman and child was far from lacking tenderness. We get the same impression from a bucolic scene engraved on a mirror: Aphrodite releasing a dove, which flies away (fig. 16). The impression is strengthened when we examine the brief accompanying inscription: *tifanati* (B). Trombetti inferred that this was an epithet of Venus; but the facts are otherwise:

ti is the Albanian verb "to know", *di*.

fanati is Albanian *banese*, "house, residence" (M. 19). The letter *f* in Etruscan, as we have already said, corresponds to Albanian *f*, *p* or *b*, according to context. We have pointed out *θuflθas* = *θubaltas*, *frontac* = (Greek) *bronté*, and shall adduce further examples.

The inscription means: "She knows the house (knows her home)."

By means of this laconic commentary the artist has succeeded in giving his picture more meaning. But if we want to take the meaning of the tiny inscription somewhat deeper we can extract from it a further and more accurate shade of significance. Another word for "house" in Albanian is *banë*, whence *bana*, "the house". The ending *ti* (*θi*) is a locative. The first *ti* will be of another kind, namely the Albanian *tej*, "far; get away! shoo!" (M. 511). *tifanati* now becomes: "Shoo! Go home!"

Youth was loved among the Etruscans, and much was forgiven to it. Let us glance at a little scene of a somewhat nudist character: a young

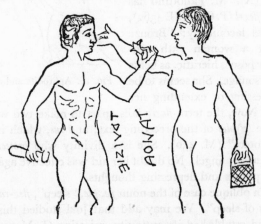

FIG. 17. After bathing

man holding in his right hand a bottle (doubtless of eau-de-Cologne) offers a flower to a girl who is carrying the little basket containing the things she needs for bathing. With her free hand the girl is either caressing his cheek or dealing him a slap in the face (fig. 17).

This flirtatious spectacle incited Gerhard,[1] to whose book we are indebted for the drawing, to address a retrospective reproof to the two young people:

[1] Gerhard, *Etr. Spiegel*, III, t. CXV

The frivolous encounter of the sexes directly after a bath, which is what seems to be taking place here, was doubtless in no way foreign to the loose morality of Etruria. The erotic meaning of this drawing is, in any case, more comprehensible than the inscription beside the man, *truisie*, and that beside the girl, *talitha*.

Let us note at once that this *talitha* is not the Aramaic word of the Gospel (Mark v. 41), which means "maiden", though Bugge thought it was and compared the Etruscan word with Armenian *talitaj*, "girl", which is borrowed from Aramaic. As for the morality of the Etruscan scene! . . . Besides, it may, on the other hand, be a representation of virtuous chastity. The young man boldly offers the girl a flower; but she, indignant, punishes him by saying: "How dare you, sir? Go and ask my mother for permission first!" [1]

However, what is the meaning of *truisie* and *talitha*?

Trombetti thought that in *talitha* he had found the name of a goddess.

But Gerhard was right in thinking the scene took place just after bathing. Here is the meaning:

truisie (A) is the Albanian *druejshëm*, "terrible". But it is connected with the root *druej*, "to fear, adore" (M. 84). So its meaning in Etruscan this time, naturally, is "adoring". Cf. *drouna* (already discussed).

taliθa (A) is the Albanian *tallit*, "mockery, raillery"; *tallës*, "ironical" (M. 509).

So there is no need of proper names here. The scene is entitled: "adoration and mockery", or "an adorer and a mocker".

But reality was not always so cheerful. There were wars, there was mourning. We are reminded of this by an inscription on a black ceramic tablet bearing a drawing of a lion. M. Pallottino comments: "A lion or a dog" (*Testimonia*, p. 92), despite the fact that not far from the animal the word *liuna* is written. Need one be so mistrustful of Indo-European "infiltrations"? The same author says this inscription is suspect. But such was not the opinion of M. Buffa, who declared the creature was a lion, and wrote that the inscription's authenticity was suspect for one reason only, the difficulty of interpreting it.

M. Buffa was right. I have managed to surmount the difficulty and can affirm that the inscription has nothing suspect about it. Chance has willed that this should be one of the most powerful, spontaneous and poignant inscriptions which I have had the opportunity of

[1] Igerhard, *Etr. Spiegel*, IVa, t. CDXIII, p. 74.

deciphering. It would have been enough by itself to make me completely reverse my opinion of the Etruscans, if I had previously thought poorly of their vitality and fundamental sincerity.

We feel how close to us they are, the members of this archaic, complicated, ingenuous people. And we shall feel it all the more in that the essential features of this inscription are confirmed by another document which I shall exhibit directly after it, and which will corroborate my interpretation beyond any possibility of doubt.

Here is the text of the tablet in question, which was probably deposited in the tomb of a young warrior, and in which the grief of his mourning relations and friends is expressed without restraint:

(P. 744, NRIE 1061) *mi feʃ me timχa naeʃirm peʃanl liuna*
emfeʃame śuθina (A)

Let us begin with those elements whose interpretation is already quite clear: *mi*, "this, this is"; *peʃanl liuna*, an individual name and a family name: "Pepan the Lion". In Albanian "lion" is *luan* (M. 251). *suθina*, "tomb". *Grosso modo*, the meaning is: "This is the tomb of Pepan the Lion". What does the rest say?

feʃ: to be read as *beʃ* or *bef*, and linked with Albanian *befë*, "surprise"; *bef*, "to happen by chance"; *befët*, "sudden" (M. 24).

timχa: two words: *tim* is Albanian *dhimbe*, "grief" (M. 91); *χa* is the Albanian *ka*, "there is", from the verb *kam*, "to have" (already noted). Another *kâ* is derived from the verb *jam*, "I am". If the latter is the word present here the meaning will be "it is", with only a tiny shade of difference from the first version.

naeʃirm is relatively more difficult, since several solutions can be envisaged. The simplest of them is this: *na* is Albanian for "we, us" (nominative and accusative). *eʃir* is Albanian *eperu*, "higher, superior"; we shall meet the Etruscan word again in our chapter on the market-place. The meaning is: "superior to us", "surpassing us".

emfeʃame is an epithet referring to *śuθina*, "tomb". It is certainly one of the most instructive words in Etruscan epigraphy. It throws a special light on the Indo-European character of Etruscan grammar. Its construction is exactly the same as that of the Albanian word *ënbeftaeh*, "taken by surprise", and of *ënbegat-em*, "to become rich" (from the root *begat*, "rich") and, at the same time, "enriching".

This word *emfeʃame* is analysable into three elements, exactly like analogous word-formations in Albanian, Latin and French

(*embellir*, etc. [And in English.—Tr.]): *em* (preposition) + *fep*
(the root already noted) + *ame* (a suffix?). The meaning is:
"astonishing, surprising, stupefying".

Here, then, is the translation, very slightly modified by the substitution of "What" for "This is": "What astonishment, what surpassing grief: of Pepan Liuna this dumbfounding tomb."

And what a human document! Confronted with texts like this one,

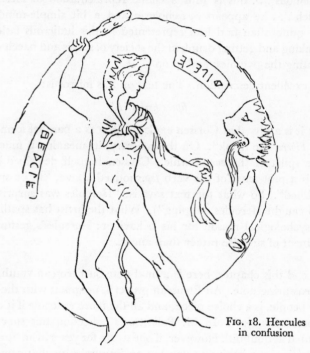

FIG. 18. Hercules
in confusion

can anybody go on grumbling about Etruscan epigraphy—which has
sometimes been presented to us as a mass of stereotyped magical
formulae through which the Etruscan sorcerers used to mutter their
way casually, automatically?

Philologically, the important point in this inscription was *fep*,
"surprise". It occurs again in a quasi-mythological scene, which I am
bringing up now so that its weight can be added to the scales. This
scene was created by the artist merely in order to amuse the beholder.
The drawing is an excellent one, engraved on a mirror, and has been
published by Corssen. The author explains it as follows (fig. 18):

Hercules is thirsty and comes to a fountain to fill his amphora.
The jet of water from the fountain overturns it. The hero gets into a

temper, thinks the culprit is the lion from whose head the water gushes, and brandishes his club to deal a blow just as if the lion had been a living monster; at the same time he holds in front of him part of the skin of the lion of Nemea, which he is wearing, so as to protect himself against the teeth of this carved, fountain-head lion. Hercules' blind rage, as he challenges the harmless mouth of the fountain and assumes a conventional position of combat . . . is ridiculous . . . this is thus a comic representation of Hercules, in which . . . he appears . . . choleric and a bit simple-minded. . . . We quite often find him represented in this ludicrous fashion . . . drinking and getting drunk in the society of satyrs and bacchantes . . . fighting the pygmies, and so on . . .[1]

An excellent description. The text on this mirror is:

fipece hercle (A)

But it is a pity that Corssen explains *fipece* as a parallel formation to Latin *bibere*, "to drink". On the contrary, its meaning is much closer to the spirit of the scene which Corssen himself described so well. *fipece* is a past tense of the verb *fep*, noticed above: "to be surprised, astonished". So what the text says is: "Hercules was surprised" (or "This caught Hercules napping"). What the artist has spotlighted is the psychological reason for his behaviour: Hercules's gesture was a movement of surprise rather than anger.

To end this chapter, here is a final note on Etruscan youth, a clear and reassuring note. An Etruscan proverb, pregnant with the wisdom of the people, is a choice piece; and all the more welcome if it concerns our present subject. In M. Pallottino's collection this short text is presented as doubtful. However, if one works for years in an atmosphere of suspicion one begins to develop an immunity to that atmosphere. The inscription is on a drinking cup from Clusium:

(P. 486, CII 802) śenulis rite (A)

śe: Albanian *shé*, "torrent, fast-flowing stream" (M. 470). In Etruscan circumstances this would be a mountain stream.

nulis is two words fused together: *n* is Albanian *ne*, "in, into"; *ulis* stems from an Illyrian root of the first importance, *ul*, "to descend", *ulje*, "descent" (M. 539). Here, the terminal *s* indicates an oblique case.

rite is exactly the Albanian *rit* (*të rit*), "young days, time of youth" (M. 427).

[1] *Über die Sprache der Etrusker*, 1874, Vol. I, p. 324.

Putting all this together: "A stream rushing down, such is youth!"

Ah, these Etruscans, who discovered a philosophical urge in themselves when they were in their cups! This dictum charms and disarms me; it is at once a willing and an unwilling tribute, a sigh of admiration and resignation. And the comparison with the stream rushing down evokes Tuscany itself, crouching with the ramparts of the mountains at her back.

Thus did Italy stamp her imprint on the very soul of this rough, alien stock. The Etruscan people fused itself with the very landscape it had acquired; the development of the Etruscan ethnic character was influenced by the sky of Italy; and when the Romans later adopted some of the Etruscan customs they must have felt themselves lapped in the very atmosphere of the ancient Italic civilisation.

V

MEALS AND THE KITCHEN

WE now find ourselves enclosed in a circle of everyday, material interests, a domain so straightforward and humdrum that it seems closed *a priori* to everything "gloomy", or even symbolic.

An imaginary dialogue between reader and author begins to take shape in one's mind:

AUTHOR: Would you like to come and have a look at an Etruscan butcher's shop with me?

READER (*attracted by a juicy subject, especially after a protracted regimen of alternate Etruscan and Albanian vowels, and perhaps with the secret thought of comparing the escalopes and steaks of the Etruscans with those of our own day*): I would indeed.

(*They start out.*)

READER (*cautiously*): It's not far, is it?

AUTHOR: Oh no, only as far as the cemetery.

READER (*stops dead, speaks in a cold, steely voice*): Sir, I don't see how——

AUTHOR (*in confusion*): But really, I assure you——

READER (*icily*): I fail to see——

AUTHOR (*pulling himself together*): I'm so sorry. But do look: it's a really high-quality butcher's shop. Only it happens to be in the necropolis. It's painted on the wall of a burial-vault. You really must understand, we're in Etruria now.

And in fact we are looking at a fresco from a vault which dates from the 4th or 3rd century, and which was discovered near Orvieto in 1863, by Golini. Each of the nine wall-surfaces of this vault is decorated with a picture (fig. 19).

On wall No. 6 (the least accessible to view, incidentally) there are two pictures of the infernal deities; to the right of the entrance, scenes from a funeral banquet; to the left of the entrance, preparations are being made for the banquet, which, certainly, have nothing of a funerary nature about them and which admit us straight into that part of the Etruscan nobleman's household where the slaves and servants can be watched as they go about their daily tasks. The middle of the vault, wall No. 5, is occupied by a monkey. Nothing

symbolic about him, either. He is led on a leash by someone whose
face has yielded to the depredations of
time. Except for the one depicting the
lords of the Underworld, all these
frescos are clearly intended to surround
the dead with their normal way of life,
the environment with which they were
familiar and all the pleasant things they
had enjoyed.

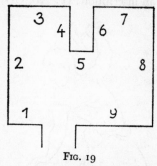

FIG. 19

To this intention we owe the pleasure
of finding, on wall No. 1, a butcher's
display of animals hung up, dominated
by an enormous ox, a worthy ancestor of the one painted by Rem-
brandt. The sight is described in the following terms by G.
Conestabile:

> An animal with its belly opened-up . . . an ox's head, two pigeons,
> a hare, a roebuck with its belly opened . . . two other birds, larger
> than pigeons . . .

No inscription. But this plentiful display helps us to understand
what comes after. On wall No. 2 work is in full swing. In the left-
hand part of the picture is a wooden block at which a male figure,
half-naked, stands with his cleaver raised; he is leaning forward and

FIG. 20. Etruscan butcher's display

is on the point of energetically dividing a joint of meat. Here there is an inscription: (P. 220, CIE 5058) θar . . . kaθ (A).

FIG. 21

There is nothing doubtful about the meaning: Albanian darë is the infinitive of daj, "to divide, share", which we have previously encountered. If kaθ is gja (plus the t of an oblique case), "game" (M. 140), all is well; if not, it means something no less meaty. It is perfectly clear that the butcher is cutting the meat into pieces.

Another character provides a counterpart to the butcher, in the right-hand part of the same panel (fig. 22). He is a muscular young fellow, bending over a small round table with three legs which looks like a trough with an outlet in the form of a spout. The accompanying inscription is: (P. 225, CIE 5083) pazu muluane (B).

Conestabile says the young man is—

pressing down on this table, with the help of the two little pads held in his hands, as if he was grinding up pigments or mixing a variety of substances together.

Feeling this description to be a little vague, the writer decides to season it with a generous spoonful of symbolical substances:

What is going on is an operation required for the proper execution of the sacrifices . . . in a religious ceremony . . . an office of which we do not recall any other example . . . [and which is,] nevertheless, in harmony with the general scheme . . . since the individual is preparing substances which will subsequently be consecrated on the table used in the funerary banquet or libation . . . in the sacred place which is characteristic of the whole spirit of the rite depicted here . . .

(Pitture murale, p. 55)

Personally, I think the substance concerned is cheese.

For, indeed, an exact counterpart to pazu is found in Albanian bazho, "cheese-maker" (M. 23), and baç, "derived from milk" (M. 16).

muluane is nicely interpreted by Albanian mollis, "to weigh down on something, oppress" (M. 291); "to press", we can say. The verb is related, indeed, to the Albanian root mul-, which is found in the words *mulli*, "mill", *mullis* "miller", etc., words deriving from the archaic Indo-European verb which appears as *malla* in Hittite, *molo* in Latin (*molere*, "to grind in a mill"); cf. Greek *mulon*, "mill".

The young man is probably pressing a cheese so as to expel the liquid from it; hence the spout of this trough-like table. Is it fresh cheese? The ancients were also fond of grated cheese, which was one of the ingredients in the *libum*, a special cake used in sacrifice. Thus the Osco-Umbrians used to regale themselves (as appears from the Tables of Iguvium) with a kind of cake called *mefa* which was the same as the Latin *libum*. It was made of grated cheese, eggs and flour. Similarly, we read in the *Works and Days* of Hesiod: "Drink wine from Byblos, choose, for your meal, cakes made with cheese."

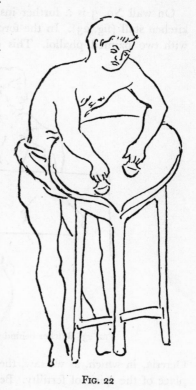

FIG. 22

Perhaps, however, the substance was some symbolical one, with a ritual purpose only? Etruscans who had been awarded a triumph had the privilege of coating their faces with minium, an oxide of lead which was mixed with oil to yield a red paint. O. Müller connects this custom with the traces of minium noticeable on the faces of the carved figures with which funeral urns are decorated, and concludes that this was a sign of the deification of the dead. The Romans took up the custom and periodically coloured the effigy of Jupiter Capitolinus with minium. Moreover, the Tables of Iguvium contain a puzzling word, *pistunire* (II b, 15). We know only that *pistum* means the same as Latin *molitum*, "crushed, ground"; *nire* makes me think of Albanian *ngjyrë*, "colour" (M. 324), such a contraction being quite possible. However, in the funerary frescos the guests' faces are not very strikingly red.

The question remains open; but it seems to me that the coincidence of *pazu* and *bazho* is more than fortuitous. I believe the substance is some kind of cheese. Poulsen reinforces my contention by saying:

The table with raised edges [in this fresco] reminds us of a recipe given by Cato the Elder, in which a table of this kind is recommended for mixing honey and cheese and making good cheesecakes.[1]

On wall No. 3 is a further instalment of the tireless work of the kitchen staff (fig. 23). In the foreground is a large oven, decorated with two painted phalloi. This can be explained by the story of

FIG. 23. Butcher behind an oven (after Conestabile)

Ocresia, in which, as we saw, the domestic hearth was the dwelling-place of the spirit of fertility. Behind the oven is a second butcher, a powerfully built man, vigorously wielding a chopper. The inscription is intact:

(P. 227, CIE 5085) *tesinθ tamiθuras*

tesinθ: "ten", which we discussed in the chapter on numbers. (If not "ten", it will mean "of the sheep" (sing.); cf. Albanian *dёshinj*, "sheep" (plur.), M. 67.)

tamia is Albanian *damje*, "division", which, like *damas*, "separately", comes from the root already noted: *daj*, "to divide", whose infinite is *damё* (M. 66). The meaning of *tamia* in the present context is "separate" (adjective).

θuras is the word dealt with in the chapter on the family: "kind, sort, species".

[1] *Etr. Tomb Paintings*, p. 40.

The meaning is: "Ten different kinds!" or, alternatively: "Lamb! Different kinds!"—these being, apparently, the words spoken with professional pride by the brawny fellow as he slices off a cutlet or what-not at each blow of his arm.

At the foot of the oven, on the left, a boy, clad only from waist to knee, has come to draw wine from a large amphora. The inscription announces:

(P. 226, CIE 5084) *klumie parliu* (A)

I spent a long time on this sentence. In the end I managed to unearth the meaning of the first word:

klumie consists of two elements: Albanian *kluaj*, "to call" (M. 200 and 420); whence *klu. mie* is Albanian *mijë*, "only" (M. 288). But *parliu* stood out against all my attempts to decipher it.

S. Bugge considered *parliu* to be the name of a receptacle, connected with *patella*, "plate"; but this is unconvincing. O. A. Danielson mistook the very subject of the picture; he imagined that a man called *klumie* was putting a frying-pan on the fire, and he therefore suggested, for *parliu*, the translation "cook", an honour which the poor fellow does not seem to have deserved.[1]

One day, mechanically turning over the pages of the little Albanian–German dictionary I had bought by the Seine, I came across the magical word I needed: *barl*, a local variant (in the dialect of Gjakova) of the word *bardh*, "white", which is standard Albanian.

So now the text became clear: "(They) ask only for white!" In other words, "These gentlemen are asking for white wine and nothing else"—a remark not without humour.

Later, I found support for this interpretation in an observation of Kretschmer's, to the effect that the difference between the two names Odysseus and Ulysses could be attributed to the transition from *d* to *l* which is found to have occurred among the Illyrian tribes of Epirus, among whom the change Lasimos–Dasimos, for example, has been noted (*loc. cit.*, p. 281). To which I add the fact that E. Vetter, in one of his reviews of the year's work in Etruscology, mentions the proper name *parla atrus*.[2] This in no way invalidates my interpretation, since proper names, such as the Bardulius we have already met with, are sometimes derived from the root *bardh*, *barl* (like Laban in Hebrew and Blanche in French).

Thus the two inscriptions, the one applying to the butcher and the other to the young cup-bearer, are neither proper names nor impersonal explanatory notes, but conversational remarks uttered by

[1] *Glotta*, XVI, 1–2, p. 91.   [2] *Ibid.*, XV, 1926, 1–2, p. 229.

these two characters themselves. Having, by housebreaker's methods, entered back-stage while a domestic drama of Etruscan daily life is going on, we find ourselves overhearing these busy people as they exchange their customary backchat.

But this is merely a prelude. We shall witness another, much livelier exchange.

No longer are we in an ordinary kitchen, with smells of garlic and of meat roasting. We are confronted with something almost like a short theatrical scene. A curtain rises (after a slight delay, much regretted by the management), revealing to our delighted and intruding eyes one of the most graceful impromptus that can be imagined.

FIG. 24. Head cook between two serving-women in a hurry (after Conestabile)

I return to wall No. 2, for it is there, between the first butcher and the cheese-maker, that we see preparations for the banquet going on at a higher level. The cooks, scullions and so on have finished their part of the work. The dishes ready for serving have been placed at a distribution-centre, as it were, to which the serving-women come hurrying to transmit orders and to carry them back forthwith to the dinner-table. This picture is the *pièce de résistance* of the extraordinary spectacle which is known as the Golini Tomb.[1] (Fig. 24.)

In the middle of this scene, and fortunately in a good state of preservation, are some small tables loaded with cooked dishes and with fruit. Behind the tables is a young man overwhelmed with work; the summer heat, and the necessity of answering the simultaneous requests of two serving-girls, seem to have brought him near to exasperation. For he is flanked by two charming girls, one on each side, who are

[1] Conestabile, *loc. cit.*, t. V.

ABOVE: Flezru, the tutelary goddess of sleep.
OVERLEAF: Sarcophagus of Laris Pulena, a nobleman and civil
dignitary of Tarquinia.

Amphora from Formello, with alphabet and the words *mi
atianaia*.

running up, panting, each clamouring at him to be served immediately.

They are so prettily dressed that the mere sight of them would have made a Roman grind his teeth; the Romans were hard-hearted and stingy in the way they treated their slaves. They used to criticise the folly of the Etruscans in dressing their slaves too well, "in contrast to their condition", as Diodorus Siculus says.

The girl on the left is wearing an amber necklace and a red tunic. She is holding a small vessel in her right hand and arrives in a hurry, crying: *θrama mliθuns*! But she has been beaten a short head in the race by another serving-girl, a blonde with a classical profile, a necklace, a hair-do with a bandeau and dressed not a bit less elegantly. This one imperiously demands: *re(e)miiśmeθumfs . . .*

What are the comments of Conestabile on these circumstances? Seeing fruit and eggs on the tables, he naturally remembers that the egg is a symbol of resurrection, and the pomegranate, sacred to Proserpine, of reproduction; and that grapes are closely connected with the worship of Bacchus. In all of which he is perfectly right. But the Etruscans did not live on symbols alone! What was the blonde girl really saying?

(P. 223, CIE 5081) *re(e)miiśmeθumfs* (A)

re is Albanian *ri*, feminine *re*, "new"; here: "anew, again".

miiś is Albanian *mish*, "meat", a word which goes back to Sanskrit *masa* and emerges in Lithuanian as *mesa*, and occurs in all the Slavonic languages (*miaso*, etc.). *miiś* therefore cannot be whittled down to a borrowing from Armenian *mis*, as G. Meyer believed (*loc. cit.*, p. 280).

me is Albanian *me*, "with".

θumfs is Albanian *tumb*, "cream" (M. 274).

The final *s* evidently denotes an oblique case.

Obviously, it cannot be sworn on oath that the last word does not mean "sauce" or "gravy". For the time being we are above such petty details. The main facts are what counts. What some greedy Etruscan diner was demanding was neither more nor less than "Some more of that meat with cream!"

And what a tasty dish, too, for Etruscologists, nourished hitherto on a dry diet of sibilants, hushing-sounds,[1] prehistoric substratum and the rest!

---

[1] The phoneticians' name for the voiceless *sh*, as in "ship", and its voiced counterpart, as in "pleasure". (*Tr.*)

This inscription has let us in one of the secrets of the Etruscan cuisine, so highly appreciated by the Romans.

At the same time we have put a finger right on one of the "Indo-European implantations" in the Etruscan language.

So eat some *miś*; and thereby taste at once Etruscan, Illyrian, Albanian, Sanskrit, Armenian and Balto-Slavonic! With the addition of a few more words of this kind the printed collections of Etruscan inscriptions may assume a somewhat surprising supplementary function: that of guide-books for tourists visiting Albania. Go to Scutari or Tirana and ask in a restaurant for *mish me-tumbs*. Perhaps there will be a moment of embarrassed silence, while the proprietor seems to be saying to himself, "Whatever will these tourists think of next?" But after that he will reply with great dignity, "Sir, this is not one of the dishes we are acquainted with. But since you ask for it, I can certainly bring you some *mish* on one plate and some *tumb* on the other, for you to mix together in whatever way takes your fancy." Never mind— from a strictly Etruscological point of view this is an entirely satisfactory answer.

But what is being asked for by the servant on the left, who is not quite so good-looking and who is casting a somewhat suspicious glance at her rival?

(P. 221, CIE 5079) *θrama mliθuns* (B)

At first I thought this servant was holding in her left hand a small basket which she intended to fill with cakes and fruit. However, the object seems too small to contain even the smallest of the bunches of grapes lying on the table; they would get crushed in it. Besides, she is also carrying a small goblet.

Should we therefore be thinking in terms of a drink? If so, I shall interpret *θra* as "milk", which appears in the Book of the Mummy as *trau* (with the definite article *u* at the end):

> *pevaχ vinum trau pruχś* (IV, 22)
> *vinum trau prucuna* (IX g I)

In these fragments, *pevaχ* probably means "beer", and *pruχ* and *prucuna* are taken over from Greek and denote a vessel of some kind. The three drinks mentioned are thus beer, wine and milk. The meaning of *θra* will be confirmed, moreover, when we come to a mythological scene depicting Hercules putting himself on a milk diet. *mli* or *mliθun* is clearly "honey"—Greek *meli*, Hittite *melit*, Albanian *mjalt*. *ma* is Albanian for "more, again, yet". So, although there is still room for discussion about details, the general sense of the inscription is clear enough: "More milk with honey!" This is the same as the Greek *melikraton*, a drink well known in ancient times.

The debatable point is the question whether *mliθuns* should be divided or not. The rendering "honey" is obviously only a working hypothesis. "Honey" in Etruscan may have been *mli*, not *mliθun*. And, moreover, we cannot rule out in advance the possibility of interpreting *ma* as *me*, "with", and of taking *mliθuns* as *mli-θuns*, in which the syllable *θuns* would be the same as *θunz*, meaning "twice", as we already know. In which case the meaning of our text will be: "Milk (*θra*) with (*ma*) honey (*mli*), twice (*θuns*)!"

This is curt, but we must be understanding with this waitress: she is vexed.

Moreover, this interpretation has the advantage of bringing her into line, professionally speaking, with waiters in restaurants at the present day, who habitually give their orders in the same style: "Steak and spinach, twice!"

What is the reaction of the poor devil of a cook, under fire from both flanks at once? He would never dare defy these two Graces, for their necklaces and their rustling embroidered dresses show what flattering attentions are paid to them in the household.

Overworked and exasperated, striving to preserve the remains of his masculine dignity, all he can do is to growl, like Topaze [1] confronting a turbulent class of schoolboy tormentors:

(P. 222, CIE 5080) *θresu f. siθrals* (A)

θresu is the Albanian verb *thrres*, "to call, convene, summon" (M. 536); an important verb in the interpretation of the Book of the Mummy.

f. is *b*, once again, and allows us to infer *bâ* (*bâj*), which is Albanian for "to make" and has been encountered already.

siθrals is Albanian *sedër*, "dignity, prestige" (M. 447). A word of prime importance, since it also occurs in an inscription which concerns a temple. The same word yields us the meaning of the Etruscan proper noun *seθre*, *seθra*, "worthy, dignified".

The literal meaning of the sentence is therefore: "(Make) orders with dignity"; or "I demand dignity" (for *u* can mean "I"); or "Behave in a dignified way when giving your orders." The implication of his words is undoubtedly: "You ask me for meat and drink, and you make a lot of noise about it. All I ask you for is this one thing: behave properly and don't rush me."

[1] The schoolmaster in the comedy *Topaze*, by Marcel Pagnol. (*Tr.*)

Surely a scene worthy of the pen of a Courteline? [1] Restaurant proprietors the world over ought to have a vignette made of it as a decoration for their menu-cards. If such are the pearls to be found in the funerary inscriptions left by Etruscan artists, what must have been the qualities of their stage-plays—all of which, alas, are lost; what treasures of the human spirit, impregnated with finesse, humour and psychological understanding, crushed for ever beneath the marching feet of the Roman conquerors?

However, the possibility cannot be excluded, it seems to me, that these inscriptions in dialogue were taken from comedies which were popular at the time.

There are more things yet for us to see in this cave of wonders. But the fresco on wall No. 4 is badly damaged. Apart from its three inscriptions, all that remains of it is a figure in the centre of the composition, and the heads of two other characters, one on each side (fig. 25).

FIG. 25. A steward comes into the kitchen (after Conestabile)

The central figure is a half-naked man. In his left hand he holds a vessel with a handle; he may therefore be a wine-server. With his right hand he is making a gesture which might mean, "It's not true", or "It doesn't matter".

Perhaps he is addressing a character who stood in the extreme left-hand part of the picture but who has now disappeared. Let us take the left-hand inscription for a start:

(P. 228, CIE 5086) aklχis muifu

[1] French comic and satirical dramatist of the late 19th and early 20th centuries. (Tr.)

akl is perhaps *acil*, a word which occurs frequently in LM and which means "receptacle made of terra cotta" (according to Corssen), "urn".

χ*is* may be either an abbreviated form of Albanian *hitishem, hitas*, "to hurry" (M. 160), cf. *qitas*, "at full speed" (M. 419); or else the verb *qis, qes*, "to furnish, provide" (*ibid.*).

mui seems to be the Albanian *muj*, "to be able" (M. 297), whose antiquity is attested both by G. Meyer and by Jokl (*Studien zur alb. Etym.*, p. 58).

fu can perhaps be interpreted by way of Albanian *buj*, "to spend the night" (M. 41).

Taking a line from the previous fresco, we can suggest that the meaning is something like: Bring wine so that they (the guests) can spend the evening.

Let us look at the speech allotted to the central character:

(P. 229, CIE 5087) *run*χ*lvis papnas*

*run*χ*lvis*: one thinks of Albanian *rrungullis*, "to roll, roll down" (M. 443), or possibly of Germanic *ringeln*; alternatively, of Albanian *rreng*, "trickery" (M. 434).

papnas seems easier. It can be divided into three short words:

pa is an Albanian negative particle, "not, im-, in-, -less", etc., e.g., *pa-bes*, "faithless".

pn, if read as *ben*, is the present of Albanian *bêj*, "to make, to do". The whole tense is as follows:

bëj	bën
bën	bëjmë
bëni	bëjnë

(From the Albanian–Russian dictionary, p. 530)

as is another negative particle: "neither, nor", etc.

Alternatively, the word can be divided thus: *pa-p-nas*, in which *pa* is "not", *p* is *bê bêj*, "do", and *nas* is an abbreviated form of the verb *ngas*, "to hurry, hasten" (M. 318) (just as *nga*, "from", equivalent to Latin *ex*, M. 316, shortens to *na*, M. 303). Hence *papnas*, word for word, would mean: "Don't make such a rush", i.e., "Don't be in such a hurry".

papnas may also be an expression on the lines of "It doesn't matter". It seems to me that the cup-bearer is indicating that there is nothing particularly urgent in the requests for wine which are brought to him: "They (the guests) are rolling, wallowing on their couches; they aren't doing anything." Or, alternatively: "There's no point in hurrying like that."

My interpretation, at least in its general intention, is confirmed by the third inscription, the one by the person on the right, of whom nothing remains but a vigorous profile. It is really he who plays the leading part in this little scene, which, while it has not the rich flavour of the preceding fresco, is nevertheless remarkable in its way. The man is a steward, an overseer who comes up unexpectedly, confounds the wine-server and contradicts his rash pleasantries:

(P. 230, CIE 5088) *θresu penznas* (B)

θresu: this is the same *θresu* as we heard uttered by the cook, but this time it is spoken coldly and imperiously: "I demand . . ." Or perhaps: "The orders" (those given by the guests).

penz is the subjunctive of *bej*, *ben*, the verb noted in dealing with the last inscription: "May you do!" (*bensh*).

nas is Albanian *ngas*, also noted in the last inscription.

The meaning will be: "I demand that you do it at once", or rather: "Carry out the orders at once!"

This completes the little dramatic scene. Even in the smoke of a kitchen you can't say what you think; the master's eye is on you, he pops up like a djinn from a bottle and calls you to order. Slavery, really. . . .

So our little impromptu in two tableaux ends on a tragi-comic note. Think of it: this gamut of feelings, impatience, disappointment, resignation, suppressed irritation, "don't care", tyranny, has been condensed into half a dozen very brief speeches! How human it all is!

On walls 6 and 7 we are shown scenes from the funeral feast. The guests, men and women together, are sitting or carelessly reclining round the tables, which are loaded with fruit and cooked dishes and lit up by tall candelabra. Side by side, the god Hades and his spouse (a charming lady) preside over the meal. Amid the noise coming from the butcher's room, the kitchen and who knows where else, while the music of flute and cithara mingles with the din, the lord of the world beyond the tomb seems to be relishing the fragrance of the roast meat, and caresses Proserpina with all the affection of a good Etruscan husband.

We see also the portraits of two brothers, Vel Leinie and Arnth Leinie, the masters of the house, and a little fellow aged seven who is the son of one of them. But the character who holds most interest for us is a four-footed one, because of the interesting inscription which refers to him. He is a tame leopard, standing with his supple spine in a curve, and devouring something. Facing him is a dwarf. Both of them are under the banqueting-table. Over the carnivore stands written (fig. 26)

(P. 235, CIE 5095) *krankru* (A)

This graceful creature of the wild has been the subject of much comment. Gerhard took him for a panther and thought his presence was an allusion to the worship of Bacchus. Another author was

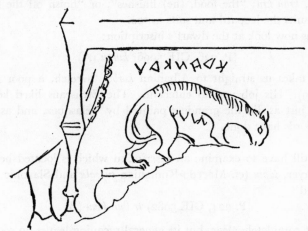

FIG. 26. krankru: "finish up the food"

reminded by *kra* of the cawing of crows! Bugge provided *krankru* with a replica (but a dubious one, surely?) in the Armenian word *kerakur*, "food", just as he explained the dwarf's inscription, *kurpu*, by Armenian *krup*, "a punch with the fist"; hence the dwarf was "he who gets punched". And Poulsen considered *krankru* was the leopard's name, because in Egyptian frescos the proper names of the favourite animals of the deceased are often given.

But *krankru* is one of the most informative Etruscan inscriptions. It explains, with all the clarity we could wish, not only the mechanism of the epigraphy of the Etruscans but also the rules of their spelling. It allows us to observe how what appears to be a single word is built up organically from distinct elements, and how these elements are presented in an abridged, purified form, reduced to essentials and expressed in the simplest possible way.

kran is Albanian *ngranë*, an irregular verb meaning "to eat" but also "food, nourishment" (M. 320). The initial *n* in this Albanian word is not dropped, as it can be in *ndegjoj-degjoj*, "to hear";[1] but there is every

[1] And, for example, in *ndaj, daj*, "to divide"; *nep, ep*, "to give".

likelihood that, in Etruscan, it was. The Tuscans, great eaters as they were, used the word so much that they wore out its first letter!

kru is the Albanian verb *kryej*, "to complete, finish" (M. 217). Thus, in Lambertz, I, p. 279: *me e krye kët shërbim*, "at the end of this service". In the *Lingua Albanese* of F. Cordignano (Milan, 1931), p. 138, we read of an Albanian Penelope, who was weaving a length of cloth and asked her suitors to wait for "when she should have finished it": *kuer t'a kryej*.

Thus, *kran kru*: "the food, (he) finishes", or "finish off the food". Which suits the leopard and suits us too.

Let us now look at the dwarf's inscription:

(P. 236, CIE 5096) kurpu (A)

This takes us straight to Albanian *korbe*, "wretch, a poor devil" (M. 209). His job was to entertain. The Etruscans liked keeping dwarfs, just as did the grandees painted by Velasquez, and as other feudal lords have done.

We still have to examine an inscription which is located beside a flute-player, *śuplu* (cf. Macedo-Rumanian *supeala* and Slavonic *sopél*). We read

(P. 224, CIE 5082) tr θun śunu (B)

It is not completely clear, but its general meaning leaves no room for doubt.

ter is Albanian *tërë*, "all".

θun is very probably "the house", as we shall see later; cf. Albanian *dhomë*, "room".

sunu corresponds to Albanian *sy*, "eye", *syni*, "the eye"; *syna*, in the plural. We shall meet the word again in the chapter on Medicine, when we describe Etruscan ophthalmology. Another possibility is that *nu* means "knows, is acquainted with", corresponding to Albanian *njo*, which is connected with the root *njoh* (M. 332).

The only problem is this: should we translate *sunu* as "(in) the eyes" or as "(these) eyes know"? In the first event the inscription means: "The whole house is in his eyes"; in the second: "His eyes know the whole house." In either case the sense is: "He sees everything which goes on in the house." We already know that the flute-player attended all ceremonies and even assisted at ordinary events of daily life.

Before leaving this unexpected little world which the Golini Tomb has shown us, we shall stop for a moment on the threshold and glance

back. Contemplating this crowd of slaves busy round their banqueting
masters, we are surprised to discover among them an atmosphere of
understanding, humour and trust. We have found that these short
inscriptions were, for the most part, neither proper names nor some
other kind of labels, but exclamations and retorts set down direct from
life, human documents which neatly hit off the butcher's satisfaction
("What variety!") and the little altercations which go on among the
servants and in which they do not fail to imitate the dignified, measured
language of their masters.

This atmosphere will seem all the more striking, and this page of the
history of class-relationships all the more surprising, if we consider the
matter against its historical and literary background.

According to M. Pallottino, the Golini Tomb dates from the 4th or
3rd century B.C. Plautus, who on occasion inspired Molière and other
great modern European writers, and who depicted the circumstances
and atmosphere of slavery among the Romans better than any
other author, was born about 250 B.C.; he must therefore have composed his plays towards the end of the 3rd century. The society described by Plautus is nearer to us than that of the Golini Tomb by
some eighty years. But what a gulf separates the two pictures, even if
we remember that the Golini Tomb represents a comparatively
isolated society, deeply devoted to its own traditions, where, as in the
Rome of Plautus, there was already a mixture of all the ancient
peoples of the peninsula, levelled-down by the dissolute morals of the
capital.

Plautus reveals a world in which the slave, debased and degraded,
was no more than a piece of furniture and could extricate himself from
this condition only by becoming a worse knave than his master; a
contest in which human dignity had no place.

The reader will perhaps remind me that even in Plautus there are
noble characters, among both the masters and the slaves. But Plautus
presents typical cases for the most part, not the exceptions. In his
comedy *The Deceiver* we are shown a slave-dealer, Ballio, beating his
slaves and shouting at them:

Come along out of it, get a move on, you lazy scoundrels, you
worthless property. . . . I've never seen men more like donkeys,
their flanks are too hard to feel blows. . . . They've only one thought:
pillage, steal, hide things, snatch, drink, eat, run away. . . . Wast-
rels . . . idlers, always forcing me to remind you of your duty with
my whip!

(Act I, Scene 2)

Ballio later goes in search of a cook. This gives us a glimpse of another kitchen, a Roman one:

BALLIO (*complaining*): It's not Cooks' Square, it's Thieves' Square. . . . I couldn't have got a worse man than this: a chatterbox, a boaster, a cheeky fellow.

COOK: . . . Then why did you engage me?

BALLIO: Labour-shortage. There wasn't anyone else. But why were you still in the forum?

COOK: . . . People take the one who asks the lowest wages. . . . I don't make dinners like the others' . . . They give you a whole meadow as seasoning . . . as if the guests were so many oxen. Their dinners are just fodder, just forage . . . with ground mustard; poisonous stuff . . .

Now *I* cook meat with spices. . . . When my pots boil I take the lids off all of them . . . the smell goes up to heaven . . . and that's what Jupiter has for supper every day.

BALLIO: And when you don't go out to cook anywhere, what supper does Jupiter get?

COOK: He goes to bed empty.

In short, Ballio regards this master of the culinary art as a certified thief and consequently has his every action spied upon by his slaves, the very individuals whom he habitually calls "thieves and robbers".

An atmosphere which makes a decided contrast with what we have seen among the Etruscans.

Mommsen writes:

The portraits of the cook and the parasite, in Plautus's comedy, . . . which are executed with such vivacity . . . are comprehensible enough if one knows that the Greek cooks of that time used to offer their services daily in the Forum.

But we also know that Plautus's Greeks were, for the most part, only Romans adorned with Greek names. Plautus knew that the Roman public preferred to laugh at others' expense rather than its own. These two samples of the facts, set side by side, give us to understand why it was that the Romans, when they saw Etruscan slaves better treated and dressed than their own, accused the Etruscans of "softness" and "dissolute customs": their neighbours' relatively humane way of life seemed to the Romans to strike at the foundations of the "established order" of society.

We started out from little things, a few sparkling fragments of Etruscan humour kept alight in the Golini Tomb; and this has carried us insensibly to the point where we can gain a better understanding of a major event in Etruscan history, namely the "revolt of the slaves" which took place at Volsinia, in 265—that is to say, between the period of the Golini Tomb and that of the comedies of Plautus. This revolt was crushed by the Romans.

It is most instructive to compare three divergent accounts of this event. They contradict each other and reveal how partial some authors can be.

According to Valerius Maximus (about the beginning of the Christian era):

Volsinia was opulent and regarded as one of the capital cities of Etruria; but through its luxury and vice it had to submit to the power of its slaves, who became impudent enough to enter the ranks of the senators; they took over every position of power; they made wills, married their masters' daughters, etc.

According to Orosius (4th century A.D.):

The Volsinians used to free their slaves in the most immoderate fashion, allowed them to take part in their banquets and honoured them with advantageous marriages. These former slaves frequently possessed themselves of the inheritance of their masters, whom they expelled and who took refuge at Rome, exiled and destitute. Having displayed their poverty, they were avenged and restored to their former position.

Finally, according to Zonaras (Byzantine, 12th century):

The Romans were obliged to undertake a punitive expedition against Volsinia after the effeminate inhabitants of that city had entrusted its government to the slaves.[1]

As can be seen, the degree of goodwill evinced by the Volsinians towards their former slaves proceeds in a *crescendo* from one version to the next. We almost feel justified in hoping that a fourth source of information on the slaves' revolt will be discovered some day, an account which will be even more objective than the foregoing and in which, perhaps, we shall read:

Disgusted by the intrigues and cabals of their statesmen, the Volsinians one day liberated all their slaves, giving them at the same

[1] Quoted in Buonamici, *Fonti di Storia Etrusca*, pp. 275-7.

time strict orders to assume administrative power at once, to occupy the curule chairs, and so on. Overcome by fear, the slaves threw themselves at their masters' feet and begged them to reverse this unfeeling decision. But the unhappy wretches found their lords inflexible and were compelled to obey. At the sight of this iniquity the Romans were smitten with compassion, and arrived incontinent to raze the city walls and to flog, behead or sell, in a properly conducted auction, all who fell into their hands.

However, pending the appearance of this "limit", as it were, of the series of the historians' testimonies, we beg leave to surmise that no definite *coup d'état* had taken place at Volsinia; but that at one juncture in the struggle for power there was in that city a clan which requested the Romans to intervene; and that, to incite the Romans, attention was called to certain facts which were likely to shock them: the facts that slaves were treated humanely, and that in many cases they were liberated and thereafter enjoyed the rights of free citizens.

An event of this nature would be hard to interpret as anything more than a result of the demographic problem with which the Etruscans were faced.

Not being indigenous, and in many cases not having evicted the original population of the districts they occupied, the Etruscans were more susceptible than any other people to the need for reinforcing their social framework and increasing the number of their free citizens, who in those days were the city's only defenders. Generous in their outlook and influenced by the Greeks, by whom a slave was regarded as a servant and not a dumb chattel, the enlightened circles of Etruria eventually turned their slaves into freedmen, *lautni*; but, as we have already seen, this name denotes "him who is of the family", and every path to advancement was consequently open to these Etruscan *clientes*. In this respect the Etruscans came close to the spirit of the Old Testament, which laid it down that slaves should be set free after seven years' service, and that any slave who refused liberty should have one of his ears marked as a sign of opprobrium.

But what is there in this to astonish us, seeing that the very inception of Roman democracy was due to Etruscan initiative and was imposed on the Romans only by force? Let us see what is said about the Etruscan king Servius (Mastarna) by a writer as little given to exaggeration as Fustel de Coulanges:

> The traditions and records of antiquity tell us that the social progress of the plebeians was initiated under the rule of Servius. The hatred which the patricians thereafter felt towards that kind is a

sufficient indication of his policy. His first reform was to give land to the plebs.

(Loc. cit., p. 338)

For the first time, all the men, without distinction as between patricians, *clientes* and plebeians, were gathered together in one place. The king made the round of this mixed assembly, driving the victims before him and chanting the solemn hymn. The ceremony over, all the participants had one citizenship in common.

(Ibid., p. 340)

It is true that the patricians took their revenge. The first step was to slay Servius; later, they expelled Tarquin. The royal line and the plebs were vanquished together. This defeat of the royal house was also the defeat of the plebs.

The patricians exerted themselves to recover from the plebs all the gains which the plebs had achieved under the kings.

(Ibid., p. 342)

It is clear that the Etruscan kings were driven out of Rome not because they were kings but because they were Etruscans.

It is equally clear that they brought a new spirit with them to Rome, a spirit inherent in the Etruscan civilisation whose standard-bearers they were. That civilisation, rudimentary though it was in some ways, had a humanitarian, democratic tendency. This explains the Volsinian "revolt" and much else besides.

Rome had to wait several centuries for the revival of these humanitarian ideas, namely until the appearance of the Gracchi, those noble brothers who were to pay the same price for their generous impulses as had the Etruscan reformer.

The invaluable service which 15th-century Italy rendered to humanity was precisely this, that at the same time as it rediscovered the heritage of Greek science and Greco-Etruscan art, it also recovered the seed of Etruscan humanism and planted it once more in the fertile Italian soil.

VI

THE TAVERN

FROM the nobility's banquets we pass to the people's. If you were hungry or thirsty you went to a tavern. The word "avid" or "famished" appears in a scene engraved on a mirror and published by Gerhard,[1] in which there is a naked man holding a large amphora while another man stands in front of him eagerly drinking (fig. 27). The inscription to the left is badly preserved. It might be *ulanc*. In this case it could be

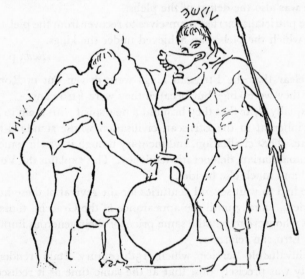

FIG. 27. "Avid"

connected with the Albanian root *lang* (with an initial *u* indicating a past tense of the passive voice), from which are derived in Albanian the noun *lâng*, "liquid", and the verb *langaros*, "to sprinkle, spatter" (M. 236), which are differentiated by a nasalised *n* from the verb *lag*, "to wet, to water" (noted in the chapter on Numbers). The inscription to the right, on the other hand, is clear: *urθe* (A), which is elucidated by Albanian *urtoj*, "to be hungry", *urt(i)*, "hunger", *urtuar*, "hungry, famished, avid".

Gerhard took *urθe* for Orpheus, was *überrascht* ("taken aback") by

[1] Table CCCLIV.

this and insisted that further inquiries were necessary, in case the inscription itself was wrong. But let us leave Orpheus to his melodies and content ourselves with the discordant voices of reality.

In the drink-shops these voices were certainly noisier and hoarser than elsewhere. There you could quench your thirst, lament your lot and find consolation in a cup of wine; songs, jokes and insults were mingled in confusion; people shouted at one another *helluo! bargena! dalius!* and various other pleasantries which our ignorance of Etruscan still covers with the veil of modesty.

helluo, in M. Ernout's list of words, which we have mentioned already, means "glutton". Probably the word should be grouped with Albanian *hell*, *hej*, "spit for roasting"; *hell-mishi*, "meat-skewer" (M. 157); there is a cross-check on this in G. Meyer. Hence, perhaps, *helluo* is "lover of grilled meat"?

bargena, *bargus*, from the same list, is "lout, blockhead". It is possibly a counterpart to Albanian *parregjun*, "untanned" (negative particle *pa* with *regj*, "to tan", M. 424), with the sense of "raw, uncultured".

dalius (A), which I quote following von Hahn (p. 276, note 288), is a gloss preserved by Festus and meant in Oscan "madman"; this is explained by the Albanian root *dal*, "to go out": the man who is "out of his mind", exactly as the expression goes in Albanian, *dal menç*, and also in Russian, for example. The presence of this Illyrian root in Oscan should be noted; we shall revert to it at the end of the book.

Drinking only a little wine, on the other hand, did not lead to insults. This principle is stated in an inscription on a drinking-cup. I have no formal proof that cups of this kind, which we shall be studying in this chapter, were part of the fragile and often mistreated equipment of Etruscan taverns; but certainly the spirit of the inscriptions on them would not be out of place in such establishments. Here is one which promised good humour:

(CIE 3627) *tisein naime* (B)

tise: Albanian *disa*, "a little". We shall meet the word in the chapter on the Market: *mantisa*.

in: "wine" (like *en* and *vinum*); of Aegean and Oriental origin (Phoenician *yaïn*).

nai corresponds to Albanian *ndaj*, "to grant" (M. 305). (The *d* in Albanian can be dropped, as for example in *ndën* = *nën*, "under", M. 306).

me corresponds to Albanian *mej*, "to soothe, pacify" (M. 275).

Thus: "A little wine is soothing."

This inscription leads on naturally to the next, which is in the same spirit and comes likewise from a cup:

(CIE 3266) *larivia tesin*

lari is the Albanian verb *laroj*, "to polish, to smooth" (M. 237).
via in Albanian is "channel, furrow" (M. 557).
tesin is in fact the same as *tisein*, which we have just examined. Instead of *tisa* we find *tes*. Which proves that, where spelling was concerned, the Etruscans were sturdy individualists and would shape a word according to their own fancy.

Word for word the inscription runs:

"Smooths the way a little wine"

—or, in our own word-order:

"A little wine smooths the channel" (the throat, the way).

The word *via* evidently demands more explanation, for while in Albanian it means only "channel", in Latin it has two meanings, "channel" as well as "way". How did *via* get into Etruscan? Is it a late borrowing from Latin or, on the other hand, an old Illyrian and Etruscan root? It will be remembered that roads and canals in Italy were, above all, the work of the Etruscans. But of course I am not going to take it on myself to discuss the origin of these words.

Another patera bears a dictum whose truth is beyond dispute:

(CIE 3268) *vinimia leniace*

One's instant demand is, "Don't translate this as 'Wine is lenitive'." That would be to carry the Indo-Europeanism of Etruscan to absurdity. The inscription does, however, express a proverb which is as old as the world and which looks like the essence of banality; but which earns renewed attention as soon as we realise that we have inherited it from the Etruscans:

vinimia: this word presents a slight difficulty. There is no doubt that it is concerned with wine. But I do not know if the word should be divided into *vinim ia* or *vini mia*. If the former is the case, *vinim* is the familiar *vinum* and *ia* means "here you are!" or "look!", or an interjection (M. 168 and 303) which occurs in the Capuan Tile, l. 12, etc. (*vacil ia leθamsul*) (?). Or else it is a sign of the direct object. In the second eventuality, *vini* is wine and *mia* is Albanian "my" (preceding a feminine noun in the plural). This is less probable.

lenia (B): here we are on sure ground: Albanian *lenje*, "abandonment, leaving" (M. 244), from the root already noted, *la*, "to
leave, abandon".

ce: a demonstrative particle, "this"; Albanian *çe*, "which, what"
(M. 53) (cf. *suθce*, "this tomb"?, LM, V, 7); or else it is equivalent
to *se*, "what, that" (M. 477).

Thus: "In wine, abandonment is to be found." The word is evidently
used here in the sense of "oblivion", "escape from reality".

We possess another inscription of the same kind which is full of
humour. It comes from a small shallow bowl, only 3 cm high, which
formed the lid of a larger vessel. Both were found in a tomb. M. Buffa,
from whom I borrow the inscription, thinks it concerns the name of
the deceased: a child of three months. But if, on the other hand, we
conjecture that the bowl was not originally intended for a tomb and
was placed in it only because it belonged to the dead person or his
family, the whole situation changes. In this case the owner of the bowl
could have been an old inn-keeper, for example. Here is the text in
question:

(P. 494, NRIE No. 420) klenase citia (B)

klen: Albanian *klenë* is the infinitive of the verb *jam*, "to be"; (të)
    klenë, "existence" (M. 199).
ase: Albanian *as*, "Eh? Isn't that so?"
citia: *kithi*, "askew, awry, crosswise, crookedly" (M. 199).

Assembling this, we find it is an exclamation of combined fear and
astonishment: "What a cross-grained place the world is!"
I think that this, like other Etruscan aphorisms, has a double meaning. On the other hand, its author—after a good long session of
libations—sometimes began to see the world leaning over to one side,
like the Tower of Pisa or its poor relation, the Tower of Bologna.
But at the same time he found these occasions propitious to a summing-
up of his opinions on this life of ours, all unjust as it is. But no doubt
this did not prevent him, whenever he found himself contemplating
this dual phenomenon of morals and geophysics, from being filled with
a sense of wonder not far removed from beatitude.

An invitation to drink, addressed imperiously to drinkers in general—
such is the content of the next sentence we shall study. It is inscribed
on a handsome patera, of which an illustration has appeared in the

F

Studi Etruschi.[1] This vessel holds out its two large handles to all comers with cheerful and disarming arrogance. To solve the problem it is sufficient to cast a glance at the last word of the inscription and at the vessel's welcoming handles. This is the inscription:

(P. 774) *kapemukaθesa kapes sli* (B) (fig. 28)

kape is the Albanian verb *kap*, "to seize" (M. 182). I was intimidated at first by G. Meyer's assertion that this verb was borrowed from Turkish *kapmak*, "to seize". But Jokl reacts vigorously against this opinion, and attests that the word in question is related to Latin *capio*, "to take, seize", and is an "idg. Erbwort", an element of the Indo-Germanic linguistic heritage.

Fig. 28. Patera with an inscription

kapes is Albanian *kapëz*, "handle, hilt" (M. 183).

sli is Albanian *shlej*, *shlyej*, "to efface, wipe out", which we have already seen in *caraθsle*.

Caught between its two poles: "Seize ... (my) handle and clean me out!" the sentence is now held firm. The question is to unriddle the meaning of the intermediate element, *mukaθesa*.

mukaθesa? It may be that the first syllable, *mu*, belongs to the preceding word: *kapemu* would then be the 1st person plural of the present tense of the verb; thus, in Albanian, *A dalëmë?* ("Are we going out?"), and *Dalëmë!* ("Let us go out"). *kapemu*, on this reckoning, is an invitation: "Let us seize!"

kaθesa: in Albanian, *kade* is "barrel" (M. 173). But as this word goes back to Phoenician *kad*, "pitcher", it may designate the very vessel which we are studying.

In any case, the general sense amounts to: "Let us seize the handles of the cup and empty it!"

In the same volume of the *Studi Etruschi* there is another interesting inscription of the same species, published by M. Michel Lejeune.[2] It is written on a black-glazed earthenware jar; but it is arranged in a circle,

[1] Vol. XXII, 1953, fig. 12.   [2] P. 147, fig. 20.

so that it is not easy to decide where to begin reading. Moreover, three of its letters are badly preserved. Here it is, with the words in the order indicated by M. Lejeune:

paχeis lavθr peiare vθ] /tar if evnuχrcv

Let us begin by studying the clearest parts of it:

peiare (A) relates itself automatically to the idea of "to drink", which tallies with a cup; more particularly, it is related to an Albanian root we have seen before, *pi, pij*, which is the same as the Slavonic root *piti*. The termination *-ar* indicates a profession or habit; we find it, for example, in *capesar*, the Etruscan cobbler. What is really odd is that *pejare* has an exact counterpart in modern Albanian, where it means "spa-guest" (M. 384).

paχeis is, of course, Bacchus. This is confirmed by another inscription (P. 336), in which he is designated by the same word.

lavθur (B): the interpretation of this word follows on from "Bacchus": *lav* is Albanian *lav*, "to turn foolish" (M. 238); *θur* was examined in the chapter on the family: "kind, species, race". So we get "Bacchus's mad tribe".

vθ.ar (A) can be identified with Albanian *udhëtar* (with the same ending as in *peiare*), "passer-by, traveller", from the root *udhë*, "way" (M. 537–8). G. Meyer analysed this Albanian word without so much as mentioning Greek *hodos*; he compared it with other ancient Indo-European roots (*loc. cit.*, p. 455).

So we know now to whom the appeal is addressed: ". . . Of the frenzied race of Bacchus, a drinker or a wayfarer . . ." But what is being asked of him?

if may be *ip*, "put!", from the verb *ap, ep, ip*, already encountered ("to put" and "to give").

evnu can be divided as *e venu*, another word for wine, like Albanian *vënë*, preceded by the article or else by an initial inflection denoting the complement.[1]

χ in this context may be an abbreviation of Albanian *kejo*, "this" (rather than the conjunction *-c*)?

rcv is, in all likelihood, "receptacle, vase". Albanian *rrex (rredz)* means "horn" (M. 435). A rhyton, perhaps? After all, was not an animal's horn the very prototype of all containers for liquids in archaic times? But the word is perhaps no more than an adaptation of the Greek word *urcha*, "earthen vessel". In order not to stray from our inscription we shall study the word *rcv* (*rku, rtzu*) in a separate paragraph.

[1] Cf. Cretan *ibena* (*i-vena*), "wine", according to Hesychius.

The text from *Studi Etruschi* can perhaps be expressed as follows: "Drinker, (whether you are) of the frenzied crew of Bacchus or (simply) a passer-by, put wine into this vessel!"

Let us return to the word *rcv* (*rcu*, *rku*, *rdzu*), which justifies a digression, since it occurs in other Etruscan texts as well. We must note for a start that this noun seems to be related to Latin *urceus*,

FIG. 29. Female figure carrying a pitcher

"pitcher, ewer" (and its diminutive, *urceolus*), which is connected with Greek *urcha*. In Albanian the form taken by the word is *rrëxhuell*, "small jug, mug, tankard" (M. 438) (pronounced *rëdjouel*). We may add that in an epitaph, P. 425 (NRIE 1092), *reχu* probably means "urn".

Let us next consider an Etruscan "illustration" involving the word in a slightly modified form, *rcu* (*retzu*). Plate CCXV of Gerhard's *Etruskische Spiegel* (II) shows a fragment of the engraving on a mirror (fig. 29). Next to the goddess Turan, who is preoccupied with the toilet of another goddess, Malacis, there is a servant or assistant. In her right hand is an object which Gerhard says is a coronal of flowers. The drawing of this so-called coronal is partly effaced; one can, however, pick out the handle of a pitcher (or a pail); and this seems all the more likely in that the woman's head is inclined a little in the opposite direction, just as if she was carrying something heavy. To one side of her head we read the inscription *resχuale*: the Albanian *rrëxhuell*. The meaning is probably "pitcher-bearer" (fem.).

Another Etruscan mirror, with a somewhat similar inscription, shows us a mythological scene or what appears to be so. This is Plate CLXVI in the same collection. Gerhard identifies Minerva lavishing her care on two babies of lofty birth. With the goddess are the babies' fathers, the Dioscuri, and Turan-Venus (fig. 30A). We seem to have found our way unexpectedly into an Etruscan *crèche*! Leaving aside the other details of the scene and confining our attention to the infant in the centre, we observe that he is enthroned in a somewhat suspect fashion on a large vase of what is intended to be a majestic appearance. These Etruscan draughtsmen often had a decided sense of mischievous humour. It may well be that this august child, under the eye of the daughter of Zeus, is doing what his likes have always done, since whenever it was that pots and babies were first invented.

So one and the same root is recognisable in this series of Greek, Etruscan and Albanian words:

urcha—rcv—reχu—rezχual (c)—recial—rrëχhuell

—whose meanings run through a wide gamut but all express the notion of a vessel or receptacle.

FIG. 30A. Minerva with divine children

We pass on to a spirited, comparatively perspicuous inscription from a small black earthenware patera:

(CIE 3264) *limatis ene cavire vemati turesa* (B)

limatis seems to correspond to Albanian *lum-madh*, in which *lumë* means "blessed" (*të lumtë*, "good luck") (M. 252), and *madh* is "great". *limatis*, then, is *beatus*.

ene, en, in, vene, vinum—"wine".

cavire is Albanian *gavër*, "empty" (M. 123).

vemati can be looked at in two different ways:

1. *vema ti*: *vema* is the 1st person plural of the present indicative of the Albanian verb *ve*, "to put" (M. 547): *vemë*, "let us put". *ti*, already encountered in *tifanati*: "to know", "knows", etc.

2. *ve mati*: *ve*, "to put", *mati* as in *limatis*, "large, much".

turesa (A) is Albanian *turizë*, "muzzle, snout", *turéçke*, "nose, snout" (M. 529).

G. Meyer, who suspected every Albanian word of being borrowed from somewhere, could find nothing to mention in this instance except a ridiculous resemblance to Slavonic *rot*, "mouth" (*loc. cit.*, p. 452).

Broadly speaking, the meaning of the inscription is this:

(*a*) keeping the Etruscan word-order: "Happy (he who) wine (into) empty shall put much mouth." Or,

(*b*) more comprehensibly: "Happy is he who, into his empty mouth, shall put much wine."

It is possible that the construction of the sentence takes us to one of the sources of Latin syntax.

We often find ourselves faced in this way by texts which remain relatively incomprehensible; but, in compensation, one text helps us to elucidate another. We shall now look at one which is clear and vigorous and will give us real pleasure because of its construction, its firm verbal and grammatical outline, and also because of the poetry with which it is imbued; a poetry tinged with sadness, however, the poetic charm of mimes and comedians. We shall steal a quick glance behind the scenes and gain a glimpse of the feelings of those actors whom the Romans so despised. We could not deal with these entertainers of the multitude elsewhere than in our chapter on the Tavern, because their lowly social position did not allow them to mix with loftier company.

The inscription is a dedication written on what is known as the "Paduan palette", which was used in making-up for a stage performance. It has been published by V. Wanscher among his "Rhaetian texts":

na ki nata risakvil (A)
et sual euti kukaian (A)

And the decipherment:

na: means "we", in Albanian; here it is in the accusative.

ki: "have!" (2nd person singular imperative of Albanian *kam*, "to have"). Here, the meaning is "to keep, maintain". In Albanian, it would be *ke*.

nata is "the night". Cf. Latin *nox, noctis*, and Albanian *natë*. We shall see it again, in the form of *nac*, in LM.

ri, both in Albanian and here: "young" (in singular or plural); or "fresh".

sa: is Albanian for "as . . . as . . ."

kvil is Albanian *kvillë*, "brightness, clearness" (M. 232), here probably "the dawn". Cf. P. 644, *tinścvil*.

et: unless this is the extended form of the conjunction *e* (as seen in the chapter on Numbers: *etve*), it is an interjection translated by Mann as "Enough!" (M. 97).

sual: an important landmark: the Albanian verb *shuaj*, "to efface" (M. 505). We have already noticed interchangeable *i, j, l* in both Etruscan and Albanian.

eu: one of those little words which are often traps. It may possibly be an Albanian interjection *heu* (M. 158) and *ehu* (M. 94), in which the *h* is unimportant.

ti: the shortened form of *tin*, "day"?

kukaian: redness, red (as a noun), like Albanian *kuq*, "red" (*kuqilar*, "purple", etc.) (M. 228); a root borrowed, but very early, from Greek. *kukaian* may be the accusative of *kukaia*.

The whole is an eloquent appeal to the palette, which was one of the tools of the actor's trade: "Keep us, during the night, as youthful as dawn; and, alas, when dawn appears, efface our red complexion!" [1]

Here is another of these "Rhaetian texts"; it has much more dash and brio than the preceding example; its author seems to have discovered the secret of eternal youth and is not in the least afraid that he will look pale and old when morning comes. We are back in the Tavern now, attending a solemn occasion, moreover: a Declaration of the Rights of Drinkers for all time, the proclamation of the Magna Charta of Drunkenness, conceived in terms both charming and forceful, and at the same time cunningly stressing the purely medicinal advantages of drinking Etruscan wine:

(a) *peva śniχe siu*
(b) *pi kitiu tisaχvil* } (A)
(c) *ipi peri snati*

D. Lattes has tried to divide this text differently: *pevas niχesiu*, with *niχesiu* taken as a proper noun. But the truth is otherwise:

[1] Or, perhaps: "Efface it, our redness", if *e* (in *eu*) denotes the direct object.

(a) *peva*: close kin to *peiare*, which was discussed earlier in this chapter. Connected with Albanian *pi*, "to drink", the aorist of which is *piva* (M. 383).

ś: Albanian negative particle *s*, placed in front of verbs. Thus: *s'due*, "I don't want" (M. 444).

niχe: Albanian *njoh*, *njof*, "to know"; its imperative is *njih* (= *njikh*) (M. 332, 331).

siu: here I recognise Albanian *zi*, "black, unhappy, miserable, sorrow" (M. 581), with the article *u*.

"He who has drunk knows no sorrow"?

(b) *pi*: "drink!"

kutiu: *ku* should be compared with Albanian *qi të*, "so that" (M. 417). It is, in any case, a conjunctive particle. *tiu* seems to come from the root *di*, "to know" (already encountered), and to mean "for knowledge", "in order to know".

tisa: Albanian *disa* (already encountered), "a little". (Cf. *mantisa*.)

χvil: "brightness" (joy), as in the preceding text.

(c) *ipi*: yet another demonstration of the elasticity of Etruscan spelling: *e pi*, "and drink".

peri: either a preposition common to Latin (*per*) and Albanian (*për*) (M. 364), "for"; or else a "nut with two kernels", *per rri*, *rri* being "to live" (M. 439): "in order to live".

snati: a remarkable word, in which I recognise *znate*, the Albanian verb *znjatem* (*znjas*) (M. 583), an equivalent of *ngjatoj*, "to prolong, continue". The commonest Albanian greeting is *t'ungjatë jeta*, "may your life be prolonged!" We should note that the Faliscan farm-labourers used to offer flowers and wine to the Genius *who does not forget the brevity of life*.[1]

It is possible, however, that *snati* is a noun ("duration") with a definite article at the end; but this makes little or no difference, if true. The meaning of the exhortation as a whole is now clear:

(*a*) "Drink in order to know no sorrow!"
(*b*) "Drink so as to know a little brightness!"
(*c*) "And drink to live long!"

Since these incisive slogans are inscribed on a jar, one cannot help wondering if the Etruscan wine-merchants had come to an understanding with the potters to launch a major propaganda campaign.

However that may be, the importance of this threefold inscription for our understanding of Etruscan requires no emphasising.

[1] R. Bloch, *Le mystère étrusque*, p. 158.

Before we leave this refreshing place and go to the Market, from which we can hear a certain amount of noise already, the exigencies of deciphering demand that we make a slight detour; and, of course, this will take us to a tomb. We must visit the so-called Typhon Tomb, in Tarquinii, which will show us again one of the words we noted in the Tavern. Inscription P. 100, CIE 5401, which has survived only in part, speaks of the last "sacred dwelling-place" (*eiθ fanu*) of a freedman (*latvn*) Pumpus (Pompey) Scunus and his sons. The inscription contains several points of interest. The most interesting of them to us, at

Fig. 30B. The final sleep—detail from an Etruscan urn (L. Heuzey, *Recherche sur les lits antiques*, p. 18)

this moment, is the fact that it uses the word *flenzna*, twice, and *fleśzneves*, once. First comes the statement *Pumpus Scunus suθiti in flenzna*: P. Scunus in this tomb (ensured for himself) "a long sleep"; for *flen* is "sleep" (2nd or 3rd person singular of *flej*, "to sleep"; M. 111), and *zna* is obviously from *snati*, "to last", which we met in the Toper's Charter. Next comes this beautiful sentence: *aθis θnam flenzna* (A), "In Hades, with the fathers (*etnam*), (he enjoys) a *lasting* sleep." Of which the moral is, if your conscience is clear you can sleep anywhere!

Confirmation exists, moreover, for our interpretation of the verb *θna, zna, sna* as "to last". This confirmation comes from another drinking-cup inscription. The text is incomplete, but the fragment is a gem none the less:

(P. 484; SE, XXII) *la . θna rite*
clani ciani sθ (B)

la, "let".
θna, "to last".
rite (already examined:) "youth".
clani, ciani, the imperative of a verb which we shall meet later: "to call by name" and also "to weep".
sθ = suθ, "tomb".

Interpretation: "Let youth last. Weep when you invoke the tomb." In other words, "There is a time for all things".

VII

AT MARKET

THE town market-place was an important institution among the Etruscans, for it was there that on every ninth day the peasants came flocking to sell their produce; there, too, that matters of administration and of business were conducted and, according to tradition, that the Etruscan kings granted audience to petitioners and dealt out justice.

The market was called *treg* or *terg*, as in Albanian (*treg*, M. 523); in Russian (*torg*); Polish (*targ*); Serbian and Bulgarian (*t'rg*); and Lithuanian (*turgus*). Perhaps it was also called *tergeste* (as in Russian and Bulgarian, *torzyshtshe*, and as in Lithuanian, *turaviete*).

I found this out by comparing the following three texts:

(1) An Illyrian inscription, a bilingual example from Pannonia, dating from Roman times, an epitaph quoted by Jokl in connection with the links between Illyrian and Albanian:

(CIL, III, 4251) *P. Domatius P (f) Tergitio Negociator*

Jokl observes:

In my view, this shows us that *tergitio* is the Illyrian equivalent of the Latin *negotiator* . . . whose root (Albanian *treg*, "market") and whose grammatical form are in perfect harmony with Albanian.

Jokl goes on from this to compare Illyrian place-names: Tergeste (Trieste), Bigeste (in Istria, on the north coast of the Adriatic), with Albanian names having the same termination: *kopshte*, "garden", *venesht*, "vineyard", etc. This is an excellent piece of observation. Jokl came within inches of the secret of Etruscan; he need only have gone a little farther in the same direction and encountered the same word *treg* in Etruscan; but he rested content with the study of suffixes. Yet, be it noted, Illyrian *tergitio* is exactly reflected in Albanian *tregyeti* (and *tregtar*), "merchant" (M. 523).

(2) An Etruscan inscription from Volterra, on a square stone. I believe it has to do with an agreement between the municipal authorities and a contractor to whom (perhaps) land is being granted,[1] in return for services past and future:

---

[1] This land is perhaps indicated by the word *letem*, which can be compared with Albanian *ledïnë*, "meadow, unploughed land" (M. 239).

θui: "here, of here, local" (adjective).

araśa: *ar* is probably "fire" and "place where fire is", i.e., "altar", like Latin *ara*. We shall revert to this.

θent is the exact counterpart of Albanian *dhëndë*, "sheep" (plural, from the singular, *dele*).

mase is the word already encountered in the forms *mish, meso, miaso*, etc., "meat". It can be seen that *mish* is not the only form, and that Etruscan was not borrowing from Armenian. *θentmase* is "sheep-meat"; *anglicé*, "mutton".

laei is either a parallel formation to, or a loan-word from, Greek, viz., *laoi*, "people" (in the plural sense); *laos*, "people" (singular). In the dative case here?

trecś: the word which concerns us, *trec*, i.e., *treg*, "market"; in the genitive here.

θenśt: connected with *θent* (above), but perhaps used with a collective meaning, "flock of sheep"?

menaθa: the construction of this is pure Illyrian. *Me*, "with"; *naθa* is, of course, the *nata* of the actors' palette, "night"; *menaθa*, "with the night", is paralleled by Albanian *menatë*, "in the morning" (M. 280).

In other words, a certain Larth Titus is to provide "mutton for this altar, and also for the people of the market, (bringing) the sheep as soon as night is past". There was therefore probably in the market-place itself an altar on which livestock were slaughtered and from which the butchers, or the people of the market-place, drew their provisions. This seems to be indirectly confirmed by a somewhat sinister piece of information:

... Tarquinii, Caere, and Falerii ... attempted to revolt against the Roman encroachments, and the deep exasperation which these had aroused in Etruria was shown by the slaughter of the whole of the Roman prisoners taken in the first campaign, three hundred and seven in number, in the market-place of Tarquinii ...

(Mommsen, *History of Rome*, Book II, Chapter 4)

To which we may add that among the Romans:

... the general was wont to present the tenth of the spoil which he had procured, and the merchant the tenth of the substance which he had obtained, to Hercules at the chief altar (*ara maxima*) in the cattle-market.

(*Ibid.*, Book I, Chapter 12)

(3) Finally, inscription P. 411, CIE 14, on a stone, is visibly related
to the same root *terg*, *targ*:

mi mal tarcste (A)

tarcste is the same as Tergeste, mentioned above, and is therefore
"market". *Mi mal tarcste*: "This is the mountain of the market". At
first I was much put out by this: where would I be expected to go
climbing next? And who would consent to go mountaineering for the
sake of a pound of tomatoes? Eventually I capitulated in the face of an
observation by Mommsen:

> . . . The most important of all the Italian fairs was that which
> was held at Soracte in the grove of Feronia. . . . That high isolated
> mountain . . . lay on the boundary which separated the Etruscan
> and Sabine lands . . . and it was likewise easily accessible from
> Latium and Umbria. Roman merchants regularly made their
> appearance there . . .

(*Ibid.*, Book I, Chapter 13)

So these "mountain fairs" were reasonably accessible after all.

The Etruscan tradesman knew how to put his customers in a good
mood. When he was weighing up goods he took care to remember

FIG. 31. Prayer written on figurine of a bull

mantisa (B), an Etruscan word which, according to Festus, meant "a
small addition to the weight". On this point there is a difference of
opinion between Thomopoulos and myself. My forerunner explained
mantisa by Albanian *mbanë disa: mb'anë*, "aside", being contracted to
manë, and *disa* meaning "a little, something". Before becoming
acquainted with this solution I had already thought of an Albanian
verb which is found in two forms: *mbaj*, *maj*, "to hold" (M. 267). "I
hold, thou holdest, he holds" is *maj*, *man*, *man*. This present tense
might well serve as an imperative; *man disa* would mean "hold (i.e.,
have, or take) a little (more)". The difference of opinion between
Thomopoulos and myself is only a small one.

An Etruscan market must have been full of goods of every description.

By way of livestock there were bullocks and horses as well as sheep. The word "bull" can be elucidated with the help of two pieces of documentary evidence:

(a) A short but persuasive prayer, inscribed on a rudimentary (and damaged) representation of a bull, and published by Corssen (fig. 31):[1]

pelθurinu petrual (A)

pel: Albanian pjell, "to produce, beget, bear" (M. 383).

θurinu: "bull", as shown by the figurine itself.

petrual: probably "of Petru"—some worthy farmer who was alarmed by the shortcomings of his bull made this simple work of art with his own hands, briefly inscribed his supplication and his name on it, and hurried to the temple to present it to the appropriate deity.

"May Petru's bull be fecund!"

(b) The Etruscan name of the Minotaur, Minos the Bull:

(P. 755) θevrumines

The word for "horse", cal, caius, was mentioned in the chapter on Numbers. Hesychius has preserved another word for it: damnos. This might be related to an expression for a thoroughbred horse; Albanian kalë damas, in which damas means "set apart" .

The presence of wine-merchants in the market-place seems to be indicated by an inscription on a wine-pourer (oenochoë):

(P. 272, NRIE 498) aplueparusis (A)

aplu is one of those words whose meaning was irresistible at the first glance, both to Thomopoulos and, later, to myself: it is quite clearly Albanian ambël, amël, ëmbël, "sweet, pleasant" (M. 5).

eparu is Albanian epër, "upper; superior" [2] (M. 95).

sis, "of the taste", corresponds to Albanian shijë (in which the last two letters are secondary).

The wine was therefore "sweet, of superior taste". M. Buffa came to the conclusion that it was wine consecrated to Apollo, but I believe myself that the author of the inscription was a devotee of Bacchus.

---

[1] Über die Sprache der Etr., Taf. XIX B, I.

[2] In parenthesis, it seems natural in this context to wonder whether the name of the mountainous region of Epirus should be explained by means of this same root epër, "the higher country".

Besides, the month of May was called *ampiles* (P. 805), "sweet", in Etruscan.

Different kinds of oil could be bought, too; as is shown by an inscription from an amphora:

(P. 720) trskmetr LXXVI s (B)

The following interpretation may be suggested:

trsk: Albanian *draskë*, "butter-brine" (M. 85).

me: "with".

tr: either Etruscan *θra*, "milk", or Albanian *drâ*, "lees of melted butter" (M. 81).

Obviously, the meanings of Illyrian culinary terms are likely to have developed somewhat in the course of the ages. I must leave gastronomical historians to attend to the problem.

Cheese must have been sold in the same row of shops. M. Ernout considers *caseus* to be an Etruscan word which passed into Latin. He says that where this word is concerned, scholars have been—

> too easily content to trace a relationship with Old Slavonic *"kvasu"* ("yeast"), which suits neither the form nor the meaning.

(Loc. cit., p. 114)

We should note, in parenthesis, that Slavonic *kvas* is also "acid, sour". Still, the difference separating *caseus* from Albanian *gjathë* is small indeed. However, there were certainly different names for different kinds of cheese; we have already discussed *pazu*.

When we come to poultry we recall Deecke's mention of an Etruscan surname, *pataks*. *Patak* in Albanian is "a gander" (M. 356). But there were predators as well as poultry: (P. 99) *capys*, "falcon", is Albanian *shkabë* (M. 477), Serbian *kobac*, Polish *kobiec*, Russian *kobtchyk*. A whole Indo-European word-family!

Coming to vegetables, we find that beetroot was already on the scene. As Buonamici has observed, it was called *gigarum* (A) by the Etruscans. A word in an excellent state of preservation, since it is immediately recognisable as Alban *kukerem*, *kuqërruem*, "reddish; blushing" (M. 228). I was slightly alarmed by G. Meyer, who associated this Albanian word with Latin *coccinus*, "scarlet"; but I felt better when he went on to say that the Latins themselves had purloined it from the Greeks (*kokkos*, "a kind of insect which yields a scarlet dye"). Everyone pillaged the Greeks, why deny this privilege to the Etruscans?

There was no lack of flowers in the market, either. Buonamici cites *garuleum* (A), a kind of chrysanthemum (*Fonti* . . ., p. 123). This word is elucidated by Albanian *garule*, "heap, pile" (M. 123). Is not the name justified by the heaped-up petals, one on top of the other, of this flower?

Flowers and vegetables, obviously, depended on the seasons; so we can take this opportunity of mentioning the Etruscan names for the months.

Sacrilege! The arrangement of the nine-day Etruscan weeks in their proper order, and the attribution of the right date to every religious ceremony, was the prerogative of the priests. How dare we deprive them of this sacred task and drag it down to the level of the market-place? It hurts me to suggest such a thing. Tracing the course of time was a function carried out in the temple of Nortia, where old nails were driven in to mark the passage of the years. And yet—how can we refrain from discussing these matters here? Some of these names of months exhale such freshness, such a good smell of the fruitful earth and wheat-fields and blossoming cherry-trees, that we really cannot leave them entirely to the priests. These names are reminiscent of the Canaanites' names for the months, such as the month of the first wheat (*aviv*) or that of the new blossom (*ziv*); reminiscent, too, of the Judaean calendar of Gezer (8th century B.C.): the sowing month, the month of the flax-harvest, the month of pruning the vines.

Thus in the Etruscan May, *Ampiles*, we cannot but recognise *ambël*, "the sweet", as Thomopoulos did before us. We find the same freshness in the Etruscan April, *Cabreas* (P. 818), which Thomopoulos explained by a reference to the Albanian verb *kaboj*, though I prefer *capra*, which meant "goat" in Etruscan (P. 820) as well as in Latin. A month of "caprine capers", perhaps?

The same author and myself are also at odds over *Velcitanus*, "March". He connects it with Albanian *mbiell*, "to sow"; but I think rather of *vejk* (*velk?*), a kind of small fig (M. 548). His ideas on June, on the other hand, are more acceptable: he matches *Aclus* with Albanian *kali*, *kallëz*, "ear of corn",[1] with prothetic *a* (as in *agaletora?*).

(P. 854) *Traneus*, "July" (B), is said by my Athenian predecessor to be "a month of dryness", because of Albanian *ter*, "dry". But I doubt this; I suggest Albanian *trahan*, "cereals" (M. 521).

Thomopoulos and I also have a bone to pick with one another in the form of *Ermius*, the Etruscan August. He says it is the month of Hermes, one of the gods of fertility. But I notice that no other Etruscan month seems to be dedicated to a deity; I shall connect *Ermius* with Albanian *ermoj*, "to rake, rummage" (M. 96). In the country in August you can search wherever you please, you will find fruits and crops everywhere.

[1] Cf. Russian *kolos*, "ear of corn".

(P. 824) *Celius*, "September", is derived by Thomopoulos from *caljis* (which is perhaps the word given by Mann as *kalis*, "to cut", M. 176), taken in the sense of "to hoe, to weed". But for my own part I look to Albanian *gjellë*, "food"; a food-giving month.

Finally, for the Etruscan October, (P. 858) *Xosfer* (B), Thomopoulos has nothing but uneasy conjectures to offer. I interpret it by Albanian *kusp*, "to twist; knit" (M. 231). October would be the month in which every good Etruscan housewife busied herself with the same work as the good housewife in the Old Testament: "She seeketh wool, and flax, and worketh willingly with her hands. . . . |She layeth her hands to the spindle, and her hands hold the distaff" (Proverbs xxxi. 13, 19).

Note: My contention is based not only on Albanian *kusp* but also on Latin *cuspis*, "the smooth head of a lance, and hence every pointed weapon", concerning which M. F. Martin observes: "A word probably borrowed from the Etruscans" (*Les Mots latins*, 1941). In Etruscan the word could also have meant a knitting-needle.

However, Mme E. Fiesel suggested in 1936 that χosfer be interpreted through Etruscan *cezp*, "eight", on the analogy of Latin *October*, "the eighth" (*Studi Etruschi*, X, p. 324).

It seems to me that in addition to the change of vowel in χosfer-cezp, this view comes up against the following obstacle: it is hard to believe that only one month, the eighth, should have got its name from the corresponding number. In Latin we have not only the group September, October, November and December but also July and August, which were previously called Quintilis and Sextilis. In Etruscan, on the other hand, neither the month preceding χosfer, namely *Celius*, "September", nor the rest of those that are known to us, namely Aclus, Ampilus, Cabreas, Hermius, Trabeus and Velcitanus, have anything in common with the Etruscan numerals.

Obviously the market offered things made as well as things grown, such as chrysanthemums and beetroot. Etruscan metalwork comes to mind. Since weighty transactions were recorded on lead, the price of that metal, which, moreover, was essential for producing bronze, must have fluctuated rather as it does in the metal market today. This thought is prompted by an inscription on a lead ingot, published by M. Lejeune in *Studi Etruschi* (XXII, 1953, p. 133): *cenise neis* (A).

ceni I connect with the Albanian verb *cenis*, "to value, fix the price of" (M. 47) and to *cena* (already discussed). Hence *cena* is "price". The same meaning had already been given to it by Trombetti (*La lingua etr.*, p. 5).

se represents the Albanian pronominal adjective "hers".
neis is Albanian *nejse*, "the same" (M. 313).

Thus: "Its price is the same." The ingot was a sample sent to a customer, with a note to say that the price had not altered.

Pottery being on the scale of a national industry among the Etruscans, pyramids of pots must have been on view in the market-place. On an elegant pot with a handle, described by Corssen, the following inscription [1] appears:

mirianaśplenianaś (A)

Corssen read this as: *mi Rianaś Plenianaś*, "This (is dedicated) by Rianaś, son of Pleniana." Being a trifle tired of proper nouns invented *ad hoc*, I interpret it differently:

miri: Albanian *mirë*, "beautiful". The alternative is to make two words of it: *mi*, "here is", and *ri*, "new". But we are dealing with pots; and nobody sells old pots. Though one might, in the last resort, conceive it to be a new pattern, a "new line", as shopkeepers say.

anaś is Albanian *anë*, "vessel, pot, crock" (M. 7).

pleni is perfectly clear; it is Albanian *bleni*, the 2nd person plural of the imperative of the verb *ble*: "Buy!"

Thus: "Fine pots! Buy some pots!" This one was probably put out on show, as an advertisement. It is tempting to imagine an Etruscan travelling salesman, driving a small and apathetic donkey in front of him along the sunny streets, and uttering a long-drawn, plaintive cry of

mi-ri a-naś! ble-ni a-naś!

Incidentally, it should be noted that this display of pottery may well lure us unexpectedly into the consideration of much larger problems.

On a black earthenware amphora there has been found an inscription of some length which contains the Etruscan alphabet twice over (with the addition of the Latin *b*, *d* and *o*), and also a disorderly accumulation of syllables such as *uar* and *uas*. So far the thing gives the impression of a writing-exercise. It is followed by a few words which make sense:

(P. 49, NRIE 841) . . . *mi atianaia aχapri alice venelisi velθur zinace*

venelici velθur are proper names. *zinace* has already been interpreted by some other authors as "wrote", from the root *zi*, "black", which

[1] Vol. I, Taf. XXIII B.

has been seen already (literally, "has blackened"). Here we shall examine only the two first words: *mi atianaia*. M. Buffa divided this as *ati anaia*, "the mother Anaia". Elsewhere he did in fact find a proper name Anaia (Fabr. I, 384 b). His division may be right.

But, if not, it will be remembered that Etruscan inscriptions some-times begin with the word *mi* ("I" or "this") directly followed by the name of the *container* which bears the inscription: (P. 63) *mi qutun*; (P. 3) *mi culiχna*; (P. 11) *mi putiza*; etc. So it is legitimate to inquire whether *atianaia* denotes the amphora itself. Now, be it noted, in an article on "The Pelasgians and the Greeks", P. Kretschmer refers to the Greek word *attana*, meaning a vessel which was used in sacrifices. The word is thought to be of pre-Hellenic origin. The goddess Athena was the original patron of the potters in pre-Hellenic times. Kretschmer therefore asks whether the name of the goddess, and that of the city, are not related to the name of the vessel in question. He goes on later to establish resemblances between the earliest inhabitants of Athens and the Etruscans.[1]

And it does seem that Etruscan *atianaia* is connected with *attana*. Recalling what Kretschmer also wrote about Huttenia, another pre-Hellenic name (see the chapter on Numbers), we have a twofold indication, which we should do well to bear in mind, of the links between the Etruscans and archaic Greece.

Etruscan footwear, which was famous, must have been among the features of the market. The shoemakers constituted one of the eight corporations of craftsmen recognised in Latium in the remote times of King Numa. It is known that the sandals with golden thongs with which Phidias supplied his statue of Minerva were called "Tyrrhenian", and that the cothurni of Greek tragedy were described by Ovid as "Lydian". Finally, the Roman senators adopted the kind of sandal worn by the lucumons, the Etruscan chieftains.

Now the profession of a dead person is sometimes inscribed on the vault; an example is the following:

(P. 468, NRIE 373) *larθ cae capesar* (B)

—in which I have identified Albanian *kapucar* or *këpucar*, "shoemaker, cobbler" (M. 184). This identification put me to a certain amount of trouble, however.

G. Meyer (*loc. cit.*, p. 188) asserts that the word comes from Turkish *papush*, "slipper". But I must submit the following observations in opposition to his view:

[1] *Glotta*, XI, 1921, pp. 282–5.

(*a*) The Turkish word made its way into other Balkan languages without any change in its initial consonant: Bulgarian *papuć*, Macedonian *paputs*, Modern Greek *paputzi* and so on. (*b*) Numerous Turkish words have been incorporated into Albanian without any modification of their initial *k*: *kaïmak*, "cream", *kalaï*, "pewter", etc. (*c*) G. Meyer himself derives another Albanian word, *mammuze*, from Turkish *papush*. (*d*) In his dictionary, S. E. Mann does not give a Turkish origin for the word *këpucë*, "shoe, boot" (M. 193).

In view of these points I was prepared to take up the cudgels against Meyer in the matter of *capesar*, but I was not altogether happy about it. What finally solved the problem was *Sardis*, Bückler's collection of Lydian inscriptions. There I found the Lydian word *kupassis*, "a kind of footgear", according to Harpocration. This gave peculiar force to my own view. And it was only at this point that it occurred to me to see whether the root of *capesar* and *këpucë* was to be found elsewhere in Albanian. And in fact it is. *Këpucë* may well be derived either from the verb *kep*, "to hew" (M. 190) or, if this is not accepted, from *qep*, "to sew" (M. 414). Thus Etruscan *capesar* strictly corresponds to Albanian *këpucar* (*këpucëtar*), in which the ending -*ar* denotes occupation (*detar*, "seaman"; *zyrtar*, "functionary"; *udhëtar*, "traveller, wayfarer"), and whose meaning in Lydian, Etruscan and Albanian is "he who cuts (leather)" or else "he who *sews* (leather)"; the latter is exactly analogous to Polish and Ukrainian *shvetz*, "he who sews". The problem is thus solved.

Summing up, the term in question (and also the fashion, in this basic craft) may have come to Etruria from Lydia. This is an added confirmation of the early links between the two countries. We shall examine those links again at the end of the book.

Not far from the master-shoemaker a carpenter must have been at work. Our notice is drawn to woodworkers by a Latin word, *grosa*, "plane", whose antecedents have been well sifted and scrutinised. The word is preserved for us by Arnobius, a writer of the 3rd century B.C. Jokl says:

> Walde wondered where this word came from. But G. Meyer had already given the answer in his assertion that the word *gërresë* (scraper, plane) was one of the basic elements of Albanian. Thus *grosa* is one of the oldest Albanian words for which we have a written attestation.
>
> (*Studien zur alb. Etym.*, p. 22)

And indeed the word is connected with the Albanian root *gëruanj*, "to grate, to rasp". But Jokl coldly announces that the word passed *directly* from Albanian into Latin. I am therefore obliged once again to curb the excesses of Illyriomania, by postulating that Latin inherited the word from Etruscan, the latter having drawn it from ancient Illyrian; Albanian, on the other hand, being a neo-Illyrian language. Besides, the Etruscans were great carpenters, boat-builders and cabinet-makers.

Not far from these other artisans may well also have been found the workshop of a sculptor or a letterer. When a master-craftsman in this line had finished one of his works he sometimes inscribed it with the word *cana* (A), next to his name. This is found on a weight in the form of a beetle (P. 260), and on a marble statue representing a goddess with her child (P. 260, CIE 76) (*idem*, P. 284, 328, 681, 731).

FIG. 32. Etruscan cup

The word may equally well mean "sculpta" (carved) or "sculpture, image". I compare it with Albanian *qanë*, "plane" (M. 411), and with *çan* (*tshan*), whose aorist is *çani*, "to split, cleave" (M. 54), both of which notions are essential to the sculptor's craft. We have already noted interchangeable *k* and *ç* in Albanian: *dorak* = *doraç*, "handle, lever" (M. 80).

But the sculptors were not the only craftsmen who signed their work, as may be seen from a beautiful cup of the 7th or 6th century B.C., which has an inscription, and which was described in 1934 by M. Pallottino (*Studi Etruschi*, VIII, p. 343, tav. XLI). The large perforated handles of this cup are boldly conceived, and M. Pallottino justly remarks that "the unusual shape and fine workmanship of the cup do indeed justify its being signed". The inscription says:

mini urθaneke aranθur (A) (fig. 32)

M. Pallottino compares *urθaneke* with *muluvaneke*, "consecrated, offered", which occurs so frequently in votive texts; he postulated that the word *ur* was a verb meaning "to make" or something similar. The text would therefore mean "Aranθur made this".

However, the inscription can be precisely interpreted thanks to two elements: *raθ*, "order", Hammarström's elucidation of which has been quoted earlier; and the passive form of verbs, as established in the present work. As we have seen, the passive in both Etruscan and Albanian is formed by adding a *u* at the beginning of the verb. *Radhis, radhoj* mean in Albanian not only "to line up, arrange" (cf. Slavonic *riaditi, poriadok,* "order") but also "to draw" etc. (M. 422). *U-radh* will therefore be its passive form, and the inscription becomes clear: "This was designed by Aranθur" (or: "I was designed by Aranθur").

It would be a pity to leave the market-place without taking a glance at the crowd, who are surrounding a set-up stage in a corner and admiring the talents of a company of mimes or comic actors. A strolling player was called *histro, histrio, hister* or *ister*.

A bilingual inscription in Etruscan and Latin was the epitaph of

(P. 541, CIE 2965) *aθ trepi θanasa*
Ar Trebi histro

From this it is to be inferred that the Etruscan, though Latinised, word *histro* is a translation for another Etruscan word, *θanasa*. I rendered this latter word as "*diseur*", availing myself of the Albanian verb *tha*, "to speak". Two years later I came on it again in Thomopoulos, coupled with a mention of Greek *apangélia*, "narration"; hence, "narrator". But we must bear in mind that Arnth Trebi was also a *histro*. It seems to me that Thomopoulos has successfully explained this word by means of Albanian *heshtur*, "silent"; in which case the player was a mime, acting in silence. But the situation is now rather odd: the epitaph designates the dead man's profession by two words, of which one means "narrator" or "*diseur*" and the other means "silent", speechless. I do not know whether Thomopoulos noticed the contradiction.

But perhaps this tragic dilemma, in which the actor has post-humously involved the decipherers of his epitaph, is more apparent than real; it is merely the last amusing trick he has performed on the stage of time. To his fellow-Etruscans he was, above all, a bard or actor reciting their epic poems—the epic of Mastarna, perhaps. To the Romans, on the other hand, that side of his talent presented no interest, since they did not understand his language. They lumped all such entertainers together under one name, *histrio*. The scribe, who composed this bilingual epitaph, did not attempt to re-educate the Romans by informing them of details which would only have made them yawn; for their benefit he simply used the Latinised word which was known to them all. Hence the dual role which this actor of ours,

Arnth, having played it in his lifetime, went on playing after his death.

But is this the end of our troubles?

I originally followed the way marked out by Thomopoulos. However, in his *Researches in Comparative Historical Philology* (Moscow, 1958), V. Georgiev reminds us of a Thracian word, *istr(o)*, "speedy, strong", from which came the ancient name of the Danube, Istros. Ought we to relate *istro* to *ister,* and infer that agility and strength were what the Etruscans especially admired in their acrobats? This is something for future investigation to determine.

VIII

VISITING THE DOCTOR

THE Etruscan doctor, who was a dentist, gynaecologist, oculist and pharmacist all at once, had an arsenal of remedies at his disposition with which to wrestle with his patients' ills. If you went and told him you were feverish and tired he could offer you a decoction of gentian-root, which figures in M. Ernout's list as *Cicenda*, *Kikenda* (A) and was a tonic, a stimulant and a febrifuge. Its Etruscan name nicely matches the Albanian verb *kyq*, *kyç*, "to fasten" (M. 232).

But if the trouble was over-excitement and nervous tension the doctor could dose you with a potion of *apium*, "parsley", which the Etruscans called *apium raninum* (A), the meaning of the latter word being "calmative, *sedative*" (Buonamici, *Fonti* . . ., p. 364). *raninum* is well explained by the Albanian verb *rri*, "to seat, to sit down", whose imperfect is *rrinja*. Note the expressions: *dielli rrie*, "the sun *sits down*" (i.e., sets); and *rróbat më rrijnë*, "the clothes suit me" ("*sit* well on me", as the English expression goes) (M. 439). It is evident to what a degree interpretation via Albanian *sits well* on Etruscan.

In addition to tonics and calmatives, more powerful herbs were available; notably the poisonous and narcotic henbane, which was known to the Tuscans as *fabulonia* (B) (Buonamici, *ibid.*, p. 365). This word can be elucidated. Its initial element is *fa*, that is to say *ba*, the verb *bâj*, "to do, to make", which we have met before; the second element, *bul*, is connected with the Albanian group *bubullij*, *bubullis*, in the sense of "to thunder, rumble" and *buburitem*, "to play the fool" (M. 40). The meaning of *fa-bul(onia)* is thus "to cause to roar", which is not far from "to make mad".

We must believe that recourse was not often had to this philtre, for Etruscan pharmacology and hydrotherapy were renowned. There is, moreover, an inscription which bears witness to the Etruscan doctor's solicitude for his patient. It consists of two words written on a little receptacle which M. Buffa has described as a "piccolo balsamario":

(P. 343, NRIE 703) ip siune (A)

This remarkable little inscription is the counterpart of the kind of label with which we are familiar ourselves: "EYE OINTMENT. For external use only." Thus:

ip is the Albanian already encountered *ep*, *ip*, "to give", with the sense (as in some other languages, the Hebrew of the Bible, for instance) of "to put". Albanian *ip*, with this meaning, occurs in Deuteronomy xxi. 5: "*epete funt*", "you shall put an end . . ."

siu: *si* is "eye", in Albanian; *u* is the definite article.

ne: Albanian preposition "in". As can be seen, it is put at the end of the word which it governs. Alternatively, *siune* is an oblique case, and plural; cf. *e ka synë*, "there are eyes" (M. 465).

So the meaning is pellucid: "To be put in the eyes." The owner of the bottle had something wrong with his eyes, and the doctor took the trouble to ensure that the patient did not swallow the drug in his eagerness.

Let us note in passing that the use of eye-salves was much practised in Rome (Paoli, *Vita romana*, p. 331).

This is one of the most convincing inscriptions which it has been my lot to decipher. More than two thousand years ago the remedy contained in this little bottle helped to clear the misty sight of some unknown Etruscan; it would be pleasant to hope today that the last atom of the precious salve, lingering in the bottom of the bottle, might help to remove the scales from the eyes of those who are still unable to discern the roots of the Etruscan language.

As for the preposition or article coming after the noun, let us remind ourselves that this phenomenon is common to several Indo-European languages: Bulgarian, Roumanian and the Scandinavian languages.

The Etruscan doctors were a "new wave" who, little by little, drove the old sorcerers out into the shadows and encroached on some of the prerogatives of the soothsayers and priests. Which does not mean that no one went to a sorcerer any more when he wanted to put a spell on an enemy. I want to mention here just such a negative "remedy", of "external" application indeed; I shall present it with reservations, my intention being merely to lay down one or two surveyor's marks with an eye to full decipherment at some future time.

There is a vase (aryballos) with a drawing of a snake. The inscription is written on the body of the reptile, which seems to be moving towards an unseen enemy; its forked tongue is out, and it seems prepared to strike. It has been reproduced in *Studi Etruschi*, 1953, pp. 307–8.

The first part of the inscription forms a single, long, agglutinated word, with a lacuna near the end. The second part is not divided up either. So the difficulties are great:

(P. 331)

hefmasuveitesalevarearavapeisnislarekasiais . . . emal . . .
uθikemaluvekavisiazili ziχina ein suθueas

Let us try to pick out some recognisable words in this amorphous mass:

hef is Albanian *hep*, "to bend", *hepoj*, "to curve", *hepur*, "curved, bent" (M. 157). The word therefore conveys the sense of "to wind, to twist".

maś: cf. Albanian *mas*, "to take aim" (M. 265).

uveiteś: cf. Albanian *vej, vejtur*, "to twist, weave" (M. 548); passive form denoted by initial *u*?

aleva: Albanian *allavitem*, "to grope along, feel one's way" (M. 5).

re: "anew" (already encountered).

ara: *ar*, "fire", will be studied later.

va: the verb *bâ*, "to become", already seen.

peis: cf. Albanian *pêiz*, "sinew, string" (M. 358).

isnis: cf. Albanian *ishnushëm*, "justly, according to law" (M. 167 and 207).

uθi: *udhe*, "way", seen already.

ke: "may you have!", from the verb *kam*, "to have".

maluve (A) is Albanian *maleve*, "of the mountains", a common expression;

FIG. 33

uθi ke maluve: a fragment about which there can be no doubt, "take the mountain road".

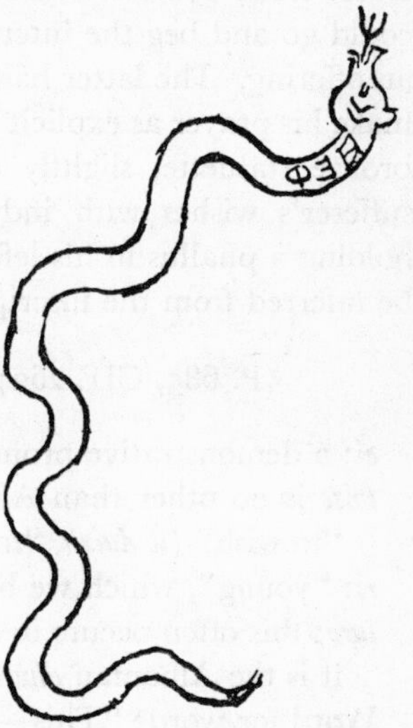

ziχina: a known Etruscan root, *ziχ*, "to cut", etc.; here "to wound"? "to bite"?

suθu: "the tomb".

eas: cf. Albanian *eia*, "go!"? Or perhaps rather it should be assimilated to *eius* ("his", adjective or pronoun) which occurs on the Stele of Novilara.

Analogies can be found in Albanian for other words in this inscription besides the above; but for the time being it is sufficient to note that the general sense of the text takes shape as follows: "Crawl; coil like a cord, grope your way along, seek out your way over the mountains and strike to his very tomb!"

The name of the person for whom these charming attentions were intended is not indicated. Perhaps the text was a pro-forma which the sender was supposed to complete, just as a form is filled in when one sends a registered letter.

Continuing this series of medical inscriptions (and taking the word
"medical" in a pretty broad sense), let us now look at a text which is
rather less gloomy, despite the fact that it concerns a grave infirmity
which still persists in mowing down millions of human beings: old age.
When a highborn Etruscan who was still young in heart found none
the less that he could get no substantial help against this complaint,
either from doctors or from sorcerers, he had one resource left: he
could go and beg the intervention of a god, to whom he would make
an offering. The latter had to be chosen so that its very nature would
make his prayer as explicit as possible. The present example is a small
bronze statuette, slightly damaged, which does indeed express the
sufferer's wishes with indubitable candour, for it portrays a man
holding a phallus in his left hand. The petitioner's advanced age can
be inferred from the inscription on the statuette:

(P. 685, CIE 2627) *eitviscri ture arnθ alitle pumpuś* (B)

ei: a demonstrative pronoun.
tvisc is no other than Albanian *duesh*, the optative of the verb *due*,
"to wish" (*të duesh*, "may you wish") (M. 95).
ri: "young", which we have met already. Here, "youth".
ture: this often occurs in dedications, in the form *turce*, "has given";
   it is the Albanian *dhuroj*, "to offer, present, give" (M. 93).
Word for word: "This—may you wish—youth—to give . . ."

So the text means: "This, in order that you may consent to give
youth back to Arnth Allidius Pompey."
From the Etruscan point of view, this notability's way of stating the
problem had nothing comic about it.

The Etruscan name for a malady of the respiratory passages has
been preserved down to our own times in the Rhaeto-Romance dialect
of the Grisons. The word is *candarials*, thanks to which we are able to
define the linguistic ambiance to which Etruscan belonged; for it was
by analysing a Lydian divine and royal name, *Kandaules*, "wolf", that
Ellis, in 1886, was enabled to notice the identity of the two terms.
Now, *Kandaules* is made up of two elements: *kan*, which means "dog",
and *daules*, which means "strangler"; hence "strangler of dogs". The
Armenian word, *kheldavl*, meant the same.
Kretschmer also studied the Lydian word in question and observed
that *daules* was related to the Slavonic word *dav(iti)*, "to strangle"
(*loc. cit.*, p. 388). We thus have concordances between that very ancient
language, *Lydian*, and the Slavonic languages, which are less ancient,

with no question of any borrowing from Slavonic. These concordances are similar to those which are found between *Etruscan* and Slavonic.

We see that the name of the malady in question must have had precisely the meaning of "strangling" or "suffocation". What is equally interesting is that Kretschmer, in the same context, points to the designation for a wolf in *Phrygian*: *daos*, which he associates with the root *dav*, "to strangle", which is evidently common to Lydian, Phrygian and Slavonic.

The other element, *kan*, "dog", belongs at once to Latin (*canis*), Greek (*kuon*), Albanian (*kan*), Sanskrit (*çvan*), and to the language of the Carians.

We have already met *cna* (*cuicna*) (p. 116).

Here, possibly, is an instrument used by an Etruscan doctor. A short inscription on a bronze strigil (scraper) says:

(P. 612, CII 1925) *śatnaślθac*

śatnaśl: "From Satan's house".
θac (A) is *zac*, *zaχ* (cf. *zaχri*, LM, I, 4); i.e., Albanian *gjak*, *dzjak*, *dzak*, "blood".

In the present instance, "to bleed, to let blood"? So the interpretation is: "From *śatna*, (to let) blood". The instrument was therefore not intended for cleansing the skin, but for bleeding, an operation whose importance in the medical practice of past ages is well known.

The tip of this scraper was perhaps sharpened in the appropriate manner.

We shall mention here also a curious object described by Buonamici. It is a "small bronze, perhaps a medical instrument in the form of a stethoscope", with the word *luaś* (A) inscribed on it. The author adds that it may be the upper part of a candlestick, "in which case the word *luaś* might afford material for interesting etymological inquiries" (*Epigr. etr.*, p. 408).

This Etruscan word is perfectly comprehensible and, moreover, confirms Buonamici's fine stroke of intuition. *luaś* (P. 266) is not connected with Lua, the wife of Saturn, as M. Buffa supposed (*loc. cit.*, p. 149), but simply corresponds to the Albanian verb *ljej*, "to anoint", in the subjunctive. (We shall meet the verb again on pp. 239 and 320.) The meaning of the word is thus "for anointing".

We can end this chapter suitably by invoking Skutona (A), the Illyrian goddess of health. Among the Etruscans she is unlikely to feel that she is in a strange land. The meaning of her name is made clear by Albanian *skutoj*, "to dress (wounds)" (M. 454, 455). For lack of any portrayals of Illyrian doctors we show here a contemporary of theirs, a Scythian doctor, dressing a soldier's leg (detail of vase from Kul-Oba,

FIG. 33A. Scythian doctor

after Rostovtzeff, *Greeks and Iranians*, pl. XXII). The art of dressing wounds must of necessity have been an important matter to the Etruscans.

IX

ETRUSCAN ART AND ITS MYTHOLOGICAL
SUBJECT-MATTER

THE study of the art of any ancient people always implies the study of
that people's origins. Consequently, the study of Etruscan art will be
carried on to the best advantage only when all the new material made
available by the present decipherment has been taken into consideration. In this chapter, works of art will be treated only from the strictly
epigraphical point of view; in other words, we shall occupy ourselves
almost exclusively with the inscriptions accompanying certain mythological scenes executed by Etruscan artists, or by Greek artists working
in the Etruscan style.

Several authors have complained of the levity with which the
Etruscans treated subjects from Greek mythology. Gerhard raises his
hands to heaven when, on a mirror, he sees the Gorgon Medusa
depicted as a man, and bearded into the bargain; and he talks of these
artists' capriciousness, their lack of decency, and criticises pretty plainly
the gaps in their education. Of one of these scenes he says:

> The creator of this drawing . . . has quite obviously arranged or
> modified any of the figures in his composition whenever he found
> it convenient to do so in order to fill up the circular form of the
> mirror, without any respect for the meaning of the scene, which he
> clearly only half understood . . .
>
> (*Loc. cit.*, p. 148)

It is a fact that the Etruscan artists sometimes showed themselves to
be poor mythologists. In this respect, surprisingly enough, they
resembled their customers. Thus the engraver would confect an
eclectic scene, a sort of mythological pot-pourri in which the heroes of
assorted legends were given an unexpected chance to get to know one
another; and the public would cheerfully buy his little masterpiece,
provided there was some familiar figure for the eye to rest upon, an
Apollo, as it might be, or a Hercules or a Venus. After all, the customer
was neither a Greek nor a pedant.

And yet these mythological scenes present a whole range of feelings
and attitudes which are by no means devoid of interest. Like every
ancient work of art, they are always narrative in character; sometimes

they appeal to the spectator's noblest emotions, his admiration, pity or compassion; in other cases they confine themselves to telling him the story of some interesting adventure; or, finally, they set out merely to amuse him by the display of situations comic, grotesque or even obscene.

Let us begin by examining a mythological scene on a vase, a scene whose accompanying inscription visibly tends to underline the tragic nature of the legend. The subject is Alcestis offering her life to the Underworld in order to save the life of her husband, King Admetos. Husband and wife, surrounded by demonic spirits, are seen embracing for the last time (see photograph between pp. 208 and 209). The text says:

(P. 334, CII 2598) *eca ersce nac aχrum flerθrce* (A)

eca: "here is", "this is".

ersce: an interesting word, both semantically and morphologically. For the meaning, I recognise here the Albanian word *errshëm*, "dark" (M. 96). As for the form, it is instructive in three ways: (*a*) the double *r* is reduced to a single one; (*b*) we see that Etruscan *sc* can be equivalent to Albanian *sh*; (*c*) the final *m* of this class of Albanian adjectives is always absent in Etruscan.

nac: "night", already studied (with Etruscan *naθa*, Albanian *natë*).

aχrum: Acheron, a river in the Greek Underworld and hence, by extension, the Underworld itself.

fler: "vow". This is the outcome of the long controversy which has been waged about this word. Practically speaking, the meaning amounts to "image, statue", etc., but the real, intrinsic meaning is *votum* (a vow, but also the thing vowed or promised) and hence also an *ex-voto*, since, originally, every work of art represented someone or something vowed as an offering to a deity.

θrce: *turce*, "has given, had given, gave" (Albanian *dhuroj*).

"This is (how), in the darkness of night, she gave (executed) a vow to Acheron" (or, "acquitted herself of her vow").

Another scene, also intended to touch the spectator's emotions, represents two helmeted heroes conversing peacefully in the foreground and failing to see two women in a state of agitation and movement, in the background. This is Gerhard's illustration CCCLX (fig. 34).

Gerhard thought these figures were three heroes and a fury. He wrote of the figure on the left: "The young man to the left (our left) . . . wearing a Phrygian cap, is raising his right hand as if he had been contradicted in argument and wanted to give lively emphasis to what he is saying." This is obviously a quite arbitrary interpretation. This supposed young man is the second Fury, standing behind the central figure and not taking part in any argument but, on the contrary, apparently guiding the fatal blow about to be inflicted by the Fury with the axe upon the two figures in the foreground. The Furies are presumed to be invisible, which explains why the two heroes are so calm.

The inscription, three words long, is difficult. Gerhard mistakenly

FIG. 34. Furies and heroes

read it from left to right: *lamn (?) amira npheil*, and came to the conclusion that it was indecipherable. I take it to be *nfsil amira lamni*:

amira is the only clearly comprehensible word. It is connected with Albanian *amër* (M. 5) and *emër* (M. 94), "to designate". Thus the Fury on the left is designating what must be done and guiding the arm of the other Fury (or goddess).

lamni may possibly be Albanian *lamjë*, "bogey, spook" (M. 235), or "monster", as we may say. G. Meyer connects the word with modern Greek, but it may be derived from ancient Greek *Lamia*, a cruel monster with a woman's form.

nfsil (?) should perhaps be referred to Albanian *fshij, mpshij*, "to sweep; to cancel" (M. 116); or to *fsheh, fshih*, "to hide, dissimulate".

If these deductions are correct the meaning, in outline, is: "Lamni directs the murder", or else "The invisible Fury designates". The problem remains unsolved.

However, this need not prevent us from mentioning a feature of Basque folklore. The Basques used to believe in goblins and other legendary creatures, which were thought to inhabit prehistoric caves. These creatures are sometimes known as *lamina*.

"It seems," writes Philippe Veyrin, "that the word *lamina* is sometimes used to cover all varieties of fantastic creatures. . . . The *laminas*

FIG. 35. Abduction of Thetis

are innumerable and may be of either sex" (*Les Basques*, Arthaud, Paris, pp. 233–4).

Another scene engraved on a mirror, eventful, violent even, but less grim than the preceding one, presents the abduction of Thetis by Peleus[1] (fig. 35). The essence of the situation is summed up in a single word, *parsura* (A), which is perfectly clear, since it directly corresponds to the Albanian verb *përza*, whose aorist is *përzura*, "to seize, chase away, deport, expatriate" (M. 382). However, it is possible that what we have here is the past participle, with the *a* of the feminine ending, like Albanian *dashur*, "loved", *lodhur*, "tired" (curiously similar to Russian *lodyr*, "idler"), etc. In the first event, the translation will be, "He abducted"; in the second, "The abducted one" (fem.).

After Peleus, let us look at his son Achilles, that hero of the Trojan War whom every ancient people venerated. A mirror-engraving depicts him dashing along in his chariot, but does not make it clear where he is bound or why. M. Pallottino thinks it is the sun-god, not Achilles. Gerhard also thinks the picture shows that god in his quadriga, and explains the inscription as being the name of the owner of the

[1] Gerhard, *loc. cit.*, Taf. CCXXVI.

mirror; but one of the words is a verb in a past tense. All in all, despite having elucidated one or two points, I can give only a conjectural interpretation of the text accompanying this dynamic drawing (fig. 36):

(P. 329, CII 2175) aχlei truies . θesθufarce

FIG. 36. Achilles in his chariot

aχlei: this name differs only slightly from aχle, inscribed beside the head of the same hero in a fresco of the Francois Tomb. So it undoubtedly is Achilles.

truies . θes: this is probably two words, of which the second has lost its initial letter. I take it that the letter in question was u; that the second word was udhës (of the way, to the way) which we have seen before; and that the two words together mean "on the way to Troy" or something of the sort.

θufarce: should this be divided so as to produce θuf, "army" (cf. P. 137, zilc θufi tenθas and Albanian tubë, "troop", M. 528, which G. Meyer derives from Latin tumba, "heap", loc. cit., 452) and arce, "made, has made"?

For my own part I look rather to Albanian thupur, thupër, "rod, lash" (M. 538).

So the translation is possibly: "Achilles whipping (his horses) on his way to Troy."
G

After these disappointments we shall be rewarded by the following scene, which has nothing doubtful about it; moreover, it will arm us with a new argument which is striking in more senses than one. I have, indeed, every reason for calling it a delightful scene—especially as it is by no means lacking in humour. Like the preceding examples, it comes from a mirror,[1] and its purpose is to entertain simple mortals by

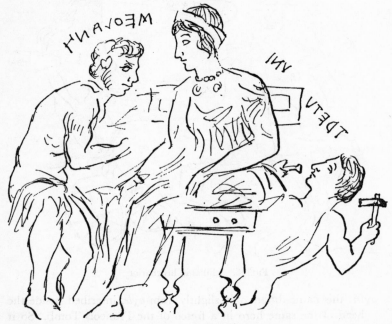

FIG. 37. Juno's chains broken

reminding them of a scandalous incident in the annals of Olympus; one of those affairs, however, which allowed their beholders to feel particularly close to their gods (fig. 37).

The story is that of Juno fixed immovably on her own throne; the said throne being nothing but a trap, devised, patented, constructed and sent to the goddess by her own son, Sethlans, the Etruscan Vulcan. The smith-god was mollified only with the help of wine. The picture shows him in the act of setting his mother free. He is being helped in this task by a brawny assistant, a mechanic who is hammering off the chains without meddling with family affairs which are no concern of his.

By this assistant is the one word *tretu* (A).

[1] Gerhard, *loc. cit.*, Vol. V, Tafel 49.

This is the Albanian verb *tres*, aorist *treta*, past participle *tretun*, "to crush, pound" (M. 523).

Remember the old peasant who held forth in front of Martin-Leake, Napoleon I's Enemy Number 1. Among other things, he said that a grave should be opened three years after the burial to see whether the bones were *i tere a i treture*, "whole or fallen into fragments" (*loc. cit.*,

FIG. 38. Seθlans' handiwork

p. 398). The past tense of the same Illyrio-Etrusco-Albanian verb is found in Cimochowski (*Study of the Dushmani Dialect*, p. 138): *treta, trete, treti*. So the meaning of *tretu* is clear: "break" or "broken to pieces". The assistant's name was unimportant; his action, on the other hand, was underlined.

The smith-god figures on another mirror; the scene [1] this time is eclectic or, to put it bluntly, a muddle (fig. 38). The god is on the left, with his name in a caption: Sethlans. In the middle is a horse; here again the name is given: *Pecse*, Pegasus, the courser of poets and heroes,

[1] Corssen, I, p. 613.

born of Medusa's blood. In the right-hand half of the engraving is an individual wielding a hammer; like his colleague in a similar pose in the preceding example, he is unnamed. Corssen decided that the picture showed the construction of the Trojan horse by Epeos (the unnamed figure) under the supervision of Sethlans. O. Müller, on the other hand, considers the subject to be the chaining of Pegasus. We might observe that the horse would need wings (which it has not got) to be a proper Pegasus, and that to be the Trojan horse it ought to be under the guardianship of Athena. However, let us leave the mythologists to unravel whatever legends may be woven together in this sample of the Etruscan popular tradition. What we are interested in is the inscription:

huins etule pecse seθlans

huins is connected with Albanian *hyjni*, "divinity"; *hyjnueshëm*, "divine"; *hyineshë*, "goddess'; *hyjnoj*, "to deify" (M. 164). (On the other hand, however, it might mean "well, store of water"; cf. Albanian *uje*, "water").

etule: probably an adjective *tul*, connected by the conjunction *e* to the preceding adjective *huins*; *tul* being "fine, delicate" (M. 528).

pecse is Pegasus; probably here used as an epithet, however.

seθlans: the god already mentioned.

Summing up, then: the words are an exclamation on the part of the man with the hammer; and it should be noted that the last word may be a separate item from the rest. The meaning is either:

(*a*) "(What a) divine and delicate Pegasus, (O) Sethlans!" Or

(*b*) "A divine and fine Pegasus."—Sethlans.

We shall now study a mythological scene devoted to the divine twins, Castor and Pollux, the Dioscuri. This scene has long been known, but was interpreted incorrectly until 1935, when M. F. Chapouthier established its real meaning. By elucidating the short inscription which accompanies it we shall also be corroborating that author's opinion. The scene is depicted in one of the engravings published by Gerhard,[1] and shows the Dioscuri on either side of a giant, with whom they are fighting. Over the giant's head is the inscription χaluχasu (fig. 39).

Roscher considers the character in the middle, "called χaluχasu", to be a drunken man whom Leda's two sons are either gripping or supporting. Pauly-Wissowa recalls that the brothers had a white horse and a black one, and that they symbolised day and night; but that they cannot be regarded as representing the morning star and evening

[1] *Loc. cit.*, I, Taf. LVI.

star, since the legend has it that they were inseparable. But M. Chapouthier has succeeded in proving that at a late period the Dioscuri were conceived as having vowed eternal separation and were

FIG. 39. The Dioscuri separated

thought of as being two stars, one shining by day, the other by night:[1] "When one is rising, the other is setting. . . . Our triad often took the form of the Moon between the Dioscuri . . ." (*ibid.*, p. 279).

FIG. 40. Morning star and evening star

In the illustration in M. Chapouthier's work which confirms his thesis, the Moon is to be seen separating the rising star (symbolised by a lighted torch) from the setting star, whose torch is upside down

[1] *Les Dioscures au service d'une déesse*, 1935, p. 272.

(fig. 40). The thesis acquires further corroboration from another piece of evidence, from an Etruscan source, moreover; it occurs in Gerhard's collection (III, t. CCLV). A male figure whose head is surmounted with a crescent moon is holding apart the Dioscuri, over one of whom there is a star. This clarifies the meaning of the other example from Gerhard, the scene with the supposed drunkard in the middle. In very fact, an altercation with a drunkard is involved in neither of them. The myth of the forcible separation of the two brothers, who resist in vain, was evidently well understood by the Etruscan engraver. But what is meant, in the first example, by the word χαluχasu (B)?

FIG. 41. The brothers separated

Does it designate Night, or the Moon, or Fate, or some other sublime and grandiose idea? Not a bit of it. We are on the frontier separating two worlds; behind us lies Greece, here in front of us is Etruria. Our artist is not in the least interested in lofty dramas connected with Fate, or anything of the sort; he ignores such things with royal unconcern. What he has seen and shown is a wonderful feat of strength and skill, by means of which the athlete in the middle has succeeded in neutralising the efforts of the two lusty lads who are tussling with him to no purpose. He is a wily wrestler; with his powerful arms he is executing a simultaneous double hold. The term for this feat is χaluχasu; a duplicate for this is to be found in Albanian—a duplicate, moreover, which runs through such a rich gamut of variations that it cannot be a recent addition to the language: kalikaç, kalapiç, kalakuç, kalapesh, kalaqa, all of which mean "on the back" or "pick-a-back" (M. 175,

172, 176). In all of these we can recognise *kal*, "horse" (already mentioned more than once). "On horseback"? The second part, *kaç*, means "on the back" (M. 172); however, G. Meyer relates it to Turkish "kitch, ketch" (*loc. cit.*, p. 182), "the croup" of a horse; but it is equally possible that the Etruscan syllable *kas*, in *kalukas-u*, is connected with Osco-Umbrian *kasit* (*decet*, "it is fitting or suitable"), which is Albanian *gjaset*, "it is fitting" (M. 142): "as befits a horse", "in the manner of a horse".[1]

FIG. 42. Adonis, goddesses and treasurer

The atmosphere in which we find ourselves is one of such physical health and emotional equilibrium that the empty fears of the mind can never succeed in eclipsing the purely sporting interest of any encounter.

In other scenes engraved on mirrors (and let us remember at this point that a mirror is not a moral treatise or a compendium of civil law), the artist represents the Greek divinities in a spirit of sly humour.

Gerhard's illustration CCCXXIII (Vol. IVa) shows us a magnificent bevy of Olympian beauties. These saucy young deities come before us here in a scene which almost belongs to the world of operetta—say, Offenbach's *La Belle Hélène*. Eris, Euterpa and Alpnu are competing

[1] Indeed, *gjasë*, in Albanian, is "similarity" (M. 142).

for the favours of Adonis, who is standing half-clad in the centre of the group and is evidently finding the pace a hot one.

On both sides he is being besieged with efforts to dazzle him with gems or promises. All this is too clear to require any commentary. There is only one puzzling point: the presence, at the right-hand extremity of the picture, of a highly serious gentleman, fully and soberly dressed, who needs only a large white stiff collar to become an eminently respectable person. His bare, wrinkled forehead and his whole deportment make us sure that he is hard working, meticulous and entirely reliable. With one bony forefinger he is delicately touching the shoulder-blade of the young person who is deploying such ardour and persuasiveness in her advances to Adonis. Is the confidential agent trying to remind the lady of something? Trying, perhaps, to add weight to her arguments?

We do not know. All we do know is that he is designated here as *arxate* (A).

This name, which is unknown to mythologists both ancient and modern, rather embarrassed the learned editor of the collection. He muttered something about Arkas, who flourished long ago in Arcady. However, since *arca*, in Latin, meant "coffin", among other things, the author was somewhat inclined to regard the intruder as "a dweller in the realms of the dead".

Hades is a god who has sometimes had to suffer when Etruscology has been in difficulties. Meanwhile, in this picture in general and the behaviour of the serious gentleman in particular, it is not easy to discern anything at all macabre. For, to put it briefly, this special point allows Mann's dictionary to perform yet another of its miracles and to transport us from the gloom of Hades to the hilarious world of Offenbach. *Arkë*, in Albanian as in Latin, also means "cash-box, safe, treasury". *Arktar* is "treasurer, cashier", forming a parallel to Latin *arcarius*. The ending -*te*, in Albanian, can sometimes mean "pertaining to"; thus from *thekër*, "grain (wheat, etc.)", is derived the adjective *thekërte*, "of grain, in grain, pertaining to grain" (Albanian–Russian dictionary, 419; M. 533).

So the enigmatic character in this mirror-engraving of ours is a treasurer; probably a freedman promoted to that office; and being well aware of the resources available in cash and in kind, he is always ready to provide such information as may hasten the conclusion of a deal.

Is *arxate* a Latinism which made its way into Etruscan? Was it a noun common to both languages? Did it originally denote any and every coffer, hollowed out of the trunk of a tree and provided with a *vaulted* lid, as well as denoting a *vault* or arch in general, as *arcus* did in Latin? We must not forget that the vault was an Etruscan innovation.

But such problems as these go beyond the purely pragmatic intentions of this book; they are not in my field.

We shall now examine an excellent series of four texts, all of which turn upon one and the same word. The sense of that word will thus be elucidated and confirmed beyond any possibility of doubt.

The first three of these texts are all devoted to Bacchus. Here, for a start, is a tiny inscription which is written across the hair of a Bacchante and which Gerhard [1] declares to be illegible, but which can

FIG. 43. Bacchantes and satyr

nevertheless be read as the word *iθnin* (A) (fig. 43). This word, which is characteristic of the whole group, is perfectly in tune with the picture in which it is incorporated. In Albanian it presents the following gamut:

> *idhun*, "bitter"
> *idhnak*, "irascible, choleric"
> *idherim*, "anger, bitterness"
> *idhnoj* ⎫
> *idheroj* ⎭ "to vex", etc.   (M. 165)

"Angry", then, or "irascible", is the word with which this Bacchante is labelled; the very word which denotes the sacred rage in which the devotees of Bacchus executed their dances.

[1] *Loc. cit.*, I, fig. XLII, 5.

The second inscription refers to a scene illustrated in Gerhard (LXXXV), who describes the central portion of it (fig. 44) thus:

Bacchus, walking unsteadily, is apparently supported . . . by Ariadne. . . . Eros, accompanying the god, turns towards Bacchus, raising his arms and looking heavenward as if to execrate this divine intoxication, which was a rare but not unfamiliar phenomenon.

(Vol. III, p. 89)

FIG. 44. Bacchus drunk

The inscription is *itχrani* (A) (or *itχrui*?), a word which is quite clearly related to the verb *idheroj* and cannot mean other than "anger", "indignation" or "indignant". If you open F. Cordignano's little manual of the Albanian language at p. 246 you will find: "Mos m'u *idhno* per ket punë", "Don't get *angry* about this." An *n* has been added to the root *idh* exactly as, in the noun *cemnac*, it was added to the root *gjem*, *gëm*, "to thunder".

The third of our inscriptions is part of the only known Etruscan text of any length other than the Book of the Mummy: the Tile of Capua, of which only some thirty lines have survived. This document, like the others, is concerned with religious ceremonial. For the moment let us consider only two words of it: (P. 2) *faca iχnak* (line 5) (A), which means, of course, "Bacchus the wrathful", *iχnak* being an exact repro-

FIG. 45. Hercules at the breast

duction of *idhnak* (see above), with the same termination denoting habit or provenance as in the words *cemnac, romaχ*, etc., which have been studied already.

For the fourth and last text in this group we return to the mirror-engravings. This time another wrathful character is brought before us: Hercules. In Gerhard, p. 60 (Vol. V), we see Hercules thirsty and apparently preferring a healthy and economical milk diet to all the masterpieces of Etruscan cooking. Juno is giving the breast to this mature and surprising "infant", while in the background several of her Olympian colleagues, taking no notice, continue their worldly conversation (fig. 45).

Perhaps these deities were not very particular about strict accuracy in matters of Greek mythology. Hercules, at any rate, is usually known as Alcmena's son, not Juno's. Gerhard writes:

> It is most surprising . . . to find Hercules described in our description as the son of Juno. The only writer who alludes to his being so is Ptolemy Chennus. . . . The contradiction between this assertion and the whole drift of the myth of Hercules is too great for us to renounce, on the sole authority of the fraudulent Ptolemy, the Greek tradition in the matter. We can only surmise that what we have here is an Etruscan tradition.
>
> (*Loc. cit.*, p. 73)

Finally, M. Buffa (no. 288) mentions that, according to a legend recorded by Diodorus Siculus, Juno once gave suck to the infant Hercules. In Etruria there used to be a fine group by a Greek sculptor, which is now preserved in the Vatican and which represents this very scene (Victor Duruy, *Histoire des Romains*, p. 75). An Etruscan engraver could have inferred from this that Juno was the demi-god's mother. The text I shall now quote has been studied successively, but unsuccessfully, by Körte, Tropp, Trombetti, Goldmann, Lattes, Menicucci, Buonamici and Ducati. Trombetti took the word θra to mean "milk"; M. Buffa was wrong in rejecting this stroke of intuition.

Here is the text:

(P. 399) *ecasren tva iχnac hercle unial clan θra sce*

eca: "here is", etc. Cf. archaic Latin *ecca* (as distinct from the later *ecce*).

sren: a difficult word. It has an Albanian replica: *shëroj*, "to heal, cure" (M. 474), whence *sherim*, "remedy"; but G. Meyer thinks, questionably perhaps, that the root is from Latin *sanare*.

Another possibility is Albanian *rënje*, "prostration", with an initial negative *s*, hence equivalent to "putting an end to fatigue", "refreshing oneself". There is an analogy for this in Albanian: *lodh*, "to tire, fatigue" (M. 249), and *shlodh*, "to relax, repose" (M. 486).

tva is simply *dua*, from the Albanian verb *due*, "to like, want" (M. 85). G. Meyer's opinion that this verb was derived from Latin *debere*, "to owe, ought", is no obstacle; for there is a separate verb in

Albanian for this, namely *duaj*; besides, there were words which were common to both languages.

iχnac (A): "irascible, wrathful".

hercle unial clan: "Hercules, of Juno son".

θra (A) cannot mean anything but milk—for this reason for a start, that the next word means "was sucking" or "sucks". *θra*, with the definite article, occurs in the Book of the Mummy in the form *trau*: *pevaχ vinum trau pruχs*, in which the first and second words are "beer" and "wine" and the fourth denotes a vase (IV, 22); and again, *vinum trau prucuna* (IX, g, 1). And if, in Albanian, *tra* is the lees of melted butter, as we have seen, we can at least feel glad that it refers to a lactic product. But it is also possible that the word *θra* comes not from Illyrian but from Thracian, especially if (as may well be the case) it was pronounced *dzra*. I am prompted to say this by a Macedo-Rumanian word: *dzar* (*dzaer*), "whey", which Pascu includes among the Thracian terms inherited by Macedo-Rumanian[1] (cf. *zerum, Lat. *serum*).

sce (A): this little world solves a number of problems and reminds us anew of the place occupied by Etruscan among the languages of antiquity. We find this Illyrian word almost unchanged in neo-Illyrian, that is to say Albanian: *thith*, "to suck" (M. 535). The same onomatopoeia is obviously present in Latin *suxit*, Lithuanian *zisti*, Russian *sosati* and Serbian *sisati*, etc. It would be ridiculous to look for a borrowing where there is only a single, common, very ancient source. Thus the word *sce* proves that the Etruscans sucked in their Indo-Europeanism with their mothers' milk!

The translation, if we keep the word-order of the original, is:

"Here is to restore himself likes wrathful Hercules: milk (he) sucks."

In other words:

"Here is how wrathful Hercules likes restoring himself: he sucks milk."

It should be remarked that at the same period, in the comedies of Aristophanes, Hercules is presented as a comic character and a glutton.

On the other hand, a hypothesis has been put forward that Hercules is portrayed here being ritually adopted by the Olympian gods. But in that event the word *tva*, for example, remains unexplained.

There is a further alternative for consideration. It is thought that our Hercules sucked Juno's milk to become immortal. Now the Albanian verb *renë* (the infinitive of *bie*), "to fall; to strike", has a

[1] *Dict. étymologique macédo-roumain*, 1925, p. 16.

further meaning: "to wane" (of the moon) (M. 28). If the Etruscans used *renë* to express the idea of "dying" the negative form *s-ren* might correspond to our *immortality*. In which case our inscription runs: "Here is how wrathful Hercules wished (to obtain) immortality: by sucking milk."

On this occasion we must be allowed to draw a conclusion. Consider how clear is the testimony contributed by these four texts containing the same radical, *idhn*; how coherent it is from the grammatical point of view (as is confirmed by the suffix *-ak*); and, finally, the information conveyed so unequivocally by the drawings which the inscriptions accompany (for, in fact, what is expressed by those arms, raised at the sight of Bacchus drunk, if not the displeasure, indignation, anger and bitterness which are so well attested by the corresponding term in Albanian)? We can say without exaggeration that, where decipherment is concerned, these four texts are as valuable as a bilingual inscription—even so explicit a bilingual inscription as the famous Rosetta Stone. Those who have lamented the relative absence of Etruscan bilinguals have simply failed to observe what resources were at their disposition, in the form of Etruscan epigraphy and the Albanian language.

The prestige of Hercules will not be much enhanced by the next scene we shall consider, which is Table 88, I, in Vol. V of Gerhard's collection. Its inscription, which is very legible, is of great interest from the point of view of Etruscan syntax. In it we shall see a sentence-construction in which the object comes at the beginning and the subject at the end, which is common in the *Eastern* European languages of our own day.

The picture (fig. 46) portrays a group in which Hercules, who can be recognised by his club, is listening to Peleus holding forth. Now Peleus was a person of consequence: grandson of Zeus, husband of the goddess Thetis, brother of Telamon, who was a great friend of Hercules, and so on. So there is nothing strange in his appearing in the company of Hercules. But what does the inscription say?

slia hercle puris pele (A)

Gerhard wondered whether *slia* might not be a vestige of the name of the fair Penthesilea, that Amazonian queen who took part in the Trojan War.

Once again we shall resist the fatal preference of Etruscan studies for proper names; we shall not disturb the shade of the fair Amazon, especially since, even without her help, this little text unveils before us certain perspectives which lead into the far distance and are not less ancient than the Trojan War.

FIG. 46. Peleus telling stories

Its deciphering is as follows:

slia: here I recognise the Albanian verb *shllíj*, "to salt", from which are derived the adjectives *shllimë* and *shllishëm*, "salted, pickled", etc. (M. 487) (with the additional meaning of "spicy, piquant", naturally). Thus we have here the archaic Indo-European root *sal, sol*, "salt".

puris is reproduced exactly in Albanian *purris*, "to poke (a fire)" (M. 409), which we saw earlier and connected with the functions of the *prytanis*, originally the guardian of the fire.

Thus the whole becomes clear. If we wanted to keep the word-order of the Etruscan sentence we should get:

"(With) salty things Hercules stirs up Peleus."

But, evidently, the word *slia* must be understood in the ablative and Hercules in the accusative, which would be easy enough to render in Latin and in the languages of the *satem* group. In English the sentence becomes:

"Peleus excites Hercules with salacities."

But what about those perspectives which were to "lead into the far distance"?

We have been discussing *slia*, that so-called "Indo-European implantation" in the Etruscan language, which is certainly implanted pretty firmly in your own kitchen. You can ask our imaginary Albanian restaurant-proprietor for some *shli*. He will not bring you salt (for which there is a different name in present-day Albanian), but there is a good chance of your getting some salted gherkins.

However, G. Meyer stands right across my path, telling us curtly that Albanian *shëllij* derives from Latin *salire*, "to salt".

The situation would be a tricky one were it not for the figure of Professor H. D. F. Kitto on the horizon, with his study *The Greeks* (Penguin Books, 1951).

He has something instructive to tell us about the Greeks' name for the sea: *thalassa*. The word was not of Greek origin; it came from the language of the indigenous population, whom the ancestors of the Greeks, arriving on the sea-shore for the first time, asked in astonishment, "What's that?" In the language of the natives, *thalassa* meant "brine", "salty water". The word can be instantly recognised in, for example, Albanian *shëllishëm*, "briny, saline" (M. 473).

These natives were of the stock called "Pelasgic", which was related to the Illyrian stock. It can be seen that neither of these peoples had any need to wait until the emergence of the Latins to borrow the word *salire*. They had been familiar with this "salt water" for a very long time, for the brine of the spacious Mediterranean had carried them as far as Crete, Egypt and Palestine several centuries before the foundation of Rome.

The foregoing observations do not mean that we wish to deny the frequency with which proper nouns figure in the Etruscan texts. Here, for example, is a mythological scene in which every word is a proper noun. The interest of this mirror-engraving is twofold: first, two of the names are enigmatic; second, it poses an interesting problem, that of the Etruscan theatre.

The scene (which is reproduced by Gerhard, CCCLXXVIII; Vol. IVa) takes us back again to *La Belle Hélène*; it is executed with the maximum Etruscan sparkle. Six characters appear in it, but names

ABOVE: Votive statuette of Apollo-Svulare.
OVERLEAF: Alcestis and Admetus: fulfilment of a vow,

The *tanasar* chanting the praises of the deceased. Tomb of the
Augurs. Tarquinia,

are inscribed over the heads of only five of them: Tevcrun, Irisis, Crisiθa, Menle, Turan (fig. 47).

Gerhard identified the scene as "Menelaus before his departure for Crete". King Menelaus is Menle in the inscription; Turan is Aphrodite; Paris, a handsome young man holding a lance, is Tevcrun, after his people, the Teucri. The names Irisis and Crisiθa remain enigmatic. As Paris and Menelaus appear together, the occasion must be that of

FIG. 47. "La Belle Hélène"

their first meeting. To reward the prince from Troy for her golden apple, Aphrodite has just brought him to Menelaus's palace in Sparta, where the latter's wife, the most beautiful woman in Greece, will be delivered into his hands. Helen is therefore to be identified in the young woman who seems to be trying to restrain Menelaus at the very moment when, as naked as the day he was born, he is addressing the goddess. Perhaps he is telling her how very sorry he is to have to abandon his distinguished guest for the time being because of urgent business elsewhere. Helen seems to be emphasising the inconvenience of his going away, so as to saddle him with the responsibility for everything which is going to happen. The comedy of the situation lies in the glance exchanged between Venus and Paris; it is as if they were saying, "What a bit of luck!" They are as thick as thieves and the understanding between them is perfect. These are true pantomime effects, which must have given great pleasure to their Etruscan beholders.

In parenthesis, be it said that the name Crisiθa reminded Gerhard of *chryse*, "the golden", a stock epithet for Aphrodite; but no such epithet is associated with Helen. It might be Chryseia, one of the daughters of Thetis.

Now, it seems that I was not alone in supposing that the theatrical art of the Etruscans might well be reflected in their decorative art. Speaking of the beautiful Etruscan krater with a spiral decoration, on which the farewell of Alcestis and her husband Admetus is painted, Professor Beazley observes:

> Lesky and L. Weber think that the picture records an earlier, simpler version of the story than the Euripidean. . . .
> [Certain details] had caused Giglioli to ponder . . . whether the whole picture may not have been inspired by an Etruscan dramatic performance. Surely not.
>
> (*Etruscan Vase Painting*, p. 134)

For my own part, and pending fuller information, I incline towards the opinion of one of the fathers of Etruscan studies, Antonio Gori.

FIG. 48. Etruscan stage

In 1737, at Florence, that author published a collection of drawings engraved on Etruscan mirrors, under the title *Museum Etruscum*. He reproduces three of them in his Plate CLXXXVI with the legend: *Histriones mimi. Etruscae scaene*. A glance at one of these leaves no doubt that it does portray a theatrical scene. Though the drawing is sketchy, we can distinguish an elegant, stylised stage setting and two characters without masks or cothurni, who seem to be gesticulating as in a panto-mime (fig. 48).

The mocking humour often manifested by Etruscan artists, in the treatment of mythological subjects, sometimes breaks into caricature. Evidence of this will be found in t. 104, 2, in Vol. V of Gerhard (fig. 49). The picture shows us a hero, of low and disreputable

FIG. 49. Etruscan caricature

appearance, in the company of three women who are slightly more decent. Perhaps it represents the judgment of Paris? Gerhard says:

This picture gives an impression of thoroughgoing parody. . . . The young man is unclothing himself in a thoroughly indecent manner. . . . The artist is visibly allowing himself to ridicule, not a myth, but some image which was beyond his comprehension.

(p. 136)

I suppose just the opposite: I think the Etruscan artist was very much alive to the incongruity of some of the classical stories, and that the good sense of him and his colleagues sometimes inclined them to sarcasm; especially in a late epoch, when they had been drawn into the world of Roman indifference and the last remains of ancient piety were in a state of dissolution.

This does not mean that these artists were necessarily cynics. The mythological scene with which we shall close this chapter demonstrates that they were capable of loving the poetry which is inherent in so many of the Greek myths. In Table CXI (Vol. V) of Gerhard we see Apollo, who can be recognised by his lyre and a swan, protecting the love of Turan (Venus) and Adonis (fig. 50). Adonis spends six months of every year in the Underworld; it is clear that Apollo's role in this scene is a decisive one, since it is only in spring, when the sun begins to resume

FIG. 50. Apollo's consent

its sway, that Turan can take Adonis to her arms. Beside Apollo can be read the word *pultisph* (A). This is Albanian *poltis*, "to accept, consent" (M. 394). The *ph* at the end can be identified with the Albanian preposition *mbë*, "in", contracted to *bh*. The meaning is thus "In agreement". The lovers' meeting was made secure by Apollo's consent.

Once again, we note that the preposition comes at the end; it is a postposition.

SOME GENERAL TERMS OF ETRUSCAN RELIGION

LET us begin with three glosses. Every religion essentially consists of certain *ceremonies* (A). M. Ernout writes:

> The Latin word *caerimonia* with its strange diphthong *ae*, a word which neither Latins nor moderns have succeeded in explaining properly, may well have derived from an Etruscan word *caerimo* (cf. *lucumonius* from *lucumon*; Populonia; etc. . . .). And we ought perhaps to regard it as the prototype of the Latin formations in *-monia*, *-monium*, and to infer that such formations made their way first into religious language (*castimonia, matrimonium*) or technical language (*testimonium . . . patrimonium*).
>
> (Loc. cit., p. 40)

This *caerimo*, of which M. Ernout had a presentiment, receives undeniable confirmation in Albanian, in the verb *kremtoj*, "to celebrate", whence *kreme*, "holiday", and *kremtim*, "festivity" (M. 214). Jokl studied this verb and found parallels for it in Sanskrit, Old Slavonic and even Old Icelandic, always with the meaning "to glorify" (*loc. cit.*, p. 40). To which we must add that Hittite *karimmi* means "temple".

Let us turn our attention to another of these inherited words, drawn from the same list: *silicernium*, a meal which was a feature of funeral rites (and consisted of salt, lentils, eggs, etc.). M. Ernout presents it as "another of the desperate cases of Indo-European etymology".

Well, this is a lost cause which can be saved. Looked at from the Albano-Illyrian point of view, *silicernium* (A) falls into two parts:

sillë: "mid-day meal, lunch" (M. 450).
qerm: "edge, outside" (M. 415).

It was therefore "a meal (eaten) on the edge"—at once at the graveside and at the border of the next world; a meal eaten near the tomb, in honour of the deceased. It was also a meal eaten "outside"; for Etruscan tombs were outside the town, the cemetery being some distance from the city walls; at Tarquinii it was on the nearby hill of Monterosi; at Caere, more than a mile from the city walls; and so on.

As for the third word, it occurs in the title of certain of the Etruscan sacred books, Libri *Bacchetidis* (B). O. Müller identifies them with the *libri fulgurales* attributed to a legendary Etruscan nymph, Begoë, whose name, in his conjecture, was subsequently Hellenised to Bacchetis.

In *Bacchetidis*, however, can be recognised the Albanian common noun (obsolete, moreover, be it noted!), *bagëti*, "cattle, livestock" (M. 17). Jokl places this word in the "inherited" category and connects it with Sanskrit *bhaga*, "goods". I think therefore that these books were concerned with animals suitable respectively for sacrifice in various circumstances. A sacrifice of this kind had to be carried out in a place which had been struck by lightning; it is thus possible that the books which specified such animals were related to the *libri fulgurales*.

It is disturbing to find a chthonic goddess with the name of *Bacchetis*. Such is the inscription in Latin characters under a statuette representing a goddess (or priestess) holding two snakes in her hands (Gori, *Museum Etruscum*, I, Tab. XIII, III). But this piece of evidence is of late period.

We pass now to religious terms preserved in Etruscan sources, as distinct from glosses. One of the ceremonies most frequently mentioned in LM (the Book of the Mummy, often known as the *Liber Linteus*, the Book of Linen), and also on the Tile of Capua, is *vacl* (A), *vacil*.

In his *Elementi di lingua etrusca* (1936, p. 90), M. Pallottino reviews the meanings which have been successively proposed for this word: invocation (Torp, Trombetti), augury (Ribezzo), offering (Goldmann, Corssen), etc.; and he emphasised the fact that *vacl* is found in directions for the rituals connected with different deities: *vacl* in honour of θesan (the Dawn), *vacl* of the god Veltha, and that of Culśu and so on. The writer concludes by defining *vacl* as a sacred act, perhaps "libation". My own conclusion is that this is close to the truth, but that *vacl* represents a wider conception than this. The deities' names do not enable us to solve the problem, because a variety of things can be offered to a deity. In deciphering the word I have been guided by a different association: *vacl lunasie* (A) in the text of the Tile of Capua (P. 2, 5), in which I have no hesitation in recognising the Albanian noun *lojna*, "game; sports event" (M. 250). *lunasie* therefore means "games" or "followed by games"; the termination -*sie* corresponds directly to Albanian -*sh*, the ending of the genitive and ablative plural (thus, *nji sasi librash*, "a quantity of books", Mann, Grammar, 57).

It is immediately apparent that the suggestions quoted above for *vacl*: invocation, augury, libation, genuflexion (which has also been put forward), do not fit with *lunasie* in such a way as to make a stock formula out of the two words. Against this, we know that there were often *funeral banquets followed by games*, gladiatorial contests and so on, as described by Homer and portrayed in the Etruscan frescos. Poulsen mentions, for example, the singing, dancing, athletic games, horse-races and regattas which took place during royal funerals in Cyprus, in the 4th century B.C.

Now this same notion of *banquet* or *meal* comes up in Albanian in the form of *vagjëtoj*, "to feed carefully", with a modern derivative, *vagjët*, "diet" (M. 543). Thus *vacl* seems to correspond to the Greek *symposion*. But a meal at what time of day?

In order to answer this question and at the same time to define the etymology of *vacl* more closely, we must make a choice between two possible paths: one which leads by way of Lithuanian, the other by Albanian. The first points to an evening meal; the second, to a banquet held during daytime. In Lithuanian we find the word *vakariene*, "to have supper", derived from *vakaras*, "evening". In this we recognise *vetcher*, *vetchor*, "evening", in all the Slavonic languages, *vetchera*, "to sup", and so on.

Obviously, this fits very well with the fact that the main meal among the Romans was dinner or supper and that, in the Etruscan frescos, we see the banqueting tables lit up with candelabra.[1]

However, two considerations militate in favour of a banquet held earlier, in the daytime:

(a) the fact that *lunasie*, the athletic contests and races, could have taken place only in daylight;

(b) the Albanian word *vagul*, "daybreak" (M. 543): but also morning, for I find it in the Translation of St John: *mbë të* vaguluarët *erdi përsëri ndë hjeroret*, "And early in the morning he came again into the temple" (viii. 2).

Obviously, an "early morning meal" could in time have come to mean simply a "meal taken at some time during the morning", just as the French *déjeuner* [lunch; literally, "breaking one's fast"] does not mean that one fasts until midday; and as a theatrical matinée, literally and originally a morning performance, now takes place in the afternoon. Besides, the time of a solemn *vacl* held in honour of the deities and the dead may well have been different from that of an ordinary banquet. In any case, a banquet is what the word denotes.

Finally, it is possible that the connection between *vacl* and eating is corroborated by another association of words which occurs frequently

[1] It is true that the interior of the Etruscan house, as of the Roman house, did not admit a large amount of daylight.

in LM: *vacl araś*. It is true that there is an Etruscan verb *ar*, "to make, to do"; we have already mentioned one of its past tenses, *arce*. Is *araś* perhaps an optative, "may you make!"? I can only repeat, in passing, that *araś* might also be a genitive from the noun *ara*, "altar", a word which we have seen already and which may have been an Etruscan as well as a Latin word. In this case *vacl araś* would be "a banquet at an altar", in conformity with the following observation of Fustel de Coulanges:

> *The eating of a meal prepared on an altar* was, to all appearances, the first form ever given by mankind to the act of worship [our italics].
>
> (*La Cité Antique*, p. 179)

We have now found ourselves confronting another important religious term: *ara*. Here is an archaeological document which may help to elucidate this word for us: a drawing published by S. Reinach in his *Répertoire des vases peints grecs et étrusques* [*Repertory of Greek and Etruscan Painted Vases*], I, 1899, p. 276. (Fig. 51) (fragment).

The learned author comments thus on the part of the scene which concerns us here:

> Purification of Orestes at Delphi; on the right, Apollo holding a branch, a cup and two laurel leaves. . . . The inscription on the altar at which Orestes has taken sanctuary appears to be apocryphal. . . .

This inscription is: *ceaarvc*. Is it necessarily apocryphal?

Against the menacing upraised forefinger of the great archaeologist I have but one shield: M. Buffa's remark about an inscription which was suspect *because* no one could understand it.

ceaarvc is no more absurd than any other Etruscan word. If it has not the transcendent clarity of *ip siune* or *miiś meθumfs* or *krankru*, its general meaning is in no way dubious and leaves me hesitant only about certain details. I reason as follows:

(a) *ceaarvc* is *ceaaruc*.

(b) *ceaaruc* is *cea aru* + *c*.

(c) *cea* is exactly the same as *cea* in *cea sutve*, which is part of an inscription on a funerary urn P. 758, CII 2596, an inscription which is perfectly comprehensible and which we shall be meeting later on. The two words mean "this tomb"; so *cea* is "this".

Failing this, I would have thought of *ceia* (LM, ch. VII) which seems to mean "Call!", but that is too abstract for the present context.

aru is the main item which concerns us here: *ar*, "altar", with the
article.

c usually means the conjunction "and"; but might be a demonstrative pronoun, or the word "also".

The meaning of the sentence is therefore not, "I appeal to this
altar" but, rather, "This *too* is an altar." The reason for the words is
the fact that the altar was a place of refuge and that Orestes, having

FIG. 51. Orestes at an altar

killed his mother, is being relentlessly pursued by the Erinnyes, the
avenging Furies. To cling to the altar of the temple of Delphi therefore
represented his last chance of survival. That is why, as Aeschylus tells
the story, Orestes sat down there beside a sacred round stone. He
hastens to legalise his position with a formal declaration: "I am beside
an altar and no one may touch me."

A similar adventure also befell Paris, Priam's son. On his return to
Troy he was not recognised by his brothers, who were on the point of
running him through; he succeeded in escaping only by fleeing to the
altar of Zeus.

Let us add that the altar shown in Reinach's illustration is not
round. The Etruscan artist had not read his Aeschylus!

From the conception of an altar we pass to that of fire, that sacred
element which, as we have seen, was the dwelling of the family genius.
An altar is essentially "a place of fire". There are two reasons for

supposing that in Etruscan these two ideas, "fire" and "altar", were
expressed by the same root: *ar*, "fire", and *ara*, "altar":

(1) In a bilingual (Etrusco-Latin) inscription there occurs the word
ar, which in that context seems to us to be equivalent to "red", that is
to say "fiery, of the colour of fire":

(P. 545, CIE 3023) *aθ unata varnal ar* (B)

Mn Otacilius Rufus Varia natus

According to Deecke:[1]

aθ is Arnth. But in the translation this Etruscan name is replaced by
a Latin one, Manius.

unata is rendered (for no visible reason) as Otacilius.

varnal is translated exactly, as "born of Varia".

ar is the only Etruscan word in the inscription to which the Latin
name (or cognomen) Rufus can correspond. And Rufus means
"red, reddish, red-headed". On this topic Deecke plunges into a
sea of conjectures. For my own part I see no other solution than
to translate *ar* as "red".

(2) According to Festus, a Latin writer of the 2nd or 3rd century of
our era, an Etruscan expression, *arseuerse*, meant "to avert fire, to turn
fire aside". Festus explains *arse* as "to turn aside" and *uerse* as "fire".
This interpretation probably springs from a long-standing confusion.
I believe the two words should be explained just the other way round:
arse is "fire" and *uerse* (*verse*) is "turn aside". Here are my reasons:

(*a*) The root *vert, vers*, "to turn", is part of the very basis of the Indo-
European languages. We find it not only in Latin (*verso*, "to turn
round", and *verto*, "to turn, turn something aside") and Slavonic
(*verteti*) but even as early as among the Indo-Iranians of the 18th
century B.C., whose instructors in the handling of war-chariots in the
country of the Mitanni used the term *teravartanna* for a "triple turn".
Vartanna is *verto*.

(*b*) There is an absolutely explicit pointer in Osco-Umbrian *uersus* [2]
and Latin *versura*, "place where the plough is turned at the end of a
furrow".

Thus, indications press in on us from all sides that *uerse* is "turn" and
nothing else. Consequently, *arse* cannot be other than "fire", *ar*. The
ending *-se* must be attributed to Etruscan *ś*, an oblique-case termination.

Written on house-doors, the phrase in question was meant to protect
houses against fire (Paoli, *loc. cit.*, 398).

---

[1] *Etr. Forsch. und Stud.*, V, 1883, p. 105.

[2] R. von Planta, *Grammatik der osk.-umbr. Dialekte*, 1897, p. 590.

What do we know about Etruscan sacrifices:

Here let us appeal to the Magliano strip, on which we found the word χimθ "hundred". One of the periodical sacrifices which it enjoins is the offering to be made four times a year (*IV avils*) to the goddess Mlaxθanra: (P. 359b, CIE 5237) *menicac marcalurcac*.

Let us begin with the second term, which can be explained as follows:

marca (A) is Albanian *maraq* "fennel" (M. 263).

lur (A) is Albanian *lyrë*, "fat, grease" (M. 254).

ca an important little word: Albanian *ca* (tza), "a little"(?).

What is set before us here is a refined (or perhaps not so refined) dish which was much appreciated in ancient temples: *marcalurcac* (B) is "fat with a little fennel". So we are sure of getting our vitamins.

This interpretation of *lur* appears, moreover to be confirmed by an epitaph: the inscription on the sarcophagus of Larθ Aleθnas, P. 172, CII 2058, which ends with the words *luri miace* (see C. Battisti, *Studi Etruschi*, VII, p. 495). They indicate the periodical offerings which are due to the shade.

We interpret *luri* as "fat". *miace* is in effect something we have seen already, the "contract for the supply of meat", in the chapter on the Market. *mish, mase, miace* corresponds perfectly to *miaso* in modern Slavonic languages. *Luri miace*, "fat (and) meat".

Finally, another mention of fat, or a fat animal, to be sacrificed to Tinia, occurs on the Magliano strip, P. 359b, in the form *lursθ*.

menicac appears to be a harder case. The root involved is possibly the same as in the word *menaχe*, which is found as an inscription on many offerings. Thus on the statuette of a child, which was presented to θuflθaś, are written the words *alpan menaχe* (P. 652, CIE 446). *alpan* has been interpreted as "gift, offering"; the second word can therefore perhaps be regarded as an epithet. According to inscription P. 447, a citizeness named θa(na) Cencnei presented to the same deity the statuette of a goddess (or a woman) on which is inscribed the short supplication already examined (p. 77), *śuv luśi* ("look thou on my prayer"), ending with this expression, *menaχzi*. Can we connect the element *menaχ* with Albanian *mënoj*, "to put off, adjourn" (M. 281)? *zi*, which we have seen already, is "black; wretchedness, misfortune, evil". *menaχzi* would thus be an exhortation: "Avert evil!" The first word of inscription P. 359b, *menica(c)*, therefore meant "averting evil" (it may be added that the Etruscans had a strong belief in the possibility of postponing evil, "putting off the evil day" as the English expression goes, by means of religious practices); in other words, one offered fat mixed with fennel as a propitiatory sacrifice to Mlaxθanra. G. Meyer, however, connects *mĕnoj* with Latin *manere*, "to wait". Ought we to regard it as a borrowing from Latin; or rather, perhaps, interpret *mena(χ)* by means of the Indo-European root *men*, "less", to give the sense of "to lessen, diminish"? The question remains open.

On the conjectural level, another favourite dish of the Etruscan deities may be mentioned. In the *vacil* (which is the older form of *vacl* and corresponds still better to Albanian *vagjel*) of the Tile of Capua, there is a mention of *tule apirase* (P. 2, 13). *tule* is probably Albanian *tul*, "tender". For the meaning of *apirase* we can inquire of Deecke, who quotes a short Etrusco-Latin inscription from a charnel-house.[1] In this text there is an Etruscan name, *hapirnal* (from *hapirna*), which is rendered in the Latin as *nigri* (P. 455, CIE 272). Thus hapirna was "black" (masculine or feminine). *hapir* will be equivalent to *apir*, initial *h* being secondary in Etruscan (cf. *hercle* and *ercle*, etc.). So *tule apirase* would be "tender black lambs".

As for other sacrificial animals, let us take note of just one more, for the moment; but a weighty one this time, the bull. We have met him already: *tur, turinu* (*pelθurinu*). But he also appears on the Cippus of Perugia, under a much less perspicuous name. In my estimation he is disguised there in a disquieting group of words: *intemamer* (P. 570, l. 18).

It is generally agreed that the inscription on the Cippus, to which we have often referred in this book, is a kind of contract between two families, the Afuna and the Velθina, mentioning an apportioning of lands and a funeral vault (*spel-*) which appears to constitute a common burial-place.

It has been noticed that names of gods do not figure in the inscription. Nevertheless, such words as *θaura* ("tomb"), *araś* ("altar"?) and *θunxulθe* (*θun*, "house; funerary edifice") point to an ancestor-cult. There were periodical ceremonies to be carried out there.[2]

What was afoot? My mind prowled round this group *intemamer*, a collection of sounds as haughty as the name of a Pharaoh or a first-class hotel. It disconcerted me to such an extent that I did not even dare to detach the particle *in*, well known though it was ("this", as adjective or pronoun). *intemamer* seemed to me like a sort of stone

---

[1] *Etr. Forsch. und Stud. Die Etr. Bilinguen*, p. 52.

[2] In Ch. XII we shall see the survival of ancestor-worship among the Albanians. At this juncture we may quote L. Heuzey: "One Sunday morning, as I was travelling through a Christian canton of Albania, I was astonished to meet on the path some women who were going to the church, carrying on their heads baskets in which were a jug of wine, bread, and different kinds of food: I was told that this was a meal for the dead and that they were going to spread it round in the cemetery, beside the tombs of their relations" (*Le sanctuaire de Bacchus*, p. 11).

obelisk, smooth and dumb, round which I could walk as long as I pleased without eliciting any sign of a reaction.

But, one day, I happened to read the Albanian translation of the Book of Job, a present from Professor S. E. Mann. I found a striking verse:

merrni tashi (per vetëhenët' uaj) shtatë dêma

"Therefore take unto you now seven bullocks . . ." (xlii. 8)

These words began to slide round and arrange themselves in different ways in my mind as if in a kaleidoscope:

"Take . . . bulls"
merrni . . . dema
dêma . . . merrni
tema . . . mer
in tema . . . mer
"Take these bulls!"

The obelisk melted, and in its place appeared three words whose engaging simplicity would recommend them to any beginner in Etruscan studies. *Dêm(a)* was in fact "bull" in Albanian (M. 70); *mar* was *marr* (imperative: *merr*), "to take" (M. 264). Chance willed that the two words of my enigma should be found embedded in a command to proceed to a sacrifice, a command figuring in the Book of Job, that optimist in spite of himself.

But, I wondered, what was this isolated sacrifice doing here, among the clauses of a contract? Why do we not see the verbs *raχ* or *ziχ*, to "smite" or "slaughter", which are usually found keeping company with the names of animals to be killed? If there is a sacrifice where is *vacl*, "banquet"? For one thing is certain: when they paid a visit to the ancestors the Etruscans were not in the habit of coming home hungry. They had no liking for palavers unaccompanied by refreshments. Indeed, they showed considerable perseverance in the way they persisted in fortifying their constitutions against the vagaries of the climate, the unfriendly attitude of the Romans, the piracy of the Sicilians, the commercial competition of the Carthaginians and their wives' expensive taste in Oriental jewellery.

Was there no mention of a banquet at all? Still, the banquet's nodal point, the place where libations were poured, was indicated: *tularu*, the stone which might mark either a tomb or the boundary of consecrated ground. In line 8 there is the expression, *epl tularu . . .*

epl . . . When all is said and done, this may, perhaps, take us back to the Latin *epulum*, "religious feast"; *epulum*, in reference to which my

Latin dictionary by Smith and Hall (1910) admits "Etymology
unknown".

Daremberg describes it as a public meal at which a libation was
poured to a god. In the Odyssey the people of Pylos ate in groups, at
an *epulum*; each group had sacrificed nine *bulls* . . . *Dêma!* . . . Ritual
meals; everyone dressed in white; meat roasted over the open fire——

Now, an *epulum* took place on various occasions, and in particular at
funerals, when the whole town participated. So there we are!

The etymology of the noun in question [1] is probably explained by
the ubiquitous root *ep*, "to give". As will be seen, the sentence *clen
θunχulθe falaś χiem* (lines 12–13) seems to indicate the place where the
banquet will be held:

clen: "to be" (cf. Albanian *klenë*).
θunχulθe: *θun*, "house"; *χul* is Albanian *ngul*, "to establish, set up";
    θunχul, "mausoleum"; *θe*, "in". *θunχulθe*, "in the mausoleum".
falaś: from Albanian *balle*, "front": "in front of".
χiem: cf. the Albanian verb *hyj*, "to enter" (M. 164); "the entrance"?

Thus: "To be—in the mausoleum—in front of—entrance."

In other words: "To take place in the mausoleum, facing the
entrance."

This legal text from Perugia is beginning to lose its dryness. The
Afunas and the Velθinas, though exigent and particular about the
terms of their agreement, seem to be setting up a fund to cover the
expenses of periodical funeral banquets, in a sort of jointly owned
mausoleum.

A religious concept which took precedence over all others was that
of the *temple*. Hence the marking-out of the boundaries of a temple
was at once a rite and a science. The Etruscans have left us an impressive delineation of this ceremony—all we have to do is to understand it! The picture is a fresco on the right-hand wall of the celebrated
Tomb of the Augurs which dates from 530 B.C. and, as we shall see in a
moment, commemorates the marking-out of the bounds of a *templum*.
This act of religious surveying is what is being performed by the two
priests whom we see in Fig. 52.[2]

Their backs are turned on each other. The priest on the right is
holding in his right hand a lituus, the curved staff of the augurs; he
wears a black toga. The one on the left, in a red toga, is looking in the
direction of a boy carrying a folding chair. Both are making approxi-

---

[1] For which a connection is commonly sought with *op-s*, "abundance".
[2] After *La Peinture Etrusque*, Introduction by P. Ducati, 1943, pl. V.

mately the same gesture, with one arm bent and the other extended forwards. By the head of each is written the same word: *tevaraθ*.

Obviously this name holds the clue to the whole. Before translating it, I must observe that in his excellent study, already mentioned, Poulsen has mistaken the augur on the left for a spectator who is signing to the boy to bring him a chair; while the man on the right becomes "evidently not an augur, but an umpire", *tevaraθ*, supervising a

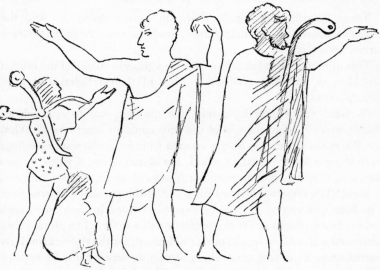

FIG. 52. Marking the bounds of a "sacred place"

wrestling-bout which is taking place in front of him, farther to the right. P. Ducati has adopted this mistaken interpretation, and in his album has described the fresco as a wrestling-contest in the presence of the *agonothetis* [judge] and a spectator.

But neither Poulsen nor Ducati has inquired why spectator and judge should be designated by the same word, *tevaraθ*. And why should the character on the left, who is supposed to be giving an order to a boy, be making at this moment such a balanced, rhythmical, gymnastic movement? Or are both these *tevaraθ* umpires? In that case why is the *agonothetis* on the left turning his back on the wrestlers; does he think his job is a sinecure?

In short, Luigi Dasti, who described the Tomb of the Augurs eighty years ago, was nearer the truth. He speaks of the character holding

one of those staves . . . which the augurs used for *determining ideal divisions in the heavens* and for predicting the future [1] [our italics].

[1] *Notizie storiche archeologiche di Tarquinia e Corneto*, Roma, 1878, p. 348.

Dasti nearly found the key to the enigma.

(P. 81 CIE 5331–2) *tevaraθ* (A)

teva: either Albanian *daj*, aorist *dava*, "to divide" (M. 65), or
Albanian *thej*, aorist *theva*, "to break" (M. 534).
raθ: Albanian *radhë*, "line, order", a word whose meaning in
Etruscan has been settled once for all by Hammarström.

Thus: "divides the lines". Both augurs are doing it. And the
adjacent scene, a wrestling-contest, had no connection with these
sacred geometers.

This quest for "ideal divisions" leads us straight to one of the crucial
problems of Etruscan civilisation, that of their religion and their
conception of life.

As Guhl and Koner have said, the question was to establish an
"observatory" where the will of the gods could be ascertained. What
the Etruscans did was to isolate an area from its profane surroundings
by tracing a square on the ground, the square being divided by two
medians, of which one ran from north to south and the other from east
to west. The observer took up his stand at their point of intersection.
The four quarters of the square were subdivided in their turn, each
section being placed under the protection of a deity. The ground thus
delimited was, as it were, the mirror of heaven, for the sky was similarly
partitioned. By noting over which section an omen made its appearance it was possible to determine by which deity the omen had been
sent. So the augur could always tell what god was taking a hand in
events, rather as we can look up a name in the telephone directory.

Such was the peculiar mould in which Etruscan civilisation cast a
universal idea, an idea which is as old as the world itself: the need to
learn the will of the gods.

This system of communication was not without drawbacks, however.
If you failed to get through there was no pleasant female voice, faintly
tinged with asperity, to tell you: "The number of the subscriber you
are calling has been changed. Consult the Liver of Piacenza!" Worse
still, if you happened to have chosen a bad moment for the person at
the other end of the line, he was quite capable of replying with a flash
of lightning.

Nevertheless, this "checkering" of the Etruscan sky was a wonderful
feat of innovation. The Etruscans dared to forge a link between earth
and heaven. They made them, in a sense, *commensurable*. Towards the
abyss overhead, now blue and now filled with darkness, and inhabited
at all times by forces both menacing and incomprehensible, they sent

up the first companion-way of human reason—of science, logic, calculation, which from henceforward they could use to complete the work begun by prayer and sacrifice.

There is no need to compare their conceptions with the heavenly regions of the Greeks, inhabited by country gentlemen who were always running after women, or drinking, or laughing, perpetually quarrelling and bearing grudges, delighted if there was a chance of a banquet or of participating in some squabble among mortals. But what would a Biblical character have said of the Etruscans' audacity? Did not Jeremiah remark ironically, "If heaven above can be measured . . ."? (xxxi. 36). And did not the Psalmist exclaim, "The heavens declare the glory of God"? (xix. 1). They would undoubtedly have been shocked. Who dares measure what it is permitted only to admire? They would surely have asked, "Do you dare to come with your rule in your hand, like a tailor taking the measurements of a customer?"

The Etruscans were far from rising to the moral level of the Prophets. The imperative of justice was relegated by them to the Underworld, where the god Hades settled accounts with (metaphorically speaking) the insolvent debtors who came to him with heads hanging in shame.

This does not mean that the Etruscans' religious awareness was anything less than keen. The very brevity of the Tuscan votive inscriptions attests the strength and simplicity of the appeal they were intended to convey: "To Juno the Mother", or "Hear my prayer!"

Like all gods, those of the Etruscans were more than a mere reflection of their worshippers. Every man bears in his heart a salutary need to *idealise* some being or other of his own choosing, otherwise life would turn to chaos; beside which, this device makes it possible for him to evade the role of active idealism which is due from him. Thus, like everybody else, the Etruscans were bound to imagine their gods as being better than themselves and to turn towards them in the hope of gaining added strength, intelligence, generosity and (we must grant the Etruscans this) justice. Someone has said that if triangles had a god he would be a triangle; but this celebrated aphorism has always seemed a little pessimistic to me. If the triangles had to choose a god they would choose a circle. Some of the gods of the Etruscans were benevolent, certainly. But, just as in Egypt, justice and fraternity were ideas which had not yet been sufficiently matured to gain a firm hold.

However, they were a youthful people, fresh and lively of soul, without the weight of thousands of years of tradition to paralyse them. And they gave to their watchful consciousness of the divine omnipresence a novel, clear, comprehensive expression—a "modernised"

H

expression, one would almost say. Moreover, as a people emerging from the Bronze Age, they constitute the transition between an older civilisation and that of Roman Italy. And the time was not far distant, relatively speaking, when an Alexandrian Greek of genius, Eratosthenes (3rd century B.C.), under a sky already swept bare of its native Egyptian deities, would measure the earth (by taking the position of the sun and the length of a shadow), and do it as coolly as if he were dealing merely with some enormous lantern suspended above a stadium.

But among the Etruscans the act of "dividing the lines" was a sacred rite, no less sacred than the *templum* which resulted from it. But what was the origin of this Latin notion of the *templum* (the augurs' "observatory") and of the temple? According to Guhl and Koner, the noun is "derived from an old Italic root which is identical with that of the Greek verb *temnein* (to cut, demarcate) . . ." (*La Vie Antique*, p. 7).

Thus, to our surprise, we find in this "cutting" or "demarcating" an echo if not a faithful translation of our *tevaraθ*, which is the very source of the Roman *templum*.

In the immediate vicinity of an Etruscan temple there was sometimes a trench which was regarded as an entrance to the Underworld, and into which offerings were put. The Etruscans and the Romans called it *mundus*. The true meaning of the word (which coincides with *mundus*, "world") is perhaps explained by Albanian *mund*, "torture, torment" (M. 298). This corresponds closely to the Etruscans' idea of the beyond. We shall come across *mund* again, in the form of *muθ*, in the chapter devoted to the Book of the Mummy.

In order to mark out the bounds of a temple the sun had to be observed. The sun, in Etruscan, is called *usil* (B). It has been observed that this word was common to several of the Italic peoples: *ausel* (Sabine), *ausar* (Samnite).[1]

Let us pass on to another Etruscan word for the temple. Latin has the word *aedes*, "temple, house, chamber". This is very similar to the Etruscan word *eθ*, "sanctuary, edifice". Herbig translated *anu eithi* by "in the temple of Janus"; here are my reasons for believing his translation confirmed:

(*a*) On a statuette of a goddess, in the Florence Museum, we read:

(P. 739, CIE 301) *larce lecni fleres uθurlaneiθi* (A)

---

[1] We may note in parenthesis that, in Albanian, "to turn" is *sillem* (M. 450). Cimochowski mentions the imperative negative, singular and plural, of this verb: *mos usiell*! and *mos usillni*! "do not turn!"

larce lecni: a nomen and praenomen.

turce: offered (i.e., dedicated).

fleres: (this) ex-voto.

uθuri: according to Bugge, this is the genitive of the name of the goddess Uturna. As she was a water-goddess, I refer this word to Albanian *ujë*, "water", from which is derived *ujetore*, "tank, cistern" (M. 539).

anu: Anu, Janus. The sanctuary therefore housed a divine couple: Juturna and Janus.

And it would be difficult to understand the words in any other way, since Janus was Juturna's husband.

eiθi was wrongly explained by Bugge and Pauli as a demonstrative pronoun.

To identify it with Latin *aedes* we resort to Albanian, in which I find *ajet* and *hajat*, "vestibule, hall, porch, enclosed court" (M. 3 and 152).

Thus: "Larce Lecni offered (this) ex-voto in the temple of Juturna and Janus."

(*b*) In one of the inscriptions which we have already considered, P. 359b, where fat seasoned with fennel is offered up to a goddess, there occur the words *eθ tuθiu*: meaning that the offering is being made "in the temple of the city".

We may add that in inscriptions P. 100 and P. 619 the expression *eiθ fanu* appears; *fanu* is Albanian *banë*, "residence, dwelling" (M. 19), which we met with in the affair of the dove (or carrier pigeon), *tifanati*; *eiθ fanu* means something in the nature of "sacred dwelling-place". Jokl connected Albanian *bane*, *banoj*, "residence, to reside", with Sanskrit *bheua*, *bhavanam*, which mean the same things.

Corssen, on the other hand, considered *fanu* to mean "sepulchre" and emphasised the close identity of this word with Latin *fanum*, "temple, place consecrated to the infernal gods";[1] in which case *ar*, *eθ* and *fanu* form a set of religious terms common to Etruscan and Latin.

In connection with *eθ fanu* we shall now proceed to examine a remarkable inscription, at the end of which we shall see *fanu* again, but in a modified form, *fave*, or (to be precise) *phave*, which must be read as *bhave*, a word which is astoundingly close to the Indian word *bhavanam* quoted by Jokl. It is an attractive text, but a desperately tantalising one. It is full of movement, one seems to hear the din of hammers and saws wielded by muscular arms, and to watch Etruscan

[1] *Über die Sprache der Etr.*, I, 449.

builders carrying heavy slabs of stone and the trunks of trees as they raise a temple worthy of their zeal—but to what deity? and where? These details and many others remain hidden from us.

The greater part of this inscription from Volterra, engraved on a strip of lead, is taken up by a list of generous donors, some twenty of them, a whole co-operative society of donors. Some letters are missing. Several words or sentences were subsequently intercalated in the list. In several cases it is difficult to know whether we are dealing with proper names or building materials. M. Pallottino accompanies this inscription (P. 401, CIE 52a) with a stern warning:

> legendi ratio difficillima apparet propter scriptorum negligentian, adjecta ac interpolata vocabula, obscurum versuum ordinem.

However, some parts of the text are enough to overwhelm us with concrete, precise information and to make us understand what a valuable piece of evidence it is.

The text is divided into two parts, which we shall call (a) and (b). First of all we read a series of proper names. Then come lines 11–14:

> cure malave laristna v eθa putace zv i cap fuluna (p)utace

cure malave, anyway, is not a donor's name!

cure (A) is Albanian gur, "stone", one of the foundation-stones of this piece of deciphering, a word as unshakable as pava, and iχnac, and tretu, and enqten and so many others.

This word is sufficiently related to the Indo-European family by Polish gora (to be read as gura), Russian gora, "mountain", although G. Meyer rejected this comparison; gur is also an ancient Italic word, since it occurs in a Samnite inscription (written, that is to say, in Oscan) studied by C. D. Buck. This is an amusing morsel, a dialogue written on a missile (an oval stone). Buck presents it as follows:

1. pis tu	who are you?
2. iiu kuru	. . . acorn
3. puiiu baiteis	from whom? from Meaeti
4. Aadiieis Aiifineiis	Adii Adeini

And Buck complained (in 1905): "iiu is absolutely incomprehensible, and no etymological antecedents are known for kuru."[1]

What a slander on a poor little Osco-Etrusco-Illyrio-Albano-Indo-European word! Nothing more sensitive than a stone could have stood up to it—which we may accept as additional proof that guru means

---

[1] Elementarbuch der Osco-Umbr. Dial., p. 151.—It may be noted that guru is "heavy" in Sanskrit.

"stone". And in *iiu* it is impossible not to recognise Albanian *u*, "I" (M. 537). But this same lapidary dialogue has been re-examined in our own day by M. Pisani. He has made a forward step, presenting it thus:

1. pis tu	Who are you?
2. iiu kuru	I am an acorn (a missile)
3. puiiu baiteis	From whom do you come? (Taking the second word for Latin *vadis*.)
4. A. A.	from A. A.[1]

The word *kuru*, however, raised doubts in M. Pisani's mind. He compared it with Sanskrit *carus*, "javelin", and Sabine *curis*, "lance". But why not have thought first of a nearer neighbour than Sanskrit, Albanian? Would it not have been logical to ask: In what language is there a word meaning "bullet, projectile" or something of the kind? He might have found a stone to remind us of a verse in the Psalms, "The stone which the builders refused is become the head stone of the corner" (Ps. cxviii. 22).

The translation which imposes itself is this (A):

1. Who are you? 2. I am a stone. [Could any self-respecting stone answer otherwise?] 3. From what sling? [More exactly, From the sling of whom? Albanian *bajzë* means "sling" (M. 17).] 4. From A. A.

Buck had made *baiteis* into a third name for the slinger. M. Pisani was quite right in doing away with this luxury article. The soldier must rest content with two names. He knows enough to scribble a dialogue, but that is no reason why he should give himself the airs of a Plautus.

Finally, to bring this little mineralogical digression to a dignified close, let us quote a sentence from the Albanian translation of the Old Testament. In Exodus xvii. 4 Moses speaks with the Lord, telling him of the "murmurings" of the people, who are in the midst of the desert, have no water, and are suffering from thirst: *janë gati të më vrasënë me guri*, "they be almost ready to stone me". In this sentence we find two Etruscan words: *vras*, "to kill", which we found in the inscriptions on missiles; and *gur*, the word with which we are concerned now. This is an example of the way in which everyday Albanian is, as it were, inlaid at times with Etruscan words.

malave (A), already seen in the "snake incantation", is "from the mountains, of the mountains". We have already emphasised the

---

[1] *Elementarbuch der Osco-Umbr. Dial.*, p. 98.

importance of the word *mal*. Buonamici mentions an Etruscan
king Malcos, the legendary inventor of the trumpet; and Mount
Malea; and so on.

In the Albano–Russian dictionary of Kostallari, p. 471, the
declination of the noun *mal* in the plural is given (without the
definite article):

> Nom. male
> Gen. *maleve* (instead of Etruscan *malave*!)
> Dat.   „
> Acc. male
> Abl. malesh

Thus the donors whose names are recorded have procured, for
the future temple, *cure malave*, "stones from the mountains"
("marble"?).

One begins to feel dazzled by the richness of Etruscan grammar.
Little Etruscan schoolboys must have been given a good deal of
trouble by it. It is true that corporal punishment was administered
to the accompaniment of the sound of a flute; but we are not well
informed enough to be able to say whether the scholars regarded
this as an adequate compensation.

laristna (A): Is this really a name? Since we are dealing with
building materials, we want them to be of the highest possible
quality. We have already met the verb *laroj*. It has two meanings:
"to polish" and "to speckle, variegate" (M. 237). Note that what
gives marble its variegated colours is polishing. Moreover, *larisk*
is "spotted, dappled" (*ibid.*). So we are sure of getting stones with
shimmering colours for the façade of our temple. Malachite,
perhaps? That would certainly add charm to the pediment.

tna: Albanian *tna, tene*, "them" (masculine or feminine), in the
accusative (M. 512).

eθa: *eθ, aedes*, "temple", etc.

v: perhaps a passive augment belonging to the next word?

putace (A) is identical with *puts* (LM, XII, 6 and P. 131), *putz* (P. 133)
and *puθce* (*śutu puθce*) in P. 188; it is the past of the Albanian verb
puthis, "to adjust, fit, join" (M. 410); in Etruscan, very probably,
"to build". "Was built"?

zv i: two words or one? A difficult question. Ought we to think of
Albanian *zôjë*, "lady, mistress; wife (*obs.*)", which comes from
zônjë, which comes from *zôtnje*, which, finally, comes from *zôt*,
"god, master, lord" (M. 583)? Mann quotes an interesting
expression which is surely an echo from the past: *Zoja e Dheut*,

"Goddess of the Earth". Does this part of the text indicate the name of the deity to whom the building is consecrated? This would fit nicely, but, alas, is far from convincing. The epithet *zot* does not seem to occur in association with any of the Etruscan names of deities. There is only one case in which this root may possibly be pertinent, namely in the last part of the following sentence: *ara ratum aisna leitrum zuθeva* (LM, X, 20), whose meaning is largely obscure.

The truth is probably something less impressive: *zv i* is probably *zui*, written alternatively for the usual *θui*, *θu*, which means "here". *z* and *θ* are sometimes interchangeable. Cf. *ravnθu* and *ravntza*; note, also, the word *zauri* in the remarkable inscription P. 498, CIE 1546, which will be quoted later; the word seems to mean *θauri*, connected with *θaura*, "tomb".

cap: "to take, seize" (already encountered, in the chapter on the Tavern).

fuluna putace: the second word indicates that *fuluna* is not a proper noun and that the topic is more likely to be building materials. All the more so in that the word recurs in the second half of the same inscription, thus: *acap fuluna mazutiu*. *acap* is certainly connected with the verb *cap*, "to take". *mazutiu* is only a slight disguise for *matu*, "large", the Albanian *madh*, already seen (cf. *matu manimeri*, in "The Family"). These *fuluna* were therefore big or even very big. Taking all the indications together, I see these *fuluna* as beams, forest trees, tree-trunks, corresponding to Albanian *pyll*, "wood, forest", *pyllinë*, "grove, copse", *pyllnaje*, "woodland" (M. 410–11).

It is true that G. Meyer connects *pyll* with Latin *palus*, "marsh, swamp" (*loc. cit.*, 360). But, to begin with, "forest" and "marsh" are rather wide apart; and, to go on with, there was in the island of Lesbos a mountain with the Pelasgic name of Pulaion (von Hahn, II, p. 237). A "mountain of marshes" defeats imagination; a "forested mountain" would be more natural. There is one other possibility for *fuluna*: "enclosure" (cf. Albanian *mbyll*, "to close").

It is a pleasure to escape from these nebulous entities and cling to something as safe and solid as the *gure maleve*, whether they be mottled or merely polished.

We can now pass on to the second piece of flotsam rescued from this epigraphical shipwreck—but what flotsam! We shall find in it the term *fave*, "residence", equivalent to the usual Etruscan form *fanu*, and excellently elucidated already by Jokl. And we shall find ourselves interpreting a vigorous sentence which sums up the intention of the inscription as a whole, gives it scope and eloquence and rewards us for having had to struggle in the quagmire of conjectures.

We start by noting that part (*b*) of the inscription, like part (*a*), consists mainly of donors' names. Yet a few technical terms are found inserted into it here and there: for example *larθu fuluna*, "tall trunks" or "long beams". Here are the last lines (12–13) of the inscription:

> *fave setra fvi θuścu fvimv larθu pacv*

Let us draw up a balance-sheet of things known and things unknown:

fave (A): this we have seen already: Latin *fanum*, Etruscan *fanu* (*bhanu*), Albanian *bane*, "dwelling-place, sanctuary".

setra (A): this takes us back to the word *f.siθrals* (from the Golini Tomb), "with dignity"; it is the same as Albanian *sedër*, "dignity" (M. 447).

> Here, "worthy".

fvi: ?

θuścu (A): a sparkling and invaluable word which illuminates the whole of this fragment. It is Albanian *dushku*, "the oak" (M. 87). I quoted *dushku* in an earlier passage but did not reveal its brilliant future. I now own up to this little deception.

fvimv: ? The form is that of the verb in the 1st person plural of the present. Cf. Albanian *dalem*: "we go out" or "let us go out".

larθu: "high".

pacv: *pacu*. Is this the Albanian *pake*, "rare", from Latin *paucus*? "Of rare height, of unusual height"? Or is it the name Bacchus (elsewhere called *faca*)? *larθ* is sometimes found with the name of a deity: cf. Larth Vel(χ)unus.

"A sanctuary made of oak, worthy of the great Bacchus (?)." There are still two gaps: *fvi* and *fvimv*. But when one has accumulated a store of building materials—slabs of polished marble, long beams, tall oak trunks—what is there left to do, in the name of Heaven, in order to have a fine temple? Why, build! The conclusion is unavoidable. *fui* (*bhui*) is bound to take on this meaning, which, after all, is in line with *putace* in the first part of the inscription.

The ending *mu*, in *fuimu*, can, moreover, be assimilated to the Albanian preposition *me*, "with", placed after the noun which it governs, in the Etruscan way: "with oak, (made) of oak".

Thus this capital fragment of our document says: "To build a worthy temple, of oak to build it for great Bacchus."

This reminds us irresistibly of a remark by O. Müller, that Etruria's principal export to the Romans was wood for building with, planks and long beams.

So, then, our inscription from Volterra was commemorative, its chief contents being the list of those who had untied their purse-strings to send for stone and tree-trunks. Other details were interpolated later. Despite their terse, lapidary style the sentences convey the pride the builders felt as they looked at their finished work, as tall as the oaks and pines of Etruria.

Although I attribute most of my difficulties to the shortcomings of my knowledge of Etruscan, I believe none the less, with M. Pallottino, that this inscription is fairly incoherent in itself. It was composed by a carpenter rather than by a scribe. He knew his grammar (*gure maleve!*), having no doubt often listened to the flute in his boyhood, but his style remained poor.

Poor, yet powerful.

There is nothing fussy or precious about his three closing phrases; he hewed them out with three firm blows of the axe.

Let us ponder once more on this verbal triptych:

fave setra fui	"A temple worthy to build
θuścu fuimu	Of oak to build (it)
larθu pacu	For great Bacchus (?)"

These are the three final chords of a powerful symphony ringing forth from an organ. In its own laconic way it is a little masterpiece of rhythmical prose; superior, surely, to many a more verbose effusion?

It certainly deserves a moment's further thought.

What, after all, was the primary objective of these people on the outskirts of Volterra, with their lopped oak-trunks promoted to the dignity of columns?

They wanted their temple to be worthy; dignified.

May we not have stumbled here on another of the keys to the Etruscan enigma? The dignity of the lucumons sitting opposite one another and talking of affairs of state; the dignity of husband and wife, smiling serenely on their marble couch in the course of a timeless banquet; the dignity with which a rough Etruscan peasant moves along behind his plough, accompanied by his wife, the sower; the dignity of a magistrate unrolling the scroll which lists the services he rendered to his city—is not this dignity one of the dominant features of the Etruscan character?

These ingenuous souls wanted dignity, no more and no less. They had none of the servility of the Egyptians or the Assyrians, those slaves who kissed the ground before their masters' feet.

Were not all of them like that head cook in one of the frescos of the Golini Tomb who, at the end of his patience, called for "More dignity, please!"?

In all deference to these good people, I am reminded by them of the heroine of one of Tchekhov's comedies, a midwife who during a wedding banquet confides in her neighbours at table, in languishing tones: "I ask so little of men: be noble!"

They wanted to keep their dignity. And when their conquerors refused them that dignity they felt doomed to disappear.

Now to return to P. 401. As it has given us a chance of basing our inferences on hard, strong materials—tree-trunks and mountain stones—let us continue in the same vein and tackle two other texts: four short inscriptions on stones, testifying for the most part to the liberality of devout donors who had contributed to the adorning of a temple. On a plinth we read the following:

(P. 256, NRIE 558) *larθ paiθunas prezu turuce* (A)

What was it he offered (*turu-ce*), this man Larth Paidunas? *Prezu* is not a proper noun. It is elucidated by *brezar* (in which *ar* is merely a suffix), a "wooden beam running through mudbrick walls" (M. 37). There seems no doubt that what this Larth of ours offered was a massive wooden pillar to strengthen the wall of a brick-built temple, or to support its roof. And his name has been perpetuated in consequence.

On another plinth we read:

(P. 707) *arnθ veiane . . . lariza ma turunke* (A)

turunke means the same as *turce*: "(he) offered".
lariza is very close both to the word *laristna*, which we met in connection with the building with the small sanctuary owned in common, and also to the Albanian verb *laroj*. In Albanian we find *larzoj*, "to cover with designs", and *larzim*, "ornamentation carved in stone" (M. 237). Albanian, poor country though she be, has retained an echo of the Etruscans' luxuriant decorations!

So the stone perpetuated the name of one Arnθ Veiane, who of his liberality embellished the place of his devotions.

On yet a third stone plinth, some ten inches high and therefore of a very adequate size to support a statue, for example, we read:

(P. 257, NRIE 541) *mi peθns ae titi vucinas turce* (A)

This probably concerns someone who, at his own expense, offered an object called *peθn(s)*. Buonamici thought this word was the sculptor's name; Buffa took it for the name of the deity to whom the presumed statue was dedicated. But Bugge and Pauli had already interpreted it as "stone"; Pauli added, "This word occurs only on tombstones."

I think that *peθns* is very likely explained by Albanian *betimë*, "slab, marble block" (M. 26). This is in perfect agreement with an interesting observation by Ribezzo, who drew a comparison between Etruscan *petna*, *penθna* and the Sicilian word *penta*, "a stone detached from a rock" (*Studi Etruschi*, 1953, p. 119). So the meaning is certainly a plinth or a slab.

These conclusions enable us to understand an inscription carved on a slab at Perugia:

(P. 575, CIE 4540) *suθis eka penθuna cai velś caiś θareś lautni* (B):

"This is the tombstone of C. Vel, freedman (or client, in the Roman sense) of C. θare."

The same meaning is necessarily correct for the noun *penθna* in texts P. 621 and 626.

Finally, the term "temple" itself is inscribed on the massive capital of a column, found at Tarquinii: *panzai* (A) (CII 2321 bis). Looking through its typically Etruscan "disguise", *p* for *f*, *ai* for *e*, *z* for *ś*, I recognise *fanze* and hence *fanuśe*, "building, residence", *fanu*, a term already known to us and to be encountered again when we study the Book of the Mummy.

After the temple, let us look to its accessories.

Speaking of votive statuettes M. Pallottino observes that they were kept in chests or stores; or, let us say, in a treasury. We are reminded of this fact by the Etruscan word *cver* (A), which occurs frequently in the votive inscriptions. Thus, according to P. 752, a woman named *Tite Cale Atial* (daughter of Ati?) *turce* (offered, dedicated) *malstria* (a mirror) *cver*. *atial* may be "To the Mother Goddess." But *cver* leaves no room for doubt, since, in Albanian, *quer* (M. 420) and *kjuer* (M. 199) mean "pantry, larder"; a store. Thus the mirror was brought to the temple treasury, the second of these having replaced the idea of the temple itself, in the minds of the simpler sort of people.

Another mention of *cver* comes in an inscription engraved on a statuette of a child holding a bird:

(P. 624, CIE 4561) *fiereś tec sanśl cver* (A)

fiereś: "ex-voto, statuette".

tec is likely to be the Albanian preposition *ndek*, "towards, to, with" (M. 306) or *tek*, "by, at" (M. 512).

sanśl cver: the treasury of the temple of Sancus.

Thus: "An ex-voto (to be placed) in the treasury of Sancus."

Various ceremonies gravitated round the temples. If we want to find out something about the solemn processions held in Tarquinii and other details of the different cults maintained there we cannot do better than to go and pay our respects again to Laris Pulena. Let us salute this pillar of the capital, saturated with the respect his compatriots pay to him, full of the memories of his services to the City. He is *parniχ*, "one of the first", the son of such an one, nephew of such another, and he does not forget to emphasise that he is the grand-nephew of Creice, "the Greek".[1]

His epitaph is a chapter in the history of religions.

Etruscan is a conglomerate of enigmas, and the struggle with it is an arduous one; however, let us ask this paunchy Sphinx respectfully but firmly for a little light to guide us.

Light to disperse the darkness which has been allowed to persist indefinitely under the most luminous sky in Europe.

L. Pulena is, in any case, by no means unwilling to receive our visit. His unrolled parchment is, after all, simply a bond certifying a loan which he made long ago in good ringing coin and whose value has been somewhat depreciated by the 2,200 years of wars and revolutions which have elapsed since. Politely, he asks us to restore its value . . .

But from whence will come the light we need?

> (P. 131) *creals tarχnalθ spureni lucairce*
> *ipa ruθcva caθas hermeri* (lines 3–4)
> *slicaχeś aprinθvale*
> *luθcva caθas paχanac* (lines 4–5)

Starting with the first line: *creals* and *lucairce* are unknown; *tarχnalθ* is "at Tarquinii"; *spureni* is "of the city", "municipal", etc.

According to Devoto (*Studi Etr.*, X, p. 278), Ribezzo had already produced a brilliant proof that *lucairce* meant "was lucumon" (cf. *zilaχce*, "was a *zilaχ*", etc.). Was Laris a king? Dumbfounded, I made haste to read Ribezzo's article. But that author confers the insignia of royalty on Laris for no better reason than the juxtaposition of *tarχnalθ* and *spureni* with *lucairce* (*L'epitafio etrusco di Pulena*. *Rivista indo-greca-italica*, 1932, I–II, pp. 69 *et seq.*). In addition, though he makes several interesting observations, he does not explain *creal*.

[1] Pauli translated *creice* as "Greek". Corssen (*Beamtentitel* [Titles of Officials] p. 48) writes that this is "unlikely". We shall see later that *crece* = Greek.

It is certain that the inscription concerns the career of our eminent civil dignitary. But *lucair(ce)* contains an *r* which is missing from a designation of the "lucumonia" which occurs in the Book of the Mummy, *lauχumneθi* (Ch. X, 2).

Is it a case of *r* having been added to the root?

I think *lucairce* will be easier to interpret if we first concentrate our attention on the words *ipa . . . caθas hermeri.*

caθas is the genitive or dative of caθ, the Sun God. So the phrase must be conveying something directly related to the cult of that attractive deity. This is our first step towards the light. At least we are sure not to lose ourselves in the darkness of Hades.

Laris was visibly concerned to maintain the cult in question and to enhance its splendour. Laris *ipa.* Laris *gave* (*ip*, already mentioned) something to *caθas hermeri*; or else he offered this *caθas hermeri* to the city. The ending *eri*, in *hermeri*, seems to be one of the inflexions denoting the plural: cf. Armenian *dounere*, "houses", and Albanian *dorberi*, "flock", and *fquinjëri*, "neighbours" (M. 113, etc.). What are these *hermeri* of *caθ*? The plural indicates that there is no question of the god Hermes in person. If there is we shall have to conclude that *hermeri* is an oblique case of the name Hermes.

I feel almost embarrassed at being able to suggest only a very straightforward means for solving the problem: let us open the dictionary of Daremberg-Saglio.

An article by P. Paris will remind us that the cities of classical antiquity were profusely adorned with—HERMAE, columns or miniature columns, originally consecrated to Hermes and bearing his symbol, later modified and used as "mascots" of the cities:

> The phallic column has a head at the top . . . these boundary-stones at street corners, in front of the doors of houses . . . *rows of hermae erected by the good offices of pious citizens. . . .* Hermes protector of streets . . . god of the market-place . . . of propitious meetings and prosperity rapidly attained. . . . The surfaces of the pillar are orientated to the cardinal points . . . *lamps were kept alight, and incense was burnt, before the hermes of the market-place* . . . the centre of festivals and ceremonies . . . endowed with a clearly marked Bacchic character . . . [there were] hermae of Dionysos and . . . hermae of the gods . . .

We are beginning to see a little, by the light of those little winking lamps burning piously by night and day before these columns, these *hermae.* There were many *hermae: hermeri.* There were *hermae* of different gods, Bacchus for example. It was even possible for two gods to be associated with one *hermes*; a picture accompanying the article shows one of these columns surmounted by a *pair of gods*. We can therefore presume the existence of a *hermes* of the *Sun God*; moreover, at a later point in our inscription Caθ and Bacchus are found in association: *caθas ραχanac.*

But all this refers to Greek and Roman cities. Where do the Etruscans come in?

Let us go on reading:

> The Etruscans, in our opinion, do not appear to have made much use of *hermae*. There is one representing Dionysos. We ought probably to identify in the same way a curious figure which Gerhard tries to identify with *a Sun God*. This figure is a tall, slim pillar. . . . The upper part represents a torso ending in a head. . . . One arm is extended to the right, bearing a patera; on the left a hand emerges from the sheath, supporting an incense-burner . . .
>
> (Daremberg, fig. 3818)

It is startling to realise that this is probably the very image of the *caθas hermeri*, *hermae* of the Sun, which through the generosity of Laris

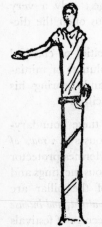

Pulena were erected in, as it were, Temple Square (or Market Square, or Government Square) at Tarquinii.

In pursuing our objective we have incidentally, I believe, elucidated the nature of certain Etruscan works of art representing gods or goddesses with slender, much-flattened bodies; these have often been described as "bizarre" votive figurines (cf. *The Art and Life of the Etruscans*, Cologne, 1956, pl. 50). These are probably "column divinities", of which our *hermeri* must have been the prototype.

But what about *lucairce* and some other obscure words in the fragment we are studying? Here I can offer only conjectures.

FIG. 53A. Hermes

It seems to me that *lucairce* is part and parcel of the special context in which it occurs. Laris Pulena adorned his native city with these monuments, which had *lamps* kept burning in front of them. Consequently, I think of *light*. Here is the linguistic background of *lucair(ce)*, (*lukair, luker*):

luk: Indo-European root, "light".
lucerna: "lamp" (Latin).
lux: "light" (Latin).

luqere: "lamp" (Albanian; M. 253).

lusχnei: "moon" (Etruscan; on a patera on which the moon is represented, P. 290).

luχnia: "lamp" (Greek).

luχnos: "torch" (Greek).

lusnkay: "moon" (Armenian); *lusnak*, "moonlight" (Bugge).

Roksané: a Bactrian princess, Alexander's wife ("the Shining One").

losk: "brilliance" (Russian).

—from which the conclusion is that *lucairce* may mean "has illuminated" or "has added splendour". *creals* seems to be the genitive of *crea*. One's thoughts go to Albanian *kré*, "head", plural *krere* (M. 213). "Capital, centre?" In view of these considerations, *creals tarχnalθ spureni lucairce* could mean: "He illuminated the centre of the city of Tarquinia", or "he added splendour to the most important points in the city of Tarquinia", etc.[1] The next line explains how he did it: by providing the city with the *hermeri* of *Caθ*, and the *ruθcva*. This is a difficult word; is it perhaps a plural form of *ruθ*?

In Albanian, *rud* means "curly, curly-haired" (M. 430). In our text, does the word *ruθcva* mean "crowns" (with their curled, intricate forms)? The Etruscans used them a great deal in their religious ceremonies. Crowns were hung on the *hermae*.

slicaχeś aprinθvale

I have the impression that the verb *ipa*, "offered", also refers to this, the third line of the fragment; Laris offered *sliχaces aprinθvale*:

sli is a verb we have met already, Albanian *shlyej*, "to rub, wipe".

caχeś: appears to be the genitive of *caχ*, which is also written *θac* and *zaχ* and which occurs a number of times in the Book of the Mummy; it is Albanian *gjak*, *dzjak*, "blood" (M. 140).

slicaχeś would therefore be a term of Etruscan ritual: the term for an offering which consisted of applying the blood of the sacrificial animals to a tombstone, an altar or any other place of sacrifice.

This is exactly the term I subsequently found in the pages of M. A. Piganiol. He has written of the earliest worship in Rome: the cult of fire, and the cult of "the stone which is rubbed with blood". "Boundary-stones are stones and gods at once: anyone who removes them . . . becomes the prey of the gods of the nether world; the sacrifice accompanying the erection of these stones has the effect of rooting them in the soil."

(Essai sur les origines de Rome, 1917, p. 95)

[1] See fig. 53B.

We now see why the word *slicaχes* was used: the *hermeri* had to be rubbed with blood.

aprinθvale specifies what kind of sacrifice was offered.

aprin: the accusative of *apir*, a word we studied in discussing sacrifices among the Etruscans. Black lambs? Let us add that the pig also played an important part in the rites of the Italic peoples; its names, Latin *aper* and Umbrian *apros*, are very reminiscent of *aprin*. *Apir* and *apirase* are frequently mentioned in the inscription of the Tile of Capua.

θvale, derived from *θu*, "two", may mean "twofold". *le* is found as a termination of derived adjectives in (for example) *lautnescle*, "familial".

The general lines of the meaning of *slicaχes aprinsvale* may be: "offerings of the blood of a pair of lambs (or young pigs)".

This interpretation is confirmed, moreover, by a Roman rite: after a funeral, the house was purified by the sacrifice of *two* rams (Daremberg: *lares*).

luθcva caθas paχanac

In *luθcva* we can recognise the root *lut*, *lus*, "to pray" (śuv lusi!). *caθas paχanac*: "to Caθ and Bacchus". There is certainly no question of *prayers* offered by Laris to these two deities, for that would not have earned a mention in his epitaph. I see *luθva* as "places of prayer", little chapels containing images of deities, such as were built in Greek and Roman towns (*sacrarium*) at crossroads and by the road-side and in private houses (*lararium*). I therefore believe that Laris endowed his city with *hermae* and made many sacrifices in shrines containing images of Caθ and Bacchus.

The columns or boundary-stones in question were, moreover, above all landmarks of property, agrarian and otherwise, symbolised later, among the Romans, by the god Terminus, the protector of boundaries. So it is clear that the action taken by L. Pulena was not dictated by purely aesthetic considerations. By causing these signs of Hermes to be erected he was strengthening Tarquinii both religiously and as regards the city's economic stability.

But let us go on gleaning in the rich field of our inscription:

(Lines 5–6) *alumnaθe hermu melecrapicces*
puts χim culsl leprnal

This is the continuation of the list of the gods whom Laris Pulena had particularly honoured. *alumnaθe*, which we shall meet again and examine a little farther on, denotes, I believe, the goddess Fortune.

She is followed by Hermes, not his columns this time but the god himself. The epithet applied to him is very interesting:

> *melecrapicces*: mele seems to correspond to Albanian *mëlle*, "mouthful, morsel" (M. 280). It is legitimate to suppose that in Etruscan the word could also mean "a share". *crapicces* I connect with Albanian *krapis*, "to flourish, prosper" (M. 213 and 119).

Thus we have the luck to find an expression which corresponds exactly with the role of Hermes, the god of fortunes quickly made, whom we mentioned a short while ago. *melecrapicces* nicely expresses the character of the god who grants "a substantial share" or a life of prosperity. *puts χim culsl* perhaps means that L. Pulena offered incense to Culśan. The problem of *χim* will be studied later (in Ch. XII, "The Book of the Mummy"). What we must study now is the epithet of *Janus-Culśan*: *leprnal*. Remembering Janus's solar antecedents, one thinks of the Albanian verb *lëbyr*, "to dazzle, fascinate" (M. 243). Thus Hermes is the god "of good fortune", and Culśan's origins are duly underlined.

(Lines 6–8) *pśl varχti cerine pul alumnaθ pul hermu . . . pśl ten . . .*

> *ci meθlumt pul hermu*
> *θutuiθi mlusna ranvis mlamna . . .*

pśl should probably be connected with the number *pes, peś*, "five", which we consider we have identified in *peslialχ* (P. 195). Is this a reference to a five-day feast, or to something else? The Romans held a feast in honour of *Minerva*, the *Quinquatria*, a name which the ancients considered was derived from *quinque*, 5. But the Roman triad of Jupiter, Juno and *Minerva* came from Etruria (Altheim, *La Religion Romaine*, p. 176).

varχti (A): this word is interpreted perfectly by Albanian *vark, varg*, "chain, *procession*" (M. 546), which has, moreover, a Slavonic equivalent: Bulgarian *veriga*, Russian *verigi*. The syllable -*ti*, the locative inflexion, probably indicates the part played by Laris Pulena *in* the sacred processions.

cerine remains obscure. I think of Albanian *ther*, "to slaughter" (M. 534). *cerine* also occurs on a cippus, P. 315, perhaps indicating the part of the tomb on which the periodical sacrifices were made. We shall return to the problem when we discuss ancestor-worship, in Ch. XI.

pul may be Albanian *pyll*, "forest". Does it refer to the sacred groves to which processions made their way, consummating a sacrifice when they got there? The alternative is Albanian *mbyll*, "to close". Initial *m* sometimes falls away, as for example in the Albanian *mbar*, *bar*, "to carry" (M. 267). Jokl has found a counterpart to Albanian *mbyll* in Lithuanian *pilis*, "fastening". In this eventuality *pul* will be a sacred *enclosure* in which the Etruscans kept stags destined for sacrifice. We have just seen the same root in *fuluna*.

alumnaθ: an enigmatic word. As *pul alumnaθ* comes as a parallel to *pul hermu* and as *hermu* is Hermes, we may conjecture that there were two groves sacred to two deities. In line 5 there seem to be the names of four gods in succession: Caθ (sun), Bacchus, Alumnaθ and Hermes. One's mind turns to the Albanian root *lumë*, "happiness, fortune".[1] Is *alumnaθ* the Etruscan Fortuna? Or an epithet of Juno? Note that according to O. Müller the Faliscans had a grove which was sacred to Juno. Carpets were spread in the path of processions making their way to it.

The cult of the goddess of Fortune was set up in Rome by the Etruscan king Servius Tullius.

pśl ten(u): I made the supposition above that *peśl*, derived from *pes*, "five", referred to the processions in a "five-day feast". *pśl tenu*, if we keep the same meaning, "of five", is much more explicit: L. Pulenas would be a *quinquevir* of the city (*tenu*), one of the members of a college composed of five members of the priesthood, or of five civil dignitaries.

We pass on now to the second part of the fragment we have selected, in which the words *pul hermu* are used again:

ci: "three".

meθlumt: considered as equivalent to *meχlum* (whose derivation should perhaps be traced to *maχ*, "one"), *meθlumt* means "federation" or "community", comprising a metropolis and the small towns in league with it. The final *t* may be the sign of a possessive adjective. Perhaps, then, "federal"?

ci meθlumt pul hermu may mean three groves which belonged to the confederation and were sacred to Hermes.

θutuiθi (B): a most interesting expression, which seems to confirm our interpretation of *pul* as grove or sacred enclosure, and which decomposes into three elements:

  θu, "here" or "there", a word whose meaning is already established, rather than *θu*, "two".

[1] Connected by Walde-Pokorny to the Indo-European root *leubh* (*love*, *lieben*, *lubitj*), II, 419.

tui therefore cannot mean "here" on this occasion, as we have got a "here" already. This prompts me to compare *tui* with Albanian *tuis*, "to keep, reserve" (M. 528).

θi will be explained by Albanian *dhi*, "goat"; *dhi e egër*, "chamois" (M. 91); perhaps in the sense of (sacred) "stag". *θutuiθi* therefore emerges as "the place where the sacred stags are kept".

mlusna (A) can be interpreted with certainty. *m* means "with". In *lusna* we immediately recognise *lusχnei*, from inscription P. 290, which we mentioned a short time ago; it is the Etruscan *losna*, "moon".[1] *lusna* can mean "month, moon, new moon, feast of the new moon", and so on. As there is in the Book of the Mummy an expression *tiurim avils* which by general consensus is translated as "the months of the year", we can interpret *mlusna* for the time being as "with the new moon".

ranvis: this should probably be read as *ranuish*, which could be connected with Albanian *ranë*, "to strike" (from the irregular verb *bie*) (M. 423). Here, "to slaughter, to sacrifice", "to be sacrificed"; cf. *ranem*, LM, Ch. VIII.

mlamna: as in *mlusna*, *m* is a preposition. *lamna* is probably Albanian *lâmë*, *lëmënj*, "threshing-floor"; or perhaps, by extension, a public place or square? The leading role played by the threshing-floor, in archaic rites and sacrifices connected with fertility-cults, was emphasised by me in 1935.[2]

The second part of the selected fragment therefore appears as follows: "three (sacred) groves of the confederation, consecrated to Hermes, where are kept the stags (or mountain goats) which are sacrificed, at new moon, on the threshing-floor."

So it was to the groves of Tarquinii that the processions went, finding at the end of their journey the animals which were kept ready for sacrifice. If I have hit the mark, this text is of great interest for the study of Etruscan religion in general and of moon-worship in particular. It will perhaps be felt to indicate a link with pre-Hellenic Greece, in which Artemis-Diana was the goddess of the moon and the stag was one of her animals.

The two last words in the inscription perhaps bring out once more this Tarquinian aristocrat's chief benefaction. *lese hrmrier*: *lese—lece*, aorist of the verb *le*, "he left"; *hrmrier*—a different form of *hermeri*, "Hermes-columns".

---

[1] Bugge, *loc. cit.*, p. 3.
[2] *L'Arbre sacré et le rite de l'alliance chez les Anciens Sémites*, pp. 14–15.

To sum up, here is the portion of Laris' epitaph which we have discussed:

> *Iris pulenas . . . prumts pules larisal creices ancn ziχ neθśrac acasce creal tarχnalθ spureni lucairce ipa ruθcva caθas hermeri slicaχeś aprinθvale luθcva caθas paχanac alumnaθe hermu melecrapicces puts χim culsl leprnal pśl varχti cerine pul alumnaθ pul hermu . . . psl ten . . . ci meθlumt pul hermu θutuiθi mlusna ranvis mlamna . . . parniχ amce leśe hrmrier.*

Our suggested translation, though it rests on certain key-words of whose meaning there can be no doubt (*creices, slicaχes, varχti, θutuiθi, mlusna, parniχ*, etc.) and on words whose meaning is assured by other texts, cannot be regarded in its entirety as being more than an approximation:

Laris Pulenas, son of Larce . . . grand-nephew of Pule . . . He illuminated the centre of the city of Tarquinii (or: the capital of the cities of Tarquinii). He adorned with crowns the *hermae* of the god Caθ. He anointed with the blood of two sacrificial sheep the shrines of Caθ, Bacchus, Fortune, and Hermes who grants prosperity. He offered incense to Culśan the shining one. He was a *quinquevir* of the sacrificial processions (which go) to the (sacred) enclosure of Fortune and the (sacred) grove of Hermes. . . . He was a *quinquevir* of the city . . . three enclosures of the (Tarquinian) federation (which were consecrated) to Hermes, in which are kept the wild goats (for sacrificing) at (new) moon, on the threshing-floor (or: in the public square). . . . He was a patrician. He left (to the city) the columns (of Hermes).

On turning to the priesthood, we find ourselves once again thrown back upon conjectures. Let us begin with a well-known bilingual Latin–Etruscan inscription cut on a tombstone, in which three Etruscan words are given for two in Latin. This fact by itself is enough to cast doubt on the accuracy of the translation. The text is this:

> (P. 697, CII 69) *L Cafatius L f Ste   haruspex fulguriator cafates lr lr*
> *netśvis trutnvi frontac*

netśvis: must perforce denote some sacerdotal function. The element *svis* is perfectly clear: Etruscan *śuv*, "to see, look at" (*suvluśi*, "see the prayer").[1] Is *net* the god Neθ, Neptune? A suggestion of long standing is that the word be interpreted by Greek *nédys*, *nédyïa*, "entrails". In that case *netśvis* would be "he who inspects the entrails".

---

[1] The reader will remember *tshovish*, "to see", in Arbanas's little dictionary which I used to consult in the early days of my investigations. "See" assumes here the sense of "Behold!" or "Pay attention!"

trutnvt: Thomopoulos explains this by Albanian *trut*, "brain" (which he interprets as "head, chief", by analogy with Athene's epithet, Tritogeneïa, born from the head of Zeus) and by Albanian *vetoj*, "to lighten, flash". But the title "chief of the senders of lightning" leaves me dubious. I regard the syllable *nvt* as *not*, equivalent to Albanian *njotje*, "recognition" (*njojtës*, "expert") from the verb *njoh*, "to know" (M. 332). As for *trut*, my first thought was of (sacred) *trees*, *dru* being "tree" in Albanian; for the wife of the *flamen* used to deck her head with a branch from a *tree of good omen* (the Etruscans had a lore of trees of good omen and trees of evil omen). Later, however, I changed my mind, associating *trut* with the root *druej*, "to fear, adore", which we have encountered already and which, to the Etruscan mentality, must also have meant "to be religious", just as in the Old Testament "to fear the Lord" also, and simultaneously, means "to be pious". *trutnvt* would thus be "expert (in the rules) of religion". I fall back on the authority of Mommsen, according to whom the Roman pontiffs, who were the heirs of Etruscan tradition, "described the sum of their activities as 'the science of things human and divine'." (I. 12.)

However, we shall come back to the question of *nvt* later on.

It may be added that in the votive inscription which appears on a statuette dedicated to θuflθa (P. 740) the expression *trutvecie* may mean "faithful (to the behests) of the faith", since the Albanian verb *vegoj*, "to keep, observe" (M. 548), gives an adequate interpretation of the word *vecie*.

frontac we have already examined; it is interpreted by Greek *bronte*, "thunder". I must, however, mention that there is an Albanian root *frunj*, "to blow" (M. 115). Etruscan *front* may have had some connection with *thunderstorms*, which according to O. Müller are of frequent occurrence in Etruria. In any case, the function of Larth Cafates was to conjure or call forth lightning, but, especially, to interpret its meaning. All the more so in that we already have another designation for "thunder" in Etruscan, namely *cemn(ac)*.

Before ending this chapter we shall mention two other Etruscan religious titles: *tanasar* and *cepen*, of which the second occurs frequently in the inscriptions. Two *tanasar* can be seen in a fresco in the Tomb of the Augurs, the tomb in which we have already admired the two *tevaraθ* laying out a *templum*. The Etruscans had a decided habit of seeing double! Their serious demeanour and their professional fondness for

meditation give the *tanasar* a close resemblance to the *tevaraθ*. Right
hand outstretched, left hand striking forehead,[1] they stand facing each
other and look as if they were praying. But their official title points to
their having something in common with their humble brothers the
θanasa, the actors in the market-place who with their rhymes and
songs amuse the peasants who flock to the city on every ninth day. The
meaning of the word *tanasar*, like that of *θanasa*, must be sought in
Albanian *tha*, "to say, speak, relate". But in this instance it was
visibly a matter of striking a statuesque pose and improvising a eulogy
of the deceased, mourning his premature death in rhythmical prose.

FIG. 53B. Street-lighting in Tarquinia?—A
lamplighter of antiquity

In Albanian, *Zanë* is the "mountain fairy, pixy, *muse of heroes*"
(M. 573; our italics). A cousin of *θana*?

It is worth noting that the inscription beside one of the *tanasar* (in
which word the ending *ar* denotes a profession) includes the words
(P. 82) *apas tanasar* (B). It seems to me that this indicates a distinction
in rank. *Apa* in Albanian is "elder brother" (M. 9). He was a "senior"
or "higher" *tanasar*. The word is interesting because we come across it
again in the epitaph of a magistrate, Avle Aleθnas, who was

zila χ . . . spureθi apasi svalas marunu χva (P. 171, CII 2057).

Note, first, that M. E. Benveniste puts *zila χ* in the category of nouns
ending in *ac, aχ*.[2] It ought therefore to be quoted along with *cemnac,
i χnac, roma χ, velzna χ*, etc. As for the sentence containing *apasa*, I
understand it to mean: "During his life (*svalas*) he served as *marun*
(*marunu χva*), supreme (*apasi*) *marun*, in the city (*spureθi*)." It might be
possible to interpret *spureθi apasi* as "in the upper city" (?). M. S.
Mazzarino, quoted by M. J. Heurgon (*loc. cit.*, p. 97), gives an in-

---

[1] This interpretation came to my mind when I read a passage from the *History* of
Nicholas of Damascus (1st century B.C.): when Croesus was about to be burnt on the
pyre the *Lydians* among the crowd of onlookers began weeping, groaning and *striking
their heads* (see photograph facing p. 209).

[2] *Notes Etrusques* (*Studi Etr.*, VII, 1933, p. 251).

geniously precise turn to *svalas* by translating it as *perpetuus*: Avle Aleθnas was a *marun* for life.

As for *cepen*, whose general meaning is attested by the Sabine noun *cupencus*, "priest", I compare it with Albanian *cip*, "tip, peak" (M. 50). This recalls the more archaic form, *cipen*, in which the word appears in the Tile of Capua. And it accounts for the possibility that the word means "chief".

XI

GODS, DEMONS AND HEROES

WE have already met *ais cemnac*, the "thundering god" or perhaps the "hurler of thunderbolts". While the Etruscans knew nine divinities who had the prerogative of sending lightning, Tinia was the most important of them, "a god whose utterance is a lightning-flash", as O. Müller puts it. Tinia's name has often been explained by reference to Etruscan *tin*, "day", which we find in a sentence used frequently in the Book of the Mummy: *tinsi tiurim avilś*. The context refers to the days and months of the year (?), or perhaps to the consecration of the months of the year to Tinia. In either case I can confirm "day" as the meaning of *tin*, thanks to a sentence which also comes from the Book of the Mummy:

heci nac va tinθasa (VI, 6) (B)

heci is Albanian *heq*, "to take away, remove, subtract" (M. 157).

nac we have seen before (in *ersce nac*): "night".

va is the Albanian verb *bâj* and *bâhem*, "to make, make oneself, become", already encountered.

tinθasa is a form developed or derived from *tin*, "day", in the same way as *zilaχnθas* comes from *zilaχ* (P. 92 and 136), and *trinθasa* from *trin* (LM, VII, 6); perhaps with the sense of "the day's doings, the content of the day" [i.e., French *journée* as distinct from *jour*. Cf. Eng. "Have you had a good day?"—*Tr.*].

The sense of the whole sentence is thus: "Night retires, day dawns."

To return to Tinia. In the following line:

ais cemnac truθtraχs rinuθ (LM, V, 18)

we believe the "thundering god", *ais cemnac*, is accompanied by his other conventional epithets. But they cannot be translated with certainty.

truθ is probably Albanian *druej*, "to be afraid", already examined, with the adjectival suffix *θ* (*t*); it will mean "frightening, redoubtable, terrible".

traχś reminds us of Albanian *tarak*, *taroq*, *taroc*, "bullock, steer (about two years old)" (M. 510). In Etruscan this could be another name for "bull", connected (as is *θurinu*, *θevru*) with Greek *tauros*,

Latin *taurus*, Slavonic *tur*. Does *truθtraχs* mean "redoubtable bull"? Is not thunder the bellowing of a celestial bull? *cem, gjem* is not only "to thunder" but also "to bellow". *Bull* is a familiar epithet of Zeus. *Tarak* may be the very origin of the name Tarχies, Tarquin.

rinuθ: We have already interpreted *ri* as "young" and *nuθ* (*njojt*) as "knowing" (*trutnuθ*). But this association does not yield a satisfying interpretation in the present instance. We must therefore think of other Albanian words for *rinuθ*; for the phonetic nature of Etruscan transcription is bound to involve overlapping from time to time.

ri: Albanian *re*, "cloud".

nuθ is close to Albanian *nodh* (M. 326), equivalent to *ndodh*, "to chance to be; happen; take place" (M. 310). For instance, we read in Mann's grammar: *boçe në të cilën* ndodhet *sendet*, "a receptacle in which objects *are to be found*" (p. 108). *Nodh* can thus mean "to be" or "to dwell".

Does *rinuθ* mean "who dwells in the clouds"?

Hence: "god bellowing like a formidable bull and dwelling in the clouds"? [1]

However, judging by an enigmatic expression *celc ceanuθ*, "fifty-five" (?), in P. 188, NRIE 770, *nuθ* can equally well dwindle to the role of a mere suffix. In which case *trutnuθ* may be "he of religion; priest", and a god who is *rinuθ* may be "he of the clouds".

Finally, *nuθ* may be connected with Albanian *nyjët*, "jointed" (M. 329); this would make *ri nuθ* into "who gathers the clouds together", which is in line with one of the known epithets of Zeus.

The question remains open.

Let us now look at two little inscriptions, each of which is two words long and refers to Tinia:

(*a*) (P. 657, CIE 371) (on a stone) *tinś lut* (A).

This consists of two known elements: *tinś* (to Tinia) and *lut* ("to pray"). A prayer to Tinia; or rather, perhaps, "Pray to Tinia"?

(*b*) (P. 270) *tinia calusna* (on a cup).

This *calu* has nothing to do with *cal*, "horse". The second element *sna*, which we have met before, warns us against that conclusion:

calu is *gjallë*, "life" (as already noted).

[1] *traχs* would be an oblique case: "as a bull, in the manner of a bull".

sna has been examined already in the form *snati*, which occurs in the
"Topers' Charter"; it is Albanian *znjatem*, "to continue, last,
prolong".

Thus, "Tinia, prolong (my) life!" A brief, pithy prayer; no one has
yet invented anything better in the same line. The cup may have been
used for making libations.

And here is the god Mars. Two Etruscan mirrors show the birth
of Minerva from Tinia's head. The father of the gods is surrounded

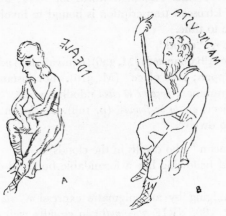

FIG. 54. Two versions of Mars

by the Olympians. The two drawings are almost identical, except for
the figure on the right-hand side in each case. On mirror B it is Mars:
maris ph usta (A). On mirror A it is a youth with a Louis Quatorze
hair-style and the caption *preale*. (Gerhard, pl. CCLXXXIV, 1 and 2.)

First inscription: *ph* is Albanian *baj*, "to carry, bear" (M. 17), or else
a particle (*mbë*); *usta* is "the pike", Albanian *ushta* (M. 542); cf. Latin
hasta. Thus, "Mars bearing a pike" or "Mars with pike". Which is
visibly true.

Second inscription: The placing and the pose of the two characters
being identical, this one is also a Mars, but an adolescent Mars. In his
youth he was so handsome that Eos, goddess of the morning, fell in
love with him (Kerenyi, *loc. cit.*, p. 198). *Preale* corresponds to Albanian
brêj, "to quarrel" (M. 36): "The quarreller". As everybody knows,
Mars was "a lover of discord".

When we discussed *θuflθa* or *θuflθaś* we mentioned the god Culśanś
in his aspect of *bifrons*, and also the goddess Culśu. B. Hrozny has
connected these two divinities with a group of Hittite gods of the

same name: Kulśaś, Kulśuś (accusative: Kulaśśana). He explains
their name by the Hittite root *kulś*, "to guard"; these were tutelary
gods, protectors of man, house and tomb.[1]

However, while Culśan does in fact figure as a beneficent god to
whom votive statues and the like are dedicated, such is not the case
with Culśu. This comes out in a fine bas-relief adorning the tomb of an
Etruscan lady of noble birth, a bas-relief of which an illustration was
published by Corssen (Vol. I, p. 381). The scene is one of farewell,
with Culśu playing a macabre role in it (fig. 55).

At the right-hand end an angel of death can be seen gently leading
off the departed woman, Tita Aunei, who is taking leave of her aged

Fig. 55. The goddesses Culśu and Venθ in a scene of farewell

father; he would dearly love to hold her back. Next to him his other
daughter (or perhaps his wife) is affectionately laying her hand on his
shoulder; and the next four figures to her right (our left) are other
members of his family. There is something official and conventionalised
in this scene of family farewells; nevertheless, the impression comes
through that these people are extremely well brought-up and are
used to controlling their feelings; they are behaving with great
dignity.

True, their attitudes make them look rather like people who have
come to see a friend off at the station and are a little bored by having
to wait for a train which is running late. But at last the signal has
changed, the train moves off, and "Bon voyage!" and a wave of the
hand are the expected gesture.

What is less comprehensible is the fact that several members of the
family have scrolls in their hands. What do the scrolls contain—
perhaps a little set speech, copied out in a fair hand by one of those
Etruscan secretaries of whom a drawing has survived, and whose
simple attire consists of nothing but a necklace, a stylus and an inkpot?

---

[1] *Civilisation de l'Asie Antérieure*, p. 211.

(Fig. 56.) Or are these members of the family freed slaves? Freedom was sometimes formally conferred by letter (Paoli, *loc. cit.*, p. 219).

Finally, the goddesses Vanθ (armed with an enormous key) and Culśu (holding a torch and a pair of shears) have their places at the left-hand end of the relief. Culśu is about to cut the thread of Tita's life; her role is the opposite of protective.

She reminds us not of the beneficent deities of the Hittites but, much more, of a kind of Fury, a female monster of Albanian folklore: Kulshedër (M. 223 and Lambertz, *loc. cit.*, I, p. 161). Is this Albanian figure an echo from a remote past?

Both the Hittites and the ancient Illyrians drew on a common archaic fund which we could call proto-Danubian. Identical motifs

FIG. 56. A Lasa ready to write

might, of course, evolve in one way in the Balkan countries and Etruria, and in another in Asia Minor.

Conjecturally, we can compare the names Culśan and Culśu with Albanian *golle*, "vault, cavern" (M. 130). It will be remembered that the gates of Etruscan towns, of which illustrations have been published so often (notably those of Veii, Falleri and Volterra; and many others), and also the inner doors of Etruscan tombs, are *vaulted* (cf. photograph facing p. 257). This Oriental feature also characterises Hittite architecture and that of Urartu (S. Lloyd, *loc. cit.*, p. 132). This being the case, *cul* may mean "gate, door", and *culś* may mean "he of the gate or door", in other words "gate-keeper" or "door-keeper" (referring to the gates of towns or those of temples and palaces). In short, θuflθas and Culśan are simply two epithets (Bifrons and "guardian of the gates") of a single deity who is also known under the name *Ani*, the same deity as we saw on coins from Velathri, but whose real name is unknown to us—as it was to every "average Etruscan", too.

We need not be particularly surprised at the fact that we are acquainted with a goddess θuflθa, who, however, never appears in the form of a *bifrons* (which would account for her name). The whole of Etruscan religion was lapped in an atmosphere of mystery. In the

earliest times the line of demarcation between some of the gods and
their consorts may not have been clearly maintained. Later, Diana
and Jovino make their appearance as the feminine forms of Janus and
Jovis (V. Duruy, *Histoire des Romains*, p. 75). A recent writer who has
studied this problem is J. Przyluski. He speaks of the primitive duality
of the androgynous Great Goddess who was later separated into two
opposite complementary elements. In the Orient and in the Aegean
region, Ashera-Astarte, the Tree-Goddess or Goddess-Tree, is symbolised by the sacred column whose capital has two volutes, one facing
to the left and the other to the right (*La Grande Déesse*, pp. 82–7 *et seq.*
and pl. III). Among the Etruscans, after a process of development in
their religious conceptions, the formidable privilege of possessing a
head with two faces fell to the lot of Culsanś; his consort θuflθa had
emancipated herself from it. As for the sex of θuflθaś, we may add that
there was another divinity in Italy, Pales, the guardian of the Roman
shepherds' flocks, who was sometimes considered to be a god and
sometimes a goddess.

Let us turn now to a deity who cares nothing for the past and the
future, living for and in the present moment, and whose origin (unlike
that of Culśan and Culśu) is unequivocally Danubian and Balkanic:
Bacchus-Dionysos. His Etruscan name is Fufluns.

For years I was baffled by this grotesque, charming name with its
rustle, its frivolity, its air of trickery and boasting. I felt it as a challenge; somehow, the fact that it belonged to the god of the Bacchantes
did not quite account for its character. When I thought of the paunchy,
jovial, elderly personage depicted for us by Rubens, the name seemed
rather too light and airy.

And then came the thunder and lightning of illumination! The
two *f*'s of Fufluns correspond to two *b*'s. We know that *frontac* is
bronte, that θ*efri* is Tiberius, and that *nefele* ("cloud" in Greek) corresponds to *nebula* ("cloud" in Latin). Just as *fanuse* has come out into
the open as *baneshe*; and as *fep*, when its mask was removed, became
identical with Albanian *bef*; and as *fvi* (*phvi*) became *buj* and θ*uflθas*
revealed his two foreheads, *du baltash*, so in his turn Fufluns declared
his true identity: *Bubluns*. Under this thunderous name he suddenly
appeared to me not only full of rage and vigour but also provided with
a *raison d'être*, for his origin, the Albanian verb *bubullij*, *bubullis*, means
"to resound, roar, bellow", etc. (M. 40).

Now among the Greeks Bacchus was surnamed Bromios: "the god of
the din of the Bacchic processions" (Kerenyi, *La Mythologie des Grecs*,
270).

However, W. Meyer-Lübke holds that the Albanian verb *bubullij* is derived from the Romanic verb *bubulare*, "to cry like an owl"; and he derives the Italian words *bubbolare*, "to shout, roll (of thunder)", and *bubbolo*, "thunder", from the same Romanic radical.

If Meyer-Lübke is correct in this we must look for a different explanation of "Fufluns".

There is no disputing that Fufluns is Bubluns and that the "bu-bu" sound in the latter is onomatopoeic. It is equally indisputable that the same onomatopoeia exists in Albanian; the interjection *"Abubu!"* (M. 1; Lambertz, I, 59) expresses terror.

But suppose, after all—suppose Meyer-Lübke was wrong?

I make bold to express this doubt because I remember how the same scholar treated another problem, one which is analogous to our own.

This concerns the *Italian* word *albardeola*, "pelican". Meyer-Lübke studies it in relation with Romanic *ardea*, "heron", which corresponds to Rumanian *barza*, "stork". The author observes that, on the one hand, the aforesaid *albardeola*, and on the other hand, the Albanian adjective *barth* ("white") both bear a phonetic resemblance to Rumanian *barza*.

Well, what about it? What is the inference?

It leaps to the eye that all these words are connected with the same root. Meyer-Lübke ought to have told us what that root was; and surely, in theory, could it not have been a putative Romanic word *bard*—since, after all, Romanic is older than Rumanian, Albanian and Italian?

But on reaching the brink of this precipice he hesitates and finally extricates himself only by launching a pathetic appeal into space:

"But who created that Italian word?" (*Ibid.*, p. 619.)

Now, Meyer-Lübke must have known that behind the Albanian root *bardh*, "white", there lay an Illyrian kingly name, Bardullos; which is to say that the inclusion of that root in the *ancient Illyrian linguistic stock* was, *ipso facto*, proved. Yet he did not deem it necessary to mention this detail—which, however, is an enlightening one. Perhaps he was uninterested in it, because, after all, it did not come within the framework of the Romance languages. It is this watertight partitioning of knowledge, carried to excess, which has so much retarded the deciphering of Etruscan. This is one of the real—as against the imaginary—disabilities under which Etruscan studies have laboured.

As for the root *bardh*, we have met it already in the form of its dialectal variant, *barl*: (P. 226) *klumie parliu*.

Coming back to Bubluns, there are two possible ways of explaining it:

(a) the Illyrian root *bubul* was present both in Etruscan and in archaic Albanian, and was inherited by Romanic as a survival from Etruscan; or, alternatively,

(b) this Etruscan root may have been missing from Albanian; but Albanian later got it back by borrowing Romanic *bubulare* or Italian *bubbolare*.

But in any case, Fufluns was *Bubluns*. What finally persuaded me of this was an article by C. Devoto, *Nomi di divinita etrusche*. For his own part, this writer comes to no conclusion on the matter; but he very appositely quotes an observation of Grotenfend, who related Fufluns to *bublinon oïnos*, the name of a celebrated wine of Naxos, on which island the worship of Dionysus flourished (*Studi Etruschi*, VI, p. 243).

In Etruscan, Fufluns is also known as *Paχa* and as *Paχies*, that is to say Bacchus. On this we have two remarks to offer: (i) the Hittite word *paχχiśa*, which resembles both of these names so closely, means "stick, rod". Is not this connected with the famous thyrsus of the Bacchantes? (ii) Bacchus was of Thraco-Illyrian extraction and, originally, was worshipped only by women. There is no doubt that the vine was regarded as a source of fecundity and that women tried to obtain fecundity from it. An ancient bas-relief from Askalon, reproduced in Perret and Chipiez (Vol. III, fig. 314), depicts women in coitus with a vine-stock. This is perhaps to be explained by the fact that Askalon was one of the five cities of the Philistines and that the latter were a branch of the Illyrians. They could thus have brought with them, into the land of Canaan, rites which went back to the archaic sources of the Dionysiac cult.

Since we have mentioned the Bacchantes, the moment is opportune for us to set about explaining one of those words which are as old as the world and which nevertheless remain puzzling: the word *satyr*. It will become evident once more what a crude, pitiless light our deciphering casts on the very heart of so many complicated and fruitless discussions. What is the meaning of "satyr"; more precisely, *satur(os)*?

The etymology of the word *Satyros* is unknown. The attempts of grammarians to explain this word, which is probably not of Hellenic origin, have not yielded any satisfactory result ... [The Satyrs'] Dorian name, *tituroï*, means "he-goats". Hence the Satyrs can be incorporated in the large family of theriomorphic spirits ... animal spirits. ... These beliefs, slightly modified it is true, still survive among the mountain-dwellers of Macedonia.

[In Arcady there was a cult of] Pan, the goat-footed god. His horns, tail and cloven hooves were borrowed and given to the Satyrs, those rebellious and wanton creatures who have always retained something of this caprine nature.

This is a quotation from Daremberg, who goes on to explain that the Sileni, who are closely related to the Satyrs, were horse-demons; and that the Satyrs were often associated with Hermes and took part in the processions known as phallophoriai.

Wissowa's encyclopaedia, however, in its article *Satyroi*, categorically denies the antiquity of the identification of the Satyrs with the he-goat, saying that it dates from the Hellenistic period. Ancient Athens, as distinct from Hellenistic Athens, knows nothing of these satyrs in the guise of he-goats; on the contrary, they are ithyphallic and have horses' tails. An argument in favour of the caprine origin of the Satyrs, drawn from the *Prometheus Bound*, is totally demolished. We are then informed that the etymology of their name was at one time regarded as being from Sanskrit *turas*, "strong". Mommsen, for his part, had suggested Latin *satur* ("sated, saturated") as the source of the word.

Finally, in our own day, Altheim attests that "Satyr" is a word of Illyrian origin (*loc. cit.*, p. 15). At the same time it is indisputable that Hermes, who is closely akin to the Satyrs, is an ithyphallic deity and that both the Satyrs and the Sileni are so represented in innumerable examples of classical iconography.

I therefore believe that the origin of the word is to be sought in Albanian *shtuar*, "erect", from the verb *shtoj*, "to stand up" (M. 501) (cf. Latin *sto* and Russian *stoiati*); *shtuar* meaning in this context no more or less than "ithyphallic". This confirms both Altheim's assertion and the manifold connections of the cult with that of Dionysos and with Thrace. The satyrs represent the worship of fertility in all its Thraco-Illyrian crudity.

We have already spoken of the god Veltun, Vertun, Voltumna, whose name is connected with one of the longest-known and most incontrovertibly established of the Indo-European roots: *vert* (*vers*), "to turn". Let us now study a votive inscription from an "askos", a vase with the shape of a leathern bottle:

(P. 60) *mi venelusi aχesi muluemknie vrtun* (B)

muluem is a verb already examined: "to dedicate". Its grammatical form (differing slightly from the more frequent *mulu*, *muluvanice*, etc.) is what requires emphasis here. Its termination *em* causes it

Etruscan censer.

The "Porta di Giove" (*circa* 200 B.C.) at S. Maria de Falleri.

to be classified as a middle-voice infinitive, to judge by what we see in Albanian:

Active	Middle voice (medio-passive)
bâj, to make	*bahem*, to make oneself, be done
lus, to pray	*lutem*, to be asked
kryej, to achieve	*kryhem*, to be achieved

This is an example of the way in which the profusion of Etruscan verbal forms becomes less confusing in proportion as our decipherment progresses.

knie is connected with the Albanian root *qenë*, "to be, exist", which we discussed earlier in relation to *klenase* (*kitia*) and *acnanasa*.

So the inscription means: "This, from Venelus Aχes, is consecrated, for as long as it lasts, to Vertun."

As a change from so many gods—and, moreover, as a mark of respect for Etruscan customs—let us speak of a goddess, Latona, Leto, lover of Zeus-Tinia and mother of Apollo and Artemis. She is a pre-Hellenic goddess whose worship was widely diffused on both shores of the Aegean: it was found in Macedonia, Delos, Ephesus, Crete, Caria, Phrygia and Lycia. According to Daremberg, her name may have been derived from an Indo-European root, *le*, "to give, procure": "*She is the goddess who procures fortunate childbirth.*"

This pointer is enough for me to suggest a new interpretation of the Etruscan word Leθam, Leθn, Leta (A). What I have in mind is the Albanian verb *le*, whose past participle is *lete* (obs.), "to bear, bring forth, beget" (M. 239). This is well suited to a goddess of maternity.

She is mentioned several times in the inscription on the Tile of Capua, which we have had occasion to mention a number of times and shall be mentioning again; a text rendered difficult to decipher by its comparatively archaic language (5th century), its poor state of preservation and the fact that it comes from Campania, where the Etruscans were a minority among the aborigines.

I consequently found it hard to understand the optimism with which this inscription was hailed by M. Buffa in 1935:

We can regard it as the oldest text of any considerable length which our forefathers have left us. But its importance becomes still greater when we reflect that the numerous Italic affinities, which are presented by the language in which it is written, may make it easier to understand.

(NRIE, 284)

I

Now since 1900, the year of its discovery, this text has obstinately resisted every attempt at decipherment. It has remained as recalcitrant as any wild bull; I shall feel myself fortunate if I can plant a few banderillas in its neck.

It mentions *vacil leθamsul*: in this we can recognise a *feast* in honour of the goddess or rather "in the house of Leθam", that is to say in Leθam's temple. We next read: *vacil lunasie face iχnac*, "a feast (or banquet) followed by games (in honour) of Bacchus the Wrathful". This naturally makes us think of the great games which were held every year at the temple of Voltumna. We have already quoted several other terms from the same source: . . . *tule apirase unialθi*, which means perhaps "(the sacrifice of) tender black lambs in Juno's temple". Now let us look at a sentence in which *Leθam* plays a leading role. If I have rightly understood them, these few words throw an unexpected light on Etruscan rites; less unexpected, however, if we admit the links between Etruscan religion and that of Asia Minor.

The words are a fragment which I arrange thus:

puiian acasri
Tinian tule leθamsul (P. 2, 19)

puiian: *puia*, "woman", a word already known; in the accusative here?

acas: in Rumanian and Macedo-Rumanian, both of which have retained a few Thracian elements (we emphasise, Thracian), *akatsa* means "to take, to grasp".

ri: Albanian "young, new", as already noted.

tinian: Tinia; in the accusative?

tule: "tender, delicate", already noted.

leθamsul: Leθam (in an oblique case).

As the words stand, the meaning emerges thus:

"woman to take young,
Tinia, in the house of tender Latona".

But what they mean is probably: "to take (the statues of) the young wife, the tender Latona, and of Tinia, her husband". In other words, the fragment refers to the images' of these two deities being carried in procession. This suggests an analogy with the periodical rite of the *sacred marriage* between the Great God and the Great Goddess, the divine pair ensuring the fertility of the country, which was the central motif in the religion of the Indo-European Hittites. This rite figures in the great bas-relief cut in the rock-face [1] at Iasili-Kaia, in Anatolia,

[1] G. Contenau, *Manuel*, I, p. 290 and fig. 131.

in which a procession of gods is to be seen. Does the Capuan text refer to a feast celebrating a marriage between the Etruscan Great God and Great Goddess, a feast which included processions? A memory of the rites of Asia Minor? These customs could have been brought over into Etruria by the Tursha, the ancestors of the Etruscan aristocracy, who were of Illyrian stock; hailing, however, from the coast of Lydia.

But the rite was Aegean as well as Asian.[1]

A general observation is necessary at this point. It appears that several important religious ceremonies were conducted in the temple of Leθam; others, in that of Uno-Uni. It has already been made clear in the chapter on the Family that Turan also belonged to the group of Mother-Goddesses.

One fact is certain. There are several pieces of evidence in Etruscan epigraphy to prove that by the side of the "official" religion, so to speak, in which the place of honour belonged to Tinia *ais cemnac*, the Etruscans' daily life was dominated by fervent worship of the Mother-Goddesses.

The name of the sun-god Cauθa was preserved in the Etruscan name of a flower, *kautam*, "Solis Oculum" (according to Dioscorides, 1st century A.D.). This deity has been mentioned already, in the chapter on Numbers, in connection with the strip of lead from Magliano. On the well-known bronze liver he appears with the name Caθ; in the Book of the Mummy he is *caθinum*. It is interesting to compare this latter name with the Lithuanian verb *kaitinu*, "to heat" (Seidel, *Grammatik der lithuanischen Sprache*, p. 119).

In the Magliano inscription offerings in honour of the god Marisl (Mars) are also mentioned: *cialaθ χimθm avilś*, "one hundred and thirty a year"? (P. 359, CIE 5237). They are to be made by *cepen tuθiu* (the chief priest—?) (of the city) *θuχ iχutevr*. In the last expression we have two verbs and a noun:

θuχ is Albanian *dukem*, "to appear; be visible" (M. 86). According to G. Meyer there is no proof that *dukem* is related to Greek *dokéo*, "to appear" (*Etym. Wört.*, pp. 76–7).
iχu is *ik*, "to go, run away, flee" (M. 166).
tevr is *tivr*, "month", a word already known.

The meaning of the phrase *θuχ iχutevr* (B) will therefore be: "at the beginnings and ends of the months", or alternatively "at the

[1] According to Diodorus, the Cretans held an annual celebration of the marriage of Zeus and Hera.

appearance and disappearance of the moon". We have already seen *mlusna* representing the second of these meanings; but it is possible that different phrases were used in different parts of Etruria.

The name of θesan, the Etruscan Aurora, recurs frequently in the Book of the Mummy. θesan (A) is explained by the Albanian root *dhez*, "to kindle" (M. 90). We read, for example, in Martin-Leake (*loc. cit.*, p. 389): *te mare kiri edhe ta dezne perpara sentit*, "to take a candle and light (it) in front of the saints". The meaning of the name θesan is therefore "Kindler", which is close to "torch". This deity appears in the Book of the Mummy as θesan tinś θesan eiseraś (V, 19–20), which means "θesan of Tinia, θesan of the gods" (or "of the goddess"—the Goddess Uni, Juno?). Both by the etymology of her name and by these epithets, θesan reminds me strongly of the Aurora of the Phoenician pantheon of Ras-shamra (Ugarit), *Nerat Elim Shepesh*, "luminary [torch] of the gods, Shepesh."

There is a little-known goddess, *Malaχe*, who is represented, according to Skutsch, on the coinage of Lemnos. She is probably the same

Fig. 57. Hercules and Mlacu

as the goddess represented on an Etruscan mirror described by Gerhard (*loc. cit.*, Table CCCXLIV). The inscription is: *herucel* (?) *mlacuχ*, "Hercules and Mlaku". (Fig. 57.)

Now this name occurs a number of times in the Book of the Mummy in the form *mlaχ*. It forms part of the phrase: *un mlaχ nunθen* (Ch. III, 19; V, 1, 20; IX, 19; and *un mlaχ* in VIII, 12).

Un, Uni being Juno and *nunθen* being *nundinae*, the ninth day, the goddess Juno figures as *mlaχ* of this Etruscan holiday. The same epithet *mlaχ* is applied to other Etruscan deities, however: to the goddess θanir (*mlaχanθra*) and to Tinia (*mlaχ tins*), in the Magliano strip (P. 359).

Now it is known that in the city of Veii, Juno was called "queen" (Müller-Deecke, II, p. 44). Does *mlaχ* mean "queen, king"?

This Etruscan word reminds me of the Illyrian and Albanian verb *mblak*, "to grow old" (M. 270), from which are derived the name of one of the cities of the Pelasgians, Plakia, and Albanian *plak*, "old" (M. 390). The Albanian *mb* is often contracted; thus *mbloj*, "to cover", can be found reduced to *mloj* (M. 271). *mblak* could have become *plak* in one Illyrian dialect and *mlak* in another.

But "old" leads us straight to the idea of a "lord", as is shown by Latin (*senex*, from which *senatus* is derived). Thus *un mlaχ* must have been Juno the Sovereign Lady, like the Lady of Byblos, widely known in ancient times. *mlaχanθra* would be "θanir the Sovereign Lady" and *mlaχ tinś*, "Jupiter the Sovereign Lord".

An inscription *mlaχ* (P. 666) on a vase would then mean "To the Sovereign Lady". We may also note another votive inscription P. 27, CIE 8413, concerning a man named Auvile who consecrates his offering to *ateri mlaχuta*. Ateri (A) is elucidated perfectly by Albanian *atër*, "fathers" (a parallel to *etna*), and *atëri*, "paternity" (M. 14), both of which are derived from *at*, "father". *ateri mlaχuta* would therefore mean, "To the lords, the ancestors".

In view of the foregoing, a sentence in the Magliano text:

aiseras in ecs mene mlaθcemarni tuθi tiv

should perhaps be interpreted as follows:

aiseras: oblique case of the noun *aisera*, "goddess".
in: "this" (adjective, feminine).
ecs: oblique case of the word *ec*, *eca*, "behold!"? Or cf. Albanian *ec*, "go!"?
mene: (cf. LM, Ch. II).
mlaθcemarni, in my estimation, consists of three elements:
  mlaθ, equivalent to *mlaχ* (cf. *meθlum* and *meχlum*), "sovereign" (feminine).
  ce: another demonstrative adjective (cf. *suθce*, "this tomb").

marni is evidently connected with the room *marr*, *merr*, "to take",
already identified (cf. *intemamer*), and has the suffix *-ni*, which
in Illyrian denotes the imperative (cf. *epni*, "give!"; *bleni*,
"buy!"). *Marrni*, "take!"

tuθi, "in(to) the city".

tiu: *tiv*, "month".

Would the whole sentence mean: "This goddess whom you see,
this Sovereign, take her (in procession) into the city, every month"?

But there are still many difficulties to be overcome.

How, for example, are we to interpret the following inscription?

(P. 42) *mi mlaχ mlakaś*
mini θanirśiie turice hvuluves

The second sentence is clear: "This (or, me) to θanir offered (cf.
Albanian *dhuroj*, 'to offer, present, give') Holaies" (i.e., "Holaies

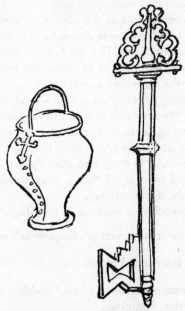

FIG. 58. The Rhaetian bucket and key

offered this to θanir"). But what is the meaning of the repetition *mlaχ*,
mlakaś in the first line?

"To the queen of queens"? Cf. the "god of gods", Janus.[1] Or does
mlaχ possess a supplementary meaning in addition to its main one;
"libation", for example? Should we be thinking of Sanskrit *mlaka*,

---

[1] An epithet of Janus in the Salian chants (Macrobius, *Saturnalia*, I, 14).

"earth saturated with water", and Lithuanian *malkas* and Lettish *malka*, "sip, mouthful" (Walde-Pokorny, *loc. cit.*, II, p. 287)?

This is something for future investigation.

On turning towards other divinities, we have the pleasant surprise of coming across a veritable "key to the Etruscan language", a palpable key of corroded bronze, enriched with an interesting inscription.

What a windfall! Have we not been told a hundred times that there was no key to Etruscan, and that to look for one was a waste of time?

Well, this deeply symbolic object does exist; though no one has paid much attention to it so far (fig. 58).

In appearance it is both simple and elegant; only its length—some fifteen inches—is at all out of the ordinary.

This product of Etruscan heavy industry was found in 1870 at Dambel in Rhaetia, near the city of Trenta. But there is better yet to come; for in the same province, but nearer to Trenta, in the valley of Cembra, not far from the River Avisio, another ancient bronze article had been found in 1828: a bucket. Now the River Avisio (rivers are important just here) joins another river, the Etch, near the town of Lavis (and Lavis is important too, as will be seen). Better still: this bucket also bears an inscription. Best of all: the inscription on the key and that on the bucket are almost identical, both objects being dedicated to the Etruscan god of springs, Lavis, whose name has miraculously survived in the name of the town of Lavis.[1]

The fact that the inscriptions are couched in the same terms proves that the objects must be assigned to a common origin. Yet neither the similar content of the two texts nor the differences between them can be easily accounted for; indeed, they set us a number of problems.

So the "key to the Etruscan language" with which that great researcher, blind chance, has supplied us, possesses a grave disadvantage: it must first be deciphered.

The text on the key is a little longer than that on the bucket. Here are the two of them, set out in such a way as to show the brevity of the latter as compared with the former:

KEY		BUCKET
1. *laviseśelk*		(a) *laviseśelk*
2. *lth velχanu*		(b) *rupinupitiave*
3. *upinupitiapv*		(c) *velχanu*
4.	*vthinrśitl*	
5. *lravinutalina*		(d) *thelnavinutalina*
6.	*thikeurais*	
7. *skuztrinaχe*		(e) *kusenkustrinaχe*
8.	*lttvralsnu*	

[1] Corssen, *Ueber die Sprache der Etr.*, I, p. 919, tab. XXIII.

Three preliminary observations:

A. Lines 4, 6 and 8 are missing on the bucket.

B. Certain words which appear on the bucket *seem* to appear on the key in a distorted or abbreviated form (*rupinu–upinu*).

C. In his juxtaposition of the two texts, Corssen reversed the order of lines (*b*) and (*c*) so as to make them come opposite lines 2 and 3 of the key, thus:

2. *lth velχanu*	(*c*) *velχanu*
3. *upinupitiapv*	(*b*) *rupinupitiave*

The bucket is archaic in appearance. It is not soldered but held together with bronze nails, which were clenched after insertion. Let us take the inscription on it as our starting-point:

THE BUCKET

laviśelk: The first part, *lavis*, "to the god Lavis", is as clear as the second part is difficult. We find ourselves placed between two equally strong temptations. On the one hand, we recognise in *śelk* the Albanian word for *key*, namely *çilc* (*tshiltz*) (also written as *çelës* and *çels*), from the root *çel*, "to open" (M. 58 and 60). This is nicely pertinent; the key and the bucket were consecrated at the same time, and the key was regarded as the more valuable of the two offerings. I may be asked how it was that the announcement "This is a key" came to be written on a bucket. But the objection is not a damaging one; for the donor may have ordered that the same dedication be inscribed on both objects, leaving himself the option of having three new words added to the key-inscription when he had had time to think about it.

On the other hand, it is possible that *śel* is a form of the Etruscan dative and genitive particle *sul, zul*, as in *leθamsul, larezul*, etc. (cf. *Fuflunsl*). A local variation? After all, we are in Rhaetia now. But in that case we shall have to find a reason for the last letter, *k*. The conjunction "and"? This would be natural enough on the key, where the opening phrase *laviśelk* is in fact followed by another name (*lth velχanu*); but, as we shall see, "and" does not fit in so nicely on the bucket.

A third possibility: *śel* may be the deity *cel* who is mentioned on the liver of Piacenza (P. 719b).

rupinupitiave (B): This brings us on to firmer ground. After the indication showing *to whom* the offering was made, there comes a prayer to the god of springs. It falls into three parts:

rupinu: here I recognise Etruscan *repine*, which can be interpreted thanks to the formula *hatec repinec*; this occurs frequently in LM and means "in Hades and in the abyss". It can also be interpreted by Albanian *rrëpinë*, "precipice, drop" (M. 437). The word will be examined again later. Alternately, *rupinu* is related to *rru*, "watercourse" (M. 442).

piti is perfectly clear: *pitë*, "to drink" (M. 388), infinitive of *pi*, which we have met several times already. This shows complete identity with Slavonic *piti*, "to drink".

ave can be interpreted with the help of its counterpart on the key, *apv*, which is none other than *apu* from the verb *ap*, "to give". The sense of the three words is "Give (us) to drink (of the water) of the depths" (that is, of the waters that issue from the depths of the earth); or, alternatively, "of the brooks"; or, again, "of the rivers" (in view of a possible parallel to Latin *ripa*, *ripula*, "river bank"). Another possible line is to regard *ave* as a counterpart to Thracian *ap*, *apa*, "water" (Tomaschek); which will give us, "From the depths (*rupinu*) to drink (*piti*) water (*ave*)."

velχanu: the counterpart of this on the key is *lth velχanu*, Larth Velχanu. It is curious to note that this resembles Larth Velχas, a name occurring twice in the inscriptions from Tarquinii (P. 91, CIE 5401 and P. 124, CIE 5554). However, I do not think the name is that of the worshipper who dedicated the key and the bucket to Lavis, because the name is not followed by a verb referring to the objects dedicated; which is contrary to the usual custom in votive texts. *Velχanu* is therefore an appeal to a second deity, namely Vulcan (?), the god of subterranean fire. Vulcan could be connected with Lavis, since both of them were gods of fertility. This occurs to me because, as we have already seen, fire was regarded by the Etruscans as a source of fecundity.

The foregoing lines had long been written when I at last perceived that there was every possibility of our Lavis' being the same deity as *lvsl* in the celebrated inscription of the bronze liver of Piacenza (P. 719). Be it noted that the latter does not appear alone; we find him in good company, *lvsl velχ*, Lavis Vulcan. So our troubles come to an end. We have two divinities here, and the imaginary donor Larth Velχas must vanish from our horizon at supersonic speed.

thelnavinutalina (B): this is fairly clear:

> *thel* tallies with Albanian *thel*, "deep", and a verb connected
> with the same root, *thalloj*, "to deepen; to expand" (M. 533).
>
> *na*: us, our, to us (as in Albanian).
>
> *vinu*: in this context, undoubtedly "vines" or "vineyards".
>
> *tali(na)* is the Albanian verb "to come out; to succeed". So
> what is asked of Velχan is: "Make our vines flourish, make
> us succeed (prosper)."

kusenkustrinaχe: this takes us back into the darkest depths of obscurity.
Extrinsically, it is true, there could be nothing simpler: *kusen*,
accusative of Albanian *kus*, "saucepan" etc., and *kusiçkë*, "bucket"
(M. 230), consequently the word is appropriate enough in an
inscription on a bucket; *kustri(naχe)* would be a verb which could
be interpreted by Albanian *kushtër*, "to dedicate" (M. 231);
putting the two together we get "this bucket is by us dedicated".
But G. Meyer is against this: according to him, *kusi* comes from
Venetian *cusina* and *kushtroj* is an early borrowing from Latin
(*loc. cit.*, p. 217). So the problem remains unsolved.

The broad sense of the inscription, based only on what is comparatively clear, is:

"To Lavis and Cel (?). From the depths of the earth, give us to
drink. To Vulcan. Make our vines flourish, make us prosper . . ."

THE KEY

laviselk: "To Lavis, the key".

lth velχanu: *larth* is "high"; hence, "to great Vulcan".

upinupitiapv: the meaning may be the same as in line (*b*) of the
bucket-inscription. But there may be a slight difference:

> *upinu* may be the middle voice (identifiable by initial *u*): "to
> quench our thirst"; *piti* could well mean "drink" (noun).
> Hence, "Give us, to quench our thirst, of (your) drink." *apu*
> is a plural; two gods are being addressed.

vthinrśitl (A): a superb composite word which gives us the courage
to go on. Thus—

> *vthi* = *udhi*, which we already know means "path, way".
>
> *nrś* corresponds to the genitive of Albanian *njer-i*, "man": "of
> man, of men".
>
> *itl*: Albanian *i dal*, which we have met before (*i* is the object
> preceding the verb), "to succeed, cause to succeed" (M. 65).

Thus: *udhi njerish i dal*, "Cause the path of men to succeed."

lravinutalina (A), another comprehensible passage:
lra: Albanian *lërej*, "to leave" (M. 244).
vinu: "vineyards".
tali(na): "to succeed" ("our").
"Let our vineyards succeed."

thikeurais (A): this is a really extraordinary fragment, and one of the most beautiful which I have succeeded in deciphering. Of its three constituent elements, *thi*, *ke* and *urais*, we have so far met only the first, in which I detected the meaning (by extension) "stag". The two others seem, at first glance, to be unique cases. But their vitality, the fact that they go so well together and, moreover, the logical way in which they are connected to each other, are such as to preclude all doubt:

> *thi*: "goats" (Albanian *dhi*, M. 91); or else *thi*, "pigs" (M. 534).
> *ke*: Albanian *qé*, plural of *ka*, "ox" (M. 171).
> *urais*: with prefixed medio-passive *u*, this is an optative of the Albanian verb *rris*, "to rear animals" (M. 439). We are decidedly in luck, for Mann gives an example of just the grammatical form we need here:

> *t'u-rrit dera!* "may your clan prosper!"

The risks we run are reduced to zero on this occasion.
thikeurais: "May (our) goats and (our) oxen flourish" (or "multiply").
skuztrinaχe: this time I shall try a different angle of attack in my decipherment, not the one used for line (*e*) of the bucket:

> *skuz* would be connected with the Etrusco-Albanian root *shkoj*, "to go" (which occurs in LM: *ścun*, *ścanin*, and also on the Cippus of Perugia, P. 570, *scuna*, *ścune*, etc.). Mann gives a noun which comes from this root: *shkuesi*, "habit, practice" (M. 485). I.e., tradition.
> *trin* is Albanian "hero", and occurs frequently in LM. We must remember at the same time that in the archaic period in Greece the dividing line between *heroes* and *ancestors* was a loose one. Ancestors became heroes; heroes were regarded as ancestors; the tombs of both, in the *agora* of the city, represented its concentrated psychological capital. This twofold meaning must be kept in mind.
> *χe*: this may be Albanian *ke*, "have!", from *ka*, "I have".

lttvralsnu (B) is, fortunately, fairly clear:

> *ltt*: the plural of the noun *lut* ("prayer"), already interpreted; or else of the noun *lot*, "tear" (M. 250). Final *t* is common to the plural of masculine and feminine nouns: *mali—malet* ("the mountains"), *nata—netët* ("the nights").
>
> *vra* is Albanian *ura*, "hunger" (M. 541).
>
> *s*: the Albanian negative particle, already encountered.
>
> *nu* is Albanian *njoh*, "to know", already encountered (cf. *trutnut*).

Thus: "Tears and hunger (may we) not know!"

Leaving out everything which is not so far clear, the meaning of the inscription on the key is as follows:

> "To Lavis . . . Let us quench our thirst with thy drink. May the way of (our) people prosper. Let our vineyards prosper. May our goats and cattle multiply. Maintain the customs of our ancestors. May we not know tears and hunger."

Our interpretation is not without gaps. So this "key to the Etruscan language" is not a master-key: we no sooner had it in our hands than we found it was by no means an "Open, sesame!" and that we must go on clambering our way up the slippery walls as before. I have been compelled, of course, to combine the data yielded by the two texts in order to make something comprehensible out of them. It will therefore be seen that my method is "combinatorial" as well as "comparative". I trust that this will gain me the favour of the adherents of both these trends, and that the interests of both parties will thus at long last be reconciled.

In any case, our toil has not been barren: these two texts have enriched us to the extent of several permanent acquisitions, both in vocabulary and in morphology. The key, in particular, has yielded a pithy, meaningful prayer, which contains two or three striking expressions.

But, if I am not mistaken, the value of this unusual item of evidence does not end here. There are historical implications to be taken into account as well.

We are in Rhaetia. This is the Etruscan Far West, on the frontiers of Etruscan expansion in the valley of the Po. That, in itself, determines a certain ambiance: a society of expatriates, anxious to make good in their new surroundings. Arriving in a new country, they look for good water and good pasturage, they plant vineyards and are determined to keep up "the customs of the ancestors". They give us a brief glimpse of

Etruscan colonisation, which was essentially agricultural in character, the work of farmers, vine-growers and shepherds.

Let us digress a little—taking as our point of departure the inscription featuring the god Lavis. That inscription helps us to open a side-door which has hitherto remained shut.

Let us take up again one of the clearest passages from the key: *vthinrsitl, udhi neris idal*, "(may) the way of (our) people succeed"; thus equipped, let us hasten back to the Tavern.

There we left, languishing in the darkness of incomprehension, a handsome cup from Vetulonia which has a curiously attractive handle and an inscription:

> (P. 366, NRIE 701) *naceme uru iθal θilen iθal*
> *iχeme mesnamer*
> *tansina mulu*

We can start by eliminating the third line from our field of vision. It means "Tansina dedicated (this cup)", and it appears to have no connection with the two preceding lines.

If we examine the first line we find one of the words from the key, *i(d)al*, "(may it) succeed"; and it is repeated insistently, *iθal . . . iθal*.

Is it, then, a vow, a wish, a toast, which someone reiterates with cup in hand?

We see that *naceme* and *iχeme* have the same ending *eme*. Amputating this, we are left with *nac* in the first line and *iχ* in the second. These two words are old friends of ours: *nac*, "night", and *iχ*, "to go, to set out". *Eme* has an exact counterpart in Albanian: *eme*, "my" (masculine or feminine) (M. 94). It is tempting to present the rest of the first line thus:

> *uru*: cf. Albanian *uroj*, "to wish", *urim*, "wish" (noun) (M. 541). Could it have been an adaptation from Latin *orare*, "to pray"?
> *θilen* seems to divide into *θi* and *len*. *len* finds an immediate echo in Albanian: *lenj*, "to be born" (M. 241). Nascent?
>> *naceme uru iθal θilen . . .*: "At night, my wish is that it may succeed when *θi* is nascent . . ." Then what must be the meaning of *θi*? What birth is hoped for, what success is looked for? Let us take care to profit not only by parallelisms but also by antitheses: *night* and *day*? Is *θi* or *di* a shortened form of *tin*, "day" (from which the name Tinia is usually supposed to be derived)? If not, does the solution lie in Albanian *gdhi*, "the dawn", cf. *u-gdhi*, "it dawned" (M. 74)?
>> On this reckoning, *iθal θilen* would be "May (it) succeed at the dawn of day".

We go on to line 2: *ixeme mesnamer*. As *ix* means "to go, to set out", the wish expressed is that something should succeed and some other thing should go or set out. May it be that good should come and that evil should depart?

> *mes*: cf. Albanian *mësyj*, "to charm, enchant" (M. 283). Something to do with a spell or enchantment?
>
> *namer*: a plural? Cf. Albanian *nâm*, "to curse" (M. 303). Curses, maledictions?

Here is the hypothetical meaning of the text as a whole:

"At night, my wish (is): May it succeed, at dawn of day, may it succeed!

"May my spells and curses speed on their way! Tansina has dedicated."

At the same time, our Etruscan key has opened our eyes to the problem of irrigation in Etruria. We have already mentioned the goddess Iuturna, whose name I compared with Albanian *üje*, "water", and *ujtore*, "cistern" (M. 539).

The question of the connections between Etruscan and the other Italic languages will be raised briefly at the end of this book. It may be remarked meanwhile that the element *utur*, in Iuturna, occurs in Osco-Umbrian, notably in the Iguvine Tables, which contain the expression *sviseve utur fertu* (col. IIb, 15).

svisve seems to denote receptacles, *fertu* means "to carry". It is interesting to see that the term *utur* has been handled with great circumspection. In his excellent commentary on this verse, M. Bréal says:

> The objects referred to as *svisveva* are three. In the first, milk is carried; in the second, wine; in the third, an unknown substance named *utur*.
>
> (*Les Tables Iguvines*, p. 268)

One may wonder whether it is not the liquid in which we wash our hands?

It is clear that the Etruscans had a high regard for that liquid. According to O. Müller, they were versed in the art of exploring underground supplies of water and possessed special rites for bringing rain. Those rites centred about Tinia, as rain-god.[1] This has to be taken into account in the elucidation of a phrase which occurs fre-

[1] *Loc. cit.* ,II, pp. 318–19.

quently in the Book of the Mummy, and whose variants are as
follows:

> *eiser śic śeuc* (V, 10, 14) (A)
> *aiseraś seuś* (II, 12)
> *eiseraś śeuś* (V, 20; etc.)

These epithets could apply to Tinia (*eiser* being perhaps a plural,
to indicate majesty?), or to Juno (*aisera*) or, obviously, to various other
deities; but it is pertinent to mention that they may refer to the souls
of the ancestors. We are reminded of this important point by the study
of M. F. Bayet on the Etruscan Hercules. We read in that study of an
archaic rite which was current in Rome and which consisted of bearing
in procession the *manalis lapis*, a sacred stone. This object was supposed
to block up the entrance to the infernal abode of the *Manes* (corresponding to the Etruscan *Mund*), and the purpose of the rite was to re-open
the entrance. But the rain escaped at the same time as the Shades.
In the eyes of the ancients the souls of the dead possessed an "immense
power" over the production of rain.[1]

This digression over, let us interpret the epithet *śic śeuc* or *śeuś* which
was applied to the deities or to the divinised dead:

> *śic* is *si* + *c*. *śi* is Albanian *shi*, "rain" (M. 476). *c* is "and".
>
> *śeuc* is *seu* + *c*. *se* (with the definite article *u*) is Albanian *shé*,
> "torrent", which we have seen already in the proverb *śenulis
> rite*.

Thus *eiser śic śeuc* means "gods of the rain and the torrents".

Let us review several more divine names and glance rapidly at their
etymology.

Nortia was the goddess of destiny. It was in her temple, as we have
already indicated, that a nail was periodically hammered in to mark
the passage of time or perhaps to "nail down" misfortune. According
to Livy (VII, 3), there was a belief at Rome that on one occasion a
dictator had caused an epidemic to cease by driving in a nail. This is
an illustration of the fact that, for the ancients, the idea of destiny was
closely linked with that of death. Now, Nortia was identical with
Decuma, whose name recalls the Albanian verb *dekun*, "to die" (M. 69).
Finally, according to a collection of Old Albanian literature, there used
to be an Albanian verb *ngurdhitur*, "to kill";[2] the descendant of this
word in modern Albanian is *ngordh*, "to die off, die (of animals)"
(M. 320), which perhaps takes us back to the word *Nortia*.

---

[1] *Hercle*, 1926, pp. 247, 248, 255.

[2] *Letersya e vjeter Shqipe dhe arberesthe*, Tirana, 1952, p. 75.

There was, however, another goddess of destiny, Libitina, a portrayal of whom is presented by Gerhard (*Etr. Spiegel*, tab. LXXVII). The word may have been only a subsidiary name; in any case, not much is known of Libitina. But the Albanian language rudely tears away the veil which seems to float about this name, and reveals it charged with truly implacable significance:

> *lebeti*, "fright, terror"
> *lebetis*, "tremble, shudder"
> *lebetitje*, "fright, alarm"   (M. 239)

There is a well-known votive inscription, from the helmet of an Etruscan warrior, which says: *aisiu himiu* (A). In Albanian, *himë* is an "abyss" (M. 159). So the helmet was dedicated to the god of the Underworld or the gods of the Underworld. We shall meet the word *him* again when we discuss the Book of the Mummy.

It may be noted that the word *aisiu* appears in the inscription on the Tile of Capua (P. 2, 21) as *aiuzie*.

Turning now to the world of demons, we find that the Gorgon Medusa was called *Tarsu* in Etruscan. The name would seem to be explicable with the help of Leotti's Albanian–Italian dictionary, which gives the following:

1. *ters*: "fateful, of bad omen" (p. 1469).
2. *turrem*: "to assault, to hurl oneself at somebody", whence *i turrëshem*, "violent" (p. 1514).

Tuχulχa, the terrifying demon, hurls himself on the dead; he is either armed with a mallet or brandishes serpents with gaping mouths. His name may have a connection with the Albanian verb *tëhelk*, "to drag, draw along", whose aorist is *tëholqa* (M. 515–16).

The name may also be connected with the number *θu*, "two", and with the weapons wielded by this demon. In the frescos he is shown holding a fork with *two* tines. Now, in Albanian, *dyqel* is "a two-pronged fork" (M. 88 and 92). Moreover, he is often shown holding *two* snakes (as in the Tomb of the Ogre, for example): the Albanian verb *ngul* means "to stick in, thrust home" (M. 321); and since *ngul* could well change to *gul*, a composite word *du-gul* could mean "two fangs".

It would perhaps be well to compare (from the morphological point of view) *tuχulχa* with *aclχa* in Ch. V, 18 of the Book of the Mummy, and with *simlχa* in Ch. X, 5, in which *-a* means "has, possesses".

Let us note in passing that it is enough to glance at the frieze of an Etruscan tomb of the 3rd century B.C., the Tomba de Cardinale (described by Poulsen, *loc. cit.*, p. 57), in which demons armed with forks are pursuing a crowd of young people, to become aware that it presents the very prototype of the devil with his fork and his cloven hooves, who was to play such a prominent part in the history of European ideas and beliefs until the approach of modern times. As we have already pointed out, it is possible that the Etruscans borrowed the notion of these demons from an Eastern source, the Mazdeism of Iran.

A note on a hero. As did so many other episodes from the *Iliad*, the tragic death of Ajax, Achilles' friend, who killed himself to expiate his own fratricidal anger, provided the subject-matter for several engravings on Etruscan gems. These drawings show the hero bent double, his head nearly down on his knees, at the moment when he is preparing to throw himself on his sword, which he has stuck point upwards in the ground.

One of these gems bears the inscription: *aiax viet* [1] (B).

I read the second word as *ujet*, connecting it with the Albanian verb *ûj*, "to bend, bow oneself" (M. 538–9). The meaning will thus be: "Ajax bent double" or "Ajax bowed".

It is noticeable that the Etruscan engraver was sometimes content to emphasise the purely external aspect of the scene, as in *tretu*, "break to pieces", or in χαλυχασu, "on horseback", which we examined earlier. Certainly Ajax's posture is very unusual.

Hercules we have already mentioned.

But we must find a place of honour for the great Hellenic or rather pre-Hellenic deity, Apollo. His cult is propagated in Italy from the 9th century B.C. onwards, by the Greeks of Cumae; by the 8th century he is venerated in Etruria, as is proved by his statue at Veii. We shall study the following votive inscription from a bronze statuette of the god (see photograph facing p. 208).

(P. 737, CII 2613) *mi fleres̆ svulare aritimi fasti ruifris trce clen ce a* (B)

The statuette (*fleres̆*) is consecrated to Svulare (an epithet of Apollo) and to Artemis (Diana), his divine sister. A woman, Fasti, daughter or wife of Ruifri, gave it (*trce, turce*) in order to be (i.e., in order that it should be; *clen*, Albanian *klenë*, previously studied) here (*ceχa*, Albanian *keha*)—"here" meaning "in this temple".

What gives one to pause is the word *svulare*. It would be vain to try and equate it with "solar", for the sun is designated in Etruscan by the terms *usil* and *caθ*. I think the basic, uninflected form of the word is *svular*, with the termination *ar* denoting (as do *ac* and *aχ*) profession,

[1] Beazley, *loc. cit.*, p. 139.

place of origin, etc., both in Etruscan (*kepucar*, "shoemaker", *uθetar*, "traveller", etc.). But which of Apollo's qualities did this epithet express? We know that for the Etruscans, as for others, he was the god of divination above all else. The oracles of the Pythia, his priestess, made it possible to foresee the future. The same function was sometimes performed by a *sibyl*. According to Daremberg, "there is no Greek etymology for *sibylla*". But it seems to us that the words *svular* and *sibulla* have a common root. Daremberg quotes Plato, according to whom the sibyl and the Pythia "rend the veil which hides the future". Are we to accept this definition just as it stands? Was the notion one of "unveiling" or "discovering" something?

Certainly, in Etruscan an *s* preceding a verb gives the verb a negative sense. We have already seen (in the chapter on the Tavern) the word *sniχe*, "not to know"; and the same thing happens in Albanian. Did *svul* mean "to unveil", and *svular* "he who unveils"? There does in fact exist in Albanian a verb *zbuloj*, "to reveal, discover" (M. 575), which is the contrary of the verb *mbuloj*, "to cover" (M. 273) and which seems to us to hold the key to *svular* and *sibylla*, whose role in the history of Greco-Roman civilisation was so important.

Since I wrote the foregoing I have had my doubts on the matter swept away by a word which figures in the *Additions* to Mann's dictionary:

> *zbulues*, "discoverer" (p. 601). Thus *svulare* really is "he who reveals".

It has been established by Jokl that this verb *mbuloj* belongs to the ancient Albanian stock; he connects it with Ancient Indian *pur*, "walled city", Greek *pyle*, "gate", Lithuanian *pilis*, etc. (*loc. cit.*, p. 54).

In conclusion, let us pay homage to von Hahn and his efforts to elucidate certain pre-Hellenic names by means of Illyrian, that is to say, Albanian. Some of his comparisons deserve to be recalled here. *Uranos*, "sky", he explained by Albanian *vranoj*, "to cloud, overcast" (M. 564). *Rhea* is *reja*, "cloud" (M. 424). *Thetis*, the sea-goddess, is *det*, "the sea" (M. 71).

Perhaps this item holds the key to the name of a group of deities which figures on the liver of Piacenza (P. 719 d): *tetlvmθ*, thus:

tet = *det*, "sea".

lvmθ = *lumt*, corresponding to Albanian *lumë*, "river" (M. 215) (not to be confused with *lumë*, "fortunate").

The meaning would thus be "seas and rivers"—which were in fact regarded as divine.

XII

THE BOOK OF THE MUMMY

THE Book of the Mummy, which we have already mentioned so often, is an expression of the Etruscans' religious ideas. Its main subject seems to be ancestor-worship. This cult is represented in it, above all, by sacrifices, libations and periodical funeral banquets. Sacrifices to the infernal gods are also made. To invite the souls of the ancestors to take part in these banquets was one of the constant preoccupations of the priests in charge of funeral ceremonies.

We must note, however, that the Book of the Mummy is not a book in the usual sense of the term. It is a sort of calendar in which ritual prescriptions (the sacrifice of an animal on such and such a date or at such and such a time of day; prayer; the pouring of libations, and so on) are interspersed with expressions of encouragement to the dead.

At present, our progress in decipherment enables us at the most to extract from it a few general ideas and one or two proverbs or, perhaps, verses from litanies. One clear feature, on the other hand, is the frequent repetition of certain set phrases.

Some of these phrases, though they seem to come out incoherently and jerkily, touch on one of mankind's most agonising religious problems.

As we have already said, frequent and regular prayers, sacrifices and libations were meant not only to prevent the souls of the dead from being hungry and thirsty but also to promote them to the rank of beneficent spirits and even tutelary deities, protecting home, family and city-state.

Thus there was continually created a circle of defence-works behind which man sought to shelter; and this circle became a cycle in which past and present, the living and the dead, stretched out their hands to one another for mutual help in their struggle against the forces of destruction.

By this means human beings provided themselves with divine protectors.

It was the same elsewhere. Among the Hittites the word to "die", when used of a king, meant to "become a god". When an Egyptian pharaoh died he was received as a friend by the gods. The Romans referred to the dead as gods, *dii Manes*: "Render to the *dii Manes* what is due to them," says Cicero . . . "look upon them as divine beings."

Certain passages in the LM stipulate clearly that the offerings be made periodically, on fixed dates. The same characteristic seems to be indicated in the opening words of a curious inscription on a stone; though only a little of this inscription has survived, the approximate meaning can be worked out:

<blockquote>(P. 498, CIE 1546) mina tiurke . . . zauri . . .</blockquote>

mina: equivalent to *mini* ("this", etc.)?

tiur is surely the Etruscan *tivr*, "month"; but with the meaning here rather of "the first day of each month"; just as in the Old Testament *hodesh* (literally "new") means both "month" and "the new moon", the ceremonies of the first day of the month.

ke: Albanian *ke*, "thou hast", "mayest thou have" ("mayest thou celebrate").

zaur(*i*): would be another transliteration of *θaur*, "tomb" (cf. *θaurχ* in LM, Ch. VII). An indication of the funerary character of the offerings which are to be made.

In short: "This (is to be done here): celebrate the first day of every month (by this) . . . tomb."

If the dead were to benefit by these offerings they had first of all to be invited. But they had already lost the habit of keeping human society. Living in darkness and the fear of demons, they had become shy and distrustful. It was necessary to coax them along and persuade them to appear.

Fustel de Coulanges describes the funeral rites of the Romans:

> The milk and wine were sprinkled on the earth of the grave. . . . A hole was dug to let the solid food get through to the dead person. . . . Certain set formulae were uttered to invite him to eat and drink. . . .
>
> (*Loc. cit.*, p. 13)

In the same fashion an annual meal was provided for the warriors who had been buried after the battle of Plataea:

> The Plataeans uttered a formula which invited the dead to come and take this meal.
>
> (*Ibid.*, p. 15)

It is curious to find that these beliefs survive in certain contemporary customs: and, in particular, in an Albanian community which for generations past has lived in Southern Russia. This is what we are told in an article by the Academician N. S. Derjavine on the Arnauts, who are settled on the coast of the Sea of Azov, in the district of Melitopol:

> The Thursday of Holy Week is a great day among them. On the evening before, at midnight, they make a fire in the courtyard, a table is set up by the brazier and laid with traditional dishes, and candles are lit; cushions are placed on the seats; incense is burnt. God releases the dead for 40 days. . . . Every Thursday the graves are sprinkled with water. On Ascension Day the dead go back to their places.
>
> (*Ethnographie soviétique*, 1948, 2, p. 156)

These data harmonise perfectly, moreover, with von Hahn's account of the funerary customs of the Albanians, which he observed in the country itself:

> When a relation dies the Albanian women cut off their hair, scratch their faces till the blood comes, strike their bosoms and throw themselves on the ground, uttering fearful shrieks. Funeral litanies are chanted for 40 days. A plaint composed in couplets is sung by one of the mourners and is instantly taken up by a chorus of women. A coin is placed in the dead person's mouth. Three years later the bones are taken out of the grave and put in a charnel-house.
>
> Nor are bloody sacrifices lacking. When an old man dies one or more ewes are slaughtered. If someone is ill, black lambs are slaughtered. . . .[1]

It will be recalled that among the ancients this blood-sacrifice was part of the very foundations of the cult of the dead. We shall see later that the Book of the Mummy sometimes refers to it euphemistically: *tei zivas fler*, "dispense *life* to the effigies (of the ancestors)". But in archaic times this species of offering must have produced a very vivid and moving atmosphere. We catch a reflection of this in the Odyssey. Ulysses tells how he went down to Hades to seek the advice of the soothsayer Tiresias. First he dug a trench one cubit square and addressed prayers and supplications to the dead. Then:

> I took the sheep and cut their throats over the trench so that the dark blood poured in. And now the souls of the dead who had gone below came swarming up from Erebus—fresh brides, unmarried youths, old men with life's long suffering behind them, tender young

[1] *Loc. cit.*, Vol. II, pp. 150 *et seq.*

girls still nursing this first anguish in their hearts, and a great throng
of warriors killed in battle, their spear-wounds gaping yet and all
their armour stained with blood. From this multitude of souls, as
they fluttered to and fro by the trench, there came a moaning that
was horrible to hear. Panic drained the blood from my cheeks.
I turned to my comrades and told them quickly to flay the sheep
I had slaughtered with my sword and burn them, while they prayed
to the gods, to mighty Hades and august Persephone. But I myself
sat on guard, bare sword in hand, and prevented any of the feckless
ghosts from approaching the blood before I had speech with
Teiresias.

. . . Next came the soul of my dead mother . . . who had been
still alive when I said farewell and sailed for sacred Ilium. My eyes
filled with tears when I saw her there, and I was stirred to compassion. Yet, deeply moved though I was, I would not allow her to
approach the blood out of turn, before I had had speech with
Teiresias. And the soul of the Theban prophet now came up, with a
gold rod in his hand, saw who I was, and saluted me.

"Royal son of Laertes, Odysseus of the nimble wits, what has
brought you, the man of misfortune, to forsake the sunlight and to
visit the dead in this mirthless place? Step back now from the
trench and hold your sword aside, so that I can drink the blood and
prophesy the truth to you."

I backed away, driving my sword home in its silver scabbard.
And when Teiresias spoke, after drinking the dark blood, it was the
voice of the authentic seer that I heard.

(*Odyssey*, XI, trans. E. V. Rieu)

These preliminary remarks will help us to understand the texts
about to be presented. But, as many of them can be interpreted no
more than tentatively, we shall content ourselves with studying only
certain extracts from them, in the order in which they occur in the
Book.

LM, *Chapter I*

Barely a dozen words of this chapter have survived. We shall deal
only with these three, which are of undeniable interest:

spanza . . . *zaχri* (B)

spanza we can hardly fail to recognise as Greek *sponde*, "libation",
and *spendo*, "make a libation", likewise Hittite *šipand*, which also means
"to make a libation" (according to J. Friedrich, *loc. cit.*, p. 193); all the

more so in that *zaχri* is Albanian *dzjak* (*gjak*) *ri*,[1] "fresh (?) blood", which corroborates our rendering of *spanza*. The latter does not seem to occur in any other text, but is no less important for that. Indeed, coming at the beginning of the Book of the Mummy, it takes on a peculiar prominence, both as a demonstration of the Indo-European nature of the Etruscan language and as a proof of the connections between the ritual terminology of the Etruscans, the Greeks and the Hittites.

As for the function of the blood of the animals sacrificed for libations, we shall meet it in every chapter of the Book, and especially in Chs. VII and VIII.

LM, ch. I: Supplementary Material

Sacrificial blood is also mentioned at the beginning of the text of the Capuan Tile. Two banquets are announced. The first is a *vacil lunasie faca iχnac*, "banquet (accompanied) by games, (consecrated) to Bacchus the Wrathful", which includes *picasri* and *picas śiiane*: these we shall identify in due course as "fresh roasts" and "tasty roasts". The second is a *vacil leθamsul*, a banquet in honour of the goddess *leθam*, Latona, or, at least, in her temple.

The mention of the second is followed by three interesting words:

scuvune marzac saca (line 7)

This is an invitation or a specification. We do not know to whom it is addressed, but its meaning is clear:

scu: imperative of the Albanian verb *shkoj*, "to come, go".
vune is very probably Albanian *vonë*, "softly" (M. 563).
scuvune: "Come softly" or perhaps "Go softly". In procession?
marzac: *marr* in Albanian is "to take"; *zac* is *dzjak*, *gjak*, "blood". Cf. *intemamer; mlaθcemarni*.
saca: even this little word is really two, in all likelihood: *sa* "as much, how much", and *ca* "a little" (already seen in the word *θapicun*). I shall translate *saca* as "just a small amount", "*pochino*".

"A banquet in the temple of Leθam. Come softly, to take just a little (new?) blood!"

We note in passing that in the language of the Scythians *saca* means "stag" (Abayev, *Langue ossète*, p. 179). But *saca* occurs only once in our texts; and in Ch. II we shall propose another Etruscan word for "stag".

---

[1] It may be noted that Walde-Pokorny connects *gjak* with the Indo-European root *suaqo*, "juice" (*Vergleich. Wörterbuch der indog. Sprachen*, I, p. 515).

LM, Chapter II

At the beginning of this chapter comes an instruction to proceed to sacrifice. Certain *set formulae* are repeated in this chapter and in the subsequent chapters. In some cases they are supported and amplified by the context; in others they appear in somewhat shortened form. It is obviously the former category which will interest us the more.

> (a) *cś mene utince*
> *ziχne śetirunec*
> *raχθ tura nunθenθ* (lines 9–10)

cś: Albanian *qysh*, "as, how, when" (M. 421).

mene is the weak point in this passage of interpretation. The word may be related to Latin *minuo*, "I diminish", *minor*, "smaller", *minus*, "less"; Greek *meion*, "less"; Russian and Bulgarian *ménéié*, *menjché*, "less"; Polish *mniej*, "less"; and Serbian *manje*, "less". The meaning of Etruscan *mene* would be "little (adv.), a little". But this is only a conjecture. It may be added that in Lithuanian the word for "a little" is *menkai*.

utince (B): an interesting formation, made up of three components: *u*, the sign of the passive; *din*, the Albanian verb "to dawn" (M. 75) or *gdhin* (M. 124); and finally the suffix *ce*.

The meaning of the three first words is therefore: "When the day dawns a little" (i.e., begins to dawn).

It was probably a moment of the day which was specially indicated or certain rites or ceremonies. Unless I am mistaken, the position of the rising sun, in the drawing on the celebrated Tuscan mirror which we have already discussed, and which shows Tarxies examining a liver, implies an early hour of the morning. And, be it noted, among the Greeks any sacrifice to a deity was usually made *at dawn*.

It is encouraging to see that *mene* and *utince* are not isolated instances. There are interesting analogies to both these words: (*a*) *mene* is corroborated by *mele*; (*b*) *utince* both by *mutince* and by *mutinum*.

Thus, (*a*) LM, Ch. IV (lines 4, 16–17) contains a sentence similar to the present one: *cs mele θun mutince*, literally "when—partially—(in) the house..it shall be light . . ."; for the word *mele*, "part, share", is known to us already from Hermes's epithet *melecrapicces*, "of the Prosperous Share" (P. 131, inscription of L. Pulena). The meaning here is "at the first gleam of light".

(*b*) *mutince* differs from *utince* only in having the preposition *m* ("with") prefixed, which does not alter the general sense of the sentence. It is just an example of the Etruscans' craze for duplicating their determinative particles: "when" and "with" appear simultaneously here and fulfil the same function as each other (in the manner of the double genitive: Fuflunsl, etc.).

But *utince* is also supported by *mutinum*, in the formula *tarc mutinum*, in LM, Ch. III, 13, which is studied below, and in Ch. XII.

ziχne: *ziχ*, "to engrave, incise, write, cut"; perhaps related to Albanian *çik(as)*, "to mark" (M. 48). In this passage, *ziχne* means "slaughter, sacrifice!" (imperative, singular or plural), with the same termination for the imperative as has been seen already in *epn*.

śetirune(c) (A): a beautiful word, and so characteristic that in itself it should have been enough, long ago, to open the eyes of Etruscologists to the real nature of the Etruscan language. Yet even those who believed, rightly, in the Indo-European character of the language did not notice the existence of this argument in their favour. *śetirune* is undoubtedly Albanian *sheterunë*, "heifer". G. Meyer related the Albanian word to Sanskrit *stari*, "a barren cow", when Armenian *sterj*, "sterile", Latin *sterilis* and Greek *steira* (*loc. cit.*, p. 416). There are thus two branches to this theme: "young animal" and "sterile animal". In Mann we find them both: *shtere*, "heifer" (p. 499) and *shtjerr*, "castrated" (pp. 501 and 495).

It is appropriate to add here that the *taurea sacra* ceremonies introduced by Tarquinius Superbus, in conformity with the Etruscan *libri fatales*, included the sacrificing of *sterile cows* to the underworld gods (O. Müller, *loc. cit.*, p. 101, note 66).

It is also pertinent to recall that Odysseus, when he descends to Hades, makes a sacrifice to the dead and promises them that as soon as he returns to Ithaca he will sacrifice a *barren heifer* to them.

raχθ (A) is Albanian *rrah*, "to beat" (here "to slaughter") (M. 431).

tura: the meaning of this word was established in the chapter on the Market, thanks to the inscription *pel θurinu petrual*. A bull or a bullock.

nunθenθ is "he of *Nundinae*", he of the feast of the 9th day. We should remember that final *t* is a way of forming an adjective in Albanian: *teker*, "wheat", *tekerte*, "wheaten".

The broad sense of our fragment is therefore as follows:

"When day begins to dawn,
Slaughter a barren cow,
Smite a bull of Nunθen."

(b) *fašei zarfneθ*
zušle nunθen
farθan aiseraš šeuš (lines 11–12)

The word *fašei* is Albanian *bajsh*, "may you do". *zar* is identifiable as Albanian *zjarr*, "fire". *f* is a preposition (*bë*, contracted from Albanian *mbë*). *neθ* has been encountered already (in *neθšvis*) and assimilated to *nedyja*, "entrails". The expression *fašei zarfneθ* thus appears to mean "Make the entrails (burn) in the fire", which is the immediate sequel to the sacrifice.

zušle seems to confirm this supposition, for *zuš* makes us think, first of all, of Albanian *zushë*, "heat" (M. 584); perhaps a verb, "to heat"? Thus the second line would mean: "heat (the meal) of Nunθen". The third line adds that *farθan* must be made for the "gods of rain", in other words the souls of the dead. *farθan* seems clear. It is probably connected with Albanian *bardh*, "white, happy". *farθan* frequently occurs in the inscriptions, with the sense of *beatus*. Thus, in P. 321, CIE 5313, there is a woman named Tanχvil Tarnai, *farθnaχe*, perhaps "the blessed". In P. 583 there is a woman called Afli with the word *farθana* after her name. Does *farθan aisera šeuš* mean: "the happiness (or delights) of the gods of rain"? (*šeuš* instead of *six šeuc*, V, 10). Or does it refer to something which is literally white: white bread or flour for the deities and the divine shades? Might it be the food of Nunθen, duly warmed in the oven? The question remains open.

Anticipating our programme, here is a phrase from Ch. IX, lines 15–16, which we quote here because it is related to the extract just given:

estrei alfazei zusleve

estrei: this was an attractive riddle in itself, quite apart from its context. *es* may be *esi*, "blood" (by analogy with Hittite). *trei* corresponds exactly to Albanian *dre*, "stag" (M. 82), followed by the definite article. "Stag's blood"?
al: cf. Albanian *alë*, "trifle, jot, tittle" (M. 4)?
fazei should be read as *fashei*, *bâjshë*, "may you make".
zusleve, which occurs elsewhere in the form *zusleva*: *leve*, *leva* seems to be identifiable as Albanian *leva*, the aorist of *lyej*, "to smear, anoint" (M. 254).
Cf. *luaš*, in Ch. VIII, "Visiting the Doctor".

Thus this verse of Ch. IX probably concerns stag's blood and an anointing with something warm (?). The reader will remember the part played by *dhi* (stag or chamois or roebuck) in the sacrifices mentioned in the inscription of Laris Pulena.

LM, Chapter II: Supplementary Material

Given that *zar* means "fire", we are enabled to elucidate a formation derived from the same root: *uzarale* (B).

This word is part of an inscription on the wall of a sepulchre, which begins: (P. 108, CIE 5507) *carsui ramθa avils XXX lupu*. Next come some words in which almost nothing can be understood, and from which several letters are missing. The last word but one is intact: *uzarale*. The initial *u* shows that we are dealing with a medio-passive. We must therefore visualise the word as *u-zara-le*, "was burnt" or "was cremated" (cf. *lautnescle, ratele,* etc.). I believe the burial was that of a woman called Ramtha Carsui, who died at the age of thirty and whose body was cremated.

This is also an opportunity for inquiring whether another Etruscan word *aizaruva* (which should be read as *ezaruva*) does not express the same idea as *(u)zara(le)*, though there is a difference in the suffix, which in this case is *va*, denoting a verb in the past (cf. *pava*). *aizaruva* occurs on a vase, in an inscription which is probably funerary and consists of some twenty words, mostly jumbled into each other and difficult to interpret. The first of them can be picked out: *eθa*, "small religious building"; farther on there is *ati*, "mother"; then *akaraisi*, which is vaguely reminiscent of Ukresia (P. 160, NRIE 736). M. Buffa wondered whether *aizar* might be a translation of *sacre uvem*, from the Iguvine Tables. For my own part I am afraid that nothing to eat or drink is in question here. *zar*, "fire", in association with an urn, takes our appetite away and makes us think of cremation.

LM, Chapter III

In this chapter there appear several important formulae which are repeated later on:

(*a*) *vinum husina* (line 4); cf. *husina vinum* (VIII? 5); *huslne vinum eśis* (line 20); cf. *huslne vinum esi* (VIII g 4).

> *vinum* and *esis* are "wine" and "blood". *hus* is Albanian *hudh*, "to spill, scatter" (M. 162); undoubtedly, therefore, "libation". *husina* (A) also contains the article *i*, and the suffix *-na*, which denotes pertaining (as in *rasna, suθina,* etc.). *huslna* also signifies libation; cf. Martin-Leake, *lien me miel*, "I scatter flour" (*loc. cit.,* p. 295).

The formula therefore indicates a libation of wine, or of a mixture of blood and wine.

(*b*) After *vinum husina* there is a short lacuna followed by these two words: *clucθras caperi*, which I analyse thus:

cluc seems to be connected with Albanian *kuluq*, "gulp" (M. 224), *kullufis*, "to gulp down, swallow" (*ibid.*).

θras we have seen already, on a mirror depicting Hercules; a drinker of milk, *θra*.

caperi must be "cups". The sentence is incomplete. We find it in its entirety in Ch. VIII, 9–10: *clucθras caperi zamθic*, "gulp down milk from golden cups". We find ourselves having to raise once again the problem of the termination *eri*. M. Pallottino judged it to be a sign of the dative *singular*, giving as his reason: "It is enough to cite these two names of divinities, *hermeri* and *tineri*."

(Il plurale etrusco, Studi Etr., V, 1931)

But we have already pointed out that, in Albanian, *eri, er, era* are a sign of the collective (*dorberi*, "flock") or the plural (*vlla*, "brother", plural *vëllezër*; *kré*, "head", plural *krerë*; cf. Armenian *dunere*, "houses"). In addition, we have already seen in the inscription of Laris Pulena that *hermeri* could, on occasion, mean "columns of Hermes", as well as being the dative of the god's name. *caperi* cannot be a singular; the sentence is addressed not to one person but to the shades of the ancestors. It is plural again in the sentence *sal cus eluce caperi zamtic* (LM, XII, 12), which we shall come to later on; and in the verse *tul θans hatec repinec meleri sveleri* in the next chapter of LM. The same is true of *manimeri*, which we have already studied. In other instances, however, the situation is less clear. The forms *sacnicleri, spureri, meθlumeri*, which occur frequently in the LM, may be in the singular, although *śaclineri* can mean "sanctuaries", *śpureri*, "cities", and *meθlumeri*, "leagues, alliances"—not only "the (Etruscan) confederation", since every Etruscan city must have formed a kind of league with the small towns in its vicinity. It is therefore possible that the suffix *eri* had more than one function.

(*c*) We come next to a twofold formula, a very important one because it expresses an appeal subsequently repeated in Chs. VI, VIII and X: *etnam tesim etnam celucn* (line 12).

tesim is related to the Albanian irregular verb *due*, "to love", whose aorist is *deshi* (M. 71). Cf. the past particle *dashëm*, "loved"

(M. 68). *etnam tesim* is (keeping the original word-order) "fathers beloved".

celucn brings us back to *cluc*, analysed above. There are temptations lurking, it is true, to drag us in other directions. We could explain *celucn* by way of the Albanian verb *ngëlleqem*, "to carouse" (M. 319) or "tipple" (*ibid.*), which might convey no more than the basic idea of "to drink". Or, on the other hand, we could try to divide *celucn* into *celu-cn*, in which *celu* would be the equivalent of Albanian *gjell*, "dish, food" (M. 144), and *cn* would be an accusative termination. This rendering of *cel(u)* fits nicely in a sentence from the Tile of Capua, for example (lines 12–13): *celu tule apirase unialθi*, which I translate "dishes (of meat) of black lamb (*apir*) in (the temple) of Juno (*unialθi*)". But in *etnam celucn* this rendering does not answer nearly as well ("O fathers! These dishes!"?): because *celucn* ought to be a *verb*. I come to this conclusion in the light of a formula which will be studied in LM, Ch. VIII:

> etnam hanθin
> etnam celucn
> etnam aθumitn.

The obvious parallelism between these three lines, in which the words *han(θin)* and *aθumitn* are verbs, invites us to interpret *celucn* as "to drink, drink!", etc.

To sum up: we translate *etnam tesim etnam celucn* as "O beloved fathers! O fathers, drink!"

This heartfelt cry, directed time and again into the darkness, becomes a veritable leitmotiv resounding through the whole of the Book.

(d) cletram srenχve (line 13):

Since *cletram* refers to a litter or chariot on which offerings were carried, *srenχve* poses a problem. *Sren* may be the same word as the *sren* we saw previously, in the description of the milk diet which Hercules resorted to in moments of impecuniosity. We translated *sren* by "refreshment, restoration". But it is equally feasible to relate it to the Philistian word *seren*, a royal title which has been preserved in the Old Testament. The Philistines, like the Etruscans, belonged to the Illyrian family.

In the first eventuality, *cletram srenχve* would be "a comfortable chariot"; in the second, "a lordly chariot".

(e) In a description of a *vacl ara nuθene*, a banquet at the altar of Nundinae, we read:

hetum ale vinum uśi trinum flere in crapsti (lines 17–18)

hetum is identifiable with Albanian *het* (and *et*), "thirst" (M. 158 and 97), all the more so in that it is followed closely by *vinum*, "wine".

ale seems to be composed of the direct object in the form used before the verb (*a*, "him, it") and the Etruscan, Albanian and Hittite verb *le*, "to leave"; *ale*, "leave it", in the sense of "give it". *hetum ale vinum*: "according to thirst (that is to say, *ad libitum*) give (or: provide) wine."

uśi perhaps represents Albanian *ushëm*, "hungry" (M. 542); in the present passage it may mean "hunger", which makes a complement to "thirst".

Alternatively, we might relate the word *uśi* to *uceti*, in the formula:

vacl aras θui uceti (LM, X, 18)

to which we must perforce devote a little attention now. *vacl aras* is probably "a banquet (at) the altar". *θui* means "here". So we are led to regard the suffix *ti*, in *uceti*, as a sign of the locative; and hence to take our formula as meaning "an altar-banquet here, in *uce*". In which case it is legitimate to think of Albanian *uxhë*, "cave, cavern" (M. 543 and 490), here obviously with the sense of "funeral vault". So for the time being we stand at a crossroads between several possible solutions, as in the case of a number of other words in LM. Later, indeed, we shall suggest other possible solutions for *uceti*.

trinum also poses a dilemma. It makes us think of two different Albanian words: *drenzë*, "doe, hind" (M. 83), and *trim*, "bold, brave" (M. 524).

If "hind" is right, fragment (e) comes out as: "Wine according to thirst, hind (i.e., hind's meat) according to hunger, for these (*in*) images (*fler*) *crapsti*" (the last word will be studied in Ch. VI).

But why should we think of hind's meat for the *pièce de résistance*? As we have seen, the sacred stags, kept in sacred enclosures or groves, were a specially choice offering. There are echoes of this in Albanian folklore. We read, for example, in a ballad by G. Fishta, of the feast provided by the good fairies for heroes who have won a fight against a dragon: they are given *dy dréj të majmë*, "two fat stags" (M. Lambertz, I, 170).

Besides, *sutë*, which also means "hind", is mentioned several times in connection with sacrifices in LM.

However, there are instances in which this rendering of *trin* or *trinum* presents difficulties. So we can have recourse to *trim*, "hero". In Irish, this word is *tren*. Moreover, the difference between *trim* and the Etruscan *trin* is no obstacle, as is shown by Etruscan *matam, matan*.

If we take *trinum* as "heroes", the rendering should perhaps be: "Wine according to thirst, for the hungry heroes (who have returned into the) sacred images." The meat or game to be selected may have been indicated in an earlier passage. In any case, the food and drink had to be served in front of the sacred images, into which the souls of the heroes who had returned from the underworld were invited to enter, in order to share in the funeral banquet.

In Mann's inexhaustible dictionary I find a further argument in favour of this interpretation of the word *trin*. Dealing with *trim*, Mann adds (p. 525): *trimth*, "little hero (term of endearment for *deceased husband*)" (our italics). He acquired this precious detail from the dictionary of *Bashkim* (an Albanian national society); it is all the more precious in that the very same formation, *trimth*, is also found in Etruscan: *ceia hia trinθ etnam* (VII, 4). That expression, as we shall see, deals with *heroic ancestors*.

Finally, this solution of the problem seems to be definitively confirmed by the rigorous parallelism (something which does not often happen in Etruscan) between two formulae which we shall meet again when we discuss LM, Ch. VII:

hia etnam ciz (line 2)
hia ciz trinθasa (line 6)

hia means "shades". Whatever may be the meaning of *ciz*, which we shall study below, it can be seen that *etnam* and *trinθasa* must signify much the same thing as one another. The latter therefore cannot represent a sacrificial animal. *etnam* is "fathers"; *trinθasa*, "heroes".

(f) faśei spureśtres enaś
eθrse tinśi tiurim avilś (lines 21–22)

This is one of the most frequently repeated refrains in these litanies, but its meaning is still rather obscure.

faśei: we have seen this before; it means "may you make".

spureśtres: *śpure* is "city"; *tres* may be related to *θres*, "to ask", from one of the inscriptions of the Golini Tomb; "according to the wishes of the city"?

enas: a difficult word, because several analogies to it can be found. Trombetti translated it by "our" (adjective singular or plural; the genitive of the Etruscan and Albanian pronoun *na*, "we"). But it would be equally logical to regard it as the genitive of *ena(c)*, "wine", a word we have already met. There are other conjectures which could be taken into account as well. I think, however, that the solution will be reached by studying a sentence in Ch. XI, g 4, in which the subject once again is the good things lavished on the ancestors in a funeral banquet:

tei rinuś streta satrs enas.

tei: "extend, offer" (already studied).

rinus: "those who have lain down"; cf. *rrinsh*, the optative of the verb *rri* (infinitive *rrinja*), "to sit, remain" (M. 439).[1]

streta: cf. Albanian *shtratë*, "bed" (M. 502). A borrowing from Latin *stratum*? The LM is a late text.

tei rinuś streta: "give to those who are reclining on the couches"?

satrs is composed of *sa* and *tras*.

sa, "how many, as many", which we recognised in *teśamsa* (P. 135) and in *venθical . . . saχs* (P. 299).

trs is probably *θresu*, "ask" from the Golini Tomb (*θresu penznas*). The resemblance between *satrs* and Satres, the Etruscan Saturn, is a coincidence.

satrs: "as much as you ask, as much as you want".

enas cannot mean "wine" because, in the sentence *faśei spureśtres enaś*, the word *faśei* indicates that directions are being given for something to be *done*; this might apply to a meal or dish, etc., but not to wine. So I adduce the word *haena*, which is "food" in Albanian (M. 152). Cimochowski has paid special attention to this noun and quotes, moreover, an ablative plural, *haenash* (*loc. cit.*, p. 63). The initial *h* is unimportant, for, in an Albanian litany published in 1555 by Gjon Buzuk, we read (as S. E. Mann points out) *a* instead of *ha*, "to eat". Thus, in place of *haenash*, we may legitimately postulate an ancient word *aenash*, *enash*. So *satrs enas* becomes "as much food as you want".

The first line of fragment (*f*), *faśei spureśtres enaś*, thus assumes the following meaning: "Prepare food according to the wishes of the city."

[1] We shall see this word again in LM, Ch. XI: Supplementary Material.

Banqueting scene. "Tomb of the Leopards", Tarquinia.

"Ponte Sodo" and the underground channel which supplied
water to the defenders of Veii.

eθrse: it seems pretty plain that this is related to the Albanian verb *jetersoj*, "to change" (M. 170).

tinśi tiurim avils: in this expression we see a succession of three ideas: days, months of the year. But what does it mean? Must we attribute a profounder meaning to *eθrse*, something to do with the renewal of the year, the germ of the New Year, or the renewal of life in general? Or ought we to stay closer to the material side of the very down-to-earth religion of the Etruscans? If the latter is the case we shall be guided by the immediate proximity of the word *enaś*, "food"; I would be inclined to see in it a recommendation to change (to renew, that is) the offering meant for Tinia, every month of the year, in other words at the beginning of each month.

> (g) *tul θans*
> *hantec repinec*
> *śpureri meθlumeric enaś* (lines 22–24)

The final chord sounded in this chapter reiterates the necessity of providing the god Hades with his habitual food. Hades, who is here called *hante*, reappears in LM, Ch. IV, under the name *hate*.

The difference between *hate(c)* and *hante(c)* is to be accounted for by a nasal *a* which was transcribed on some occasions by *a* and on others by *an*. The same phenomenon can be observed in the Tables of Iguvium (Osco-Umbrian), in which the words *hutra* and *hondra* both express the idea of "lower".

The rite which is referred to here is pre-Hellenic in origin and was in use everywhere: the rite of a sacrifice to the Underworld. Thus, in the *Argonautica* of Apollonius Rhodius, when Jason implores Medea to show him how to carry off the Golden Fleece she makes him come by night to the bank of the river Phasis, bathe in the river, put on black clothes, then *dig a deep hole in the ground* and sacrifice a black ewe to Hecate, queen of Hell. Later, when Medea comes to Jason's own country and undertakes to restore his father's youth, she erects two altars, digs a trench before each of them and sacrifices black ewes to the same goddess of darkness and magic.

At Potnia, near Thebes, the Greeks, to honour Demeter and her daughter, used to cast young *pigs* into a ravine; at Athens they used to throw them into a fissure which was said to have appeared when Hades carried off Persephone. At Syracuse bulls and other animals were thrown into the waters of a deep spring. These offerings date from a very remote era. In some cases a hole was dug in the earth and the blood was allowed to flow into it. (Daremberg–Saglio.)

K

And now, back to our text:

tul: there are instances in which this can be identified with Albanian *tul*, "tender"; but in the present instance we should not exclude the possibility that *tul* is the imperative of the verb *tulas*, "to shake, rock" (M. 528), with the sense either of "casting" (the animal sacrificed) into the trench or of "presenting" the offering. The latter is an archaic rite which is mentioned in the Old Testament and was probably inherited from the Canaanites (Leviticus xxxiii. 17–20); loaves, and after them a goat and two lambs, are sacrificed: "And the priest shall *wave* them with the bread of the firstfruits for a wave offering before the Lord. . . ."

θans: visibly the same word as we recognised in inscription P. 381, in connection with the sheep supplied to the market, *θentmase*, *θenst*; Albanian *dash*, "sheep" (M. 67), with nasal *a*; cf. *Kater Ungijte*, the Four Gospels in Albanian, St Matthew vii. 15, *veshura densh*, "sheep's clothing" (Constantinople, 1879).

hantec: *hante*, with the conjunction *-c*. (Note, incidentally, Albanian *hendeqe*, "trench", M. 157.)

repinec: *repine* is Albanian *rrëpine*, "precipice" (M. 347).

It may be noted that *hantec* and *repinec* seem to confirm each other.

The broad meaning of the fragment as a whole is thus as follows:

"Cast sheep
Into Hades, into the gulf,
(That is) food (offered up) for (the safety of) the city, for (the safety of) the confederation."

LM, Chapter III: Supplementary Material

1. Having established that *hus* means "to make a libation", we shall have no difficulty in reading a short funerary inscription (P. 364, CIE 5214): *husl hufni θui* (A), in which *hufni* is "grave, tomb". The meaning of the text is clear: "Libation of the grave here", that is to say, "This is the place at which to make the libation intended for this grave." The meaning of *hufni* is made explicit by the following inscription: (P. 442) *mi hupnina larθ acrnis* (A), in which the word *hupnina* can be understood with the help of Albanian *hup*, "to coagulate, thicken", which implies the idea of "drying up". *hupnina* means a receptacle for containing bones. Finally, in a third inscription of the same kind, *husl* appears as *husiur*: (P. 566, CIE 3754) *arnθ larθ velimnas arzneal huriur suθi acil hece*,

"Here (?) the libation (*husiur*) to the funerary (*suθi*) urn (*acil*) of Arnth Larth Velimna, son of Arzne."

As we see, the exact place was often indicated where the libation should be poured out. This is indirectly confirmed by the following lines of Fustel de Coulanges:

> Among the Greeks, every tomb had in front of it a place intended for the sacrifice of the victim and the cooking of the flesh. Similarly the Roman tomb had its *culina*, a kind of kitchen of a special kind, used only for the dead.
>
> (*Loc. cit.*, p. 14)

2. In fragment *g* of LM, Ch. III, there occurs the word *enaś*, whose meaning we have attempted to establish with the help of two words borrowed from Ch. XI, *satrs enaś*. The hinge, in this short but important phrase, is the little word *sa*, "how much, as much". We shall now quote two inscriptions whose meaning we have been able to extract as a result of having definitively settled the meaning of *sa*.

As will be clearly seen, both these texts have their own intrinsic interest, especially the first of them. This is an epitaph; one, moreover, whose words have something fond and intimate about them, and allow us to see the Etruscans' ancestor-worship and funerary customs in a new light. We see once again that these customs and rites were not based on compulsive magical spells, a fact which has already been made evident to us by the epitaph of Pepanl Liuna. Here is the text; it comes from a sarcophagus:

(P. 135, CIE 5470) *camnas larθ larθals atnalc clan an suθi lavtni zivas ceriχu teśamsa śuθiθ atrśc escuna calθi suθiti munθ zivas murśl XX.*

camnas larθ larθalś atnalc clan tells us that the dead man was Camnas Larth, son of Larth and Atna.

an suθi lavtni: "of Camnas Larth, this is the family tomb".

zivas ceriχu teśamsa (A): this is a new phrase and full of interest; it is not a stereotyped formula:

zivas: "life, of life, from life"; the word is recognisable as Sanskrit *givas*, Lithuanian *gyvas*, Slavonic *zivati*, etc. Bugge was slightly mistaken in explaining it by *vivus*; but, as we have already mentioned, he did not fail to draw an accurate inference from it: "Etruscan is an Indo-European language and, moreover . . . not an Italic language . . . it occupies, rather, a place apart."

(*Etr. For. u. Stud.*, IV, 57, 1883)

ceriχu: Albanian *gjer ku*, "how far" (M. 221).

teśam: this certainly belongs to the group *dashëm*, "loved", *dashës*, "loving", *dashje*, "affection" (M. 221).

sa: Albanian "how much".

Thus *zivas ceriχu teśamsa* (A) means "from life how much loved" (i.e., from life which he loved so much).

suθiθ atrsc escuna completes the preceding phrase:

suθiθ: "in the tomb", with *θ* = *θi*, the locative termination; or rather (with final *t*, *te*), an adjective, "funerary".

atr is certainly a derivative of *at*, "father", whose plural in Albanian is *atër* (M. 14).

suθi(θ) atrś(c) means: "(and) (into) the tomb of the fathers". The element *rc*, however, opens the way to various conjectures. *rc* recalls *rcu*, "receptacle, urn"; and, probably, "sarcophagus". An open question.

escuna (A): from the root *shkoj*, "to go" (already noted). The sentence means: "He departed into the tomb of the fathers", or "into the ancestral funerary urn departed".

calθi suθiti: two words which we already know: "into the (funerary) chamber, into the tomb".

munθ zivas mural XX (A): this final phrase of the inscription has raised a storm of argument in its time. Having translated *zivas* by "living", Bugge inferred that Camnas, while still alive, *dedicated 20 funeral urns* (*mural XX*).

But since our friend Mr. Camnas appeared to be the only possible tenant of the said urns, other authors protested that such a posthumous love of luxury was incredible in a young man, however extravagant. And in fact we are now going to rehabilitate his reputation.

munθ, which we have met before, means, in Albanian, "sufferings, torments" (*mundus*).

zivas: "of (his life)".

mursl (A), obviously, is the key-word. It is usually translated by "urn". But with the help of Albanian I have been able not only to "place" the etymology of this root but also to follow its evolution. It is a matter of dialectal variations in Albanian (and probably in Etruscan too). It was only by studying C. Tagliavini's work on the Dalmatian dialects of Albanian that I was able to get the following information.

In those dialects there is a verb *mshil*, "to shut"; and because of an epenthesis (the intercalation of a letter) another root has developed from it: *mrshil*, also meaning "to shut, to shut in". Thus *mrśl* is something which encloses: "*coffin*, urn, ossuary, sarcophagus". But in the present inscription it is not a noun but the verb itself, "to close", corresponding to our concept, "to conclude".

munθ zivas murśl: "the torments of life he concluded". XX indicates his age, in the briefest manner possible. He was twenty years old, and that is the reason why he *loved life so much* and why there is no mention of his having any children.

The general meaning of the text can be rendered thus:

"It is Camnas Larth who is in this family tomb. He, who loved life so much, descended into the ancestral tomb. In the sepulchral chamber he concluded the torments of life. (Aged) 20 (years)."

As for the second of the two texts whose meaning depends on the word *sa*, it is a real Etruscan riddle. It consists of a term which, being preceded by one lacuna and followed by another, has nothing much to tell us. But, in Etruscan, no torch which we throw into the darkness ever falls to the ground without lighting up some new feature. At the same time I do not consider I have achieved more than a nominal deciphering in the present case. The text consists of a single word (four, in reality) which has always seemed to me the height of absurdity, a challenge thrown out to Etruscologists: *satirasaχiia* (B).

This is one of the first words in the inscription of the Tile of Capua. The first legible word is *vacil*. So the subject of the inscription is a banquet, or perhaps several banquets, some of which are accompanied by games and various ceremonies. It is therefore possible to envisage two different explanations of the word:

(a) *sa*: "as much, how much".
tiria may correspond to Albanian *thirrje*, "invitation", from the verb *thirr*, "to invite" (M. 535). See the Albanian translation of St Luke xiv. 16:

> *Nje njeri bëri darkë të made ede thiri shumë*,
> "A certain man made a great supper, and invited many."

sa: "as many".
χiia: "shades".

The sense appears to be: "(There will be) as many invitations as there are shades." This would be explained by the fact that, on specially solemn occasions, each dead person was summoned by name.

(b) *tiria*, the essential part of the fragment, may be Albanian *turë*, "bolster" (M. 529).

According to this interpretation the meaning is: "There will be as many cushions [round the banqueting table] as there are shades."

The second interpretation is decidedly more matter of fact: a question of making sure that the shades get the degree of comfort which is their due. But to the Etruscan way of thinking this was no mere trifle, it was deeply important. Remembering what we noted at the beginning of this chapter—the cushions placed on the seats at the funerary meals of the Arnauts—I incline towards the second solution. All the more so in that the Arnauti custom seems to be an echo from the distant past. It is enough to recall how important cushions were considered to be in the preparations for a Roman banquet. The central seat on each of the three couches surrounding the table was separated from the two other seats by cushions, on which the guests reclined on an elbow when they wanted to rest (J. Carcopino, *Daily Life in Ancient Rome*, p. 265).

3. In fragment (*h*) of this chapter we saw an offering being made to the god Hades. These offerings and libations were intended not only for the dead themselves but also, very largely, for their immediate superiors, the gods of the lower world. This is illustrated by a drawing engraved on the handle of an Etruscan mirror which has been reproduced by

FIG. 59. Libation to Hades

Corssen (I, p. 311). It exhibits a young creature, human in form but possessing a tail, who is pouring wine on to the ground from an amphora, and it bears the one-word inscription *haθna* (A). (Fig. 59.)

Disapproving of this waste of an indispensable product, Corssen comments:

A satyr named Hathna, a plump young fellow, has tipped an amphora on to its side; with one knee resting upon it he is watching, with an expression of childish wonder, the wine run out on the ground . . .

Much though it pains me to display, for once, a stronger bias for the "gloomy" side of the Etruscans other than scholars have done, I must bring the following corrections to bear:

(*a*) The satyr is not called *Haθna*. Neither his name nor those of any of his friends and relations have come down to us.

(*b*) *haθna* means "belonging to Hades", "him of Hades", "to Hades", etc. The termination -*na*, denoting pertaining, is the same as in *suθina* ("pertaining to the tomb"), *hupnina* (*idem*), *rasna*, *aisna*, *husina* ("to do with libations"), *lautna*, *spurana* ("of the city"), etc.

So there is nothing childish in the matter at all. It is a perfectly regular libation. The gods of Hell as well as its human population were, like a certain character in Jerome K. Jerome, always thirsty.

If there were any doubt at all about the meaning of *haθna* it would be enough to open one of the first large volumes ever devoted to Etruscology, the *Museum Etruscum* of Antonio Gori, published at Florence in 1737, and study the reproduction of a bas-relief from a sarcophagus (I, Tab. LXXXIV). A man and a woman have just entered Hades. On each side of them is a winged demon, armed with a mallet and a sword. The inscription is *ecatna* (A), that is to say, *ec haθna*, "Behold Hades!"

4. We have seen how vital, as it were, was the part played by offerings and libations to the underworld gods and the dead. This gives us some idea of the horror with which the ancients regarded the profanation of a tomb. To profane and pillage a tomb, and scatter the bones abroad, meant brutally interrupting the libations and rites without which the dead person could not be supported in his life beyond the threshold. The same preoccupations dominated the religious life of several peoples of ancient Anatolia.

A comparison has often been made between the rock-tombs of the Etruscans and those of the Lycians and Lydians. Now the inscriptions on the tombs in Asia Minor, which are contemporaneous with those in Etruria, often contain *curses* laid in anticipation upon any future profaner of the tomb. We shall see an example shortly. It will be readily understood what a shock of pleasant surprise I felt on discovering an Etruscan inscription of just this kind: the inscription confirmed my view that the Tursha and the Lydians had once been neighbours and that there was a real, though much more distant, relationship between the Etruscans and the Lydians.

Here is the text. It is inscribed on a jar from a sepulchre ("*olla sepulchralis*", says M. Pallottino) but refers to the tomb as a whole:

(P. 758, CII 2596) *mi riθcea sutve mi stes napaptece auneuptali cali θ* (A)

Some of these terms occur here for the first and only time, but the general coherence of the text is such that they do not occasion any doubts:

mi: "he who". An interesting grammatical form.

riθ is Albanian *res(is)*, "to destroy, obliterate", whence *resitje*, "deletion, cancellation, etc." (M. 426).

cea, beyond doubt, is Albanian *kjo*, "This" (demonstrative adjective, feminine), as the context proves.

sutve is *sut + ve*, ("to this tomb shall put").

mi: "he who".

stes is Albanian *stic(oj)*, "to offend, irritate, annoy" (M. 461); here, it evidently means "to profane, damage".

na: several suggestions are possible; provisionally, we can adopt *na* = Albanian *nga*, "to, towards" (M. 316).

tap: a verb in the past? Analogous to *de*, *dhe*, the past of the Etruscan and Albanian verb *ap*, "to give"? ("to put"). Or it may be equivalent to Albanian *tek*, "at, towards".

auneuptali is about as composite as an Etruscan word can be; but at the same time it is as logical and comprehensible as the mechanism of a watch. The elements of which it is built up are *aune*, *up*, *tali*.

aune is Albanian *aynë* (obsolete, the usual form being *ay*), "he" (M. 16).

up: *u* is the sign of the passive; *p* is the only (and valuable) residue left by the verb *bâ*, *bê* (*bâj*), "to do, make"; *up* is therefore an Albanian subjunctive passive, namely that of the verb "to make oneself, to be made, to become": it means "may he become", "may he be made".

tali is *dal*, an Albanian root which we have met a number of times already, "to go out, leave".

cali θ, paradoxically, is a single word, despite every appearance of being two words. From the epigrapher's point of view (though not from that of a prospective despoiler of tombs) it provides a happy ending, for it is identifiable as the word *gjallit*, derived from *gjallje*, "life" (M. 141), which is an old friend of ours and which explains all.

Apart from the role of the word *tece*, everything in this inscription seems clear, to me. What it says is:

"He who shall demolish this tomb or he who shall profane it by damaging it, may he be compelled to depart from life" (or, literally, "to go out of life").

5. Reverting to the subject of libations to the dead, which have been the subject of so much scholarly discussion, I shall end this Supplementary Material to Ch. III of the Book of the Mummy by examining an interesting term: *sacni*. This word, which is often used in LM from Ch. II onwards, designates the "sacred", the "sanctuary" and the like. Whence comes the difference between this word and *sacri*, which occurs in the inscription on the Tile of Capua (P. 2, 10) and is identical with Latin *sacer*, "sacred", and *sacrum*, "rites" or "sanctuary"? Obviously it may be only a matter of rhotacism (the substitution of an *r* for another consonant), a purely phonetic phenomenon not corresponding to any change on the historical or religious plane; a similar phenomenon is the couple *nunθen* (LM) and *nunθeri* (Tile of Capua).

Nevertheless, it is worth noting that there are certain parallels to the word *śacni* in the religions of Asia Minor. In Hittite, notably, *śakuni* means "source, spring". And the temples of Asia Minor, at the end of the 2nd millennium B.C. and during the 1st, were built in the vicinity of *sacred springs*.

In his study, *Ancient Anatolia*, Seton Lloyd mentions the views of R. D. Barnett on what were presumed to be Phrygian tombs hewn out of the rock but which are in fact shrines. Barnett observes that they are sited in an area which

covers the sources of all the principal rivers of Phrygia . . . the monuments stand near to, if not actually facing, springs of fresh water . . .

Lloyd adds:

[Concerning] the Hittite rock monuments . . . almost every single one of them, from Yazilikaya beside its dried-up spring at Boghazköy

to the Sirkeli relief overlooking the waters of the Jeyhan river in
Cilicia is in some way closely connected with a supply of fresh water.
Finally when one recollects that the Younger Storm God of Hittite
mythology was 'a god of rocks and waters', it becomes more and
more hard to regard this as a coincidence and one is driven to the
conclusion that, both by the Hittites and later by the Phrygians, a
bare vertical rock beside or near a source of water was deemed
holy and a cult set up there . . .

And the writer concludes:

> If, then, we are to see in the Hittite rock monuments the symbols
> of a fresh-water cult . . . we shall then find ourselves contemplating
> one of the most striking phenomena of Anatolian archaeology—the
> extraordinary vitality of local [religious] beliefs . . .
>
> (*Loc. cit.*, pp. 202–3)

We have seen the very same beliefs in Etruria. They were manifested in the cult of Iuturna, in that of the god Lavis, to whom the
Rhaetian key was consecrated, and finally in the invocations which in
the Book of the Mummy are repeatedly addressed to the gods of rain
and streams, *eiser śic śeuc.*

S. Cles-Reden observes:

> We know practically nothing of the cult of water among the
> Etruscans, but no one will deny that it occupied an important place
> in religious ceremonial. That is why, on the sites of the ancient cities
> of Etruria, archaeologists in search of buried treasures have only to
> take the springs as sign-posts; in almost every case they were within
> the temple precincts.
>
> (*Les Etrusques*, p. 114)

Decipherment, indeed, gives us no little information on the matter.
We thus have yet one more thread connecting Etruscan religious
tradition to that of Asia Minor. This makes it easier to understand
how it was that a divine name, Tarku, which is diffused throughout the
Hittite kingdom—Lycia, Cilicia and other countries of Asia Minor in
the 1st millennium B.C.—became the national name of the Etruscans.
A borrowing of this kind could have been an isolated exception. We
have already mentioned, in an earlier chapter, the influence of Asia
Minor on the funerary architecture of Etruria, on Etruscan customs
and material civilisation. It is incontrovertible that the Anatolian
peoples retained the imprint of Hittite civilisation long after the fall
of the Hittite Empire (towards the end of the 2nd millennium).

This cult of springs was, then, the heart and soul of archaic Anatolian religion; but, in Etruria as elsewhere, it must in the early days have been inseparable from ancestor-worship; and the need to be beside a spring, for the proper accomplishment of the periodical libations to the dead, must at a certain period have been part of the foundations of Etruscan religion. To the evidence already quoted we can add that of a Greek inscription, discovered in Southern Italy. It was on a small gold plaque and was intended to guide the soul in its descent to the Underworld. And it said: ". . . You will find a spring of cold water, with guardians. Say to them: . . . I am burning with thirst . . . quick, give me some cool water" (S. Reinach, *Traité d'épigr. gr.*, p. 173).

It is therefore not surprising that P. Aebischer, in an outline study of water-worship in ancient Tuscany (*Studi Etruschi*, VI, 1932), assembled various data which agree nicely with the observations recorded here.

In Aebischer's article we learn that many Italian abbeys are sited near ancient springs, which are known in common parlance as *acqua santa*, *fonte benedetta* and so on. Thus the abbey of S. Salvatore at Capo d'Arno stands near the Lago di Ciliegeto; another abbey of the same name, in the Val di Paglia, is near some springs known as *acqua santa*; a third, in the valley of Ombrone, is at a place known as Fontebuona; a fourth, between the source of the Limenta and a brook, the Bure, is named Abbazia di Fontana Tanona. The abbey of S. Trinita dell'Alpi stands at the source of a torrent, the Talla, to which pilgrimages used to be made. A shrine with the name of Madonna dei Tre Fiumi stands at the spring of Elsa. Finally, a rivulet issuing from the Caverna dell'Acqua (where several *ex voto* offerings have been found) and flowing towards the Tiber, in the Agro Falisco, is called Fosso dell'Acqua Santa (pp. 139–40).

To sum up, the cult of the god Lavis, described above, the observations of Seton Lloyd on the cult of running water in ancient Anatolia, and the remarks of S. Cles-Reden on springs at Etruscan sites, are all complementary to one another and form so many links in a single chain of archaic tradition: the adoration of springs, *śakuni*, a term which is a parallel to Etruscan *sacni*.

LM, Chapter IV

(*a*) Here, first of all, is a formula referring to sacrifices to Hades. We saw the first part of it in the previous chapter of LM:

> *tul θans hatec repinec*
> *meleric svleric* (lines 3–4 and 16–17)

meleric: *meleri* closely resembles Albanian *melore*, "goat which has not yet borne young" (M. 275); and also the Aroumanian word (possibly of Thracian origin?) *miluar*, "sheep", of which Sandfeld writes:

> "Aroumanian has supplied all the neighbouring languages with a certain number of words relating to pastoral life, such as, for example, Greek *miliori* and Albanian *miluar*, young sheep."
>
> (*Linguistique balkanique*, p. 63)

It therefore seems (and here G. Meyer agrees, though unenthusiastically) that this word is a piece of flotsam from the archaic idiom of the Danubian and Balkan shepherds. This idiom must have been anterior to the formation of so highly developed a language as Etruscan.

sveleric seems to have no counterpart in Albanian, but it would be hard to deny its kinship with *sus*, which means "pig" in Greek, Latin and many others of the languages related to Sanskrit. It is sufficient to recall the frequent sacrifices of pigs among the Osco-Umbrians and the Romans. There is thus a series of mammals to be sacrificed.

The verse as a whole therefore seems something on these lines:

"Cast ewes into the gulf of Hades, and young sheep, and pigs."

(*b*) In the following sentences, which are chosen from lines 19–22, and which come after the description of the funeral sacrifices and banquets, the subject is still the gratifications offered to the deities and the divinised ancestors. Let us note particularly the word *śin*:

> a. *śpureri meθlumeric enaś* . . .
> b. *śin flere in crapśti* . . .
> c. *śin aiser faśe*
> d. *śin aiś cemnac faśeis*
> e. *raχe sutanaś celi suθ aisna*
> f. *pevaχ vinum trau pruχs*

Let us take a closer look at the text. There are plenty of words that we know already. Line *a* means: "For the city, for the federation, (here is) food." As for lines *b*, *c* and *d*, the word *śin* evokes either *si*, "taste" (*aplu eparu sis*, in the chapter on the Market), or else a *hypothetical* word *shin*, meaning "red" and related to the Albanian root *shêj*, "to turn red, take on colour (of fruit)" (cf. the sentence *dielli shen pemët*, "the sun is reddening the fruit"; M. 470).

THE BOOK OF THE MUMMY

Since we were confronted by *fleres* [1] *aiser* and *cemnac*, in other words by assorted statues (those of the ancestors, those of the gods and that of the god of thunder), it is at least plausible that they were to be tinted with red—a sacred colour, the use of which is a feature of archaic rites.

Does *śin* mean "to colour red"?

These lines had been written for a long time before I was able to answer the question. At last one day I perceived that the word *śin*, with the sense of "red", really was there, in front of my nose; the only difficulty had been to notice it! In line 5 of Ch. VI of LM there is an

Fig. 60. An Etruscan priest sacrificing to Fufluns-Bacchus at an altar on which the sacred fire is burning (Gerhard, V, Taf. 36)

expression which solves the problem in summary fashion: *θaχśin*. The word *θaχ* is recognisable as *zaχ*, *zac*, *θac*, "blood" (Albanian *gjak*); and this is made all the more certain by the fact that *caper(c)*, "cups", are mentioned just after it. *θaχ śin* cannot mean anything other than "red blood".

So now line *c*, *śin aiser faśe*, must be translated as: "make red the statues of the gods", or else "prepare red (paint) for the gods".

Let us examine lines *e* and *f*:

raχθ sutanaś: already translated: "strike (sacrifice) a hind" (M. 564).

celi suθ eisna: Taking a hint from the similarity in rhythm between these two lines:

> *raχ θ sutanaś*
> *celi suθ eisna*,

[1] The epithet *crapśti* will be examined later.

I was tempted at first to attribute to the second of them a meaning very similar to that of the first. *suθ* would then have been translated once again by "hind" (and not "tomb") and *celi* would have been explained by the Albanian verb *qëlloj*, "to strike" (M. 416). The meaning would then have been:

> "Slaughter a hind,
> Strike a fawn, for the divine beings (?)".

However, parallelism seems to be much less definite in Etruscan texts than in the Old Testament or in the Phoenician poems. So a different interpretation seems more convincing:

celi would be connected with Albanian *gjell*, "life, food, victuals"; the three words together may mean "food for the divine tomb", since *eisna* has the suffix *na*, denoting pertaining, as in *suθina*, *haθna*, etc.

In parenthesis, this interpretation of *celi* seems to me to be confirmed by verse 2 of Ch. XI:

> *vacl vinum śantiśts*
> *celi pen trutum* (A)

śantiśts appears to be the genitive of *zamθi, zamaθi*, "gold" (P. 489) and of *santi(c)* (*θapna*) in Ch. XII, 21 ("golden cups"). The first line therefore means

> "a banquet with golden wine"

pen can be connected with Albanian *bënj*, "to make" (M. 17); in the imperative here: "make!"

trutum is *trutu* + *m* ("with"); *trutu* is Albanian *truatje (trutje)*, "fear", that is to say "religion", from the root *droj, druej*, "to fear" (M. 84), which has been noted previously. Thus *trutum* comes to mean "with religion, according to religion". The second line means: "Prepare the ritual foods" (according to the prescriptions of religion), and the meaning "strike, slaughter", for *celi*, does not seem possible in this context.

Coming back to fragment (*b*) of Ch. IV, line *f*:

pevaχ vinum trau are three drinks. The two poles of the meaning of the fragment are, therefore, eating and drinking. *pevaχ*, that is to say *peva* + *k*, is completely identifiable with Albanian *piva*, the aorist of *pi* "to drink", and with Slavonic *pivo*, which means "beer", in practice, but whose fundamental meaning is simply "drink" (as a noun). The last line of the fragment can therefore be interpreted either thus: "(As) drinks [*ak* is probably the same suffix as in *romaχ*, *iχnac*, *cemnac*], wine (and) milk"; or thus: "beer, wine, milk".[1]

pruχs, already noted, denotes a kind of vase.

To sum up, our fragment (*b*) now emerges as follows:

"For the cities, for their federations, (here is) food . . .
Put red (paint) on these images (of the ancestors) . . .
Make the deities red;
Make red the god of thunder;
Slaughter a hind as food for the divine tomb;
Beer, wine and milk in the cups . . ."

(*c*) In another extract, from the end of Ch. IV, we find a very important formula which is subsequently repeated at intervals throughout LM, and all of whose constituents we met before, with the exception of the second word:

> *śacnicestreś cilθś*
> *spurestresc enas*
> *eθrese tinsi tiurim avilś* (*g*, lines 1–3)

cilθs is one of those dangerous words, in dealing with which one feels tossed about helplessly by the waves of a stormy sea. *cilθ*, obviously, makes one think of a locative of Etruscan *cella*, a chamber in a tomb or a sanctuary: *clθ* (*suθiθ*) (P. 159) or *clθi* (P. 93, 97), etc. However, in its more extended form the word has a different vowel: (P. 135) *calti* (*suθiti*). Moreover, in Lambertz' chrestomathy I find an expression *në krie të ciltesë* (Vol. I, p. 336), of which his translation is "*in der Spitze des Essteppichs*", "at the head of the table-cloth" (i.e., in the place of honour). In Arbanas's little dictionary, p. 73, I find *çilim*, "cloth" and *çilimat*, "table". And since our text is so largely concerned with eating and drinking, surely a table is fairly apposite?

On the conjectural level only, the solution I suggest here is to regard *stres* (in the first and third words) as an optative of the verb *shtrij*, "to spread out" (M. 503), which we have seen in an inscription on a missile: *streuc*. The verb "to spread out" applies reasonably well to "laying a table" or "laying a cloth".

[1] With reference to *trau*, we may add that the word *travaiuser* (Tile of Capua, P. 2, lines 16, 17) is undoubtedly *trau aiser*, "milk for the gods".

Provisionally, then, we translate fragment *c* as follows:

"Lay the cloth in the sanctuary;
Lay (on it) the foods of the city:

Change (them) (before Tinia) every month of the year."

LM, Chapter V

(*a*) This excerpt describes sacrifices to be made in conjunction with
a *vacl* in honour of θesan-Aurora. All the words in it are ones we have
studied before, with the exception of the last:

raχθ sutanaś celi suθ vacl θesnin raχcresverae (line 16)

sutanas, as before, is the genitive of Albanian *sut*, "hind" (M. 564)
and *shutë* (M. 507). G. Meyer mentions *shut*, "animal without
horns" and *shutë*, "hind" (*loc. cit.*, p. 420), adding that these
words were introduced into the Slavonic languages and Magyar
by "nomadic shepherds".

celi is Albanian *gjelle*, "life, food" (M. 144).

suθ: "tomb"; not to be confused with *sut*, "hind".

vacl θesnin: a feast in honour of θesan.

raχ is obviously connected with *raχθ*, at the beginning of the line,
but also with *cresverae*, which follows immediately, at the end.
"Sacrifice!" (imperative).

cresverae: I thought at first of Albanian *verë*, "wine", and this put me
on the track of a Greek expression, *kriθinos oinos*, "barley wine".
We may speculate whether *kres* is not an Etruscan adaptation of
Greek *kriθe*, "barley"; and whether, in consequence, *cresverae*
represents a kind of beer or whisky.

However, Albanian *verë* has another meaning too: "spring,
springtime", etc. And I think it best to assimilate *kres* to Albanian
krriç, "colt" (M. 219); hence, a "colt of the spring". There are
four arguments inclining me to this choice:

(*a*) Later in this chapter we shall deal with a sacrifice of
"autumn lambs"; they would probably be new-born or at least
very young; one thinks of the sacrifice of new-born piglets to
Hades; (*b*) we have formal evidence of a colt-sacrifice among the
Messapians, whose culture was related to that of the Etruscans;
it was an offering to their god Jupiter Menzana; we shall come
back to it when we discuss the Messapians; (*c*) an animal sacrifice
(and not a drink-offering) fits much better with what goes before,
namely *raχθ sutanaś*, the sacrifice of a hind, at the beginning of

the excerpt; (*d*) the meaning of the name θesnin being confirmed by the fact that θesan is subsequently mentioned four times in the same chapter of LM, I shall remark that an offering of *beer* (to θesan) seems unconvincing; whereas, on the other hand, the sacrifice of a *colt* to θesan appears to be justified in some sort by Etruscan iconography: Dawn is often shown riding in a chariot (*biga* or *quadriga*), like her great patron, the Sun himself.

Thus the sentence we are studying may mean this: "Sacrifice a hind for the funeral meal; at the banquet of θesan, sacrifice a spring foal."

LM, Chapter VI

(*a*) The beginning of the chapter looks like a dangerous quagmire; we must move carefully. The subject seems to be the same as before: appeals and invitations addressed to the shades of the dead. One is tempted to single out the following words for scrutiny:

śnutuf iχ reuśceśc   aniaχ urχ   hilχvetra hamfeś (line 2)

śnutuf: this word divides into *ś-nu-tuf*:
> *s* is the negative particle which we met in the exhortation *peva aniχe siu*, in the chapter on the Tavern: "Drink, that you may know no distress!" As for the verb *niχ*, *niaχ*, "to know", we shall meet it again here, in LM, Ch. VI.
> *śnu*; we met this on the key dedicated to Lavis: *ltt ural śnu*, "tears—hunger—not to know".
> *tuf* may be connected with Albanian *dufëm*, "fear" (to be afraid?), *dufitun*, "in low spirits" (M. 85).
>> *śnutuf* thus comes to mean "have no fear, be of good courage".
iχ: "go, come".
reuśceśc seems to be explained by Albanian *rryeshëm*, "urgent, hard" and the verb *ryej*, *rryej*, "to train, accustom" (M. 444). Thus: "Have no fear, approach with practised step."

It seems that in the second part of line 2 the dead are being reminded of the drawbacks of their life in the Underworld; the milk which they lack there is mentioned:

aniaχ is the Albanian verb *njoh*, *njah*, "to know". "Does one know?" "Do you know?" (*a*, in Albanian, indicates a question.)
urχ: it is most tempting to equate this with Orcus, the infernal deity of the Latins, corresponding to the Greek Pluto and therefore also to the Etruscan Aita, Hades. But it is quite possible that it is

merely the Albanian word *uri*, "hunger" (*urët*, "hungry"), M. 541, with the conjunction χ, *k*, "and".

hil vetra must be divided into *hilχve* and *tra*. *hilχva* reminds us of *hil*, *hilar*, "dead". The ending χve is the same as in *srenχve*, *flerχve*, etc. A collective form? Cf. Oscan *sviseve*, "receptacles".

tra will be the same as θra, the "milk" which Hercules drank, and *trau*, "the milk" used in libations.

hamfeś is reminiscent of Old Albanian *amvis*, "master of the house" (M. 6). Jokl writes: *amvise* is Albanian for *Hausmutter*, "mistress of the house".

In its main lines the end of the inscription seems to say: "Does (*a-*, interrogative particle) the Underworld (*urχ*) know (*-nia*) milk (*tra*) for the dead (*hilχve*), O masters (*hamfeś*)?"

It should be added that Horace describes Charon as *satelles Orci*, "servant of Orcus". According to Pauly-Wissowa (*Orcus*), the name Orcus appears in Latin inscriptions as Orchus on two occasions out of every nine. Perhaps this has a bearing on the Etruscan form, *urχ*. According to Schulze, indeed, the form Orchus indicated the Etruscan origin of the name. Among the Romans the name sometimes meant the lord of the Underworld, sometimes the realm of the dead and sometimes the demon who carried his victims to that realm.

(*b*) In the latter part of line 3 and in line 4, we read:

> θui stretet face apniś
> aniaχ apniś urχ peθereni

θui stretet face: θui, "here"; *stretet*, "beds, couches" (discussed in connection with LM, Ch. III); *face* is probably Albanian *bâjshë*, "may you make". Thus: "Arrange here beds (or couches)."

apniś: in view of the previous line, this may well be explicable by Albanian *ambnis*, "to rest", *ambni*, "repose" (M. 5). The word *apniś* must, of course, be read *abnish*; its *a* is nasal, a fact which is not registered by the Etruscan notation, but which is expressed in Albanian by *am*. The idea of *rest* is thus juxtaposed with that of the *beds*, or couches, of the banquet. So perhaps the meaning is: to prepare couches so that the souls of the guests may repose?

peθereni: a difficult word. Some commentators have made it out to be the name of a month, because on two occasions (out of a total of four), in X, 2 and XI, 8, the word is found linked with a number. But in the other two cases (VI, 4 and X, 4) there is nothing to make us take it for a month. Consequently, it seems more appropriate to divide *peθereni* into *peθe* and *reni*. *reni* corresponds nicely to Albanian *rrini*, the imperative of the verb *rri*, "to lie, stretch out". *peθe*: there are two explanations from which to choose:

1. *peθe* should be read *bete*, corresponding to Albanian *mbete* imperative of the verb *mbes*, of which the infinitive is *mbetum*, and the medio-passive *mbetem*: "to stay, remain" (M. 269). In Albanian, *mb* is frequently reduced to *b*; thus *mbar*, "to carry", becomes *bar* (M. 267). *peθereni* would thus mean "to remain lying".

   The excerpt given above could then be translated: "Here, on beds, may you be assured of [*face*, Albanian *bajshë*, 'may one make' for you] rest. Are you acquainted with rest? When you are with Orcus, do you lie and rest?"

2. Alternatively, *peθe* could be explained by the Albanian verb *petoj*, "to roll out, make layers of" (M. 362), from which comes the noun *petë*, "layer". In this case *peθereni* will mean "to lie flat, to take one's ease". This fits well with the mention of bed and rest in the verse as a whole, *θui stretet face apniś aniaχ apnis urχ peθereni*, which I would translate on the following lines: "Here (*θui*) the beds (*stretet*) are made (*face*), you will know (*aniaχ*) rest (*apnis*), you will take a rest from the Land of the Dead (*apnis ur*). Take your ease (*peθe*), lie down (*reni*)."

(c) After this, in lines 5–6, there seems to be a reference to a funeral rite:

θaχśin θeusnua caperc

θaχsin: we have met this word already; and it comes again in Ch. IX, g, 2, where it is written *θaχsein*. The excerpt now under consideration refers to a *libation of blood* in honour of the Underworld. *θaχsin*, therefore, is "of red blood".

θeusnua is composed of *θe-usnua*. *θe* is Albanian *dhe*, "earth". *u-snua* would be a medio-passive form (or the past participle?) of the verb *shej*, "to redden", which we encountered a short time ago. *θeusnua* means "let the earth be reddened".

caperc might make us think of an Etruscan gloss (P. 820) which states that *capra* meant "goat" in Etruscan; but it may be preferable to be guided by an expression which is frequently used in LM, *caperi zamθic*, which we can recognise as meaning "golden cups". So fragment (c) can be translated thus: "The earth will be reddened with cups of red blood" (or, "with goats' blood").

(d) There now comes an important statement, likewise addressed to the souls of the dead, followed by a date (with no indication as to the month), directions for a rite and another statement:

> heci nac va tinθasa
> etnam velθinal etnam aisunal
> θunχerś in śacnicla.
> zaθrumsne. lusaś fler hamfisca . . .
> lustreś fler vacltnam . . .
> etnam eisna iχ flereś crapśti
> θunśna θunś flerś

(lines 6–13)

heci nac va tinθasa (A): Literally, this means: "Went out night, became day." heci is Albanian heq, "to withdraw"; nac is "night", as we have already seen.

va is Albanian bâ, bâj, "to make". tinθasa is probably an oblique case of tin, "day".

The verb va (ba) is used here, in all probability, in the passive sense: u-bâ, "to be made".

I have come across this twofold formula, almost unchanged, in modern Albanian. Thus, on the one hand, hiku nata (in a poem by Asdren, Lambertz, I, p. 178, translated in Lambertz, II, p. 82); and, on the other hand, u bë dit (Lambertz, I, p. 356; which he translates as "es ist Tag geworden", "it has become day", II, p. 290).

etnam velθinal: this recalls Albanian velje, "satiation, fill, surfeit" (M. 549), which may be related to the Slavonic root vele, viele, "much". Di is Albanian for "to know". So velθina(l) may mean "much known, famous" (?). A moot point.

etnam aisunal: "(O) divine fathers!"

θunχers in śacnicla: an unexpected statement, and an important one: θun is "house", as we have seen.

kërsh is "cliff, rock" (M. 196).

in is "this" (adjective).

cla is probably "to call". We are forced to this conclusion by the expression cla θesan, which we believe to mean "call to θesan", "appeal to θesan" (V, 23), and also by the analogy of the Greek verb kaleo and Hittite kalliś, both of which mean "to call"; finally, Albanian klaj (of which another form is qaj) means "to call by name" (M. 199).

Later we shall introduce another Albanian verb, kjaj. It is possible that cla must be translated "begs, asks for permission".

The meaning of the third line seems to be: "This house of rock, this sanctuary calls (you)." It would appear to refer to the tombs which were hewn out of the rock and which, because of the rites which were celebrated there, became sacred places. But, though the epithet is magnificent, must we not remember that there were imposing underground constructions of masonry? And, at the same time, the meaning we suggested for *urχ* (Orcus) reminds us that the points of similarity between the rites of the Etruscans and those of the Greeks and Romans were perhaps more numerous than is usually believed. In addition, we notice that the element *χerś* in the word *θunχerś* (*θunkers*) is singularly close to *Ker* (plural *Keres*), the name by which the Greeks knew certain goddesses or evil spirits of death and destruction. Now this same name sometimes denoted "the souls of the dead" (*Oxford Classical Dictionary*, p. 475). If we accept this interpretation, *θunχers* will mean "the house of the souls of the dead". *Kers*, moreover, is also found in Thracian: Cerzula, Kersoblephtes (Heuzey, *Le Sanctuaire*, II).

The next part of the text begins a new paragraph.

zaθrumsne: the *ne* at the end is an Albanian preposition *ne*, "in, to, at" (M. 313). So what we have here is a date: "On the 20th day of the month", "on the 20th". A month is named a little farther on.

lusaś fler hamfisca: "ask the statues of the masters"?

lustres fler vacltnam . . .: *tres* is "ask". *Vacltnam* has been explained by T. Klugge as *vacl etnam*. My own supposition is that it is connected with the Albanian verb *vagjëloj* ("to feed carefully, nurture", M. 543) (which, however, might originally have meant "to give supper" to somebody), in Etruscan "to feast, to banquet", to which, in the text, a pronoun and a preposition are added, *me na*, "with us". A further invitation follows:

etnam eisna iχ flereś crapśti: much has been written about the word *crapśti*, in an attempt to assimilate it to a name which is applied as an epithet to several divinities in Umbrian, *krapuvi* (for example, Jupiter Grabovius). Jokl mentions an ancient Macedonian word, *grabion*, "candle, torch", which he explains as "the wood of a kind of oak" or "a torch consisting of this wood". The tree concerned is probably the Latin *carpinus* (hornbeam) and the Slavonic *grab*, the wood of which is hard. Was it some kind of sacred wood, reserved for making idols? But if this suggestion is wrong, may not *crapśti* be the Albanian word *krapis*, "to prosper", which we met in the phrase *hermu melecrapicces*? Were *fleres crapśti*, "images which bring prosperity", the prototype of the Roman Lares, which were statuettes with cornucopias? (Paoli, *Vita*, 233). Did not both rain and prosperity depend on the spirits of the dead?

Next, there comes another statement, brief yet striking, about the funerary shrine at which these ceremonies take place: θunsna θuns flers (B): "our house is the house of the images (of the fathers)". Nothing is left undone that will reassure the *hia*, the shades, that this is their house and that they are the masters here.

Excerpt (*d*) can be translated as follows—with heavy reservations, and on the understanding that this is a provisional rendering only:

"On the 20th of the month. Pray before the images of the masters!
Pray and ask the *flers*: Be at the banquet with us . . .
O divine fathers, enter the images which bring prosperity!
Our house is the house of the *flers*."

(*e*) Ch. VI brings us back on to solid ground by putting the motif *raχ tur* in front of us once more:

sarve luθti raχ ture acil catica (B) (Line 15)

śarve is no doubt Albanian *zjarr ve*; *zjarr* means "fire, flame" (M. 582) (so there is more than one word for "fire")—this is related to Slavonic *jar* ("fire, fervour"); and *ve* is one of the basic verbs in Albanian, "to put" (M. 547).

luθti we know: "in prayer, at prayer". *Tinś lut* (P. 657) and *śuvluśi* (P. 447) have been valuable landmarks guiding us towards the meaning of this term.

raχ ture: "strike a bull". In parenthesis, Albanian *torishtë* means "paddock, fold" (M. 520).

acil: this word must come down from its pedestal now; all it means is "pot".

catica: an informative word. The root to be recognised in it is Albanian *gat*: *gatis*, "to prepare"; *gati*, *gadi*, "ready"; *gatim*, "preparation", etc. (M. 123). G. Meyer invokes only the affinities of *catica* with Russian *gotov* and Lithuanian *gatavas*, "ready, prepared".

ca: one line of approach is Albanian *ka*, "some" (adjective, plural); or one might even cast one's mind to the *admirative* mood of Albanian verbs, which gives strong emphasis to the meaning of a verb; thus Albanian *hap* is "to open"; *hapka* means "to open right up", "how well it opens!", and so on. But the simplest solution is *ka*, "ox" (M. 171).

But a problem crops up: how ought I to translate *śarve luθti*? Shall I translate it morally, as it were.."put fervour into your prayer"..or materially, "light the fire, praying at the same time?" The second is to be preferred, even if only for the reason that the Etruscans always did pray fervently and that there consequently was no need to spur them on. So the whole line means:

"Light the fire, praying the while. Sacrifice a bull. Prepare pots with (the meat) of the ox."

LM, Chapter VI: Supplementary Material

The word θun, "house", which we have studied above, will perhaps enable us to restore to the Etruscans a relic of their past which has been taken away from them and presented to the Celts. The relic in question is one of the simplest, most archaic monuments of Etruscan funerary art: the Zignano stele, which was found in 1828 in Liguria, not far from the ancient city of Luna, and which is now preserved in the Musée Historique at Geneva. It is merely an oblong stone surmounted by something like a head, on which a few sketchy lines were intended to represent the face. The stele carries an inscription in regular Etruscan script: mezunemusus.

Similar but more elaborate steles, representing warriors, were discovered later in the same part of Italy. J. Vendryes examined these finds and wrote of them:

> I doubt whether these objects are Gaulish. . . . But if these monuments do represent Gauls . . . the hypothesis of a Celtic inscription can be upheld.
>
> (*Revue celtique*, 1913, pp. 418 *et seq.*)

In the opinion of Vendryes the text in question could be divided into *mezu*, which would be the Gaulish *medio*, "middle" (cf. Mediolanum), and *nemusus*, the Gaulish word for "temple" (cf. Nemossos, the ancient name of Clermont-Ferrand). The name meant "the temple of the centre" or "the centre of the temple".

It was emphasised at the same time that this Celtic name could refer only to a temple; and that the monument was not to be regarded as a funeral stele.

Nevertheless, the author himself considered it to be a *cippus*.

H. Hubert, whose observations completed the article in question, added the information that another cippus, *strikingly similar* to the first, had been discovered near Bologna: "It is to be supposed that it surmounted a grave, but the grave has not been excavated." One can see that Hubert was struggling in an inescapable dilemma: the Gauls are not attested in Italy before the 4th century B.C.; but the Hallstattian daggers portrayed on the cippi in question are earlier (700–500) than the appearance of the Gauls. And the author asks: "Did the Gauls come earlier? Or are the Lunigiane steles not Gaulish?" (*ibid.*, p. 432).

To sum the matter up, these are funerary steles rather than steles of any other kind. The cippus of Zignano is more archaic in appearance than the steles on which warriors are represented. None the less, the inscription *mezunemusus* can perhaps be divided into *me-zune-musus*. *me* would be the classic *mi* of the Etruscan steles; *zune* would be an archaic transcription for *θune*, "house" (cf. *zimiθe*, the Etruscan transcription of Diomedes); and *musus*, possibly the genitive of a name, *Musu*, a name analogous to Mucius, for example. But in this event, *zune* or *θune* would mean not only "house" but also "grave, tomb". Moreover, Etruscan tombs are often built in the form of houses. It may be noted that in Old Russian, *domovina* (derived from *dom*, "house") was used to denote a coffin. It may be this aspect which is brought out in the expressions *θunχerś* and *θunśna* in LM.

A final remark on the subject of *θune* or *θuni*. The deity with the double-barrelled name *ani θne* (A), which is inscribed on the liver of Piacenza, is certainly none other than *ani θune*, Janus of the house. In the Odyssey, during the massacre of the suitors, the bard Phemius and the herald Medon, whom Odysseus has spared, take refuge in the courtyard at the altar of *Jupiter of the House* (Od. XXII).

LM, Chapter VII

This chapter is different from the others: there is something like violent surf running through it, a to-and-fro tumult of waves which break, recoil, return and break once more; such is the impression we have as the priest intones his litany, or rather his passionate appeal, six times over in his desperate attempt to rouse the souls of the dead from their torpor. We cannot speak of translation; it is, rather, a matter of clearing the ground, for beneath these stones which have remained untouched for two thousand years there are plenty of scorpions lurking. Still, we shall find that the first shadow of a solution does begin to appear.

(*a*) Here are the first six lines of the text as they appear in LM (there is a lacuna in the first):

1. *ceia hia . . .*
2. *ceia hia etnam ciz vacl trin velθre*
3. *male ceia hia etnam ciz vacl aisvale*
4. *male ceia hia trinθ etnam ciz ale*
5. *male ceia hia etnam ciz vacl vile vale*
6. *staile itrile hia ciz trinθaśa śacnitn*

It is noticeable that a dominant motif, the formula *male ceia hia etnam ciz*, occurs, with variations, in most of these lines. Several words in this excerpt are already known to us. Nevertheless, certain obstacles (which, for that matter, are the ones we are constantly encountering) make it difficult to interpret:

1. The division of the above sentences into six lines is arbitrary—as is almost always the case in Etruscan texts. For example, there is no doubt that the words *vacl vile vale staile itrile* constitute a single entity; but the scribe has put the first half in the latter part of line 5 and the second half (*staile itrile*) in the first part of line 6. Furthermore, it is possible that the last word, *śacnitn*, really belongs to a new section.

2. With the advent of our method the situation in the deciphering of Etruscan has undergone a curious change. Previously, every Etruscan word wandered alone in the desert, abandoned by God and man. But today it is in danger of being stifled by several Albanian words whose loving arms open simultaneously to welcome it.

Thus each of the key words in the refrain *male ceia hia etnam ciz*, namely *ceia*, *ciz* and *male*, constitutes a dilemma.

We shall see how true this is when we study the text line by line. But first of all here is a conjectural rearrangement of the sentences; needless to say, it does not involve any change in the order of the words:

1. *ceia hia . . .*
2. *ceia hia etnam ciz*
2a. *vacl trin velθre*
3. *male ceia hia etnam ciz*
3a. *vacl aisvale*
4. *male ceia hia trinθ etnam*
4a. *ciz ale*
5. *male ceia hia trinθ etnam*
5a. *vacl vile vale staile itrile*
6. *hia ciz trinθasa*

Line 1: How are we going to translate *ceia*? Since *hia* is "shadows", does *ceia hia* mean "these shades"? We might be led to think so by comparing *ceia* with Albanian *këjo*, *kjo*, "this, the latter" (M. 199), and with the word *cei* is one of the comprehensible sentences in the inscription of the Tile of Capua: *ara epni cei* (P. 2, 14), "put (*epni*) on this (*cei*) altar (*ara*) . . ."

Or ought we to translate *ceia hia* by "call the shades"? This involves assimilating *ceia* to the Albanian verb *kjaj*, "to weep; to call by name" (M. 199 and 411, *qaj*, with the same meaning).

We have already seen that when they carried out funeral rites, the ancients summoned the shades of the dead to partake of the meal. Fustel de Coulanges writes:

> It was a custom, at the end of the funeral ceremony, to call the soul of the dead person three times by the name he had borne in life.
>
> (*Loc. cit.*, p. 9)

It is true that we translated the formulae *cla θesan* and *clevanθ* by "call θesan" and "call Vanθ". But Etruscan was not lacking in fine shades of expression, and *cla* and *cle* may well have meant "implore, invoke" or the like.

In other words, *ceia* may have been used in one set of circumstances and *cla* in another.

In short, *ceia* confronts us with two words to choose from. Provisionally, let us adopt "to call" as the meaning.

Line 2: Here the problem is *ciz*. Are we to interpret *ciz* as "thrice", deriving it from the number *ci*, by analogy with *θunz*, "twice" (derived from *θu*) and with *cizi* (P. 99)? The latter certainly does mean "thrice". Does *ceia hia etnam ciz* mean "Call the shades of the fathers three times"? This translation looks right; but it comes up against two obstacles:

(*a*) The formula *ceia hia etnam ciz* occurs five or six times in our short excerpt. To say five or six times running, "Call the shades of the fathers three times", seems excessive, however much the mentality of the Etruscan priests may have differed from our own.

(*b*) Moreover, if we take *ciz* to mean "thrice" we shall be in difficulties when we come to elucidate the last line of the excerpt, *hia ciz trinθasa*, which is a sentence clearly isolated from the rest. It would then appear to mean: "Shades— thrice—of the heroes" which is not particularly comprehensible.

Both these difficulties will disappear if we explain *ciz* by the Albanian verb *kizoj* (M. 199), "to revive" (Leotti, p. 459: *lulet . . . u-kizuan*, "the flowers . . . revive")—a verb which is apposite enough in this Etruscan spiritualistic seance. In this event, *ceia hia etnam ciz* will mean: "Call the shades of the fathers: 'Live again!'"

This will give the last sentence in our excerpt, *hia ciz trinθasa*, the following meaning: "Shades—live again—of the heroes", that is to say: "O shades of the heroes, live again!" The meaning will be even more explicit if we take *hia* to mean "effigies" [1] of the ancestors. "May these effigies of the heroes live again!"—such may have been the invitation addressed to the ancestors, to induce them to incorporate themselves with their own images and, so accommodated, to take part in the banquet.

The use of this device—the reawakening of life in the ancestors' images by means of incantations and libations—seems to me to be confirmed by a verse from Ch. VIII which we shall examine in due course (excerpt *c*): *tei zivas fler*, "extend (i.e., give) *life* to the *fler*! (i.e., to the effigies of the fathers)". [2]

Line 2a: *vacl trin* is "the banquet of the heroes". *velθre* divides into *vel* and *θre*. *vel* is probably to be explained not by Albanian *vlla*, "brother" but, rather, by *vel*, the Indo-European root to which are related Slavonic *vele* ("great; much"; *velki*, "tall"; *velikan*, "giant") and German *viel*, "much". [3] *θre* is probably Etruscan *θur* and Albanian *döre*, "lineage, family". Hence *velθre* would be: "of high birth, of a mighty family". Failing this, possibly "brothers, companions"?

Line 3 brings us a new word which is also a new snare: *male*. Albanian *male* means "tip, top", and hence such things as "the strongest". Thus *në malë të thirmës* means "at the top of his voice" (M. 261). So it may be an injunction addressed to the keening priest. But *male* also means "fat" (M. 260).

Line 3a: *aisvale* or *aisuale*: "divine".

Line 4: *trinθ* was discussed in our study of LM, Ch. III. *trinθ etnam*: either "beloved fathers" or "little heroes".

Line 4a: *ale* has been studied already.

Line 5a is specially interesting.

vacl vile vale staile itrile: Can this, by any chance, denote a banquet accompanied by the frenzied dancing in which the Etruscans seem often to have sought inspiration? The passage is an obscure one indeed. We can hardly help being influenced by the insistent rhythm of the words, and also by the frescos which make it clear how important were dancing and the sound of the flute in the conduct of Tuscan ceremonies. The Etruscan priests, descended as they were from the shamans of the Euro-Asiatic steppes, which reached as far as the Danube, used to whirl round and round in order to attain a state of ecstasy. This can be seen in one of the

---

[1] Which in fact the word does mean, as well as "shades".
[2] Meaning, to give them the blood of the animals which were sacrificed.
[3] Cf. Walde-Pokorny, I, pp. 295–6.

frescos reproduced by Poulsen. Moreover, this dancing was a feature common to all the Italic peoples in archaic times. Mommsen writes of:

> ... ancient and primitive religious litanies which were sung and danced by the Salii and other priestly corporations; the only one which has come down to us is a chant accompanied by dancing, performed by the *fratres arvales* in honour of Mars:
>
> (To Mars) *satur fu fere Mars!*
> (To the brothers) *limen sali! sta! berber!*
> Be satisfied, cruel Mars!
> Dance on the threshold! Halt! Advance!
>
> (*History of Rome,* I)

Fig. 61. Hieratic dance

If we compare the following two lines we begin to ask whether there is not a similarity in their emphatic rhythms:

limen sali! sta! berber!
vile vale! staile! itrile!

vile is reminiscent of Albanian *velet*, "to turn" (M. 549; 82). Later, we shall meet *vilatos* (Stele of Novilara).

vale resembles Albanian *valoj*, "to heave, surge", etc. (M. 544) and Greek *ballo*, "to throw, throw oneself", etc. An open question. The passage seems to match Plutarch's description of the dancing of the Salian priests:

> Their steps are graceful and varied and they make quick, rhythmical *turns* and *returns*, both vigorous and nimble.
>
> (Plutarch, *Numa,* I)

staile: Trombetti compared this word with Oscan *stai-t* and Lithuanian *stoju*, "to stop"; cf. Albanian *shtoj*, "to stand upright" (M. 501).[1]

itrile may be connected with Albanian *jetër(soj)*, "to change" (M. 170).

We get the impression that four different movements or dance-steps are indicated; back, round, open out, modify. Since these are technical terms we cannot know exactly what they meant, of course; but in any case they do not appear in any of the descriptions of sacrifices and libations, which occur so frequently in LM.

trinθasa is the genitive of *trin*, "hero", as we postulated earlier. Cf. *tinθasa*, "of the day".

To sum up our explorations, here is a tentative sketch of the meaning of the excerpt:

1. Call the shades . . .
2. Call to the shades of the fathers: Live again!
2a. A feast for noble heroes!
3. Loudly, call the shades of the fathers: Live again!
3a. This is a feast of the divine (shades).
4. Loudly, call the shades of the heroic fathers.
4a. Let them live again (?).
5. Loudly, call the shades of the fathers: Live again!
5a. A feast! Revolve and dance! Halt! Change the pattern!
6. O shades of heroes, live again.

(*b*) What sort of welcome awaited these eminent guests is made clear in line 9:

renχzua etnam cepen ceren

renχzua: possibly Albanian *rrun ë (rrundze)*, "ewe-lamb" (M. 443).
ceren: this word raises a number of problems. In Albanian the verb "to eat" has two forms: *ngranë* and *ngrënë*. But in 15th-century Albanian the word was *garun*; from which it follows that *ngrënë* may have been *geren (ceren)*. We may also think of the verb *ther(oj)*, "to sacrifice" (M. 534). In the Albanian translation of Exodus, xxii. 1, we read: "*Ndë vjethte ndonjë njeri ka a dele edhe t'a thernje . . .*", "If a man shall steal an ox, or a sheep, and kill it . . . [*t'a thernje*: slaughter it? sacrifice it?]." *Thernjë* is not far removed from Etruscan *ceren (theren? tzeren?)*.

[1] *Studi Etr.*, IV, p. 216.

If we accept the latter derivation the line means: ewe-lamb—
fathers—priest—sacrifice—in other words, "The priest shall
sacrifice a ewe-lamb to the ancestors."

This translation of *ceren* seems to be finally confirmed a little
farther on, by the first half of verse 19:

cnticnθ in ceren cepar

cnticnθ may be a reduplicated form of the word *kmt* (χims, χimθm),
"hundred", studied in the chapter on Numbers.

in: "this, these".

ceren: "sacrifices (noun), to sacrifice".

cepar: cf. *clenar*, *eisar*,—*cepar* looks decidedly like the plural of *cep*,
which I identify as Albanian *gjebë*, "animal which has not yet
given birth to young" (M. 143).

Thus, *cnticnθ in ceren cepar* will mean: "A sacrifice will be made
of hundreds of animals which have not yet had little ones."
Hecatombs of specially chosen offerings were promised to the
ancestors. This rendering fully accounts for the juxtaposition of
the words *ceren* and *cepar*.

The reading "sacrifice, to sacrifice" seems to be further supported by the word *cerine*, probably a term derived from *ceren*;
it occurs in inscriptions P. 131 and 315, appropriate excerpts from
which we shall analyse in the Supplementary Material to LM,
Ch. VII.

(*c*) Though the text announces the ancestors' arrival from the Underworld and the welcome with which they were received, this was not to
say that their summoning by the priest had been effective: pious wishes,
and prayers and promises, were in vain. So, as the ancestors are
reluctant to appear, the invitation is renewed in a few words which
are, indeed, very beautiful, but which remain obscure and end, moreover, in a lacuna. These words occupy line 11 and the beginning of
line 12:

hecia aisna clevanθ
χim enac
usil repine tenθaś

hecia can probably be explained with the help of the formula *heci nac
va tinθasa*, which we discussed in LM, Ch. VI, assimilating *heci* to
Albanian *heq*, "to go out" (M. 157). In Etruscan, obviously, this
root may occur in the form of a noun meaning "an exodus, a going-
forth". The ancestors must implore Vanθ to grant them the means
of temporarily leaving her realm.

clevanθ is visibly constructed on the lines of *cla θesan*, "call θesan; implore θesan". The meaning of *clevanθ* will be, rather, "beg permission (to come out) from *Vanθ*" ("implore *Vanθ*"). I am prompted to put forward this interpretation by an interesting note on Ossetic folklore which occurs under the signature of M. G. Dumézil in the collection *La Civilisation iranienne* (Payot, Paris, 1952, p. 332).

Ossetic folklore has supplied me with many details which repay study. The present example concerns funeral customs and in particular the setting up of a doll which symbolises the dead person. M. Dumézil writes: "A week after New Year's Day, the dead man's soul *asks and obtains, from the Lord of the Dead, permission to return to his earthly home* and there to amuse himself in the guise of the doll" [our italics].

χim enac: this phrase will come up again in LM, Ch. XII. "Incense and wine"?

usil repine tenθaś: this unusual phrase, which is unfortunately followed by a lacuna, dazzled me to begin with. I almost decided that it described the sun, *usil*, plunging into the depths, *repine* (the reader will remember *hatec repine*). A poetic touch, perhaps? I was about to enthuse over Etruscan lyricism; but second thoughts restrained me. One remembers the verb *siell*, "to bring". *Sillem* (the medio-passive) consequently means "to be brought". *Usil*: "may it be brought . . ."? (cf. M. 540).

tenθas is a genitive form of *ten*, in connection with which we cannot help remembering (Hut)*tenia* (in the chapter on Numbers), stated by Ostir and Kretschmer to be a pre-Hellenic expression for *tetrapolis*; *tenia*, moreover, is in line with Albanian *ndenjë*, "residence, dwelling" (M. 3–6). Although we already have two Etruscan words to express the idea of a city or town, *subura* and *suθi* (P. 359, *a* and *b*, CIE 5237), there is no reason for trying to resist this multitude of synonyms, the precise distinctions between which are beyond our grasp (cf. our words capital, city, town, hamlet, village, county town, stronghold, etc.).

To gather the threads together, our excerpt (*c*) may be translated literally—and conjecturally—as follows: "(Your) departure, O ancestors, beg (it) of Vanθ! Incense and wine will be brought to the abyss (near) the city (to soften the heart of that goddess?)."

(*d*) But now a further appeal to the ancestors is made, in the next line (line 13):

> *zelvθ murśś etnam*
> *θacac usli*

zeluθ (A): Albanian *zë* is "to begin" (M. 572); *luθ*, "to pray, prayer" (already discussed); *zeluθ*, "begin to pray".

murśś etnam: "(beside) the urns of the ancestors".

θacac: *θac* is *dzjak*, "blood"; the final syllable *ac* corresponds to Albanian *ak*, an essential part of such Albanian words as *akçili*, "someone, somewhere", etc., and implying "something, a little, some indeterminate quantity (no matter how much or how little)", etc. Perhaps *θacac* means "a little blood"?

usli: medio-passive of Albanian *shlyej*, "to efface, wipe out"; here, "to rub" or "smear".

To sum up, the excerpt is perhaps to be interpreted as follows:

"Begin praying before the urns of the ancestors.
Let an anointing be performed with a little blood."

(*e*) The translation of the end of the chapter (lines 21–3) should perhaps run as follows:

vacl ar (Banquet of the altar) *var* (of tomb, *varr*, M. 546). *scun* (Go) *zeri* (begin, *zërë*, M. 579) *ceren* (to sacrifice?) *cepen θaurχ* (O priests who are in charge of the tombs) *etnam iχ matam* (and the fathers will come from below) *śuic firin* (dressed in togas? We shall meet the expression again in LM, Ch. XI) *ceren enaś* (to the sacrifice, to the meal) *ara θuni* (at the altar of the House). *etnam ceren* (O fathers, a sacrifice).

(Perhaps we had better piece this together again for the reader's benefit: "Banquet of the altar of the tomb. Go; begin sacrificing, you priests who are in charge of the tombs, and the fathers will come from below, dressed in togas, to the sacrifice, the meal at the altar of the House. O fathers, a sacrifice!")

LM, Chapter VII: Supplementary Material

1. Returning to the word *ceren* in excerpt *b*, we shall review two texts in which there appears the word *cerine*. This is probably identical with *ceren*.

The first inscription concerns our old friend Laris Pulena, whose epitaph (P. 131) records that he was *pśl varχti cerine pul alumnaθ pul hermu* (line 6). I have already put forward the view that he may have exercised a supervisory function "at the sacrificial processions" (*varχti cerine*) which made their way to the sacred groves of two deities, Alumnat (fortune?) and Hermes.

The second inscription comes from a cippus at Vulci: (P. 315, CIE 5321) *eca suθic velus ezpus clensi cerine*—word for word, "This is the tomb and, of Velu, of Ezpu son, *cerine*"; more comprehensibly, "This is the tomb and the *cerine* of V. son of E''. It is virtually impossible to link the word *suθi(c)* with anything else than *cerine*. I therefore deduce that, in this instance, *cerine* must represent something concrete whose presence the composer of the inscription *wanted to emphasise*. This was, incidentally, the reason why I could not try to relate *ceren* to Albanian *kerr*, "chariot" (an ancient word, of Celtic origin), despite the fact that funeral chariots play a capital role both in Etruscan funeral rites and in the furnishings of numerous Etruscan tombs. There was no cause for the presence of a chariot to be recorded on a cippus. On the other hand, emphasis was sometimes given, as we have seen, to a different sort of detail: "This is where a libation must be made." *cerine* may well be an indication of this kind. To be precise, my analysis of the word leads me to translate it as a "place of sacrifice". The termination *ne* is characteristic of some of the derived adjectives in Etruscan: *raśne*, *θvene* (the latter is derived either from *θu*, "two", or from *θuë*, "to love"), etc. The essential function of a *cippus* was just that, to mark the spot at which periodical offerings to the souls of the dead were to be made.

2. We examined the possibility of interpreting *ceia hia etnam* by the expression "*call by name* the shades of the fathers". I originally based my decision not only on philological probabilities but also on the confirmation of this ancient rite by Fustel de Coulanges.

Another positive indication was given to me a year later, when I read the interesting observations with which Mme S. Cles-Reden has enriched her book, *Les Etrusques*. She has studied contemporary Italian folklore in out-of-the-way places, where echoes of the Etruscan past still miraculously survive. She writes, for example, this passage on the village of Barbarano Romano, an "eagle's nest" which is not far from the remains of Sutri, a fortress situated between Tarquinii and Veii. The inhabitants of the village,

> if they have forgotten their origins, have nevertheless retained several customs which go back to pagan times. . . . They still pay honour to the dead in various ways. . . . On All Saints' Day they decorate the tombs with large portraits of the dead, the portraits being hung with flowers; in front of these images a curious ceremony takes place, a survival of the rites of invocation which were part of the funeral liturgy of the Etruscans. Old women, chosen for the occasion, invoke the dead; conversing with the departed, *whom they call by their names*, they supply both the questions and the answers. They ask the dead what their news is, inquire after their wants and comfort the souls in purgatory. [Our italics.]

(P. 150)

This reminds us of the same customs among the Arnauti (Albanians of Southern Russia) and the Ossetians. But they are also found among some of the Balto-Slavs. Thus, according to A. Bastian, the ancient Letts used to invite the dead to a meal at home on the day of the feast of Semme, the Earth Mother (*Ethnolog. Forschungen*, Jena, 1871, p. 102).

LM, Chapter VIII

(*a*) At the beginning of this chapter we find a description of rites, sacrifices and libations, preceded by a date: *celi huθis zaθrumis*, June, four (and) twenty, the 24th.

> . . . *scara priθaś raχ*
> *tei menas cltral*
> *mulaχ husina vinum*
> *paiveism acilθ ame*
> *ranem scare*
> *reuχzina*
> *caveθ zuślevac*　　　　　　　(lines 4–7)

scara (A) is Albanian *shqera*, the irregular plural of the word *kingj*, "lamb" (M. 495), perfectly preserved. Those astonishing pastoral nomads of the Danubio-Balkan region spoke, ate cheese, played the flute and, probably, danced, three thousand years ago, in exactly the same way as those of today.

priθas comes, I think, from the root preserved in Albanian *britëm*, "autumn" (M. 38). Thus *scara priθas* would be "autumn lambs", on the same lines as *cresverae* (discussed on an earlier page).

As the date is September 24th, are we to suppose that these "autumn" lambs are new-born? In that case they would certainly be the latest-born lambs of the year.

raχ: "smite, sacrifice".

tei menaś dtral mulaχ: if the distribution of the sentences which I have made (and which is, of course, provisional) is correct, I do not think these four words refer to an animal to be sacrificed. *Cletra*, a word known to us from Osco-Umbrian, is the litter in which a slaughtered sacrificial animal was carried to the altar. *tej* is Albanian *dej*, "to stretch". *menaś* has an exact counterpart in Albanian, namely *mënash* (also *mëndash*, *mëndafsh*), "silk" (M. 280). This Albanian noun was studied by G. Meyer. In its Latin form, *metaxa*, it was used in the Eastern countries of the Roman Empire. It meant "raw silk". *mula(χ)* is evidently connected with the litter in some way. The four words together seem to mean "stretch [or 'cover'] with silk the consecrated litter".

paiveism: a delicate matter. It is a question of "hair-splitting" once again, or rather of splitting the Etruscan atom, that source of energy. Perhaps the constituents of the word are: *pa*, "not"; *i*, "it" (as object); *veis*, a formation derived from the verb *ve*, "to put"; *m*, a suffix (possibly "with" or "in"). Since the following word means "receptacles" *paiveism* may denote receptacles "which were never put", "which had never been used".

acilθ ame: *acilθ* is "urn, receptacle, container" (especially one made of terracotta, according to Corssen); the word *ame* is a whole vast problem in itself, which we shall be content to indicate and no more. It has long been known that the Etruscan verb *amce* meant "was, has been". To which we can add that *am* corresponds exactly to Albanian *jam* ("to be", or, more precisely, "I am"). But *ame* is more ambiguous—because Albanian also has *amë*, "mother". Let us briefly examine two possible explanations of *ame* in Etruscan:

1. *ame* = "mother".

Earlier, we translated a votive inscription, *turis mi une ame*, as "This is a present to Juno the Mother" (taking *ame* as a parallel to *ati*).

Moreover, it is tempting to translate the phrase *ame vaχr lautni* (at the beginning of the inscription on the Cippus of Perugia) as "the mother-in-law of the freedman".

Finally, in the sentence *θucu aruś ame acnesem ... ipa ... ais ...* (LM, M, 5), *θucu* seems to be Albanian *dukem*, "to appear" (M. 86); *aruś* is "sun" in Etruscan; and *acnesem* can hardly be divorced from *acnanasa*: *clenar zal acnanasa*, "brought into the world six sons" (P. 169 and 170); so that *ame ascnesem* (LM, X, 5) will be "the mother who brought (us) into the world"; and the whole sentence in LM, X, 5 will be "At the appearance of the sun ... god ... will give ... to the mother who brought us into the world ...", etc.

2. *ame* = "to be" ("that it may be", etc.).

This translation seems plausible in some cases. Thus, in 1954, R. Pfister proposed to read *vinum acilθ ame* as "May the wine be in clay pots!" (*Etruskische Toepferstempel. Studi Etr.*, XXIII, 2nd Series, p. 273). It is relevant to add that in an *epulum*—a subject we have touched on in an earlier part of the book—clay vessels were used.

ranem (A) raises no doubts: it is Albanian *me-râne*, in which *râne* is the infinitive of the verb *bie*, "to strike" (M. 422). *ranem* therefore means "by slaughtering". Cf. *ranvis* in P. 131 (Laris Pulena).

reuχzina: a difficult word. We might divide it into two elements, *reuχ* and *zina*. *Zina* is identifiable as Albanian *zi*, "black". *Reuχ* perhaps denotes a receptacle, a vessel. G. Meyer discusses an Albanian word *rugën*, "vessel", which he regards as an adapted form of a Greek term (*loc. cit.*, p. 370). Does *reuχzina* denote the black pottery which the Umbrians employed when casting ritual spells on their enemies? We have also seen that sacrifices to the Underworld deities required the use of black pottery. Cf. *rcu*, "vessel", already studied.

What does Albanian tell us? In the translation of Ecclesiastes vii. 2 I find the expression *shtëpi zie*, "house of mourning" (Hebrew *beth-evel*), in which *shtëpi* is a word of relatively recent formation, but *zi*, as we have noted, goes back to Illyrian. The Albanian word *zi*, "black, unfortunate", corresponds to Etruscan *zi*, whose derivatives are *zina*, *sineθi*. Thus *reuχ-zina* is a construction conceived in exactly the same way as *shtëpi-zie*, and means "vessels of mourning" or "funeral vessels".

I would add that in line 8 there is a word-group *surθi reuχzineti*, in which *θi*, the sign of the locative, "in", occurs twice. We therefore take the group to mean "in the *sur*, in the funeral vessels". Is the word *sur* the same as Albanian *zhurr* (pronounced like French *jour*), "sand" (M. 588)? In other words, are we to think of black pots, intended for the Underworld, being buried in the sand? On the contrary, it is more likely to be an offering vowed to *suri* the god of the Underworld (Corsten, *Beamtentitel*, p. 117) and placed in his temple or shrine: *surθi*, like *unialθi* (in the house of Juno).

caveθ (A) is Albanian *gjavet*, an oblique plural case of the noun *gja*, "livestock, game" (M. 140), a form similar to *malevet* (which has been studied already).

zuslevac (B) consists of two parts:

> *zus* is Albanian *zushë*, "heat" and the verb *zhuzhis*, "to burn, roast".
>
> *levac* (A) is connected with the Albanian verb *ljej*, "to smear", studied previously, whose past is *leva*; *lyem* is "unction; ointment" (M. 254). The Albanian translation of Isaiah lxi. 1, "The Lord hath anointed me", is ". . . me ljeu". Cf. Buonamici, *luaś*.

zuśleve is therefore probably a "warm anointing". We saw earlier (p. 228) that *θacac usli* probably meant to smear with the blood of a sacrificial animal. Cf. the expression *zuśleve zarve* ((IX, II), in which the second word means "sets on fire" or "put into the fire", the expression as a whole probably referring to an offering poured into the fire of the domestic hearth, the home of the genius of the house.

Leaving aside the terms not yet elucidated, the excerpt as a whole seems to say something very like this:

"... sacrifice the autumn lambs.
Spread the silk on the litter.
Let the offerings and the libations of wine
Be (put) in vessels never used.
By means of the sacrifice of lambs
(In) black pots,
Heat the smeared (fat) of the animals."

(*b*) Shortly afterwards, in line 9, the interesting expression *puruθn vacl* occurs.

This introduces us to a new epithet characterising a certain kind of *vacl* (ritual banquet). One is inclined to trace *puruθn* to the Albanian word *mbrujtun*, "fattened", from the verb *mbruj*, "to feed, fatten" (M. 273). This reminds us of the burnt offerings of fatted calves which the prophets denounced with such determination; one thinks especially of Isaiah's phrase, "a feast of fat things" (xxv. 6) (Hebrew *mishte shemanim*).

(*c*) In another passage, which also we shall not quote in full, and which likewise mentions a *vacl*, a banquet, offered to the *fler* (images of the ancestors), there is a very characteristic phrase which means approximately "to restore life to the statues", and then some references to customs which we shall fortunately be able to check by means of evidence other than that of the LM:

... *θaclθ θar tei zivas fler* ...
    ruze nuzlχne zati zatlχne   (lines 12–13)

θaclθ: at first I identified this *θac* as *gjak*, "blood"; but it may be more logical to read it as "in the *cella*" (in the shrine, the chapel, etc.), since in Ch. III, 19 we have the same expression but with an explicitly locative termination: *θaclθi (ar)*, and since, in addition, we find similar expressions in tomb-inscriptions: *ta suθi* and *ta suti* (P. 158, 431 and 387) and *θui clθi*, meaning, respectively, "in this tomb" and "in this *cella*".

θar is Albanian *darë*, "to divide, distribute" (studied in the chapter on Numbers).

tei zivas fler: "extend (sprinkle, pour) life to the *fler*". I interpret *tei* by Albanian *dej*, "to expand" (M. 69).

It is something of a euphemism, although the Etruscans have no objection to saying what they think. I think that in reality it denoted the blood of sacrificed animals, mixed with wine; but, as we have seen, human blood was not absolutely excluded. We have already mentioned a sort of Etruscan harakiri, and also the sacrificing of prisoners of war; moreover, there is a fresco in

FIG. 62. Phersu "ensures a bleeding"

the Tomb of the Augurs depicting a man who is inadequately armed and even deliberately hampered (by another man standing behind him with a thong or lariat) and who is being bitten by a huge dog, a Molossus (perhaps the man is a condemned criminal?). In this way the letting of blood was assured for the benefit of the dark gods of the Underworld. The Romans later transformed this rite into a spectacle, an entertainment, and a much more blood-thirsty affair at that, for the Molossus was replaced by a lion or tiger.

It remains to note, that, in my reading of the excerpt, the words *θar tei* are two verbs coming in succession: "distribute, extend". This worried me somewhat. On mature reflection, I think the first verb must refer to a libation, and the second to daubing the ancestors' effigies with blood, as used to be done to the face of Jupiter Capitolinus and to the face of anyone receiving a triumph (to quote O. Müller's judicious observation). This was an in-heritance from Neolithic times: to daub oneself with a victim's blood or to eat the heart of an enemy was to acquire the virtues of whoever it happened to be. This recalls the word *śin*, which we discussed earlier.

ruze nuzl ne zati zatl ne: note that the two first words also occur in Ch. IV (5 and 18). They are more difficult than the third and fourth words. *ruze* leads us into various temptations: (1) *rruzë*, "one-year-old ewe-lamb" (M. 444), which seems very suitable; (a) *rryesë*, "training, drill, exercise" (*idem*), which is still more suitable in view of the rest of the sentence, as we shall see.

nuz may be either Albanian *ngus* (we remember that Albanian *nga* is sometimes reduced to *na*), "to urge, incite, *drive (a cart, etc.)*" (M. 322); or *nguzoj* (and *guzoj*), "to incite; to dare" (M. 140). Both these words are held by G. Meyer to belong to the ancient treasury (nucleus) of the language. And in either case, *nuz* may well suggest the idea of races and other competitive sports.

lχne is probably traceable to Albanian *le qenë*, "to allow to be" (M. 574), in other words "to cause to be done", "let there be made".

zati (A) is Albanian *zatis*, "to pounce on, seize" (M. 574), i.e., "fight" (as verb or as noun). We shall make a separate study of this word.

The two lines as a whole appear to mean:

". . . in this *cella* distribute and extend life to the divine images. . . . Let races be held. Let fights be held."

LM, Chapter VIII: Supplementary Material

1. Looking again at *zati*, we note that its meaning is corroborated both by a fresco and by the very explicit inscription by which that fresco is accompanied. We return to the celebrated Golini Tomb, which has already done us such good service with its tragi-comic kitchen, its expert on grated cheese and its leopard finishing up the *miiś meθumfs* under the table. After so many airless discussions and so long a period of that doubting agony of mind in which these studies involve us, a fresco with a text comes as an oxygen-apparatus to revive us. The fresco is in sepulchral chamber No. 2 and forms a sequel to Golini Tomb I. In that chamber there is a sarcophagus leaning against the back wall, and on the wall itself are the remains of a much-damaged fresco, with three perfectly preserved words:

P. 241, CIE 5106 *zat laθ aiθas* (A)

The fresco represented a pair of young warriors with another pair facing them. Of those on the left there remain only two helmeted heads and part of a buckler; of those on the right, two pairs of legs protected by greaves, and part of a round buckler. These soldiers are not fighting; they are eyeing one another, ready to begin. The character of the scene is, moreover, brought out by that of the scene depicted next to it. This shows a couple of two-horsed chariots, likewise facing each other. The drivers are leaning forward, whip in hand, only waiting for the signal to let their horses go; the horses, capering, striking the ground with their hooves and trembling with impatience, are rendered with extraordinary mastery and vivacity. In his *Pitturi murali*, Conestabile is resolutely determined to regard this as the start of a journey to the next world. But it is in fact a horse-race. As for the warriors, Conestabile does consent to describe their activities as "funeral games and combats". It is possible that the symbolic representation of two detachments of warriors drawn up ready for mutual combat confirms my interpretation of the word *ruze* as *rryesë*, "training, exercise". The matter is visibly one of groups of fighters waging some kind of combat in the presence of spectators; and it may be that the two pairs of soldiers in the fresco are picked combatants delegated by opposite camps, as in the time of Homer or of David and Goliath. In any case, the fight was to end in bloodshed which was an offering to Hades; the text is explicit on that point:

zat: "combat".
laθ: this is *lat*, from the root *la*, "to let"; here, "vowed, dedicated".
aiθas: "to Hades".

laθ is an important word, because it is possible that the first word in the inscription on the Cippus of Perugia, (p. 570) *eulat* (*Tanna Larezul*) . . . means "This is *left* (by T. L.)", in other words "This is the legacy (of T. L.) . . ." Cf. *θuia*, a past participle, "beloved".

zar is a clear case. We may note in addition the epithet of Mars on the Etruscan sky-map (Pallottino, *The Etruscans*, p. 165): *Maris zaθ*, "Mars (god) of combats", or, probably, "Mars (god) of combatants".

We also know the Etruscan word for the *arena*. An Etruscan vase of the 8th or 7th century (known as the vase of Tagliatella) shows an episode in the equestrian game which the ancients called "the Troy game". A labyrinth is marked out and the word *truia* is inscribed inside it. Giglioli and Toutain took this to mean "arena". And it is in fact Albanian *troje*, *truej*, "ground, area, space" (M. 526) (cf. *SE*, III, 1929).

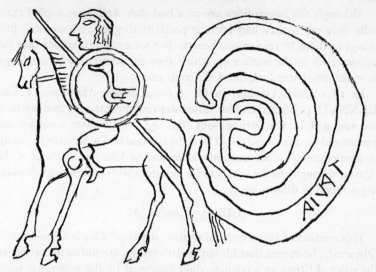

FIG. 62A. Pitcher from Tagliatella (SE III, Table XXVIC)

Yet one more case in which the intuition of Etruscologists is confirmed by Albanian. This detail from an archaic Etruscan vase shows one of the mounted participants in the funeral games, apparently emerging from a labyrinth. Some of the Etruscan royal tombs have labyrinths. The word *truia* means "area, precincts", or, as had already been supposed, "arena" (P. 74, NRIE 892).

2. Before leaving these combats in honour of the dead it will be a pleasure to glance at a racy page from the daily life of the Etruscans. To find it we must once again enter the Tomb of the Inscriptions at Tarquinii, which we have mentioned before, and whose lively frescos are accompanied by revealing dialogues.

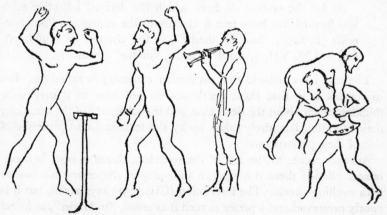

FIG. 63. Boxing and wrestling scenes (Tomb of the Inscriptions)

Although the inscriptions are in a bad state and were copied carefully only when they had become partially illegible, we can still find things in them to rejoice our hearts. But we must remember that the tiniest crack in the surface on which they are written may be enough to make any letter look like a different one.

In 1851 Luigi Canina, in his *L'antica Etruria Marittima*, Tavola LXXXVII, published an illustration showing several men, two of whom are engaged in a wrestling-bout (fig. 63). Two short speeches are exchanged by the wrestlers. The fight has reached a decisive moment. A gentleman with an uncomfortable feeling that he is about to be thrown through the air reacts to his situation with a comment displaying a touch of disapproval:

(CIE 5350) *eicrece* (A)

This consists of two words, of course: *ei greke*, "This is Greek stuff!" Obviously, he means that his opponent's tactics are unfair according to the rules of Etruscan wrestling, duly approved by the governing body of the sport. But his adversary retorts, politely but firmly:

(CIE 5349) *nucrtele* (A)

—which is, being interpreted—

nuc: Albanian *nuk*, "no", and Greek *ouk*.

rtele is undoubtedly *radele*, "regular". We keep coming back to Hammarström's word *raθ*, which he translated so accurately by "order". *radele* means "it is in order"; or, to read between the lines, "I don't need to resort to foreign tricks to get the better of you!"

As for the ending *-le*, from which the derived adjective *ratele* was formed, we have met it already in the expression *θaure lautneścle* (P. 619), "familial tombs" (in the chapter on Numbers), and in LM, VII, 3, *aisvale* (*aisuale*), "divine" (from *ais*).

The text is so pellucid that no further comment is called for. Let us remark only that these gentlemen do not look as if they were thinking much about the dead man and the solemnity of the occasion; their attention is entirely taken up by the technical and professional side of their performance.

Another scene, to the left of the wrestlers, shows a bout between boxers. Beside them is a *suplu*, a flute-player, dispensing his *fioriture* with swelling cheeks. The inscription (CIE 5351) says *anθasi*, but it is poorly preserved and I prefer to read it as *aiθasi*, "to Hades", as in *zat laθ aiθas*; this is apposite to the circumstances.

The boxers, craftily taking advantage of the sound of the music, seem to be exchanging propositions and counter-propositions of a highly practical nature, rather than mere meaningless punches. Unfortunately the two speeches are in a somewhat mangled state, but a fair amount of comprehensible material has survived. As we can see from CIE 5352, the boxer on the left is saying *fivan*. Fabretti read this as *fiun* (No. 2316). The first three letters are perfectly clear; they are *fiu*. This *f* being a *b* or *bh*, we can identify the Albanian verb *bie*, "to hit" (M. 28; cf. the Albanian–Russian dictionary, p. 530). *fiun* must be *bi un*, "I beat"; that is to say, "it is I who am beating", or, more precisely, "I'm determined to be the winner."

His adversary's reply to this declaration is terse; it is also, probably, in the best interests of them both and, what is more, of the front teeth of them both:

(CIE 5353) *vecenesmei* (A)

which is good Etruscan for "put my price"; thus:

ve corresponds to Albanian *ve*, "to put".
cenes is the same word as *cenis* and *cena* (P. 65), which we studied in the chapters on the City and the Market, and which means "price"; *cina*, in P. 381.
mei: "mine, to me".

In other words, he is saying: "What is it worth to me (or, accept the price I'm asking) if I pretend to be beaten?"

If the dear departed had been able to put a word in he would probably have shouted indignantly: "Come on now, I know your tricks!" But as no such troublesome interruption was possible, we may assume that the affair was amicably arranged.

Turning to Canina's Fig. 1, we see five people—two serving-men bringing wine and, in the left-hand half of the picture, three *histriones*. The combined stress of performance and the heat of the day has made the actors thirsty, and they are delighted to see refreshments coming. They are dancing for pleasure, like children; they raise their arms and run to give the good news to the rest of the troupe (fig. 64a). The scene itself is clear enough; but the inscriptions in CIE leave me somewhat perplexed. Thus, the man on the extreme right, who seems to be the head cup-bearer, is accompanied by the inscription (CIE 5338) *punpu*. From the deciphering point of view it would be more convenient if this was *punru*, *pu-n-ru*: *pu*, "drink!"; *ne*, one of the Albanian conjunctions, "and" (M. 313); *ru*, Albanian *rroj*, "to live" (M. 440). Taken together, this would yield: "Drink and you shall live", or, "Drink, to be revived."

FIG. 64A. Actors being given wine (Tomb of the Inscriptions)

That this termination *-u* is perfectly possible for the imperative in Illyrian is proved by, for example, the Albanian irregular verb *dal*, "to go out"; as well as its usual imperative *dil! dilni!* this verb has an alternative form *delu!* "get out!" (M. 69).

There is one argument in favour of my reading. Fabretti informs us

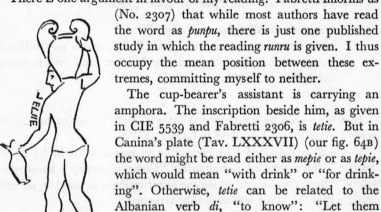

FIG. 64B. A cup-bearer

(No. 2307) that while most authors have read the word as *punpu*, there is just one published study in which the reading *runru* is given. I thus occupy the mean position between these extremes, committing myself to neither.

The cup-bearer's assistant is carrying an amphora. The inscription beside him, as given in CIE 5539 and Fabretti 2306, is *tetie*. But in Canina's plate (Tav. LXXXVII) (our fig. 64B) the word might be read either as *mepie* or as *tepie*, which would mean "with drink" or "for drinking". Otherwise, *tetie* can be related to the Albanian verb *di*, "to know": "Let them know!", i.e. "Tell everyone (that the wine has come)!"

Above the actor with upraised arms is an inscription which is recorded in CIE (5340) as *araθvinacna* (B); this yields a satisfactory reading, as follows:

araθ is Etruscan and Albanian *ardh*, "has come" (cf. *arθ vaχr ceus*) (LM, VII, 7–8).

vinac: "cup-bearer"; one simply cannot interpret it in any other way; the termination is the *-ac* of *cemnac*, *romaχ*, etc.

na: "our".

Above the man who is running along and holding a cup an inscription *avilerec iienies* (CIE 5344) is to be seen. This should be compared with another fresco from the same site (Fig. 4 in Canina's plate) which we shall consider shortly. In this second fresco we shall find an inscription beside another running actor: *arauθlec ieneies* (CIE 5344).

Aule or *Avle* is a known Etruscan name. As we said earlier, there were two brothers in Etruscan legend, named Caile Vipinas and Avle Vipinas. But what are we to make of this unusual form, *avilerec*? Must we suppose it to be an example of a hitherto unknown *diminutive*? Or are we to say: *rec* is "a pitcher"; *iienies* means "of the wine"; and *avilerec iienies* must mean "a pitcher of wine for Avile"?

Or are we to suppose that there were two brothers, Avilerec and Arauθlec? But then, what are we to make of the name Arauθlec, which is even more unusual than the other? Are we to suspect it of being a distorted form, or even merely a faulty reading, of the name *Arnθ*? Fabretti, indeed, does give an alternative reading (n. 2308), *aranθlec*.

M. Pallottino has not included these short inscriptions in his collection. In view of their state of preservation, it would be premature to base any conclusions on them. The characteristic feature of the Tomb of the Inscriptions is that some of its characters are accompanied by their names and others by speeches, and it is not always easy to tell which is which.

Finally, coincident forms are always a possibility in Etruscan because of the frequent omission of a letter here and there; and also because of our own lack of knowledge and the fact that we are still just clearing the linguistic ground. So let us leave this particular problem to the future.

Returning to Canina's Fig. 1, let us contemplate the figure on the extreme left of the drawing. He is naked except for his shoes; and if I am not mistaken he is juggling with some crowns. The inscription (CIE 5342) indicates his name: *Larth Matves*. And to our great confusion, this same name seems to appear also in another fresco in this tomb.

This other fresco, a neighbour of those we have just been considering, is also reproduced in Canina's Tavola LXXXVII (his Fig. 3, on the left). It shows us two characters: "a priest or god" as M. Pallottino says, making a sign of blessing with his right hand and holding a long stick, forked at the end, in his left; and in front of him a worshipper bowing down, offering with his left hand a fish and holding in his right hand something which looks like a knife. Between the two figures stands a kind of altar. Both characters are naked. The drawing is rather carelessly executed. An inscription, starting from the worshipper's head, describes an arc of a circle in the direction of the deity (fig. 65).

It should be noted that only the first word of the text is written as a separate entity; it is followed by two groups of agglutinated words. The last syllable of the first word is not clearly legible. CIE 5536 gives it as *civesa* . . . M. Pallottino reads it as *civesaśa* (P. 79). But in the copy taken by Canina I can clearly distinguish *civesana*, and this is the version I adopt. The inscription then appears as follows:

(P. 79) *civesana matvesicalesece eurasvclesvafesθi va a*

This is an abracadabra and, for the time being at least, eludes decipherment. The observations I shall pass on it are merely marginal notes, which may or may not prove useful at some future time:

1. *civesana* seems to be clear: it is *ceuś* (LM, VII, 8), "grandfather" or "ancestor", as we saw previously. *civesana* will be "our ancestor". This word might enlighten us about the scene, which apparently shows an offering being made to a divinised ancestor (to whose family the tomb belongs). Lured on by the misleading fish, I originally took this august personage for the god Neptune and his stick for a somewhat defective trident. I remembered, moreover, that the name of Neptune came up frequently in LM. But if the figure is an ancestor, why is he naked?

2. *matvesicalesece*: we are in the dark again. It seems reasonable to pick out the elements *matves* and *calese*. *Matves* is the same name as that of the "leader of the *histriones*", Larth Matves. And we have met *calese* in the Market-place (P. 381, the contract between an Etruscan "municipality" and a contractor named Larth Tite Cale). The same name occurs in a votive inscription, in which it may be a woman's name: (P. 752, CII 2852) *tite cale atial turce malstria cver*; this I translate as "Tite Cale to the Mother (Goddess) (*atial*) gave this mirror, to the Treasury (*cver*) (i.e., the treasury of the temple)". Matvesi Calese is probably the dative of the name. The particle *ce* (*ke*) must be a demonstrative pronoun. So far, so good. But why have Larth Matves and Matves Cale a name in common? This is a very worrying point. Are they perhaps one and the same person? Or is there a vexatious coincidence: two Matves as neighbours in one tomb, although not a single Matves is known from elsewhere? Finally, their profiles and beards do not seem to be the same; but that argument is not decisive. To make confusion worse confounded, there is an Albanian word *gjallesë*, "life" (M. 141) ("victuals"?), which may be lurking disguised in *calese*. In that case, the worshipper offering his fried whiting to the divinised ancestor may be declaring, "To Matves, these victuals!"

And if this is so, the Matves in question will be the same as the other, Larth Matves, naked as usual. But why should he climb to such a giddy eminence and proclaim himself an ancestor, merely in order to receive so meagre an offering?

The second half of the inscription gives us nought for our comfort, and I shall confine myself to studying the last elements in it, since these do allow themselves to be teased out into recognisable parts. I shall take the last of these first:

vaχa: the expression *heci naχ va tinθasa* (LM, VI, 6), with its word *va* (*ba, u-ba*), "made itself, became", has shown us that the Etruscan *v* sometimes corresponds to *b*. If that is the case here, *vaχa* will be *baχa*, Bacchus.

fesθi, with its locative ending *θi*, corresponds to Albanian *besë*, "faith, creed" (M. 26), an ancient word vouched for by G. Meyer.

fesθi(χ)vaχa: does the expression mean "in the worship of Bacchus", "in our fervour for Bacchus", etc.? The idea would not be altogether alien to the actors, whom we have seen jubilating at the arrival of the wine.

FIG. 65. Sacrificial scene

To make an end of the matter, when I scrutinise this scene and compare it with the other frescos I do not think it is a real sacrifice at all. This god is not a god; not Neptune, not Bacchus. He lacks their noble bearing. Nor is this divinised ancestor a real ancestor; there is nothing of the venerable shade about him; and he is really rather too naked. Nor is the sacrificant a real priest, or an augur. And the sardine he is offering to the "deity" is not a real offering; it is merely playing the part of one. All three of them are merely playing their parts. It is a piece of play-acting which forms part of a *vacl lunasie* on the same level as the boxing and wrestling bouts and which entertains the spectators, living and dead, as much as those contests do, or more so.

To convince ourselves of this we have only to remember that, among the Etruscans, actors took a prominent part in funeral ceremonies. It need only be pointed out that an actor wearing a *mask* of the deceased person's face was one of the members of the procession and impersonated the deceased. And no doubt "props" were not allowed to become a problem. Any sort of stick could replace Neptune's trident or the sceptre of Hades, indifferently. A play would be improvised, full of touching or comic situations; and the fresco which puzzled us so much may be a snapshot of such a play.

My suggestion, moreover, tallies with Mommsen's description of Roman funerals:

> First in the line of march came mourning women, musicians, and dancers; one of them wore clothes similar to those of the dead person and a mask reproducing his features and, no doubt, brought back the memory of his living self to the attendant crowd by appropriate gestures and bearing. Then came the most magnificent part . . . of the ceremony, the procession of the ancestors . . . each of them being dressed in the clothes he or she had most commonly worn during life. . . . In this manner the procession made its way into the Forum . . . the ancestors descended from their chariots and seated themselves in the curule chairs. . . .

Thus, in Rome, we find ourselves watching a striking pantomime, a play, with a number of actors taking part. And yet the play is not amusing, or intended to amuse; it is a funeral rite.

But where did the play come from?

The testimony of Valerius Maximus is explicit:

> During the consulship of C. Sulpicius Beticus and C. Licinius Stolon a violent plague swept the republic. . . . Hymns were composed to appease the god . . . the young mingled lascivious dances . . . with the signs of respect paid to the deities. This occasioned the introduction from Etruria of a kind of pantomime whose nimble grace . . . was an agreeable novelty in Roman eyes.
>
> (Bk. II, 4)

The theatre in general and pantomime in particular, including funerary pantomime, could have come only from Etruria.

We must not forget that even in this remote epoch the theatre is already a well-developed art, carried on by professionals. The theatre, be it noted, is a sacred reality which has been turned into a secular one. Originally, it was sacred and nothing else. There were no actors; the whole tribe, city or clan "played", that is to say religiously performed a rite, evoking the ancestors and becoming at one with their very being, so as to feel them come back to life.

Thus a simple Etruscan fresco whose first word is *ceus*, "grandfather", has lighted our path towards one of the sources of the art of the theatre —an art which was in the beginning a rite, a mystery, a pantomime sacred or merry.

Jensen, moreover, has written: play is older than civilisation. Kerényi regarded some rites of primitive peoples as a repetition of the deeds of the ancestors. Both these authors regarded play as a certain psychological condition, a "creative state". What the deciphering of Etruscan will enable us to do is to bring out the primordial function of the cult of the dead in the act of play, a cult which is older than the interest taken by early man in cosmogony.

I find indirect confirmation of my point of view in another phenomenon of Roman religious life, described in Daremberg-Saglio. This refers to a ceremonious institution, the epulum, which we have mentioned already: a sacred meal offered to the deities during the funeral of a person of consequence, and on similar occasions. Here is a summary of some observations by G. Bloch concerning the *epulones*, the priests who organised these sacred banquets.

The Romans used to hold an *epulum* of Jupiter and an *epulum* of Minerva and Juno. This "Capitoline triad, who had immigrated from Etruria with the Tarquins, were in themselves of a decidedly exotic character".

Jupiter's *epulum* bears an anthropomorphic character. Puppets representing Jupiter, Juno and Minerva were displayed, reclining on cushions. This character, says Bloch, "arises, and is developed, through contact between Etruria and Greece".

But the Roman believers who look on at these simulated meals and who, as far as can be seen, are inspired by an Etruscan tradition, do much more than just look. They participate in the game themselves, fervently. Their "passionate devotion" excites the disgust of Seneca, who describes this "exoticism" at once with precision and distaste:

Enter the Capitol. . . . You will blush to see such folly. . . . One man announces to Jupiter the names of those who have saluted him; another tells him what time it is . . . and there you can see his perfumier, whose mimicry reproduces all the actions of those who massage and groom the bathers at the public baths. Women go through the motions of arranging Juno's and Minerva's hair . . . others hold the looking-glass. . . . A clever arch-mime, a decrepit old man, played his various parts day by day at the Capitol. . . . You see women [there] who imagine to themselves that Jupiter is in love with them. . . .

What was really there? A crowd of worshippers communing with their divinities, surrounding them with affection, and acting. But it was sacred acting, a rite, an archaic pantomime which was much older than the "theatre". It was the source from which the theatre was born.

And this brings us back, after a detour, into Etruria. Our glance

Fig. 66. Actors and performing dog

at Roman experience has enabled us to sense the very quick of the Etruscan *vacl* and *epl*, those banquets in which the deities and the ancestors, and the worshippers of both, took part side by side.

The actors portrayed in our frescos were an organic part of this somewhat Dionysiac atmosphere.

After all our efforts, inscription P. 79 has remained inscrutable in places; but we shall not abandon the Tomb of the Inscriptions on this note of defeat. There is something else there which will give us new courage. This something is only a little dog—but a dog of unique pedigree, one which existed nowhere else and has never since been seen on earth.

He is to be found in the right-hand fresco in Canina's illustration (Fig. 4 in that plate), a fresco which exhibits our three actors, with *Aruθlec Ieneies* at their head. The odd thing is that he is preceded by a dog more or less like a fox terrier, which has halted with one leg lifted (a front leg!) and beside which there is an inscription (CIE 5345) *aefla* (B) (fig. 66).

Since his master, the exuberant Arauθlec (?), already has an inscription to himself, we can allow this one to the dog. We shall see in due course that it is not an order ("Find it!") which is being given to the dog. And those who delight in proper names will be disappointed: it is not the name of the dog. On the contrary, it is a speech by the dog himself—the only "talking dog" in all antiquity.

The generous decorators of the tomb gave him this chance of expressing himself, but in a reasonable way; that is to say, within the bounds of the job for which he had been trained. He does not look particularly interested in the problem of the survival of the soul as conceived by the Etruscans, and the real or pretended sacrifice of a sprat (or gudgeon or whatnot) leaves him unmoved. He has scented the presence of something and he is telling his master. "I've found it!" he says.

On what is our translation based?

FIG. 67. Apollo and Mercury

In order to elucidate this brief and unexpected canine utterance I plunged without hesitation into the depths of Greek mythology, in the form in which it is presented on Etruscan mirrors. Plate LXXIX of Gerhard's *Etruskische Spiegel* reproduces a mythological scene in which there are three characters and a short inscription, *aplu*. The learned author comments:

> *aplu* means Apollo. Apollo is holding in his right hand an animal's foot, perhaps a cow's. This may indicate one of the oxen which were stolen from him by Mercury. Apollo is holding this proof before Mercury's eyes so as to convict him of the theft.
>
> (Vol. II, p. 82)

The character on the right in this fine drawing is therefore Hermes, who, as usual, is pretending he knows nothing at all about it.

It is well known, on the one hand, that Hermes, while still a babe, stole his brother Apollo's cows; and, on the other hand, that Apollo could not find them and that it was Hermes himself who subsequently showed Apollo where they were hidden. Thus Apollo had no grounds on which to nail the theft on Hermes.

So what we have here is an Etruscan variant of the myth. But what has this scene on a mirror got to do with the little dog of the fresco in the tomb?

The explanation is that *aflu*, in Macedo-Rumanian, means "he has found". In Rumanian, which also inherited a few Thracian elements, the verb *a afla* is "to find, to discover"; *a se afla*, "to find oneself"; *aflator*, "finder".

Juxtaposing this Macedo-Rumanian word with the word from the mirror, *aplu*, and remembering the affinities between *p* and *f* in Etruscan (*pupluna* and *fufluna* on coins from Populonia, P. 378 and 379, θαpna and θafna, θuplθas and θuflθas), I conclude that the artist who engraved the mirror was making a pun: *aplu* seems to be saying two things at once, Apollo and "I have found".

Coming back to the fresco with the little dog, I consider that the word in it, *aefla*, can be interpreted by means of Macedo-Rumanian *afla*, which is so to speak corroborated by the scene on the mirror. Is not this confirmed by the dog's attitude? He is a well-trained dog who has been taught to stop and "point" as soon as he finds game or whatever else is being looked for. If he was running along and then one of his paws was raised he could but stay motionless in that position. And he is saying, "I've found!"

Our understanding of the texts in the Tomb of the Inscriptions is not without gaps. But let us remember that we have translated not only the fox terrier's little speech and the word *araθvinacna*, but also several texts of high value: *eicrece, nucrtele* and *vecenesmei*—revelations, all of them—and we have scored a real "bull's eye" in getting a glimpse of the knavish tricks of the boxing champions of the time. Better still, we have seen and sensed the ambience of a troupe of players; their world has been gradually unveiled before us.

And so I have no hesitation in concluding that the Tomb of the Inscriptions really ought to be accorded an exalted position in the work of decipherment, second only to that of the Golini Tomb.

Egyptian tomb-frescos also often portray the daily life of the incumbents of the tombs; and the idea of such portrayal undoubtedly derives from Egypt. But in this impressive setting the Etruscans re-created their own beliefs, the spirit of their time and the liveliness and vividness of their scenic art, with the result that their frescos are an incomparable spectacle.

In their filial love, their *joie de vivre* and their longing for survival after death they succeeded in preserving, in their very tombs, a fresh and ingenuous image of their daily lives.

The literary genius of Etruria has not disappeared; its traces are there.

LM, Chapter IX

In this chapter we shall content ourselves with selecting and juxtaposing two sentences, of which the second comes almost immediately after the first (lines 16 and 17–18) and which are couched in identical terms; this will illustrate the continual repetition of the same formulae in LM:

(a) *raχθ eim tul var nunθenθ*
(b) *faśi eim tul var cel suθ nunθenθ*

eim can be identified with Albanian *éjë*, "ewe or goat which has lost its young" (M. 94). *raχθ eim*, "strike, sacrifice a ewe"; *faśi* (*bâjshë*), "prepare". *tul*, in this instance, will be "tender"; and as for *var*, ought we to identify it with Ossetic *waer*, "sheep", which G. Meyer identifies with Albanian *berr*, "ewe", "an old word from the Alps" (*loc. cit.*, p. 33)? *nunθenθ* is an adjective denoting the day of the week (like French *dominical*, "of Sunday", for example). Thus line (b) may mean: "Prepare a tender ewe and a sheep as food on Nundinae for the tomb." But this is not the only possible translation.

We should note that, in Albanian, *varr* means "tomb, grave, burial place" (M. 546).

LM, Chapter IX: Supplementary Material

It is worth observing that in this chapter another of the formulae we have previously studied is also used again:

tul θans hantec repinec

We found this in Chapters III and IV, and it occurs frequently in LM. It speaks of offerings to Hades being thrown into an abyss, *repine*. There is reason to believe that this rite was performed throughout Etruria and that it is related to the fact that, in that country, cemeteries were in many cases separated from towns by a deep ravine. S. Cles-Reden writes of the town of Caere, for example:

> As in the case of most Etruscan cities, a ravine separates it from a hill of the same height, which was occupied by the city of the dead.
>
> *(Les Etrusques,* p. 21)

And of the plateau where Vulci once stood, she writes:

> Suddenly, the scene changes. . . . A ravine unexpectedly appears, a narrow slit nicked into the surface of the plateau. Over a bed of black stones of volcanic origin the river Fiora winds its way . . .
> . . . Over the wild gorge, at the height of a hundred feet above the torrent, hangs the rounded arch of the bridge which for more than two thousand years has connected Vulci with its necropolis. . . .
> The bridge, though useless now, still straddles the abyss.
>
> *(Ibid.,* p. 81)

These ravines, with their rocky beds and their streams, were probably chosen as *repine*, "abysses" into which offerings were thrown, because of their proximity to the kingdom of the dead. But in other cases the *mund*, the trench in the centre of the city, could be used.

LM, Chapter X

(*a*) A remarkable invitation is addressed to the "beloved fathers" (*etnam tesim*) in line 10 and the lines following it, in which they are once more requested to take part in a *vacl*. They are asked, in terms at once affectionate and poetic, to profit from this chance of a brief spell of oblivion:

θimitle caθnaim elfaci θimitle unuθ huteri

This is a double sentence, with a marked degree of parallelism in its construction.

θimitle: *le* is "let, leave" (imperative). *θimit* offers us a choice between *gdhime*, "dawn" (M. 124) and *dhime*, "pain" (Leotti, p. 149); *dhimt*, "it hurts, it aches" (M. 91). Let us assume provisionally that *θimitle* is "leave (your) pains, abandon (your) cares".

caθnaim: *caθ* is the sun; *naim* is probably connected with the Albanian preposition *ndaj*, "towards", whence comes the Albanian word *ndajnatë*, "dusk, evening" (literally "towards the night"; M. 305); so *caθnaim* must be interpreted as "dawn, daybreak" ("towards the sun"). "Abandon your cares till dawn", in other words "Make merry all night long".

elfaci: is *el* Albanian *ill* (also *hyll*), "star" (M. 166)?

    faci: Albanian *pashi*, "vision" (M. 355), which is connected with the verbal formations *pashë*, *pash*, the past of the irregular verb *shof*, "to see", previously encountered (M. 355).

unuθ: *u* being the sign of the passive, this will be the verb *njoh*, "to know", whence *njojt* (studied in connection with the word *trutnvt* in the bilingual inscription): "to recognise oneself, to know oneself".

nuθ, *nut* appears to have more than one meaning.

huteri: I am inclined to detect in this the plural of the Albanian noun *hut*, "owl" (M. 164), a night-bird which is easier to see at dawn. Otherwise, would it be *hut*, "four" (P. 570, a 16)?

Thus the ancestors were summoned to come and feast all night long and to "forget their sorrows till daybreak, when the morning star is seen; and to leave their cares behind them till the time when the owls can be seen" (?).

We must pause for a moment to look at the Albanian verb *pashë*, the past of *shof*, *shoh*, "to see". *Pashë* is identical with Polish *patrz* and Ukrainian *batsh*, "look". Cimochowski, moreover, has found several affinities between the morphology of Polish and that of Albanian. N. Jokl and other writers have brought out the many points of contact between Albanian and Lithuanian. The essential Indo-European character of Albanian cannot be doubted. Walde-Pokorny, for example, connects *shoh* with the Indo-European root *segn*, from which *see*, *sehen*, etc., are derived (II, p. 477).

(*b*) Chapter X has been saving up a surprise for us. From line 20 onwards we feel a song emerging with an undeniable rhythmical beat, a song which was perhaps taken up by a chorus; we imagine ourselves hearing a procession winding slowly round an altar beside which tables have been set up for the ancestors; the priests' voices, growing ever more solemn, remind us of the beyond yet do not fail to touch on the paltry consolations obtainable in this present life:

(a) *ara ratum aisna*
leitrum zuθeva

(b) *zal esic ci halχza*
θu esic zal mula santic θapna
θapn zac lena esera

(c) *θec veisna hausti*
fanuse neris
sane ipa θui neri . . .

(lines 20–23. These lines are followed by a lacuna.)

Interpretation:

(a) *The appeal*:

ara: "the altar, this altar".

ratum (B): this is *raθ*, "order, row, line", which is known to us already. Albanian *radis* is "to arrange" (M. 422). *ratum*: "arranged, ready".

aisna: "O divine beings!"

leitrum:

lei: "leave it, abandon it", from the verb *le* (already encountered a number of times).

trum is Albanian *druhem* (medio-passive), "to fear" (M. 84).

zuθeva: a difficult matter. Is it Albanian *zot*, "god, master, lord" (M. 583) (which has been mentioned already), with *va* (*ve*), the suffix of collective nouns; cf. *pleqve*, "the old (people)", and *svisve* (which was discussed earlier)? In this case, *leitrum zuθeva* will mean "Abandon fear, O masters!"

But if not, does the ending indicate an oblique case of a noun in the plural, cf. *mulave, malave, maleve*? "Abandon the fear of your masters"?

Or again, is it the termination of the past of Etruscan verbs, cf. *eprθieva*, "he was a prytanis"? "Cast off the fear which was dominating you"?

Or, finally, is it an unusual transcription of *suθ*, "tomb", cf. P. 69: *zuθina = suθina*? "Fear the tombs no more"?

Putting these findings and suggestions together: "O divine beings! The altar is ready. Abandon your fears."

(b) *The libations.* The numbers 2, 3 and 6 appear here:

zal eśic: "six times, blood"?
ci halχza: "three times . . ."

> *halχ*: a drink? One thinks of Hittite *ualki*, a drink mentioned in the Hittite rites (Friedrich, *loc. cit.*, p. 293); but also of Etruscan *aliqu*. Inscription P. 27, CIE 8413, begins with the words *mi aliqu*, in which *aliqu* appears to designate a vase. We shall nevertheless give the preference to *halica*, Latin *alica*, "spelt; a beverage brewed from this species of grain"; in other words a kind of beer.
>
> *za* is Albanian *zâ*, "to take" (M. 572).
>
> Thus *zal esic ci halχza*: "six (times) of a drink and three (times) of beer to take."

θu eśic: "twice of blood" (?).
zal mula santic θafna: "six times to offer a gold (*santi*) patera (*θafna*) of it".
θapn zac: "a patera of blood" (?).
lena esera or, probably, *lena eisera*, "make a libation to the deities".
> *lena* is explained elsewhere.

(c) Here a conclusion is reached, compounded of resignation and melancholy, yet with the love of life in it too:

> *θec veisna hausti fanuśe neriś* (A)
> *sane ipa θui neri*

θec is the Albanian root *dek, vdek*, "to die"; *dekë*, "death" (M. 69).
veis is the Albanian verb *ve, vej*, "to put" (M. 548), often encountered already. *veis* appears in modern Albanian in the form of the present subjunctive *të vejsh* and the future *do te vejsh*.
na: us, to us, for us.
hausti: as we have seen, this means "in the abyss" (the suffix *ti* is that of the locative). It can be seen that the word is not of Turkish origin.
fanuśe, which has been studied already (*eiθ fanu*, P. 100; *eθ fanu*, P. 619; *fanusei*, P. 2, 26, etc.), "dwelling".
neriś: (previously encountered) "man"; here, "to man".

Thus the first sentence says: "For us, death places man's dwelling in the abyss."

sane is a harder nut to crack.

> If *ipa θui neri* can be deciphered as "give here to man", the meaning of the whole sentence depends on the word *sane*.

My first thoughts were of the Albanian verb *shaj*, "to sigh" (M. 467). In this case the meaning of the second sentence would be, "(Only) sighs are given to men here." But is this pessimism really Etruscan? I next preferred a Scythio-Thracian word, taken from V. I. Abayev, *La langue et le folklore ossètes* (p. 180): *san(a)*, "wine", quoted from a mention by Apollonius Rhodius (3rd century B.C.). *sanaptis*, "wine-drinker", is a Scythian word preserved by Hesychius. In Ossetian, wine is *saenae*.

Provisionally, we can adopt "wine" as the meaning of *sane*. The drawback of this solution is that we already possess other names for this drink; but a rare, archaic name always stands a chance of surviving within the protective shell of a proverb, and the aphorism with which we are dealing is undoubtedly a proverb. We have already quoted one word which is common to Etruscan and Scythian, *cena* and *cina*, "prize".[1] Finally, the spirit of the proposed solution goes well with the moving inscriptions on the drinking-cups in our Tavern. This conclusion brings us back abruptly to the *vacl*, the funeral banquet.

The end of fragment (*b*) thus assumes the following meaning:

"Death prepares man's dwelling-place for us in the abyss (of the beyond); but (meanwhile) it is here that wine is given to us."

It seems to me that these notions have lost none of their freshness since the days of the Etruscans.

(*c*) I believe the same idea is put forward, in a quieter and more poignant style, in a poetic touch a little further on:

> *θumsa cilva neri*
> *vanva farsi putnam*
> *θu calatnam*   (g, 2–3)

θumsa: this is reminiscent of an Albanian expression, *thomse*, "perhaps, maybe" (*thom*, "to say", *se*, "that") (M. 536). But it is possible that *θum* is the same root as in Greek *thymiama*, "incense", and in Slavonic *dym*, "smoke"; *sa* is "how much, as much". "Like smoke" (?).

cilva (A) is Albanian *qilve*: *kam qilve*, "I am weak" (from hunger); the expression comes from the verb *qillem*, "to linger" (M. 417). Cf., in a poem by G. Fishta: *pse kam qillue*, "since I am weak" (Lambertz, *loc. cit.*, p. 152); cf. Russian *khileti*, "to languish".

---

[1] Cf. Etruscan *maθ* ("great") and Scythian *maz*.

neri: man.

vanva: a reduplicated form of the verb *va* (*bâ*, "to make, to make one-self"), evidently meaning "See, he becomes" or "Lo, he becomes", etc.

farsi (A): the word gives us the key to the whole of this interesting passage. I relate *farsi* to the Albanian verb *faros*, "to destroy, exterminate, confound", *farosje*, "destruction", *farohet*, "goes out, is extinguished" (M. 102).

putnam is identical with Albanian *botë*, "earth, soil, world, people". Jokl has connected this noun with the Indo-European root *bheua*, ancient Indian *bhumi-h*, "earth", Lithuanian *buti* and Slavonic *byti*, "to be", etc.

calat(nam) is the root *gjall*, *ngjall*, "to live, cause to live" (seen already).

Summing up, a possible translation of this passage is:

> "As is smoke, so is man feeble;
> See, he becomes a ruin under the earth;
> Would that we might live (again) here!"

Is not the whole Etruscan mentality epitomised in this reaffirmation of the will to enjoy life in the here and now, just as it is?

LM, Chapter X: Supplementary Material

It is in this chapter that the names of two divinities are mentioned: *Velθa* (*Veltun*) and *Sancus* (*velθe sancve*) (lines 8, 10, 15). The sentence *iχ velθa etnam tesim etnam celucn* perhaps contains a direct invitation to the "beloved fathers" to come to the temple of Velθa (?), there to participate, of course, in a banquet.

The Etruscan "community" or "confederation" is constantly men-tioned in the Book of Zagreb (LM). *meθlum* is perhaps derived from the Illyrian and Albanian root *madh*, "great", on the same lines as Slavonic *gromada*, cf. Czech *hromada*, "community"; cf. Russian *gromadny*, "huge". We may therefore speculate whether the LM is not connected in some way with the only common temple of the "twelve peoples" of Etruria, that of Velθa, Fanum Voltumnae, near Volsinia. However, the cults of Tinia, Juno, Neptune, θesan, Culśu, etc., occupy a larger place in LM than does that of Velθa.

LM, Chapter XI

This chapter is mainly taken up with a description of a great *vacl*. We are given a certain amount of detail about these sumptuous sacred

dinner-parties which are dangled as a lure before the eyes of the unhappy, hungry, thirsty shades. They will have as much wine and meat
as they want. They are invited to come "in hundreds", which reminds
us of the shades rushing to enjoy the sacrifice offered up by Odysseus.

(*a*) In the opening passage we read two sentences which have been
already explained (in Ch. IV):

> *vacl vinum santists*
> *celi pen trutum* (A)   (line 2)

So there is a *vacl*, with wine. The second line means: "Prepare the
food prescribed."
Other details of the ceremony follow:

> *hanθin celi tur hetum vinum* (lines 3–4)

han: "they eat", from the Albanian verb *ha*, "to eat". Thus, in the
Albanian translation of Ecclesiastes v. 11: *kë han ato*, "they eat it".
θin: the meaning of this cannot be directly determined, for we
already know two Etruscan words *di* which could be taken into
consideration here: *di*, "day" (*iθal θilen iθal* on a cup; and *di* on
the make-up palette, where it is contrasted with *nata*, "night");
and the *di* which is *dhi*, *thi*, an animal to be sacrificed.[1]
Thus *hanθin* appears to mean either "they eat today", or "they
eat venison" (or "pork").
celi tur: "dishes of the meat".
hetum vinum: "according to thirst, wine" (i.e., as much wine as they
want to drink).

> *vacl heχz etnam iχ matam cnticnθ* (lines 4–5)

heχz is Albanian *heqsh*, "to draw, pull": "that it may attract".
cnticnθ: possibly "by hundreds", with *cnt* for *χimθ*, 100; cf. *canθce*,
"was a centurion".
"May this *vacl* attract the ancestors, may they come from below
in their hundreds."

> *etnam hanθin etnam celucn etnam aθumitn* (lines 6–7)

aθumitn: *tn* is Albanian *tene*, "him" (accusative of "he") (M. 512).
a is either prothetic, or else a particle emphasising the direct
object, as in Albanian; the basic constituent of the word is *θum*,
which in this instance will be Albanian *thom*, *them*, "to say, tell"
(M. 533). G. Meyer connects this word with an ancient Indian

---

[1] The third *di*, "to know", has been studied elsewhere.

root meaning "to recite, praise" (*loc. cit.*, p. 91). If we are on the right lines here, the meaning of the verse is: "The fathers eat . . . the fathers drink, the fathers utter praises."

Which is what well-bred guests ought to do.

(*b*) To this description of the funeral banquet a detail is added, it seems to me, which lacks neither realism nor humour:

> . . . *slapiχun slapinaś*
> *favin ufli*
> *spurtn eisna hinθu*
> *cla θesns*   (lines 9–11)

slapiχun (A) took me years to understand, but is really quite simple. *sla* is the verb *shlyej*, "to efface", which did us such good service in the Tavern; *piχun* is Albanian *pjek*, "to cook, roast" (M. 388), whose infinitive, and past participle too, are *pjekun*. It goes without saying that it is related to *piek* and *piec* (*pietz*), in all the Slavonic languages, just as Etruscan *miis* is related to Slavonic *miaso*, *mieso*, and Albanian *mish*. These things certainly amount to "solid Indo-European implantations"; and how very solid they are! There is no gainsaying them.

slapi un means: "we demolish (efface, i.e. eat up, to the very last mouthful) the roast meats"[1] (or: "you will swallow", etc.).

slapinaś (A): "we efface (swallow to the last drop) the drinks." In Albanian the same word *pina* means "drinks" (M. 386). It is astounding to observe to what an extent the trail has been blazed for us by Mann.

favin: conjecturally, I suggest "we shall make wine" (*fa, bâ*, "to make"), meaning "we shall savour our wine after drinking it", let it "sink in", as it were (on the lines of the French expression *cuver son vin*).

ufli (A): after that, of course, they "go to sleep". The verb is *flé* (imperative *fli*), "to sleep" (M. 111), which we have also met in the medio-passive but with an orthographical deviation which is purely Etruscan, in P. 193 ("The Family"), *uples* ("may you sleep!").

spurtn eisna hinθu: "O Infernal Gods of the city!" (i.e., the ancestors).
cla θesns: "call θesan!" (or "pray to θesan", etc.).

Thus, the excerpt as a whole means: "We eat up all the roast meats, swallow all the drink, savour our wine and then sleep . . . O gods of the world below! Call to θesan!"

[1] Cf. M. Lambertz, *loc. cit.*, I, p. 135: *keta derkuca, do t'i pjekëmë ndë hellt*, "these piglets, (we) shall roast them on spits."

(c) Let us now tackle an interesting but difficult subject: the sentence *veives θezeri etnam aisna*, which occurs in lines 14 and 15 of Ch. VII. It will be appropriate to compare it with similar passages in Chs. VI, VII and VIII, as this comparison will enable us to detect an ancient Etruscan rite which is parallelled in certain historical data.

Let us look at these data first:

The Etruscan king Servius Tullius used to clothe the image of Fortune in numerous togas, and these were preserved for a long time in her temple. According to J. Przyluski, these garments were made of a valuable woollen fabric with a long pile, of Eastern origin (*kaunakès*). That writer believes the stuff was an imitation of foliage, which was a symbol of the renewal of nature; but he is obliged to acknowledge that it is usually regarded as an imitation of a ram's fleece (*La Grande Déesse*, Payot, 1950, p. 56). The second point of view is the one we adopt, since, for one thing, the Etruscans were formerly nomadic shepherds and, for another, the view is supported by the epigraphical data which we shall now study.

These epigraphical data can be divided into two groups:

FIRST GROUP

veiveś θezeri etnam aisna (XI, 14)
zaθrumsne lusaś fler hamfisca θezeri laivisca (VI, 9)
flerχva neθunśl śucri θezeric (VIII, 4)

The word *θezeri* is used in each of these three lines. The first and second have a further element in common: *veives*, *laivisca* (*laivisa*). *θezeri* corresponds to Albanian *desh*, "rams" (M. 67), followed by the collective suffix *eri*, which we have met already (cf. Albanian *dorbëri*, "flock"). Will *θezeri* mean "ram's fleece"? *veives* is composed of the verb *ve*, "to put", and the noun *veś*, "garment", a familiar Indo-European root; cf. Hittite *ueś* and Latin *vestio*, "to clothe". The first sentence may mean: "Put cloaks (made of fleeces) of sheep on the divine fathers." The wardrobe of the ancestors' statues was renewed from time to time, just as S. Tullius renewed the goddess's robes.

The second sentence, nearly all of whose constituents we know, appears to mean: "Twenty (i.e., on the 20th of the month). Pray before the *flers*, the masters. (With cloaks) of fleece let them be clothed."

The third sentence is visibly on the same lines as the other two, but at the same time presents us with a new element: *śucri*. Since *ri* is "new", one turns either to Albanian *shokë*, "belt, girdle" (M. 488) or to *shag*, "serge" (M. 467). It is obvious that the word *shokë*, "belt", may have to be taken in a wide sense (loincloth, sash, etc.). *śucri* can be translated as "a new belt". The sentence may mean: "For the *flers*, in Neptune's temple, new belts (or tunics), and fleece."[1]

This interpretation is corroborated by the context, for *flerχva neθunsl śucri θezeric* is followed soon after by another injunction, *tei menas cletral*, which we have already studied: "cover the litter with silk." These two rites are similar; it is clear that the accessory equipment of the temple was periodically renewed.

As for the part played by the belt or girdle in certain rites, we may consult Guhl and Koner, *Ancient Life: Rome* (1885):

> In accordance with their traditional custom, the early Romans wore the toga when they fought . . . and they wound round their bodies the panel of the garment which was thrown over the left shoulder, knotting it firmly below the chest like a belt. This way of wearing the toga, known as *cinctus Gabinus*, was no doubt copied by the Romans from the Gabians . . . who in turn had borrowed it from the Etruscans. It is incontrovertible that it dates from the military organisation carried out by Servius Tullius, and it was kept up in a variety of ceremonial usages, such as the founding of towns . . . and the opening of the temple of Janus; at the beginning of a campaign, the consul, dressed in a toga worn in this way, . . . was required to carry out the usual sacrifices.
>
> (Pp. 296–7)

This has brought us back into a thoroughly Etruscan atmosphere, and we begin to see the line of demarcation between the ancient toga and the sash or belt of modern Albania.

Under the republic, be it noted, the Roman soldiers wore a cloak of coarse stuff, the *sagum* (*ibid.*, p. 300).

The last sentence (Ch. VIII, p. 4) constitutes a transition to the texts which remain to be examined: five sentences of Ch. VII, all of which contain the element *suc*:

SECOND GROUP

(Line 7) *sal śucivn firin arθ vaχr ceuś*
(,, 9) *śucic firin tesim*
(,, 16) *ic clevanθ suciχ fir . θvene*
(,, 20) *etnam śuci firin etnam velθite etnam aisvale*
(,, 22) *etnam iχ matam śucic firin ceren enaś*

Two observations to begin with:

In lines 7, 16 and 20 the phrase *śuci firin* is used in association with

[1] It may be noted that in the earliest times the Romans wore only a loincloth or short tunic and an animal's skin (Paoli, *Vita*, p. 191).

the verb-forms *ic* (*iχ*), *arθ*, "to go, to come", with which we are already familiar. It refers to the march of the ancestors. Invited to the funerary banquet, they must come from Hades.

In lines 9, 16 and 20 the words *suci* and *firin* are connected by *c*, *χ*, the conjunction "and". This may be an indication that *fir*, *firë*, *firin* contains some idea related to *śuc*, "belt, tunic, toga".

Among the several possibilities which Albanian offers us for *firin* is the following:

> *birini*: "(prob.) handkerchief". *birinisem* "to equip oneself for a journey" (M. 30).

Given that *birinisem* is derived from *birini*, we must try to look through this modern Albanian form (in which tunics and togas are no longer within our field of vision) to discover a possible ancient nucleus from which the modern word arose. We may well imagine that "equipping oneself for a journey" in ancient times was not a matter of a hand-kerchief merely; all the more so in that handkerchiefs cannot have been widely used. The piece of material involved must have been something in which the traveller could cover his body or his head, a plaid or a neckerchief. This would bring the Albanian *birini* closer to the togas inherited from the Etruscans, for the primitive toga consisted of an "oblong piece of stuff" (Guhl and Koner, p. 294); and the Etruscan shades needed it, for they had a long journey to make on their way to the banquet.

We are far from having defined the terms *śuci firin* with any precision. We should be glad even to have made sure of their general drift. However, the meaning of the second group of lines seems to be broadly as follows:

(Line 7): "Together (?), girding on (their) togas, come the parents-in-law, the grandparents."

(Line 9): "Gird on your togas, O beloved!"

(Line 16): "Go and implore (leave of) Vanθ and gird on your double garment."

θvene is probably *θuene*, a derivative of *θu*. Note that Guhl and Koner, writing of the Romans, say: "The women, like the men, wore a double tunic" (p. 303).

Line 20 deserves a separate mention because of its parallelism:

> *etnam śuci firin*
> *etnam velθite*
> *etnam aisvale*

velθite is relatively clear. *vel* has already been interpreted as "much". *θite* is probably derived not from the noun *θi*, "day", but from the verb

Pillars in tomb with ornamented reliefs, in the Necropolis of
Cerveteri.

Votive vase with the word *suθina* ("funerary") written from right to left.

θ*i*, "to know" (already studied). The construction of θ*ite* resembles that of θ*uta*, "loved" (derived from the verb θ*u*). Taken in its entirety *velθite* must mean "well-known, famous". In fact, since it is used as a parallel to *aisvale*, "divine", *velθite* is bound to be a laudatory epithet. It would thus correspond to the Latin *nobilis*, which meant at once "known, famous, noble". Summing up, the second and third fragments of line 22 yield this:

> "O celebrated fathers!
> O divine fathers!"

Now the first fragment can be expected similarly to emphasise the virtues of the ancestors. I conjecture that it means:

> 'O fathers, garbed in togas!"

This interpretation harmonises with the following data:

> The toga was the dress . . . which only a free man had the right to wear. It was forbidden to any stranger, and anyone else not in enjoyment of all the prerogatives of a Roman citizen, to appear dressed in a toga.
>
> (*Ibid.*, p. 291)

As for the *toga praetexta* (edged with purple), we read that it was "an old fashion, imported by the Etruscans" and that it was reserved for the principal officials: "No tribune or aedile . . . was allowed to appear dressed in this honorific toga" (P. 298). Thus among the Etruscans, before the Romans, the toga must have been a sign of nobility. Since the ancestors were divinised heroes, they could not make their appearance otherwise than "garbed in togas".

All the more so, in that the banquet to which they are bidden is by implication a sacrifice (line 20). As we have just seen, it was in this fashion, with his toga girt round him like a belt, that a consul was required to perform sacrifices.

The importance of the toga wound round the torso, in the Etruscan cult of the dead, is, moreover, confirmed by a piece of visual evidence published by Körte. His picture (fig. 68) displays just the detail which is relevant to this discussion: the garb of an ancestor (or of an image representing an ancestor), *l'ombra del defunto*, as Körte says (*I rilievi delle urne etrusche*, Roma, 1890, Tav. XLV, 2; cf. XXXVIII, 4). I consider this shade, who is perhaps arriving from Hades for a *vacl* or an *epulum*, to be a remarkably dignified figure, very different from the spectres described by Homer.

Line 22: "O fathers, come from below, girding on your togas, to the nourishing sacrifice (*ceren*)."

We must admit, however, that other solutions remain to be discussed.

M

For example, another possible derivation for *śuci* is the Albanian verb *shukoj*, "to look, watch" (M. 505), which can be compared with Slavonic *shukati*, "to seek"; while *firin* recalls Lydian *bir, pir*, "house" (Messapian *bouria*), with the addition of *in*, "this", which we have met

before. In which case line 7 will become: "Together, to see this house again," etc.; and line 16: "Go and implore Vanθ that you may see again this loved house . . ." (*θuene* from *θu*, "to love"); and line 20: "O fathers, see once more this house", etc.; and line 22: "O fathers, come from the beyond and see once more this house", etc.

(*d*) In lines *g* 2–4 of the same chapter there is another description of a banquet; all the words in it are ones we already know. There is once again a libation (*lanti*) of blood (*eśi*) to be shed (*tei*) for the ancestors who are reclining (*rinuθ*?) on their beds (*streta*), and to whom as much food as they want (*satrs enas*) is promised. From all this we select a group of three words:

etnam aθumica θluθcva

etnam: "fathers".

FIG. 68. Effigy of an Etruscan ancestor

aθumica is doubtless related to the word *aθumitn*, which we studied at the beginning of this chapter. In Albanian, *ca* means "some, a few". Does *aθumica* denote "saying something"?

θluθcva (A) evidently corresponds to Albanian *dlutun*, "prayer, appeal" (M. 78), which is connected with *lus, lutem*, to pray.

Summing up, the phrase seems to be a suggestion: "O fathers, have you something to say? Prayers?"

LM, Chapter XI: Supplementary Material

1. Our decipherment of excerpt (*a*), in which the remarkable words *slapiχum slapinaś* occur, is pleasingly corroborated by a text inscribed on a leaden tablet, P. 380, a text we discussed in the chapter on Numbers. We spoke of a list of contributions, which may have been given for the periodical celebration of a common cult. Now the interpretation of the tablet and that of excerpt (*a*) support each other quite invaluably. Thus—

The individuals mentioned in P. 380 seem to be of modest estate. Among them we see a *lautnita*, "freedwoman", and, more especially, two *suplu*, "flute-players". We may fairly doubt whether these representatives of Etruria's Bohemia were very well off. Some of the contributors were more prosperous than others. Some undertake to contribute money; as for the others, it is stipulated merely that they *inpa θapicun θapintaś* (or *θapintaiś*), or again, *inpa θapicun* and no more. Now, *inpa* (A) represents *i* (the object) and *nep* (*ep*), "to give, shall give"; *θa* is Albanian *ca* (*tza*), "some, a few" (cf. *lautniθa-lautnica*); *picun* (A) is *piχun*, "roast meat"; and finally, *pintas, pintaiś* (A) is "some drink", i.e., some wine.

These donors, then, are to make their contribution in the form of necessary provisions for the sacred banquet: "some roast meats and some wine", each according to the size of his purse. In this little religious congregation the expenses shared out judiciously. The temple is not an imposing, official one, ruled by the patrician families.

2. When we were studying excerpt (*f*) in LM, Ch. III, we mentioned the words *rinuś streta* from Ch. XI, g, 4, in which *rinuś* corresponds either to the Albanian verb *rri*, "to stay, remain", or to *rënë* ("to lie"). This verb helps us to elucidate the inscription on an ossuary: (P. 454, CIE 267) *θana lecne amθnial renine*, and also an important term on the Cippus of Perugia (P. 570, b, 7), (*spelθi*) *reneθi*.

renine (A) means "the place where rests" (or "lies", "remains" etc.) someone (a feminine someone) named *θana*. *spelθi* is "in the vault"; *reneθi* (A), "on the funeral couch". Cf. Albanian *rënë* (infinitive of *bie*; M. 28), "to lie down".

LM, Chapter XII

The final chapter of LM does not sin by excessive clarity any more than the others do. Here are a few excerpts, taken from lines 1–13 (line 13 being the last):

(a) *etnam aisna*
    iχ nac reuśce aiseraś śeuś
    θunχulem muθ hilarθune

(b) *caθre χim enac*

(c) *unχva meθlumθ puts muθ hilarθuna*

(d) *muθ nac θuc . unχva hetum hilarθuna*
    θenθ hursic caplθu
    ce am enac eisna hinθu   (lines 1–7)

(e) *sal cus eluce*
    caperi zamtic
    svem θumsa matan
    cluctraś hilar   (lines 12–13)

(a) *etnam aisna iχ nac reuśce aiseraś śeuś* has been discussed already; it means: "O divine fathers, come by night with firm tread, gods of rain!"

θunχulem: *θun* is "house"; *χul* I have interpreted by means of Albanian *golle*, "vault" (M. 130), in my discussion of the "gate-keeper", the god Culśu; *θunχulem* perhaps means "through the door of the *house*" (of the temple, the tomb, etc.).

The word *muθ* plays a large part in the whole of this ritual. We explain it by the phenomenon of *nasalisation*, which is so often to be observed in Etruscan vowels. We have already seen how, for this reason, the word *hate(c)* can assume the form *hante(c)*. This time it is a *u* which is nasalised:

muθ: "*mund*", the opening leading into the beyond, the trench.
hilarθuna: "the house of the souls of the dead".

Thus the dead are invited to come through the "door of the House", through the *mund* which is in the "House of the dead".

(b) *caθre χim enaχ*

Our main purpose in isolating this phrase is to remark briefly on the word *χim*, which we have met both in LM, Ch. VII, and in the Laris Pulena inscription (P. 131).

The very pronunciation of the word is doubtful. Should we say *him*, or *kim*, or *khim*? We remember that, for example, the Etruscan word *hia*, "shade, effigy", also appears as *χie* (in a phrase in Ch. VII of LM, *scuχie*, as we shall shortly see).

We shall examine five extracts containing the word *χim*.

First of all, three cases in which the meaning of *χim* seems to be clearly defined:

(1) LM, VII, 11, already studied: *χim enac usil repine tenθaś*.

(2) LM, XII, 4: *caθre χim enaχ*, above.

(3) P. 100, an inscription from the "Typhon" Tomb which we have quoted already: *eiθ fanu . . . lavtn pumpus scunus suθiti in flenzna . . . enac celi* (line 6) . . . *enac χim* (line 7) . . .

As the word *ena* means "wine", and we see in these examples two couplings of "*χim* and wine", and one of "wine and *χim*" (*enac χim*) alongside "wine and food" (*enac celi*). From which we must conclude that *χim* was a material object offered to the ancestors on the same level as wine and food. Consequently, we are tempted to explain *χim* by Albanian *kam*, *qem*, "incense" (M. 413). It is in fact known that in ancient Italy incense was burnt before the ancestors' images.

Obviously, *χim* may equally well be a verb, "to burn incense before . . ., to praise with incense".

This being so, the next of our five examples:

(4) χim fler tarc mutinum anac veś (LM, III, 13) should perhaps be
interpreted as follows:

tarc is a very interesting word, for it is effectively represented in
Albanian by darkë, "supper, dinner" (M. 67); drekë, "lunch, mid-
day meal; supper given in honour of the dead" (M. 83; Leotti, 130).

mutinum: the initial m seems to be a preposition, "with"; the second
element, utinum, marches in line with the expression utince, which
we studied earlier and in which we detected u + tin, "to become
light, to dawn" ("become day"). Hence the meaning of mutinum
emerges as "with the beginning of the day"; and our meal, tarc,
becomes a "lunch" or even a "breakfast", in Etruscan circumstances, at least: a meal taken at dawn.

enanc has probably nothing to do with the Greek ananke (Fatum,
necessity); the word is probably connected with anë, which means
"side" in both Etruscan and Albanian. ananc: "from one side
and the other; all round", etc.

veś, in this context, is likely to be the subjunctive of the Albanian and
Etruscan verb vê: "that thou put".

The extract may mean: "Burn incense before (χim) the images
(flers). Arrange (veś) a morning meal all round (the banqueting-
room)."

The last of our examples:

(5) χim scuχie acil hupnis painiem (LM, VI, line 16) comes out as
follows:

χim: "incense".

acuχie: "come, O shades!"; cf. Albanian shkoj, "to come" (M. 482).

acil: "vase, receptacle"; a long-established rendering.

hupniś: "has dried up" (cf. hup, "to dry", and hupnina in LM,
Ch. III).

painiem:

    pa: an Albanian negative.

    ini: "the wine, of the wine".

    em: "in, inside".

"There is no longer any wine inside."

So the broad sense of the sentence will be: "Come towards the
incense, O shades! The wine-pitchers (of your tombs) are already
drained dry: there is no wine left in them."

A further observation is needed here, however. The possibility cannot be excluded that *scu* (in *scuχie*) is, after all, a plural imperative from *sce*, "suck", which we studied in the inscription featuring the wrathful Hercules (*θra sce*). In this event *scuχie* will mean "suck the incense!" or "drink the fragrance of the incense, O shades!" This may sound odd; but I am in fact guided here by Albanian, in which the expression is not "to smoke" or "to inhale smoke" but "to drink smoke", *pi duhan* (M. 383). If the Albanians have simplified the notion of "to inhale" in this fashion there is good reason for supposing that the Etruscans did too.

We now come back to the extract from LM, Ch. XII, with which we are concerned:

caθre χim enaχ

caθre may contain a number of problems. If the word *caθ* can be connected with the Albanian root *gat*, *gad*, "to prepare" (encountered in LM, Ch. VI: *acil catica*) *caθ re* will be "prepare-new", "prepare anew".

In which case the sentence as a whole will mean: "Once more, prepare incense and wine."

(c) *unχva meθlumθ puts muθ hilarθuna*

unχva: cf. Albanian *unët, unshëm*, "hungry"; *unshim*, "hunger", *unshoj, untohem*, "to be hungry" (M. 540). *Un*, in the Etruscan word, designates hunger.

unχva meθlumθ puts muθ hilarθuna may mean: "For the hungry ones, the community places a *mund* in the House of the shades."

(d) *muθ nac θuc. unχva hetum hilarθuna*
θenθ hursic caplθu
ceχam enac eisna hinθu

θuc. probably stands for *θucu*, "appear" (imperative), which we have met already (M. 86).

muθ nac θuc. unχva hetum hilarθuna: "at the *mund*, by night, appear, O ye hungry and thirsty, in the House of the shades."

θenθ: I see this as *dënt*, "sheep" (plural); cf. the Albanian translation of St Matthew x. 6: *shkoni ndëpër dënt te humbura*, "But go rather to the lost sheep . . ."

hursic: Albanian *hurdhë*, "dike" (M. 164).

caplθu: cf. Albanian *kapërdij*, "to swallow" (M. 183).

ceχam enac: the reader will remember our suggesting, in the chapter on the City, in connection with Valθur Parθunus (P. 126), that *ceχa* is a derivative of *θaχ*, "blood".

We must pause for a moment to consider the expression *θenθ hursic caplθu*. *hursic* could be differently explained, namely by Albanian *ursi*, "hunger", *urshëm*, "hungry" (M. 541). In which case the whole expression would be rendered: "The hungry ones will swallow (meat) of sheep." But we prefer "precipice" for the meaning of *hursi(c)*, seeing that Mann renders *hurdë* as "pit", which in English has associations with "trench, well, abyss, grave". And we are in an ambience in which *repine*, *mund*, trenches, precipices, play a leading role, since they convey offerings directly into the next world. This rendering throws the parallelism of the following two lines into bolder relief:

> *θenθ hursic caplθu*
> *ceχam enac eisna hinθu*

"Meat of sheep the precipice will swallow,
Blood with wine, the infernal gods."

The difference between the two renderings rests on a point of minor importance.

The next two lines are:

(e) *sal cus eluce caperi zamtic* (**XII**, lines 11–12)

sal: "one, one alone, together"?

cus: cf. Albanian *gushë*, "throat; craw, crop" (M. 139).

eluce is made up of two elements:

> *e*, which is either prothetic or else a direct object preceding the verb;
> *luce*, Albanian *luçë*, the aorist of the verb *lutem* (studied already), "to ask, pray" (M. 251 and 253). In Etruscan *luce* may be some other form of the same verb.

caperi zamti(c): "cups of gold".

In other words: "With a single throat (with one voice) ask for golden cups"?

svem will be *shuem*, "to efface", already studied.

θumsa: *θum* "smoke" (cf. Albanian *tym* and Slavonic *dym*); *sa*, "as, like". Not *θum*, "to speak".

svem θumsa matan: "will be effaced, like smoke, the beyond".

cluctraś: this occurs in Ch. VIII, 9 (in association with *caperi*) in the form *clucθraś*. We are already familiar with *θra*, "milk". We discussed *cluc* in connection with *etnam celucn*. The meaning is, "taste milk". The passage refers to a libation carried out in the normal way, a classical libation.

The five excerpts given above will thus have the following meaning, broadly speaking:

(*a*) "O divine fathers, come by night with firm tread, gods of the rain, through the entrance which is in the House, through the *mund* of the House of the Lares."

(*b*) "Let wine and incense be prepared anew."

(*c*) "Let there be put, for the hungry (dead) of the community, a *mund* in the House of the Shades."

(*d*) "Appear by night at the *mund*, O ye hungry and thirsty! The abyss will swallow sheep. Blood and wine (shall) the infernal gods (have)."

(*e*) "With one throat, call for cups of gold! The after-world will dissolve like smoke. Savour milk, O shades of the dead!"

PART III

THE ETRUSCANS AND THE ITALIC PEOPLES

In general, it will be necessary to determine what is the relation between the many Illyrian masculine nouns in -*a*, on the one hand, and Etrusco-Latin surnames in -*a*, on the other. G. Herbig says: "-*na* is a kind of 'buried conductor', the sign of an Etruscan ethnic stratum, in the names of towns (formerly the names of tribes) ending in -*ina* (Mutina, Felsina), -*enna* (Ravenna), -*ona* (Verona, Cremona, Crotona)." But Illyrian place-names presented a similar appearance: Azina, Kanina, Narona, etc. What was the connection between these two groups of nouns? There are, moreover, equivalences between the basic elements of which they are composed.

(H. Krahe, *Lexikon altillyr. Personennamen*, 1929, p. 160)

WE have seen, in a short dialogue in the Samnite language, the word *gur*, "stone"—which has been a stone indeed, a stumbling-block, to so many scholars. There is nothing to lead us to believe that this was a unique or exceptional case of contact between Etruscan and the languages of the neighbouring peoples. On the contrary, several words which are at once Osco-Umbrian and Etruscan have long been known: *kletra*, "chariot or litter", *touta*, "city, people", *honto*, "lower, inferior", *ais*, "divine", *ner*, "man", etc. It is also known that in Umbrian the plural is sometimes indicated by the suffix -*ar* (*anglar*, "birds"), that *o* and *u* are interchangeable, that *fiktu* is written for *figitu*, "to fix", etc. Finally, we have learnt that the Oscan word *hurt*, "sacred wood", is related to Etruscan *caraθ* as well as to Latin *hortus*, Hittite *gurta*, "city", Slavonic *grad*, Germanic *gart*, etc.; and we have seen that Ombrian *kasit* is identical with Albanian *gjasët*, "it is fitting". However, Osco-Umbrian is much closer to Latin than to Etruscan. What interests us here is to inquire whether certain words from Italic languages, words which have hitherto remained obscure, can be illuminated to any extent with the help of Illyrian.

This will be a legitimate hope, in the first place, with regard to the Messapians, whose language (as scholars have known for centuries) was a branch of Illyrian.

Messapian poses a riddle, one of the great riddles of Etruscology to which we have already called attention: how did it happen that Etruscan was not deciphered?

The problem, which we have glimpsed already, is as follows:

1. Bugge affirmed the identity of Messapian and Illyrian.
2. Deecke showed that there was a link between Etruscan and Messapian grammatical forms (*Etr. Forsch. und Stud.*, V).
3. Finally, according to Pauly-Wissowa, there are substantial resemblances between Messapian and present-day Albanian.

What other conclusion could be drawn than this: Messapian being related at once to Illyrian, Etruscan and Albanian, these three languages must belong to the same family?

One would think some kind of taboo had prevented this deduction.

According to Kretschmer, the Messapians reached Italy from Illyria; their language is related (as Albanian is) to Lithuanian and Slavonic. Hrozny pointed out that their name was abundantly represented in Greek toponymy. Pascu, studying the Macedo-Roumanian word *mindzu, mandzus,* "foal", connected it with Albanian *mëz, maz,* also meaning "foal", and with the name of a deity, Jupiter *Menzana,* to whom the Messapians used to sacrifice a foal. This reminds us of the sacrifice of a foal which the Etruscans may have made to θesan-Aurora, and which we mentioned in our discussion of Ch. V of LM.

Finally, F. Altheim has added an interesting detail to our knowledge of the Messapians by detecting a relationship between: (1) the Messapian god Messapos or Metabos; (2) the Etruscan god Neptune (Poseidon); and (3) the horse, the animal common to these two deities.

This being so, it seems to me that the name "Messapian" is connected with the Illyrian root *mëz,* "foal", which has been preserved in Albanian and which, in all probability, denoted the primitive totem of the tribe.

Consequently, it is this association of Poseidon and the horse which definitively explains the frequency with which the "horse from the sea", Neptune's symbol, is found on Etruscan funerary steles. My view is, moreover, in agreement with F. Altheim's definitive description of Messapus as a "deity who retained the most ancient of Poseidon's forms, that of the stallion . . ." (Rel. Rom., 167).

Messapian texts are few. As an example we may take No. 77 in M. V. Pisani's *Le lingue dell'Italia oltre il latino,* a Messapian inscription consisting of a deed in which a woman makes a donation to a temple of Aphrodite. The first words in the text indicate what was given:

plastas moldatθehiai . . . We are told that the meaning of these words is unknown. Let us therefore observe that in Albanian, *pullas* is "roof" (M. 408) and *mullezë* is "a kind of elm" (M. 298), a tall tree which yields strong timber.

Surely, then, this liberal Messapian lady presented the temple with a fine elm-wood roof?[1]

Mention may also be made of an inscription in Oscan from a wall in Pompeii, giving the names of several young people who were members of a society and are referred to as *vereiai*. As there is also a reference to a palestra, Professor Buck and M. Pisani deduce that the society's purpose was military education. They quote Bücheler's opinion that the *vereiai* were the defenders of the city gates (from Osco-Umbrian *vero*, "gate"). Perhaps we ought rather to think of Albanian *ber*, "javelin, arrow; bow" (M. 15). If this assumption is correct the *vereiai* were a Pompeiian archers' club.

A document of the 5th century B.C., richly interesting but desperately difficult, a thicket of allusions and pitfalls: such is the celebrated stele from Novilara, on the Adriatic shore, in Picenum. Framed by various clumsily carved scenes, this inscription might stand as the very symbol of confusion. Herbig wrote in 1927:

> The reverse side shows a wheel, then two battle scenes . . . five foot-soldiers and three dead men . . . underneath are a kind of lizard or crocodile, and a bear fighting a bull . . .

> The language of the inscription has been thought by some to be Etrusco-Tyrrhenian (Lemnos), and by others to be Etrusco-Italic, Ligurian or Illyrian. Only E. Lattes has had the courage and persistence to pursue, right down to details, his conception of this document as an Etruscan one; and his undertaking has ended in failure. The language gives the impression of not being Etruscan . . . Certain geographical and historical considerations indicate that it is, rather, an Illyrian dialect, which, to judge from certain Hellenisms, may perhaps already been subject to Greek influence. . . . The hypothesis of an Illyrian dialect is based, for the time being, not on any convincing linguistic resemblances, but on the feeling that a geographical and linguistic continuity runs through the Siculian and Messapian pre-Sabellian inscriptions which have been collected from Novilara and the country of the Venetians.[2]

---

[1] Cf the Macedonian nobleman who presented four hundred bricks for a temple roof (Heuzey, *Miss. Arch. de Macédoine*, p. 74).

[2] *Eberts Reallexikon*, IX, pp. 128–9.

I have translated this extract, which was written at a time when very little indeed was known of Illyrian, to bring out the fact that Herbig asserted

(a) that this inscription was Illyrian in character, and

(b) that it was not Etruscan.

The whole record of elucidation which is presented in the foregoing pages makes it clear that to oppose Etruscan to Illyrian in this fashion was to fall into gross misunderstanding. It is this error which has been responsible for the impasse in Etruscan studies.

While Herbig's utterances are somewhat vague, Whatmough is more precise and observant. He remarks that the ornamentation of the stele consists of spirals and that this constitutes

> a strong argument for regarding the people who left these monuments behind as somehow connected with the Illyrians. [There is] ornamentation of a kind which seems to find its closest analogy in the spiral decoration of architectural fragments found in an Iron Age cemetery at Nesazio in Istria and also have a five-spoked wheel . . .[1]

It is worth while to emphasise, in passing, that the Picenum region was a centre of Illyrian influence. There were, in fact, three Illyrian centres in ancient Italy: in the north, the country of the Venetians (west of Tergeste–Trieste); in central Italy, Picenum; in the south, the Illyrian tribes settled in Apulia and Calabria. These were the Iapygians, the ancient Messapians and several small tribes speaking Messapian, which is an Illyrian idiom. Helbig proved that there were strong connections between the place-names and personal names of these peoples and those of their kindred in Illyria itself. It is enough to say that these same Iapygians (or Iapudes) inhabited Northern Illyria.

This Illyrian population was sufficiently large and vigorous to prevent the Greeks from colonising the east coast of Italy, although it was nearer their own country than were the shores of Cumae and Marseille. Fighting against the Messapians, the Greek colonists of Tarentum suffered military defeat in 473 and 338 B.C., and this checked their expansion.

If we add that the people of Novilara were regarded as a Sabellian population, and that Pauli considered them to be *Illyrian* immigrants into Picenum, the Illyrian stamp displayed by the stele of Novilara becomes undeniable. Nevertheless, both the bas-reliefs and the texts of this monument have remained obscure.

[1] *Prae-Italic Dialects*, II, pp. 207 and 212.

Trombetti even expressed doubts as to the authenticity of the text. He says the inscription is anonymous and that we are surprised by its presenting four languages at once, promiscuously: Etruscan, Latin, Umbrian and Greek. Trombetti estimates that the friable stone of the stele is in too good a state of preservation; and that its alphabet is Etruscan, the simultaneous use of *k* and *c*, and the presence of *g* and *d*, are in contrast to Etruscan epigraphy.

E. Lattes, on the other hand, considered the text to be authentic.

In 1953 the state of progress with regard to the question was summed up thus by M. Pisani:

> The attempts made both in the interpretation of the inscription, and in the identification of its Greek words, are fanciful, or at least very dubious.
>
> (*Loc. cit.*, p. 218)

And now, after this long preamble, here is the Novilara text:

mimnis (1) *erut* (2) *caareśtadeś* (3) *rotnem* (4) *uvlin* (5) *parten* (6) *uś* (7) *polem* (8) *iśairon* (9) *tet* (10) *śut* (11) *trat* (12) *nesi* (13) *kruśtenac* (14) *trut* (15) *ipiem* (16) *rotneś* (17) *lutuiś* (18) *θalu* (19) *iśperion* (20) *vulteś* (21) *rotem* (22) *teu* (23) *aiten* (24) *taśur* (25) *śoter* (26) *merpon* (27) *kalatneniś* (28) *vilatoś* (29) *paten* (30) *arniuś* (31) *baleśtenac* (32) *andś* (33) *et* (34) *śut* (35) *lakut* (36) *treten* (37) *teletaunem* (38) *polem* (39) *tiśu* (40) *sotriś* (41) *euś* (42).

According to Herbig, the idea that this is an Illyrian text is not based on "convincing linguistic resemblances"; he could not see any such resemblances in it.

For our own part, we do detect a few such in this confusion, and we shall point them out here. They will not put us in a position to *translate* the text, even in its main lines; but the ground will have been cleared a little.

This is to say that the text contains words, and even phrases and sentences, which become intelligible with the help of Etruscan and Albanian. Thus:

(23–25) *teu aiten taśur*:

> *teu*: Albanian *dhe*, *dhe-u*, "the land, the country".
>
> *aiten*: Hades, cf. *zat laθ aiθas* (P. 241).
>
> *taśur*: (A) is undoubtedly Albanian *dashur*, the past participle of the verb *due*, "to love", already encountered. Cf. St Mark xii. 6: *një bir të dashurin*, (having yet therefore) "one son, his well-beloved" (an accusative).
>
> *teu aiten taśur*: "loved by earth and by Hades"?

(39–41) *polem tišu sotriś euś*:

> *polem* and *sotriś* would appear to be two of the Hellenisms remarked on by Herbig. *polim* is from Greek *polis*. *sotriś* is from Greek *soter*, "saviour".
>
> *tišu* (A) is derived from the root *due* cited above; according to Buzuk, *desh* is the aorist of that verb (M. 85).
>
> *euś* is either Latin *eius*, "his, of him" or else Albanian *hyjeshëm*, "divine" (encountered previously).

"The people adored its hero" or "The people adored the divine hero".

We shall now pass on to single Etruscan words, which we shall detach from the context without regard for their connection with the rest of the inscription:

(5) *uvlin* is Albanian *uvill*, "star" (M. 541, 543).

(6–7) *partenus*: is this Albanian *bardh*, "white, fortunate" [1]?

(11) *sut*: this does not seem to be *suθ*, "tomb", but, rather, the Albanian word *sytë*, "the eyes" (M. 466), or *syth*, diminutive of *sy*, "eye" (*ibid.*) (cf. *sunu*, P. 224).

(13) *nesi* makes one think of Albanian *nesh* ("our") or of *njerzi*, "people, kinsmen" (M. 330).

(14) *kruštenac* (B): *krus* is the genitive of Albanian *krye*, "head" (already encountered); *tena(c)* is *tenu*, "town" (?). Patron of the town, chief of the city? We shall meet the word *kruś* again a little later on, in the form *crousa*, in unexpected surroundings, namely one of Aristophanes' comedies.

(15) *trut* (already studied): "fear, faith" (*trutnvt*).

(16) *ipiem* (B): the root *ip, ep*, "to give", can be recognised here.

(18) *lutuis* (A): here we cannot fail to recognise *lut, lus*, "to pray" (*θuluter*).

(19) *θalu*: from the root *dal*, "to go out, succeed"?

(27) *merpon* is materially identical with Albanian *merpunoj*, "to undertake", which is composed of the words *mer, marr*, "to take" (cf. *intemamer*) and *punë* (derived from Greek *ponos*), "matter, affair" (M. 278, 264).

(32) *baleštenac* (B): the same termination -*ac* as in *kruštenac* (cf. *rumaχ, cemnac*?). The word is composed of Illyrian *ballë*, "forehead, front" and *ten(u)*: capital?

(33) *andś*, cf. Albanian *andshëm*, "pleasant" (M. 7).

(36) *lakut*, cf. Etruscan *lacθ* (P. 359), *laχuθ* (P. 2, 25), "libation";

---

[1] *partenus* perhaps corresponds to Etruscan *farθan. uvlin partenus*—"of a lucky star" (i.e., born lucky)?

perhaps "liquid, wet, damp"; *śut lakut*, "eyes moist (tearful)"? Cf. Greek *lekythos*, "oil-flask, oil-bottle".

(37) *treten* recalls Albanian *tretem*, "to break" (cf. *tretu*, on a mirror).

(38) *teletaune*: *tele*—Albanian *dele*, "sheep"; *tau*—aorist of Albanian *daj*, "to divide", "divided" (M. 68); "sheep broken in pieces"?

Evidently, all I have succeeded in doing here is, as it were, to get a glimpse of a few of the little cubes of a mosaic which is lying dispersed in a jumbled heap. It does seem clear, however, that the text is concerned with glorifying a hero who is referred to as "star", "saviour", "beloved chief", etc. Is it a votive inscription, an epitaph—or what?

If the individual referred to is a god, surely the stele may be consecrated to Apollo? The wheel which appears as an ornament on this class of monument may be the sign of a solar cult. Apollo was in fact known as *soter*, "saviour", a word which occurs twice here. According to one of the myths, this god soared up out of a Cretan ship in the form of a *star*. The word *θalu* may be an allusion to *talos*, which meant "sun" in the language of the ancient Cretans (Altheim, *loc. cit.*, p. 110), and which also reminds us of *diell*, "sun", in Albanian. Apollo could be "loved by earth and Hades". In his comments on the *Cratylus* (one of Plato's dialogues) Proclus, an Alexandrian philosopher, speaks of Apollo's marriage to Persephone, the goddess of the Underworld. But was not Apollo beloved above all "of gods and men"? Besides, the gods are not mentioned; and many other details remain unelucidated.

As for the scenes depicted on this stele, might the "crocodile or lizard" be Python, who was killed by Apollo? But these "rupestral" drawings are too vague.

Then is the inscription the epitaph of a leading citizen? Is his name concealed from us in the word *mimniś*, *mi Mniś*, "This is Menius" (or Arnius, in word No. 31)? Menius is a known name. There was a Menius who was son of king Lycaon, grandson of *Pelasgos* and nephew of Iapyx, the eponymous hero of the Iapygians, an *Illyrian* people. The individual to whom this epitaph seems to be devoted was *kruśtenac* and *baleśtenac*, "chief of the capital" (?). Was he a lover of horse-racing? Several words in the text seem to gravitate round this subject, which was an important matter in the lives of the Etruscans and their neighbours. Notably, *rotnem* (4), *rotnes* (17), *rotem* (22) are reminiscent of Latin *rota*, "wheel", and the wheel is depicted on the monument.[1] Since *rotne* has the same adjectival termination *ne* as in *raśne* and *θvene*, does it perhaps mean "driver"? Does *caareśtadeś* (3) mean "pertaining to the auriga", from *caresta* (?) (cf. *lanista*), with the same genitive

[1] Unless, on the other hand, *rot* is *ruθ* (inscription of Laris Pulena), "crown".

termination as in *trinθasa* and *tinθasa* (in LM), and derived from *car*, *carrus*, "wagon", a word of Celtic origin?[1] Is not *erut* (2) a replica of Albanian *erët*, "wind", a word borrowed from Greek? *erut carastadeś* seems to convey "the whirlwind of the racetrack", "the speediest of chariots", etc. *vulteś* (21) and *vilatos* (29) recall Albanian *velet*, "to turn" (M. 549 and 82) and Latin *voluto*. Finally, *treten*, "to break" (?), may be an allusion to a fatal accident, a smash in which the victim was the hero now buried beneath this stele.

It is also possible that the wheels adorning the stele, at the same time as being solar (and therefore religious) symbols, indicate that similar steles were sometimes erected to the winners of races. Was not horse-racing itself a religious institution in the first place, and did not the ellipse of the track, round which the horses galloped—the horse, moreover, being a solar attribute—symbolise the solar ellipse?

The text as a whole remains obscure. Some of the terms we have salvaged from it may, however, be useful as surveyor's marks in future deciphering.

How was it that Novilara became a crossroads of civilisations? The district round it was peopled by Illyrian tribes. Speaking an idiom related to Etruscan, this city borrowed the alphabet of the Etruscans; and, on the other hand, its relations with the Greeks and the Latins must have been equally peaceful and stable. The geographical situation of Novilara, not far from the Adriatic shore, near the mouths of the Po and, consequently, near the great market for amber from the Baltic, may throw much light on the subject. Greek merchants were doubtless free to come and settle there without interference. Although Greek military expansion from Tarentum was curbed, Greek commerce and civilisation must always have found a welcome in the region of Novilara.[2]

Etruscan elements can also be discovered in one of the most interesting documents of ancient Italy, the Tables of Iguvium, which we have already mentioned several times. These are seven plaques of lead, measuring 50 cm. by 30 cm., with an engraved text mostly written in the Osco-Umbrian alphabet and language, and a summary in Latin characters. The text describes a series of ceremonies consisting in processions carried out by a religious congregation, and in sacrifices to the local deities, before the gates of Iguvium. This little town lay to the north of Perugia, near the eastern frontier of Etruria. The object of the

---

[1] Or may not *care* be Albanian *ngarë*, "horse-races" (M. 317), which might fit in extremely well: a "stadium for horse-racing"?

[2] Cf. the town of Spina, farther north, inhabited by Venetians, Etruscans and Greek merchants (Heurgon, *La vie quot.*, p. 170).

ceremonies was the purification of the town; and maledictions were pronounced at the same time against hostile neighbours.

As an example we may take a significant Umbrian word (column VI a, 8), *uerfale*, "augural temple" (according to M. Pisani) or "place reserved for omens" (according to Buck). All commentators agree that the word denotes a space marked out by an augur. It can be seen how similar were the religious practices of the Etruscans and those of the Umbrians: *uerfale* means exactly the same as *templum*, which we studied earlier and which was represented as "the division of lines" (*teva raθ*). Now it is possible that *uerfale* was pronounced *verdhale* (just as Umbrian *capif* amounted to *capides*), and this enables us to find a counterpart in Albanian: the verb *vërdallos*, "to surround, encircle", and *verdallë*, "round, about; circle" (M. 555). This clearly refers to the operation we studied before: *tracing the boundaries of the temple*; and *uerfale* is seen to mean "an encircled space", or a place bounded by intersecting lines.

The description of the route followed by the procession swarms with puzzling words. Four or five different words denoting certain places, or certain points on that route, are invariably regarded by Buck as "the name of a building or open space in Iguvium". This is the explanation given by Buck for the word *persoliaf*, which is accompanied in the text by the word *ooserclome*, translated as "observation-point". What was observed there? I assume it must have been mainly the flight of birds, that is, the direction from which they came and the place at which they *turned*. For, in fact, the element *sol* in the word *persoliaf* is identical with Albanian *soli*, the past of the verb *siell*, "to turn", which we detected in the word *usil*. *per* recalls Albanian *prej*, "towards". "Towards which (they) turn . . ."? I have nothing to suggest for the element *af*: for although *avis* is "bird" in Latin, the bird of omen in Umbrian is *angla* (plur. *anclar*). But it does seem to me that *sol*, "to turn", may guide the study of the term *persoliaf* in a more appropriate direction than does the Slavonic word *selo*, "village", which has been invoked in this context by M. Pisani, but which is totally absent from Illyrian.

Another stage on the processional route is denoted by the words *praco pracatorum*, which we are also told is the name of an open place or square in the town. *Pracatorum* has the structure of a genitive plural. It would seem to denote a place where there were large numbers of those mysterious things called *praca*. Could these be, perhaps, the steps of a stair? I am thinking of Albanian *prag*, "step, stair" (M. 397), which is related to Slavonic *prag*, "threshold, step".

We come next to *carsome uestisier*. According to M. Pisani, *carsome*

means a spring; according to Buck, a square or place. It may be connected with Albanian *geresa*, "as far as". The second word being a
proper noun, *carsome uestisier* may mean "as far as the Vestisier". The
procession thereafter goes on its way towards *randeme Rafrer*. Buck
makes his usual imperturbable announcement: "*randeme*, name of a
building or square in Iguvium." This little town seems to have been
riddled with public squares; an anticipatory masterpiece of town-
planning! However, Albanian will enable us to do without this
unexpected luxury, for *randeme* corresponds to *rrandë*, "channel, flow
(of water)" (M. 432). Another signpost follows: *pertome Padellar*, in
which *pertome* is probably Albanian *përte*, "beyond" (M. 379). Later
there is a mention of *popler anferener* (*ibid.*, a 19), "populi circumferendi",
in which *anferener* is satisfactorily interpreted by Albanian *aferm*,
afermeni, "near, neighbouring".

We subsequently come on a detail in the religious service which has
caused a considerable divergence of opinion among the commentators.
It concerns an instruction to the priest carrying out the sacrifice: *perca*
(*arsmatia habitu*), "Put on a ritual perca" (?). The word *perca* is accompanied, moreover, by *puniciater*, "purple". Devoto consequently
translates *perca* by *toga*, admitting at the same time that there is no
etymology to support this interpretation. M. Bréal wrote:

> One is therefore led to think that the word denotes clothes (dyed
> with purple) . . . white toga with a purple border . . . *praetexta*. . . .
> The priests wore the *praetexta* at sacrifices only.

Buck, however, translated *perca* by "perch, rod", by analogy with
Latin *perticam*. M. Pisani is of the same opinion.

It is possible that the contention will be resolved by Albanian, in
which we find the word *përgac* (with suffix *tch*), "apron", from the verb
përgoj, "to soil" (M. 388). While apologising for being so *terre à terre*,
we suggest that the rod or pole which has been offered to us would,
in the circumstances, be more of an encumbrance than a help; an
apron, on the other hand, would be of direct practical use to anyone
about to sacrifice lambs and piglets.

Farther on (VI a, 23), in connection with animal sacrifices, the term
purdouiti is used. This has been translated, in accordance with the
general drift of the document, as *porricito*, "thou shalt offer in sacrifice . . ." The Umbrian word would seem to be very close to Albanian
përtetoj, "to dedicate, consecrate" (M. 379).

Three wild sows (the female of the wild boar) are next sacrificed to
the god *trebe iuvie*. A somewhat desperate attempt has been made to
relate this to Greek *teremnon*, "house". Ought we rather to look towards

Albanian *trepo*, "downward, downhill" (M. 523), and to imagine a Jupiter of the Underworld?

In line 57 a puzzling word occurs: *uatuo*. On the strength of the general meaning of the text, the sentence *uatuo ferinu fertu* has been translated as "Cause the victim to be struck". But M. Pisani, concentrating on *uatuo*, mentions Latin *statua*. However, *uatuo* ought perhaps to be read as *vaduo*, and this form of the word makes us think of Albanian *vadim* (in which *im* is merely a suffix), "experience", and *vaditur*, "experienced" (M. 543). Did not the sentence in question mean, rather, "cause to be adroitly struck"? We know how much importance was attached to the actions of the sacrificing priest and that, if he made a blunder, the rite was thought to be ineffective in consequence.

In line 58 mention is made of a rite which seems to take us back to a prescription occurring frequently in the Book of the Mummy. The expression *persae fetu* is explained by the commentators as an order to throw the sacrificed animal into a trench, *persae*. But the latter word also appears in the form *perum*. And in *perum* we can recognise Albanian *prue*, "mountain stream, bed of torrent or stream" (M. 405). We may add that at Syracuse it was customary, as part of the sacrificial procedure, to throw bulls into a deep spring (Daremberg, *Sacrificium*). This, of course, is reminiscent of Etruscan *hatec repinec*, which we have studied in earlier pages.

If we turn to column VI b, line 50, we find a reference to certain persons who took part in the sacrifice: *prinuatur*, which has been translated as "delegates". Buck adds the observation: "Etymology unknown." M. Pisani accepts this translation, but, to justify it, appeals to Old Bulgarian *prijati*, "to be favourable", and Old Irish *riar*, "to desire".

I think Albanian is more likely to reveal the source of the word in question. In that quarter we find, indeed, the verb *prij*, "to go ahead; lead", from which is derived the noun *prinj*, "pioneer, leader" (M. 402). "To go ahead" is much more appropriate to a delegate than is "to desire" or "to be favourable".

We must now embark on one of the most touching passages in the Tables of Iguvium, a passage, moreover, which will reveal to us certain hitherto unknown historical perspectives. The passage is concerned with the maledictory spells which the inhabitants of Iguvium launched on a mass-production scale against their possible aggressors. These spells are rained upon the heads of tribes of whom half are unknown to us, but among whom the place of honour is kept for *tuscer* and *iabuscer*, in other words the Etruscans and the colony of the Iapodes in

Picenum, as M. Pisani explains. The terms in which these un-
favourable wishes are expressed are often obscure, and Albanian will
be a great help in our understanding of them.

Thus in column VI b, 53 *et seq.*, a wish is transmitted to these enemies
that they be *etur*, a term which, like a number of others occurring after
it, has been translated by "exterminated". To justify this rendering
M. Pisani is obliged to resort to a word *e-tudes-to*, "expelled from the
frontiers". This is complicated; a much more probable idea is that
the word is the Illyrio-Albanian *etur*, "parched, dried up" (M. 97).
Next, the wish is expressed that the Iguvians' evil neighbours be
tursitu, "shaken, trembling", a word which is accounted for rather
poorly by Latin *tremare*, but very well by Albanian *trazoj*, "to agitate",
traz, "commotion" (M. 522), a root common to Slavonic and Albanian.
This is followed by a no less cordial wish: that they be *holtu*, which
M. Pisani explains by means of Greek *oleto* (*oleter*, "murderer"). But I
prefer to turn to Albanian *holloj*, "to thin, attenuate, reduce to powder",
and (*të*) *hollët*, "faint, swoon" (M. 161), which adds a pleasing diversity
to the list of calamities compounded by the spiritual leaders of Iguvium.

Next comes "to be *ninctu*". Some writers having seen this as an
allusion to snow (from Latin *ningere*, "to snow"), M. Pisani retorts that
this is a stupid explanation; he proposes Latin *nectum*, "to put to
death". We might also suggest Albanian *nink*, "not" (M. 325):
perhaps "in no wise" (?), which would give *ninctu* the sense of "an-
nulled, annihilated". The enemies are next offered the prospect of
being *preuilatu*, in which M. Pisani would like to identify Latin *pre-
vinculato*, "to be fettered" (*loc. cit.*, p. 174). Albanian offers either
përviel, "to fling out" or *përvëloj*, "to boil, to burn" (M. 381). It is a
matter of taste which of these one chooses.

Yet another wish is formulated: that the enemy be *preplotatu*. This
has been interpreted for us by means of Latin *praeplauditato*, "to beat
noisily". But it is by no means certain that the Iguvians were concerned by the amount of noise the operation involved. I would rather
look for the explanation in Albanian *përplas*, "to burst, crash" (M. 376),
which is a good deal more explicit.

A place which is frequently mentioned (and this fact in itself inclines
us to think the word is not a proper noun) is *rubinia* (II b, 44; VII a,
6). This may be something rather similar to Etruscan *repine*, "the
precipice", and Albanian *rrëpinë* (M. 437), at least if the passages
concerned deal with sacrifices to the infernal gods. It is noteworthy
that Umbrian religion seems more archaic and sombre than Etruscan.

Moreover, *repine* occurs on the bucket dedicated to Lavis (studied
in an earlier chapter), its form there being *rupinu*.

In column II a, 15–16, which deals with a sacrifice, an expression is used which has given rise to some awkward renderings:

sume ustite anter menzaru çersiaru

ustite is translated as *tempestate*, "weather, storm". Buck's comment on this word is: "Etymology unknown." M. Pisani says: "Etymology obscure." *Anter menzaru* is given the meaning of "between the months". Buck considers it denotes banquets held between the months.

Conjecturally, we can interpret this sentence with the help of Albanian, as follows:

sume: Albanian *shumë*, "much"; the Albanian word, moreover, is derived from Latin *summa*, "sum" or "highest".
ustite: "noise"; cf. Albanian *ushtoj*, "to resound", and *ushtim*, "noise" (M. 542), and also Lithuanian *oshti*, "to rustle, murmur".
anter: "in front of" (Latin *ante*).
menzaru: "moon" (cf. Greek *mene*, Gothic *ména*).
çersiaru corresponds to Albanian *kërthi*, "late", *kërthinenj*, "to become old, to weaken" (G. Meyer, *loc. cit.*, p. 188).

Taken in its entirety, this seems to be instructions to make a lot of noise before the weakening (or disappearance) of the lunar crescent. This is a universal practice which has survived among primitive tribespeople in our own day. It is possible that a sentence in the Book of the Mummy, X, 18, refers to a similar ceremony:

uceti cepen caθinum zaneś

cepen: "the priest".
uceti: "to rustle, murmur"? "The priest will make a noise"?
caθinum: from the deity's name *caθ*, "sun".
zaneś: Albanian *zanë*, which is so close to the Etruscan word, means "eclipse"; it is derived from *z*, "to occupy, seize" (M. 573).
 caθinum zaneś (B) is: "at the eclipse of the sun".
 There is all the more reason for accepting this in that the Romans likewise, "in order to bring an eclipse to an end, used any and every means of making a noise" (Paoli, *Vita*, 109).

Earlier, when discussing the words *pazu muluane* (Golini Tomb), we mentioned the expression *pistunire fertu*. This comes from II b, 15, of which M. Pisani says: "*Di che cosa si tratti è difficile dire*" (it is difficult to say what this is about). *Pistu* is "to grind" or "pound"; but does *nire* come from *nigrum*, "black"? I have suggested Albanian *ngjyrë*, "colour, dye" (M. 324). It may be noted that the women of one of the

Messapian tribes, the Daunians, dressed in black and put red make-up on their faces.[1]

To conclude this brief glance at Umbro-Illyrian affinities, here are two more words from the Tables of Iguvium:

(1) *kukehes*, a term whose meaning M. Pisani says is uncertain, is perhaps composed of Albanian *ku*, "when", and *kohë*, "time".

(2) *acrutu revestu* (V a, 9), an expression which has been translated as "without interruption to look", can be interpreted with the help of Albanian *akkroj*, "to glare at, scowl at" (M. 4). The difference between the two renderings is small; the point about the second is that it turns conjecture into reality.

Perhaps the few soundings we have taken in this chapter will be a contribution towards defining the problem of the ancient connections between Osco-Umbrian and Etruscan.

[1] *P.I.D.*, II, p. 263.

XIV

ILLYRIAN IN RELATION TO LANGUAGES OVERSEAS

THIS chapter will contain a few summary notes, mainly concerned with the points of contact between Illyrian and the languages of certain other peoples.

The chief Illyrian dialects are Etruscan and Albanian.

I. ALBANIAN, THRACIAN AND MACEDONIAN

According to Pauly-Wissowa, the Albanians are one-third Illyrian and two-thirds Thracian. Conway, in 1933, repeated this definition. But the results of deciphering, as set out in the present book, render these computations precarious.

G. Meyer's opinion, recorded in 1885, was that the Albanians were Neo-Illyrians; he added that we knew almost nothing about the ancient Illyrians. Ellis, in 1886, established that Albanian belonged to the eastern part of the Indo-European linguistic system.

Thus, for example:

Sanskrit	*putra*	"son"
Persian	*pisar*	"child"
Ossetic	*furth*	"son"
Albanian	*pizere*	"little"

According to G. Weigand (1924), the Albanians are descended from the Bessi, a Thracian tribe who were still speaking their own language as late as the 6th century A.D. and who do not emerge as Albanians until 1079, after emigrating towards the south-east. Weigand did not perceive that many elements in the Albanian language, which he looked on as having been borrowed from Slavonic in the 6th century A.D. and subsequently, belonged in fact to an archaic Indo-European vocabulary, contemporaneous with the Hittites.

Finally, holding that the Albanians could not be Illyrians because the latter were a maritime nation, whereas the Albanians are a continental people, Weigand was forgetting that the Illyrians were a vast family of peoples, in which there was room for both categories at once.

On the other hand, when Weigand notes that after the disappearance

of the Macedonian language (which was related to Thracian) the
Thracian language continued to be used by the mountain shepherds,
we recognise in these latter the nomadic shepherds so often mentioned
by G. Meyer.

In his important work, *La linguistique balkanique* (1933), Sandfeld
affirms that Albanian is a modern development of Illyrian and
Thracian. Meillet and Cohen, in their capital work *Les langues du
monde* (1952), put forward this view:

> Some have thought that modern Albanian was a continuation of
> ancient Illyrian. This is not certain. Only its geographical position
> has caused it to be so classified.

(p. 44)

This view must now be revised.

It was established by Jokl that the Albanians are descendants of the
ancient Illyrians who passed from the north-east towards the south-
west [1] and that their language is related both to Illyrian and to
Thracian. Finally, Jokl, Walde-Pokorny, M. Lambertz and S. E.
Mann have demonstrated that Albanian is a separate, independent
member of the Eastern Indo-European linguistic family.

In fact, the many concordances between Etruscan and Albanian
enable us to regard the former as an ancient branch of the old Illyrian
tree, and the latter as its most recent branch.

The continuity of this Illyrio-Albanian idiom has already been made
clear. Von Hahn saw a connection between the Zeus Sullanios of the
ancients, the tribe of the Selli who lived near the sanctuary of Dodona,
and the people of Suli, the Albanian Souliots of our own times. The
place-name Pardhos is explained by Albanian *bardh*, "white". With
this can be ranked the name of an Illyrian king, Bardullis, and that
of a locality in Apulia, Barduli. To this series I should like to add two
terms which further attest the diffusion of the root *bardh*, namely
Lithuanian *baltas*, "white", and Russian *bérioza*, "birch".

As for other ancient Illyrian names, Sandfeld quoted the identification of the name Dalmatia with Albanian *delmë*, "ewe", and of
Dardania with *darde*, "pear". Jokl identified the name of a river in
Carinthia, the Maltein, and of another, in Arcadia, the Malus, with
Albanian *mal*, "mountain"; and a deity's name, Jupiter Menzana,
who was worshipped by the Messapians, with Albanian *mëzi*, "foal",
as we have seen.

Julius Pokorny juxtaposed the name of a locality, Nomisterion, stated

[1] This is confirmed by the observations of the Coon expedition (*Mountains of the Giants*).

by Ptolemy (2nd century A.D.) to be in Bohemia, with the Etruscan place-name Numistro, in Lucania.

Speaking of a name dating from Roman times, Aquae Balizae (in Pannonia), Jokl remarks: "This is truly Illyrian." [1] In Albanian, *baljtë* means "marsh". This is obviously related to Slavonic *blato*, *bloto*, *boloto*, but it is several centuries earlier than the appearance of the Slavs on the right bank of the Danube.

It is instructive to compare this with a brief note by J. Brüch on the Latin words *blatea*, *balatro*, which are mentioned by Festus. The author notes their identity with Albanian *baltë* and adds that their common origin has been rightly attributed to Illyrian. "The Illyrian word penetrated into Latin."[2]

Finally, Vasmer's elucidation of the name of the Carpathians is of special interest. He writes of the Albanian word *karpë*, "rock":

> I recognised this word in the name *Carpates*. Meyer-Lübke wondered from whence came the root of the Romanic terms *krepp*, *krapp*, "stone". We can now answer that it came over from Illyrian.[3]

This gives us the northern limit of the Illyrians' expansion. The centre of this multitude of tribes must have been on the two banks of the middle Danube; this accounts for the points of contact between Albanian and the Balto-Slavonic languages, especially Lithuanian.

Krahe situates the Illyrians between the middle Danube, on one side, and Italy (Venetians, Iapygians, Messapians), on the other, and regards them as having gone so far afield as Asia Minor (including Troy), Crete and Palestine. It is generally agreed that the Philistines can be recognised as Illyrians. According to F. Altheim, it was the onward drive of the Illyrian tribes which set off the Dorian migration into Greece. These ethnic movements implanted everywhere the Illyrian names and terms which we have so far mentioned and to which we shall add, for example, the word *teuta* ("people"). But Pannonia too, according to Jokl, is an Illyrian name, while the ancient name of the Danube, Istros, is Thracian, and thus belongs to a language related to Illyrian.

G. Battisti has recently consented to see a "remarkable assonance" in a juxtaposition made by Krahe: on one hand, the mountain of Bulsinius in Illyria, and the Illyrian personal names Volsius, Volsouna, Valussius; on the other hand, the Etruscan city Vulsinii-Bolsena, and Vulsana, a town of Rhaetia (*Studi Etr.*, XXIV, 1956, p. 291).

---

[1] "Albaner" (*Eberts Reallex.*, I, p. 86).
[2] *Glotta*, VIII, 1917, p. 83.
[3] *Studien zur Albanesischen Wortforschung*, 1921, p. 25.

We have pointed on several occasions to the diffusion of other Illyrian roots, such as *mal*, "mountain", *gur*, "stone", *ballë*, "forehead, head, chief", and so on.

As for *gur*, I shall point out one more case of it, a curious one. The old etymological Russian dictionary of V. Dal gives an old Russian word *guriy, gurey*, which he explains as meaning "heap of stones". They used to be erected at the water's edge, to mark places where a boat could come alongside. The word is the same as Albanian *gurishte*, "stony place" (M. 139).

In moments of discouragement, unable to get used to the idea that Etruscan had now been partly deciphered (and still less, that it was I who had done it), I sometimes felt like saying: "But really! *gur* may be just an archaic Slavonic word which the Albanians borrowed. All this deciphering is just a mirage. I give up. Let me out of here!"

But the master-carpenter of P. 401 (*cure malave*), and the little Samnite with his sling, who used to scribble dialogues or the name of his fiancée on his missiles, were waiting beside me, ready to lay a hand on my coat-collar and shout, "Halt! We were writing *gur* a thousand years before your Slavs came on to the scene at all."

But what really is astonishing is the omnipresence of *ballë*. We have exhibited the following cases:

(1) *θuflθas̀*, Bi-frons, *du-baltas̀*;
(2) *ballen*, "king", "he who is at the head", in Phrygian;
(3) *Balla*, which, as we shall shortly see, is the name of a Macedonian town, "chief place";
(4) *bales̀-tenac* on the Stele of Novilara (a parallel formation to *krus̀tenac*), "chief" (of the "dwelling-place");
(5) *Triballe*, "a mountain with three peaks".[1]

We must pause for a moment to consider *Triballe*. In ancient times there was a tribe known as the Triballi, on the lower Danube; we mentioned them in an earlier section of this book. Aristophanes (in *The Birds*) speaks of them as barbarians. Philip of Macedonia and Alexander the Great fought them. Pauly-Wissowa (*Triballi*) informs us that among modern authors Kerenyi considers them to be Illyrians, and Jokl, Thracians. Their home has been identified as the Vitos mountains, to the south of present-day Sofia. They have a reputation for bravery, explained by their belief in the immortality of the soul. This was probably connected with an ancestor-cult. The very name of this people has been a source of embarrassment to philologists. Jokl

[1] It may be that *tri*, "three", and *mal*, "mountain", are present in the name Trimalchion, the hero of the *Satyricon* of Petronius Arbiter. Is *Trimalc* a parallel to *Avilerec*?

tried dividing it into *Trib* and a suffix *-al*, a suggestion dismissed by Pauly-Wissowa as "unconvincing"; the latter's alternative suggestion, however, is not far from ridiculous. In all probability the name stands for the inhabitants of a valley or plateau at the foot of a mountain with "Three Summits" (*Tri Balle*), a term which we have already related to the name of the deity Du-Baltash.

I therefore believe that this ethnic title is Illyrian: and I am all the more sure of it because, however strange this may seem, we possess a sample of the people's language. In *The Birds* a Triballian god figures among the characters; he pronounces two sentences which the Greek poet's commentators have declared to be an "unintelligible jargon": *nabaisatreu* and *saunaca bactaricrousa*.

It is thought that Aristophanes was merely aiming to amuse the Athenian public. This reminds me of the fact that in one of Plautus's comedies there is a Carthaginian who frequently utters complaints in his own language. To the Romans, this was merely a comic rigmarole. But Orientalists have detected perfectly clear Phoenician words in it: *ilanim, ilanot*, "gods, goddesses", and a number of others. Similarly, the speeches of the barbarian god are no mere jumble of ridiculous syllables. Aristophanes seems to me to have noted several Illyrian words eight centuries before Hesychius of Alexandria. *Nabaisatreu* has an Illyrian stamp. In it I discern: *na* ("us, to us, our"), *baisa* (Albanian *bâjshë*, "may he make"), *treu* (possibly the Illyrian sacrificial offering, which is already known, "the stag", *dre-u*, M. 82). Indeed, in the Greek speech which follows this there is talk of "offering a sacrifice". As for the Illyrian god's second speech, I shall content myself with pointing to its final element, *crousa*, which is strongly reminiscent of the word *kruś* ("head, chief") on the Stele of Novilara, and of Albanian *kryesi*, "leadership", *kryesoj*, "to head, lead; preside" (M. 218). Surely, after all, it is the normal thing for an Illyrian god to speak Illyrian?

A sixth, and very interesting, case of *balle* can be added to the list, for the word comes up unexpectedly in several modern languages to denote a class of animals with which we are familiar—at least, those among us who devote their time to hunting the whale: *la baleine*.

This revives a controversy which was presented to the attention of the readers of the review *Glotta* (X, 1920, p. 198), and which concerned the origin of the Latin words *ballaena* and *ballo*, meaning "whale" and bearing a resemblance to Greek *falaina*, which also means "whale".

According to Walde, these Latin words do not come (for reasons known to him) from a Greek source, but represent a borrowing from Thracian or *Illyrian*. J. Brüch objects to this that for phonetic reasons (which are known to *him*) these words cannot have come from true Illyrian, but at the most from Thracian.

We might take this chance of asking a question whose importance, indeed, is not of the first order, but which is nevertheless not without interest: was not the original whale, the first whale in all the world, called *ballaena* because of his *balle*, his enormous head or forehead? Every time I have had the chance (which has not been often, I admit) of seeing a whale, it has always seemed to me to have an outsize head.

To end this muster of the various instances of *balle*, it remains to add, first, that the word *falzaθi*, in the opening lines of the Magliano strip (P. 359), seems to mean "at the start" or "in front" (*ballëz*); and second, that I believe the idea of *balle*, "summit", is slumbering undisturbed in one of the oldest conundrums of Etruscan studies, *falado*, "sky" (P. 831)—for the sky is in very fact the *summit* and crown of the visible world. Having said this much, we refuse to climb higher.

So much for the glorious yesteryear of the Illyrian language. In the Roman imperial epoch the three Illyrian provinces which lie successively between the Danube and the Adriatic, namely Pannonia, Illyria and Dalmatia, were Romanised through the agency of Roman colonies and military camps.

The connections between Illyrian and Albanian were recalled in 1950 by C. Coon, the leader of the ethnographical expedition sent to Albania by the University of Harvard.

He in his turn mentions three words common to the population of that country in ancient times and the present-day Albanians: *peligo*, "old, ancient" (*plak*), *Emathia*, "the great" (feminine) (*e madhia*, the name of a tribe), and *Molotti*, "mountain-dwellers" (*maltsor*). He adds: "The Gheg [Albanian] language is basically Illyrian" (*The Mountains of the Giants*, pp. 39 and 41).

Some Etruscologists nevertheless refuse to have recourse to Albanian, because it is a modern language which has had time to evolve and change.

Does this general rule remain absolute when we are concerned with comparing an ancient language with a modern language belonging to the same family? I note that when Hrozny was deciphering Hittite and proving the Indo-European origins of that language he did not hesitate to compare the Hittite word *eizateni* not only with Greek *edein* and Latin *edere* but also with Old High German *ezzan*, "to eat" (E. Doblhofer, *Le déchiffrement des écritures*, Arthaud, 1959, p. 176). It is true that certain specialists in comparative philology rose in protest against the "absurdity" of Hrozny's discovery. But it was he who was right, not they (*ibid.*, p. 178).

Likewise, in the course of his remarkable decipherment of the Etruscan word *raθ*, "order", to which the only reply that Etruscologists could make was an embarrassed silence, Hammarström-Justinian (whom we have mentioned a number of times) allowed himself to compare the word not only with Latin *ordo* but also with Swedish and Danish *rad*.

Again, it was through the study of Coptic—which, as the inheritor of Egyptian, had gone through a considerable evolution—that Champollion deciphered the Egyptian hieroglyphics.

The objection does not hold water; for all the borrowings which have occurred in Albanian through the centuries have done nothing to alter a cardinal fact: the fact of *continuity* between ancient Illyrian (Etruscan) and modern Illyrian (Albanian). It is thanks to this continuity that Albanian has retained from Etruscan so many notions which are basic to life, in words which have been elucidated in this book: to be (*klenë*), to eat (*granë*), to drink (*pi*), to go (*ik*), to give (*ap, ep*), to take (*merr*), to go out (*dal*), to see (*shof*), to pray (*lus*), to sleep (*fle*), to break (*tret*), to fear (*dru*), to buy (*ble*), to kill (*vras*), to roast (*pek*), to be irritated (*idhn*), to thunder (*gemn*), father (*at*), blood (*gjak, zak*), meat (*mish*), stone (*kur*), eye (*sy*), rain (*shi*), mountain (*mal*), wolf (*uc*), shade (*hia*), enclosure (*gardh*), forehead (*balle*), young, new (*ri*), worthy (*seder*), big, great (*madh*), etc. etc.

The fact is clear, and denial is vain.

We know now for certain that *pava tarχies* is not a proper noun but "Tarχies *has seen*". Even while sketching out working hypotheses, we have succeeded in setting up a collection of Etruscan terms whose meanings compel acceptance.

Finally, let us note that the name of the Albanian town Ulqini explains that of Etruscan Vulci. The root of both is ancient Illyrian *ulk, ujk*, "wolf". In Illyria there was a place called Oulkinion, and, in Pannonia, one called Ulkisia. And the Illyrian mountain, Bulsinius, has the same name as the Etruscan city of Volsinia (Krahe).

The Thracians, in their time, were a powerful group of tribes; it is enough to mention one such tribe, the Dacians. According to Altheim, their original habitat was the Pannonian basin, where they were neighbours of the Illyrians. They were the first people to fight on horseback. It was from them that the Greeks and the Etruscans acquired the cult of Dionysus. Their language, like Illyrian, belonged to the *satem* group. Here are some comparisons between Thracian, Illyrian and the Balto-Slavonic languages:

(*a*) Thracian *zelta*, "gold"; cf. Slavonic *zlato* and Lettish *zieltz*.

(b) According to Weigand, Roumanian *barza*, "stork", comes from Thracian; cf. Albanian *bardh*, "white".

(c) The Thracian names *Torkuatos*, *Torkos* are close to Etruscan and Hittite Tarku, Tarχies.

(d) Thracian *Manegordum*, "the city of Mane",[1] is related to Etruscan *caraθ*, Hittite *gurtha*, Albanian *gardu*, etc.

(e) The name of a Dacian king Orolos, "eagle", is Slavonic (and is earlier than the appearance of the Slavs in the West); so is the name of an Etruscan soothsayer, Olenus ("stag", Slavonic *olenj*, *jelenj*).

(f) The Dacian name Tautomedes belongs to the Umbrian–Etruscan series *touto*, *tutim*, *tuθiu*, etc. We may also note two words quoted by O. Hoffmann (*Die Makedoner*): *vetes*, "of the same year", in which I see the genitive of Albanian *vit*, *vjet*, "year"; and *esterikai*, an epithet for dogs. The later corresponds to Greek *trapezes*, "eating from the table, domestic". In *esterikai* I detect Illyrio-Albanian *eshtera*, "bones" (M. 97); hence "eater of bones, domesticated".

(g) According to Ellis, the name of an Etruscan beneficent spirit, *lasa thimrae*, is akin to the name of a river in the country of the Thracians, the Thymbrians.

Finally, we may add to this list the following Thracian words: *dardë*, "pear"; *dala*, "lamb", like Albanian *dele*; *maro*, "great", like Etruscan *maru*; *uis*, "water"; *din*, "day", cf. Tinia; *bounon*, "hut, cottage", like Albanian *bunë* and Etruscan *fanum*; *istro*, "swift"; *drenis*, "stag", like Albanian *dreni*, etc.

References to the Macedonian language are rare, but they will help us none the less to discover some more ancient Illyrian roots:

(a) Herodotus, VII, 137, and other sources, record two Macedonian names of princes: *Gavane* and *Perdiccas*. Their etymology seems to me to be explained by Albanian: *gavanar* means "proud" (M. 123), *gavni*, "pride"; and *përdëgjëj*, "to encourage" (?) (M. 366).

(b) *Korannos*, a Macedonian king. Kretschmer says this name is explained by *kara*, "head". Cf. Albanian *krue*, "head" and *kren*, "chief".

(c) According to von Hahn, there was a Macedonian town with the name of *Balla*. This lengthens the list of names founded on the notion of *ballë*, "forehead", and, by extension, "chief, king; capital", etc. This should be compared with *Kruja*, a town in Albania, whose name comes from *krye*, "head". We have met this word already. We meet it again in a verse of Ecclesiastes (ii. 14) translated into Albanian:

syt'e te urtit jane nde kryet t'ati
The wise man's eyes are in his head

[1] P. Kretschmer, *Einleitung*, p. 203.

Bronze Etruscan head. Parma Museum.

"Men of bronze": the future Etruscans make their appearance
in Italy as formidable bronze-clad warriors.

(d) *lisson*, in Macedonian, "upper, higher". Cf. Albanian *ljiss*, "oak" ("very high"?).

(e) According to Kretschmer, Macedonian *indea* meant "midday". I explain it by means of the Albanian verb *hinj* "to enter" (M. 164), "the entrance (start) of the day", since according to O. Müller the Etruscan day began at noon.

(f) Finally, a Macedonian word of great interest is that used by Alexander of Macedonia in one of his letters: *skoïdos*, which von Hahn interprets as a kind of manager or administrator whom Alexander was anxious to engage. Von Hahn compares the word with Albanian *skutër*, "head shepherd" (I, p. 227). I originally thought of the Albanian verb *shikoj*, "to look after, see to" (M. 476; cf. Polish and Ukrainian *shukatj*, *szukac*, "to seek"); this would have made an inspector of the *skoïdos*; note may also be taken of Albanian *shkues*, "messenger; mediator" (M. 485); but the verb *shquaj*, *shqoj* (aorist *shqojta*), "to choose, determine, decide upon" (M. 496), is probably more suitable. Alexander's word, in the latter event, will mean "director, administrator".

It may be added that, according to Hirt and G. Weigand, Macedonian was close to Illyrian. Such is also the opinion of Kretschmer, who remarks: "a Macedonian could not understand the speech of an Illyrian, but that proves nothing; in the same way, a North German does not understand a Swabian peasant, but the peasant is no less a German for that" (*loc. cit.*, p. 285). We shall have occasion to mention Macedonian again.

2. ILLYRIAN AND HITTITE

In 1929 B. Hrozny published an article on "Etruscan and the Hittite Languages",[1] pointing out certain common features between the one and the other. He compares the Etruscan genitive termination *-al* (*larthal*, etc.) with Hittite *Alisal*, "(inhabitant) of Alisa" etc., and also mentions the other genitive suffix, *-s*, which is common to both languages. He examines an Etruscan "family name", *hatili*, and finds a counterpart to it in Hittite *hattilis* ("Hattite"). He next draws a connection between the Etruscan god Culsan and the Hittite deities known as *culses*, as we said in an earlier section.

Some concordances between Hittite, Etruscan and Albanian will be included in a table at the end of this book; but they are not based on the study by Hrozny, who was concerned but very little with the vocabulary of Etruscan. Except for his observations on the morphology

[1] *Zeitschr. für Assyrologie*, 1929, B, 4, pp. 172–85.

N

of the two languages, his attention was devoted to the community
of religious ideas as between the Etruscans and the Hittites. He
emphasises that the latter, like the former, sought to discover the
will of the gods from the flight of birds, from lightning and from the
livers of animals, and he concludes by saying: "The Etruscans came to
Italy from a region in the immediate vicinity of the Hittite lands,
that is to say from Asia Minor." This, in our view, gives an inadequate
picture of the situation.

3. ILLYRIAN AND LYDIAN

According to Herodotus and Strabo, the Etruscans were Lydians
who had migrated to Italy. The Romans ironically called them
"Sardians", from the name of the Lydian capital, Sardis. After the
fall of Veii the cry of "Sardians for sale!" was heard in Rome.

Horace, stressing the noble origins of his Etruscan friend Maecenas,
refers to him as a Lydian.

But when we turn to the results of Lydian epigraphy in the hope of
gaining a little light on Etruscan we are quickly disappointed. They
confront us with yet one more enigma, one more gaping hole in the
history of ancient civilisation. We find ourselves back again in a
cemetery, surrounded only by funeral vaults with inscribed steles.
But these are not like the Etruscan tombs, with their colourful frescos
and entertaining dialogues. We no longer feel ourselves to be standing
in the full light of history, at the heart of the civilised world, admiring
beautiful statues, vases with stories in picture-form and cups with
pithy and amusing inscriptions. All these are lacking.

However, on six of the handsome 6th-century Lydian steles of fine
white marble, which were found during the American excavations at
Sardis, there are poems. Whole poems engraved in handsome calli-
graphy (whose letters, alas, are Lydian!), from ten to fifteen lines
long, perfectly preserved. Funereal poetry, of course. One surmises
that the local undertakers' firms employed (for first-class funerals, need
we add?) teams of poets, of tried and infallible eloquence. These
things offer plenty to see—and nothing to understand. Nevertheless,
E. Littmann, who in 1916 published the first account of these excavations (*Sardis*, VI, 1), waxed so enthusiastic over these epitaphs as to
proclaim that they were samples of the oldest poetry in the world, no
less!

One of these inscriptions, moreover, is bilingual, consisting of some
ten lines in Lydian and Aramaic.

In conception it is like the funerary inscriptions of the Phoenician
kings of archaic times; it consists of a mutter of assorted curses aimed

at anyone who should disturb the repose of the departed. This inscription has, indeed, helped in the elucidation of several Lydian words. Several Lydian glosses have also been preserved. From these materials a small Lydian vocabulary and a few notions of Lydian grammar have been built up. But even in this restricted field there is no lack of disagreement among the philologists, and the language as a whole remains obstinately dumb. So far from helping us, it asks to be helped; it does not even refuse to profit from the often pale and intermittent gleams which, with such labour, we have elicited from Etruscan. But this in itself proves a certain community of origin between the two languages, however vague that common origin may appear as yet; the fact that Dionysus of Halicarnassus considered there was no resemblance between Lydian and Etruscan does not constitute a decisive argument. In ancient time, moreover, there was always a lingering memory of the relationship between the Lydians and the peoples who lived in, or came from, the Balkan peninsula. According to Herodotus (I, CLXXI), Lydus, the eponymous king of Lydia, was the brother of Mysus. And the Mysians, like the Phrygians, were related to the Thracians (*Les Premières Civilisations*, 1950, p. 347).

The points of contact so far discovered between Lydian and Etruscan have amounted, in the main, to the following:

(*a*) The only alphabet, besides Etruscan, which contains the symbol 8 (f), is the Lydian. On the other hand, the Etruscan letters χ, θ, *ph* (*f*) are lacking in Lydian, while *b* and *d* are used in Lydian but not in Etruscan.

(*b*) In Lydian, as in Etruscan, we meet the endings -*s* and -*l* for the genitive, -*k* as a conjunction and -*ak* to denote pertaining: *sfardak*, "inhabitant of Sardis", like Etruscan *romaχ* and Albanian *romak*.

(*c*) In inscriptions the name of the deceased's mother is given as well as that of the father.

(*d*) As we have seen, the Lydian word *kandaulos* also occurs in Rhaetian.

(*e*) Lydian *pir*, "house", occurs in Messapian as *burion*, again meaning "house".

Lydian, however, differs from Etruscan in possessing signs for several nasal vowels. Littman draws an analogy with modern Albanian, which possesses the nasal vowels *â, ê, i, o, u, y*. The Etruscans denoted their nasals by simply adding an *n*: *hatec–hantec*.

We may note also that the name of a Lydian deity, *levs*, was connected by Littmann with the name of the Etruscan deity *lvsl* (P. 719) (the god Lavis!), and that a royal title, *palmus*, has been connected with Phrygian *ballen*. Finally, thanks to the bilingual inscription, Lydian *pel* has been identified with Phoenician *meara* ("cave, vault"); which enables us to render Etruscan *spel* (Cippus of Perugia, P. 570 a 23, b 4, 6) as "vault".

The following new considerations can be added concerning the account of the American excavations:

(1) In the list of Lydian glosses (*Sardis*, VI, 2, Index III) there is an expression *baske pikrolea* (13), which expresses the idea of things being *brought together*. This reminds us of Albanian *bashke*, "together" (M. 22).

(2) In Index V there is a Lydian name for Dionysus: *Breseus*. This recalls Albanian *verë*, "wine". "He of the wine"?

(3) In the same list there is a Lydian place-name: *Kaira*. A pencilled note in the margin of page 93 of the copy of *Sardis* which I studied at the Bibliothèque Nationale, Paris, says "cf. Caere in Etruria". A judicious annotation!

(4) *Ibid.*, p. 8: *baki* is Lydian for Bacchus. Cf. Etruscan *paχi(es)*.

(5) We have already discussed *kupassis*, "footgear", in Lydian.

(6) In inscription No. 10 (*Sardis*, VI, 2), we read:

> *es mrud karok katovalis bilu vora* . . .
> This (is) the stele and *Karo* (of) Katova . . .

It has been suggested that *bilu* may correspond to Albanian *bilu*, "daughter". An important consideration is that M. Pisani has found the same word, *bilia*, "daughter", in a Messapian text and compared it not only with Latin *filia* but also with Albanian *bijë* and Venetian *vhiila*. A root common to Latin and to the Illyrian languages: Messapian, Venetian, Lydian (*N.B.!*) and Albanian.

But here is yet another possible point of contact between Lydian, Etruscan and Albanian: *karo(k)*, *Karo(l)* would seem to be identical with an enigmatic Etruscan word (*slelet*) *caru* in the inscription of the Cippus of Perugia (P. 570 a 3). Note that, in Albanian, *karu* is "phallus", which is appropriate on a cippus erected to the memory of a man;[1] however, in Lydia the word may have denoted some other element in funerary architecture.

(7) Inscription No. 50 is the epitaph of one Timles *Brdunlis*. This is recognisable as the Illyrian root *bardh*, "white", which is as widespread as *ballë*.

(8) *Cibyra*, the name of a Lydian town, seems to be the same as that of the Etruscan quarter in Rome, Subura, and as *spure*, "city", in LM.

---

[1] This is evidently an indication of a fertility-cult fused with a cult of the dead. Thus the cippus of Vetulonia is a phallus (*Studi Etr.*, V, 1931, p. 401, fig. 6).

(9) Finally, the word *vanaś*, *wana*, which occurs frequently, recalls Etruscan *fanu*, "dwelling-place, building, sacred place".

The foregoing remarks are merely preliminary. We shall now concentrate on two important Lydian words: *enslifid* and *uqbahent*, which, in my opinion, also take us back into Illyrian. Both of them occur in the bilingual, Lydian–Aramaic inscription (No. 1 in *Sardis*, VI, I, and in *Sardis*, VI, 2).

The inscription consists of nine lines, in Lydian (where the first has been restored) and Aramaic, the second text being intact. The meaning is this:

> On the 5th day of November in the Xth year of King Artaxerxes, in the city (or: citadel) of Sardis. This portico (?) and this funeral vault, and everything in it, are the property of Mane son of Kumli. If anyone damages or destroys anything in this tomb, may the goddess Artemis of Ephesus and of Koloë drive him out of his house and his land and everything he possesses.

The two Lydian words quoted above have been the subject of controversy; there are doubts not only as to the rendering but even the reading; some scholars read them as *ensuifid* and *uqbapent*.

Obviously, our understanding either of these terms or of their grammatical structure will depend partly on the spirit in which the study of Lydian is approached. To what language should it be compared?

We are thus compelled to ask a question, to which we have already given part of the answer.

E. Littmann was not slow to declare:

> We can say with certainty that Lydian is neither Hamitic nor Semitic.

> (*Sardis*, VI, 1, 77)

He would seem to have been filled already with dark premonitions concerning the methods of future commentators.

M. Cuny, undeterred, examined these Lydian texts in 1926 from a point of view which can be summarised thus: linguistically speaking, the position of Lydian is between Hamitic, Semitic and Southern Caucasian. Given that the meaning of *enslifid*, thanks to the Aramaic inscription, was fixed by the verbs *khabel* and *parok*, "to damage, to destroy", M. Cuny saw in *enslifid* one of the Semitic grammatical forms, a *niphal*, that is to say the medio-passive, of a verb in classical Arabic meaning "to cut to pieces". We shall take a fresh look at this word.

E. Vetter observes that M. Cuny confuses the issue by introducing Semitic and Ancient Egyptian.[1]

I believe that any attempt to characterise Lydian as a language with Semitic tendencies, or influenced by Semitic, rests on a misunderstanding. Not only does Lydian not resemble Aramaic; it is also a fact that none of the proper nouns in *Sardis*, VI, 2, is of a Semitic cast. Borrowings are always possible, but these exceptions only prove the rule.

One wonders upon what grounds Lydian was declared to have undergone a Semiticising process. We know that when Gyges sent an embassy to Assurbanipâl the king's regular interpreters were unable to understand the language of the emissaries. But these interpreters, among the Assyrians, were Aramaeans. They would therefore have had no difficulty in understanding a Semiticised language, even without a "combinatorial method" to help them.

The reason for the existence of the Lydian–Aramaic text is that the Persians, who were the masters of Lydia at the time, propagated Aramaic through all the countries of their empire, as far as Elephantis, using it as the official language of diplomacy.[2] Sardis was not only a nodal point on the caravan-routes but also the location of a satrapy, and this satrapy had been created following a sternly contested war between the Persians and the Lydians. The Sardian satraps must naturally have surrounded themselves with scribes and mercenaries, both Aramaeans and others. S. A. Cook tries to show that the latter included Judaeans. The prophet Obadiah, indeed, mentions "the exiles of Sephared" (Sardis); but neither the repeated invocations of the goddess Artemis which are found on the funerary steles nor the names of the incumbents of tombs yield any argument in favour of Cook's thesis. It was only later, in the Hellenistic epoch, that any significant number of Jews were settled there (by Antiochus II).

To return to Lydian, Perret gives a straightforward summing-up of the testimony of the ancients on this subject by saying that the Lydian dialect was related to Phrygian (Perret and Chipiez, V, 242).

It is true that the same author speaks of the "marked influence of Semitic civilisation". Commerce with Syria, Phoenicia and Assyria undoubtedly played a considerable part in Lydian life. But this did not necessarily leave an imprint on the language, just as commerce, navigation and war, carried on in concert with the Carthaginians over a period of centuries, did not result in giving the slightest Semitic cast to the Etruscan language.

[1] *Glotta*, X, p. 238.
[2] M. Lidzbarski, *Die lydisch.-aram. Inschrift von Sardes. Z. fur Assyr.*, XXXI, 1918, p. 122.

Finally, Perret mentions the influence of the Semitic religions: the Lydians' practice of sacred prostitution and their worship of Attis, who was the counterpart of the Phoenician Adonis and the Babylonian Tammuz. But the Lydian religion remained essentially Anatolian, consisting first and foremost of the worship of the Great Goddess— Cybele, at Smyrna, and Artemis, at Ephesus.

In short, Lydian was not a Semitic idiom, and the word *enslifid* can be explained through Illyrian. In the element *slif* I recognise the Albanian verb which we have met a number of times already, *shlyej*, aorist *shluva*, "to efface, destroy" [1] (M. 486). The construction of *enslif* is the same as that of the Etruscan verb *empefame*, "to surprise, surprising", which we studied in a moving funerary inscription and which I compared with *ënbegatem* and to *enrich*. It will be more logical to look for analogies in this direction than in classical Arabic; and the sense of the word in question will be found to be in perfect accord with the Aramaic part of the text.

As for the reading *ensuifid* (for *enslifid*), it does not affect the argument. Its vowel *u* is a special symbol which is neither an ordinary Lydian *l* nor an ordinary *u*. It stands for a nasalised *u*. Nevertheless, Littmann recognises that this symbol must be connected with *l*, since it takes the place of *l* in the name Alexander. Littmann writes:

We may recall the change *l>u* in Umbrian, and in many other Indo-Germanic languages and dialects. In Naples, the article *lo* is pronounced *uo*. (*Loc. cit.*, p. 16)

I will add that in Polish there are two sorts of *l*: a hard *l* and a soft *l*. If the *first* of these is compared with a Russian *l* its pronunciation will seem not far removed from the sound *ou*.

In the same way, it is hard to accept another of M. Cuny's interpretations, his rendering of the termination *lid*, in the names of the owner of the "Lydio-Aramaic" tomb. This individual is called Manelid Kumlilid Selukalid. Cuny suggests identifying *lid* with *yelid* (or *yeled* or *walad*), "the child", in Hebrew and Arabic. But the Aramaic text describes the deceased as *Mane bar* (son of) Kumli. *Manelid* therefore cannot mean "son of Mane".

Let us turn to the second of the two words on which we have thrown a spotlight, *uqbahent* (Littmann's reading) or *uqbapent* (Sayce's and Bückler's reading). It comes in the fifth and last line of inscription No. 5 in *Sardis*, VI, 2. Thanks to the Aramaic translation, we are able to understand the words of the curse:

pirau peluk uqbapent

[1] Cf. *caraθsle*.

pirau we know already; "the house" or "his house".

peluk: *pel* "vault", *u* the article, *k* "and"; "and his vault".

uq is, of course, Albanian *nuk* and Greek *ouk*, "not".

bapent is *bahent*. The disputed letter is a Lydian symbol, + to be precise, which Littmann reads as *h* and Sayce as *p*. Littmann said, in effect: I cannot be wrong, for I find this letter *h* at the beginning of a word which must be read as Hudans. If it is not an *h*, then it is—well, a catastrophe, because the letter *h* would be missing from the Lydian alphabet.

Sayce said, in effect: I cannot be wrong, for I find this letter *p* at the beginning of the word which I read as *palmas*, "king". If it is not a *p*, then it is—well, the end of the world, because the letter *p* would be missing from the Lydian alphabet.

A tragic situation! It looks as if we must sacrifice one or other of these innocent little letters, *h* or *p*, both of which are indispensable. But what rash mortal would dare place his head between the Scylla and Charybdis of philology? In other words, I believe that Littmann and Sayce were both right and that the disputed letter was a true Illyrian *θuflθaś*, a bifrons, which could be read either as *p* or as *h*, or perhaps as *ph* or *bh*. In any case, I shall read it as *uqbahent*, since I recognise in it the Albanian verb *bâhem*, the medio-passive of *bâ*, "to make, to do" (M. 17), which has served us so often and so well.

Kostallari's Albanian–Russian dictionary gives yet another very explicit meaning for *bâhem*: "to take place" (p. 52).

Cordignano gives an Albanian expression of which the last part is *nuk bâhet kurrgja*, "nothing happens" (literally "nothing makes itself") (*Lingua albanese*, p. 18); he follows this with an Albanian proverb, *anëmik plak s't'bâhet kurr mik*, "an old enemy never makes himself into a friend" (*ibid.*, p. 301).

Lydian *uqbahent* must have a negative meaning, for the putative profaner of the tomb is promised nothing but negative, unpleasant things; furthermore, *uqbahent* is identical with *uqbahet*, since the *e* in it is nasal and can therefore be transcribed as *en*. To sum up, *uqbahent* is "may it not happen, may it have no place", and the Lydian sentence which we are studying means "may his house and tomb not endure, not subsist".

Thus Lydian grammar joins hands with Etrusco-Albanian grammar, and the Lydian language re-enters the fold of the basically Illyrian languages.

Still on the subject of the curses at the end of these inscriptions, we would call attention to inscription No. 26 (*ibid.*), of which the last words are:

> . . . *artimuk aśbluvaś viś* . . .

The first of these words means "and Artemis". The inscription evidently mentions a deity whose name is now lacking, and Artemis; and it seems that these two will punish whoever profanes the tomb. It may be conjectured that *bhuvaś* is connected with the Albanian verb *bluej*, aorist *blova*, "to grind" (M. 32).

I identify the *aś* of *aśbluvaś* with Albanian *asht*, "bone", a well-known Indo-European word which occurs in Greek, Latin and elsewhere.

The threat levelled at the pillager of tombs is that the gods will shatter his bones to pieces or grind them to dust.

Farther on, the arsenal of calamities prepared for looters contains an expression which has caused a good deal of bewilderment: *klidal kofulk*. M. Cuny remarks that these words probably correspond to the "clay and water" of the Aramaic half of the text, "but," he says, "we cannot find that they have counterparts either in ancient Hamitic or in Semitic".

But we have learnt from our experience with the Etruscan bilingual inscriptions that one cannot always expect an exact translation in these cases. It is possible that the word *klidal* is related to Albanian *klith*, "outcry, clamour" (M. 200), and *kofulk* to *kopili*, "servitude" (M. 208). We shall meet the latter word again.

We note, finally, an interesting observation by Bückler on the subject of Lydian place-names (*Sardis*, VI, 2, Index IV): Grimenothura, Timenothura, Mastaura, etc. Bückler's inference is that *tura* means "town", from whence would be derived the nouns *tyrannos*, "ruler of the city", and *Turrenoï*, "the people of the cities". Such a people would thus be the inhabitants of fortified towns, as against the native population whom they had brought under subjection. It will be recalled that the Etruscans belonged to this species of town-dwellers. Is this the explanation of such enigmatic names as the *Tursha* (an Aegean people who took part in an attack on Egypt in the 14th century B.C.), the Tyrrhenians and so on?

Now these conjectures receive an unhoped-for confirmation from the information furnished by Albanian. It is quite unusual to see a purely philological phenomenon so closely intertwined with the shadowy, almost unreal fabric of historical reconstruction, and endowing that reconstruction with the vitality which belongs to fact.

The Albanian root which provides the confirmation is *thur*, which I stumbled upon while thinking about a verse in the Book of Job (i. 10), in the Albanian translation. In the dialogue between the Lord and Satan, God vaunts Job's integrity and piety. Satan retorts that it is easy enough for Job to be a good man, because God has heaped so many blessings on him: "Hast not thou made an hedge about him, and about his house, and about all that he hath on every side?" [R.V.].

This is very close to the original Hebrew, which says "Hast thou not made a *fence* . . ." The Albanian translation is equally faithful:

> *a nuk' e ke thururë nga të githë anëtë atë?*
> "Hast thou not *fenced* him on all sides?"

The Hebrew word for the verb we have italicised is *soukh*, "to erect a fence". The Albanian verb *thur*, *thururë* means "to fence in, enclose". *thurës* (noun) means "enclosing" (M. 537).

This word *thurës* compelled me to a kind of horrified admiration. The Tursha, the Etruscans, the people who lived in the fortified enclosures which they constructed in the countries they had conquered, subdued or colonised, were standing before me, almost in the flesh.

Having been nomadic shepherds in the first place, like the Hyksos before them, they must in their early days have built *enclosures* to protect their flocks, herds and carts, rather than towns in the real sense.

But let us return to the Lydian language.

In spite of showing these various signs, which we have enumerated or discovered, of a common basis with Illyrian, Lydian taken as a whole seems to be fairly remote from Etruscan. The Tursha can have been Lydians only because, and only to the extent that, they lived for several generations in a certain sector of Lydian territory or of the Anatolian coast which was ruled by the Lydians, to whom they were related and who must have behaved in a hospitable, friendly manner towards them. They would seem to have adopted certain of the Lydian cultural forms without, however, fusing their own identity with that of the Lydians or assimilating their language. It was possible for the Tursha to come to Italy from Lydia and yet not be Lydians, as is proved by the divergence between their respective languages. The earlier Lydians, the former Meanians, must have been the result of a fusion between a proto-Illyrian or proto-Danubian wave of migration and the native Asianic inhabitants of Anatolia, as appears to have been the case with the Hittites (Nesites).

4. ILLYRIAN AND CRETAN

According to Homer, the great island of Crete was inhabited by at least five peoples: the Achaeans, Dorians, Eteo-Cretans, Kydonians and Pelasges. At any rate, the presence there of an Illyrian element is attested by the river Messapios and a mountain, Messapion. Jokl connects the name of another locality of ancient Crete, Dordhannai, with the name of Illyrian Dardania.[1] Hrozny enumerates several toponymical terms which are common in Crete, and shows that the same terms are found among various peoples of Illyrian stock elsewhere.[2] We have already mentioned the identity of the Cretan word *piva* and Albanian *piva*, "he drank".

There is another Cretan word of great interest to us: *ibena*, "wine", according to Hesychius;[3] I recognise in it the article *i* (with which the proverb on the Autun dice begins: *i va est orti caius volote*) and Albanian *venë*, "wine". The word proves the antiquity of this article, *i*, of which there are not many instances and which appears to be absent from the text of LM. We may note, lastly, that according to Deecke the name of the god Velχanos is found on coinage from the Cretan town of Phaistos as well as in Etruria[4] (cf. our "key to the Etruscan language").

Perhaps we should also mention Rhadamanthus, a king of Crete who became one of the three judges in the Underworld. *Rhada*, the meaning of which was discovered by Hammarström, has survived in the Albanian verbs *radis* and *radhis*, "to inquire; to arrange, dispose" (M. 422). Manthus, among the Etruscans, was an Underworld god, possibly lord of the Underworld. According to one ancient writer, Rhadamanthus was an expert in procedure. Does his name mean Counsellor (or Ruler) of the Underworld?

However this may be, it is certain that Crete acted as a springboard for Illyrian expansion in the Mediterranean. It was from there that the Philistines set sail; their sojourn in the island preceded their attack on Egypt and their subsequent landing on the shores of Canaan (cf. Amos ix. 7).

5. ILLYRIAN AND PHRYGIAN

The Phrygians were a people of Thracian origin who, after leaving Paeonia, crossed the Bosphorus into Asia Minor; they are thus an example of the Illyrians' expansion eastward. Neighbours and allies of Troy, these shepherds and farmers, hard-working and inventive, occupied a large part of western Anatolia; but their disunited kingdoms could not stand up to the attacks of the Cimmerians and the Lydians.

The Phrygian language is related, according to Kretschmer, to

---

[1] *Illyrer, Ebert Reallexikon*, VI, p. 38. [2] *Histoire de l'Asie Ant.*, pp. 281–301.
[3] Corssen, *loc. cit.*, p. 735. [4] *Etr. Forsch. u. Stud.*, IV, p. 53.

Lithuanian, Slavonic and Albanian. We know that *ballen* meant "king" in Phrygian; *bedu*, "water" (cf. Slavonic *voda*); *beret*, "he carries", is the same as Albanian *bjer*, which also means "he carries". According to Hesychius, the Phrygian Zeus was surnamed Bagaïos. Torp and Kretschmer explain this name by Phrygian *bage*, which is Latin *fagus*, "beech"; this recalls Jupiter Grabovius.

We should note at the same time that the Phrygian place-name *Kudrara* is reminiscent of Albanian *kodra*, "hill". We have already seen that *daos* ("strangler") was the Phrygian for "wolf".

E. Kirsten, in Pauly-Wissowa, mentions another surname of Phrygian Zeus, *Mazeus*. In my opinion the root of this is Etruscan *maθ*, *mat*, "great", which we have studied already. In Phrygian the word may have meant "supreme".

A Phrygian funerary inscription quoted by the same author ends with the words *eda es*. *Eda* is probably connected with *eiθ* (*fanu*), "sacred building", in Etruscan; *es* will be "he, that", as in Lydian. *Bekos* is Phrygian for "bread", reminding us of Albanian *bukë*, "bread", a word which G. Meyer says was borrowed from Italian.

The name of the important city of Pessinus, the centre of the worship of the great goddess Cybele, remains unexplained. Its resemblance to Pession (a town mentioned in the chapter on Numbers) takes us back to the Illyrian root *pes*, "five". Some have tried to derive Pessinum from Greek *pessos*, "dice". If the streets of the city intersected at right angles it may have been likened not so much to a die as to a checker-board; all the more so in that the type of board used by the ancients for backgammon was composed of *five* lines up and down and *five* across.

To end this brief account, I shall adduce one further fact pointing to the kinship between the Phrygian and Etruscan languages. The capital of 7th-century Phrygia was called *Gordium*. Here we can recognise the root *carθ*, whose importance has already been emphasised. *Gordium* meant "the City". It therefore seems that a lengthy chain of names of towns or fortified places,[1] a chain spanning three thousand years, beginning with *gurta* (Hittite), Cortona (Etruria), *caraθ(sle)*, Manegordum (Thracian) and Gordium, and ending with Novgorod, Belgrad, Ushorod, Novogrodek and Leningrad, has been built up from the Thracio-Illyrian and Slavonic root to which *curt*, the Etruscan sacred enclosure, also belongs.

---

[1] M. Pallottino, moreover, quotes a series of these towns with Pelasgian names: Gurton (Thessaly), Gortyna (Crete), Gortynia (Macedonia), Gortys (Arcadia), Crotona (Southern Italy) (*The Etruscans*, p. 54).

6. ILLYRIAN AND LYCIAN

There is no doubt that links existed between Etruria and Lycia. The Lycian tombs, hewn out of the rock, bear some resemblance to Etruscan tombs constructed in the same way. Lycia was, moreover, one of the principal centres of diffusion of the divine name Tark, in the forms Trqnta, Trokondas, Tarkudimme, etc., a name connected with Hittite, in which the same root means "to be strong". This ancient name, whose presence in Thrace we noted in the first part of this chapter, was still in use in Asia Minor in the Byzantine period; there was a Byzantine marshal called Trokoundes. It is from this source that the Etruscan national name, Tarχies-Tarquin, is derived.

The name of the Lycians has come down to us in a form influenced by Greek, and is related to Greek *Lykos*, "wolf"; but also to Albanian *ujk* and Etruscan *uc*, "wolf" (cf. the inscription on a missile, *streuc*).

G. Pauli grouped the Lycians with the Pelasgic peoples. In their documents the Lycians put the mother's name, not the father's, after their own; and it was the daughter, not the son, who inherited.[1] As for Lycian religion, let us insert here a detail noted by S. Reinach: a Lycian slave, in the 2nd century B.C., founded a little temple in honour of the lunar god *Men Tyrannos*, whose cult was widespread in Asia Minor.[2] This Tyrannos is related to the Etruscan goddess Turan (Venus).

Finally, among personal names and place-names, mention may be made of the Lycian town of *Krya*, whose name is a parallel to *Balla* and identical with that of the Albanian town *Kruja*; and Maleius, a place-name in which we recognise *mal*, "mountain"; and the personal name Troballissos, which seems to take us once more to the omni-present root *balle*.

For my own part, I have observations to offer on a few Lycian words:

(1) The name of the Lycian town *Arna* was rendered in Greek by *Xanthos*, "yellow" or "golden". *Ar* in Etruscan is "fire", "altar" (place of fire) and "gold" (metal of the colour of fire), though there were other terms as well for gold: *santi*, which we have mentioned already (*zamaθi*, P. 489), and perhaps *śalθn* (P. 646).

(2) "Mother" in Lycian is *knna*; this is connected with the Etruscan term *acnana(sa)*, which we have examined already and which proceeds from the Illyrian verb *qene*, "to be", and, by extension, "to beget, to give birth to". *Knna* means just this, "she who gave us birth".

[1] Perret et Chipiez, *La Lycie*, pp. 349–51.
[2] *Traité d'épigr. grecque*, p. 127.

(3) The Lycian word *nte*, "in", which Pauly-Wissowa compares with Hittite *andan*, is exactly like Albanian *ndë*, "in".

(4) Like Hittite, Lycian possesses a certain number of words of a Slavonic stamp: *lada*, "woman" (Old Russian *lada*); *kupa*, "tomb" (Slavonic *kupa*, "heap", tumulus); *isba*, "sarcophagus" (Slavonic *izba*, "house"); *olen*, "stag" (Slavonic *olenj, jelenj*). There was an Etruscan soothsayer named Olenus. We might add that Lycian *tideimi*, "child" (son or daughter), bears a slight resemblance to Slavonic *ditià*, plural *dieti*, which means the same and is likewise of the neuter gender. Finally, we note: *du*, "two"; *qla*, "family, lineage", cf. Etruscan *clan*, "son" (?); *se*, "that, he" (cf. *suθ-ce*?).

7. ILLYRIAN AND THE LANGUAGES OF THE CAUCASUS

The Caucasus, in the wider sense, takes in not only the mountains known by that name, and Armenia, but also the vast plains of the Kuban to the north, including Maikop, that important centre of pre-historic civilisation, where the earliest Indo-Europeans mingled with tribes who were later pressed back into the mountains. Connected at once with the proto-Danubian world and with Asia Minor, and also with Mesopotamia, the region was the setting for incessant population-movements involving various ethnic groups. Among the many attestations of such movement is the diffusion of black pottery (lustre ware in many cases) coming from the Euro-Asiatic steppes. This pottery travels through the Northern Caucasus, where it has been discovered by excavations in recent years and has been given the approximate date of 1500–1200 B.C.[1] But between 1710 and 1580 it had made its way as far as Egypt, with the Hyksos. A few centuries later, other types of this black ceramic ware, from the western part of the great steppe, infiltrated with the Etruscans into Italy.

Religious ideas follow the same routes. The dancing Etruscan priest recalls the shamans of the proto-Scythian tribes. One of the sources of the ecstatic cult of the Thracian and Etruscan Dionysus (Fufluns) is probably the archaic cult of the vine, which was centred on the Caucasus as well as on the banks of the Danube. In Erivan, for example, at an altitude of well over 3,000 feet, the vine-stocks are covered with earth for the winter; at Kizlar there is a formal "inter-ment" of the vine. Exactly the same precautions are taken in Thrace, where the winter is harsh. The awakening of the vine must have been the signal for clamorous rejoicings.

It may be added that, according to Byhan, certain customs are

[1] Kisselev, *The Ancient History of Southern Siberia*, 1949 (in Russian).

common to the Touches of the Caucasus and to the Albanians, and that the wooden furniture of some Georgian tribes is very similar to that found in Albania.[1]

Etruscan has been compared with the Caucasian languages by Pauli, Ellis, V. Thomsen and other scholars, with special reference to morphology; in vocabulary there is almost nothing in common between the two.

It has been found that the genitive suffixes, -sa, -isa, -al, are common to both; so are the plural terminations -er, -ar; but we must remember that this latter feature is also common to Gothic and the Scandinavian languages.

Some of the numerals in the language of Kabarda, tu (2) and shtchy (3), and Georgian hut (5), show a close similarity to the Etruscan numerals θu, ci, huθ. Georgian thve, "month", is reminiscent of Etruscan tiv. The Kabarda word pśatar, "townsman", makes one think of Albanian fshatar, despite the fact that the latter is related by G. Meyer to Latin massatum, massa, "domain".

We learn that the name Tarkh was preserved in the Caucasus not only longer than in Byzantium but even almost down to our own day. Visiting Georgia in 1814, J. von Klaproth noted the name of a district on both sides of the River Koura (Kyr, Kour), Ssa-Tarchno, a domain belonging to the aristocratic Tarchni family.[2] The same writer mentions a Georgian prince George Tarchanoshvili who lived at the beginning of the 18th century.

Among the inhabitants of the Caucasus is a very interesting people, the Ossetians. They are the descendants of a Scythian tribe, the Alains. In their language, which is of Indo-Iranian mould, "fire" is art. V. Abayev, an authority on the language, says:

Fire, the holy element of the ancient Iranians . . . has retained its old Iranian name in Ossetic: art (from atr), which is equivalent to Ancient Iranian atar and is athar in Ancient Indian, atr in Soghdian, and ar in Kurdish.

What rivets our attention here is the last word, ar. No one is going to make out that the Etruscans were an Iranian group; but, like all the Illyrians, they belonged to the same vast family of Eastern Indo-European peoples as the Indo-Iranians. We can therefore regard this Indo-Iranian word ar as indirect confirmation of the meaning we have attributed to Etruscan ar, "fire", and, by extension, "altar with fire" and so on.

[1] La civilisation caucasienne, Payot, 1936.
[2] Kaukasische Sprachen, p. 47.

As a result of having made this detour through the Caucasus we are in a better position to understand an Etruscan word whose meaning is in any case indicated by an "illustration". There is a patera bearing an inscription of which two words, *erus lusχnei*, are perfectly comprehensible: beside them are depicted the sun and moon (P. 290). *erus*, "sun" (an alternative to *usil*), probably contains the root *ar* (Etruscan *e* and *a* being interchangeable). *lusχnei*, on the other hand, is elucidated by Greek *lukhnos*, "torch", but can be interpreted much more closely with the help of an Indo-European language from the Caucasus, Armenian, and, even were this not so, with the help of other Eastern Indo-European languages. Notably, (*a*) *lusnkay* is "moon" in Armenian, and (*b*) *rauxsna* is "light" in Scythian (whence the name Roksane) (cf. *lucairce* in P. 131). And it may be added that, in Sanskrit, *aru* is "sun" and *aruśa* is "of the colour of fire" (Tomaschek, *Die Alt. Thrak.*, II, p. 55).

There is nothing surprising in the fact that Armenian can show counterparts for several Illyrian terms, for according to Herodotus's testimony, the Armenians are Thracio-Phrygian in origin (or descended from the Bryges, an ancient Balkan people). A few points of contact between Armenian and Albanian may be noted: (1) both languages have a definite article in postposition; (2) *erthal*, in Armenian, is "to go"; cf. Albanian *ardh*; (3) *ges* is "half"; cf. Albanian *gjysmë*; (4) *gtanem*, "I find"; cf. Albanian *gjet*; (5) *tzain*, "voice"; cf. Albanian *za*; (6) Armenian *medz*, "great", is *madh* in Albanian. Other resemblances have long been known, the most important being that the Armenian plural is formed by the ending *-er*, *-eri* (*doun*, "house", plur. *dounere*). We have already compared this with Etruscan *-ar*. (As for *-eri*, cf. Albanian *shoqeri*, "society", *vëtëra*, "years".)

G. Kapantzian drew attention recently to an *ancient* Armenian suffix in ethnic names, *-ali*: *Manali*, the country of the Man (who lived near Ararat and are the Mini of the Old Testament); *Aramali*, the country of Aram (which was conquered by the Assyrians in the 9th century), and so on. This is the same as the well-known Etruscan genitive termination *-al*.[1]

It is interesting to note the survival of *Tark* in Armenian. We find it in the form of Torqom. According to Hommel, Armenian legends of pagan times speak of a gigantic shepherd named Tork.[2]

Another proper name, feminine this time, deserves our full attention, for it is not only Armenian, and Caucasian in general, but also an

---

[1] *Historico-linguistic Studies in the Ancient History of the Armenians*, Erivan, 1956 (in Russian).
[2] *Ethnologie u. Geogr. des Alten Orientes*, 1926.

Etruscan gentilitial name. *Satenig*, or *Satinik*, is the word in question.
It occurs among the Ossetians too, as the name of a legendary soothsayer or sorceress closely connected with the epic of the Nartes,
legendary heroes whose origin is a confused memory of the first Indo-
European irruption into the Caucasus.[1]

That is all we know about the origin of these Nartes. In parenthesis,
it may be noted that the same ethnic name appears in the designation
of an Illyrian locality, Nareste (near a river, the Naron). Among the
Ossetians, Satanay was also the name of a Nart, as Abayev attests
(*loc. cit.*, p. 304). The name appears in Kabarda in the form of Sotenej.
Finally, we also find it in Etruria and among the Osco-Umbrians. The
CIE contains an inscription (4939), *mi ramnunas šatanas*.

The Tables of Iguvium mention sacrifices made for the prosperity of two *gentes*: Satanes and *etre* Satanes (the latter term perhaps
meaning "other" Satanes, or a collateral, "inherited" branch of the
family?).

The Ossetians would seem to have much else to tell us. The definite
article *i* is common to Etruscan, Ossetic, Scythian and Albanian (cf.
Abayev, p. 169). *Zian* is "misfortune" and also "dead", in Ossetic;
cf. Ossetic *saw*, "black", Avestan and Scythian *syava* (Abayev, p. 183),
"black", and Albanian *zi*, "black; misfortune"; the latter word also
occurs in Etruscan. *Akhour, akhowyr* means "knowledge, teaching", in
Ossetic, *akhourgond* is "wise", etc. (Kassayev, p. 49). This makes one
think of the Etruscan *libri acheruntici*. And we note in passing that
Ossetic *tharχon* means "judge"; *saer* (*ser*) is "head", and *saeron* is
"chief" (cf. *cletram srenχve* in LM?), etc. Our chief reason for drawing
attention to this material is that the study of Ossetic takes us towards
the eastern limits of the early Indo-European expansion into Asia;
and here a surprise awaits us. I am thinking of the researches of
S. Tolstov, according to which the Ossetic language is related to
ancient Soghdian. Tolstov points out Thracian–Cimmerian–Choras-
mian affinities and devotes special attention to two branches of the
Massagetes of Scythia: the Tochari and the Kouchans.[2]

The language of the Tochari, who are an outpost of the aforesaid
expansion into Central Asia, presents connections with Hittite:

	Tochari	Hittite
blood	*ysar*	*eshar* (cf. Etr. *eśi?*)
light	*luk*	*luks*

[1] Mayani, *Les Hyksos et le monde de la Bible*, p. 216.
[2] *Ancient Khorasmian*, Moscow, 1948, p. 325 (in Russian).

Now it is very notable that the language of the Kouchans, of which so little is known, is suddenly illuminated when we apply our "Geiger counter", the Albanian language. I am thinking of the names of two "Indo-Scythian" kings who repeated (successfully, for a few generations) Alexander the Great's undertaking, by founding, about the beginning of Christian times, a Scythian kingdom in Northern India; the kings in question are called *Kaniska* and *Huviska*. Astoundingly, it appears possible to interpret these names with the help of Illyrian: *kanisk* is Albanian for "gift, present" (M. 182); and *hovisk* would seem to be connected with *hovshëm*, "dashing, impetuous", from the verb *hov*, "to dash" (M. 162). *Kanisk* is so striking that one hesitates to reject the whole notion out of hand, as a coincidence. Names ending in -*isk* are not rare in Albanian.

Let us think again of the mountains bordering on the Caucasus. Brandenstein has drawn attention to a feature which is common to the *khaldu* language, in the country of Urartu (adjacent to ancient Armenia), and Etruscan grammar. The name of the city of Khaldina, "that of the god Khaldi",[1] has the same ending, -*na*, as *suθina*, *haθna*, *rasna*, *spurena*, *surina*, etc.

A language related to the Caucasian group is Basque. According to a theory of Trombetti, this language is a residue from ancient Caucasic, whose area stretched originally from the Caucasus to the Pyrenees, and of which there now remain only the two extremities, the Basque language and the Caucasian languages.

Nevertheless, a few points of contact can be detected between Basque and Albanian. Thus, in Basque, *a* is an article which comes after the noun, as in Etruscan and in Albanian. And here are some Basque words and their relevant affinities:

aita: "father", as in Etruscan (*at*), Albanian and the language of the Tcherkess.

ama: "mother", as in Albanian. A very widespread root.

giltz: "key"; cf. Albanian *çelës*.

hil: "dead"; cf. *hilar? hie?*

huntz: "owl", cf. Albanian *hut*.

ithurri: "spring, fountain", cf. Juturna, the goddess of waters.

orein: "stag", cf. Anatolian *olen* and Etruscan *olenos*.

so: "glance", cf. Albanian *shoh*.

zerri: "pig", cf. Albanian *derr*.

lamina: "evil spirit", cf. Etruscan *lamni*, etc.

---

[1] *Die Herkunft der Etrusker: Der Alte Orient*, 1937, p. 36.

8. SOME "EURO-ASIANIC" TERMS

To conclude this chapter, we shall pass in review several words which seem to occur in a vast gamut of languages extending both east and west of the Bosphorus. These words are:

(a) *djale*, (b) *kopil*, (c) *lar*, (d) *θafna*, (e) *rasna*.

(a) *djale*: In Albanian this means "child, young man", and we have had the luck to rediscover it intact in Etruscan: *ati sili θial*.

It is noteworthy that Ellis succeeded in identifying this Albanian word with Ossetic *syvaellon*,[1] which has the same meaning (cf. Kassayev, *Osseto-Russian Dictionary*, Moscow, 1952, p. 317). What is more, the same word had previously been noted in the Istro-Roumanian dialect by F. Miklosich: *deyely*.[2]

We are therefore in the presence of a Balkano-Caucasian word. This gave me the idea of pursuing my researches in the direction of the Caucasus, and I had the pleasure of meeting the word again, slightly disfigured, as was only to be expected, in a non-Indo-European language of the North-eastern Caucasus, namely that of Kabarda, which has been mentioned already, and which belongs to the Tcherkess group. This time the word comes to us in the form of *shtchale*, "young", *shtchalag*, "youth"; *shtchalen*, "to be young", etc.[3]

Thus the initial consonant oscillates between *θ*, *d*, *s* and *shtch*.

This observation prompts a query: should not a new examination be made of the meaning of the word *fokiasiale*, from the stele of Lemnos, whose text is regarded as being Etrusco-Aegean or "provincial" Etruscan, or, quite simply, Pelasgic?

According to von Hahn, *djalje*, "adolescent", is applied particularly to the "armed servant of a dignitary" (*loc. cit.*, III, p. 28). Usually, the element *siale* in the word from the stele of Lemnos is interpreted in the same way as, for example, the last syllable of *Fluflunsl*, which is probably simply an abbreviation of *sul* (*Leθamsul*, P. 2, 8) and denotes pertaining. According to this interpretation, *fokiasiale* meant "from Phocaea", "Phocaean". But it is within the bounds of possibility that a different translation will be adopted, namely "child of Phocaea", "son of Phocaea"; without, however, necessarily going so far as to accept "young warrior of Phocaea" (although *maryannu* of the Mitanni, for example, means "young" and "warrior").

(b) Albanian *kopil* is stated by G. Meyer to mean "henchman, serf, illegitimate child, bastard". "The origin of the word is obscure,"

[1] *Sources of the Etruscan and Basque Languages*, 1886, p. 157, n. 1.
[2] *Istro und macedo-rumunische Sprachdenmäler*, 1881, p. 64.
[3] *Kardanov, Dict. kabardino-russe*, Moscow, 1957, p. 451.

writes Meyer. In Mann the chief meaning given is "bastard" (p. 208). Pascu notes the presence of the word in Macedo-Roumanian, Serbian and modern Greek, and says it is derived from Sanskrit *kopil*, "boy".[1] Sandfeld, in his *Linguistique balkanique*, places *copil*, *kopil*, "child, bastard" (the word occurs in Roumanian, Bulgarian, Serbian and Cretan), in the category of words whose origins are unknown (p. 93).

However, I have found a curious etymology for it in the language of Kabarda, which we have called to our aid more than once already, and in which the verb *kypyl'el'yn* means "to fall", in a very special sense. It is used in speaking of fruit which falls *of itself* from a tree. *Kypyl'el'a* is said of a fruit which has fallen without the tree being shaken (*Kabard-ino-Russian Dict.*, p. 218). The image of a fruit falling unexpectedly is decidedly pertinent to *kopil* in the sense of "bastard". However, if I was right when I connected the Lydian word *koful(k)* with the same source we shall have to prefer the translation "serf, slave". But are the two renderings incompatible? Among the ancients, the son of a female servant or slave was "bastard" and "serf" at the same time.

What is no less important, there seems to be confirmation of the existence of a stratum of words which are at once Asiatic and European.

(*c*) *lar*: The *lares* were the souls of the dead. We glanced briefly at this word when discussing Etruscan *hilar*. Now, in another language of the autochthonous inhabitants of the Caucasus, namely the language of the Ingoush, who belong to the Tchetchen group in Daghestan (in the heart of the Northern Caucasus), the verb *aelaer* means "to die"; (*so*)*lar* means "(I) die".[2]

(*d*) *θafna*: (in P. 341 and 488, but *θapna* in LM, X, 22, and in P. 375 and 646), is the Etruscan name of the Roman *patera* and Greek *poterion*. It came in our description of Hammarstrom's article on the word *raθ*. The etymology of *θapna* is clarified by Ossetic, provided we first refresh our ideas by returning to primitive, archaic sources. The relevant word in Ossetic is *t'aepaen*, which means "flat, flattened, squashed" (*Dict.*, *loc. cit.*, p. 333); and in the language of Kabarda there is *teup'eshtchen*, with the same meaning (*Dict. Kab.*, p. 343). And in very fact a patera is a wide, *flat* drinking-cup. The word in question must be related to Greek *tympanon* ("drum"), Macedo-Roumanian *tonpanu* and Bulgarian *tapan*, since one of the chief things about a drum is that it is flat.

(*e*) *rasna* is undoubtedly the most important, but also the most involved, of this short list of "Euro-Asianic" words.

[1] *Dict. étym. macédo-roum.*, p. 188.
[2] Z. Malsagov, *Grammar of the Ingoush Language*, Vladikavkaz, 1925, p. 12 (in Russian).

The Etruscans were known as *Rasna*. The name has never been explained. The ancients, indeed, put forward hypotheses (or quoted legends) concerning the Etruscans' other name, "Tyrrhenians". This has been connected with Tyrrhenos, the leader of the Etruscan wave from Lydia. Not a very convincing explanation. Some modern writers have derived it from the name of the city of Tura, in Southern Lydia, a region where the Etruscans spent some time, if they did not hail from there in the first place. In our treatment of Lydia we pointed to several names of Lydian cities with the termination -*tura*. And we found a rational explanation for this in Albanian (*thurës*, "fence")—that is to say, in Illyrian itself.

Now the Egyptians of the 14th and 13th centuries are acquainted with the future Etruscans under the name *Tursha*. How did *Tursha* become *Ras(na)*? Are these names known to us from any external source?

I do not know whether Etruscologists have ever made use of this source, but it seems to me that the name is mentioned in the Bible.

Chapter X of the Book of Genesis gives a terse geographical and political account of Asia Minor, as it appeared in the early centuries of the 1st millennium B.C. We read of an unknown people or country coming after Meshek and Tubal: *Tiras*—"The sons of Japheth; Gomer, and Magog, and Madai, and Javan, and Tubal, and Meshech, and Tiras" (verse 2).

Meshek and Tubal are two peoples known to history; they lived in the south of what is now Georgia and are referred to by the writers of antiquity as the Moschi and the Tibareni. Their homeland was in the mountains to the south-east of the Black Sea and in north-eastern Phrygia (Herodotus, III, 9). It can be inferred that Tiras may have been adjacent to Phrygia.

Thus there is, south of Colchis, a group of three countries: Tubal, Meshek and *Tiras*.

Some two centuries after the historical account given by Genesis, we hear the voice of a great prophet, Ezekiel, who was deported about 587 B.C. from Jerusalem to Babylon.

He is well aware of current events in the political life of the surrounding countries. Asia Minor is part of his horizon. And he utters a harsh warning to the warlike Gog (Gyges) the Lydian, ruler of *Rosh*, Meshek and Tubal (xxxviii. 2–3, and xxxix. 1–2).

The word *Rosh* in this passage is sometimes translated by "chief, sovereign" (since elsewhere the word does in fact mean "head, chief"), and the possibility is rejected that it is a proper name coinciding with similar names in other contexts. In the French translation of the *chanoine* Crampon, for example, we read: "Gog, prince *souverain* de Mosoch et de Thubal . . ." But this cannot be accepted: the idea of sovereignty is expressed already by the word "prince" (*nassi, nessi*) and, moreover, the double title, "sovereign prince", has no parallel elsewhere. There is no escaping the fact that *Rosh* denotes a people of a country. But what people or country?

Delitzsch found, in an 8th-century cuneiform inscription, a country called *Raśu*, situated east of Elam. But as early as 1902, Hastings' *Dictionary of the Bible* rejected the identification of this Raśu with Rosh in Asia Minor, on the grounds that Raśu lay too far to the east. Bochart, in the 18th century, decided that Raśu meant the Russians, to whose history he thus added some fourteen hundred years.

Whatever view is taken, the disturbing fact remains the triad appearing in Genesis x, Tubal, Meshek and *Tiras*, reappears in Ezekiel as the triad Meshek, Tubal and *Rosh*.

Must we conclude that Rosh (which it would be equally justifiable to read as *Rash* or *Ras*) became synonymous with the earlier word, Tiras?

Are we to see merely a coincidence in the identity of these two equations: *Tiras = Ras* (Asia Minor), and *Tursha = Ras(na)* (ancient Italy; and strictly contemporary with the first equation)?

On the other hand, are we not falling into self-contradiction when we suggest identifying the Biblical *Ras* with *Rasna*?

The objection will be raised that we adopt Hastings' argument for the country of *Ras* mentioned in the cuneiform inscriptions, the argument being based on the remoteness of *Ras* from the Caucasus; and that we simultaneously accept a *Ras* in the vicinity of the Moschi and Tibareni, that is to say decidedly remote from our presumed Rasna of Anatolia, who are generally thought to have lived in Lydia.

But the contradiction is only apparent. Since Ezekiel's triad, Rosh, Meshek and Tubal, were collectively under the dominion of a Lydian prince, Gyges, a historical personality whose existence is attested by the Assyrian chronicles, the country of Ras could not but be fairly close to Lydia.

This view is strengthened by the fact that Meshek gives us a strong pointer towards Phrygia. For example, Mita, the king of the Mushku (8th century), is generally regarded as being Midas, king of the Phrygians. Whether this be correct or not, Seton Lloyd, in his *Early Anatolia*, writes that the Mushku on whom the Assyrians made war in the 11th and 9th centuries must be identified with the Phrygians of Greek tradition (p. 191). Finally, M. G. Contenau, speaking of the

Hittite heritage and the destroyers of the Hittite empire, defines the latter as *Mushki who had come from Thrace and were related to the Phrygians* (*Les Premières Civilisations*, p. 293).

Thus *Meshek* seems to be of the same stock as the Phrygians, the Lydians and the Hittites; but this must apply with equal force to Ras (or Rosh, or Tiras), since Ras is mentioned on the same footing as Meshek.

Moreover, as regards the mysterious correlation Tiras–Rasna, I believe it confronts us not merely with a normal example of phonetic development, but, better still, with the two faces of a single phonetic phenomenon.

This needs elucidating. Philologists have long ago pointed out an important feature of Anatolian and Eastern Aegean phonetics, and have also pointed to the survival of that feature in the Caucasian languages of our own day; the feature in question being the fact that, in certain cases, initial *t* sometimes disappears.

Thus, for example, Hrozny writes of Cretan *labru* ("double axe"), which also took the form *tlabru*. It was from the word *tlabrun(th)* ("house of the double axe", decorated with *bipennes*) that the Greeks had derived their "labyrinth", writes Hrozny, and he adds that the Anatolian languages had, among other peculiarities, that of possessing the sound *tl* which was simplified sometimes to *l* and sometimes to *t* (*loc. cit.*, p. 288).

Beside this we may set an observation by Ellis on the Avarian language of the Caucasus. Ellis finds in it a counterpart to the Lycian word *lada*, "woman"; and the counterpart exists in two forms, *tlyadi* and *lyadi*.

It is legitimate to suppose that a similar simplification may have given rise to the change of the name (or surname) of the Tursha (recorded in Genesis in the form of Tiras) into Ras.

The latter name would have become *Rasna* in Etruscan by the addition of the possessive suffix *na* (cf. *suθina, haθna*). The difficulty is that the language of the Tursha was not Aegean: it was Illyrian. It must nevertheless have undergone, in the course of several centuries, Aegean and Anatolian influences.

We therefore think it possible that this evolution of the name Tiras (*thures*) into Ras should have taken place in Asia Minor.

But in the margin of this problem another one rises up unexpectedly: that of the relation between a *Caucasian* word *rasna, ryzna*, meaning "silver", and the Etruscan words, which probably mean the same thing, *raśne* (Cippus of Perugia, P. 570, line 5) and *riθnai* (Tile of Capua, P. 2, 12).

So we have not yet closed the account of our dealings with the Anatolian and Caucasian world. And this is the reason why:

If "silver", in "Aryan–Italian–Celtic", to borrow Kretschmer's expression, is *rajata, errezata* (whence are derived *argentum, argyros,* etc.) (Kretschmer, *loc. cit.*, p. 137), the essential element of the word *errezata*, in the Avesta, is *reza*; and this "nucleus" is also found in the Caucasus. A hundred and fifty years ago Klaproth noted in his *Kaukasische Sprachen* (in the chapter entitled "*Abassische Sprachen*") that, in the language of the Abkhazes, a people belonging to the Tcherkess group, silver was *rasna, risna*. And in fact I find this word recorded in the modern *Russo-Abazine Dictionary* (Moscow, 1956, p. 452) in the form (which is probably the ancient one) *ryzna*.

At the same time, we must remember that ancient Anatolia was the Peru of antiquity, the realm of precious metals. This was the ambiance not only of Colchis and Lydia but also of the Hittite lands.

Legend says that the Golden Fleece, which had belonged to a golden ram, travelled through the air to reach Colchis. This legend is not an isolated motif as far as Colchis is concerned. According to the Old Testament, Tubal-Cain, the eponymous leader of the people of Tubal, was the ancestor of all metal-workers. According to Homer, the country of the Khalybes was the land of *silver*; but these Khalybes were subject to the Moschi (Meshek). According to Pliny, the metal-working Dactyli came from Colchis. And the Biblical (and Phoenician?) word *paz*, "pure gold", seems to be connected with the name of the Colchian river Phasis.

As for Lydia, the ancients' general feeling was that it was replete with gold and silver. Its river Pactolus was thought to bear gold along in its current. Its legendary king Midas turned everything which he touched into gold. Perret writes that there was "an enormous mass of gold and silver" in Lydia. Its riches came not only from its auriferous streams and its gold-mines (on Mount Tmolos) but also from the tribute paid by neighbouring peoples who had been brought under subjection by the celebrated Lydian cavalry (reminding us of the Etruscans' Tities, Ramnies and Luceres); moreover, the Lydian soil was fertile and well cultivated; and the country carried on a flourishing trade with both East and West. The Lydians could wear purple robes on occasion, and the Ionians acquired this fashion, from them, just as the Romans were indebted to the Etruscans for the use of the crimson chlamys.

Thus it was that the Lydians were the first to mint coins, especially gold coins. And Croesus (or so it has been calculated on the strength of the information supplied by Herodotus) offered massive gifts of gold to the temple at Delphi to a total weight of over 6·3 tons. It may be added that the Assyrians called Taurus the "Mountain of Silver".

The Hittites themselves confirmed in effect the ancients' opinion of their country's wealth in gold and silver, for the very name of the country, Hatti, meant "the land of silver" and their capital, *Hattusha*, was a "city of silver".

Instead of writing Hattusha, the Hittites used two Sumerian symbols meaning respectively "city" and "silver" (*ku-babbara*). J. Friedrich remarks in his Hittite dictionary that this identification has been accepted by such authorities as O. Schroeder and M. Ch. Virolleaud (*loc. cit.*, pp. 316 and 281).

To sum up, it is not impossible that the term *ryzna*, originating in those lands so rich in metals, should have made its way into Etruscan; and this would explain the words *raśne* and *riθnai*.

In spite of its resemblance to Rasna, *raśne* does not mean "Etruscans". It is *raśne* which occurs on the Cippus of Perugia.

We have already said that the inscription on the Cippus mentions religious banquets, and also some land whose extent is defined and which is probably, in my view, valued in terms of coin. This is the conclusion to which one is led by the frequent association of the words *tesan* and *raśne*. Thus we read, in lines 4 and 5:

(a) *tezan fuśleri tesnś teis raśneś*

Later (lines 21–22), between the words *θaura* ("tomb") and *spelθ* ("cave, vault") the same words are intercalated, except for *fuśleri*:

(b) *tesne raśne . . . tesnś teiś rasneś*

The word *fuśleri* (a plural, perhaps?) reminds one of two similar nouns in Albanian: *fuśe*, "field" and *bushat*, "property, farm" (M. 44). G. Meyer examined the former of these words, connecting it first with Latin (*campi fusi*); but he saw obstacles to this connection and did not make any definitive pronouncement.[1] One gets a strong impression that units of area, or specifically of land-measurement, are involved. In the context it is difficult to attribute any other meaning but "ten" to the words *tezan, tesne, tesnś* (cf. the chapter on Numbers). It would be impossible to understand *tesne raśne* and *tesns . . . rasneś* as "ten Etruscans" or "of ten Etruscans", since the affairs of the Etruscan people as such would appear to be quite alien to a document of a personal nature. Such being the case, *tesne raśne*

---

[1] *Etymol. Wörterbuch*, p. 115.

could be interpreted as the price of the land or fields in question: "ten (pieces of) silver" per unit of land. *raśne*, in this interpretation, is "silver".

As for the word *riθnai*, we read, in the text of the Capuan Tile (P. 2, line 12), a description of a banquet:

> *vacil ia leθamsul nunθeri*
> *vacil ia riθnai taeθ aθenei*

ia is Albanian *ja*, "here is" (M. 168).

nunθeri is *nuθen*, the feast of the ninth day, as in LM.

ta eθ: "in this temple"?

aθenei looks as if it was the name of one of the vessels used in sacrifices; it may be identical with *atianaia*, from inscription P. 49, NRIE 841, a word which we discussed in the chapter on the Market.

If these deductions are correct the lines in question will read as follows:

> "(Here is) a banquet of the ninth day in the temple of Latona,
>   (This is) for her, a banquet *with silver vessels*,
>   In this temple." [1]

---

[1] We do not imply that *ras, riθ* was the only name for silver in Etruscan and Illyrian. Von Hahn, in his list of ancient Macedonian words, cites *sirbénon* (*topanon*) and compares it with Albanian *sirmë*, "silver" (II, p. 227). But we note that according to Mann, *sërmë*, "silver", comes from Turkish. If von Hahn's pointer was valid it would send us to an expression in LM: *śerfue acil ipei θuta* (X, 6–7), in which *acil* is "vessel", *ipei* is connected with drinking, and *θuta* is "loved" (participle or adjective); so that the passage would perhaps describe ancestors or mothers with silver cups for drinking.

XV

THE ILLYRIANS AND THE WORLD OF THE OLD TESTAMENT

A. THE PHILISTINES

IT is an established fact that the Philistines are a branch of the Illyrian stock. Several parallels to their name occur in the West. MM. Meillet and Cohen mention the town of *Palaiste* in Epirus. Ribezzo speaks of *Palaistine* in connection with the Sicanians (ancient Sicilians). F. Altheim recalls that the lower part of the course of the Po was known as *Philistina fossa*. The Philistines were one of the "peoples of the sea" who attacked Egypt, and the Egyptians knew them as the *Poulousati*. There is, moreover, an Egyptian bas-relief in which these Poulousati are represented with an adornment of feathers, like American Indians. And in ancient Italy the heroes of archaic days depicted on an amphora or in certain rock-carvings are represented in just this way.

From the 12th to the 10th century approximately, a Philistine garrison was stationed in the Palestinian town of Beth-Shan, having been placed there by the Egyptians. In the tombs of these mercenaries gold masks have been discovered which portray the dead and which closely resemble the bronze masks of the 9th century B.C. that have been found in tombs in central Italy.

A curious episode from the period of the Philistines' domination of the land of Canaan will serve us as a bridge between the Philistines and the Etruscans. Fearing a revolt, the Philistines forbade the Hebrews to have smiths, ". . . lest the Hebrews make them swords or spears". And when a man of Israel needed to sharpen a ploughshare, an axe or a mattock, he shouldered his tools and went down into Philistia (1 Samuel xiii. 19–21).

Now, as Pliny the Younger attests, these were exactly the tactics of the Etruscans towards the conquered Romans, some six centuries later: Porsenna laid a ban on their using iron for any except agricultural purposes.[1]

The Philistines oppressed the Hebrew tribes of peasants and shepherds, but they were a powerful civilising factor nevertheless. David served an exacting apprenticeship in their country and must have

---

[1] Buonamici, *Fonti di Storia Etr.*, p. 20.

profited by their example when his own time came to organise the
royal power, the army and the state.

One fact will suffice to illustrate this. David ordered that a census
be made of the population of his kingdom, an action which shocked
the most devoted members of his entourage, who regarded it as a daring
innovation (2 Samuel xxiv).

This administrative measure must have been imitated from the
Philistines; for the Illyrians treated census-taking as an act of great
importance. The city was sacred; and the purpose of the census was to
promote the safety of the city. According to Livy (I), the census was
initiated in Rome by the Etruscan king Servius Tullius. About 577
B.C. the whole Roman Army—in other words, all the citizens of Rome
—were gathered together in the Campus Martius and purified by a
sacrifice; a census was taken and 80,000 names were inscribed.

Fustel de Coulanges describes the purification-rite as it took place
both in Athens and in Rome. Every citizen was obliged to be present,
so the ceremony had to be preceded by a general roll-call.

Further, M. Bréal notes that the same ceremony was in use among
the Osco-Umbrians. It seems that in Iguvium lustration was accompanied by a census. The same religious and administrative procedure,
in an earlier, more rudimentary form, may well have been practised
by the Philistines.

Philistine proper names and other Philistine words are preserved in
the Old Testament: *kova* (helmet), *seren* (prince), *argaz* (coffer).
Gaster connected *kova* with the Hittite word *kupahi*,[1] but it seems to me
that it can be explained differently. In Albanian, *kove* means "bucket"
(M. 211). This was probably the Philistine soldiers' slang expression
for a helmet. The Hebrews could have taken the word over without
concerning themselves with its antecedents.

The classical example of this species of word-borrowing is well
known. The Roman soldiers stationed in Gaul used to say *testa*
("earthenware pot") for *caput* ("head"). The Gauls adopted the word
testa, but not its ironical overtones, and that is how the French word
tête, "head", came into being. A similar process may have taken place
in Palestine.

Seren has been compared with *tyran* or *turan*, which is of Anatolian
and Etruscan origin. It also recalls Parthian *surena*, which was a
proper name and later became a dignitary's title. An obvious comparison is with Etruscan *srenχva*, which occurs so often in LM and is
perhaps the plural of *sren*; cf. *pleqve*, "the council of the elders", which
we have studied already.

---

[1] In Koehler's *Lexicon of the Old Testament*, 1953, p. 425.

Finally, *argaz* has been compared with Latin *arca*, which we detected in Etruscan *arχate*, "treasurer".

These three are far from being all the Philistine words which have survived in the Old Testament. Before looking at others, let us take note of a Philistine word which was preserved in more ancient records, those of Egypt. There was a king of the city of Dor whose name was *Badra*. This is an Etruscan name Petru (or Bedru). There was a family called Petruni in Etruria. There was an Etruscan woman called Petru. And we have studied *pelθurinu petrual*.

Coming back to the Bible, we can start with Sisera, one of the generals of king Yabin, who ruled from the great fortress of Hazor in Canaan (see Judges iv and v). *Sisra* can be recognised as Etruscan *Seθre*, a name which was much used and which meant "worthy". It is also found in the feminine, *Seθria*.

But the place of honour in this list undoubtedly belongs to that proverbial giant, Goliath the Philistine, David's adversary. We have had the satisfaction of dredging up this choleric person's name in one of the inscriptions in the Tomb of the Ogre (4th–3rd centuries B.C.), where we read that among the many owners of the tomb was a certain Galiath: *caliaθesi* (P. 84, CIE 5357). It's a small world!

And what about *urim*? In Hebrew the word stood for a means of divination by which it was thought possible to find out whether such and such a course of action was sanctioned by Providence (Deuteronomy xxxiii. 8).

The term has remained cryptic. Koehler puts forward three hypotheses:

(a) *urim* is derived from the Hebrew verb *aror*, "to curse";
(b) it can be connected with a verb meaning "to uproot, extirpate";
(c) *urim* is simply a meaningless word which was made up as a counterpart to *thummim*, its opposite in the technique of divination.

The upshot is that the word is said to be "unexplained".

But it may well be that the word is an echo from the art of the soothsayers. It reminds one first and foremost of two Hittite words: *uraianni* ("bird of omen") and *urianni*, the title of one of the higher ranks in the priesthood (Friedrich, 235).

Thus this word is perhaps one more facet of a long historical process: the refinement and sublimation of the various archaic ideas which, as the centuries went by, Israel borrowed from her neighbours (such as *sabbath*, originally "an evil day" in the vocabulary of the Babylonians); ideas into which she breathed new life.

In any case, the idea of "cursing" does not seem to go well with *urim*, at least if we are to judge from a verse in the Bible: "And when Saul enquired of the Lord, the Lord answered him not, neither by dreams, nor by Urim, nor by prophets" (1 Samuel xxviii. 6).

Another interesting word is *beri*, which is used only once in the Bible, in the Book of Job. This is one of those Old Testament words which have been discussed for the last two thousand years, but without result. It seems to be almost as enigmatic as an Etruscan word.

The author of Job was a poet and a thinker. His language is concise and varied, moving rapidly from image to image and sometimes dovetailing one image into another.

The word *beri* occurs in chapter xxxvii, verses 10 and 11, where one of Job's friends, Elihu, tries to bring Job back into the right way of thinking by praising the Almighty's works and His Self-manifestation in the wonders of nature.

Elihu says that even if *beri* makes a cloud heavy the cloud will be dissipated by the light of God. Some commentators have tried to interpret *beri* by relating it to Hebrew *ri* ("dampness, vapours")—a term which does not exist. Perhaps the answer lies in an Illyrian word which has survived in Albanian: *veri*, "the north wind", which brings the clouds with it; a near relation of Greek *boreas* (M. 551). I conjecture that *beri* was borrowed from the Philistines. At no time did the development of Hebrew take place in a watertight compartment, a fact which is illustrated by the words *pilegesh*, "concubine", and *mekhera* (*machaïra*), "cutlass"; both of these passed fairly early into Hebrew from Greek.

The Assyrians' and Babylonians' campaigns of devastation in Palestine, the exile and homecoming of the people of Judah, the beginnings of the Diaspora, the empire of the Achaemenides, the irresistible expeditions of Alexander the Great—all these upheavals shook the Old Testament world, widened its horizons and abruptly opened the eyes of the Jews to the vicissitudes of life in far countries. Proof of this is visible in Ezekiel's utterances, and in the current of Greek thought which is to be found emerging in the Bible, in Ecclesiastes and elsewhere.

It is therefore within the bounds of possibility that a short passage in Ecclesiastes (ix. 14–15) is an echo from such a large and resounding event as the Median wars. Those two verses tell us that: "There was a little city, and few men within it; and there came a great king against it. . . . Now there was found in it a poor wise man, and he by his wisdom *delivered* the city; yet no man remembered that same poor man."

The word for "delivered", in the Hebrew, is *milet*. Some have regarded this as an allusion to Miltiades, with a play on words, *milet–Miltiades*, since the vanquisher of the Persians at Marathon was later condemned to pay a heavy fine and died in obscurity.

There is also, for example, the undeniable testimony of the Book of Daniel, in which the political upheavals of the Hellenistic epoch are reflected.

A passage in the Book of Proverbs, which for the most part is no earlier than the 3rd century B.C., seems to contain allusion to events which specially interest us, namely the affairs of Etruria.

Proverbs xxx (the penultimate chapter) begins with a private dedication, something after the manner of a title-page, giving the chapter the appearance of a separate work; one is almost inclined to call it an independent collection of precepts which was introduced into the Book of Proverbs at some later time from a different source. At the same time nearly the whole of the chapter contains the same ideas as the preceding chapters and expresses them in the same style: the same exhortations to piety, the same wise counsels, the same warnings against temptation. We say "nearly" the whole, because verses 22 and 23 stand out from the rest; and they are the part which catches our attention.

The dedication is confused: "The words of Agur, the son of Jakeh, even the prophecy: the man spake unto Ithiel . . ." Who was Agur? No one knows.

Ancient writers sometimes provided themselves with mysterious names.

We have in fact just seen an example of this practice in Ecclesiastes. The title Ecclesiastes is a translation of the Hebrew *Qohelet*. But what does the rather baffling *Qohelet* really mean? It is thought to be connected with the verb *qahal*, "to assemble", and hence to mean "he who assembles the people"—evidently for the purpose of inculcating his own ideas. But this is a very odd explanation. Does this world-weary philosopher, who has considered everything under the sun and found it vanity, this refined sceptic who, by comparison with his contemporaries is almost an atheist, really want to "assemble" the people and "preach" to them? Not in the least. He is an individualist who says that happiness lies in living unobtrusively. His ideas are not intended for the majority, the public, the ordinary man.

The ancients did not know who wrote the book. The author begins by saying that he was "king in Jerusalem" and ends his book saying that he taught his wisdom to the people. It is not easy to imagine a teacher-king of this kind. I therefore believe that the work, at the same time as it is an expression of individual views, is a *collection* of aphorisms drawn from various sources, and that *Qohelet* means not "he who assembles", but "he who collects, he who composes an anthology".

Let us return to the Proverbs and the sayings of the mysterious Agur:

21 For three things the earth is disquieted, and for four which it cannot bear:

22 For a servant when he reigneth; and a fool when he is filled with meat;

23 For an odious woman when she is married; and an handmaid that is heir to her mistress.

It may seem that there is nothing out of the ordinary here and that the evils enumerated are just the common social ills of the time; Agur is merely denouncing them in the style of any conservative, almost reactionary, moralist in any country and period. But could this have happened in Judaea, where, after the return from exile, the freeing of slaves had become not only a legal obligation but even a matter of religious dogma?

I cannot get rid of the notion that in Judaea at that time there was nothing happening which could have given cause for these complaints about slaves holding power and handmaids inheriting, as if such things were remarkable social phenomena. If there was anything of the kind which could have made an impression on "public opinion" anywhere round the Mediterranean it could not have been happening in Judaea but—in Etruria. The famous "social revolution" at Volsinia springs to mind. We have seen how it appeared to different observers. Rumours of it must have travelled as far as Judaea. The further removed from the source, the cloudier and vaguer must the outlines of the event have become. Certainly, there it is, this so-called revolt, reflected in the most reactionary terms of all by the Book of Proverbs: ". . . Servants reign." In other words they are no sooner liberated than they dare to set about becoming notables, senators, *zilaθ*, what you will. And the rogue who is "filled with meat"—does this mean that the poorer classes have begun to taste prosperity? The "hated woman is married"—no doubt to the son of a good family? Translators and commentators do violence to the Biblical text at this point by rendering "hated" as "odious" or "disdained" or "morally base". What are their grounds for this rendering? What are the woman's faults? We are never told. Certainly there is plenty of room for conjecture. But the reason why she is hated is perhaps that, once given her freedom, she dares to enter the family of the *patronus*. By looking at this passage from the social (as distinct from the moral) point of view we restore its homogeneity, and the sentence about the hated woman fits in with the sentence before and the sentence after.

The "handmaid that is heir to her mistress" takes us right back to Volsinia: we recognise the servants "dictating their masters' wills", to the indignation of public opinion at Rome.

Thus there is a striking parallel between the complaints of Roman historians and those of Proverbs xxx.

To bring to a close this account of trends in Hebrew life which can be attributed to Philistine influence, we must say a few words about Philistine religion. In our view this religion may have retained a few features of its originally Illyrian character. We say "traces", because this people from overseas was essentially a body of warriors who were absorbed by the Canaanites after a few generations, and adopted their language.

The chief god of the Philistines was called Dagon, and his temple is mentioned in the Old Testament as Beth-Dagon (House of Dagon). In 1 Samuel v we are told that the Philistines, after defeating the Israelites and sacking their simple temple at Shiloh, carried off their Ark of God to their own country and placed it in their principal temple. But the results were most upsetting: Dagon's statue was found prostrate before the Ark every morning. Worse still, on the second morning the god's head and hands were found cut off and lying on the threshold of the temple, and only his *dagon* was in its original position.

So there were two things: Dagon, the god and the name; and *dagon*, which was part of his image. Some commentators explain this by referring to Hebrew *dag*, "fish"; others refer to *dagan*, which means "corn" in Phoenician (Canaanite) and Hebrew. There is no doubt that the Semitic pantheon did include an agrarian god called Dagan, a leading deity among the Assyrians and in the Amuru territory. The Philistines could well have adopted his worship. There was also a Hittite or Anatolian deity called *daganzipa*, a genius of the earth, who protected the crops. Accordingly, M. E. Dhorme considers Dagon to have been "divinised corn". But the narrative in Samuel tilts the balance in favour of the first hypothesis. It is difficult to imagine how an image of "divinised corn" could be part of a statue. Hence the *chanoine* A. Crampon translates the end of the verse in question thus: ". . . there remained only the stump of him, in the form of a fish." ("*. . . Il ne lui restait que le tronc en forme de poisson.*") The same interpretation is given by a modern Hebrew dictionary, that of A. Even-Shoshan (Jerusalem, 1953): "*Dagon*, the name of the Philistines' god . . . His lower part was that of a fish." And I have found the same point

O

of view in an English translation of the Bible: "*dagon* . . . the fishy part" (The S. S. Teacher's Edition, Oxford).

It is, of course, possible that the Philistines developed a syncretistic religion, a partnership of the original Illyrian deity with the local gods. The Etruscans avoided pronouncing a deity's name: they used epithets instead. So also in Canaan, as time went by, the indigenous population imposed a fitting epithet in their own language on this Philistine god with a fish's tail. For we are bound to recognise Dagon as being essentially a marine god: as Neptune, in fact, to whom so much honour is paid in LM. It was he who conducted the Philistine fleet to Gaza, just as, five centuries later, he was to conduct the fleet of the Tursha to the site of the future city of Tarquinii; for which the Etruscans subsequently showed their gratitude by decorating their funerary steles, such as those which are to be seen in the Museum of Bologna, with his sea-monsters.[1]

B. JEBUSITES AND GIRGASHITES

The attacks and onward surges, which were the form in which Illyrian expansion took place, were carried out by groups of tribes rather than by the isolated action of any one tribe. This can be seen as clearly in Italy as in Asia Minor and Palestine. In their landing on the shores of Canaan the Philistines were not alone; they were accompanied by a small number of Teucri, a well-known tribe from Asia Minor and, like the Philistines, of Illyrian stock. But a third tribe, of the same extraction, seems to have escaped the historians' notice.

Before discussing them, we should recall that in the Tables of Iguvium an abundance of curses is directed at the Iguvians' neighbours; these being the Etruscans, and others who are named variously as the Iapuzkum, Iabuscom, Iabuscer and Iapudikum. These were a colony of the Iapydes from Istria, who had settled in Picenum. Kretschmer has drawn attention to their Illyrian tattoo-marks.

Those whom we shall discuss now are their namesakes in an earlier period, a people who were part of the same Illyrian tribe: the Jebusites or *Yaboussi* inhabiting ancient Jerusalem, which was known as *Yebous* until the time of David. Their name is identical with Iabuscum and reveals their origins. They were not a numerous people. They are mentioned in the following ways among the peoples inhabiting Canaan before the arrival of the Israelites; (*a*) with the Girgashites (Genesis xv. 21); (*b*) as mountain-dwellers, like the Hittites and Amorites

[1] It may be added that, at a later period, Atargatis, the Syrian goddess of Hieropolis, was represented half as a woman and half as a fish at Askalon, an ancient city of Philistia.

(Numbers xiii. 29); (c) as the tribe whom Judah could not overcome (Joshua xvi); (d) as a people whom the tribe of Benjamin could not drive out (Judges i. 21), the chronicler adding: "But the Jebusites dwell with the children of Benjamin in Jerusalem until this day."

Finally, the capture of their city by David is mentioned in 2 Samuel v. 8. It was a redoubtable fortress on a high plateau. Excavations in Jerusalem have shown that its Cyclopean walls were like the walls of Etruscan towns. The siting of the citadel resembled that of many of the towns of Etruria, crowning rocky plateaux which had steep sides and allowed only one way of approach to the main gate. It will be recalled that the Romans, though better armed than David's fighters, took some ten years to subdue Veii. They finally succeeded only by going underground and sapping the defences. The same thing was done six centuries earlier by David, who penetrated the besieged citadel through a "sap" already dug by the capable hands of the Jebusites themselves, a subterranean gallery which enabled the beleaguered defenders to steal out and replenish their water-supplies at the spring of Gihon.

This underground working is mentioned as something unique in its kind in all Palestine; and it helps us to identify the Jebusites as much as their name does. The Jebusites did in their city what the Etruscans were to do both in Rome and in every place where they gave free rein to their talents as builders. This tunnel in Jerusalem makes us think of the vaulted sewers with which the Etruscans endowed Rome. And we can with equal justice liken it to undertakings of exactly the same kind which had been carried out in Asia Minor by the Phrygians, a people of the same Thracio-Illyrian stock. Seton Lloyd writes that in the Phrygian "city of Midas" (6th century B.C.), which stands on a rocky height, some of the houses were built over the blocked-up entrances of underground staircases constructed in an earlier epoch and leading to the springs running out at the foot of the rock (*Early Anatolia*, p. 195).

But for the best example of these artificial underground watercourses we must go to Veii. By tunnelling in the rock on which their city was built the Veians diverted the river Cremere into a canal; this canal was overhung at one point by a natural bridge whose name today is "Ponte sodo", the solid bridge. Some interesting details concerning it are to be found in Mme S. von Cles-Reden's work, from which we have quoted before:

It is not known whether the Romans broke into the city by making use of an existing underground gallery, or whether the sight of one

of these passages gave them the idea of making a tunnel themselves. . . . The admirable network of channels constructed by the
inhabitants of Veii brought about their undoing.

(p. 120)

The former bed of the Cremere, sheering aside from the rock of
Veii and describing a vast sinuous curve, can still be seen. . . . The
foundations of walls and fortified towers were supported on the
vault of the tunnel. The diversion of the Cremere, as well as making
the city easier to defend, provided the inhabitants with a reliable
water-supply in time of siege. A circular opening which was made
in the vaulting of the tunnel, and which is still visible today, made it
possible to dip pitchers into the water.

(*Ibid.*, p. 127)

If we compare these three defensive constructions, that of Yebous
in the time of king David (10th century), of Veii (7th–5th centuries),
and of the "city of Midas" (7th–6th centuries), the resulting picture
shows a striking unity. These three are focal points of the archaic
Thracio-Illyrian tradition in different corners of the ancient world.
Their character can but confirm our identification of the Jebusites.

We can now see the purpose of David's campaign more clearly.
He was hemmed in between Illyrian powers: in front of him, on the
coast, were the Philistines; and to the rear he had the Jebusites. Only
when he had dealt with the latter could he attack five strongholds on
the coast. By his victories he liberated from oppression not only the
tribes of Israel but also the towns of Phoenicia.

The Teucri, an important pre-Hellenic tribe, make their first
appearance in Cyprus, where the legendary Teucer founded the city of
Salamis. But part of the tribe moved westward and settled in Troas.
Another tribe of the same stock, the Girgashites, set up a small colony
to the south of Troy; its name was Gergitha. They also expanded
southwards along the Anatolian coast; they had settlements at Miletus
and near Cumae.

Homer's Trojans (who, according to Kretschmer, originated in
Thrace), and the Teucrians and the Girgashites, represent different
facets of the same phenomenon, the Thraco-Illyrian expansion. But
the Girgashites had already taken part in the Aegeo-Illyrian incursions
eastward, at an earlier period; they had attacked the Egypt of
Rameses II at the same time as the Lycians, Trojans and other
"peoples of the sea". Scholars as early as Rougé and Brugsch identified
them with the *Girgashi* of the Bible (Maspéro, *Les premières mêlées des
peuples*). They appear in Palestine under the same name, Girgashi.

Dictionaries of the Bible describe them as "an ancient people of Canaan". But there is no reason for thus detaching them from their original kindred in Asia Minor, Cyprus and Philistia. The Girgashites of Canaan are mentioned twice in connection with the Jebusites, twice with the Hittites and three times with the Amorites. Their city Gergesa, whose name is identical with that of Gergitha in Anatolia, was on the shore of Lake Tiberias. In the Talmud the record of a curious fact is preserved, namely that the Girgashites complained to Alexander the Great that they had been driven out of the land of Canaan. They could not have made such a complaint unless they had retained the memory of a twofold tradition: that of having come to Palestine at an early period (perhaps with the Philistines), and that of belonging to the same stock as the Macedonian conqueror.

C. THE MACEDONIANS

Did the historical events of the 2nd century B.C.—the conflict between the Macedonians, the heirs of Alexander in Syria and Palestine, on the one hand, and on the other hand, the Jews of Palestine, on whom the Macedonians were trying to impose paganism—cause any Macedonian words to make their way into the scriptural books composed at that time, namely Daniel and Esther?

For the Jews, the period of Seleucid domination in Judaea was at times a period of bloody persecution; the cause of persecution being the Jews' resolve to cling to monotheism and reject idolatry. It was like trying to make a grown-up go back to childhood and play with dolls. The pretext given for this oppression was the propagation of Hellenism, but this was only a sinister piece of nonsense; for the Jews of Jerusalem were fervent Philhellenes. This savage play-acting had in it something of the clownish, fantastic personality of Antiochus IV (Antiochus Epiphanes, "the Illustrious"). Soldier though he was, the character of Antiochus was a curious anticipation of that of Nero, that mountebank whose only wish was to become the darling of the multitude, like a fashionable actor or a successful gladiator.

Thus Antiochus was constantly to be seen in the streets of his capital, mixing with the crowd, flattering people and embracing them, canvassing their votes for himself as a prospective aedile, turning up unexpectedly at banquets and sometimes causing all the guests to leave, disgusted by his excesses; and sprinkling perfumes about him when he appeared at the public baths. Polybius nicknamed him Epimanes, "the madman".

Defeated and fined 15,000 talents by the Romans, driven out by them from Asia Minor and subsequently from Egypt, Antiochus vented his fury on the people of Judaea. The revolt of the Macchabees swept the Syrians out of Jerusalem, but the struggle, lasting from 165 to 140 B.C., was long and harsh. It was in these circumstances that two short books appeared, Daniel (about 164, according to A. Lods) and Esther (about 142). Both of them narrated the trials supposedly undergone by the Israelites in Persia and Babylon in times gone by, and their deliverance by divine intervention. The sole aim of these writings was to encourage the persecuted Jews and strengthen their will to resist.

Despite the fact that the Book of Daniel records the vague, immense visions of a mystic, while the Book of Esther is a terse, sober, unemotional, orderly account of events (which, however, had never taken place), there is much in common between the two. Mordecai refuses to bow down before Haman; correspondingly, Daniel's three companions refuse to bow down before a golden image and are cast into the fiery furnace. The Jews in Persia are threatened with massacre because their religion is "diverse from all people"; correspondingly, Daniel defies the ban on praying to any God except the king and is cast into the den of lions (i. 7).

There is no lack of inconsistencies and blunders in the Book of Daniel; indeed, the inconsequential way in which the characters behave sometimes makes one think of an apocalyptic *Dreigroschenoper*. Its kings are innocent of all logic, and unfailingly forget today what they proclaimed or saw yesterday. When Nebuchadnezzar finds that Daniel has interpreted his dream he worships Daniel's God; but this does not stop him from raising an idol the next day and condemning to torture the worshippers of the one true God. After which the king has another dream; Daniel interprets it; and the impenitent idolater once more glorifies God. His son Belshazzar is a backslider of the same inconsistent sort. It is no use expecting the story to be logical; its readers were thirsty for the miraculous. What we must remember above all is that Nebuchadnezzar and Belshazzar are names, not real figures; phantoms from a remote past which had long since faded from people's minds; and, in any case, no one was concerned with the past when the Macedonians and Syrians, all too urgently present, had filled life full of grievous problems. No one could write or speak openly. Yet is it not possible that these two short works reflect at least a touch here and there of current reality—a touch, if not of the oppressors' cruelty, then at least of their languages?

Scheftelowitz has analysed the names of the characters in the Book of Esther.[1] Mordecai (Mardocheus) and Esther are commonly connected

---

[1] *Arisches im Alten Testament*, pp. 45 *et seq.*

with two names of deities, Marduk and Ishtar. But Scheftelowitz has suggested a new identification: *Vashti* (the name of the wife repudiated by Ahasuerus) is paralleled by ancient Indian *vashti*, "the desired one" or "beauty". On the other hand, he has neither discovered the origin of the name *Haman* nor explained the word *pur*, "lot, fate".

This word plays an important part in the book, and is, moreover, the origin of the name of the feast of *Purim* ("the lots"), which was instituted to commemorate the survival of Judaism.

A. Lods quotes J. Lewy's opinion that the Assyrian word *puri* means "lot".

We must point out that *Vashti* was one of the commonest feminine names in Etruscan: (P. 580) *fasti cvinti*; (P. 587) *fasti capznei*; (P. 564) *fasti kainei*; (P. 690) *fasti ve*.

Better still: an inscription which has been studied by Pauli mentions a woman *fasti hamana lautni nuf*, which Pauli renders as *Fasti die Hamanerin*, "Fasti of the family of Haman" (*Etr. Forsch. und Stud.*, IV, p. 9). We thus have the quite unexpected pleasure of meeting these two names, Vashti and Haman, at once; Illyrian, even Macedonian, names. In Albanian, *vashë* means "girl"; and its plural is *vashta* (M. 546). Fasti or Vashti would be a name on the same lines as "Virginia".

But *pur* also exists in Albanian, in the form of *porr*. Mann gives this as: (1) "round pebble, marble"; (2) "a game played with stones" (M. 396). Though I wish I knew what this game was, it would be still more to the point to know in what form it was played by the ancients. It seems to me that these marbles would be very suitable for taking a *sors*, predicting the lot or fate of something; for instance, for finding out whether such and such a day was favourable for the execution of some project or other. A game of this kind would be just right for soldiers, since the equipment would cost little or nothing; and if this Illyrian word *porr* is of sufficient antiquity the Macedonian soldiers may have made it known in the countries where they were stationed. In this connection one thinks of Aqra, their citadel in Jerusalem.

As a prop to the Illyrian word *por*, here is an analogy: the Greek word *kleros*, which means "an object used for drawing lots; originally, a small stone".

The stay of the Macedonian and Greek soldiers in Jerusalem was a long one, and in the course of wars, sieges, parleys and so on the Jews of Syria and Palestine had plenty of chance to get to know their enemy at close quarters and perhaps to learn something of his language. A word of Macedonian and Illyrian stamp seems to me to be lurking disguised in the famous phrase, *mene mene tekel upharsin* (Daniel v. 25).

A mysterious hand wrote these words on a wall in the presence of king Belshazzar, and the prophet translated them as "counted, counted, weighed and divided" (meaning that this was what would happen to the kingdom of Babylon).

Now the Book of Daniel was intended to show that God always punished those who profaned His Temple. As we have said, the writer of the book wanted to encourage the persecuted Jews to resist Antiochus.

The sentence in question, according to Daniel, is composed of three Aramaic words. But the commentators are doubtful about their exact meaning; they are not sure whether the words are the three verbs given above or three nouns denoting coins of different values. There is general agreement that *upharsin* is a play on words, because two meanings have been detected in it: the verb *paras*, "to divide", and the name *Paras*, the country of the Persians, Belshazzar's conquerors (this twofold interpretation being that both of Koehler and of the eminent Semitologist H. L. Ginsberg, who was kind enough to write to me on this point).

Let us therefore note that this play on words may take in more than has so far been suspected. *upharsin* is also the subjunctive of the Albanian verb *faroj, faros*, "to destroy" (M. 102). We have already met this verb in a melancholy Etruscan aphorism:

neri vanva farsi putnam (LM, X, g, 2–3)

upharsin means "May they be destroyed!" It is constructed in the same way as *u-goditshin*, "May they be smitten!" (from the verb *godis*, *goditem*), or *u-falshin*, "May they be excused!" (from the verb *fal*; cf. Mann, *Gramm.*, p. 33), etc. It may be an echo of the threats and curses which the insurgents, under the leadership of the brothers Macchabeus, exchanged with their oppressors.

XVI

CONCLUSIONS

WE have now reached the end of this incredible journey through the shadows. There is still an enormous amount to be done; much, too, to be done again and to be made clearer than it is now. But, before our dazzled eyes, pictures have risen out of a past whose colours have faded hardly at all, and whose voice reaches us with a strangely moving ring after its two thousand years of melancholy silence.

The moment has come to cast a glance back along the road we have travelled—progressing sometimes in leaps and bounds, but at other times faltering or wandering off the track—and to draw what conclusions we can, however incomplete and precarious they may be. I am thinking of a problem which is of secondary importance in a study of this nature, but which nevertheless cannot leave us indifferent: the origin of the Etruscans.

The testimony of the Etruscan inscriptions, in so far as we have interpreted them in this book, seems to confirm the presence, as we have already noted, of two currents intertwining and forming a counterpoise to each other in that strange civilisation: one from the Danube basin and one from Anatolia. A reservation is needed here: if we are not to be shackled by geographical fictions we must avoid thinking of the Balkan peninsula and of Anatolia as two separate worlds, a "Europe" and an "Asia". In dealing with folk-migrations and the epoch of the Thraco-Illyrian settlement of Anatolia this would be an anachronism.

The Euro-Asiatic Steppe, stretching from present-day Bohemia and Hungary to the north of the Black Sea and of the Caucasus, taking in the Caspian region and extending into Southern Siberia, was Europe and Asia at once. Similarly, a constant coming and going of various ethnic groups must, from an early age, have taken place across the Bosphorus.

The fact that the Steppe was near was important. The Steppe produced a great deal more than an abundance of grass. On the contrary, it was the seat of a remarkable civilisation which had been built up on the periphery of the great centres of human culture: prehistoric India, Sumer, Elam, Mesopotamia and various others. The civilisation of the Steppe had its own religious themes, its favourite pottery (the black or grey lustre-ware of which we have spoken already), its art, its means of locomotion. What is more, there were, within its bounds, archaic centres of mining and metal-working (Bohemia, Hungary); it could therefore supply itself with weapons, and its peoples' future expansion both eastwards and westwards became a matter of certainty.

Etruscan prehistory will never be understood unless these important factors are taken into account. Its antecedents must be considered in the light of the seasonal migrations of the proto-Danubian shepherds, with their heavy, leather-hooded wagons plodding over the Steppe, along the banks of the Danube and its tributaries. Etruscan civilisation never threw off the marks of its origin; the curule chair was probably one of them. Was not this "seat on a wagon" (Altheim, *La religion romaine*, p. 19) a symbol of the powers of justice exercised by the chiefs of these cattle-raising peoples, in the vicissitudes of their nomadic existence?

The migratory expansion of the future Etruscans would have come to nothing had they not entered the world of the Italics as "men of bronze", with irresistible weapons in their hands. These weapons were what opened the route Middle Danube–Bosnia–Bosphorus–Troy, the route Danube–Bosnia–Greece–Italy and so many others.

D. Randall-MacIver, writing of the ancient bronze-producing centres (in the 2nd millennium B.C.), observes:

> In the lake-dwellings in Switzerland (2,000–1,500) there have been found numerous weapons and implements of cast bronze. These could not have been manufactured in Switzerland which did not possess the metals, so it is clear that they must have been derived, directly or indirectly, either from Spain via the Riviera or else from Hungary and Bohemia.
>
> (*Italy before the Romans*, p. 30)

> The copper of Hungary and the tin of Bohemia had created a populous and flourishing series of stations along the Danube, which became the principal source of the Bronze Age culture of Europe. The Proto-Italici formed the liaison between the Danube and Italy.
>
> (*Ibid.*, p. 37)

> Occasional objects of Aegean or Trojan origin, such as spiral-headed bronze pins, must have travelled by way of the Danube. . . . Some entire Bohemian deposits of the period [1,600–1,500] are so precisely like the Italian that it is difficult to say which owed most to the other.
>
> (*Ibid.*, p. 39)

It is evidently from the Steppe, though at a much later date, that
Etruscan art is enriched by those motifs of animal portraiture which are
so characteristic of the Scythians and kindred peoples in the lands east
of the Danube. This animal art is distinguished by acute observation
of its subjects, by the violent contortions of the animals depicted, by
a "fear of empty spaces" which often results in small animals being

FIG. 69A. Etruscan decorative motif

included in the composition along with big ones and, at the same time,
by a stylisation which is at times very bold.

To realise this we have only to compare a motif from the border of
an Etruscan mirror, in which we see a horse being attacked by two
carnivores, with a golden clasp from Siberia, representing a bison. The

FIG. 69B. Scythian decorative motif

position of the leg stretched out to the rear is the same in both (figs. 69A
and 69B). To take another example, we may study a model of a stag's
head which was found in a tomb of the Etruscan period at Vetulonia,
and which has been published by Montélius (fig. 70).[1] The style is pure
Scythian, all the more so in that a little animal is slung, with charming inconsistency, from the underside of the stag's neck, in defiance of

---

[1] *La civilisation primitive en Italie*, Stockholm, 1910, pl. 188.

the laws of gravity. This stag's head originally adorned the prow of a small Etruscan ship.

We shall juxtapose this curious work of art with another, which is older and comes from Northern Mesopotamia. The Tell Halaf site, which was excavated some thirty years ago by M. von Oppenheim, yielded bas-reliefs dating from the 11th century B.C. and displaying Assyrian and Hittite inspiration yet belonging to a different type of style, at once rough and powerful (G. Contenau, *Manuel d'archéologie orientale*, II, p. 1007). We believe the sculptors of Tell Halaf were

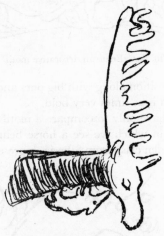

FIG. 70. Stag's head (Etruscan decorative element)

under the artistic influence of the Euro-Asiatic Steppe. Consider this powerful effigy of a lion (fig. 71), which at once catches the eye with a significant detail, the little stag running upside down along the belly of the impassive lion, once again in defiance of gravity. It is clear that the problem of Etruscan borrowing from Oriental art is fairly complex. In some cases what we must look for is not a straightforward transplantation of artistic motifs from East to West, but rather the result of the fertilisation of Anatolian and Syrio-Hittite art, on the one hand, and Etruscan art, on the other hand, by the same initial conceptions, infiltrating from the Great Steppe over a period of centuries.[1]

Here is more evidence of the Oriental influence in Etruscan art. It is most informative to compare the detail of the pillars which are to be seen inside several Etruscan tombs (at Cerveteri and elsewhere),

[1] This is illustrated by M. R. Ghirshman's publication of the Scythio-Assyrian finds at Sakis.

and whose bas-reliefs represent shields, weapons, utensils, etc., with the
pilasters of a temple in Anatolia. The latter is the temple of Musasir,
near the region of Ararat, which the Assyrians pillaged in the 8th

FIG. 71. Sculpture from Tell-Halaf (after von Oppenheim)

century and subsequently depicted on a bas-relief found at Khorsabad
(fig. 72). Its pilasters appear to form part of the façade, but this was
merely a convention of Assyrian art: in reality they are inside. The
decorations with which they were covered consisted of carvings of

FIG. 72. Temple of Musasir (fragment)

circular shields, like those in Etruria. (See G. Contenau, *Manuel*, III, p. 1266; Seton Lloyd, *Early Anatolia*, p. 189).

It is equally interesting to note that the Hyksos type of horse's bit (preserved at the Rockefeller Museum in Jerusalem), which consists of a single unjointed bar, continued much longer in use among the Etruscans than among the Scythians, who adopted a bit made in two

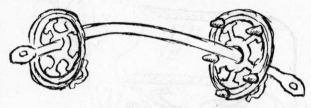

FIG. 73. Hyksos horse's bit

pieces. The centre of diffusion of the single-bar type was, naturally, neither Egypt nor Etruria; it was in the north, in Luristan, which was one of the outlets from the Steppe and a crossroads of migration-routes. That Luristan was the centre can be seen from a Kassite bit of the middle of the 2nd millennium, illustrated by M. G. Contenau.[1] (See figs. 73, 74 and 75.)

The polychromy of Etruscan decorative art is also of Eastern origin.

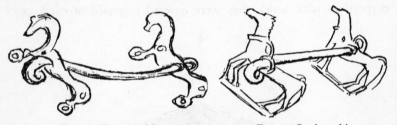

FIG. 74. Etruscan bit   FIG. 75. Luristan bit

It is known that the façades of Etruscan temples and patricians' houses were covered in multi-coloured tiles which gave them a gay, inviting air. And G. Körte gives a description of an alabaster funerary urn decorated with bas-reliefs and a portrait of the dead man: the whole is coloured blue, blue-green, vermilion, dark red and brown.[2] The cyma of the temple at Cerveteri was adorned with a winged goddess; her face was tinted red, her hair brown, necklace yellow, wings bright red and mantle dark red. The culminating figure, in the central position on the cyma, was a stockily built god, at once good-natured and truculent in expression, with eyes like a doll's and a little pointed nose,

---

[1] *Manuel d'arch. orientale*, IV, fig. 1202.
[2] *La Glyptothèque Ny-Carlsberg (Musée Jacobsen)*, 1912, II, fig 173.

doing his best to appear at once frightening, magnificent and generous. A useful comparison can be drawn between these Etruscan polychrome ceramics and those of Carthage, which are more hieratic but almost as highly and variously coloured—judging, for example, by a fine statuette (some 6 or 7 inches high) representing a goddess with a tambourine, coloured ochre, blue and red, which was illustrated by M. A. Merlin in 1921. The author notes that a band of red cloth hung from the goddess's waist to her feet, and adds that the Etruscans wore a similar band of stuff; they had inherited this custom from the East, and it is found later among the Romans.[1] (Fig. 76.)

M. André Piganiol has provided the thesis of the Oriental origin of the Etruscans with some new arguments. He rejects as unfounded the theory of Wiesner, according to which the Etruscans were mounted shepherds who, setting out from the confines of Iran and the Caucasus, passed through Thrace and Illyria. But he points out numerous links between an important Anatolian site, Toprakkale, and Etruria, such links being the presence, on that site, of a typically Etruscan monument, namely three sacred stones on a cylindrical base; the practice of irrigation; funeral chambers with benches running round the walls; etc. This

FIG. 76. An Etruscan god (terra cotta)

enables him to reach the conclusion that "the kinship between the Etruscans and the ancient peoples of Asia Minor admits of no doubt" (*Les Etrusques, peuple d'Orient*,[2] p. 338). The archaic Etruscan temple, the podium, a lofty artificial platform, is of Chaldean origin. The god Janus comes from the same source. And M. A. Piganiol adds:

> Despite the brilliant cloak of Greek influence which Etruria wears, the originality of an Eastern people shows through.
>
> (*Ibid.*, p. 349)

We shall conclude that it is useless to seek a solution of the Etruscan enigma if the seekers persist in looking for the origins of Etruscan civilisation either north of the Alps, or among the native peoples of Italy.

(*Ibid.*, p. 352)

---

[1] *Monuments et Mémoires publiés par l'Académie des Inscriptions et Belles-Lettres*, t. XXIV, 1921.

[2] *Cahiers d'histoire mondiale*, I, 2, 1953, pp. 328 *et seq.*

It is nevertheless to the north-west of the Alps that the original home of the Illyrians is situated. Can we summarily decide such a vast question on the strength of certain iconographical motifs and architectural details, without simultaneously taking into account the character of the Etruscan language and the origins of the Etruscan alphabet, and the evidence supplied by the ceramics and tools found on the Balkan sites and along the Anatolian coast?

For our part, we have not only been at pains to assemble the arguments already advanced in support of the part played by the East in the civilisation of the Etruscans; having contributed to the deciphering of Etruscan, we have also been able to lengthen the list of those arguments by bringing further points of contact to light: contact both between Etruscan and other Anatolian idioms, and between Etruscan rites and those of Asia Minor.

It is just because we have carried out this task that we are able to see the dual aspect of the Etruscan problem: its undeniable Orientalism is only one side of the medal. The Etruscan language is related to certain languages of the East, that is, of Asia Minor. But these languages are not of Eastern origin. They are languages with an Indo-European basis which took root in Asia Minor. In the same way, Etruscan is not an Oriental language.

Its origins take us towards the Danube.

The Etruscans were partially descended from the Tursha. But the Tursha were not a people of Oriental origin. They were ancient Illyrians (or Thracio-Illyrians) who had settled in Asia Minor. We have already dealt with these facts from various points of view, and we return to them now.

The early groups of settlers, the first migration-wave of a people setting out to make a new home for itself overseas, are, as a rule, numerically small. The examples of the Hyksos, the Philistines, the Carthaginians and the Normans are enough to illustrate this. It is hard to believe that the Tursha contingents, arriving from the Aegeo-Anatolian region, could have provided a sufficiently broad ethnic foundation for the future federation of the "twelve peoples of Etruria". The greater part of the Illyrian population of the country must have been there already, before the advent of the Tursha, who were under the dominion of the Lydio-Hittite civilisation.

In speaking of that population, the conception of them which we have in mind is that of a small fraction of the Illyrian nation; a part, that is, of a vast family of interrelated peoples, connected more by possessing a common linguistic basis than by anything else. Integrated in different degrees in this family there were, besides the Illyrians properly so called, the Epirots, Macedonians, Thracians, Phrygians, Etruscans, Venetians, Liburnians, Picenians, Iapygians, Dardanians, Trojans, Lydians (perhaps), Cretans (but not all of them), Teucrians, Philistines, Jebusites and many more. Hence it would be preferable to denote this family of peoples, who are historically so disparate, by a general term such as *Proto-Danubians*, thus restricting ourselves to indicating the territory which they are known to have originally occupied together.

Nevertheless, the decisive characteristic of the Illyrian population in Italy is undoubtedly its language. And that language is essentially Indo-European. It would seem, certainly, to have borrowed a number of elements from the languages of Anatolia and the Caucasus, but it took in fewer of such extraneous additions than did Hittite or Armenian. Furthermore, we have seen that it presents numerous analogies with the Balto-Slavonic languages. Its home therefore cannot have been elsewhere than in a region between the Danube and the Carpathians.

G. Battisti recently handled the problem of Illyrian, studying it without reference to Albanian. He judges the Illyrians of the Danube area to have been, in the first place, a pre-Indo-European people whose language was connected with the Creto-Aegean centre but was later heavily affected by superimposition from Indo-European dialects. Battisti enumerates some fifteen isolated, rather obscure words which he regards as belonging to a Mediterranean substratum; and he claims to detect the presence of this substratum in Illyrian. He sums up his view as follows:

(a) he recognises that Illyrian is definitely Indo-European in character;

(b) he admits that the circumstances under which Illyrian entered the Indo-European linguistic framework demand to be made the subject of a *new study*;

(c) he is nevertheless *convinced* that Illyrian consists of a "layer" superimposed on an earlier, pre-Indo-European language.

("I Balcani e l'Italia", *Studi Etruschi*, XXIV, 1956, p. 271)

But what we are looking for is not convictions, but proofs.

According to Coon's observations, which we have quoted already, the ancestors of the modern Albanians reached their present country from Bosnia and the Danube, and Albania and Epirus have been inhabited by that race and no other from an early period onwards. Is there anyone willing to maintain that Albanian is a language of Aegeo-Cretan stamp?

Moreover, M. Battisti admitted in his study that such Illyrian as he knew was confined to place-names and personal names.

Today, the situation has altered. We have broken out of the circle of place-names and personal names and have acquired a vocabulary abounding in words with an obviously Indo-European basis. These words are basic, everyday terms: *mish*, "meat"; *vaχr*, "father-in-law", *svekor* (German *Schwieger*, "mother-in-law"); *hia*, "shade" (Greek *skia*); *cem-*, "to thunder"; *parχ*, "belly" (*briukho*); *śetirune*, "young cow"; *cena*, "price"; *nac*, *nata*, "night"; *caraθ*, "enclosure" (*grad*); *pi*, "to drink"; *uθ*, "way" (*hodos*); *neri*, "men" (*aner*); *θu*, "two"; *pic* (*pec*), "to roast"; etc. And such words, occurring in various combinations in the inscriptions so far deciphered, follow the Indo-European norms of grammatical co-ordination. Barely three years ago, K. Olzscha complained with regard to Etruscan:

> "The language's grammatical structure is non-Indo-European too. . . . The accusative is lacking. . . . We cannot tell the active from the passive. . . . We do not know the word for *father*."
>
> (*Historia*, VI, 1957)

But we now have the accusative, the article, a fine selection of passives, the past participle, the negative of verbs and so on. And it is time to start formulating conclusions from these data.

What route had the Illyrians followed on their way to Italy? Here we may take note of an observation by J. Whatmough, who, after affirming the Illyrian character of Messapian (a language which was common to several small tribes of ancient Italy), says that in his judgment the Illyrians had come by sea:

> There is not the slightest indication of a long migration by land, round the head of the Adriatic Sea, which could hardly have been accomplished without disrupting their national unity.
>
> (*Prae-Italic Dialects of Italy*, 1933, II, p. 262)

We shall take no notice of the same writer's remarks on the supposed difference between Illyrian and Albanian, and on the small amount of help which could be obtained from Albanian. Those who thought as he did (and were wrong, as he was) were legion. But we accept his opinion on the part played by the Adriatic, especially as it agrees with certain ideas of M. Hammarström, in his *Beiträge zur Geschichte des etruskischen, lateinischen und griechischen Alphabets* (Helsingfors, 1920). Hammarström's ideas are in harmony with everything new which we have succeeded in discovering, and everything valid which we have learnt from other sources.

He begins his article in the most innocent way in the world, saying that he is going to concern himself only with the history of the three alphabets—Etruscan, Latin and Greek.

He then considers the fact that "the difference between the Etruscan alphabet and the Lydian, Carian and Lycian alphabets leaps to the eye". He consequently does not believe that the Etruscans brought with them into Italy any alphabetic elements which had originated in Asia Minor; though certain borrowings, such as 8 (which is the Lydian *f*), succeeded in entering Etruria later, brought, for example, by new immigrants or Phocaean prisoners.

The writer next shows that the Etruscan alphabet was not derived from that of Italian Cumae. A close analysis of scripts from Greece and Asia Minor compels us to conclude that the Etruscans borrowed their alphabet from the Greeks of the northern shore of the Gulf of Corinth. This incites the author to consider the possibility that, for a time, the Etruscans settled opposite Boeotia, that is to say in Southern Italy (*ibid.*, p. 53). And in examining this possibility he observes that there is in fact an astonishing parallel between several place-names in Southern Italy and in Etruria: Volcei in Campania and Vulci in Etruria; the river Sabatus and lake Sabatinus; and so on. Körte, moreover, had regarded this as evidence of the Etruscans' movements. And Krahe draws attention to the following important Illyrian names in the same region: Calabria (there was a people of the same name in the Balkans), Brindia (Brindisi), Sybaris (cf. Subura), Tarentum, etc. (*Die alten balkanill. geogr. Namen*).

Finally, Hammarström identifies the Tyrrhenians with the Pelasgians who were driven out of Boeotia and who settled in Lemnos (Herodotus, VI, 137–9).

We have extracted only the main thread of Hammarström's argument; which is that the future Etruscans, emerging from the interior of the Balkans and travelling by way of the Greek mainland territories and the islands, settle in Southern Italy and later move towards their eventual homes in the north-west of the peninsula.

Such, then, was the path followed by this Illyrian migration which was destined to provide the nucleus of Etruscan civilisation. We have only one objection to make. Once settled in Greece, the Illyrian colonists from the Danube region were probably themselves assailed by a Dorian invasion (9th century) which pushed them towards Italy; a case of bronze retreating before iron. But this was no mere matter of small groups of "exiled Pelasgians". A small, scattered people is unlikely to have a sufficiently strong intellectual life to need to adapt an alphabet; besides, the future Etruscans made their appearance in Italy as formidable "men of bronze", in the same way as their kindred, the Philistines, had confronted the Israelites three centuries earlier. Otherwise the Illyrians would not have been able to dislodge their forerunners, the Umbrians, from hundreds of towns, as the ancients attest. The first wave of Illyrians to reach Italy, rough and simple but armed with Danubian bronze, must have been numerically fairly massive.

We have given here our conception of the route followed by the Illyrian ethnic nucleus, and by bronze, and the chariot, and black ceramic ware, and so on, joined on the way by the alphabet in question. Setting out from the middle Danube and the borders of the steppe, they pass through the Balkans and Greece and cross the Adriatic to Italy. This is the Western contribution; primordial and massive, the preponderant element in Etruscan civilisation. It is on to this basis that a new contribution is grafted two or three centuries later, a more brilliant and colourful element, the Eastern contribution. This element is brought by the Rasna, known as the Tursha, coming over from Asia Minor. We thus have two successive waves of a single ethnic stock, with a common language but differing from one another in the level and the tone of their respective civilisations. This original heterogeneity is probably the essential cause of the Etruscans' inability to form a single nation and to overcome the centrifugal forces of tribal organisation.

This tribal structure had come down from very ancient time, and we must not let ourselves be misled by an apparently excessive number, the "twelve peoples of Etruria"; indeed, it is surprising that there were only twelve and not a hundred and twenty. We should remember the picture presented in the Odyssey. When the representatives of the little island of Ithaca are to be called together, old Aegyptus cries: "Peoples of Ithaca! Hear me! . . ." (Book II). When the Phaeacians, the inhabitants of another small island, are to hold a council a herald goes along all the streets of the town shouting: "Princes and chiefs of the peoples dwelling in this isle! . . ." (Book VIII). One wonders how many "peoples" did dwell in these countries, which were only a fraction of the size of Etruria.

To sum up: while there is no doubting that a nucleus of Illyrian colonists passed over from Greece into Italy, it is equally beyond doubt that the Illyrian Tursha, coming over from the Anatolian coast, participated in the creation of Etruria.

Consequently, three further facts must be emphasised:

(a) Illyrian expansion into Asia Minor at a very early period;
(b) participation of the Tursha in this expansion; and
(c) subsequent arrival of the Tursha in Italy.

If we review these facts in turn we shall obtain a picture of the dual nature of the Etruscan people, composed as it was of two Illyrian elements, one Western and the other Eastern. Here is our review:

(a) *Early Expansion.* F. Altheim sees the cause of the Dorian migration and a number of others in an initial Illyrian drive which was particularly vigorous about 1500 B.C. The Illyrians and the Thraco-Phrygians penetrate into Asia Minor. This migration is of "enormous amplitude" (*loc. cit.*, p. 13).

O. Müller enumerates the peoples of the lower Danube: the Teucrian Paeonians, the Mysians and the Thracians, whose migration to Anatolia is a comparatively recent historical fact (7th century B.C.).

Ida Thallon has studied the same expansion in relation with the discovery, in a succession of sites which stretches from the Danube into Bosnia, Serbia and Thrace, of an archaic incised ceramic ware with a white slip.

This writer begins by noting Strabo's testimony (XII, 8, 3): *before the Trojan War* the Phrygians arrive from Thrace and kill a Trojan king. But, adds Thallon, the Trojan War (*circa* 1200 B.C.) was primarily a conflict between two ethnic groups, the Greeks and the Illyrians. Not only the Trojans (of Troy VI), who were Teucrians, but also their chief allies, the Phrygians of Thrace, the Thracians, Mysians and Paeonians, were Thraco-Illyrians. As for Troy VII, which is post-Homeric, it was neither Trojan nor Greek in character but typically Danubian. Axes from the Danube have been found there.

Thallon's conclusion is that we do not know who the original Trojans were; but that we do know the Danubian element came there early and continued coming at frequent intervals.[1]

M. F. Chapouthier writes that in earliest Troy (about 3000) there were tribes who may have come from Thrace (*Premières civilisations*, p. 183). Later, the Phrygian and Trojan hinterland was populated by Phrygians from Thrace (*ibid.*, p. 347).

More recently, this whole set of ideas has been incisively summed up by Seton Lloyd, who considers the Trojan War to have been an episode in the

eastward thrust of peoples from Thrace and Macedonia, which ended after some centuries of confusion in the establishment of the Phrygians as rulers of Asia Minor.

(*Early Anatolia*, p. 71)

[1] "Some Balkan and Danubian Connections of Troy", *Journ. of Hellenic Studies*, XXXIX, 1919, p. 201.

From this movement towards the south-east the first name to emerge is that of the Pelasgians. Some of their cities bear names which can be interpreted with the help of Illyrian, for example Cortona. We may also mention the *spring of Bourina* on the Aegean island of Cos, just off the Anatolian coast, and within the area of the earliest Pelasgian expansion. How can we fail to point out that *burim*, in Albanian, is "spring", and *buroj*, "to gush out" (M. 43)? The language of the Pelasgians may have had, as nucleus, a very ancient Illyrian dialect.

Furthermore, M. A. Piganiol observes that "the Etruscans followed exactly the same route as the Pelasgians". He takes note of a legend according to which the heroes Iapyges, Daunos and Peucetos, the sons of the Pelasgian Lycaon (whom we mentioned on an earlier page), landed in Italy with an Illyrian army (*Essai sur les origines de Rome*, p. 23). Moreover, the fact that the eponymous founders of three large Illyrian tribes are stated to be the sons of a Pelasgian is in itself an indication that these two ethnic groups are related. If we add that the religious beliefs prevalent in the Pelasgic countries shared with those prevalent in Etruria such important words as *prytanis* and *sibyl*, it begins to look very possible that the Pelasgians were one of the first of the Proto-Danubian waves to penetrate into the Aegean region.

So much for the first of our three points, the early expansion of the Illyrians into Asia Minor. The other two can be dealt with more briefly.

(*b*) *The participation of the Tursha* in the Illyrians' expansion into Anatolia is proved by the Illyrian names of certain towns in Lydia and Troas which we have mentioned already, and which are *connected by tradition with the Tyrrhenians*; and also by the fact that, after the attacks made by the "peoples of the sea" on the country of the Pharaohs, the Tursha are mentioned in the Egyptian sources along with the Shardana (the men of Sardis) and other Anatolian peoples. But the positions held by the Tursha in Asia Minor must have crumbled under the shock of the Cimmerian invasion, after the devastation of the Phrygian hinterland.

(*c*) *The arrival of the Tursha in Italy* is clearly attested by the fact that both the Etruscan people and its territory were thereafter known, among their neighbours, by the name of the Tursha; the reason being that, from the military and religious standpoints and also that of material civilisation, the Tursha were evidently superior to the other tribes of the same stock.

It is legitimate to speak of a common Etruscan language, without taking local dialects into account. One, nevertheless, has the impression that the basic duality, which characterises the development of Etruscan civilisation, may well have been reflected to some extent in the language. It may have been this which caused the presence of synonyms, Eastern European, on the one hand, Oriental, on the other, for several things: *vinum* and *ena*, *in*, "wine" (though both are derived from the same source); *zac*, *θac* (*gjak*) and perhaps *esi*, "blood"; *zar* (*zjarr*) and *ar* (?), "fire"; *śerfue* (?) and *ras* (?), "silver"; *pes* and *śa* (?), "five"; etc.

We are faced with a problem. The Etruscans were a courageous people. They developed a well-ordered civilisation and their attitude to life was, on the whole, optimistic. Why did both people and civilisation disappear?

Disunity was not the only cause. There is another reason, which may be formulated by saying that the Etruscans were still, to too great an extent, a Bronze Age people, whereas their aggressive neighbours the Romans were ahead of them; the Romans were part of the Iron Age.

This may seem strange. How could a past age have laid its dead hand on the Etruscans—those farmers with a mastery of irrigation; those engineers who were the first to build vaulted subterranean aqueducts, those metal-workers, those musicians, those sculptors who opened the way to the art of portraiture in Roman sculpture; those practical minds, the inventors of the anchor, the beaked prow of fighting ships, and the trumpet; those capable physicians?

However, despite the high level of their technical accomplishments, the imprint of archaic life on the soul of the Etruscan people was deep and irremovable. Their relations with the nearby Romans are an example of the age-old story of the earthenware pot and the iron pot.[1]

Their mentality is in thrall to the Bronze Age. We are reminded of this not only by the fact that tribal rivalry prevents Volsinia and Clusium from accepting Tarquinii as the capital of the country but also by their very rites and customs. Thus, for example, the rite performed at the founding of a town is valid only if the plough used in marking the boundaries is fitted with a share made of bronze (or copper).

A vestige of the primitive matriarchy can be seen in the preponderant role often played by the female line. A similar vestige is the fact that, in Etruria, the recipient of a triumph painted his face red. Livy's description of a battle between the Tarquinians and Faliscans, on one

[1] Who, according to the fabulists, set out travelling together. But the rough road caused them to knock against one another; the Earthenware Pot broke into pieces but the Iron Pot went on. See La Fontaine, *Fables*, V. 2.—*Tr.*

side, and the Romans, on the other, about the middle of the 4th century takes us back suddenly to the threshold of the Bronze Age:

The Romans were at first defeated, the Roman soldiers having been terrified by the sight of the enemy's priests advancing like furies, brandishing snakes and lighted torches. The soldiers retreated in disorder to their trenches; but the consuls, lieutenants and tribunes having begun laughing and mocking at them because, like children, they were afraid of empty shows, shame revived their courage and they rushed blindly at the very things which had put them to flight. Having scattered these ghosts, they threw themselves on the real enemy, broke his whole line, collected an enormous amount of booty and returned victorious, making fun in their own rude way both of the enemy's wiles and of their own fear.

(Book VII, 17)

"Ghosts"! In that one word the whole of the heroic, childish Bronze Age is condemned without hope of appeal. Spectres cannot put up with laughter. Fear of furies was dissolved, as a pearl dissolves in vinegar, in the laughter of the officers, with their "modern" mentality.

The struggle was thus an unequal one between these two worlds in collision, one of them trusting in the breastplate of inherited ideas and the other piercing that breastplate with a burst of laughter. It is attested that two Roman augurs could not look at one another without laughing. Augurs though they were, they thereby admitted that their lore was nonsense, a fiction based on the behaviour of the sacred chickens. There is no denying that they were several centuries in advance of their colleagues, the soothsayers of Etruria.

It is time to take another glance at Etruscan religion; a great deal has been written about it, yet a little must be added here.

The perfect "quartering" of the sky and earth which the Etruscan priests carried out as the necessary precondition of their observations, and which, as I have indicated, was not without an aspect of "modern" precision, must not deceive us; we must not mistake the real essence of the matter. These ancient rites—observation of birds in flight, of animals' entrails, of lightning and other natural phenomena—are merely a late stage in the development of an animism which goes back to Neolithic times. The cradle of such beliefs is in the caves of Altamira and the Dordogne, where hunter and sorcerer felt themselves to be surrounded by invisible forces and, in fear and trembling, did their best to tame them. Their rock paintings were the first beginnings of animal art, which, like the religion in question, was deeply rooted in an intimate relationship with nature.

Although this inheritance from the distant past held within it the seeds of the sciences of future ages, it was a weighty encumbrance to those who still adhered to it too faithfully. The Etruscans were out of date not only in political organisation but also in military tactics. Livy records that the Etruscan cavalry never learnt to dismount and fight as infantry, as the Romans did when necessary; nor did the Etruscans commit their reserves gradually to the battle, but let their entire phalanx fight from the start, until it could fight no more.

Finally, the Etruscans' swords were not as good as those of the Romans.

But the Etruscans' disunity and conservatism would not have been so fatal in the absence of a third cause of their degradation: the policy adopted by the Romans.

During the early centuries of their history the Romans displayed admirable courage, discipline, devotion and perseverance. But the same qualities became correspondingly evil when they were placed at the service of a state which organised itself for one thing, war; and whose wars had one object, wealth.

They rapidly became a kind of Western Assyrians. The Eastern Assyrians were merely butchers with curly beards and simple souls. An Assyrian king, if you had asked him, would have said that he was only obeying the orders of his god. That god, another curly-headed butcher, somewhat larger and more powerful and housed in a palace in heaven, told him to invade the neighbouring countries, burn their towns, cut down the vines and olive-trees, flay and impale some of his captives and deport the rest, and bring plenty of bronze and other metals home with him. And these religiously motivated expeditions were more or less effective in supplying the deficiencies of the native metal-working industries.

The Romans, on the other hand, were interested only in the noble metals. They felt their vitality ebbing away if they were not surrounded with luxury—the very luxury for which, when they were still poor, they so energetically criticised the Etruscans. Their dream was that they might one day succeed in pillaging India. They never did it, but they did succeed in another exploit: they ruined all the Mediterranean civilisations, one after the other. The consequences were incalculable, and some of them can still be felt today.

The venality of the Senate, bought at wholesale prices by Massinissa, and the venality of the praetors later on; the crimes of provincial governors; a story such as that of Verres, who succeeded in pillaging Sicily single-handed (and with impunity)—all these are well known. And let us also mention Epirus, Macedonia, Carthage, Corinth and Jerusalem.

Professor Léon Homo writes:

> Thus the exploitation of the world, the natural corollary to its conquest, is organised in the manner of an enormous and profitable business undertaking from which every class of the population extracts some degree of benefit.
>
> ("L'Italie primitive et les débuts de l'Impérialisme romain", *L'Evolution de l'humanité*, 1925, p. 311)

After the third Macedonian war, the Senate rewarded the victorious army by allowing it to sack the towns of Epirus. . . . On the appointed day, at the fourth hour, the signal for pillage to begin is given throughout the army; the troops . . . pillage and rob on every side. In one hour 70 towns are sacked, 150,000 men are reduced to slavery and sold. . . . Every cavalryman receives 400 denarii as his share; every foot-soldier, 200. Livy records the event without a word of disapproval; Plutarch stresses the hideousness of the operation, in which "a nation was ruined to provide only a small profit to each individual soldier . . .".

(Ibid., p. 317)

When Macedonia had been conquered it was divided into four small republics; intermarriage between citizens of different republics was forbidden, and commercial relations were restricted; the Macedonian army was suppressed, and the exploitation of the gold mines and silver mines forbidden.

The value of the gold and silver taken in Macedonia by one man alone, the *triumphator* Paulus Emilius (in 167 B.C.), is assessed by Livy at 120 million sesterces.

We know almost nothing of the scientific, artistic and literary treasures which were reduced to ashes when Carthage was levelled to the ground.[1] Mommsen, describing the Roman army-commander, writes:

> Scipio, whom nature had intended for a nobler role than that of an executioner, blushed at his own work and, instead of being filled with the joy of triumph . . . the conqueror himself was haunted by the idea that such a crime must one day be expiated.

---

[1] A treatise on agriculture, in twenty-eight books, composed by Magon, a Carthaginian, was translated into Latin.

And Léon Homo writes:

The Senate, meeting in secret session, coldly decides that Carthage
is to be suppressed, a cynical resolution rendered even more odious
by the treacherous and hypocritical manner of its execution. . . .
The Carthaginians must be induced to disarm voluntarily; they can
thereafter be informed, without danger if not without dishonour, of
Rome's irrevocable decisions, and the executioner will be able to
perform his task untroubled. . . . This destruction of Carthage
carried out with truly diabolical perfidy, constitutes one of the most
odious episodes in Rome's onward march towards the conquest of
the Mediterranean.

(*Ibid.*, pp. 318–20)

Athens having fallen into decadence, a further crime of the Romans
was to deal a death-blow to Hellas, the source of art, science and
democracy, Hellas which was humanity's teacher and to which Rome
itself owed its initiation into the values of mind and spirit. Corinth
was captured, the men were killed and the women and children en-
slaved, and a large quantity of works of art destroyed. Polybius
watched the Roman barbarians turning precious pictures into dice-
boards. Mommsen speaks of

. . . revolting treatment which was frowned on even by the
apologists for the sack of Numantia and that of Carthage . . . a
measure conceived and formally decided upon by the Senate. We
shall not be mistaken if we see in it the work of commercial interests,
which were already beginning to take a hand in politics . . . and
which by destroying Corinth had rid themselves of a trading rival. . . .
The Romans forbade any future settlement on a site so eminently
favourable to commerce.

It was Jerusalem's turn next. The Romans determined to destroy the
country from which the prophets uttered their appeal to the brother-
hood of man, and where, in the very century of Rome's foundation,
the shepherd-prophet Amos had proclaimed the equality of nations,
reminding Israel that the heathen (the Philistines, Aramaeans and
Ethiopians) had the same rights as herself:

Are ye not as children of the Ethiopians unto me? saith the Lord.
Have not I brought up Israel out of the land of Egypt? and the
Philistines from Caphtor, and the Syrians from Kir?

(ix. 7)

Merciless war was waged on the people who, in the very preamble of
the Old Testament, had raised the majestic effigy of Abraham. So

intense is Abraham's desire for justice that he even intercedes for strangers, urging the Lord to spare the city of Sodom if any just men be found there, that the innocent may not perish because of the guilty (Genesis xviii).

Illyria went the same way as the rest, and was divided into three districts (Mommsen, Book III, Ch. 10). But the Illyrian stock, despite undergoing a heavy degree of Romanisation, retained its characteristic features for centuries in its three principal territories: Pannonia, Illyria and Dalmatia. One Pannonian tribe, the Eravisci, long continued speaking its own Illyrian language. The Illyrian soldiers in the Roman Army of the Danube were distinguished for their bravery and energy and also for their tall stature, as we mentioned earlier. By one of the paradoxes of history this Romanised Illyria was to supply Rome with three emperors, including Aurelian and Constantine (b. A.D. 274, at Naïssus-Nish). Here is F. Altheim's opinion on the matter:

> The accession of the Illyrian emperors, in the middle of the 3rd century A.D., carried the Roman idea to one of its decisive climaxes . . . but, to be complete and really convincing, the renascence would have had to include the spiritual life of Rome.
>
> The Illyrian emperors did not display the requisite qualities for such an undertaking.
>
> (*La Religion romaine*, p. 132)

It should be added that these emperors were preceded by another, Gallineus (260–268), a well-educated man, but a weak character, who, according to Altheim, "was an Etruscan and had his patronymic, Egnatius, from his mother" (*ibid.*, p. 395).

The devastation of the regions surrounding Rome was not only material or political but also moral, for Rome ruled by the sword and the sword alone. The consequences of this devastation have been far-reaching.

The Greeks, in particular, showed themselves incapable of creating a powerful centralised state; on the other hand, though, they found means which were more effective than pillage and destruction for entering into relations with the Barbarians. The prestige of Greek thought and art, and Greek commerce, and the establishing of the peaceful Greek colonies (on the shores of the Black Sea, for example), set in motion a civilising influence of vast scope. New ideas and gentler ways began spreading abroad, and penetrated even into obscure corners of Europe and elsewhere, without bloodshed, and exciting curiosity, interest and admiration wherever they went. The cities which the Scythians began building in the Crimea, the thinkers and educators who began appearing in their ranks, bear eloquent witness to this influence. But this remarkable achievement in the education of backward peoples was brutally interrupted.

Blinded by the "Eastern mirage", "that land of facile triumphs and prodigious booty" (Homo, *loc. cit.*, pp. 418–19), Rome was incapable of organising the West, still less of inspiring it. Her technical progress was to her advantage. But the Greeks did not conquer at Marathon because of the excellence of their civilisation on the material side. And the Romans, having crushed all the Mediterranean peoples, rendered a European Marathon impossible. The zoological instincts of the Barbarians remained unsubdued. This is the explanation of certain sporadic outbursts of human bestiality in the Middle Ages and later, and even, alas, in our own day.

After this rapid survey can we be astonished that, in such conditions and in such an atmosphere, Etruria, once conquered, lost her will to live and felt doomed to die?

This was made the more inevitable by the Romans' sacking and destroying Veii, Perugia, Fidenac, Catena and other cities of the Etruscans or their Allies. Volsinia was razed to the ground and suffered the fate which was later to be inflicted on Carthage: its inhabitants were forced to remove and settle elsewhere.

But, for us who are alive today, Etruscan civilisation never died. Furtively, like a wounded animal, it crept away into the darkness. There it remained, crouching in the funeral vaults of Etruria, till the excavators brought it back into the light. Etruria has spoken to us through her colourful frescos, her vivid drawings, her mirrors, her drinking-cups and the stories they have to tell, her statuettes, her ruins.

Today, she is beginning to speak to us again in her very language— a language simple, direct and lapidary, but how moving!

And how articulate!

These people who had but lately emerged from the Bronze Age speak to us in short, staccato phrases. But every one of their utterances is a human document of whose meaning we are just becoming aware. Today we can follow their feats of war, understand their grief as they mourn at the graveside, enter their temples, overhear their ingenuous prayers, laugh at the dishonesty of their boxers or the flustered bewilderment of a head cook in love, accompany them on their visits to the doctor, appreciate their proverbs or share their momentary melancholy when they drink a cup of wine and let themselves go in a drinking-song.

Much remains to be done before we can grasp everything they would

P

like to tell us, after so long a silence. There have been many misunderstandings, there are many still, and there will be many more before we understand everything they have to offer.

Everything, or almost everything.

For the contractions and inconsistencies of Etruscan writing are such that they give the words a kind of mimetic quality, and the words make full use of this to elude us. Anyone who sets himself to study them, though he may score a success now and then, is always finding himself back in the position of the eminent astronomer of whom Balzac tells that, after an eclipse, an *incroyable* [1] brought some ladies to see him, with the request: "Be kind enough to repeat the performance."

We have nevertheless dared to dive into the depths of a world of silence.

The silence has been broken.

What appeared to be dead has gently returned to life; has begun to breathe, is shaking off its torpor, is beginning once more to mourn, to speak and to laugh.

These sounds, which we hardly hoped to hear, sometimes reach us with astonishing clarity and at other times remain muffled and obscured as yet. They command our full attention. They are a precious echo from the life of the past.

For archaeology is the reconstitution of life.

[1] The *incroyables*, a kind of dandy flourishing under the Directoire (1795–9), were one of the many human species introduced by Balzac into his vast novel-sequence, *La Comédie humaine.* (*Tr.*)

APPENDICES

Typical letters	Archaic forms (7th—5th cent. B.C.)	Later forms (4th—1st cent. B.C.)	Modern equivalents	Typical letters	Archaic forms (7th—5th cent. B.C.)	Later forms (4th—1st cent. B.C.)	Modern equivalents
A	A	A	a	⊞			(s)
B			(b)	O			(o)
Ɔ	Ɔ	C	c(k)	↑	↑	↑	p
D			(d)	M	M	M	ś
⧻	⧻	⧻	e	Ϙ	Ϙ		q
⅂	⅂	⅂	v	D	D	D	r
I	I	ⱡ	z	⌇	⌇	⌇	s
⊟	⊟	⊟	h	T	T	✝	t
⊗	⊗	⊙	θ (th)	Y	Y	V	u
I	I	I	i	X	X, ✝		ṡ
Ϗ	Ϗ		k	Φ		⊖	φ (ph)
↓	↓	↓	l	↓		↓	χ (ch)
⋈	⋈	m	m		8	8	f
↑	↑	∩	n				

Etruscan Alphabet

TABLE OF COMPARISONS BETWEEN CERTAIN WORDS IN ALBANIAN, ETRUSCAN, HITTITE AND SOME OTHER LANGUAGES

ALBANIAN	OTHER LANGUAGES	TRANSLATION
ama	*ama*? (Etr.)—*anna* (Hit.) *ama* (Basque)	mother
—	*ar* (Etr.)—*ar* (Kurdish)	fire
at	*at* (Etr.)—*atta* (Hit.) *aita* (Basque)	father
—	*caθ* (Etr.)—*kaitinu* (to heat, Lith.)	sun
cenis	*cena* (Etr.)—*kaina* (Scyth.)	price, to prize
deg	*zec*? (Etr.)—*deg* (Lith.)	to burn
	zeg (Slav.)—*deg* (Kabarda)	
dimer	*gim* (Hit.)—*zima* (Slav.) *tzmer* (Armen.)	winter
dru	*taru* (Hit.)—*doru* (Gk.)	tree, wood
dukem	*dug* (Hit.)	to appear
gardh	*carθ* (Etr.)—*gurtas* (Hit.)	enclosure
	grad (Slav.)—*Garten* (Germ.)	
gur	*cur* (Etr.)—*car* (Armen.) *garu* (heavy, Anc. Ind.)	stone
gjymsë, gjysmë	*ims* (Etr.)—*gues* (Armen.)	half
hyi	*siu* (Hit.)	god
hie, hia	*hia* (Etr.)—*skia* (Gk.) *hi* (dead, Basque)	shade
kishë	*kikkis* (Hit.)	was, has been
ketu	*θu* (Etr.)—*ket* (Hit.)	here
klaj = (*qaj*)	*cla* (Etr.)—*kallis* (Hit.) *kaleo* (Gk.)	to call
kordhë	*kardas* (Lith.)—*kart* (Oss.) *karta* (Avesta)	sword
kremtoj	*caerimonia* (Lat.) *karimmi* (temple, Hit.)	to celebrate
la, le	*le* (Etr.)—*la, le* (Hit.)	to leave
lepij	*lip* (Hit.)	to lick
lule	*lul* (Hit.)—*liliak* (Basque)	flower
(*luqere*)	*losχna* (Etr.)	moon
	loussine (Armen.)—*losk* (brilliance, Russ.)	
	lukkes (to be bright, Hit.) *lux* (light, Lat.)	
madh	*maθ, meθ* (Etr.) *medz* (Armen.)—*maz* (Scyth.)	great
mjaltë	*mliθun*? (Etr.) *milit* (Hit.)—*meli* (Gk.) *miod* (Slav.)	honey
ndej	*tei*? (Etr.)—*tai* (Hit.)	to put, place
njer	*ner* (Etr.)—*nar* (Scyth.) *aner* (Gk.)	man
pi, pine	*pino, piein* (Gk.) *piti* (Anc. Ind., Slav.)	to drink

ALBANIAN	OTHER LANGUAGES	TRANSLATION
puesh	*punuś* (Hit.)	to ask
puth	*puθ*? (Etr.)—*pot* (Basque)	to kiss
rrah	*raχ*? (Etr.)—*raχojyn* (Oss.)	to strike
shi	*śi* (Etr.)—*heu* (Etr.)	rain
shof, shoh	*śuv* (Etr.)—*sakuaii* (Hit.) *seqn* (Indo-Europ.)	to see, look
—	*spanza* (Etr.)—*sipand* (Hit.) *spendo* (Gk.)	to make a libation
tarak	*tarχu*? (Etr.)—*tark*	bull; to be strong
toke	*tecum*? (Etr.)—*tekan* (Hit.)	earth
ujete	Cf. *Iuturna;* *uatar* (Hit.) *hydor* (Gk.); water, *voda,* etc.	water
vesh	*veś*? (Etr.)—*ueś* (Hit.)	to clothe
vesht	*wes* (Scyth.)	vineyard
vit	*uitt* (Hit.)	year

SUMMARY OF OBSERVATIONS ON ETRUSCAN GRAMMAR

PHONETICS

1. Etruscan *f* and *ph* sometimes correspond to Albanian *b*: *frontac, fufluns, θuflθas, fanu* (Albanian *bane*, "residence"), *faśei* ("mayest thou make", cf. Albanian *bâj*, "to make, do"), etc.

2. Etruscan *sc* corresponds to Albanian *sh*: *ersce* = Albanian *errshëm* ("dark"); *tvisc* (as in *eitviscri*) = *duesh*, "mayest thou wish".

3. Etruscan *n* is sometimes Albanian *m*: *θun* corresponds to Albanian *dhöme*, "house"; *trin* = *trim* ("hero").

4. Nasal vowels: *hatec* = *hantec* (Hades); *muθ* = *mund* ("hell, underworld").

Examples of the fluidity of Etruscan: *nac, naχ, nata, naθa* ("night, the night"); *za* = *θac* ("blood"); *repine* = *rupinu* ("abyss").

5. Etruscan *l* = Albanian *j*: *sual* = Albanian *shuaj* ("to efface").

NOUNS

1. Definite article:

i.—*iduare* ("the divided"); *i va est* (on the dice of Autun); *lusi*, as in *śuvlusi* ("the prayer"); *ibena* (*i vene*, "the wine", Cretan).

u.—*aplu* ("the sweet wine"); *siu* ("the evil"); *himiu* ("the infernal"); *fanu* ("the dwelling"); *θuścu* ("the oak"); *tenu* ("the town").

a.—*θaura*, etc.

As direct object: *i-npa? e-luce?*

2. Suffix *-ac* (origin, profession, habit, etc.): *cemnac, romaχ, iχnac, vinac, veliak, fruntac* ("thundering, Roman, wrathful, cupbearer, brother?, expert on thunderstorms"); *patac* ("the gander").
Cf. *kruśtenac, baleśtenac* ("leader of the city"?) on the Stele of Novilara.

3. Suffix *-ar* (profession, habit, etc.): *tanasar, uθ.tar, peiar(e), capesar, apcar* ("diseur, traveller, drinker, shoemaker, schoolboy"); similarly, *svular(e)* ("revealer").

4. plural ending:
-er.—*θuluter* ("two who pray").
-e.—*θaura*—*θaure*.

5. Declination:

Genitive suffix: *tinθasa* ("of the day"); *trinθasa* ("of the heroes").
Accusative suffix: *aperucen* ("to open the way"); *puiian* ("the woman"); *kukaian* ("the redness") cf. Hit. *kulaśśana*.
Ablative plural suffix: *malave, maluve* ("from the mountains").

ADJECTIVES

1. Derivative adjectives with suffix *-na*: *aisna, eisna* ("divine", plural?); *Rasna; spurana* ("of the city"); *lautna* ("of the family"); *suθina* ("funerary"); *haθna* ("of Hades"); *husina* ("of the libation"); *hupnina* ("of the coffin"?); *Iuturna . . . lusna* (?); *penθuna* ("of stone slabs") (P. 575).

2. With suffix *-le*: *aisvale* ("divine", plural); *lautnescle* ("familial"); *rtele*, as in *nucrtele*, ("regular"); *uzarale* ("incinerated").

3. With suffix *-ne*: *raśne* ("of silver"?); *θvene* (*θuene*, "double"?); *śiiane* ("savoury"); *renine* ("of the dwelling", P. 454); *huslne* ("of the libation").

4. With suffix *-θ, -θe*: *arχate* ("treasurer"); *nunθenθ* ("of the Nundinae"); *trinθ*, from *trin* ("heroic"); *urθe*, from *ure* ("hungry"); *huθte*; *volote*; *alumnaθe*.

NUMBERS

θu ("two"); *huθ* ("four"); *śa* ("five"); *ims* ("half").
peś- (also "five"?) (pp. 242, 396, 439). Cf. *peslialχ* (P. 195) ("leader of fifty"?).

VERBS

1. Suffix of the past tense (aorist) *-va*: *pava*, from *śuv* ("he saw"); *teva* ("he divided"), from *tevaraθ*; *peva* ("drank").

2. Medio-passive: *upinu(pi)* ("to drink, quench thirst"); *uples* ("went to sleep" or "mayest thou go to sleep"); *uχulni* ("was erected"?); *usli* ("was wiped"); *urais*, as in *thikeurais* ("may they multiply!"); *usnua*, as in *θeusnua*; *utince* ("it dawned; day broke"); *ucnim* (P. 87) ("was created"?); *uzarale* (see Adjectives, above); *unuθ* ("to make oneself known"); *upinu (piti)*.

3. Infinitive of the medio-passive: *muluem*, as in *muluemknie* ("to be consecrated").

4. Imperative: *epn* ("surrender!"); *ziχne* ("cut!"); *pkeni* ("buy!"); *ścu*, as in *ścuχie* ("go!" or "come!"); *scuvune* ("come gently"); *ec* or *ecu*, as in *ecunzaiiti* (P. 2, 10) ("go!"); *pi* ("drink!", singular); *pu* ("drink!", plural); *ip* ("give!" or "put!"); *clani* ("invoke!"); *ciani* ("weep!").

5. Past participle: *parsura* ("carried off"); *tusur* ("loved"?); *satur* ("erect"); *tasur* (as *tuśur*); *taliθa* ("mocking, ironical"?).

6. Negative form: *sniχe* ("mayest thou not know"). *śnutuf; svulare* ("to unveil"?).

7. Interrogative form: *aniaχ* ("do you know him? do you know?").

8. Optative: *tvisc* (*tuiś*) ("mayest thou wish"); *penz*, as in *penznas* (Albanian *benjsh*, "mayest thou do"); *tace*, as in *itace* ("may be given"); *ranvis; urais; luaś*.

9. The verb "to have": *χa* (*timχa, tuχulχa*).

10. Prefix *em, en*: *emfepame, enslifid, enqten*.

PRONOUNS

u ("I"); *mei* ("me, to me"); *aune*, as in *auneptali* ("him"); *tna* ("they", masculine or feminine); *na* ("us, to us"); *se, si* ("to her, of her"); *eme*, as in *naceme* ("my"?).

ADVERBS

re, as in *ree-miiś-meθumfs* ("again, more").

PREPOSITIONS

After the noun: *ne* as in *zaθrumsne* ("on the 20th"); *ph* (*b*), as in *pultisph* ("in agreement"?); *nr* as in *siune* (?) ("in the eyes"?); *m*, as in *painiem* ("into").

Before the noun: *n* as in *se-n-ulis* (*n-ulis*, "in the descent"); *peri*, "for" (*peri snati*).

CONJUNCTIONS

e as in *etve* ("and two"); *i* as in *ipi* ("and drink").
me as in *reemiiśmeθumfs* ("with"); *m* as in *mutinum* ("at dawn").
ku as in *kutiu* ("that").
sa as in *sa-trs*, and in *teśam-sa*, etc. ("how much, as much as").

NEGATIONS

pa as in *paniem* ("there is no wine in it"); *papnas* ("do not hurry").
s as in *s-niχe* ("not"); *s-nu* ("not to know"); *svular* ("revealing").
nuk as in *nucrtele* ("not").

APPENDIX III

A FIRST CONCORDANCE OF ETRUSCAN
ROOTS AND RADICALS

(Each of which is found in two or more sources)

1. APLU ("sweet"); (P. 272) *aplu eparu śis*; (P. 805) Ampiles.
2. ARθ ("has come"): (LM, VII, 7) *arθ vaχr ceus*; (Tomb of the Inscr.) *araθ vinacna*.
3. BALLE ("forehead"): *θuflθas*; Triballoi; (P. 359 a) *falzaθi*; *ballen*; (P. 831) *falado*, etc.
4. CARAθ ("enclosure"): (P. 572) *caraθsle*; (P. 532) *iucurt*; (p. 644) *unial curtun*.
5. CENA ("price"): (P. 65) *cena mi kalaturus*; *cenise neis*; (CIE 5353) *ve cenes mei*.
6. CEUS ("grandfather"): (LM) *vaχr ceuś*; (P. 79) *civesana matvesi* . . .
7. CUR ("stone"): (P. 401) *cure malave*; (Oscan) *iu cur*.
8. FANU ("dwelling, temple"): (P. 100, 619) *eθ fanu*; *tifanati*; *panzai*.
9. FEP ("to surprise"): (P. 744) *mi fep* . . . *empfepame cuθina*; (Corssen, I) *ercle fipece*.
10. FLE ("to sleep"): (P. 193) *uples*; (P. 100) *flenzna*; (P. 629) *flezrl*.
11. HIA ("shade, effigy"): (LM, VII) *hia etnam*; (LM, VI, 16) *scuχie*.
12. IC, IΧ ("to go, to come"): (LM, VII, VIII) *ic*; (LM, XII) *iχ nac*; (P. 366) *iχeme*; (P. 359) *iχutevr*, etc.
13. IP, EP, AP, NAP ("to give"): (LM, X) *ipa*; (P. 380) *inpa θapicun*; Gerhard, CCCXC, 2) *epn*; (Lavis Inscr.) *upinu piti apv*; (P. 343) *ip siune*.
14. IΧN, IΘN ("to become angry"): (P. 399) *iχnac*; (P. 2) *iχnac*; *iθnin* (?); *itχrani*.
15. KE, KI ("well! aïe!"): (Palette of Padua) *na ki nata risakvil*; (P. 331) *uθi ke malave*.
16. KLEN ("to be, to exist"): (P. 495) *klenase citia*; (P. 652) *clen ceχa*.
17. KVIL ("light"): (Palette of Padua) *risakvil*; ("Rhaetian Text") *tisaχvilus*; (P. 749) *tancvilus*; Tanaqvil; (P. 663) *tinścvil*.
18. LUT ("to pray"): (P. 208) *θuluter*; (P. 657) *tins lut*; (P. 447) *suvluśi*.
19. MAL ("mountain"): (P. 411) *mi mal tarcste*; (P. 331) *uθi ke maluve*; (von Hahn, II, 243) *Dimallum*, "two summits"; (P. 401) *cure malave*, etc.

454

20. Maθ ("great"): (C. S. Coon) Emathia; (P. 170) *matu manimeri*; (CIE 3264) *limatis* (?); (LM) *meθlumeri* (?).

21. Mar, Mer ("to take"): (P. 2, 7), *marzac*; (P. 359) *mlaχce marni*; (P. 570 a 18) *in tema mer.*

22. Mis ("meat"): (P. 223) *remiiśmeθumfs*; (P. 381) *θenśtmase*; (P. 172) *luri miac.*

23. Nac, Naθ ("night"): (P. 334) *ersce nac*; (P. 381) *menaθa*; (Palette of Padua) *na ki nata*; (LM, XII, 2) *iχ nac*; (LM, VI, 6) *heci nac,* etc.

24. Ner ("man"): (LM, X, g, 3) *neri*; (Lavis Inscr.) *vthi nrs itl.*

25. Pi ("to drink"): (LM, IV, 22) *pevaχ vinum*; (Lavis Inscr.) *upinu piti apv*; (Studi Etr., XXII, fig. 20) *paχeis . . . peiare*; (Wanscher, p. 15) *pi kutiu tisa vil ipi peri snati*; etc.

26. Pic ("to roast, roasted"): (P. 2) *picasri . . . picas śiane*; (LM, IX, 9) *slapiχun*; (P. 380) *θapicun.*

27. Raθ ("order, line"): (P. 81) *tevaraθ*; (LM, IX, 20) *ara ratum*; (P. 488) *raθiu*; (Studi Etr., VIII, 343) *mini urθaneke*; (CIE 5349) *nuc rtele.*

28. Re, Ri ("new, young; anew"): (P. 223) *re miiś me θumfs*; (P. 2, 19) *puiian acas ri*; (P. 486) *śe nulis rite*; (P. 685) *ei tvisc ri*; (P. 485) *la θna rite*

29. Setra ("worthy, dignity"): (P. 401 b) *fave setra*; (P. 222) *θresu f.siθrals.*

30. Se ("torrent, stream"): (LM, V, 10, 14) *eiser śic śeuc*; (P. 486) *śe nulis rite.*

31. Si, Sy ("eye"): (P. 224) *tr θun śunu*; (P. 343) *ip siune.*

32. Sli ("to efface"): (P. 131) *sli caχes*; (Studi Etr., XXII) . . . *capes sli*; (P. 572) *caraθ sle.*

33. Suv ("to see"): (P. 447) *śuv lusi*; (P. 719 c) *net svis* (?); *pava.*

34. Terg ("market"): (CIE 4251) Tergitio Negotiator; (P. 381) *trecs*; Tergeste.

35. Ti ("to know"): (Wanscher, 15) *pi ku tiu tisa vil; ti fanati.*

36. Tisa ("a little"): *tisa vil*; (CIE 3267) *tise in naime*; (P. 844) *mantisa.*

37. Tra ("milk"): (LM, IV, 22) *trau*; (P. 399) *θra sce.*

38. Tru ("to fear"): (P. 829) *drouna*; (Gerhard) *truisie*; *trutnuθ*; (LM, XI, 2) *celi pen trutum*; (P. 740) *trutvecie.*

39. θAL ("to go out; to succeed, be successful"): (P. 366) *iθal*; (P. 2, 10) *ital* (?); (Lavis Inscr.) *vthi nrs itl.*

40. θu ("two"): *θuflθas*; (P. 298) *θuluter*; (P. 619) *e tve θaure*; Dimallum.

41. Uθ ("way, road", etc.): (P. 331) *uθi ke maluve*; (Studi Etr., XXII) *uθ(e)tar*; (Lavis Inscr.) *vthi neris itl*; (P. 2, 10) *ital sacri utus ecun . . .*

42 VINUM ("wine"): (LM, II, IV) *vinum*; (Tomb of the Inscr.) *araθ vinacna*.

43. ZAC, ZA, θAC, θA ("blood"): (LM, I) *zaχri*; (L, VII, 13) *θacac usli*; (LM, VI) *θaχsin*; (P. 612) *satnaslθac*; (P. 131) *sli caχes*.

44. ZAR ("fire"): (LM, VII, IX, X) *zar ve*; (LM, I, IV) *zarfneθ*; (P. 108) *uzarale*.

45. ZNA ("to last"): (Wanscher, 15) *ipi peri snati*; (P. 100) *flenzna*; (P. 485) *la.θna rite* (?) ("*let* youth last!").

46. VE ("to put"): *zar ve; ve cenes mei; ve iiu aniies*.

47. ANE ("side"): (P. 519) *sianś*; (P. 73) *huθte anaes; ve iiu aniies*.

48. SCU ("to go"): *scuχie* (LM, VI, 16); *scuna* (P. 570); (P. 135) *escuna*; (P. 2, 7) *scuvune*.

49. Aθ ("Hades"): (P. 100) *aθis*; *Haθna*; (LM) *hatec*; *Aθets*.

50. IU ("god"): (CIE 5337) *ve iiu aniies*; (P. 390) *iiulaθilin*.

51. LUAS ("to oil, anoint"): (P. 266) *luaś*; (LM, II) *zusleve*; (LM, VIII) *zuśleva*.

52. θIAL ("child"): (P. 734) *atisiliθial*; (P. 169) *θelusa*; (P. 802) *agaletora* (?).

ETRUSCAN-ALBANIAN-ENGLISH-VOCABULARY

(Words deciphered in this book and belonging essentially to category A or B)

ETRUSCAN	ALBANIAN	ENGLISH
ame (A)	ama	mother, 121, 323
ana (A)	anë	receptacle, 177
ane (A)	anë	side, 72
ape (A)	ap	to give, 104, 266
ape (B)	hap	to open, 112
aplu (A)	ambel	sweet, 173
ar (A)	(Lat. *ara*)	fire, altar, 171, 216, 286, 344
arθ (A)	ardh	came, 123
arχate (A)	arktar	treasurer, 200
ati (A)	at (father)	mother, 124, 334
atr (A)	atër	fathers, 261
aune (A)	aynë	he, 296
bacchetidis	bagëti	animals, 214
balteus (A)	bajt	"carrier", 118
ca (A)	ca	a little, 355
caerimonia (B)	kreme	feast, 213
caius (B)	kal	horse, 87
calat (B)	gjallë	life, 347
calusin (B)	kalorës	horseman, 103
cana (A)	qanë	to carve, 180
canθce (B)	qind	(was) centurion, 103
capesar	kepucar	shoemaker, 178
caraθ (A)	gardh	enclosure, rampart, 112
casθi (?)	gjashtë	six, 84
cavire (A)	gavir	empty, 165
cemnac (A)	gemon	(it) thunders, 58
cena (A)	cenis	price, 109
cenes (A)	"	price, 331
cenise (A)	"	price, 176
cep(ar)	gjebë	young animal

457

ETRUSCAN	ALBANIAN	ENGLISH
ceus (A)	gjysh	grandfather, 123, 334
cilva (A)	qilve	to languish, 346
citia (B)	kithi	askew, 161
cla (A)	klaj = qaj	to call, 314, 349
clani (A)	klaj	to weep, 161
clen (B)	klenë	to exist, be, 101, 222, 273
cnan (B)	qënun	to be; to procreate, 122
creice (A)	Grek	Greek, 330
cuicna (B)	koje, qen	dog, skin, 116
cure (A)	gur	stone, 228, 380
curte, cf. caraθ		(114)
cver (A)	quer	store, 236, 334
cvil (A)	kvillë	light, 167
dalius (A)	dal	mad, 157
drouna (A)	druhem	fear, 99, 344
θa (A)	tha	to say, 128
θa (A) cf. ca		(354)
θac (A)	gjak	blood, 101, 239, 310, 320
θanasa (A)	tha	*diseur*, 181
θans (B)	densh	ewe, 290
θar (A)	darë	to divide, 140, 326
θec	dek, vdek	to die, 271, 345
θent (A)	dhendë	ewe, 171, 355
θial (A)	djalë	boy, 124, 403
θluθcva (B)	dlutun	prayers, 354
θra (A)	(Mac.–Rum. *dzar*)	milk, 146, 205
θrce cf. turce		(190)
θresu (B)	thrres	to call, ask, 147, 150
θu (A)	du	two, 72 *et seq.*
θufarce	thupër	to whip, 193
θuflθas	du-ballesh	*bifrons*, 75, 76
θuluter (A)	du, lut	"two praying", 62
θumfs (A)	tumb	cream, 145
θun (B)	dhomë	house, 152, 222, 308, 312, 356
θur (A)	dorë	lineage, 119, 315
θurinu (A)	tarak	bull, 173
θuscu (A)	dushku	oak, 232
θutuiθ (B)	ketu, tuis, dhi	here to hold the mountain goats, 242

ETRUSCAN	ALBANIAN	ENGLISH
θuχ	dukem	to appear, 259
eluce	e luce	to ask him?, 359
emfepame (A)	ënbeftaeh	surprising, 134
eparu (A)	epër	upper, 173
epl	(Lat. *epulum*)	sacred banquet, 221, 337
epn (A)	epni	surrender, 55
ersce (A)	errshëm	dark, 190
etnam (A)	etna	fathers, 120, 285, 308, 312
etule (B)	tule	tender, 196
eθ, eiθ (A)	ajet	temple, 227, 230
evnu (A)	venë	wine, 163
fabulonia (B)	ba bullij	causes to roar, 183
falas (A)	balle	forehead, 222
fanati (A)	banë di	house knows, 131
fanu (A)	banë	house, 227
fanuse (A)	banesë	house, 345
farsi (A)	farosje	ruin, 347
fep (A)	bef	surprise, 134
fipece (A)	bef(she)	was surprised, 136
flenzna (A)	fle, znjatem	sleep long, 169
fler (A)		vow; ex-voto, 190, 308, 315
flezru (A)	fle, ruej	sleep to keep, 131
fufluns (A)	bubullij	who roars, 253
garuleum (A)	garule	chrysanthemum, 174
gigarum (A)	kuqerem	beetroot, 174
hate, hante, haθna (A)	hadh	Hades, 276, 295, 356
heci (B)	heq	to withdraw, 248, 308
hetum	het	thirst, 286, 348
hia (A)	hia	shade, 60, 287, 293
himiu (A)	himë	abyss, 272
hinθiu (A)	(Oscan)	lower, 72
hupnina (A)	hup	ossuary, 290, 357
hurtu	hurdhë	(a game), 116
hus (B)	hudh	to pour, 283, 290
huθ (B)		four, 79–81
ic, iχ (A)	ik	to go, 351, 355
iduare (A)	tuari	divided, 86

ETRUSCAN	ALBANIAN	ENGLISH
ims (B)	gjymsë	half, 85
inpa (A) cf. ip		
intemamer	in, dema, marr	these bulls take, 220
ip (A)	ip	to give, 183, 369
itχrani (A)	idhërim	vexation, 202
iθnin (A)	idhnim	vexation, 201
iχnac (A)	idhnak	choleric, 203
kapes (B)	kapëz	handle, 162
katek (A)	katoc	piece, head, 115
ke (A)	ke	hold!, 166
ke (A)	qe	oxen, 267
kikenda (A)	kyp	"tonic", 183
klen (A)	klenë	to be, 161
knie (B)	qenë	existence, life, 257
kran (A)	ngranë	to eat, 151
kru (A)	kryej	to finish, 152
kukaian (A)	kuq	redness, 167
kurpu (A)	korbë	wretched, 152
kvil cf. cvil		
la (A)	la	to let, leave, 127, 169, 328
lacθ (A)	lagët	libation, 85, 158
lari	laroj	to smooth, 160
laristna (A)	laroj, tna	to polish them, 230
lariza	larzimoj	to adorn, 234
lav (B)	lav	to be mad, 163
lena (B)	lângje	libation, 345
lenia (B)	lenje	abandonment, 161
libitina	lebeti	"horrible", 272
luaś	luej	to anoint, 187
lucairce (B)	luqere	to light up, 238
luθcva (B)	lus, lutem	prayers, 240
lunasie (A)	lojna(sh)	games, 214
lur (A)	lyrë	fat, grease, 219
lus, lut (A)	lus, lut	to pray, 72, 219, 268, 310
lutuis (A)	"	to pray, 368
malave (A)	maleve	mountains, 228, 378
maluve (A)	"	mountains, 185
marca (A)	maraq	fennel, 219
marni (A)	marrni	take!, 279

ETRUSCAN	ALBANIAN	ENGLISH
marun	maroj	to make, to perfect, 102
mase (A) cf. miis		(171)
matu (A)	madh	great, 129
melecrapicces (B)	melle, krapis	good share, 241
menas (B)	mënash	silk, 322
menaθa (A)	më natë	with the night, 171
mer (A)	merr	to take, 221
miiś (A)	mish	meat, 145
mlamna	më lëmënj	on a threshing-floor (?), 243
mlusna (A)	(losna, moon)	at new moon, 243
muluane (B)	mul-	to grind, 140
muθ (B)	mund	Underworld, 226, 355
munθ (A)	mund	sufferings, 292
mursl (A)	mrshil	to conclude, 292
nac (A) cf. nata		(308, 356)
nas (B)	ngas	to haste, hasten, 150
nata (A)	natë	night, 167
neriś (A)	njerëz	men, 101, 345
niχe (A)	njoh	to know, 168
nrś (A) cf. neriś		
nuk (A)	nuk	no, 330
nulis (A)	n'ulis	in the descent, 136
num (A)	njom	tender, 130
nuna	nënë	mother, 122
orti	urtë	intelligent, 87
panzai (B) cf.		
fanuse		(235)
parliu (A)	barl	white, 143
parniχ (A)	paranik	notable, "first", 120
parsura (A)	përzura	carried-off, 192
parχis (A)	bark	innate, hereditary, 120
pataks (A)	patak	gander, 174
pava (A)	pava	saw, has seen, 25, 97
pazu	bazho	cheese?, 140
peiare (A)	pijar	drinker, 163
pel (A)	pjell	to produce, 173
peθna (A)	betinë	stone slab, 235
peva (A)	piva	to drink, 168
pi (A)	pi	to drink, 168

ETRUSCAN	ALBANIAN	ENGLISH
pinaś (A)	pije	drink, beverage, 349
piti (A) cf. pi		(265)
piχun (A)	pjek	roasted, 349
pleni (A)	bleni	buy!, 177
prezu (A)	brezar	pillar, 234
pultisph	poltis	to consent, 212
purθ (B)	prushis	to stir up (fire), 102, 207
putnam (B)	botë	earth, world, 347
ranem (A)	rane	to strike, 324
raninum (A)	rrin	sedative, 183
ratum (A)	radis	arranged, 344
raχ (A)	rrah	to strike, 280, 301, 322
reneθi (A)	rënë	couch, 355
renine (A)	,,	of the couch, 355
ri (A)	ri	new, young, 122, 167, 186
ri (A)	re	cloud, 249
ril (A)	rillë	pea, 115
rite (A)	rit	youth, 136, 169
riθ	res(is)	destruction, 296
rtele (A)	radhe	regular, 330
ru (A)	ruej	to keep, 131
rupine (B)	rrëpine	precipice, 265
sa (A)	sa	how much, as . . . as, 167, 292
sarve	zjarr vé	put fire, 310
satrs	sa thrres	as much as you want, 288
scara (A)	shqera	lambs, 322
sce (A)	thith	sucks, 205
scu (B)	shkoj	go!, 60, 267, 279
śe (A)	she	torrent, 136, 271
śetirune	shterunë	barren, 280, 281
setra (A)	sedër	worthy, 147
sianś (A)	si anësh	from its sides, 72
sili (A)	sjell	to produce, 124
silicernium	sillë, qerm	meal (taken) outside, 213
siθrals (A)		(147)
cf. setra		
siu (A)	ziu	black, mourning, 167
si (A)	shi	rain, 271
śi (A)	shi	taste, 173

ETRUSCAN	ALBANIAN	ENGLISH
siune (A)	sy, syni	eyes (in the), 183
sle (A)	shlej	to efface, 112, 162, 310, 349
slia (A)	shllij	salty, salacious, 207
slicaχeś (A)	shlij gjak	to rub with blood, 239
snati (A)	znjatem	to last, 167
snu (B)	s'njoh	not to know, 268
spanza (B)	(Greek *sponde*)	to make a libation, 278
stre (A)	shtrij	to stretch, 117
su (A)	sy, si	eye, 152
sual (A)	shuaj	to efface, 167
sutanas	shut	(of) hind, 301, 304
suθina		funerary, 295
śuv (A)	shof	to look, 77, 343
svulare (B)	zbuloj	to reveal, 273
tal (A)	dalë	courageous, 104
talea (A)	dal	twig, shoot, 124
taliθa	tallit	mocking, ironical, 133
tali(na) (A)	dal	to succeed, be successful; to go out, 266, 296
tamia (B)	damje	separate, 142
tanasar (B)	tha	mourning, weeping (adj.), 245
tarcste (A)	treg	market, 170
taśur	dashur	loved, 367
ter (A)	tërë	all, entire, 152
tergitio (A)	tergjeti	merchant, 170
teśam (A)	dashëm	loved, 292
tesim (B)	deshi	loved (adj., plur.), 284
tevaraθ (A)	theva radh	divides lines, 224
thi (A)	thi, dhi	goats, 267
Tibre	thepuer	"toothed, jagged" (winding), 99
tim, θim (B)	dhime	grief, 134, 343
tisa, tise (A)	disa	a little, 159, 168
tna	tene	them (accus., masc. or fem.), 230
trec (A)	treg	market, 170
tretu (A)	treta	(he) hammered, 194
trsk (A)	traskë	brine, 174
truia	troje	arena, 328

ETRUSCAN	ALBANIAN	ENGLISH
truisie (B)	druejshëm	adorer, 133
trutnvt	druej, njojt	knowing religion, 245, 302
tul (B)	tul	tender, 289, 290
turce (A)	dhuroj	to offer, 76
turice (A)	„	(he) offered, 262
turesa (A)	turëz	mouth, maw, 165
turuce (A)		(234)
cf. turce		
turunke (A)		(234)
tuśur (B)	dashur	loved (adj.), 130
tva (B)	du(a)	was loving, 204
tvisc (A)	duesh	that you may wish, 186
ufli (A)	fle	to go to sleep, 340
uθi (A)	udhë	way, road, 185
uples (A)	u-flesh	that you may go to sleep, 130
urais (A)	u-rris	that they may be raised, 267
urθaneke (A)	u-radh	was traced, 180
urθe	urti	hungry, 158
usil (B)	u-siell	(it) turns, 226, 319
usli (A)	u-shlyej	that it may be smeared, 320
usta (A)	ushta	sting
utince (B)	(u)gdhin	to dawn, be light, 280, 357
uzarale (A)	u zjarr	was burned, 283
va (A)	(u)ba	was made, became, 248
vacl (A)	vagjël	sacred meal, 215, 286
vθtar (A)	udhë	passer-by, 163
varχti (A)	vark	(in the) processions, 241
vaχr (A)	vjehër	father-in-law, 123
ve (A)	ve	to put, 73, 345
vinac (A)	(vinum)	cup-bearer, 332
vc (A)	uk, ujk	wolf, 117
volote	volicem	pleasant, 87
vra (A)	ura	hunger, 268
vraθ (A)	vras	to kill, 55
vthi (A) cf. uθi		
vune (B)	vonë	gently, softly, 279
χiia (A) cf. hia		
χimθm	qind	hundred, 84
χosfer (B)	kusp	to spin, 176

ETRUSCAN	ALBANIAN	ENGLISH
za (B)	zâ	to take, begin, 320
zar (A)	zjarr	fire, 282
zati (A)	zatis	combat, 328
zaθrum (A)	zet	twenty, 83
zaχ (A) cf. θac		301
zilc (A)	zirtar	functionary, 100
zna (A) cf. snati		

TWELVE ETRUSCAN PROVERBS, APHORISMS AND DRINKING-SONGS

(For contexts and literal translations, see the pages indicated)

1. *śenulis rite*
"As a torrent rushing down, such is youth." (pp. 136–7)
2. *vinimia leniace*
"In wine, oblivion." (p. 160)
3. *klenase citia*
"A mad world, my masters!" (p. 161)
4. *kapemu kaθesa kapes sli*
"Seize this cup by its handles and empty it." (p. 162)
5. *paχeis lavθur peiare uθetar   if evnuχ rcu*
"Drinker, whether you be of the mad race of Bacchus
or simply a traveller on the road, put wine into this cup." (pp. 163–4)
6. *limatis ene cavire vemati turesa*
"Happy is he who puts plenty of wine into his empty
mouth." (pp. 165–6)
7. *na ki nata ri sa kvil*
et sual euti kukaian
"Keep us fresh as the dawn all night,
And by day, alas, take off our red paint." (pp. 166–7)
8. *peva sniχe siu pi kutiu tisaχvil ipi peri snati*
"He who has drunk knows no misery.
Drink, to know a little joy,
And drink to live long." (pp. 167–8)
9. *θec veisna hausti fanuśe neri sane ipa θui neri*
"Death has set man's dwelling-place in the abyss;
But wine is given to us in the here and now." (LM, X) (pp. 345–6)
10. *θumsa cilva neri vanva farsi putnam θu calatnam*
"Man is as weak as smoke,
And in the earth he is destroyed.
It is here and now that we live." *(Ib.)* (pp. 346–7)
11. *stre vc*
"Stretch yourself out like a wolf in his leap." (pp. 116–17)
12. *la.θna rite*
clani ciani sθ
"Let youth last while it may.
Weep when you invoke the tomb." (p. 169)

SHORT BIBLIOGRAPHY

Abayev, V., *Langue et folklore ossètes* (Moscow, 1949).
Altheim, F., *La religion romaine antique* (Paris, Payot, 1955).
Altheim, F., *Geschichte der lateinischen Sprache* (Frankfurt am Main, 1951).
Arbanas, L., *Deutsch.-alb. u. alb.-deutsch. Wörterbuch* (Vienna).
Arndt, P., *La Glyptothèque Ny-Carlsberg (musée Jacobsen)* (1912).
Bayet, J., *Herclé* (Paris, 1929).
Beazley, *Etruscan Vase Painting* (Oxford, 1947).
Bertrand and Reinach, S., *Les Celtes dans les vallées du Pô et du Danube* (1894).
Bréal, M., *Les Tables Iguvines* (Paris).
Buck, C., *Elementarbuch der Osk. Umbr. Dialekte* (1905).
Buckler, W. H., "Lydian Inscriptions", *Sardis*, VI, II.
Buffa, M., *Nuova Raccolta di Iscrizioni Etrusche* (Florence, 1935).
Bugge, S., *Etruskisch und Armenisch* (Christiania, 1890).
Buonamici, G., *Epigrafia Etrusca* (Florence, 1932).
Buonamici, G., *Fonti di Storia Etrusca* (Florence, 1939).
Canina, Luigi, *L'antiqua Etruria Marittima* (Rome, 1951).
Chapouthier, F., *Les Dioscures au service d'une déesse* (Paris, 1935).
Cimochowski, W., *Le Dialecte de Dushmani* (Poznan, 1951).
Cles-Reden, S. von, *Les Etrusques* (Arthaud, Paris, 1955).
Conestabile, G., *Pitture murali e fresce . . .* (Florence, 1865).
Contenau, Dr G., *Manuel d'archéologie orientale*.
Coon, Carleton S., *The Mountains of the Giants* (Peabody Museum, Harvard University, 1950).
Cordignano, Fulvio, *Lingua albanese* (Milan, 1931).
Corpus Inscriptionum Etruscaram (1893–1936).
Corpus Inscriptionum Italicarum (A. Fabretti, Turin, 1867).
Corssen, W., *Ueber die Sprache der Etrusker* (Leipzig, 1875).
Daremberg-Saglio, *Dictionnaire des antiquités grecques et romaines*.
Dasti, Luigi, *Notizie storiche archeol. di Tarquinia e Corneto* (Rome, 1878).
Deecke, W., *Etruskische Forschungen* (1875 ss. (I–IV)).
Deecke, W., and Pauli, C., *Etruskische Forschungen u. Studien* (1881 ss. (I–VI)).
Devoto, "Gli Etruschi nel quadro dei popoli italici i antichi" (*Historia*, VI, 1957).
Dozon, A., *Manuel de la langue chkipe ou albanaise* (Paris, 1879).
Ducati, P., *Le problème étrusque* (Paris, 1938).
Ellis, R., *Etruscan and Basque Languages* (London, 1886).
Ernout, A., *Les éléments étrusques du vocabulaire latin* (Paris, 1930).
Fiesel, E., "χ represents a sibilant in early Etruscan", *Am. Jour. Phil.* (1936), 57.
Fiesel, E., *Namen des griech. Mythos im Etrusk.* (Göttingen, 1928).
Fiesel, E., *Etruskisch* (Berlin, 1931).
Friedrich, J., *Hethitischer Wörterbuch* (Heidelberg, 1952).
Friedrich, J., *Hethitisch. u. Kleinasiatische Sprachen* (1931).
Fustel de Coulanges, *La Cité antique* (Paris, 1919).
Gerhard, E., *Etruskische Spiegel* (Berlin, 1843).
"Glotta", *Zeitschrift fur griech. u. lat. Spr.* (Göttingen).
Gori, A. F., *Museum Etruscum* (Florence, 1737–43).
Hammarström, M., *Griech.-etruskische Wortgleichungen. Beiträge zur Geschichte des etrusk., latein. und griechisch. Alphabets* (Helsingfors, 1920).
Hammarström-Justinien, M., "Etrusk. RAθ = ordo" (*Studi Etr.*, XI).

467

Hahn, J. G. von, *Albanesische Studien* (1854).
Heurgon, J., "L'Etat étrusque" (*Historia*, VI, 1957. Wiesbaden).
Hoffmann, O., *Die Makedoner* (Göttingen, 1906).
Homo, Leon, *L'Italie primitive et les débuts de l'impérialisme romain* (1925).
Hrkal (Ed.), *Der Etruskische Gottesdienst* (Vienna, 1947).
Hrozny, B., *Etruskisch u. die hethitische Sprachen, Z. für Assyr. 38* (1929).
Hrozny, B., *Histoire de l'Asie Antérieure* (Payot, Paris, 1947).
Hus, A., *Les Etrusques* (Ed. du Seuil, Paris, 1959).
Jokl, Dr N., "Albaner–Illyrier" (*Ebert, Reallexikon der Vorgeschichte*).
Jokl, Dr N., *Studien zur albanesischen Etymologie u. Wortbildung* (Vienna, 1911).
Kerenyi, Ch., *La mythologie des Grecs* (Payot, Paris, 1952).
Kluge, Th., *Etruskisch "fler"* (Pavia, 1954).
Körte, G., *I rilievi delle urne etrusche* (Berlin, 1890).
Kostallari, A., *Dictionnaire albano–russe* (Moscow, 1954).
Krahe, H., *Sprache und Vorzeit* (Heidelberg, 1954).
Krahe, H., *Die alten balkanillyrischen geogr. Namen* (Heidelberg, 1925).
Krahe, H., *Lexikon altillyrischer Personennamen* (Heidelberg, 1929).
Krahe, H., *Die Sprache der Illyrier. I, Die Quellen* (Wiesbaden, 1955).
Kretschmer, Paul, *Einleitung in die Geschichte der Griechischen Sprache* (Göttingen, 1896).
Lambertz, Maximilian, *Albanisches Lesebuch* (Leipzig, 1948).
Leotti, A., *Dizionario Albanese–Italiano* (Rome, 1937).
Librandi, Pr. V., *Grammatica Albanese con le poesie rare di Variboba* (Milan, 1928).
Littmann, E., *Sardis*, VI, I.
Lloyd, Seton, *Early Anatolia* (1956).
Mann, Stuart E., *A Historical Albanian–English Dictionary* (London, 1948).
Martin-Leake, William, *Researches in Greece* (London, 1814).
Mazzarino, Santo, "Sociologia del mondo etrusco" (*Historia*, VI, 1957).
Meyer, G., *Etymologisches Wörterbuch der albanesischen Sprache* (Strasbourg, 1891).
Miklosich, F., *Istro-u. macedo-rumänische Sprachendenkmäler* (Vienna, 1881).
Montelius, Osc., *La civilisation primitive en Italie depuis l'introduction des métaux* (Stockholm, 1910).
Muller-Deecke, K. O., *Die Etrusker* (Stuttgart, 1877).
Nogara, B., *Gli Etruschi e la lora civilta* (Milan, 1923).
Olzscha, K., "Schrift u. Sprache der Etrusker" (*Historia*, VI).
Pallottino, M., *Elementi di lingua etrusca* (Florence, 1936).
Pallottino, M., *The Etruscans* (1956).
Pallottino, M., *Testimonia Linguae Etruscae* (Florence, 1954).
Pallottino, M., "Etruskische Kunst" (*Kunst u. Leben der Etrusker*, 1956).
Paoli, U. E., *Vita romana* (1955).
Pascu, G., *Dictionnaire étymologique macédo-roumain* (Iasi, 1925).
Petrotta, Pr. P. G., *Popolo, lingua e letteratura albanese* (Palerme, 1931).
Piganiol, André, *Les Etrusques, peuple d'Orient* (Paris, 1953).
Pisani, Vittore, *Linguistica generale e indoeuropea* (Turin, 1947).
Pisani, Vittore, *Le lingue dell'Italia Antica oltre il latino* (Turin, 1953).
Poulsen, F., *Etruscan Tomb Paintings* (Oxford, 1922).
Premières Civilisations (les) (Paris, 1950).
Randall-MacIver, P., *Italy before the Romans* (Oxford, 1928).
Renard, M., *La question étrusque* (Brussels, 1941).
Ribezzo, F., "A che punto siamo con la interpretazione dell'etrusco" (*Studi Etr.* 1953).
Sandfeld, Kr., *Linguistique balkanique* (Paris, 1930).
Scheftelowitz, I., *Arisches im Alten Testament*.
Skutsch, *Etruskische Sprache* (Pauly-Wissowa, 1909).
Solari, A., *Vita pubblica e privata degli Etruschi* (Florence, 1931).

Stoltenberg, Pr. H. L., *Etrusk. Sprachlehre mit vollständigen Wörterbuch* (Leverkusen, 1950).

Studi Etruschi (Florence, from 1927 onwards).

Tagliavini, Carlo, *L'albanese di Dalmazia* (Florence, 1937).

Thallon, Ida C., "Some Balkan and Danubian connexions of Troy" (*Journ. of Hell. Studies*, XXXIX, 1919).

Tomaschek, W., *Die Alten Thraker* (1893).

Torp, *Etruskische Beiträge* (Christiania, 1906).

Trombetti, A., *La lingua etrusca* (Florence, 1928).

Vacano, O.-W. von, *Die Etrusker in der Welt der Antike* (1957).

Vasmer, M., *Studien zur Albanesischen Wortforschung* (Dorpat, 1921).

Vetter, E., Articles and notes in the review *Glotta*.

Veyrin, Ph., *Les Basques* (Arthaud, Paris, 1955).

Wanscher, V., *La langue étrusque renaît* (Copenhagen, 1951).

Whatmough, J., *Prae-Italic Dialects of Italy* (1933).

Weigand, G., *Albanesische Grammatik im südgegischen Dialekt* (Leipzig, 1913).

Weigand, G., *Die Aromunen* (Leipzig, 1894).

Weigand, G., *Ethnographie von Makedonien* (Leipzig, 1924).

INDEX